Photoshop Elements 13

the missing manual®

The book that should have been in the box®

Barbara Brundage

O'REILLY®

Beijing | Cambridge | Farnham | Köln | Sebastopol | Tokyo

Photoshop Elements 13: The Missing Manual

by Barbara Brundage

Published by O'Reilly Media, Inc.,
1005 Gravenstein Highway North, Sebastopol, CA 95472.

O'Reilly books may be purchased for educational, business, or sales promotional use. Online editions are also available for most titles (*http://my.safaribooksonline.com*). For more information, contact our corporate/institutional sales department: (800) 998-9938 or *corporate@oreilly.com*.

September 2014:   First Edition.

Revision History for the First Edition:

   2014-09-04   First release

See *http://www.oreilly.com/catalog/errata.csp?isbn=0636920032786* for release details.

The Missing Manual is a registered trademark of O'Reilly Media, Inc. The Missing Manual logo, and "The book that should have been in the box" are trademarks of O'Reilly Media, Inc. Many of the designations used by manufacturers and sellers to distinguish their products are claimed as trademarks. Where those designations appear in this book, and O'Reilly Media is aware of a trademark claim, the designations are capitalized.

While every precaution has been taken in the preparation of this book, the publisher assumes no responsibility for errors or omissions, or for damages resulting from the use of the information contained in it.

ISBN-13: 978-1-491-94721-0

[T]

Contents

The Missing Credits . . . . **ix**

Introduction . . . . **xiii**
Why Photoshop Elements? xiii
What You Can Do with Elements 13 xiv
What's New in Elements 13 xv
Elements vs. Photoshop xvii
The Key to Learning Elements xviii
About This Book xix
About the Online Resources xxiv
Safari® Books Online xxv

Part One: Introduction to Elements

CHAPTER 1: **Finding Your Way Around Elements** **3**
Getting Started 3
Organizing Your Photos 6
Editing Your Photos 8
Getting Started in a Hurry 27

CHAPTER 2: **Importing, Managing, and Saving Photos** **29**
Importing from Cameras 29
Opening Stored Images 35
Creating a New File 39
Using the Organizer 42
Searching for Photos 67
Saving Your Work 70
Backing Up Files 75

CHAPTER 3: **Rotating and Resizing Photos** **79**
Straightening Scanned Photos 79
Rotating Images 82
Straightening the Contents of an Image 84
Cropping Pictures 89
Zooming and Repositioning Your View 97
Changing the Size of an Image 105
Resizing Images for Email and the Web 105

Part Two: Elemental Elements

CHAPTER 4: **The Quick Fix** **117**

The Quick Fix Window... 118

Editing Your Photos 124

Other Fast Fixes 138

Getting Fancy: Effects, Textures, and Frames 143

CHAPTER 5: **Making Selections** **147**

Selecting Everything 148

Selecting Rectangular and Elliptical Areas 149

Selecting Irregularly Sized Areas................................. 151

Selecting with a Brush... 154

Extracting Objects 171

Changing and Moving Selections 172

CHAPTER 6: **Layers: The Heart of Elements** **185**

Understanding Layers 185

Creating Layers.. 191

Managing Layers... 196

Adjustment and Fill Layers....................................... 215

Moving Objects Between Images 219

Part Three: Retouching

CHAPTER 7: **Basic Image Retouching** **227**

Fixing Exposure Problems 228

Controlling the Colors You See 237

Using Levels... 243

Removing Unwanted Color... 250

Choosing Colors 253

Sharpening Images 260

CHAPTER 8: **Elements for Digital Photographers** **271**

The Raw Converter... 272

Blending Exposures 292

Photo Filter 299

Processing Multiple Files... 301

CHAPTER 9: **Retouching: Fine-Tuning Images**........................ **309**

Fixing Blemishes... 309

Applying Patterns.. 324

Recomposing Photos 326

Color Curves: Enhancing Tone and Contrast. 331
Making Colors More Vibrant. 334
Changing an Object's Color 339
Special Effects. 346

CHAPTER 10: **Removing and Adding Color** **349**
Making Color Photos Black and White. 349
Removing Color from Photos. 352
Creating Spot Color 354
Colorizing Black-and-White Photos 359

CHAPTER 11: **Photomerge: Creating Panoramas, Group Shots,**
and More **367**
Creating Panoramas. 368
Merging Different Faces 372
Arranging a Group Shot 375
Tidying Up with Scene Cleaner 376
Combining Photos with Photomerge Compose 379
Correcting Lens Distortion 382
Transforming Images. 387

Part Four: **Artistic Elements**

CHAPTER 12: **Drawing with Brushes, Shapes, and Other Tools** **395**
Picking and Using a Basic Brush 396
Special Brushes. 404
The Impressionist Brush 406
The Pencil Tool 407
The Paint Bucket. 407
Dodging and Burning. 409
Blending and Smudging 411
The Eraser Tools 416
Drawing with Shapes. 420
The Cookie Cutter Tool 429

CHAPTER 13: **Adding Fun and Useful Effects** **433**
Using Filters. 435
Applying Actions and Effects. 454
Adding Layer Styles. 461
Applying Gradients 465
Gradient Maps. 475

CHAPTER 14: **Text in Elements** **479**

Adding Text to an Image. 479

Warping Text. 488

Adding Special Effects 491

Type Masks: Setting an Image in Text. 496

Artistic Text 500

Part Five: **Sharing Images**

CHAPTER 15: **Creating Projects** **509**

Photo Collages 509

Photo Books 519

Greeting Cards 521

Photo Calendars 521

CD/DVD Jackets 522

CD/DVD Labels 523

Facebook Cover 523

Working with the Graphics and Favorites Panels. 526

CHAPTER 16: **Printing Photos** **529**

Getting Ready to Print. 529

Ordering Prints 530

Printing at Home. 533

Printing Multiple Images (Windows) 546

Printing Multiple Images (Mac) 548

CHAPTER 17: **Email and the Web**. **555**

Image Formats and the Web 555

Saving Images for the Web and Email 556

Creating Animated GIFs 563

Emailing Photos 565

CHAPTER 18: **Creating Slideshows** **571**

Full Screen View 572

Organizer Slideshows 574

A Few More Ways to Share. 578

Part Six: **Additional Elements**

CHAPTER 19: **Beyond the Basics** **583**

Graphics Tablets. 583

Stuff from the Internet. 586

Beyond This Book. 589

Part Seven: Appendixes

APPENDIX A: **Installation and Troubleshooting** **593**

Installing Elements in Windows....................................595
Installing Elements on a Mac 596
Scratch Disks...598
Troubleshooting 599

APPENDIX B: **The Organizer, Menu by Menu**

APPENDIX C: **The Editor, Menu by Menu**

NOTE   Appendixes B and C are available from this book's Missing CD page at *www.missingmanuals.com/cds*. (To learn about the Missing CD page, turn to page xxv.)

Index.. **601**

The Missing Credits

ABOUT THE AUTHOR

Barbara Brundage is the author of *Photoshop Elements: The Missing Manual*, an Adobe Community Expert, and a member of Adobe's prerelease groups for Elements 3–13. She's been teaching people how to use Photoshop Elements since it came out in 2001. Barbara first started using Elements to create graphics for use in her day job as a harpist, music publisher, and arranger. Along the way, she joined the large group of people finding a renewed interest in photography thanks to digital cameras. If she can learn to use Elements, you can, too! You can reach her at *barb@barbarabrundage.com* and read her blog at *www.barbarabrundage.com* (sometimes it's even about Photoshop Elements).

ABOUT THE CREATIVE TEAM

Dawn Schanafelt (editor) is assistant editor for the Missing Manual series. When not working, she plays soccer, beads, and causes trouble. Email: *dawn@oreilly.com*.

Kara Ebrahim (production editor) lives, works, and plays in Cambridge, MA. She loves graphic design and all things outdoors. Email: *kebrahim@oreilly.com*.

Julie Van Keuren (proofreader) quit her newspaper job in 2006 to move to Montana and live the freelancing dream. She and her husband, M.H. (who is living the novel-writing dream), have two sons, Dexter and Michael. Email: *little_media@yahoo.com*.

Ron Strauss (indexer) specializes in the indexing of information technology publications of all kinds. Ron is also an accomplished classical violist and lives in Northern California with his wife and fellow indexer, Annie, and his miniature pinscher, Kanga. Email: *rstrauss@mchsi.com*.

Neale Hind (technical reviewer) is a Chartered Accountant and SAP Implementation Consultant who lives in Stamford UK, "the finest stone town in England." After a career break to see his children through their schooling, he currently fills his time with a variety of charitable and community support activities. Favorite quotation: "Insanity is hereditary, you get it from your children" (Sam Levenson, 1911–1980). Email: *neale_hind@yahoo.co.uk*.

ACKNOWLEDGMENTS

Many thanks to Neale Hind for reading this book and giving me the benefit of his advice and corrections. I'm also grateful for the help I received from everyone at Adobe, especially Bob Gager, Deepak Sharad Sawant, Garima Panwar, Rahul Bansai, Akshaya Saxena, Garima Panwar, Andaleeb Fatima, Ankit Gulati, Neeraj Chaudhary, Anwesha Chaudhary, Vaishali Ahuja, and Sourabh Gupta.

Special thanks also to graphic artist Jodi Frye (*lfrye012000@yahoo.com*) for allowing me to reproduce one of her Elements drawings to show what can be done by those with more artistic ability than I have. My gratitude also to Florida's botanical gardens, especially McKee Botanical Garden (*www.mckeegarden.org*), Bok Tower Gardens (*www.boktower.org*), Heathcote Botanical Gardens (*www.heathcotebotanicalgardens.org*), and Harry P. Leu Gardens (*www.leugardens.org*) for creating oases of peace and beauty in our hectic world. Finally, I'd like to thank everyone in the gang over at the Adobe Photoshop Elements support forum for all their help and friendship.

THE MISSING MANUAL SERIES

Missing Manuals are witty, superbly written guides to computer products that don't come with printed manuals (which is just about all of them). Each book features a handcrafted index and cross-references to specific pages (not just chapters). Recent and upcoming titles include:

Access 2013: The Missing Manual by Matthew MacDonald

Adobe Edge Animate: The Missing Manual by Chris Grover

Buying a Home: The Missing Manual by Nancy Conner

Creating a Website: The Missing Manual, Third Edition by Matthew MacDonald

CSS3: The Missing Manual, Third Edition by David Sawyer McFarland

Dreamweaver CS6: The Missing Manual by David Sawyer McFarland

Dreamweaver CC: The Missing Manual by David Sawyer McFarland and Chris Grover

Excel 2013: The Missing Manual by Matthew MacDonald

FileMaker Pro 13: The Missing Manual by Susan Prosser and Stuart Gripman

Flash CS6: The Missing Manual by Chris Grover

Galaxy Tab: The Missing Manual by Preston Gralla

Galaxy S5: The Missing Manual by Preston Gralla

Google+: The Missing Manual by Kevin Purdy

HTML5: The Missing Manual, Second Edition by Matthew MacDonald

iMovie: The Missing Manual by David Pogue and Aaron Miller *iPad: The Missing Manual, Sixth Edition* by J.D. Biersdorfer

iPhone: The Missing Manual, Seventh Edition by David Pogue

iPhone App Development: The Missing Manual by Craig Hockenberry

iPhoto: The Missing Manual by David Pogue and Lesa Snider

iPod: The Missing Manual, Eleventh Edition by J.D. Biersdorfer and David Pogue

iWork: The Missing Manual by Jessica Thornsby and Josh Clark

JavaScript & jQuery: The Missing Manual, Second Edition by David Sawyer McFarland

Kindle Fire HD: The Missing Manual by Peter Meyers

Living Green: The Missing Manual by Nancy Conner

Microsoft Project 2013: The Missing Manual by Bonnie Biafore

Motorola Xoom: The Missing Manual by Preston Gralla

NOOK HD: The Missing Manual by Preston Gralla

Office 2011 for Macintosh: The Missing Manual by Chris Grover

Office 2013: The Missing Manual by Nancy Conner and Matthew MacDonald

OS X Mavericks: The Missing Manual by David Pogue

Personal Investing: The Missing Manual by Bonnie Biafore

Photoshop CS6: The Missing Manual by Lesa Snider

Photoshop CC: The Missing Manual, Second Edition by Lesa Snider

PHP & MySQL: The Missing Manual, Second Edition by Brett McLaughlin

QuickBooks 2015: The Missing Manual by Bonnie Biafore

Switching to the Mac: The Missing Manual, Mavericks Edition by David Pogue

Windows 7: The Missing Manual by David Pogue

Windows 8: The Missing Manual by David Pogue

WordPress: The Missing Manual, Second Edition by Matthew MacDonald

Your Body: The Missing Manual by Matthew MacDonald

Your Brain: The Missing Manual by Matthew MacDonald

Your Money: The Missing Manual by J.D. Roth

For a full list of all Missing Manuals in print, go to *www.missingmanuals.com/library.html*.

Introduction

When Photoshop Elements was first released back in 2001, it became a runaway success. It's easy to see why: Elements gives people all the tools they need to get the very best from their photographs. It lets you take a ho-hum shot and give it some wow.

If you run a graphics studio or a large professional photography business, then you need the full version of Photoshop. But for most people who aren't creating images for commercial printing, Elements offers a very useful toolkit at an appealing price. Even if you already have a photo-management program like Adobe's Lightroom or Apple's Aperture, you'll find that Elements offers tools for certain tasks that you can't perform with those programs.

Since Adobe introduced their new Creative Cloud monthly subscription plan for Photoshop, a lot of people are looking for an alternative that doesn't require paying every month forever. If you're one of them, Elements may be a good fit for you, but you need to be aware that a lot of features and controls are pretty well hidden in Elements. It's a capable, midlevel image-editing program, but you need to know where to find things, since Elements is laid out quite differently from Photoshop and some features have different names. (For instance, if you've used Photoshop, what you know as Smart Sharpen is called Adjust Sharpness in Elements.) Happily, you have this book to guide you.

Why Photoshop Elements?

Adobe Photoshop is the granddaddy of all image-editing programs. It's the Big Cheese, the industry standard against which everything else is measured. Every photo you've seen in a book or magazine in the past 15 years or so has almost certainly passed through Photoshop on its way to being printed. You just can't buy anything that gives you more control over pictures than Photoshop does.

But Photoshop has some big drawbacks: It's darned hard to learn, it's expensive (and now a lot of people are turned off by Adobe's new subscription-only Creative Cloud plan), and many of its features are just plain overkill if you don't work on pictures for a living.

For several years, Adobe tried to find a way to cram many of Photoshop's marvelous powers into a package that normal people could use. Finding the right formula was a slow process. First came PhotoDeluxe, a program that was lots of fun but came up short when you wanted to fine-tune *how* the program worked. Adobe tried again with Photoshop LE, which many people felt included all the difficulty of full Photoshop, but still gave too little of what you needed to do top-notch work.

Finally—sort of like Goldilocks—Adobe got it just right with Photoshop Elements, which took off like crazy because it offers so much of Photoshop's power in a program that almost anyone can learn. With Elements, you, too, can work with the same wonderful tools that the pros use. Elements has been around for quite a while now and, in each new version, Adobe has added lots of push-button-easy ways to correct and improve your photos.

What You Can Do with Elements 13

Elements not only lets you make photos look great, but it also helps you organize them and gives you some pretty neat projects in which to use them. The program even comes loaded with lots of easy ways to share photos. The list of what Elements can do is pretty impressive. You can use it to:

- Enhance photos by editing, cropping, and color-correcting them, including fixing exposure and color problems.

- Add all kinds of special effects to images, like turning a garden-variety photo into a drawing, painting, or even a tile mosaic.

- Combine photos into a panorama or montage.

- Move someone from one photo to another, and even remove people (your ex, perhaps) from last year's holiday photos.

- Repair and restore old and damaged photos.

- Organize photos and assign keywords to them so you can search by subject or name.

- Add text to images and turn them into things like greeting cards and flyers.

- Create slideshows to share with friends, regardless of whether they use Windows, a Mac, or even just a cellphone.

- Automatically resize photos so they're ready to send either as regular email attachments or in specially designed emails.

- Create digital artwork from scratch, even without a photo to work from.

- Create and edit graphics for websites.

- Create wonderful projects like collages and calendars that you can print or digitally share with friends. Scrapbookers, get ready to be wowed.

It's worth noting, though, that there are still a few things Elements *can't* do. While the program handles text quite competently, at least as photo-editing programs go, it's still no substitute for QuarkXPress, InDesign, or any other desktop-publishing program. And Elements can do an amazing job of fixing problems in photos, but only if you give it something to work with. If your photo is totally overexposed, blurry, and the top of everyone's head is cut off, there's a limit to what even Elements can do to salvage it. (C'mon, be fair.) But you're more likely to be surprised by what Elements *can* fix than by what it can't.

▮ What's New in Elements 13

The most important changes in Elements 13 are under the hood. For example, for the first time, Elements is now a 64-bit program for both Macs and Windows computers. What does that mean and why is it important?

For many years, the great majority of computer programs were 32 bit, including all versions of Elements prior to version 12 (where only the Mac version was 64-bit). The most important disadvantage of 32-bit programs is that, no matter how much RAM your computer has, a 32-bit program can only see and take advantage of about 3 GB of RAM. So even if you had, say, 16 GB of RAM, older versions of Elements might still stutter at times, because they couldn't use that extra 13 GB. 64-bit programs don't have this limitation. (There's still a limit to how much RAM 64-bit programs can use, but the formula is complex and depends on other variables besides how much RAM is in a computer. All you need to know is that it's much, much higher.) If you have a Windows computer that's still running a 32-bit operating system, no problem. When you buy Elements, you get both 32- and 64-bit versions included. (All Macs have been 64-bits for some time now.)

TIP To find out which version of Windows your computer is running, go to *http://support.microsoft.com/ kb/827218* and look under the "Automatic version detection results" heading.

Also, Elements 13 is designed to display properly on ultra-high resolution screens, like Apple's Retina Display and Windows equivalents. If you have one of these screens, you know that looking at previous versions of Elements was like watching regular-definition TV on an HDTV screen–everything looked a little soft. Now everything should be just as sharply focused for you as it is for people using lower-resolution displays, and the menus should be large enough to read easily.

But that's not all. Adobe has also found time to add a number of new features, including a couple that people have been requesting for years. Here's a brief rundown of the main changes in Elements 13:

- **64-bits for all 64-bit operating systems**. As explained above, this should make Elements perform significantly better.

> **NOTE** As part of this technical update, Adobe has written Elements 13 to require at least Windows 7. So if you're still running Windows XP or Vista, you need to stick to Elements 12 or earlier. And Macs must be running at least OS X 10.8 (Mountain Lion).

- **Content-Aware Fill.** People have been begging Adobe for years to include this popular Photoshop feature in Elements. It's available in Elements 13, but it's pretty well hidden; page 321 explains where to find it.

- **Elements Live (page 22).** If you look at the top of the Editor or the Organizer, you'll see a tab labeled "eLive." This is a new section devoted to useful tutorials, both basic and advanced, that also gives you a look at some fine photography for inspiration.

- **Effects and frames in Quick Fix**. Elements 12 brought the ability to apply special effects and frames to your photos in the Quick Fix window. Elements 13 adds several *new* effects that let you easily create popular photo styles.

- **New slideshows (page 574) and emailing (page 565) in the Organizer**. Elements' slideshow and email features got a total makeover in this version. Now both the Mac and Windows versions have the same slideshow feature, which is much simpler to use than the old Slide Show Editor. And you can now email files from Elements using any email program *without* having to hassle with aggravating Adobe Mail verification codes.

- **Facebook Cover Photo (page 523).** If you use Facebook, (and who doesn't?), you know how it's become quite the thing to create clever or amusing profile and cover images (the ones you see at the top of your personal page). Elements 13 includes a new Create project that lets you choose and customize a theme for these photos and then upload them directly to Facebook.

- **Refine Selection Brush tool (page 177)**. Elements 13 includes this brand-new brush, which helps you tweak difficult selections.

- **Photomerge Compose (page 379)**. One of the most popular uses for Elements is to move people or objects from one photo to another one. Elements 13 brings a new kind of Photomerge that walks you through this process and helps adjust the lighting in the two images for a more realistic result.

- **Updated Crop tool (page 90)**. This Elements stalwart got a significant makeover in Elements 13. Now it can suggest various possible crops for those who aren't sure just how they'd like to trim their photos.

- **Organizer updates**. Adobe has refined some of the Organizer features introduced in Elements 12. For instance, albums and folders aren't jumbled up together anymore—each has its own tab. The Tags section is now easier to use, and you get more suggestions about using Adobe's online sharing service, Revel.

- **New Organizer view.** Elements 13 brings a new way to view your photos in the Organizer: Adaptive Grid (page 6). This view lets you see all your photos edge to edge, without the gray background and all the distracting details like the image's name and date below the photo.

- **New guided edits**. Guided Edit mode—where Elements walks you through various photo projects and editing tasks—includes three great new edits for creating atmospheric black-and-white images, producing stylish effects with only a single color, or keeping a single object in color.

- **A few deletions**. A lot of traditional Elements features disappeared in Elements 12 (like Color Variations and the Magic Extractor). There aren't so many new missing features this time, but there are a few: You can no longer scan directly into Elements using TWAIN if you have a 64-bit version of Windows, or use Photo Mail in any version of Windows. The Slide Show Editor is also gone (the new slideshow feature is much easier to use, but it doesn't give you as much control over the final product).

■ Elements vs. Photoshop

You could easily get confused about the differences between Elements and the full version of Adobe Photoshop. Because Elements is so much less expensive, and because many of its more advanced controls are tucked away, a lot of Photoshop aficionados tend to view Elements as some kind of toy version of their program. They couldn't be more wrong: Elements *is* Photoshop, it's just Photoshop adapted for use with a home printer and the Web.

The most important difference between Elements and Photoshop is that Elements doesn't let you work or save files in CMYK mode, which is the format used for commercial color printing. (CMYK stands for Cyan, Magenta, Yellow, and blacK.) Your inkjet printer also uses those ink colors to print, but it expects you to give it an RGB file, which is what Elements creates. Don't worry—this is all explained in Chapter 7.

Elements also lacks several tools that are basic staples in any commercial art department, like the extra color control you can get from Selective Color Adjustment layers and the Pen tool's special talent for creating vector paths. Also, layer styles (the feature you use to create some special effects, like drop shadows and bevels) don't have as many settings in Elements as they do in Photoshop. (In Elements, you start with a given preset style and make changes to it; in Photoshop, you can create a style from scratch.) The same holds true for a handful of other Elements tools.

And although Elements is all most people need to create graphics for the Web, it doesn't come with the advanced Photoshop tools that let you do things like automatically slice images into smaller pieces so they display faster online. If you use Elements, then you'll have to look for another program to help with that.

If you're experienced with Photoshop and looking for an alternative that doesn't require a subscription, it's a good idea to download the trial version of Elements first, just to be sure it can do everything you want. If you want to be able to work with layers in 16-bit files, for example, Elements probably isn't for you. On the other hand, you won't find many alternatives that offer that capability, either, and you may need to decide how much you're willing to give up in exchange for getting away from Adobe's Creative Cloud.

■ The Key to Learning Elements

Elements may not be quite as powerful as Photoshop, but it's still a complex program, filled with more features than most people ever use. The good news is that the Quick Fix window (Chapter 4) lets you get started right away, even if you don't understand every last option Quick Fix presents you with. You also get Guided Edit mode (page 23), which provides step-by-step walkthroughs of popular editing tasks, like sharpening a photo or cropping it to fit on standard photo paper.

As for the program's more complex features, the key to learning how to use Elements—or any other program, for that matter—is to focus only on what you need to know for the task you're currently trying to accomplish.

For example, if you're trying to use Quick Fix to adjust the color of your photo and crop it, don't worry that you don't get the concept of layers yet. You won't learn to do everything in Elements in a day or even a week. The rest will wait until you need it, so take your time and don't fret about what's not important to you right now. You'll find it much easier to master Elements if you go slowly and concentrate on one thing at a time.

If you're totally new to the program, then you'll find only three or four big concepts in this book that you really need to understand if you want to get the most out of Elements. It may take a little time for some of them to sink in—resolution and layers, for instance, aren't the most intuitive concepts in the world—but once they click, they'll seem so obvious that you'll wonder why they were confusing at first. That's perfectly normal, so persevere. You *can* do this, and there's nothing in this book that you can't understand with a little bit of careful reading.

The very best way to learn Elements is just to dive right in and play with it. Try all the different filters to see what they do. Add a filter on top of another filter. Click all the different tools and try them. You don't even need to have a photo open to do this. See page 39 to learn how to make an image from scratch in Elements, and keep an eye out for the many downloadable practice images you'll find on this book's companion website at *www.missingmanuals.com/cds*. Go crazy—you can stack up as many filters, effects, and layer styles as you want without crashing the program.

■ About This Book

Elements is a cool program that's lots of fun to use, but figuring out how to make it do what you want is another matter. Elements' Help files are pretty good, but of course you need to know what you're looking for to use them to your best advantage. (Elements' Help files are online; you can download a PDF of them from Adobe's Elements support pages at *www.adobe.com/support/photoshopelements*.)

You'll find a slew of Elements titles at your local bookstore, but most of them assume that you know quite a bit about the basics of photography and/or digital imaging. It's much easier to find good intermediate books about Elements than books designed to get you going with the program.

That's where this book comes in. It's intended to make learning Elements easier by avoiding technical jargon as much as possible, and explaining *why* and *when* you'll want to use (or avoid) certain features of the program. This approach is as useful to people who are advanced photographers as it is to those who are just getting started with their first digital cameras.

> **NOTE** This book periodically recommends *other* books, covering topics too specialized or tangential for a manual about Elements. Careful readers may notice that not all of these titles are published by Missing Manual parent O'Reilly Media. While we're happy to mention other Missing Manuals and books in the O'Reilly family, if there's a great book out there that doesn't happen to be published by O'Reilly, we'll still let you know about it.

You'll also find instructions throughout this book that refer to files you can download from the Missing Manual website (*www.missingmanuals.com*) so you can practice the techniques you're reading about. And in various spots, you'll find several different kinds of short articles (a.k.a. boxes). The ones labeled "Up to Speed" are designed to help newcomers to Elements, or they explain concepts with which veterans are probably already familiar. Those labeled "Power Users' Clinic" cover more advanced topics that won't be of much interest to casual photographers.

A Note About Operating Systems

This book covers using Elements with both Windows computers and Macs, and you'll see both platforms represented in the illustrations. (Frankly, you'll see more Mac screenshots here, simply because some things are easier to read in the Mac version of the program. For example, pop-out menus are more likely to have a white background on a Mac instead of a dark one.) The Editor (the part of Elements where you tweak photos) works exactly the same way regardless of what kind of computer you're using, but there are some differences in the Organizer and the projects available to you, and those are noted as necessary. Also, most of the keyboard shortcuts you use to run commands are different in Windows and on Macs; page xxii explains how those shortcuts are notated in this book.

So remember: It doesn't matter which version of the program is shown in the illustrations; unless this book says otherwise, the differences are just slight cosmetic ones, like the fact that you close Mac program windows by clicking a button on their left, whereas in Windows the button is on the right.

> **NOTE** Adobe's video-editing program, *Premiere* Elements, also uses the Elements Organizer, and if you install both programs, your Photoshop Elements menus will show a lot of Premiere Elements choices, too. These are normally turned off when you install only Photoshop Elements, but if they get turned on by mistake and you don't care to see them, you can turn most of them off by launching the Organizer and going to Edit→Preferences→Editing on a PC or Elements Organizer→Preferences→Editing on a Mac. (Appendix B, available at *www.missingmanuals. com/cds*, explains all the Organizer's menus. Appendix C, also online, covers the Editor's menus.)

About the Outline

This book is divided into seven parts, each focusing on a different kind of task:

- **Part One: Introduction to Elements.** The first part of this book helps you get started with the program. Chapter 1 shows how to navigate Elements' slightly confusing layout and mish-mash of programs within programs. You'll learn how to decide where to start and how to customize Elements so it best suits your working style. You'll also read about some important keyboard shortcuts and where to look for help when you get stuck. Chapter 2 covers how to get photos into Elements, the basics of organizing them, and how to open files and create new images from scratch. You'll also find out how to save and back up images. Chapter 3 explains how to rotate and crop photos, and includes a primer on that most important digital imaging concept—resolution.

- **Part Two: Elemental Elements.** Chapter 4 shows how to use the Quick Fix window to dramatically improve your photos. Chapter 5 and Chapter 6 cover two key concepts that you'll use throughout this book: making selections and working with layers.

- **Part Three: Retouching.** Having Elements is like having a darkroom on your computer. In Chapter 7, you'll learn how to make basic corrections, such as fixing exposure, adjusting color, sharpening images, and removing dust and scratches. Chapter 8 covers topics unique to people who use digital cameras, like converting raw files and batch-processing photos. In Chapter 9, you'll move on to more sophisticated fixes, like using the Clone Stamp tool to make repairs, making photos livelier by adjusting their color intensity, and adjusting light and shadows in images. Chapter 10 shows you how to convert color images to black and white, and how to tint and colorize black-and-white photos. Chapter 11 explains how to use Elements' Photomerge feature to create a panorama from several photos, and how to correct perspective problems in images.

- **Part Four: Artistic Elements.** This part covers the fun stuff: painting on photos and drawing shapes (Chapter 12), using filters and effects to create artistic looks (Chapter 13), and adding text to images (Chapter 14).

- **Part Five: Sharing Images.** Once you've created a great image in Elements, you'll want to share it, so this part is about how to create fun projects like collages (Chapter 15), how to get the most out of your printer (Chapter 16), how to create files for emailing and posting online (Chapter 17), and how to make and share slideshows (Chapter 18).

- **Part Six: Additional Elements.** You can get hundreds of plug-ins and additional styles, brushes, and other nifty tools to customize your copy of Elements and increase its abilities; the Internet and your local bookstore are chock-full of additional info. Chapter 19 offers a look at some of these resources, as well as information about using a graphics tablet with Elements, and suggests some places to turn after you finish this book.

- **Part Seven: Appendixes.** Appendix A helps you get your copy of Elements up and running, and suggests what to do if it starts misbehaving. Appendixes B and C—which you can download from this book's Missing CD web page (see page xxv)—cover all the menu items in the Organizer and Editor, respectively.

For Newcomers to Elements

This book contains lots of information, and if you're new to Elements, it can be a little overwhelming. But you don't need to digest it all at once, especially if you've never used any kind of photo-editing program before. So what do you need to read first? Here's a simple five-step way to use this book if you're brand new to photo editing:

1. **Read all of Chapter 1.**

   That's important for understanding how to get around in Elements.

2. **If your photos aren't on your computer already, then read about the Photo Downloader in Chapter 2 (page 30).**

   The Downloader gets photos from your camera's memory card into Elements.

3. **If you want to organize your photos, then read about the Organizer (also in Chapter 2, starting on page 42).**

   It doesn't matter where your photos are right now. If you want to use Elements to label and keep track of them, then read Chapter 2.

4. **When you're ready to edit your photos, read Chapters 3 and 4.**

   Chapter 3 explains how to adjust your view of photos in the Editor. Chapter 4 shows you how to use the Quick Fix window to easily edit and correct photos. Guided Edit (page 23) can also be very helpful when you're just getting started. If you skipped Chapter 2 because you're not using the Organizer, then go back there and read the part about saving photos (page 70) so you don't lose your work.

5. **When you're ready to print or share your photos, flip to the chapters on sharing images.**

   Chapter 16 covers printing, both at home and from online services. Chapter 17 explains how to email photos, and Chapter 18 teaches you how to create slideshows.

That's all you need to get started. You can come back and pick up the rest of the info in the book as you get comfortable with Elements and want to explore more of the wonderful things you can do with it.

The Very Basics

This book assumes that you know how to perform basic activities on your computer like clicking and double-clicking your mouse buttons and dragging objects onscreen. Here's a quick refresher:

To *click* means to move the pointer of your mouse or trackpad cursor over an object on your screen, and then press the left mouse or trackpad button once. To *right-click* means to press the right mouse button once, which calls up a menu of special features. To *double-click* means to press the left button twice, quickly, without moving the mouse between clicks. To *drag* means to click an object and then to hold down the left button while you use the mouse to move the object.

Most onscreen selection buttons are pretty obvious, but you may not be familiar with *radio buttons*: To choose an option, click the little empty circle next to it.

In Elements, you'll often want to use keyboard shortcuts to save time, and this book tells you about these shortcuts when they exist (and Elements has a lot). In this book, unless otherwise specified, keyboard shortcuts are always presented as Windows keystroke/Mac keystroke. So if you see a sentence like, "Press Ctrl+S/⌘-S to save your file," that means that if you use Windows, you should hold down the Ctrl key while pressing the S key, and if you have a Mac, you should hold down the ⌘ key while pressing the S key. There's one slight exception to this: When you see "right-click/Control-click," if you have a Mac and a two-button mouse, you can right-click. But if you have a one-button mouse, you can *Control-click* instead—that means to press the Control key on your keyboard and then press your mouse button once.

If you're comfortable with basic concepts like these, then you're ready to get started with this book.

About→These→Arrows

Throughout this book (and the Missing Manual series) you'll see sentences like this: "In the Editor, select Filter→Artistic→Paint Daubs." This is a shorthand way of helping you find files, folders, and menu items without having to read through excruciatingly long, bureaucratic-style instructions. So the sample sentence above is a short way of saying this: "In the Editor component of Elements, in the menu bar at the top of the screen, click the word 'Filter.' In the menu that appears, choose the Artistic menu item, and then go to Paint Daubs in the pop-out menu." Figure I-1 shows you an example in action.

Mac file paths are shown using the same arrows. Windows file paths, on the other hand, are shown in the conventional Windows style, so if you see, "Go to *C:\Documents and Settings\[your user name]\My Documents\My Pictures*," that means you should go to your C drive, open the Documents and Settings folder, look for your user account folder, and then find the My Documents folder. In that folder, open the My Pictures folder that's inside it.

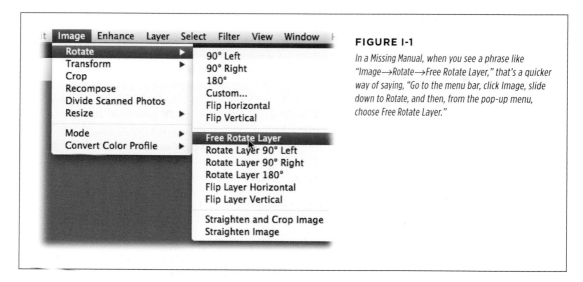

FIGURE I-1

In a Missing Manual, when you see a phrase like "Image→Rotate→Free Rotate Layer," that's a quicker way of saying, "Go to the menu bar, click Image, slide down to Rotate, and then, from the pop-up menu, choose Free Rotate Layer."

When there are different file paths for Windows 7 and 8, you'll find them all listed in this book. Like keyboard shortcuts, file paths are shown as Windows file path/ Mac file path when all versions of Windows use the same file path. Otherwise, all the different versions are specified.

If you're using a Mac, there's one special challenge to finding some of the files mentioned in this book—specifically, the ones located in the Library folders. (Figure I-2 explains.) Also, if you buy Elements from the Mac App Store, all the files are actually inside the application itself, which means your file paths will be different. (This book covers the version of Elements that was released in September 2014, so you won't see so much information about App Store version's file paths, since that information wasn't available when this book was written. Check this book's Missing CD page at *www.missingmanuals.com/cds* for updated information after the App Store version is released.)

NOTE The keyboard shortcuts listed in this book are the official Adobe shortcuts. However, if you have a Mac with an abbreviated keyboard (without a 10-key section on the right), like a laptop keyboard or the smaller Bluetooth keyboards, you need to add the fn key to shortcuts that use the F-keys on the top row of your keyboard. So, for instance, while the shortcut for Full Screen View in the Organizer is ⌘-F11, on a MacBook Pro, you would press fn-⌘-F11 instead.

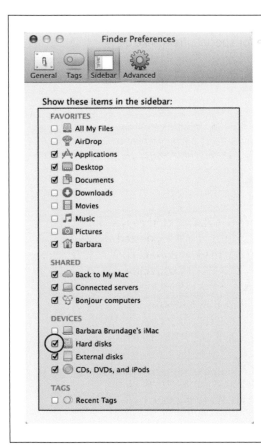

FIGURE I-2

In OS X, Apple has made it a little harder to find your Library folders.

The one you'll need most often resides at the very top level of your hard drive. This folder isn't exactly hidden, but it doesn't appear unless you change your settings to make it accessible. To do that, in the Finder, go to Finder→Preferences→Sidebar and, in the Devices section, turn on the "Hard disks" checkbox (circled). After that, you can always find the Library folder by just clicking the name of your hard drive in the list on the left side of a Finder window.

The other Library folder you may need is the one for your user account, which is a hidden file. To make it visible, in the Finder, open the Go menu and then press the Option key. Your user account's Library folder will appear in the menu just below your Home folder.

About the Online Resources

As the owner of a Missing Manual, you've got more than just a book to read. Online, you'll find example files so you can get some hands-on experience. You can also communicate with the Missing Manual team and tell us what you love (or hate) about this book. Head over to *www.missingmanuals.com*, or go directly to one of the following sections.

Missing CD web page

This book doesn't have a CD pasted inside the back cover, but you're not missing out on anything. Go to *www.missingmanuals.com/cds* to download sample files mentioned in this book, as well as a few tutorials and two additional appendixes. And so you don't wear down your fingers typing long web addresses, this book's Missing CD page also offers a list of clickable links to the websites mentioned in this book.

Registration

If you register this book at oreilly.com, you'll be eligible for special offers—like discounts on future editions of *Photoshop Elements: The Missing Manual*. Registering takes only a few clicks. To get started, go to *http://oreilly.com/register*.

Feedback

Got questions? Need more information? Fancy yourself a book reviewer? On our Feedback page, you can get expert answers to questions that come to you while reading, share your thoughts on this book, and find groups for folks who share your interest in Elements. To have your say, go to *www.missingmanuals.com/feedback*.

Errata

In an effort to keep this book as up to date and accurate as possible, each time we print more copies, we'll make any confirmed corrections readers have suggested. We also note such changes on the book's website, so you can mark important corrections in your copy of the book. To report an error or view existing corrections, go to *http://missingmanuals.com/library.html*, click the title of this book, and then click the View/Submit Errata link on the right side of the page that appears.

▉ Safari® Books Online

Safari Books Online is an on-demand digital library that lets you easily search over 7,500 technology and creative reference books and videos to find the answers you need quickly.

With a subscription, you can read any page and watch any video from our library online. Read books on your cellphone and mobile devices. Access new titles before they're available for print and get exclusive access to manuscripts in development, and post feedback for the authors. Copy and paste code samples, organize your favorites, download chapters, bookmark key sections, create notes, print out pages, and benefit from tons of other time-saving features.

Introduction to Elements

CHAPTER 1:
Finding Your Way Around Elements

CHAPTER 2:
Importing, Managing, and Saving Photos

CHAPTER 3:
Rotating and Resizing Photos

Finding Your Way Around Elements

Photoshop Elements lets you do practically anything you want to digital images. You can colorize black-and-white photos, remove demonic red-eyed stares, or distort the facial features of people who've been mean to you. The downside is that all those options can make it tough to find your way around Elements, especially if you're new to the program.

This chapter helps get you oriented. You'll learn what to expect when you launch the program and how to use Elements to fix photos with just a couple of keystrokes. You'll also find out how to use Guided Edit mode to get started editing images. Along the way, you'll find out about some of Elements' basic controls and how to get to the program's Help files.

▉ Getting Started

On a Windows computer, when you install Elements (page 595 explains how), the installer creates a desktop shortcut for you. Just double-click that shortcut to launch Elements. You can also go to the Start menu and click the Adobe Photoshop Elements 13 icon. (If you don't see Elements in the Start menu, then click the arrow next to All Programs, and you should see it in the pop-up menu.)

On a Mac, you can launch Elements as the last step in the installation process, or you can go to Applications→Adobe Photoshop Elements 13 and double-click its icon there. (Incidentally, the only other thing in that folder besides the uninstaller is a folder called Support Files. That's where you'll find the Editor application, which you'll learn about starting on page 8.) If you want to make a Dock icon for future convenience, start Elements and then go to the Dock and click the program's icon. Keep holding the mouse button down until you see a menu, and then choose Options→Keep in Dock.

> **NOTE** Elements 13 uses the same light color scheme Adobe has used since Elements 11. Unfortunately, there's no way to change it if you prefer a darker look.

Which Version of Elements Do You Have?

This book covers Photoshop Elements 13. If you're not sure which version you have, the easiest way to find out is to look at the program's icon (the one you click to launch Elements). The icon for Elements 13 is a teal square with a white, stylized outline of a camera on it.

If you're still not sure, in Windows, click once on the Elements icon on your desktop, and Windows displays the full name of the program—including the version number—below the icon, if it wasn't already visible. You can also check the Windows Start menu, where Elements is listed along with its version number. Or, if Elements is already running, go to Help→About Photoshop Elements.

On a Mac, look in your Applications folder to see the version number. If Elements is already running, go to Photoshop Elements Editor→About Photoshop Elements.

If you have an earlier version of Elements, you can still use this book because a lot of the basic editing procedures are the same. But Elements 13 has been updated in many ways, so you'd almost certainly feel more comfortable with a reference book for the version you have. There are Missing Manuals for Elements 3 through 12, too, and you may prefer to track down the book that matches your version of Elements. (For Elements 6 and 8, there are separate editions for the Mac and Windows versions.) You can get a copy from *www.missingmanuals. com*, any online bookseller, or your neighborhood bookstore.

The Welcome Screen

When you launch Elements for the first time, you're greeted by the Welcome screen (Figure 1-1). This screen is a launcher that lets you choose which part of Elements you want to use:

- **Organizer**. Click this button to start the Organizer, which lets you store and organize your image files. It's explained in detail starting on page 42.

- **Photo Editor**. Click this button to start the Editor, which lets you modify images. See page 8 for more about this part of Elements.

It's easy to hop back and forth between the Editor and the Organizer, which you can think of as the two halves of Elements. But in some ways, they function as two separate programs. For example, if you start in the Organizer, then once you pick a photo to edit, you have to wait a few seconds while the Editor starts up. And when you have both the Editor and the Organizer running, quitting the Editor doesn't close the Organizer—you have to close it separately.

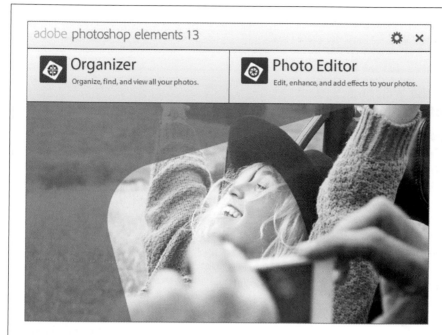

FIGURE 1-1

*Elements' Welcome
screen.*

*The images at the bottom
are dynamic, meaning
they may change, but the
buttons at the top and the
gear icon for the settings
are always the same.
Sometimes you may see
ads for special offers for
other Adobe programs.*

At the bottom center of the Editor's main window is a button that you can click to launch the Organizer (or switch over to it if it's already running). If you want to do the opposite—get photos from the Organizer over to the Editor—select the photo(s) in the Organizer, and then click the Editor button at the bottom of the screen, or right-click/Control-click one of the selected thumbnails and choose "Edit with Photoshop Elements Editor." Either way, your photo(s) appear in the Editor so you can work on them. Once both programs are running, you can also just click the Editor's or the Organizer's icon in the Windows taskbar or the Mac Dock to switch from one to the other.

One helpful thing to keep in mind is that Adobe built Elements around the assumption that most people work on their photos in the following way: First, you bring photos into the Organizer to sort and keep track of them. Next, you open photos in the Editor to work on them, and then save them back to the Organizer when you've finished making changes. You can use a different workflow, of course—by opening photos directly in the Editor and bypassing the Organizer altogether, for example—but you may feel like you're always swimming against the current. (The next chapter has a few hints for disabling some of Elements' features if you find that they're getting in your way.)

NOTE In most countries, the first time you launch either the Editor or the Organizer, Elements presents you with Elements Live (a.k.a. eLive), an inspirational and tutorial section explained on page 22. To start organizing your photos in the Organizer, just click the Media tab at the top of the screen. In the Editor, just click any of the tabs at the top of the screen besides eLive.

Say Goodbye to the Welcome Screen

How do I get rid of the Welcome screen?

If you get to feeling welcomed enough, you may want to turn off the Welcome screen so you don't have to click through it every time you start Elements. To tell the Welcome screen you don't want to see it anymore, click the Settings icon (the gear) in the screen's upper-right corner. A section of the window slides open to display controls that let you choose to have the Editor or the Organizer launch from now on instead of the Welcome screen. Just pick the program you want from the drop-down menu, and then click Done.

If you change your mind later on about how you want Elements to open, in either the Editor or the Organizer, go to Help→Welcome Screen, and then head back to the Settings menu described previously and make your change.

You can also save a little of your system resources by making direct shortcuts to the Editor and Organizer programs and skipping the Welcome screen entirely. To do that, in Windows go to *C:\Program Files\Adobe*, and then right-click the icon for the program you want and choose Create Desktop Shortcut. On a Mac, the easiest way is to create a Dock icon while the program is running, as explained on page 598.

■ Organizing Your Photos

The Organizer is where your photos come into Elements *and* go out again when it's time to print, edit, or email them. The Organizer catalogs and keeps track of your photos, and you automatically return to it for many activities that involve sharing photos, like emailing them (page 565) or creating a slideshow with them (page 571). The Organizer's main window (Figure 1-2) lets you view your photos, sort them into albums, and assign keyword labels to them.

The Organizer got a complete makeover in Elements 11, so if you're upgrading from Elements 10 or older, it's pretty much a whole new ballgame compared to the Organizer you knew before. In Elements 13, Adobe gives you a whole new way of seeing your photos in the Organizer, called the Adaptive Grid, which you can see in Figure 1-2. You can switch between this view and the old grid view found in earlier versions of Elements. Page 44 explains how. The next chapter shows you how to use the Organizer to import and organize photos, and online Appendix B covers all the Organizer's different menu options (head to *www.missingmanuals.com/cds* to download it). However, it's important to understand that you don't *have* to use the Organizer if you don't want to. Lots of people don't, for a variety of reasons. Page 48 explains some of the arguments for and against it.

The Photo Downloader

Elements has yet another component that you may have already seen if you've plugged a camera into your computer after installing Elements: the Photo Downloader (Figure 1-3), which helps get photos into the Organizer directly from your camera's memory card.

FIGURE 1-2

The Organizer lets you arrange and sort photos by the people, places, and events they represent, as well as assign keyword tags and categories.

This is Media view, which is where your photos go when you first import them to the Organizer. (Adobe calls the different areas of the Organizer "views.") This image shows Media view's new Adaptive Grid mode. Page 44 explains the Organizer's viewing options.

FIGURE 1-3

Adobe's Photo Downloader is yet another program you get when you install Elements. Its job is to pull photos from your camera (or other storage device) into the Organizer.

To use the Downloader in Windows, just click "Organize and Edit using Adobe Elements Organizer 13.0" (circled) when this AutoPlay dialog box appears.

On a Mac, you launch the Downloader from the Organizer by going to File→"Get Photos and Videos"→"From Camera or Card Reader."

After the Downloader does its thing, you end up in the Organizer.

In Windows, the Downloader is one of your options in the Windows dialog box that you see when you connect a device. If you want to use the Downloader, then just choose it from the list.

To launch the Downloader on a Mac, in the Organizer, go to File→"Get Photos and Videos"→"From Camera or Card Reader." There's no way to make the Downloader run automatically on a Mac—you have to go through the Organizer to start it.

You can read more about the Downloader in Chapter 2 starting on page 30. If you plan to use the Organizer to catalog photos and assign keywords to them, then reading that section can help you avoid hair-pulling moments.

CHANGING OF THE GUARD

Adobe Revel

For several versions of Elements, Adobe strongly urged everyone to use Photoshop.com, which let you post photos online, back them up, and sync them between computers. Photoshop.com is gone now—it's been replaced by Adobe's online service Revel.

In Elements 13, you can use Revel for many of the things you used Photoshop.com for, but it's not exactly the same. One major difference is that you can access your Revel-stored photos from many different devices, including your smartphone, not just from Elements and your web browser. You get 2 GB of free storage space from Revel. Beyond that you pay a monthly subscription fee. Page 57 has the lowdown on Revel and how to use it.

If you're looking for the video tutorials that used to be available via Elements' Inspiration Browser, they're gone, too, but you can watch tutorials at *http://tv.adobe.com* instead.

◾ Editing Your Photos

The Editor is the other main component of Elements. This is the fun part of the program, where you get to adjust, transform, and generally glamorize photos, and where you can create original artwork from scratch with drawing tools and shapes.

The Editor has four different modes:

- **eLive.** Elements Live (abbreviated "eLive" in the tab at the top of your screen) is a new feature in Elements 13. When you click this tab, you're presented with a variety of tutorials for using Elements and some examples of fancy photography and editing to help inspire you. It's a collection of interesting stuff from Adobe and from many different Internet sites. This is where you start the first time you launch the Editor. To move on to working with your photos, just click one of the other tabs at the top of the window; they're explained in the following bullet points. There's more about Elements Live on page 22.

- **Quick Fix**. For many Elements beginners, Quick Fix (Figure 1-4) ends up being their main workspace. It's where Adobe has gathered together the basic tools you need to improve most photos. You can even add frames, special effects, and textures to your photos here. This is also one of the two places in Elements where you can have a before-and-after view while you work (the other is Guided Edit, described next). Chapter 4 gives you all the details on using Quick Fix. The first time you launch the Editor, you start out in Quick Fix mode.

FIGURE 1-4

The Quick Fix window.

To compare your fixes with the original photo, fire up one of the two Before & After views, which you get to by clicking the View menu in the upper left.

NOTE   In some places, Adobe refers to Quick Fix mode as "Quick Edit mode" instead. Those are simply two different names for the same thing. This book always calls it Quick Fix mode.

- **Guided Edit**. This window can be a big help if you're a newcomer to Elements. It provides step-by-step walkthroughs of popular projects such as cropping photos and removing blemishes; see page 23 later in this chapter for an intro. Guided Edit also hosts some fun special effects and workflows for more advanced users (see page 458).

- **Expert**. This mode gives you access to Elements' most sophisticated tools. You have far more ways to work on your photo in Expert mode than in Quick Fix, and if you're fussy, this is where you'll do most of your retouching work. Most of the Quick Fix commands are also available via menus in the Expert mode window (shown in Figure 1-5).

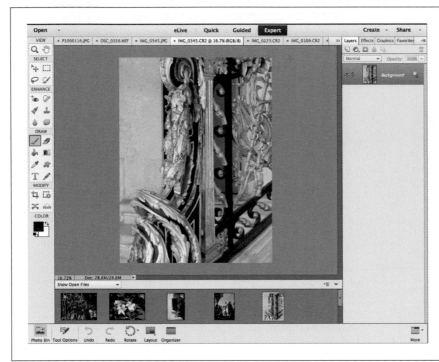

FIGURE 1-5

The main Elements editing window, which Adobe calls Expert mode. This is where you have access to all of Elements' editing features.

This screenshot shows what you see on first entering the Custom Workspace, explained in the next section (page 12). You can customize your workspace quite a bit from this starting point.

You switch modes by clicking the Quick, Guided, and Expert tabs at the top of the Elements window. The rest of this chapter covers some of the Editor's basic concepts and key tools.

> **TIP** If you leave a photo open in the Editor, then when you switch back to the Organizer, you'll see a red band with a padlock across the photo's Organizer thumbnail as a reminder. To get rid of the lock and free up your image for Organizer projects, go back to the Editor and close the photo there.

Understanding Expert Mode

Once you enter Expert mode (click the Expert tab at the top of the Editor to get there), you may be pretty puzzled as to how to proceed. There's a toolbox on the left, a row of icons across the bottom of the screen—and that's pretty much it. If you've ever used old versions of Elements, you may be asking, "Where did everything go?" Not to worry. It's all still there, you just need to know how to make things work.

■ BASIC WORKSPACE

Expert mode starts out in what Adobe calls the *Basic Workspace* (Figure 1-6), a design that it hoped would be less confusing to beginners. On the left side of the screen is a double-columned toolbox. When you open a photo, a small *thumbnail* version of it appears in the area near the bottom of the window, called the *Photo Bin*. However, what you see in this area changes depending on what you're doing. When you activate one of Elements' tools, this area is taken over by the *Tool Options*, where you see the settings for the tool you're currently using (more about that on page 20).

FIGURE 1-6

When you first use the Editor in Expert mode, the window looks like this, which Adobe calls the Basic Workspace.

The buttons at the bottom right (circled) let you switch from one panel to another. You can see only one panel at a time, which is one reason why most folks prefer to use the Custom Workspace shown in Figure 1-5. It's explained in the next section.

At the bottom right of the screen are a series of buttons: Layers, Effects, Graphics, Favorites, and More. The first four are the names of Elements' most-used *panels*. Panels let you do things like keep track of what you've done to a photo (with the History panel) and apply special effects to your images (with the Effects and Graphics panels). You'll learn about the program's various panels in detail throughout this book.

Here's the thing about the Basic Workspace: When you click one of those panel buttons, that panel appears and fills the entire right side of your screen (called the *Panel Bin*) from top to bottom, as the Layers panel does in Figure 1-6. When you're in the Basic Workspace, only the panels that have buttons at the bottom right of the screen can appear in the Panel Bin, and you can't see more than one of them at a time or resize them. To switch to another panel, you click its button at the bottom of the screen and the previous panel disappears.

But the Editor has many more panels than just those four. If you need one of the others, like say the History panel, you bring it up by clicking the More button in the window's lower-right corner. This brings up *all* of Elements' other panels in one floating group, and you click the tab of the panel you want to work with to bring it to the front. You can move the group around on your screen, but you can't put it in the Panel Bin or take anything out of the Panel Bin. You also can't remove any panels from the group, and you have no control over how big it is—it automatically resizes itself to fit the current panel. You can close the group by clicking the little X at its top right (in Windows) or top left (on a Mac).

> **TIP** If you click the tiny arrow on the right side of the More button, you can choose a panel by name, but in the Basic Workspace you still get the whole group. All choosing the name does is make sure that the panel you want is the front one when the grouped panels appear.

You can try using Expert mode's Basic Workspace, but odds are that in about 10 minutes, this setup will have you raving and beating your head on your desk. Fortunately, Elements offers a *much* better way to use the Editor: the *Custom Workspace*.

■ CUSTOM WORKSPACE

If you've ever used Elements (or any graphics program) before, you'll be enormously relieved to know that you can make the Editor work much more efficiently than the Basic Workspace does. The secret is a well-hidden menu command that restores Elements to its full usefulness. To achieve this transformation, just head to the bottom right of the Elements window, click the tiny arrow on the right side of the More button, and then choose Custom Workspace.

Voilà! You may not see much of a change onscreen, but you just regained an enormous amount of freedom to set things up the way you want them. In the Custom Workspace you can tear individual panels out of the panel group, put panels into (and take them out of) the Panel Bin, make your own panel groups, and so on.

Switch to the Custom Workspace right now. The rest of this book assumes that you'd like to see what you're doing and so are using the Editor's Custom Workspace.

Bins, Panels, and Tabs

You're not stuck with the way things are initially laid out in the Editor's Custom Workspace (explained above). You can rearrange things quite a bit from where Adobe starts you out. This section explains the various ways you can customize the Editor when you're in the Custom Workspace).

> **TIP** You can hide *everything* in the Editor except for your images, the strip of buttons along the bottom of the Editor's window, and the menu bar: no tools, panels, or anything else cluttering up your screen. This is handy when you want a good, undistracted look at what you've done to a photo. To do so, just press the Tab key; to bring everything back into view, press Tab again. (This also works in the Basic Workspace.)

■ THE PHOTO BIN/TOOL OPTIONS AREA

There's a long, narrow strip at the bottom of the Editor window that displays different things depending on what you're doing at the moment. When you first open a photo, you see the *Photo Bin* (Figure 1-7) in this area, which displays all your open files. But if you click a tool in the toolbox on the left side of the Editor window, the Photo Bin gets replaced with settings for that particular tool, called (logically enough) the *Tool Options*. There are buttons at the bottom left of the main Editor window that let you switch between the Photo Bin and Tool Options, so you can always see the one you want.

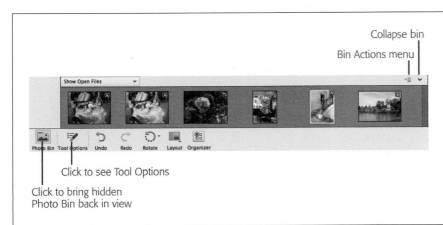

Collapse bin

Bin Actions menu

Click to see Tool Options

Click to bring hidden
Photo Bin back in view

FIGURE 1-7

The Photo Bin at the bottom of the Editor window holds a thumbnail of every open photo. Click the arrow in the bin's top-right corner to collapse it, and use the button at the bottom left to bring it back. Clicking the Tool Options button displays settings for the tool you're currently using.

The Photo Bin/Tool Options area is fixed in place: You can't move it anywhere else or resize it. However, you can hide it by clicking the down-pointing arrow at the right end of the light-gray bar just above it (labeled in Figure 1-7), or by clicking the Photo Bin button (when the Photo Bin is visible) or the Tool Options button (when the Tool Options are visible). This gives you more space, but it also hides the settings for your tools, so it's hard to do much work with it hidden. To bring it back, click either the Photo Bin or Tool Options button at the bottom of the window. (This behavior is the same in both the Basic and Custom workspaces.)

There's more about how to use the Tool Options on page 20. The rest of this section is about the Photo Bin.

The Photo Bin does a lot more than just show which photos you have open. For example, you can drag photos' thumbnails in the bin to rearrange them if you want to use the images in a project. The bin also has two drop-down menus:

- **Show Files**. This menu at the bin's upper left lets you determine what the Photo Bin displays: the photos currently open in the Editor, selected photos from the Organizer, or any albums (page 55) you've made. This menu even lets you send files from the Organizer to the bin without actually opening them. Simply click photos to select them in the Organizer, and then come back over to the Editor and switch this menu to "Show Files selected in Organizer"; you'll see the photos you selected in the Organizer waiting for you in the bin. Double-click one to open it for editing.

- **Bin Actions**. This menu is where the Photo Bin gets really useful, but it's not easy to spot: It's the little four-line square in the bin's upper right. This menu lets you print the photos in the bin or make an album right there in the Photo Bin without ever going to the Organizer. If you don't use the Organizer, then the Photo Bin is a particularly great feature, because it lets you create groups of photos you can call up together: Just put them in an album here by choosing "Save Bin as an Album"; after that, you can select the album's name from the bin's Show Files menu to see those photos. If you like things to be compartmentalized, the Show Grid menu item here puts a thin black line around each thumbnail.

> **NOTE** In the Photo Bin, you may notice little paintbrush icons at the top-right corner of your photos' thumbnails. They indicate that you've edited a photo but haven't saved your changes.

■ THE PANEL BIN

When you're in Expert mode, the right side of the Elements window displays the *Panel Bin*. (In the Basic Workspace you won't see this bin until you click one of the panel buttons in the bottom-right corner of the Editor window.) When you first switch to the Custom Workspace (page 12), the Panel Bin appears with four panels open: Layers, Effects, Graphics, and Favorites (Figure 1-8). These are the same four panels that have their own buttons in the Basic Workspace, but here you can close any of them that you don't need at the moment.

> **NOTE** In older versions of Elements and Photoshop, panels were called "palettes." If you run across a tutorial that talks about the "Effects palette," for example, that's the same thing as the Effects panel.

To pull a panel out of the bin, drag the panel's top tab (the one with its name on it); you've now got yourself a floating panel. (You can float panels even if you haven't turned on floating image windows as explained on page 99.) Figure 1-9 shows how to make panels even smaller once they're out of the bin by collapsing them in one of two ways. You can also combine panels, as shown in Figure 1-10; this works with both panels in the bin and freestanding panels you've dragged out of the bin.

FIGURE 1-8

*Two different ways of
working with the same
images, panels, and
tools. You can use any
arrangement that suits
you. (These figures show
the Mac version of Ele-
ments, in which the main
menu bar is up at the top
of the screen, out of the
picture here. In Windows,
it sticks to the top of the
workspace.)*

*Top: The panels in the
standard Custom Work-
space arrangement, with
the images in tabs.*

*Bottom: This figure shows
how you can customize
your panels. The im-
ages here are in floating
windows, and the Tool
Options/Photo Bin is hid-
den. There's no Panel Bin,
either, since all the panels
are floating.*

FIGURE 1-9

You can free up lots of space by collapsing panels accordion-style once they're out of the bin.

Top: A full-sized panel.

Bottom: A panel collapsed by double-clicking its tab (where the cursor is here). Be sure to double-click the name *of the panel, not in the blank area to the right of the tab.*

FIGURE 1-10

You can combine two or more panels once you've dragged them out of the Panel Bin.

Top: Here, the Histogram panel is being combined with the Layers panel. To perform this technique, drag both panels out of the Panel Bin, and then drag one of them (by clicking the tab at the top of the panel) onto the other. When the panel you're dragging becomes ghosted and you see the blue outline shown here, let go of your mouse button to combine them.

Bottom: To switch from one panel to another after they're grouped, just click the tab of the one you want to use. Here you see the mouse ready to click the Layers panel's tab to switch over to it from the Histogram panel.

To remove a panel from a group, simply drag its tab out of the group. To return everything to how it looked when you first entered the Custom Workspace, go to Window→Reset Panels.

The first time you call up one of the panels that's not initially displayed in the Custom Workspace (by selecting its name in either the Window menu or the menu that appears when you click the down arrow on the right side of the More button), you get the same floating panel group that you get in the Basic Workspace (page 10). Luckily, you can fix this in a jiffy. Just pull the panels you want loose from the clump. After that, Elements will remember what you did, and those panels will appear right where you left them last time. So the first time you call up the History panel, for instance, you get the six-panel group. But if you separate the History panel from the group, from then on, when you go to Window→History or click the arrow next to the More button and choose History, all you get is the panel you want, not the whole clump. You can put the panel in the bin, leave it floating, or combine it with another panel, and that's exactly how it will appear next time.

NOTE If you've floated any panels, clicking the More button closes them. You can click the arrow on the right side of this button to display the pop-out menu and make choices there, but click the main part of the button and everything is gone. Click the button again to bring everything back.

To close a floating panel, click its Close button (the X at its upper right [in Windows] or upper left [on a Mac]), or click the little white square made of four horizontal lines in the panel's upper right, and then choose Close.

NOTE Confusingly, Adobe sometimes refers to floating panels as "tabs" in Elements' menus. So, for example, when you click the four-line square on a floating panel, you see a Close Tab Group option instead of a Close Panel Group option.

In addition, when you're using the Custom Workspace, you can put floating panels into the Panel Bin. Where you drag the panel determines where it appears in the bin. If you want to see a panel's tab with the other tabs at the top of the bin, then drag the panel's tab onto the other tabs at the top of the bin and let go when you see a blue outline. Since the Panel Bin always fills the entire right side of the screen from top to bottom, you may also prefer to stack panels vertically so that you can see more than one at a time. You can't really do that, but you can get the same effect by dragging a panel's tab onto the tab of a panel already in the bin. This creates a multi-tabbed panel in the bin. Then grab the tab of the panel you want to see lower in the bin and drag it straight down. The panel is actually floating, but it will position itself within the confines of the bin, below the contents of the first panel, so that it's effectively the same as if it were docked below the first panel.

One thing that's a bit tricky about the Custom Workspace is that you may wind up losing the Panel Bin completely. If you pull all the panels out of it, the bin disappears. This can be handy because it gives you more space to spread out when working on photos, but if you want the bin back, you may find yourself dragging a panel all over the right side of the screen trying to make it dock back into the main window. The trick is to move the panel over the *far right* edge of the main Editor window.

When you do this, the blue line appears along that edge. Let go of the panel, and the Panel Bin returns with your panel in it.

All this panel organizing isn't as complicated as it sounds, and it's easier to learn by doing than by reading about it. So try dragging some panels around in the Custom Workspace. If you don't like the results of your handiwork or you move the panels around so much that you can't remember where you put things, just go to Window→Reset Panels, and Elements puts all the panels back in their original spots.

■ IMAGE WINDOWS

You also get to choose how you want to view the images you're working on. Old versions of Elements used floating windows, where each image appears in a separate window that you can drag around. Elements now starts you out with a tabbed view—which uses something like the tabs in a web browser or the tabs you'd find on paper file folders; see Figure 1-8, top—but you can still put images into floating windows, if you prefer (page 99 explains how).

The advantage of tabbed view is that it gives you plenty of workspace around your image, which is handy when you're working near the edges of a photo or using a tool that requires you to be able to get outside the image's boundaries. Many people switch back and forth between floating and tabbed windows as they work, depending on which is most convenient. All the things you can do with image windows—including how to switch between tabbed view and floating windows—are explained on page 97. (Incidentally, clicking Window→Reset Panels doesn't do anything to your image windows or tabs; it resets only your panels.)

> **NOTE** Because your view may vary, most of the illustrations in this book show only the image itself and the tool in use, without a window frame or a tab boundary around it.

Elements' Tools

Elements gives you an amazing array of tools to use when working on photos. You get almost two dozen primary tools to help select, paint on, and otherwise manipulate images, and some of these tools have as many as seven subtools. Bob Vila's workshop probably isn't any better stocked than Elements' virtual toolbox!

> **TIP** To explore every nook and cranny of Elements, you need to open a photo (in the Editor, choose File→Open). Lots of the menus are *grayed out* (unavailable) if you don't have a file open.

When you're in Expert mode, the long, skinny strip on the left side of the Editor window is the *Tools panel* (Figure 1-11). It stays perfectly organized so you can always find what you want without ever having to tidy it up. The Tools panel is fixed in place—you can't move it, resize it, or make it into a single column like you could in some previous versions of the program.

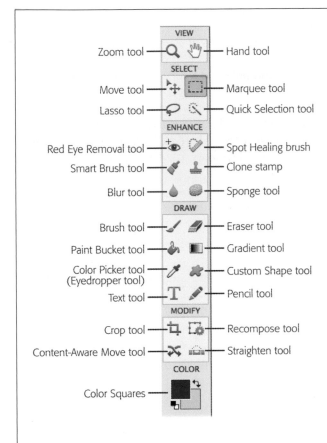

FIGURE 1-11

The mighty Tools panel is divided into six categories—View, Select, Enhance, Draw, Modify, and Color—to make it easier to find what you want. (If you don't see these category labels, see Figure 1-12 to learn why that is.)

Because some tools are grouped together in the same slot (indicated by little arrows next to the tools' icons, shown in Figure 1-12), you can't ever see all the tools at once. For grouped tools, the icon you see is the one for the last tool you used in that group.

Many of the icons in the Tools panel actually represent tool *groups*, but Adobe has chosen to play hide and seek with the subtools. Move your cursor over a section of the Tools panel, and you'll see teeny, tiny arrows above the icons of the tools in that section that have other tools nested with them (see Figure 1-12).

When you click an icon in the Tools panel, the Tool Options area (page 13) displays settings for that tool, as well as icons for any subtools nested with that tool. If you forget what a particular icon is for, just put your cursor over it—without clicking—and a label (called a *tooltip*) appears telling you the tool's name.

FIGURE 1-12

When you put your cursor over a section of the toolbox that has subtools nested with the visible tools, you see these minute arrows next to the tool icons. Here, for example, you can see that all the tools in the Enhance section except the Red Eye Removal tool have more tools grouped with them. Unlike in old versions of Elements, you can't right-click a tool's icon or hold the mouse down to see the subtools, but you can cycle through them by Alt-clicking/Option-clicking the group's current Tools panel icon repeatedly, or just by looking in the Tool Options area at the bottom of the Elements window.

Incidentally, whether or not you see the category names (like the Enhance and Draw labels shown here) depends on your screen resolution. If your screen is so short that the Tools panel would be cut off if the names were displayed, then Elements just doesn't show them.

To activate a tool, click its icon in either the Tools panel (if the icon is displayed there) or in the Tool Options area (if the tool is grouped with the currently active tool). Each tool comes with its own collection of options, as shown in Figure 1-13. The Tools panel remembers the last tool you used, so if you choose to use one of the nested tools, the next time you'll see the icon for *that* tool in the panel rather than the one for the tool that was there when you first started Elements. This may seem complicated, but after a while you'll get pretty good at remembering where each tool lives.

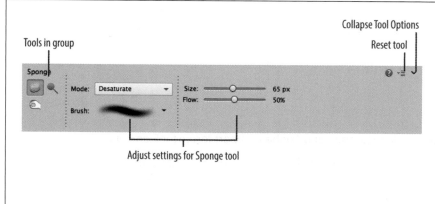

Adjust settings for Sponge tool

FIGURE 1-13

The Tool Options area displays settings for the current tool. Here you see the Sponge tool's options, and the icons for the Dodge and Burn tools, which share its Tools panel slot. Remember, the Tool Options area replaces the Photo Bin when you click a tool's icon. You can switch between the Photo Bin and the Tool Options by clicking their buttons at the bottom of your screen.

Other windows in Elements, like Quick Fix and the Raw Converter, also have tool-boxes, but none is as complete as Expert mode's Tools panel. Don't worry about learning the names of every tool right now. It's easier to remember what a tool is once you've used it. And don't be overwhelmed by all of Elements' tools. You probably have a bunch of Allen wrenches in your garage that you use only every year or so. Likewise, you'll find that you use certain Elements tools more than others.

> **TIP** You can save time by activating tools with their keyboard shortcuts rather than by clicking their icons, since that way you don't have to interrupt what you're doing to trek over to the Tools panel. To see a tool's shortcut key, put your cursor over its icon in the Tools panel or Tool Options area, and a label pops up indicating the shortcut key (it's the letter in parentheses to the right of the tool's name). To activate the tool, just press the appropriate key. If the tool you want is part of a group, then *all* the tools in that group have the same keyboard shortcut, so just keep pressing that key to cycle through the group until you get to the tool you want.

FREQUENTLY ASKED QUESTION

The Always-On Toolbox

Do I always need to have a tool selected?

When you look at the Tools panel, you'll probably notice that one tool's icon is highlighted, indicating that the tool is active. You can deactivate it by clicking a different tool, but what if you don't want *any* tool to be active? How do you fix things so that you don't have a tool selected?

You don't. One tool *always* has to be selected, so you probably want to get in the habit of choosing a tool that won't do any damage to your image if you accidentally click. For instance, the Pencil tool, which leaves a spot or a line where you click, probably isn't a good choice. But the Marquee Selection tool (page 149), the Zoom tool (page 102), and the Hand tool (page 103) are all safe bets. (When you open the Editor, Elements activates the tool you were using the last time you closed the program.)

Getting Help

Wherever Adobe found a stray corner in Elements, it stuck some help into it. You can't move anywhere in the program without being offered some kind of guidance. Here are a few of the ways you can summon assistance if you need it:

- **Help menu**. Choose Help→Photoshop Elements Help or press F1/⌘-?. When you do, Elements launches your web browser, which displays Elements' Help files, where you can search or browse a topic list and glossary. The Help menu also contains links to online video tutorials and Adobe's support forum for Elements.

- **Dialog box links**. Many dialog boxes have a few words of bright blue text somewhere in them. (Sometimes you'll see a question mark in a circle instead.) That text is actually a link to Elements Help. If you get confused about what the Remove Color Cast feature does, for instance, then, in the Remove Color Cast dialog box, click the blue words "Color Cast" for a reminder.

> **NOTE** When Elements is busy doing something that takes awhile, it lets you know by displaying a notice in a dark gray oval that says something like "Undo Paint Bucket" or whatever the particular task is.

■ eLIVE

Elements Live (eLive) is a fun new section that Adobe added to both the Editor and the Organizer in Elements 13. What's available on this tab changes constantly, and you need an Internet connection to view any of it. It's a compilation of articles from Adobe and interesting Elements-related links from around the Internet.

> **NOTE** In most countries you see the eLive tab and Elements opens to that tab the first time you start the Editor or the Organizer. However, since what Elements Live displays is geared to your language and country, it's not currently available in *every* country, especially if you use Elements in a language other than English. If eLive isn't in your area yet, you won't see the eLive tab at all, but one day it may spontaneously appear (without you needing to run any kind of update) when Adobe has it ready for your language.

Click this tab and you're presented with a smorgasbord of tutorials and inspirational articles. Some of the tutorials are very basic; others are quite advanced. Figure 1-14 explains how to filter what you see so you can focus on the type of articles you want. To read an article or tutorial, just click on its card (the graphic and synopsis you see in Elements Live). Elements opens your web browser and takes you to the page you chose. There's also a button on the right side of the screen that you can click to connect to Adobe support. There are contests and links to interesting material on other sites, like Pinterest.

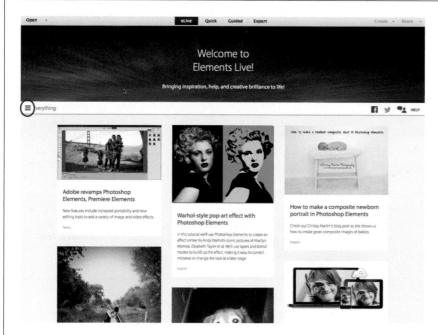

FIGURE 1-14

Click the menu circled here to filter what you see in the window by Everything, Learn (tutorials), Inspire (cool stuff to look at for ideas), and News. So if you're only interested in tutorials, just click Learn and that's all you'll see.

When Adobe updates the contents of Elements Live, a little red number appears on the eLive tab, showing how many new articles there are. When you click the tab, new cards have a New banner on them. To get rid of the number, just click over to the Everything section, a then click back to where you want to be (if you're in the midst of something and don't want to read anything right now). Doing this also removes the banners from the cards, so if you want to go back later, you won't have any easy way to tell what was changed. (Updates to Elements Live don't appear in Help→Updates. They just show up any time you open Elements with an active Internet connection.)

■ GUIDED EDIT

If you're a beginner, Guided Edit (Figure 1-15) can be a big help. It walks you through a variety of popular editing tasks, like cropping, sharpening, correcting colors, and removing blemishes. It also includes some features that are useful even if you're an old hand at Elements, like the High Key and Low Key edits (page 457). Guided Edit is really easy to use:

1. **Go to Guided Edit.**

   At the top of the Editor window, click the Guided tab.

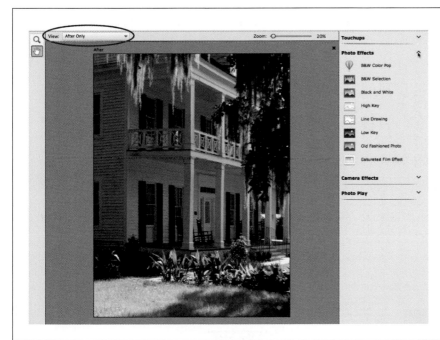

FIGURE 1-15

Guided Edit gives you step-by-step help with basic photo editing. Just use the tools that appear in the right-hand panel once you choose an activity. When you first open Guided Edit, all the different sections are closed. Just click the name of a section to expand it and see what you can do. When you click another section, the previous one collapses.

As with Quick Fix, you can change to a Before & After view by using the View menu (circled) to select the one you want.

2. **Open a photo.**

   If you already have an image open when you enter Guided Edit, then it appears in the main window automatically. If you need to open an image, click the Open button at the upper left of the window or press Ctrl+O/⌘-O and then, in the dialog box that appears, choose your photo. If you have several photos in the Photo Bin, then you can switch images by double-clicking the thumbnail of the one you want to work on. (If the Photo Bin disappears while you're working, just click its button at the bottom left of the screen to bring it back.)

3. **Choose what you want to do.**

   In the panel on the right side of the Guided Edit window, your options are grouped into major categories like Touchups and Photo Effects, with a variety of specific projects under each heading. Just click the task you want to perform, and the panel displays the relevant buttons and/or sliders for that task.

4. **Make your adjustments.**

   Simply move the panel's sliders and click its buttons till you like what you see. If you need to adjust your view of the photo while you work on it, use the Hand (page 103) and Zoom (page 102) tools in the little toolbox at the top left of the Guided Edit window.

   If you want to start over, click the Reset Panel icon circled in Figure 1-16. If you change your mind about the whole project, click Cancel at the bottom of the panel.

FIGURE 1-16

Adobe tried to make Elements easy for beginners to use, but it's a pretty good bet that you won't easily guess the purpose of this strange little icon, which appears in many places in Elements. This is the Reset button. In Guided Edit and Quick Fix, it's officially called Reset Panels, which is another way of saying, "Undo everything I've done since I entered this window."

5. **Click Done to finish.**

   Don't forget to save your changes (page 70). If you decide you don't like what you did, click Cancel. To close your photo, press Ctrl+W/⌘-W; or leave it open and switch to another tab to share it or use it in a project.

> **TIP** Guided Edit shows you quick and easy ways to change an image, but it doesn't always get you the best possible results. It's a great tool for starting out; just remember that what you see there isn't necessarily the *best* you can make your images look. Once you're more comfortable in Elements, Quick Fix (Chapter 4) is a good next step. You'll find that most of the tools there will be familiar if you've been using Guided Edit.

Escape Routes

Elements has a couple of really wonderful features to help you avoid making permanent mistakes: the Undo command and the History panel. After you've gotten used to them, you'll probably wish it were possible to use these tools in *all* aspects of your life, not just Elements.

◼ UNDO

No matter where you are in Elements, you can almost always change your mind about what you just did. Press Ctrl+Z/⌘-Z, and the last change you made goes away. This keystroke works even if you've just saved your photo, *but only while the image is still open*—if you close the file, your changes are permanent. Keep pressing Ctrl+Z/⌘-Z to keep undoing your work, step by step.

If you want to *redo* what you just undid, press Ctrl+Y/⌘-Y. These keyboard shortcuts are great for toggling changes on and off while you decide whether you want to keep them. The Undo/Redo keystrokes work in both the Organizer and the Editor.

NOTE   If you don't like Ctrl+Z/⌘-Z and Ctrl+Y/⌘-Y, you have a bit of control over the key combinations you use for Undo and Redo. Go to Edit→Preferences→General/Photoshop Elements Editor→Preferences→General. In the Preferences dialog box, the Step Back/Fwd menu gives you two other choices, both of which involve pressing the Z key in combination with the Ctrl, Alt, and Shift keys in Windows, and with the ⌘, Option, and Shift keys on a Mac.

If you prefer buttons to keystrokes, you can click the Undo and Redo buttons in the bottom left of the Elements window instead. And if you want to use the keystrokes but forget what they are, they're listed at the top of the Edit menu.

◼ THE HISTORY PANEL

In the Editor's Expert mode, you get even more control over the actions you can undo, thanks to the History panel (Figure 1-17), which you open by choosing Window→History. (In some previous versions of Elements, this feature was called the *Undo* History panel.)

FIGURE 1-17

For a little time travel, just click the step you want to go back to and watch your changes disappear.

Keep in mind that you can only go back sequentially. Here, for instance, you can't go back to the Levels adjustment without first undoing using the Paint Bucket and creating a new layer via copy. Click a step further down in the list to redo *your work.*

This panel holds a list of the changes you've made since you opened your image. Just drag the slider up and watch your changes disappear one by one. Like the Undo command, this panel works even if you've saved your file: As long as you haven't *closed* the file, the panel tracks every action you take. You can also drag the pointer down to redo changes that you've undone.

Be careful, though: You can back up only as many steps as Elements is set to remember. The program is initially set up to record 50 steps, but you can change that number by going to Edit→Preferences→Performance/Photoshop Elements Editor→Preferences→Performance and adjusting the History States setting. You can set it as high as 1,000, but remembering even 100 steps may slow your computer to a crawl if it doesn't have a superpowered processor, plenty of memory, and loads of disk space. If Elements runs slowly on your machine, then reducing the History States setting to, say, 20 may speed things up a bit.

■ THE ONE RULE OF ELEMENTS

As you're beginning to see, Elements lets you work in lots of different ways. What's more, most people who use the program approach projects in different ways; what works for your neighbor with her pictures may be quite different from how you'd work on the very same shots. But you'll hear one suggestion from almost every Elements veteran, and it's an important one: *Never, ever work on your original. Always, always, always make a copy of your image and work on that instead.*

The good news is that, if you store your photos in the Organizer, you don't need to worry about accidentally messing up your original. If you save your files as *version sets* (page 71), Elements automatically creates a copy when you edit a photo that's cataloged in the Organizer, so you can always revert to your original. Other image-management programs, like Apple's iPhoto and Adobe's Lightroom, also make versions for you if you set up Elements as your external editor (see page 36).

But, as explained on page 6, you don't *have* to use the Organizer. If you've decided not to use it or version sets, then follow these steps to make a copy of your image in the Editor:

1. **Open the image you want to copy, and then go to File→Duplicate.**

   The Duplicate Image dialog box appears.

2. **In the dialog box, name the duplicate, and then click OK.**

   Elements opens the new, duplicate image in the main image window.

3. **Find the original image and click its Close button (the X or the red dot).**

   If you're using tabs (you are unless you've changed the settings described on page 18), the Close button is on the right side of the image's tab in Windows, and on the left side on a Mac. If you have floating windows (page 18), the Close button is the standard Windows or Mac Close button you'd see in any window. Once you click this button, your original image is safely tucked out of harm's way.

4. **Save the duplicate by pressing Ctrl+S/⌘-S.**

   Choose Photoshop (.psd) as the file format when you save it. (You may want to choose another format after you've read Chapter 3 and understand more about your different format options.)

Now you don't have to worry about making a mistake or changing your mind, because you can always start over.

NOTE   Elements doesn't have an auto-save feature, so you should get into the habit of saving frequently as you work. Mac folks, pay special attention—Elements *isn't* currently able to use OS X's Auto Save feature. Page 70 has more about saving.

Getting Started in a Hurry

If you're the impatient type and you're starting to squirm because you want to be up and *doing* something to your photos, here's the quickest way to get started in Elements: Adjust an image's brightness and color balance all in one step.

1. **In the Editor's Expert mode or the Quick Fix window, open a photo.**

   Press Ctrl+O/⌘-O, navigate to the image you want, and then click Open.

2. **Press Alt+Ctrl+M/Option-⌘-M.**

   You've just applied Elements' Auto Smart Fix command (Figure 1-18).

FIGURE 1-18

Auto Smart Fix is the quickest, easiest way to improve the quality of a photo.

Top left: The original, unedited picture.

Top right: Auto Smart Fix makes quite a difference, but the colors are still slightly off.

Bottom: By using some of the other tools you'll learn about in this book (like Auto Contrast and Adjust Sharpness), you can make things look even better.

Voilà! You should see quite a difference in your photo, unless the exposure, lighting, and contrast were almost perfect before. (If you don't like what just happened to your photo, no problem—simply press Ctrl+Z/⌘-Z to undo the changes.) The Auto Smart Fix command is one of Elements' many easy-to-use features.

If you're really raring to go, jump ahead to Chapter 4 to learn about using the Quick Fix commands. But it's worth taking the time to read the next two chapters so you understand which file formats to choose and how to make some basic adjustments to images, like rotating and cropping them.

Don't forget to give Guided Edit a try if you see what you want to do in its list of topics (page 23). Guided Edit can be a big help while you're learning your way around.

Importing, Managing, and Saving Photos

Now that you've had a look around Elements, it's time to start learning how to get photos into the program and keep track of where they're stored.

As a digital photographer, you don't have to deal with shoeboxes stuffed with prints, but you've still got to face the menace of photos piling up on your hard drive. Fortunately, Elements gives you some great tools for organizing your collection and quickly finding individual pictures.

In this chapter, you'll learn how to import photos from cameras, memory card readers, and scanners. You'll also find out how to create new files from scratch and open files that are already on your computer. Then you'll be ready for a quick tour of the Organizer, where you can sort and find pictures once they're in Elements. Finally, you'll learn about saving and backing up your precious files.

Importing from Cameras

Elements gives you lots of different ways to get photos from camera to computer, but if you use the Organizer, the simplest method is to use Adobe's Photo Downloader. Later in this section, you'll learn about other ways to import photos.

NOTE Take a moment to carefully read the instructions from your camera's manufacturer. If those directions conflict with anything you read here, follow the manufacturer's instructions.

The Photo Downloader

What happens when you plug a camera or memory card reader into your computer depends on your operating system. In Windows, you get a standard Windows dialog box (shown on page 7) asking what you want to do. To use the Photo Downloader to get your photos into Elements, choose "Organize and Edit using Adobe Photoshop Elements Organizer 13.0."

> **NOTE** If you're using Windows and don't automatically see the dialog box described above when you plug your camera into your computer, then call up the Photo Downloader by heading to the Organizer and choosing File→"Get Photos and Videos"→"From Camera or Card Reader" or pressing Ctrl+G.

On a Mac, you won't see the Downloader at all unless you specifically tell your computer to use it, which you do in the Organizer: Go to File→"Get Photos and Videos"→"From Camera or Card Reader" or press ⌘-G. (You can't set the Mac Downloader to run automatically whenever you plug in a camera or card reader—you have to launch it manually.) If iPhoto normally opens when you connect your camera, open iPhoto, and then go to iPhoto→Preferences→General→"Connecting camera opens" and choose "No application," so that nothing interferes with using the Downloader.

> **NOTE** Although much of this chapter talks about importing pictures from a *camera*, most memory card readers work the same way. Use a card reader if you have one, since doing so will spare the camera's batteries and subject your camera to less wear and tear.

The Downloader's job is pretty straightforward: to shepherd your photos as they make the trip from camera to computer, and to make sure Elements knows where your images are stored. Your job is to help it along by adjusting the following settings (which are on display in Figure 2-1):

- **Get Photos from**. Your first step in downloading is to choose your camera or card reader from the list of available devices. (You may see a more generic "Camera or Card Reader" choice rather than the name of your camera; if that's all you see, then pick that option.) Just below this menu, the Downloader lists how many photos it found and how many duplicates (of images already in the Organizer) it plans to skip, if any.

- **Location**. Your photos usually get stored in a folder named for the date you shot them. In Windows, this folder lives in *C:\Users\[your user name]\Pictures*. On a Mac, it's *[your hard drive]→Users→[your user name]→Pictures*. If you want to change where your photos are headed, click the Browse button (on a Mac, it's the Choose button instead), and then pick another location. You can permanently change the standard save location by opening the Organizer and going to Edit→Preferences→"Camera or Card Reader"/Elements Organizer→Preferences→"Camera or Card Reader" and changing the Save

Files In setting; from then on, the Downloader will put your photos in the folder you chose.

FIGURE 2-1

When the Photo Downloader first launches, you see this dialog box, which lets you choose where Elements puts the photos and what it names them (say goodbye to names like IMG_0327. JPG).

To get started, choose your camera or card reader from the "Get Photos from" drop-down menu at the top of the dialog box.

If you want to import only specific images, click the Advanced Dialog button (circled) so you can choose which photos to grab and fine-tune other settings.

- **Create Subfolder(s)**. If you want to have more levels of organization, you can put your image files into a subfolder *inside* the folder you chose for the Location. Use this drop-down menu to decide what Elements uses as the subfolder's name: today's date, the shot date (in your choice of several different formats), or a custom name. If you don't want to create a subfolder, choose None.

- **Rename Files**. Here you can choose to give all the files you're importing a custom name. If you select Custom Name from the drop-down menu and then type *obedience_school_graduation* in the box below it, for example, then you get photos named obedience_school_graduation_0001, obedience_school_gradu-ation_0002, and so on. Or you can use just the shot date or today's date, the name of the subfolder, or a combination of a custom name and the date you shot the photo. No matter which naming scheme you choose, Elements adds a four-digit number to the end of each file's name (as in the obedience-school example above) to help you distinguish among them. You can also choose Advanced Rename to bring up a window where you can set a very complex group of parameters for naming your photos. If you leave the Rename Files field set to "Do not rename files," then Elements keeps the filenames your camera assigned.

- **Preserve Current Filename in XMP**. Turn this checkbox on if you want the photos' current filenames to be stored in the photos' *metadata* (page 49).

- **Open Organizer when Finished (Windows only)**. You won't see this checkbox if the Organizer is already running when you import your photos, but it appears if the Downloader opened automatically or you launched it as described at the beginning of this section (page 30). If you're going to put your files in the Organizer, leave this checkbox turned on. Turn it off if you don't use the Organizer, or if you'd rather wait until later to get organized.

- **Delete Options**. You can have the Downloader delete your files from your camera's memory card when it's done importing them. Figure 2-2 explains more about this option.

FIGURE 2-2

The Photo Downloader can delete files from your camera or memory card reader once it's done importing them. This feature seems *handy, but think twice about using it. The Downloader is pretty reliable, but it's always good to wait until you've reviewed all your photos in Elements before deleting the originals. If you really want the Downloader to delete your files, at least choose "After Copying, Verify and Delete Originals" to make Elements check that it has copied your files correctly before vaporizing the originals.*

- **Automatic Download (Windows only)**. This checkbox appears only after you've selected a device in the "Get Photos from" menu. If you like to live dangerously, you can turn on this checkbox and Elements will download any new photos it detects without showing you the Photo Downloader dialog box. It's almost always best to leave Automatic Download off so that you have some control over what's going on. If you decide to take this risky route, you can tell Elements where to put your photos and whether it should delete the originals by going to the Organizer and choosing Edit→Preferences→"Camera or Card Reader."

The Downloader is smart enough to recognize any photos that it has already imported, and it doesn't reimport those. If you want to see these duplicates and for some reason download them again, or if you want to pick and choose which photos to import, then click the Advanced Dialog button at the bottom of the Downloader window to bring up the dialog box shown in Figure 2-3. (If you change your mind and want to switch back to the standard dialog box, then click the Standard Dialog button.)

FIGURE 2-3

When you want to select which photos to import, summon the advanced Photo Downloader, shown here.

To get back to the standard dialog box, click the Standard Dialog button (circled).

NOTE If your screen is less than 768 pixels tall (if you're using a netbook, say), you won't see the option to switch to the Advanced Downloader, since the dialog box would be too big for your screen.

The advanced dialog box gives you all the options found in the standard Photo Downloader, plus a few more. The advanced dialog box is divided into two main parts. On the left side are the thumbnails of your photos, and on the right side are a bunch of settings. The little checkmarks next to each thumbnail indicate which photos Elements plans to import; just turn off the checkboxes for the ones you don't want to bring into the Organizer. If you plan to import only a few images, save yourself some time by clicking UnCheck All below the preview area and then just turning on the checkboxes for the ones you want. (If you've already imported some of the images, the Organizer tells you so and doesn't import them again.) You can also import video and sound files.

The four buttons above the preview area (next to the word "Show") let you choose which files you see. From left to right, here's what these buttons do:

- **Show/Hide Images**. If you want to temporarily hide your photos (so you can look at just your video files, for instance), click this button or press Ctrl+M/⌘-M.

- **Video files**. This button is grayed out unless Elements finds any movie or video files on your memory card. If it does, you can hide them by clicking this button. You might do that if, say, you're interested in importing only still photos right now. To see the video files again, just click this button.

- **Audio files**. This button works just like the video button, but it becomes active when Elements finds audio files you may want to import.

- **Show Duplicates**. If Elements has already imported some of the photos on your memory card and you want to see those files again, then click this button and you can reimport them (or just see them for comparison's sake). In the preview area, the thumbnails of the files you've already imported display an icon that looks just like the Show Duplicates button in their upper-right corners to indicate that they're duplicates.

> **NOTE** If you want to search for duplicates among the images already on your computer, in the Organizer, go to Find→By Visual Searches→"Duplicate photos," or click the little magnifying glass at the top of the Organizer and choose "Duplicate Photo Search." Unfortunately, either method just makes Elements perform a visually based search, and while it will probably find some duplicates this way, it's also likely to find a lot of photos you *don't* consider duplicates. However, you can put your cursor over a thumbnail to see the image's name, creation date, and size, so you have more help in deciding which images are truly duplicates. To get rid of the duplicates, select them, and then click the "Remove from Catalog" button at the window's lower left.

The right side of the advanced dialog box is where you can adjust the settings for where your pictures are stored on your computer and how their folders are named. Most of these choices are the same ones you get in the Photo Downloader's standard dialog box (page 30), but you also get a few extras:

- **Automatically Fix Red Eyes**. If you turn this checkbox on, Elements searches through all your newly imported photos looking for people with red eyes (caused by camera flash) and fixes them automatically. It sounds great, but it's not 100 percent reliable and tends to "fix" things like bright white teeth as well. Fortunately, these changes aren't permanent, because Elements makes a version set (page 71) with your original, so you can ditch the new version if you don't like what Elements did. But the extra time it takes for Elements to analyze all your photos *and* the time you'll waste looking for mistakes mean you're better off leaving this option turned off and using another method to fix red eyes later. See page 125 for more about Elements' Red Eye Removal tool. (You may find that, to keep this setting from turning itself back on again, you *also* need to turn off Automatically Fix Red Eyes in the Organizer by going to Edit→Preferences→"Camera or Card Reader"/Elements Organizer→Preferences→"Camera or Card Reader.")

- **Automatically Suggest Photo Stacks**. The Organizer lets you group related photos together into *stacks*. Turn on this checkbox to use the auto-stack feature, where Elements automatically finds photos that should be grouped together.

This feature works best for photos taken in your camera's burst (rapid advance) mode—in other words, photos of the same subject taken in quick succession.

- **Automatically Stack Raw and JPEG**. Many people like to hedge their bets by setting their cameras to create both a raw file (page 271) and a JPEG file each time they press the shutter. If you turn on this checkbox, Elements will stack the two files together so you don't have duplicate thumbnails in the Organizer for what is essentially the same shot.

- **Import into Album**. Turn on this checkbox and Elements automatically adds the files you're currently downloading to the album you choose. Click the Settings button to select an existing album or create a new one. (Flip to page 55 to learn about albums.)

- **Apply Metadata**. If you want to write your name or copyright info into the files' *metadata* (page 49) so that anyone who views your files will know they're yours, you can do that here.

Once you're done adjusting the Downloader's settings, click Get Media. The Downloader slurps down the photos and, in Windows, launches the Organizer (if it's not already running) so you can review your pictures.

> **TIP** In Windows, you can tell the Organizer to "watch" folders that you often bring graphics—or even sound files or videos—into. (Sorry, this feature isn't available on Macs.) For instance, you could tell Elements to watch your Pictures folder, which means the program will notice when you put new photos there. The program can then either import the new files or tell you that they're waiting for you, depending on which option you choose. In the Organizer, go to File→Watch Folders, and in the dialog box that appears, make sure that the "Watch Folders and their Sub-Folders for new Files" checkbox is turned on. Next, click the Add button, and then browse to the folder you want Elements to watch. (If you *don't* want Elements to watch a folder anymore, this is where you remove it from the watch list.)

If you want Elements to watch a folder that already contains photos in the Organizer, you can right-click the folder's name in the Folders panel (page 50) and then use the pop-out menu to tell Elements to watch it.

◼ Opening Stored Images

If you've got photos already stored on your computer, you have several options for opening them with Elements. If Elements isn't currently running but the file's format is set to open in Elements, then simply double-click the file's icon to launch Elements and open the image. (To change which files open in Elements automatically, see the box on page 37.) You also have several ways to open files from within Elements:

- **From the Organizer, for files not yet in the Organizer**. Go to File→"Get Photos and Videos"→"From Files and Folders" (or press Shift+Ctrl+G/Shift-⌘-G), navigate to your photos, and then select them and click Get Media. (The other options in the "Get Photos and Videos from Files and Folders" dialog box—like fixing red eye and automatically suggesting photo stacks—are covered on page 34.) Then follow the steps in the next bullet point to open your photos in the Editor.

- **From the Organizer, for files _already_ in the Organizer**. You can select an image that's in the Organizer and open it in the Editor. To do so, in the Organizer, either click the file's thumbnail and then press Ctrl+I/⌘-I; right-click the thumbnail and choose "Edit with Photoshop Elements Editor"; or click the thumbnail and then click the Editor button at the bottom of the Organizer window. You can also Shift-click or Ctrl-click/⌘-click to select multiple photos before using any of these commands, and _all_ the selected photos go to the Editor.

> **TIP** When your photos get to the Editor, they should appear in the main editing space. If you don't see anything there, go down to the Project Bin and, from its drop-down menu, choose "Show Files selected in Organizer."

- **From the Editor, for files anywhere on your computer**. Go to File→Open or press Ctrl+O/⌘-O and select your file(s). You can also drop a file right onto the Editor's main window and it'll open.

- **From other programs**. If you use another program to manage and organize your photos—like Lightroom, Aperture, or iPhoto—it's best to set Elements up as your external editor for that program and send your files to the Editor that way, rather than trying to use Elements' File→Open command. There are two reasons for this: First of all, the other program may be able to create and save _version sets_ (page 71) like the Organizer does, but it won't be able to do that unless you send your files out for editing from within your other program. Also, the program's _library file_ (the data the program stores about your photos) could get corrupted if you don't handle it exactly the way it's meant to be used. iPhoto's library is particularly resentful of being poked and prodded from outside the program itself.

The exact method for setting up an external editor depends on which program you're using, but there's typically a place to do that in the program's preferences. In Windows, you probably get to them by going to Edit→Preferences, and on a Mac, it's likely [Application name]→Preferences.

> **NOTE** People who are new to Elements often get confused by the message shown in Figure 2-4, which appears in the Organizer when you leave a photo open in the Editor.

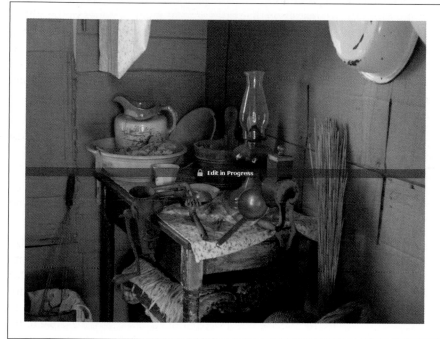

FIGURE 2-4

This red "locked" band looks kind of scary, but it just means that you left your photo open in the Editor when you came back to the Organizer.

To unlock it so that you have access to it in the Organizer, switch back to the Editor and close the photo by going to File→Close or pressing Ctrl+W/⌘-W.

Picking the File Types That Elements Opens

How do I stop Elements from opening all my files?

Sometimes people are dismayed to discover that once they install Elements, it opens every time they double-click any kind of graphics file—whether they want the file to open in Elements or not. You can fix that easily enough:

- **In Windows**: Find a file of the type you want to change (like a JPEG, for example). Then right-click the closed file's icon and, from the pop-up menu, select "Open with"→"Choose default program." In the list that appears, select the program you want to use to open the file. Turn on the "Use this app for all [file format] files" checkbox (in Windows 7, the checkbox is labeled "Always use the selected program to open this kind of file") to set that program for all files of this type.

- **On a Mac**: In the Finder, find a file of the type you want to change (like a JPEG, say). Click once to select it, and then press ⌘-I to bring up the Get Info window, which has lots of data about the file. Expand the window's "Open with" section by clicking the flippy triangle next to it, choose the program you want from the drop-down menu, and then click the Change All button.

Voilà—from now on, those kinds of files will open in the program you chose.

Working with PDF Files

If you open a PDF file in Elements, you'll see the Import PDF dialog box (Figure 2-5), which lets you control how Elements treats the file. You can choose to import whole pages or just the images on the pages, import multiple pages (if the PDF is more than one page long), and pick the imported files' color mode (page 41) and resolution, as well as tell Elements whether to use anti-aliasing (page 152).

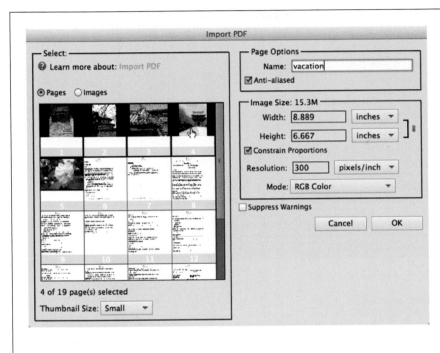

FIGURE 2-5

Elements can open multipage PDFs. To open just one page of the file, double-click the page's thumbnail. To open multiple pages, Ctrl-click/⌘-click the ones you want or Shift-click to select a range, and then double-click to open them.

You can catalog PDF files in the Organizer, too. To do that, go to File→"Get Photos and Videos"→"From Files and Folders" and, in the drop-down menu in the bottom part of the window (on a Mac it's labeled "Enable"), choose PDF Files, and then navigate to the PDF you want to import.

Scanning Photos

Scanning is a little different in Elements 13 than it was in previous versions. You can probably still scan into Elements, but if you have a 64-bit version of Windows 7 or 8, you need to use WIA, Windows' built-in scanning system. If you have a 32-bit version of Windows 7 or 8 instead, you can still use the older TWAIN option for scanning. (To figure out which version you're using, go to *http://support.microsoft. com/kb/827218* and scroll down to the "Automatic version detection results" section, which tells you whether you have the 32- or 64-bit version.) Macs can still use TWAIN if your scanner understands 64-bit TWAIN (not all scanners do).

In 64-bit versions of Windows, there's nothing you need to do to prepare for scanning into Elements except to make sure your scanner driver is up to date (if you're not sure how to do that, check with your scanner's manufacturer). If you have a 32-bit Windows computer, you need to install the Adobe TWAIN driver by going to *C:\ Program Files\Adobe\Photoshop Elements 13\Optional Plug-Ins* and then copying the Import-Export folder to *C:\Program Files\Adobe\Photoshop Elements 13\ Plug-Ins*. On a Mac, go to Applications→Adobe Photoshop Elements 13→Support Files→Optional Plug-Ins, and then copy (Option-drag) the ImportModules folder from there into Applications→Adobe Photoshop Elements 13→Support Files→Plug-Ins. (It's important to *copy* this folder rather than move it because if Adobe makes any "point updates" to Elements—from Elements 13 to 13.1 for example—Elements expects to find that folder in the original location.)

To control your scanner from within Elements, you can scan from the Editor and (in Windows) the Organizer. In the Editor, go to File→Import, and you'll see your scanner's name or WIA Support. In the Windows version of the Organizer, go to File→"Get Photos and Videos"→From Scanner, or press Ctrl+U.

TIP If you have a 64-bit version of Windows and you don't want to use WIA, one workaround is to use your scanner's software and save all your scans to a folder that you have designated as a watched folder (page 35). That way, you can easily get your scans into the Organizer.

If you have a Mac, you can also scan from Preview and then send the scan to Elements. To do that, with your scanner connected to your computer, launch Preview, and then choose File→"Import from Scanner." You can even tell Preview to send the scan to Elements when you're done scanning. You can also scan with Image Capture (also part of OS X). However, if you have a really old scanner, the scanning features in OS X may not acknowledge its existence, in which case you have to use the software provided by the scanner's manufacturer.

If these methods don't work for you or don't offer all the features you need, you'll need to use the software that came with your scanner. Then, once you've saved your scanned image in a format that Elements understands, like TIFF (.tiff, .tif) or Photoshop (.psd), open the file in Elements like you would any other photo. (Page 72 explains which formats Elements can use.)

TIP If you do a lot of scanning, check out the Divide Scanned Photos command (page 79), which lets you quickly scan in several photos at the same time. Also, to save yourself a lot of drudgery in Elements, make sure that both your scanner's glass and the prints you're scanning are as dust-free as possible before you start.

■ Creating a New File

You may want to create a new, blank document when you're using Elements as a drawing program or when you're combining parts of images, for example.

To create a new file, go to the Editor, and choose File→New→Blank File, press Ctrl+N/⌘-N, or click the Open button at the upper left of your screen and choose New Blank File. No matter which method you use, you see the New dialog box, which contains lots of settings. The Name field is self-explanatory: Simply type in a name for the file. The following sections explain all the other settings.

TIP You can't create a new, blank file in the Organizer, but Elements gives you a quick shortcut from the Organizer to the Editor so you can open a new file there. In the Organizer, choose File→New→Photoshop Elements Image File, and Elements sends you over to the Editor and creates a virgin file for you. If you want to create a new file based on a photo that's in the Organizer, select the image's thumbnail, press Ctrl+C/⌘-C to copy the image, and then choose File→New→"Image from Clipboard." Elements switches you to the Editor, where you'll see your copied photo awaiting you, all ready to work on.

Picking a File Size

After you type a name for your file in the New dialog box, the next thing you need to decide is how big you want the image to be. There are two ways to do this:

- **Start with a preset**. The dialog box's Preset drop-down menu lets you choose the general kind of document you want. If you want to create a file for printing, pick from the menu's second group. The third group contains choices for on-screen viewing. Once you make a selection here, the next menu—Size—changes to show you suitable options for your choice. Figure 2-6 shows how this works.

TIP If you're into scrapbooking, you'll be pleased to know that Elements offers some standard scrapbook page sizes as presets.

- **Enter the numbers yourself**. If you prefer, you can ignore the Preset and Size menus and just type what you want in the Width and Height boxes instead. The drop-down menus next to these boxes let you choose inches, pixels, centimeters, millimeters, points, picas, or columns as your unit of measurement.

FIGURE 2-6

Elements helps you pick an appropriate size when you use the Preset menu. Here, Photo is selected in the Preset menu, so the Size menu includes standard sizes for photo prints, each available in either landscape or portrait orientation.

(The Preset menu's Default Photoshop Elements Size option is 6" × 4" at 300 pixels per inch, which works well if you're just playing around and trying things out.)

Choosing a Resolution

If you decide not to use one of Elements' preset sizes, you'll need to choose a resolution for your file. You'll learn a lot more about resolution in the next chapter (page

104), but a good rule of thumb is to go with 72 pixels per inch (ppi) for files that you'll look at only on a monitor, and 300 ppi for files you plan to print.

Selecting a Color Mode

Elements gives you lots of color choices throughout the program, but color mode is probably the most important because it determines which tools and filters you can use on the document. Here are your options:

- **RGB Color**. Choosing this mode (whose name stands for red, green, and blue) means that you're creating a color document, as opposed to a black-and-white one. (Page 240 has more about color in Elements.) You'll probably use this mode most of the time, even if you don't plan on having color in your image, because RGB gives you access to *all* of Elements' tools. That's right: You can use RGB Color mode for black-and-white images—and many people do, since it gives you the most options for editing your photos.

- **Bitmap**. Every pixel in a Bitmap-mode image is either black or white. Use this mode for *true* black-and-white images—shades of gray aren't welcome here.

- **Grayscale**. Black-and-white photos are technically called *grayscale* images because they're actually made up of many shades of gray. In Elements, you can't do as much editing on a grayscale photo as you can on an RGB one; for example, you can't use some of the program's filters on a grayscale image.

TIP Sometimes you may need to change the color mode of an existing file to use all of Elements' tools and filters. For example, there are quite a few things you can do only if your file is in RGB Color mode. So if you need to use a filter (page 435) on a black-and-white photo and the menu item you want is grayed out, go to Image→Mode→RGB Color. Don't worry; changing the color mode won't suddenly colorize your photo; it just changes the way Elements handles the file. (You can always change back to the original color mode when you're done.) If you use Elements' "Convert to Black and White" feature (page 349), you'll still have an RGB-mode photo afterward, not a Grayscale-mode image.

If your image is in RGB and you *still* don't have access to all the program's filters, check to see if the file is 16 bit (page 288). If so, you need to convert it to 8-bit color to get everything working. Make that change by choosing Image→Mode→8 Bits/Channel. You're most likely to have 16-bit files if you import your images in raw format (page 271). Some scanners also let you create 16-bit files. JPEG files are always 8-bit.

Choosing a Background

The last choice you have to make when creating a new file setting is the file's *back-ground contents*, which tells Elements what color to use for the empty areas of the file, like, well, the background. You can be a traditionalist and choose White from the New dialog box's Background Contents menu (almost always a good choice), or select a particular color or *transparency* (more about transparency in a minute). To pick a color other than white, *before* you call up the New dialog box, use the background color square to pick the color you want, as shown in Figure 2-7; then select Background Color from the New dialog box's Background Contents menu.

FIGURE 2-7

To choose a background color, just click the background color square in the Tools panel (here, that's the aqua one) to bring up the Color Picker. Then select the color you want (the process is explained in detail on page 253). The new color appears in the square, and the next time you do something that involves using a background color, that's the shade you get.

Transparent is the most interesting option. To understand transparency and why it's such a wonderful invention, you need to know that *every* digital image is either square or rectangular. Digital images *can't* be any other shape, but they can *appear* to be a different shape—sunflowers, sailboats, or German Shepherds, for example. How? By placing an object on a transparent background so that it looks like it was cut out and only its shape appears, as shown in Figure 2-8. The actual photo is still a rectangle, but if you placed it into another image, you'd see only the shell and not the surrounding area, because the rest of the photo is transparent.

To keep the clear areas transparent when you close the image, you need to save it in a format that allows transparency. JPEGs, for instance, automatically fill transparent areas with solid white, so they're not a good choice. TIFFs, PNGs, PDFs, and Photoshop (.psd) files, on the other hand, let the transparent areas stay clear. Page 560 has more about which formats allow transparency.

Using the Organizer

The Organizer is where you keep track of your photos and start most of the projects that involve sharing images with others (like posting them online, for example). You can see thumbnails of all your photos in the Organizer, assign them keywords (called *tags*) to make them easier to find, and search for them in lots of different ways.

In Elements 11, Adobe gave the Organizer a substantial makeover, based on two main ideas: Most people find organizing and tagging photos something of a chore; and most people want to organize photos by the people, places, or events they contain. Elements 13 builds on the changes Adobe made in Elements 11.

To try to deal with the drudgery of organizing, Elements includes a lot of ways to use various *smart* features, which let Elements do a lot of the heavy lifting for you. (If you've used a recent version of the Organizer, its face-recognition system is one example of this, but there are other such features, too.) You'll read about these features in the relevant sections of this book.

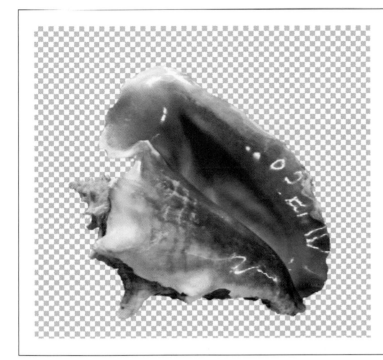

FIGURE 2-8

This checkered background is Elements' way of indicating that an area is transparent. (It doesn't mean you've somehow selected a patterned background.)

If you place this photo into another image, all you'll see is the seashell, without the checkerboard or the rectangular outline of the photo.

If you don't like the size and color of the checkerboard pattern, you can adjust them in the Editor by going to Edit→Preferences→Transparency/Photoshop Elements Editor→Preferences→Transparency.

To help you organize your photos by people, places, or events, the Organizer is divided into sections, which Adobe calls *views*. When you first import your photos, they come into Media view (Figure 2-9), which is the part of the Organizer where you can see all your photos all the time. From there, you can go into one of the other three views—People, Places, or Events—to do more organizing. You move from one view to another by clicking the tabs at the top of the window. To get the most out of the Organizer, you need to understand how all the views work together. There's also a tab for eLive, which works the same way it does in the Editor (page 22).

You can see all your tags (page 53) in Media view, although sometimes you need to switch views to use some of the program's smart features. Also, if you use Adobe Revel (see page 8) and sign into it through the Organizer, your Revel albums and libraries appear right in Media view. Page 57 explains how to use Revel with the Organizer.

In Elements 13, you have a new way to see your photos in Media view. When you first open Elements you see only your photos, edge-to-edge, so that they fill the entire space. Figure 2-10 explains how to use this new view, which Adobe calls the Adaptive Grid. To make the side panels, visible you may need to click the icons shown in Figure 2-9. In the Adaptive Grid view, you can only see the top item in version sets (page 71) and stacks (page 34), and it can be hard to deselect photos after you've selected them. Fortunately, you can also still use the old grid view (called Detail view), where your thumbnails are surrounded by gray space and you see info like the photo's date and star rating below its thumbnail. To toggle between the two views, press Ctrl+D/⌘-D or go to View→Details. You need to be in Detail view to expand stacks and version sets to see all the images they contain. In either view, while you scroll through your photos, a black pop-up appears under your cursor so that you can see the date for that particular batch of images to help you know where you are in your catalog.

FIGURE 2-9

Media view is where you usually start off in the Organizer. If you don't see the useful panels on the sides, then click the buttons circled here to display them. The panel on the left shows your albums or folders, and the one on the right displays information about your photos.

The Instant Fix button at the bottom right calls up a panel where you can perform quick image fixes in the Organizer.

This section covers only the very basics of Elements' organization system—there's lots more to it than there's room for here. Give the Organizer a good test drive to see if it works for you before you commit all your photos to it. You may hear from longtime Organizer users that they find the current incarnation of the Organizer more complicated than older versions, especially if they were used to the old setup. However, if you're upgrading from an older version of Elements, you'll be pleased to know that Elements 13 makes it easier than Elements 11 did to keep any organization you did in Elements 10 and earlier.

You don't *have* to use the Organizer. Many people use other programs to organize their photos (Lightroom, Aperture, iPhoto, or iView MediaPro, for example), or you can just create your own filing system. If you decide the Organizer isn't for you, see the box on page 46 if you use Windows or page 48 if you use a Mac to learn how to work around it.

Your Catalog

The Organizer stores information about your photos in a special database called a *catalog*. And you aren't limited to photos—you can store videos and audio files in the Organizer as well.

FIGURE 2-10

Top: Elements 13 brings this new view, called the Adaptive Grid, where you see only your photos and no background around them.

Bottom: The old Detail view, with info about your photos displayed beneath their thumbnails.

While the Adaptive Grid is more fun for showing off your photos, you'll probably want to switch to Detail view for much of your actual work, especially if you use stacks or version sets. In either view, if you click a photo to select it, the Organizer puts a checkmark in the lower right corner of the thumbnail (circled) so that you can be sure which photo's info you're seeing in the Tags/Info panel.

WORKAROUND WORKSHOP

Avoiding the Organizer on a PC

People either love the Organizer or they hate it. If you're in the latter group and you have a Windows computer, try to see if you can come to terms with the Organizer, because it does have some useful features. You'll lose a lot if you give up the Organizer, as it's the only place in Elements where you get a visual preview of your images before opening them.

If you just can't abide the Organizer, or if you prefer to use a different program like Lightroom or Windows Live Photo Gallery to organize your photos—or you just like to be disorganized—then you can sidestep the Organizer. Simply adjust your settings on the Welcome screen as described on page 5 so that Elements always takes you to the Editor. Also, in the Save As dialog box, remember to keep "Include in the Elements Organizer" and version sets turned *off* whenever you save a file. (Once

you turn off the "Include in the Elements Organizer" setting, it stays off until you turn it back on, or until you open a photo from the Organizer. You may find you need to turn it off once every editing session [maybe not, if you're lucky] but you don't have to keep turning it off every time you save.)

If you want to be extra sure that Elements doesn't interpret any of your photo-related activities as a call for the Organizer, go to your computer's Control Panel→"System and Security"→Administrative Tools→Services and find Adobe Active File Monitor V13. This is a *service*, a small program that always runs in the background when your computer is on, even when Elements is closed. Click Adobe Active File Monitor, and then go to Action→Properties and set the "Startup type" option to Disabled.

You don't have to do anything special to create your catalog—Elements creates it automatically the first time you import photos (and creatively names it *My Catalog*). It's possible to have more than one catalog, but most people don't because you can't search more than one catalog at a time. If for some reason you want more than one catalog, or if you ever want to start over with a new catalog, in the Organizer, go to File→Manage Catalogs, and then click the New button. Enter a name for it, and then click OK.

Your catalog can include photos stored anywhere on your computer, and even photos that you've moved to external hard drives and CDs or DVDs. There aren't any limits on where you can keep your originals. That's how it's *supposed* to work, anyway. But in practice, Elements sometimes has a tough time finding files stored on network drives and other externals, so you may run into trouble if you want Elements to find photos you've saved on such devices. (The Mac Organizer, in particular, can't deal with network drives at all, although it should see removable drives, like FireWire or USB drives.)

Once your photos appear in the Organizer, if you want to move them, you have to use the Organizer to do that—as opposed to using another method like Windows Explorer—otherwise, the Organizer won't know where they are.

TIP   If you want to edit photos in programs other than Elements, the Organizer lets you do that. Just go to Edit→Preferences→Editing/Elements Organizer→Preferences→Editing, turn on the Supplementary Editing Application checkbox, and then select your preferred program. This is handy if you want to supplement Elements with a program like PaintShop Pro or Pixelmator. (If you have Photoshop installed on your computer, it's automatically listed as an editing option.) Once you've chosen a supplemental editor, sending photos there is easy: Just select their thumbnails and then click the tiny arrow next to the Editor button at the bottom of the Organizer and choose External Editor.

If you decide to use a supplemental editor with the Organizer, be aware that Elements 13 doesn't automatically update your image thumbnails when you're through editing them. You need to do it manually by selecting the photo(s) and going to View→Refresh, or just pressing F5.

Media View

Media view (Figure 2-9) is where your photos make their first appearance in the Organizer. There's a lot happening in this window, but it's all laid out pretty logically.

The center of the window shows thumbnails of all your photos. On the left side of the window is a panel with two tabs (if you don't see this panel, click the Show button at the window's bottom left); this useful panel is visible in all the Organizer's views, not just Media view. One tab (Albums) includes the names of any albums (page 55) you've made. The other tab (Folders) contains, logically enough, a list of all the folders where your Organizer photos live. You can hide this panel by clicking the Hide button at the bottom of the screen. When the panel is hidden, the button changes to say "Show"; click it again to bring the panel back.

TIP   If you want to move photos that are in the Organizer from one place on your hard drive to another, use the Folder tab, which is described starting on page 50.

You can use the Sort By menu above the thumbnail area to see your photos by newest first, oldest first, name, or the batches in which you imported them. To adjust the size of the thumbnails, use the Zoom slider below the thumbnail area. You can also quickly see any image in a larger view by double-clicking its thumbnail. This enlarges the image so it's the only one on your screen. If you want to look through multiple photos in this single-image view, navigate through them by clicking the arrows above the image area. To get back to the regular grid view of all the thumbnails, press Esc or click the Grid button at the upper left of the image area. (You can also view, organize, and edit your photos in Full Screen view, which is described on page 51.)

Should You Use the Mac Organizer?

Starting with Elements 9, Adobe began including the Organizer in the Mac version of Elements instead of Adobe Bridge, which came with older versions of the program. So if you have a Mac, you need to decide whether to use the Organizer to keep track of your photos, and this is an even thornier question than it is in Windows.

If you've been using the Organizer in Windows and you just got a Mac, you probably want to use the Mac Organizer, since that's the easiest way to move everything over. However, you can move only catalogs made with Elements 9 or later from one operating system to the other, so if you have a version of Elements for Windows that's older than that, install Elements 13 on your Windows machine—you get both versions of the program in the same box—and then use it to upgrade your existing catalog. Next, make a full backup of your catalog to a removable hard drive. Then install Elements 13 on your Mac, and then restore the backup there by choosing File→Restore Catalog. Once you're sure everything's working OK, you can deactivate Elements on the Windows computer (page 594) if you no longer need it. (It's important to be aware that this process works only if you bought Elements 13 in a *box*, since a download version comes with a serial number that's only for Windows or only for Mac.)

If you have Premiere Elements, Adobe's video-editing program, the Organizer is much more important to that program than it is to Photoshop Elements. So you'll probably want to come to grips with the Organizer if you use both Photoshop Elements and Premiere Elements.

If you use iPhoto, it's easy to siphon your images into the Organizer by choosing File→"Get Photos and Videos"→From iPhoto. If you use this command, you import your *entire* iPhoto library into Elements. Elements makes duplicates of all the files, which you'll find in your Pictures folder→Adobe→Organizer→iPhoto Library Media. This is the *only* time Elements ever copies photos on import. That's a good thing, because the iPhoto library gets very cranky if you poke at it from outside iPhoto (for example, don't try to make Elements save back into the iPhoto library, or you could lose your photos entirely). Also, the Organizer has been known to make unexpected changes to the metadata (page 49) of files in the Organizer; if this happened to an image that's already in iPhoto, it's hard to say what the effect might be. So if you're feeling brave, go ahead and give the Organizer a try. Just know that there's a slight risk involved.

If you want to move only some of your photos to the Organizer or just try it out, export your photos from the photo-management program you currently use, or create duplicate files to use as your test catalog. Put them where you want to keep them, and then import them by going to File→Get Photos→"From Files and Folders" in the Organizer. (Importing this way just creates an Organizer database entry for your photos, not a separate copy.)

The two big advantages to using the Organizer are that you can use all of Elements' features, and Elements lets you save unlimited versions of your photos (see page 71). iPhoto, on the other hand, keeps only a single version plus the original. That means that if you edit a photo and then save it again, iPhoto overwrites the previous version (unless you import your saved files into iPhoto as new documents, which is a pain), and if you want to go back to your original, you lose the current, edited version. The big disadvantage of using the Organizer is that it's not as smoothly integrated with other OS X programs as iPhoto is. Whatever you do, *don't* use both the Organizer and iPhoto to keep track of all your photos, because the two programs don't understand each other very well and you'll just get confused.

If you decide to avoid the Organizer, Adobe makes it easy to ignore it on a Mac. Just turn off the "Include in the Elements Organizer" checkbox in the Save As window (it should stay off, at least for that editing session). If photos accidentally get Organized, it's not a big deal, since the Organizer is just a database, which means it's not making copies of the photos and wasting gobs of space with duplicate images. If you're a fan of Adobe Bridge that you got with an older version of Elements, you can keep using it. You just can't update it anymore, which is likely to be a problem if you shoot in raw format (page 271) and buy a new model camera whose raw format Bridge doesn't understand. (You can learn more about using Elements with iPhoto and using Bridge with later versions of Elements at *www.barbarabrundage.com.*)

On the right side of the Organizer window is another panel with two tabs at its top: Tags and Information. (If you don't see this panel, click the Tags/Info button at the bottom right of the Organizer window.) If you click a photo's thumbnail, the Information panel shows you a *lot* of info about that photo—so much, in fact, that the panel is divided into three sections. Click the name of a section to expand it and see the information it contains:

- **General**. This section includes the photo's name, caption, any notes you've made, any rating you've assigned (page 56), along with the photo's size, date, location, and any audio associated with it.

- **Metadata**. This section includes all the info that your camera stores in the file. Most notably, this is where you can see your image's EXIF (Exchangeable Image Format) data, information your camera stores about your photos including the camera you used, when you took the picture, and the various camera settings like exposure, aperture setting, and so on.

  There are two little buttons at the upper right of this section. Normally Elements starts you off showing the *brief* metadata, a short list of the most commonly used information, but if you click the right-hand button, you get the *full* metadata—all the info stored in the file. There's more about metadata on page 69.

> **TIP** You can easily edit your files' metadata in the Organizer. In Media view, just select the files you want to tweak, and then click the Edit IPTC Information button that appears in the Information panel. In the window that appears, you can add or change metadata, or click the Remove IPTC Metadata button to remove it.

- **History**. Here you can see when the file was last modified, when you imported it and from where, and the name of the volume (meaning "drive") where it's stored now.

At the bottom of the panel is a section labeled Image Tags, where you can see any tags currently attached to the selected image and add your own tags. If you switch over to the Tags panel by clicking its tab, you also see the hierarchy of your tags and categories (page 53).

At the bottom right of the Organizer window is the Instant Fix button. Click it and Elements replaces the Tags and Information panels with the Photo Fix Options panel, which lets you apply a bunch of popular one-button edits to your photos right in the Organizer, without sending the images over to the Editor. You can crop a photo here, as well as apply Auto Contrast, Auto Red Eye, Auto Color, Auto Sharpening, Auto Levels, and Auto Smart Fix. (Chapter 4 has more about how these Auto features work.) When you use any of these fixes, the Organizer automatically creates version sets with your original photo, so it's not altered at all. To bring the other panels back when you're done using these instant fixes, just click the Tags/Info button at the bottom right of the Organizer window.

If some of your images came into the Organizer on their sides or upside down, you can get them upright by selecting their thumbnails and then clicking the Rotate button at the bottom of the window. This turns the photos counterclockwise; if you want to turn them the other way, click the tiny arrow on the right side of the Rotate button and then click the button that appears. You can also press Ctrl/⌘ and the right or left arrow key.

If you want to undo anything you've done in the Organizer, click the Undo button that's always at the bottom left of your screen, or just use the regular Ctrl+Z/⌘-Z keystroke. If you change your mind about undoing something, click the tiny arrow to the right of the Undo button, and then click the Redo button that appears, or just press Ctrl+Y/⌘-Y.

In addition, no matter which of the Organizer's views you're in, you always have the option to import new files into the Organizer, start a Create project (page 509), or share your photos in a variety of ways (page 578). You can do all these things from the bar at the top of the Organizer window.

■ WORKING WITH FOLDERS

If you decide to use the Organizer, you're putting it in charge of keeping track of your photos. But it can't do that if you move or delete photos from *outside* the Organizer; if you do, your photos become unconnected, and you have to help the Organizer reconnect them. So it's much better to do all moving and deleting from within the Organizer, which includes the handy Folders panel that makes it easy to move photos around in a way that the Organizer can keep track of.

To see your folders, head to the panel on the left side of Media view and click the Folders tab. (If you don't see this panel, click the Show button at the bottom left of the Organizer window.) This tab is a big improvement over Elements 12, which combined folders and albums into one view.

Adobe gives you two ways to see folders in the Organizer. When you first start out in the Folders panel, you just see a list of the folders containing the photos currently in the Organizer. In this simple view (which Adobe calls *List view*), you can move a photo by simply dragging its thumbnail from the preview area in the middle of the Organizer window onto the name of the folder you want to put it in. In List view, you can also right-click/Control-click any folder to display a pop-out menu that lets you see where it's located in Windows Explorer or the Mac Finder, watch the folder (if you use Windows—see page 35), rename it, delete it, or create an *instant album* based on it (an album of all the photos contained in that folder; Elements names the album the same thing as the folder).

That's all well and good, but what if you want to move a photo into a folder that doesn't yet contain any Organizer photos? Simply click the little four-line square at the upper right of the Folders panel (circled in Figure 2-11), choose "View as Tree," and Elements displays an expanded view of the folders on your hard drive. This hierarchical view, aptly called *Tree view*, lets you see all the folders on your hard drive, as Figure 2-11 explains.

FIGURE 2-11

Left: Here's the basic List view the Organizer starts you out with. Click the four-line square (circled) and choose "View as Tree" to see a more complete view of the folders on your hard drive.

Right: Here's Tree view, where you can right-click/ Control-click a folder to see a menu that has all the same options you get by doing so in List view and lets you import photos from that folder, as well as see all the subfolders within that folder. These options let you move a photo from anywhere on your hard drive to anywhere else you like, as long as the photo is already in the Organizer. If not, you'll need to import it before you can do anything with it here. (To get back to List view, click the square again and choose "View as List.")

You can also search by folder name. To see the contents of a particular folder, just type its name in the search box at the top of the Organizer window. You can also include the folder's name in a more complex search if you go to Find→By Details→Metadata. There's more about searching on page 67.

■ FULL SCREEN VIEW

One of the handiest features in the Organizer is Full Screen view. Once you get your photos into the Organizer, click the Slide Show button at the bottom of the screen, (keyboard shortcut: F11/⌘-F11) or use the secret "Compare Photos Side by Side" keystroke (F12/⌘-F12) to see a larger, slideshow-like view of your photos (either singly or in pairs) so you can pick the ones you want to print or edit. You can even choose music to accompany them. Figure 2-12 shows the difference between the two views. (If you don't want anything that elaborate, just double-click a thumbnail in Media view to see that photo enlarged to fit the available space. Double-click it again to go back to thumbnail view.)

NOTE If you have a Mac with a keyboard without the 10-key pad on the right—like a laptop or the current Bluetooth keyboard—you need to add the fn key to most keystroke combinations that use the top row of the keyboard. So if you have a MacBook Pro, for example, you'd press fn-⌘-F11 for Full Screen view.

FIGURE 2-12

Top: If you press F11/⌘-F11, you get this handy full-screen view of your images, where you can tag them or make quick edits to them. There are two panels hiding on the left side of the screen (you can see only their edges here); click an edge to pop the panel open.

Bottom: In "Side by Side" view, you can choose between comparing two images next to each other, as shown here, or click the View button (circled) to see one image above the other.

Elements also lets you apply many editing commands right in Full Screen and "Side by Side" view. Just put your cursor over the Quick Edit panel's tab on the left side of the screen, and it pops out to give you access to all the one-button fixes available in the Editor's Quick Fix mode (page 117). When you use these buttons, Elements automatically creates a new version (page 71) for each edited file. You can also use the stars at the top of this panel to rate your photos (page 56). The Quick Organize panel (also on the left side of the screen) lets you apply keyword tags, or put photos into albums (page 55).

> **TIP** The Organizer's Quick Edit and Quick Organize panels close back up each time a new image appears onscreen. To make a panel stay open, click the tiny pushpin icon on its right edge. To get rid of a panel entirely, click its Close button (the X). To bring it back, use the controls at the bottom of the screen, which are described in detail on page 573.

You can even use Full Screen view as a quick slideshow to show off your latest images—see page 572 to learn how. To exit Full Screen view and get back to Media view, press Esc.

Creating Categories and Tags

The Organizer has a great system for quickly finding photos, but it works only if you use special keywords, called *tags*, that help Elements track down your pictures. A tag can be a word, a date, or even a rating (see the box on page 55). When you import photos to the Organizer, they're automatically tagged with the import date and any other tags you've specified in the Photo Downloader (see page 30). But you may want to add more tags to make it easier to search for the photo's subject later on. You can give a photo as many tags as you like.

Elements lets you group tags into *categories*. You get a few preset categories—like Nature, Color, and Travel—and you can create your own, as well as make subcategories. For example, you can make a Vacations category with China Trip and Cozumel as subcategories. Your photos in those categories could have tags like "Jim and Helen," "silk factory," and "snorkeling."

You create some tags in Media view. These basic tags are explained here, but tagging people, places, and events works a little differently (although you can *start* assigning those tags right in Media view). Those tags are explained in the following sections, beginning on page 60.

■ WORKING WITH BASIC TAGS AND CATEGORIES

As mentioned above, Elements gives you a few generic tags to help get you started, but you'll want to create your own tags, too. After all, by the time you've got 5,000 or so photos in the Organizer, searching for "Family" probably isn't going to narrow things down much. Creating a new tag is as easy as can be:

- **Just type it**. In the Tags panel (page 49), head down to the box that contains the placeholder text "Add Custom Keywords" and start typing. At first you see a pop-up menu of all the existing tags, but if you keep typing, once Elements recognizes it as a new tag, the pop-up changes to say "Create new tag '[whatever you typed].'" Select the photo(s) you want to apply this new tag to, and then click Add. Elements puts tags created this way in the Other category in the upper part of the Tags panel (you may need to click the word "Keywords" to see these categories). To put it somewhere else, drag the tag's icon to the category where it belongs.

- **Keyboard shortcut**. When you're in the Organizer, press Ctrl+N/⌘-N to display the Create Keyword Tag dialog box. The next paragraph explains how to use this dialog box.

- **Menu**. At the top of the Tags panel, click the green + sign to the right of the word "Keywords," and the Create Keyword Tag dialog box appears. (Alternatively, you can click the down arrow to the right of this + sign and choose New Keyword Tag instead; you can also create a new category or subcategory via this same menu.) Name the new tag by typing it in, and then use the drop-down menu to assign it to a category. (You can change the category later if you want.)

  If you want to assign people, places, or events tags, in the Tags panel, click the green + sign to the right of the kind of tag you want to create. If you click the + sign to the right of "Places Tags," for example, a map appears so that you can associate the photo with its location (see page 63 for details).

No matter which method you use, Elements automatically assigns the first photo to which you apply the tag as the tag's icon image, but you can edit the tag's icon, as explained in Figure 2-13. To assign the tag to a photo, simply drag the tag's icon from the Tags panel onto the photo's thumbnail. You can rearrange tags by dragging them to different categories in the Tags panel, and change tags to categories and categories to tags by right-clicking/Control-clicking them and choosing from the pop-up menu.

TIP To see all the photos that have a certain tag assigned, in the Tags panel, just turn on the checkbox to the left of its name. To get back to all your photos, turn off the checkbox or click the Back button at the top of the window.

To remove a tag you've assigned:

- **From a single photo**. Right-click/Control-click the photo's thumbnail and select Remove Keyword Tag→[name of tag].

- **From a group of photos**. Select the photos, right-click/Control-click one of them, select "Remove Keyword Tag from Selected Items," and then choose the tag you want to remove.

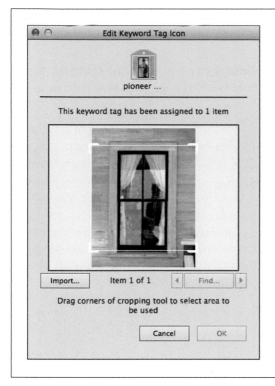

FIGURE 2-13

Some people like to edit the icons that Elements uses to represent different tags to make it easy to search for a tag visually as well as by name.

To change the picture associated with a tag, in the Tags panel, right-click/Control-click the tag, and then choose Edit. In the Edit Keyword Tag dialog box that appears, click Edit Icon, and Elements opens the dialog box shown here.

The arrows on either side of the Find button let you advance through all the photos that use that tag. (If you click the Find button itself, you see all those photos at once.) If you don't want to use any of those images as the icon, click the Import button to use a different image stored on your computer. Once you select a picture, drag the white square to choose which part of the photo appears on the tag.

TIP   In the past few versions of Elements, the Organizer has included a feature called the Auto Analyzer, which can evaluate photos and videos. In previous versions of Elements, the Auto Analyzer would evaluate your photos and assign special tags, called *smart tags*, for characteristics like high or low quality, in focus, and so on. Elements 13 still includes the Auto Analyzer, but now it runs only on video files, and even then only if you also have Premiere Elements installed or upload a video to Revel (page 57), or if you let the Organizer index your photos when it asks. If you refuse, you won't start the Auto Analyzer (which, once it runs, will always start up each time you restart your computer), but you won't get very good search results, either. There are no more smart tags in Elements, but if you used this feature in a previous version, smart tags created there are still available for searching, although they no longer appear in the Tags panel.

Albums

Elements lets you group photos into *albums*, which are great for gathering together pictures taken at a particular event. They're also handy for preparing groups of photos that you want to use in a Create project like a slideshow or photo collage (see Chapter 15).

Special Tags

Elements starts you off with two special kinds of tags:

- **Ratings**. These tags let you assign one- to five-star ratings to photos (a good way to mark the ones you want to print or edit). Ratings are a great search tool, because you can tell Elements to find, say, all your pictures rated four or more stars. To assign ratings, in the Organizer, go to View→Details or press Ctrl+D/⌘-D, and then click the star under the photo's thumbnail that corresponds to your rating (the third star from the left for a three-star rating, say); or you can rate any photo in the Information panel's General section. To search by ratings, click the appropriate star at the top right of the Organizer and then choose a qualifier (like "and higher") by clicking the symbol to the left of the stars. You can search for all photos rated four stars or higher, for instance, or those rated two stars or lower, and so on. To change or remove a photo's rating, right-click/Control-click its thumbnail, choose Ratings from the menu that appears, and then pick the number of stars you want. You can also change a rating by clicking a different star under the image's thumbnail (if you're in Details view).

- **Hidden**. When you apply this tag to a photo, the photo disappears from the Organizer window. The Hidden tag is useful for archiving photos that didn't come out quite right but that you're not ready to trash; that way, you can save these pictures (just in case) without having them cluttering up your screen while you're working with your good photos. To assign the Hidden tag, right-click/Control-click a photo and choose Visibility→"Mark as Hidden." To bring it back, go up to the View menu and choose Hidden Files→Show All Files, or right-click a visible photo and then choose Visibility→Show All Files; both methods make even your hidden files visible. Then right-click/Control-click the photo again, and select Visibility→"Mark as Visible" to keep it in view. To put the rest of your hidden files back out of sight, choose View→Hidden Files→Hide Hidden Files. See *only* your hidden files by going to View→Hidden Files→Show Only Hidden Files.

When you create an album, you don't actually make a copy of all the photos included in it; you just create a group of virtual "pointers" to each image so Elements knows where to find them. That means albums can hold lots of pictures without taking up much space and, even better, you can include the same picture in different albums. Also, photos in an album can appear in any order you choose, which is important if, for instance, you're preparing a slideshow. Albums are divided into two main sections: Local Albums, which contain photos stored on your computer, and Mobile Albums, which are for photos stored online via Adobe Revel. (Revel is explained in the next section.)

Elements gives you several ways to create albums:

- **From the Organizer**. First, Ctrl-click/⌘-click the photos you want to include to select them. Then, go to the Albums panel (page 47) and click the green + sign. In the New Album panel that appears on the right side of the Organizer window, name your album and assign it to a *category* (explained in a moment) if you wish, and then click OK. Your new album joins the list of albums.

You can also make an album from files anywhere on your computer, even if they're not in the Organizer, by heading to the Albums panel and clicking the tiny arrow to the right of the green + sign, and then selecting "Import Albums from File."

- **From the Editor**. In the Editor, you can create an album from the Photo Bin's Bin Actions menu (page 14).

> **NOTE** No matter which method you use to make an album, it will appear in the lists of albums in both the Organizer and the Editor (in the Photo Bin's Show menu).

To see the photos in an album, just click its name in the Albums panel. To return to viewing all your photos, click the Back button at the top left of the thumbnail area.

You can also create *album categories*, which are just what they sound like: they let you group albums into categories to make them easier to keep track of (handy if you have lots of albums). To make an album category, go to the Albums panel, click the tiny arrow to the right of the green + sign, and then choose New Album Category. Name your category, and it appears in the Albums list. To add albums to it, just drag their icons onto the category's name. To remove an album from it, click the flippy triangle to the left of the category's name so you can see all the albums it contains, and then right-click the album you want to remove and choose Edit. In the Edit Album panel that appears on the right side of the Organizer window, click the Category drop-down menu and choose "None (Top Level)." Then click OK at the bottom of the Edit Album panel.

You can also create subcategories within categories. To do that, in the Albums panel, click the tiny arrow to the right of the green + sign and choose New Album Category. Then name your subcategory and, in the Parent Album Category drop-down menu, choose the main category under which you want it to appear. The new category appears as a subcategory of the original one.

> **NOTE** If you're looking for the Smart Albums feature from old editions of Elements, it's gone, but you can achieve pretty much the same thing with saved searches (page 69).

Using Revel

Just below the Local Albums section of the Albums panel is the Mobile Albums section. This is the Organizer's gateway to Adobe's Revel online service, which is a way to share your photos among all your devices, both computers and mobile devices like smartphones or tablets. (You need to have the free Adobe Revel app installed on your mobile devices; it's available for both iOS and Android.)

> **NOTE** Everything in this section describes how Revel worked with Elements when this book was written. But since Revel is constantly changing, don't be surprised if some things are quite different by the time you read this. Any major changes will be noted on this book's Missing CD page at *www.missingmanuals.com/cds*.

When you first start the Organizer, you probably won't see anything in this section unless you used Revel in Elements 12. You need to sign into your Revel account (or create one) before Elements can connect and display your Revel photos. This is in *addition* to the sign-in you did when you first installed Elements, and you don't have to use the same Adobe ID for both sign-ins (though you can). However, only one Revel account at a time can be associated with a particular Organizer catalog.

> **TIP** If you have more than one Revel account and you want to switch the one you're using in Elements, first sign out of your current Revel account. To do that, go to Edit→Preferences→Online Account/Elements Organizer→Preferences→Online Account and click Sign Out. Then, sign in again by going to File→"Sign In to Online Account" and entering the information for the account you want to use.

If you used Photoshop.com in an older version of Elements, you probably already have photos stored on the Revel servers, since Adobe moved all Photoshop.com images over to Revel in June 2013. (You should have received several emails about this, both before and during the transition.) If you used Elements 12, your Revel information should have transferred along with the rest of your catalog when you upgraded it. If you've never used Photoshop.com or Revel before, no problem—you can just create a new account. Revel gives you 2 GB of storage space for free. If you want more than that, you have to pay $5.99 a month.

To sign into Revel or create a new account, in the Organizer, go to File→"Sign In to Online Account." In the window that appears, either log in with your existing Adobe ID or click "Create an Adobe ID" to make a new one.

Once you're signed in, if you already have albums on Revel, they appear in the Albums panel's list of Mobile Albums. Revel organizes your photos and albums into groups called *libraries*. You can create as many libraries as you like, but you can work with only one library at a time in the Organizer, so you see only the albums from the current library. You can delete albums from Revel via the Albums panel. This deletes only the album itself; if you want to delete the photos *within* the album from Revel as well, select them, and then right-click/Control-click one and choose "Remove from Revel." To delete a library from Revel, go to Edit→Preferences→Online Account/Elements Organizer→Preferences→Online Account, click its name in the list there, and then click the – button.

You can share your photos with other Revel users, and they can share theirs with you. When someone wants to share photos with you, a window with the invitation pops up in the Organizer so you can accept or reject the invite. If you accept, the photos appear in your Mobile Albums list. To share your own album with other people, click the "Share via Adobe Revel" icon to the right of the album's name (it looks like a rectangle with a curved arrow on it). Next, in the Album Web Share window that opens, click Start Sharing, and then enter the email address of the person you want to share with. Once you've shared an album, the icon changes from gray to blue, and you can see a list of all the people who have access to it (as well as the status of any invitations) by clicking the icon. To stop sharing with someone, click the X to the right of his name. Sharing a library works pretty much the same way, only libraries have an "Invite users to collaborate" icon that looks like a two-person silhouette. Click it, and then enter the email of the person with whom you want to share your library. You stop sharing the same way you do with albums: by clicking the X to the right of the name of the person you don't want to share with anymore.

You can upload photos to Revel by adding them to a shared album or by selecting them and then going to Share→Private Web Album. To send albums from the Organizer to Revel, just drag the album in the Albums panel and, in the Mobile Albums section, drop it into the library you want. You can also drag a Mobile Album onto the Local Albums heading to move it to that section.

It's important to know that Revel likes JPEG files best. If you send a raw file or a PSD file to Revel, it automatically creates a JPEG of the file (and in the case of the raw file, a DNG file, too, so things can get pretty cluttered after a while). If you edit the original of a file you've shared via Revel, Elements automatically creates a new JPEG and saves it as a version in the Organizer, and then shares that JPEG to Revel.

If you like, you can tell Elements to upload *all* your photos to Revel (but you probably won't want to do this unless you have a subscription). Once you're logged into Revel, in the Organizer, go to Edit→Preferences→Online Account/Elements Organizer→Preferences→Online Account and turn on "Automatically access all my catalog media in online account." After that, Elements uploads all your photos to Revel and you can use them on all your computers and mobile devices. (If you do this, then the Local Albums section of the Organizer's Albums panel disappears.)

If you want to work with photos that are only stored on Revel, you normally have just a small preview of them in the Organizer. So if you want to do something that requires a full-resolution photo—like editing or printing the image—Elements has to download it. To tell Elements to download a photo from Revel, right-click/Control-click the image's thumbnail and choose "Download original."

The *Elements Agent* is the feature that gets your photos onto the Revel servers and keeps an eye on whether there's anything new to upload. The Agent can use a lot of your computer's processor power, but there are few ways you can control it, as Figure 2-14 explains. You can also use the items in the menu shown in Figure 2-14 to view the status of your Revel uploads and downloads, and to tell the Organizer to stop syncing to Revel (although going to Edit→Preferences→Online Account/ Elements Organizer→Preferences→Online Account and setting the Elements Agent slider to Off is a better way to do this).

Here are some basics of what you can do with Revel from the Organizer:

- **Add a photo to a mobile album**. Just drag its thumbnail from the main Organizer window into the album you want.

- **Create a new mobile album**. In the Albums panel, click the green + sign to the right of the Mobile Albums label to display the New Album pane on the right side of the Organizer window. Using this pane works pretty much the same way as creating a regular album (page 56), except that the album you make here automatically gets shared to Revel.

FIGURE 2-14

Once you've logged into your Revel account you see a special icon in the Notifications area at the bottom of your screen (in Windows) or in the menu bar at the top of your screen (on a Mac); the icon is a little cloud. Click it to display this menu, which lets you tell Revel to sync your photos only when your computer isn't busy doing something else, which frees up your processor to concentrate on other things.

- **Remove a photo from a mobile album**. In the Mobile Albums section of the Albums panel, click the album's name to see its contents. Then right-click/Control-click the thumbnail of the photo you want to remove and choose "Remove from Album"→[album name].

- **Remove a photo from Revel**. Right-click/Control-click its thumbnail and choose "Remove from Revel."

- **Download a photo from Revel**. Right-click/Control-click its thumbnail and choose "Download original."

Tagging People

Elements has included *face recognition* technology for a while now. This feature lets the Organizer analyze your photos for faces and then display the ones it found so you can create tags for them. (Adobe calls this feature "people recognition," but it's designed to find only faces; it doesn't work so well on a photo of someone's back, for example.)

Here's how to use face recognition to find people in your photos:

1. **If you want to limit the photos that the Organizer analyzes, select them (this step is optional).**

2. **At the bottom of the Media view window, click the Add People button.**

   If you haven't pre-selected any photos, a dialog box asks if you're sure you want to find people. (Why else would you have clicked the button?) Click Yes. (If you selected any photos in step 1, you don't see this dialog box.) If you have any files where Elements didn't recognize anything in the photo as a person, you see a warning that Elements will skip those files; click OK. Elements starts chugging away, looking for people. When it's done, the People Recognition window opens with thumbnail images of different people that Elements found, with "Which of these people would you like to label?" at the top of the screen.

3. **Click the thumbnails of the people you want to tag, and then click Save.**

4. Identify the people Elements found.

Click the words "Who is this?" below a photo and type a name for each person. (Figure 2-15 shows what to do if Elements offers you an image that *isn't* a person.) If you need to see a larger view to be sure who the person is, right-click/Control-click the thumbnail and choose "Show in Full Size View." When you're done looking at the bigger view, click Back. Once you've filled in everyone's names, click Save.

FIGURE 2-15

If Elements makes a hopeful guess about something that isn't actually a person, right-click/Control-click the thumbnail and choose "Not A Person." If it is a person, just type the name. If you need a better look to decide, choose "Show in Full Size View."

TIP If you use Facebook, you have the option of downloading your Facebook friends list to help name people. Just click the button at the bottom left of the People Recognition window to start the process.

5. Tell Elements if it made mistakes in identifying anyone.

After you click Save in step 3, Elements shows you all the photos it found of each person and asks you to exclude anyone who doesn't belong in the group. If Elements misidentified someone—it thought one photo of your Uncle Fred was his brother Bill, say—click the arrow on the lower-right corner of the misidentified photo and choose "Not [name]." When you're done, click Save.

6. Identify more people.

Elements shows you another group of people. Repeat steps 3 and 4. It's easier this time because, when you click "Who is this?" Elements offers you a little pop-out with some of the people tags you've already created; just click a name to apply it to that photo. And if you start typing a name, you see a list of the names you've already entered that begin with that letter. When you're done, click Save.

7. Identify (or exclude) even *more* people.

When Elements is through with the people it's most sure about, it offers you a larger group of prospects that may include lots of things that aren't people and asks, "Which of these people would you like to label?" If Elements shows a photo that isn't a person you want to tag (or isn't a person at all), click the No symbol (the circle with a slash across it) in its upper-right corner. For photos that are people you want to tag, click the No symbol and choose "Is a Person." When you're done, click Save, and Elements puts you through the identification process for your selections. When you're through, Elements displays a dialog box that says, "You have labeled everyone in your selection." Click OK and, if you like, switch over to People view, shown in Figure 2-16, for a look at all the people you've tagged.

FIGURE 2-16

When you're finished tagging the people in your photos, switch over to the Organizer's People view to see all your photos of people in neat stacks for each person. To switch to this view, simply click the People tab at the top of the Organizer window.

People view includes only images tagged with people tags. You can quickly scroll through all the images in a person's stack by moving your cursor over the stack. If you want the Organizer to use a different photo as the top image in the stack, right-click/Control-click the image when it appears and choose "Assign as Profile Picture."

NOTE You can *manually* add people tags to a particular photo, but there are some limitations. Just go to Media view and right-click/Control-click a photo and choose "Add a Person." A little window pops up where you can type in the name; type it, and then click Add. When you're through adding people, click the window's Close button (the X in Windows, the red dot on a Mac) to dismiss it. If you add a new person this way, she gets a stack, but no profile photo—you just see a gray box at the top of her stack. Photos of people with existing Elements-generated People tags that you tag this way should go right into their existing stacks. In either case, to see all the photos associated with the person, expand his stack by double-clicking it and, at the top left of the preview area, clicking the Faces/Photos switch to make sure it's set to Photos.

To see all the photos in a stack at once, double-click the stack to expand it. If you want the Organizer to find additional photos of this person, click Find More at the bottom of the screen. (If you've already let the Organizer analyze all your photos for people, most likely it will just tell you there aren't any more.) Click the Back button at the top left of the preview area to go back to the main People view.

If you made a mistake naming someone—say you mistyped her name—you can fix that by clicking her photo stack and then clicking the Rename button at the bottom left of the Organizer window. A window pops up where you can type the name correctly.

Once you've tagged everyone, the People/Group switch above the photo area becomes active. Click it to set it to Groups, and a Groups panel appears on the right side of People view, where you can put people into groups. (If you don't see the panel, click the Groups button at the bottom right of the Organizer window to display it.) You get some preset groups (Colleagues, Family, Friends), and you can create your own by clicking the panel's green + sign. You add people to groups by dragging their tags onto the group's name. To remove a photo from a group, right-click/Control-click its thumbnail and choose "Move to Ungrouped." However, there's a severe handicap to using groups: Nobody can be in more than one group. So if you put a friend from work into the Colleagues group and then add her to the Friends group, she disappears from Colleagues.

Tagging Places

You can add two different kinds of place tags to the photos you take. The first kind, the ones you assign in Places view, include GPS data about the location. The second kind are ones you create in Media view, but those tags don't include any GPS info. Creating place tags in Media view is explained on page 47; this section focuses on creating them in Places view.

■ TAGGING PLACES IN PLACES VIEW

If your camera has a GPS system that automatically records the coordinates where you take each shot, then using Places view is super easy. When you click the Places tab at the top of the Organizer window, you see all your GPS-enabled photos already placed on the Google map for you. However, this *doesn't* create a place tag that you can see in Media view. If you want to make such a tag, in either Media view or Places view, right-click/Control-click the photo's thumbnail, and then choose Edit Places from the pop-out menu. Then you can create a tag by reassigning the photo to the map using the procedure explained in the following numbered list. Or, if it's not important to you that the tag appear in the Tags panel's Places category or you don't want to hassle with replacing all your photos on the map, you can just create a regular tag in Media view.

If your camera *doesn't* use GPS and you haven't added that data to any of your photos, then you see a blank window the first time you enter Places view. Not to worry, though: You can manually tag your photos here by dragging them to locations on a Google map. It's pretty easy to do:

1. **Go to Places view and call up the map.**

   Click the Add Places button at the bottom of Places view. The Add Places window appears, where you see your photos in a strip along the top of the Google map. You can preselect photos or limit your search by clicking an album or a folder in the Albums or Folders panel (if the panel isn't visible, click the Show button at the bottom left of your screen) either before or after entering Places view. If you don't, then all your photos appear here.

2. **Place your photos on the map.**

   Figure 2-17 explains how to do this. You can adjust your view of the map by using the drop-down menu at its upper right if you want a hybrid map/satellite view instead, for example. You can also search the map by typing the location you want into the search box above the map's left side.

   Once you've placed a photo, a pin appears in that spot, showing the number of photos you placed there. When you drag additional photos to the map, a little orange navigation symbol with crossed arrows appears (it's visible in Figure 2-17). If the location is close but not exact, you can drag this symbol to the exact spot you want to tag. Once you've assigned place tags, the thumbnails of the files that have already been assigned to a place show a little white tag symbol on some of them to indicate that they've already been placed.

   To see places with photos already assigned, turn on the "Show existing pins on map" checkbox.

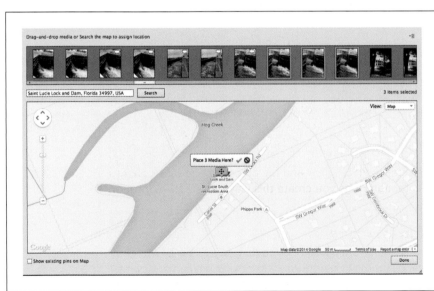

FIGURE 2-17

Zoom and drag the map to the spot where you want to place photos, and then drag a photo (or photos) from the top of the window onto the map, and a pop-up asks, "Place Media Here?" If it's the right spot, click the green checkmark or press Enter/Return. If not, click the red Cancel symbol and try again.

3. **When you finish placing photos, click Done.**

Elements takes you back to Media view, where you see the message "Places have been assigned to media."

In Media view, if you look at the Tags panel (page 49), in the Places category, you see the place tags assigned to your photos. That's at most four levels of tagging, because that's all the Organizer's map can do. So you might see something like United States, Georgia, Savannah, and Historic District-North. These tags are always visible when the Tags panel is onscreen, so you can see them in Media view and use them in searches.

> **TIP** If you're upgrading from an older version of Elements where you used the map and now you have two differently named tags for the same location—like an Elements 9 tag for "Our House" and an Elements 12 Place tag for the actual address, say—you can combine them. Just assign the older tag to the exact same location as the new tag (type out the address, if possible), and Elements will merge the old tag into the new place tag.

Once your photos have been tagged with locations (by you or your camera), you can see them on the map again by clicking the Map button at the bottom right of Places view. This opens as a regular map view, which you can drag around and search to locate your photos. Click a pin to display a pop-up that says Show Media; click that to make the photos for that location appear in the image area. There's also a search field at the top of the map where you can type a place name to find it quickly.

> **NOTE** When you don't have an Internet connection, the Places map view isn't available.

Places view also includes the Instant Fix button (page 121) so you can make quick corrections to your photos right there.

■ TAGGING PLACES IN MEDIA VIEW

You don't have to switch to Places view to add place tags to your images. You can create place tags right in Media view by clicking the Add Places button at the bottom of the window or by going to the Tags panel's Places Tags section and clicking the green + sign to the right of the words "Places Tags." Either way, Elements displays the same map you see in Places view and the process is the same. There's one important difference, though: Tags you create this way have *no* GPS location data associated with them.

■ EDITING AND DELETING PLACE TAGS

To remove either kind of place tag from a photo, in Media view, right-click/Control-click the tag icon below the image, and then choose "Remove from [name of place]" from the pop-out menu. You can also edit a tag's name by right-clicking/Control-clicking it in the Tags panel, and then choosing Rename from the pop-out menu.

To completely delete a place tag from Elements, right-click/Control-click the tag in the Tags panel, and then choose Delete. When you delete a tag, any sub-tags of it *also* get deleted. So if you have photos tagged, say, "United States, North Carolina, Linville Falls," deleting the United States tag also deletes the North Carolina and Linville Falls tags, as well as any other tags that are below the United States tag.

Working with Events

After learning about all the effort involved in tagging people and places (if your camera doesn't have GPS), you'll be pleased to know that Elements can deal with events *automatically*. The first time you enter Events view by clicking its tab at the top of the Organizer window, you see a whole lot of empty gray space with no photos, and a message suggesting you try Smart Events. Click the Events/Smart Events switch at the top left of the window and presto! Elements fills the window with piles of photos, all neatly divided based on when they were taken. As with the program's other views, you can move your cursor across an event's pile to see preview thumbnails of all the photos, or double-click one to see an expanded view.

You can name an event to make it easier to search for later on. To do that, either right-click/Control-click the event's stack and choose Name Event(s), or click the stack to select it and then click the Name Event(s) button at the bottom of the screen. Either way, in the Name Event window that opens, type a name for the event and, if necessary, use the Start Date and End Date fields to adjust the event's date(s). If you wish, you can add a description, too. (You can select multiple events before opening the Name Event window, but if you do, they all get assigned the same name. This is handy when Elements makes multiple events for one real event in your life.)

You can also create events manually. To do that, click the Events/Smart Events switch above the image area to set it to Events. Your smart events disappear, and you're back to the empty view. Next:

1. **Create a new event.**

   Click the Add Event button at the bottom of the window. (You can do this from Media view, too.) The Organizer switches you to a view where you see all your photos (or, if you preselected some images, just the selected ones) and the Add New Event panel on the right of your screen.

2. **Enter the info for your event.**

   In the top section of the panel, give the event a name, set its date(s), and enter a description, if you like. It's best to avoid punctuation like commas, which can throw off searching for the event later. Stick to letters, numbers, underscores and dashes (hyphens).

3. **Add your photos, if you didn't select them before you started this process.**

   You can control which photos are displayed in the middle of the Organizer by using the Albums or Folders panel on the left side of the screen. (If you don't see this panel, click the Show button in the lower left of your screen.) Click the name of a folder or an album and you see only the photos it contains. To get back to all photos, click the All Media button above the photo area's top-left corner. If you change your mind about creating an event, click the Cancel button at the lower right of the Organizer window.

To add photos to the event, drag their thumbnails to the lower part of the Add New Event panel (called the *Media Bin*), or select their thumbnails and then click "Add to Media Bin" at the bottom of your screen. There are also buttons in the lower left of the screen that select or deselect *all* your photos. If you want to remove a photo after you've added it to the Media Bin, click it in the bin and then click the little trashcan at the bin's lower left.

4. **When you're finished, click Done.**

Events view also lets you use a calendar to search for events by date. Click the Calendar button at the bottom right of the view's window, and the Calendar panel opens. Figure 2-18 explains how to use it. To close the panel, click the Calendar button again.

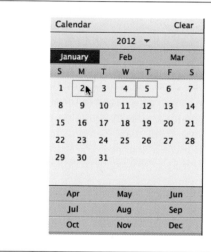

FIGURE 2-18

When you click Events view's Calendar button, this panel appears at the upper right of your screen.

Initially, the part that says "2012" here says All Years. Click it and choose the year you want. Here, you can tell that there are events for January, June, and July because those months' names are displayed in blue rather than black. Click a month to see this daily calendar, where the days with events are outlined. Click a date to see its events. (If you've used Organizer in early versions of Elements, this is as close as Elements 13 can get to the old Date view.)

■ Searching for Photos

After all that effort jumping from view to view tagging photos, you'll be happy to know that Elements makes it easy to search for photos, offering you several different methods. The most basic is to go to the search box at the upper right of the Organizer window and type a keyword into it. New in Elements 13, a slideout menu appears as you type, offering suggestions for search categories. It's explained in Figure 2-19.

FIGURE 2-19

When you start typing in the Organizer's search box, this menu slides out to help you focus your search. If you're searching for files with "Savanah" in their names, for example, click the "Filename: Savannah" menu item to see those images.

If you click the magnifying glass on the left side of the search box, you see a menu that gives you some more sophisticated ways to search:

- **Visual Similarity search**. Select a photo (or photos) before choosing this menu item and the Organizer seeks out photos that it thinks look similar. (If you didn't select a photo before choosing this item, then near the top of the window that appears, drag the photo you want to use as the basis for your search into the dotted rectangle next to the word "Find." You can also add more photos to your search this way, since the rectangle keeps reappearing to the right of each photo you drag onto it.) You can fine-tune the results by dragging the slider at the top of the window. Drag it toward Color if you want Elements to give more weight to images with similar colors, or toward Shapes if you want Elements to emphasize similar shapes more than colors. When you're done searching, click the All Media button (it may be labeled Back instead) at the top left of the thumbnail area.

- **Object search**. You can show Elements a picture of your dog, your house, or just about anything and tell it to find more photos with the same subject. Select a photo of the object, and then choose Object Search. In the "Mark an object for search" window that appears, drag the white frame so it's over your subject, and then drag the frame's corners so that it fits as precisely as possible. Then click Search Object. After that, you can drag the Color/Shape slider above the search results to tell Elements which attribute to favor.

- **Duplicate Photo search**. Choose this menu item and the Organizer finds all the photos it thinks might be duplicates. Put your cursor over a photo to see its name, date, and size. If you're sure the photos are duplicates, click the one you want to remove, and then click "Remove from Catalog" at the bottom left of the window. It can be hard to tell if the photos are really duplicates, though, since the thumbnails are pretty small. You can expand your view by using the Zoom slider at the upper right of the window. If you aren't sure, you can stack the photos by selecting them, clicking the Stack button (or, if you want to stack all the photos in a section, clicking the Stack button at the top of that section), and then expanding the stack in Media view by choosing Edit→Stack→"Expand

Photos in Stack." This lets you look through larger versions of the photos to see which one(s) you want to get rid of.

- **Saved searches**. In the search results menu, you can save any of the searches you make from the search box's menu by clicking the word "Options." After you've done that, you can choose this option from the search box's menu to call up your saved searches and use them again.

If you want to try a different search, click the Close button in the Search Results window or to the right of the Color/Shape slider in the Search Results window, or click the All Media button and try again.

In addition to searching from the search box's menu, you can quickly search in the Tags panel (page 49). Just click the box to the left of the name of a tag or category, and Elements finds all the photos associated with it. Click it again to turn off the search results.

Searching by Metadata

As explained on page 49, your camera stores lots of information about your images in the form of *metadata*. In the Organizer, you can search by metadata to find, say, all the photos you took with a particular camera model at a certain aperture and exposure. Figure 2-20 explains how.

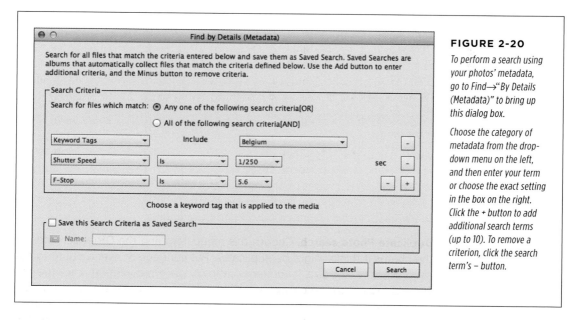

FIGURE 2-20

To perform a search using your photos' metadata, go to Find→"By Details (Metadata)" to bring up this dialog box.

Choose the category of metadata from the drop-down menu on the left, and then enter your term or choose the exact setting in the box on the right. Click the + button to add additional search terms (up to 10). To remove a criterion, click the search term's – button.

> **TIP** To share your tag information with other people, select the photos you want, and then go to File→"Save Metadata to File(s)." This transforms your tags into metadata keywords that lots of programs can read. Or you can use the Organizer's Export command (File→"Export As New File(s)"), which also writes your tags into the metadata.

■ Saving Your Work

You've heard the advice before: Save files early and often. Happily, saving your work is easy in Elements. You don't need to do anything special to save information like tags or albums in the Organizer; that happens automatically. You just need to save images you've created or changed in the Editor. When you're ready to save a file in the Editor, go to File→Save As or press Shift+Ctrl+S/Shift-⌘-S to bring up the dialog box shown in Figure 2-21.

FIGURE 2-21

Elements' Save As dialog box changes a little depending on what you're saving, but this example is pretty typical. When you click the "Save as type" drop-down menu (this menu is labeled "Format" on Macs), you'll see a long list of file formats to choose from.

The top part of the Save As dialog box is pretty much the same as it is for any program: You choose where you want to save the file, what to name it, and the file format you want (more about file formats in a moment). The settings in the bottom part include some important choices that are unique to Elements:

- **Include in the Elements Organizer**. This checkbox is turned on the first time you use Elements. Leave it on and your photo gets saved in the Organizer. Turn it off if you don't want the new file to go to the Organizer. If you turn it off, Elements should *leave* it off, at least for this editing session or until you save a photo that came from the Organizer.

- **Save in Version Set with Original**. This option tells the Organizer to save your image (including any edits you've made) as a new *version*, separate from the original. The image gets the same name as the original, plus a suffix to indicate it's an edited version.

  Elements lets you create as many versions as you want. That way, you can go directly to any state of the image that you've saved as a version, which is really handy. When you turn on this checkbox to start a version set, from then on, you'll be presented with the Save As dialog box every time you save. Elements does that to give you the chance to create a new version each time.

- **As a Copy**. When you save an image as a copy, Elements makes the copy, names it "[Original filename] copy," and puts the copy away, but the original version remains open. If you want to work on the copy, you have to specifically open it. Sometimes Elements *forces* you to save an image as a copy—for instance, when you want to save a layered image and you turn off the Layers checkbox described in the next bullet point.

- **Layers**. If your image has *layers* (see Chapter 6), turn on this checkbox to keep them. If you turn this setting off, Elements usually forces you to save the file as a copy. To avoid having to do that, *flatten* the image (page 209) before saving it. But bear in mind that, once you close a flattened image, you can't get your layers back—flattening is a *permanent* change.

- **ICC Profile**. Turn on this checkbox to make Elements embed a color profile (page 240) in your file.

- **Thumbnail**. This setting is visible only in Windows, and it's always turned on—you can't change it.

File Formats

After you've spent hours creating a perfect image, you'll want to share it with others. If everyone who wanted to view your images needed a copy of Elements, you probably wouldn't have a very large audience for your creations. So Elements lets you save in lots of different *file formats*.

What does that mean? It's pretty simple, really. A file format is a way in which your computer saves information so that another program or computer can read and use the file.

Because there are many different kinds of programs and several different computing platforms (Windows, Linux, and Mac, for example), the kind of file that's best for one use may be a poor choice for doing something else. That's why many programs, like Elements, can save files in a variety of formats. There are many formats, like TIFF and JPEG, that lots of different programs can read. Other formats—like the PUB files that Microsoft Publisher creates or the .pages files from Apple's Pages program—are easily read only by the program that created them.

File Formats Elements Understands

Elements gives you loads of file-format options in the Save As dialog box. (See the box on page 71 for a quick introduction to file formats.) Your best choice depends on how you plan to use the image. Here's a rundown of the various options in the Save As dialog box's "Save as type" menu (this menu is labeled "Format" on Macs):

- **Photoshop (.psd, .pdd)**. It's a good idea to save photos as .psd files—the native file format of Elements and Photoshop—before you work on them. A .psd file can hold lots of information, and you don't lose any data by saving in this format. It also lets you keep layers, which is important even if you haven't used them for much yet.

- **BMP (.bmp)**. This format is an old Windows standby. It's the file format that Windows uses for many graphics tasks.

- **CompuServe GIF (.gif)**. Everywhere except this menu, this format is known simply as GIF; Adobe adds "CompuServe" because CompuServe invented and owns the code for this format. This format is used primarily for web graphics, especially files without a lot of subtle shadings of color. For more on when to choose GIFs, see Chapter 17. Page 563 explains how to *animate* GIFs.

- **Photo Project Format (.pse)**. This special format is only for multipage Elements files. These days, you can create a multipage file in only a few of Elements' Create projects, like a photo book (see Chapter 15 for details). You can't create and work with multipage files in the Editor anymore.

- **JPEG (.jpg, .jpeg, .jpe)**. Almost everyone who uses a computer has run into JPEGs, and most digital cameras offer this format as an option. Generally, when you bring a JPEG into Elements, you want to use another format when you save it to avoid losing data. Keep reading this chapter for more about why that is.

- **Photoshop PDF (.pdf, .pdp)**. Adobe invented PDF (Portable Document Format), which lets you send files to people with Adobe Reader (a free program formerly called Acrobat Reader) so they can easily open and view the files. (People with Macs can also use OS X's Preview to view PDFs.) Elements uses PDF files to create presentations like slideshows.

- **Pixar (.pxr)**. Yup, *that* Pixar. This is the special format for the movie studio's high-end workstations, although if you're working on one of those, it's extremely unlikely that you're reading this book.

- **PNG (.png, .pns)**. Here's another web-graphic format, created to overcome some of the disadvantages of JPEGs and GIFs. It has its own disadvantages, though; see page 562 for details. PNG has become a lot more important recently, since it's the preferred graphics format for Apple's iOS (the operating system for iPhones and iPads).

- **TIFF (.tif, .tiff)**. This is another format that, like PSD, preserves virtually all your photo's info and lets you save layers. Also like PSD files, TIFFs can be really big. This format is used extensively in print production, and some cameras let you choose it as a shooting option.

- **Digital Negative (.dng)**. This format isn't listed in the Save As dialog box's format menu; it's available only in the Raw Converter (page 291). This format was developed by Adobe as an attempt to create a more universal way to store all the different raw file formats (page 272). You can download a special free DNG Converter from Adobe's website (*www.adobe.com/downloads*) that lets you convert your camera's raw-format photos into DNG files. DNG files aren't ready to use the way JPEG or TIFF files are—you have to run them through the Raw Converter before you can use them in projects. Page 291 has more info.

■ ABOUT JPEGS

Certain file formats are designed to make files as small as possible—and they do that by throwing out information by the bucketful. These formats are known as *lossy* because they discard, or lose, some of the file's data every time you save it, to help shrink the file. Sometimes you want that to happen, like when you need a small (and hence, fast-loading) file for a website. Because of that, many of the file formats that were developed for the Web, most notably JPEG, favor smallness above all.

> **NOTE** Formats that preserve all your data are called *lossless* or *non-lossy*. The most popular file formats for people who are looking to preserve all their photos' data are PSD and TIFF.

If you save a file in JPEG format, then every time you save and close the file, your computer squishes some of the data out of the photo. What kind of data? The info your computer needs to display and print the fine details. So you don't want to keep saving your file as a JPEG over and over again, because every time you do, the image loses a little more detail. You can usually get away with saving as a JPEG once or twice, but if you keep it up, sooner or later you'll start to wonder what happened to your beautiful picture.

It's OK that your camera takes photos and saves them as JPEGs—those are typically pretty enormous JPEGs. Just importing a photo as a JPEG won't hurt the picture, and neither will opening it to look at it, as long as you don't make any changes. But once you get your files into Elements, save them as PSD or TIFF files while you work on them. If you want the final product to be a JPEG, then change the format back to JPEG *after* you're done editing it.

> **TIP** Your camera may give you several different JPEG compression options to help fit more pictures on your memory card. Always choose the *least* compression possible. This makes the files slightly larger, but the quality is much, much better, so it's worth sacrificing the space.

Saving Options

Elements gives you several ways to save files. Before choosing one, you need to consider whether you want to create version sets (page 71) of your photos.

To tell Elements how to react when you invoke the Save command, in the Editor, go to Edit→Preferences→Saving Files/ Photoshop Elements Editor→Preferences→Saving Files. The Preferences dialog box that appears includes the On First Save drop-down menu. By making a selection here, you can control (to some extent) when you'll see a dialog box offering you options for saving a file, and when Elements will behave like any other program and just save your changes without asking you for any input.

For most people, it's fine to leave this menu set to "Ask if Original" (explained below). But if you want more control over how Elements saves your photos (for instance, say you always want the option to create a new version set without having to remember to choose Save As), you can configure Elements to suit you. Here's what the three On First Save options do:

- **Always Ask**. Choose this setting and from then on, the first time you save a file by pressing Ctrl+S/⌘-S or going to File→Save, Elements brings up the Save As dialog box—*if* this is the first time you've opened the file in this session of Elements. Close the file and reopen it while Elements is still running, and you won't see the Save As dialog box; Elements just saves the file. But once you exit Elements and launch it again, you get the Save As dialog box again the first time you press Ctrl+S/⌘-S. You can think of this option as short for "Always ask the first time I save a file during a given editing session and then don't bug me anymore."

- **Ask If Original**. If you're editing your original file (as opposed to a version) and don't have any version sets, Elements opens the Save As dialog box the first time you save the file. On subsequent saves, or if you already have

a version set, Elements just saves right over the existing version (unless you specifically choose File→Save As to create a new version). This option is meant to help you avoid inadvertently creating dozens of versions of each file as you edit.

- **Save Over Current File**. With this option selected, when you press Ctrl+S/⌘-S, Elements overwrites the existing file without offering you the Save As dialog box. This is the way most other programs behave when saving—if you save a Word document, for example, you don't get a dialog box; Word just saves your changes, writing over the previous saved version of the file. If you use Elements as the external editor for another photo-management program like iPhoto or Lightroom, this is the option you should use in order to create proper versions in the other program. If you choose this option and then, while you're working, decide you want to Save As instead of Save, press Shift+Ctrl+S/Shift-⌘-S (or just choose Save As from the Editor's File menu).

There are certain situations where Elements presents you with the Save As dialog box no matter *what* you choose in the On First Save menu. For instance, say you add layers (explained in Chapter 6) to a JPEG file. You can't save a JPEG with layers, so Elements brings up the Save As dialog box to let you choose a different file format for saving your work.

You can also use the Saving Files preferences to control how well your image file works with other programs. If you leave the Maximize PSD File Compatibility drop-down menu set to Always, Elements embeds a flattened copy of your image in the file for the benefit of programs that don't understand layers. That makes for a substantially larger file, but with disk space so cheap these days, it's usually not a problem. If you instead set this menu to Ask, then each time you save a layered PSD file, you'll see a dialog box asking whether you want to maximize compatibility.

Changing a File's Format

It's super easy to change a file's format in Elements: Just press Shift+Ctrl+S/Shift-⌘-S or go to File→Save As and, in the Save As dialog box's "Save as type" drop-down menu (labeled "Format" on Macs), select the format you want. Elements makes a copy of your file in the new format and gives you a chance to change the name, if you want.

ALL THINGS COME TO AN END

Bye-Bye, Old Formats

Elements used to be able to open a wide variety of obscure file formats, but starting with Elements 11, Adobe decided to remove the ability to open a lot of these. Mostly, they're formats hardly anyone uses anymore. And in some cases, like Photoshop Raw (which has nothing at all to do with the raw files produced by cameras), they just caused confusion.

Here are the formats you *can't* open in Elements anymore: Filmstrip (FLM), Wireless BMP (WBM, WBMP), PCX, Targa (TGA, VDA, ICB, VST), Photoshop Raw (RAW), PICT (PCT, PICT), Scitex CT (SCT), Photoshop EPS (EPS), EPS TIFF Preview (EPS), Generic EPS (AI3, AI4, AI5, AI6, AI7, AI8, PS, EPS.AI, EPSF, EPSP), IFF Format, Photoshop 2.0, Alias PIX, and PICT Resource. Also, JPEG 2000 has been gone since Elements 9.

Fortunately, there are ways around this if you need to open some of those formats. For example, here's how you can work with JPEG 2000 files (which are still used by many books that include practice images on discs and for a lot of downloadable artwork):

- **Windows**: Download the free ImageMagick program (*www.imagemagick.org*) and use it to convert your JPEG 2000 images to another lossless format.

- **Mac**: Use Preview (it's part of OS X) to open your JPEG 2000 files and save them in the format of your choice.

For the other old and obscure formats, in Windows, try IrfanView (*www.irfanview.com*), a wonderful free program that can open almost any Windows-compatible format. You can sometimes even use IrfanView to salvage damaged files, especially if you get an "invalid JPEG marker" error. If Elements balks at one of your files, first try opening and resaving the photo in IrfanView. If you're lucky, that may be all you need to do to make Elements recognize the file.

On a Mac, try GraphicConverter (*www.lemkesoft.com*), a great little program that can open darn near anything. It does great batch conversions, too, and even offers some basic image-editing features. GraphicConverter is shareware (it currently costs $40) with a generous demo period, and it's worth every penny.

■ Backing Up Files

With computers, you never know what's going to happen, so "Be prepared" is a good motto. If your computer crashes, it won't be nearly as painful if all your photos are safely backed up someplace else.

You'll be glad to know that Elements makes it easy to save files to any add-on storage device—like an external hard drive—or to a CD or DVD (in Windows, anyway). The following section explains your options.

NOTE In Windows, Elements offers one frequently requested feature for making backups: You can create *multisession* discs. That means you can tell Elements to leave your CD or DVD "open" so that you can come back later and add more files to it, instead of wasting a whole CD or DVD to save only a handful of pictures. To use this feature, in the Organizer, go to Edit→Preferences→Files and turn on "Enable Multisession Burning to CD/DVD." (Unfortunately, you can't burn discs in the Mac version of Elements.)

Organizer Backups

The Organizer includes a really helpful way to back up photos. It's one of Elements' best features, and it's certainly thorough, even going so far as to remind you to label the disc you create if you back up to CD or DVD on a computer running Windows.

You can back up your whole catalog or just specific photos. Simply follow these steps:

1. **Make sure your catalog is in tip-top shape.**

   In the Organizer, go to File→Manage Catalogs. In the Catalog Manager window, select your catalog in the list, and then click Repair. (Elements will probably tell you the catalog doesn't need repair. In that case, click Repair Anyway.) When Elements is finished doing its thing, click OK. Next, click the window's Optimize button, which makes sure your catalog's database is in prime shape. When Elements is done doing that, click OK and then close the Catalog Manager window.

   It's also not a bad idea to go to File→Reconnect→All Missing Files, although the Organizer warns you if you have unconnected files when you start your backup. (An *unconnected file* is a cataloged item that the Organizer can't find.)

   NOTE If you have multiple catalogs, you can back up only one at a time.

2. **Call up the Backup dialog box, and let Elements make sure your catalog is in backup-ready shape.**

   Go to File→Backup Catalog, or press Ctrl+B/⌘-B. If Elements is aware of any missing files, you see a window where you can choose to let Elements reconnect them, or you can click Continue to ignore any unconnected files.

3. **Tell Elements what kind of backup to make.**

   In the Backup Catalog dialog box, you have to decide whether to back up your whole catalog or to make an incremental backup. The Full Backup option backs up *everything* in your catalog. Pick that option the first time you make a backup, or if you're backing up everything to move to a new computer. The Incremental Backup option finds only the stuff that's new since the last time you made a backup, and that's all it copies—a major time- and space-saver. Make your choice, and then click Next to continue.

You have to make a full backup at least once before Elements will let you do an incremental backup, and there seem to be more problems with incremental backups, so many people think it's prudent to do a full backup every time.

4. **Choose a destination for your files.**

   Your choices in the Select Destination Drive section include all your available hard drives. In the list, click the drive you want to use. If you're using Windows and you want to back up to CDs or DVDs, choose your disc drive from this list. Elements even pops the drive open for you.

TIP In Windows, you may also find that you can back up to online storage if it has a mapped network drive letter and your Internet connection is fast enough. So, for example, you may be able to back up to your Dropbox account or to something like Microsoft OneDrive. Test this with a small catalog first to be sure it works for you. (Unfortunately, this doesn't work on Macs.)

   If you're backing up to a hard drive (your only option on a Mac), click the Backup Path field's Browse button to tell Elements where to put the backup. Navigate through the folders in the window that appears, and create a new folder if you'd like to keep your backups tidy (a good idea). Once you're done, the folder's *path* (a roadmap to where it lives) appears in the Backup window.

   If you're making an incremental backup, then you have to show Elements where to find your previous backup. Click the name of the drive where you made your previous backup, and then click the "Previous Backup file" field's Browse button to point Elements to the existing backup file.

5. **If you're on a PC and are backing up to a CD or DVD, insert a disc into the drive when Elements asks you to. (If you're backing up to any other kind of media, including internal or external hard drives, then skip ahead to step 6.)**

   Elements has to calculate how many discs it needs to create your backup. As Elements burns each disc, it asks if you want it to verify the disc to be sure it's OK. You do. Elements prompts you to feed it more discs if the backup doesn't all fit on one disc.

   If you like, you can change the write speed for your disc. (A slower speed takes longer but may be more reliable.) Just choose one of the other speed options from the drop-down menu.

TIP Always check your backup discs once you've burned them, even if you verified them during backup. Do that by putting the disc in your computer and making sure all your files are there. If there's an error, you want to know about it *now*, not 6 months from now.

6. Create the backup.

Click Save Backup, and Elements generates the backup. If you decide you don't want to make a backup, click Cancel instead.

> **TIP** These directions cover how to back up your images and your catalog. It's also a really good idea to back up your *catalog database* (the data file that the Organizer creates to keep track of where your photos are) every once in a while. To do that, in the Organizer, go to Help→System Info to see the file path to your current catalog (it's listed next to Catalog Location). Then burn those folders (including the files within them) to a CD or DVD or copy them to an external hard drive.

Be aware that a backup made using these steps is for *Elements*' use, not yours: If you look at the backup in Windows Explorer or a Mac's Finder, you'll see files with weird numerical names, and you can't just rummage around to find a particular photo you accidentally deleted. Instead, you have to let Elements handle restoring the files. Because you can't easily get individual files out of an official Elements backup, many people prefer to create their own backups, copying the catalog file (the preceding Tip explains where to find it) and their images. That way, you don't have to rely on Elements to retrieve lost photos for you.

If you want to switch your catalog to a new machine, you can install Elements and restore your existing backup. (This works even when moving from Windows to a Mac. If you want to do that, save your backup to a removable hard drive.) To restore your catalog, in the Organizer, go to File→Restore Catalog, and then follow the onscreen directions.

> **NOTE** In Windows, you can also copy just a *few* photos to CDs or DVDs rather than making a full backup of your catalog. To do that, go to File→"Copy/Move to Removable Drive." Leave the Move Files checkbox turned off, click Next, and then select your disc-burning drive in the list on the next screen.
>
> Macs don't let you do any kind of disc burning directly from Elements, but you can select photos in the Organizer and go to File→"Export as New File(s)" (page 530) to send them to the Finder for burning, if your Mac has an optical drive (one that can read and burn discs).

Rotating and Resizing Photos

I n the last chapter, you learned how to get photos *into* Elements. Now it's time to look at how to trim off unwanted areas and straighten crooked photos. This chapter will also teach you how to change the overall size of images and how to zoom in and out to get a better look at things while you're editing.

NOTE From here through Chapter 15, you need to be in the *Editor* to follow along. If you're still in the Organizer, press Ctrl+I/⌘-I to go to the Editor, and then click the Expert tab at the top of the screen.

■ Straightening Scanned Photos

Anyone who's scanned printed photos can testify about the hair-pulling frustration you feel when your carefully placed pictures come out crooked onscreen. Whether you're feeding in precious memories one at a time or scanning batches of photos to save time, Elements can help straighten things out.

Straightening Two or More Photos at Once

If you've got a pile of photos to scan, save yourself some time and lay as many of them on your scanner as you can (see Figure 3-1). It doesn't matter whether you scan directly into Elements or use the scanner's own software. (See page 38 for more about scanning images into Elements.) Thanks to Elements' handy Divide Scanned Photos command, you can save them as individual image files in no time.

FIGURE 3-1

Consumer-grade flatbed scanners are generally pretty slow, so it's a huge timesaver to scan four or even six photos at a time, since you can go do something else while the scanner works on the images. Elements can then automatically separate and straighten the individual photos thanks to the Divide Scanned Photos command.

Sometimes it pays to be crooked, and this is one of those situations. Divide Scanned Photos works best when your photos are fairly askew, as shown here, so don't waste time trying to be precise when placing them on the scanner.

NOTE If you have a Mac, the free, built-in program Image Capture often automatically creates separate files for each image in a group scan, as long as it can tell them apart.

Start by scanning in the photos using the scanner's own software (you may need to dig out the scanner's manual to figure out how). When you're done, follow these steps:

1. **Open the scanned image file in the Editor.**

   It doesn't matter what file format you saved the scanned group of photos as: TIFF, JPEG, whatever. Elements can read 'em all (with the few exceptions mentioned on page 75).

2. **Choose Image→Divide Scanned Photos, and then watch as Elements divides, straightens, and crops the individual photos.**

Sit back and enjoy the view as Elements carefully calculates, splits, straightens out, and trims each image. You'll see the photos appear and disappear as Elements works through them.

3. **Use the File→Save As command to name and save each separated image.**

When Elements is done, you'll have one file for the original group scan and a *separate* file for each photo Elements carved out. All you need to do now is import the cut-apart photos into the Organizer (if you use the Organizer, that is). To do that, just make sure that "Include in the Elements Organizer" is turned on in the Save As dialog box (see page 70). If you don't use the Organizer, just save the images as you would any other image file.

Elements usually does a crackerjack job splitting photos, but once in a while it chokes, leaving you with a file that contains more than one photo. Figure 3-2 shows you what to do when Elements doesn't succeed in dividing things up.

FIGURE 3-2

Sometimes Elements just can't figure out how to split photos, and you wind up with something like these two not-quite-separated images.

If that happens, rescan the photos that confused Elements, but this time make sure they're more crooked on the scanner. Elements should then be able to split them correctly.

Also, check for problems like you see here, where Elements can't split the photos because it can't see where to draw a straight line to divide these two pictures without chopping off the corners. Put a little more space between the photos so Elements can split them.

TIP Occasionally you may find that Elements can't accurately separate a group scan, no matter *what* you do. In that case, use the Rectangular Marquee tool (page 149) to select one of the scanned photos, copy it (Ctrl+C/⌘-C), paste it into its own document (File→New→"Image from Clipboard"), and then save it. You may also want to check your scanner's software—it may have a way to divide a group scan as part of the scanning process itself.

Straightening Individual Photos

Elements can also straighten and crop (trim) a single scanned image. After scanning the image and opening it in the Editor, simply choose Image→Rotate→"Straighten and Crop Image," and Elements tidies things up for you (if you'd rather crop the edges yourself, choose Straighten Image). Or, if you prefer, you can actually use the Divide Scanned Photos command (explained in the previous section) on a single image. (Cropping is explained on page 89.)

▮ Rotating Images

People scanning printed photographs aren't the only ones who sometimes need a little help straightening their pictures. If your camera doesn't include data in its image files that tells Elements (or any other image-editing program) the correct orientation, then you'll need to rotate your digital photos. Certain cameras, for example, send portrait-oriented photos out on their sides, and it's up to you to straighten things out.

Fortunately, Elements has rotation commands all over the place. If all you need to do is get Dad off his back and stand him upright, here's a list of where you can perform a quick 90-degree rotation on any open photo:

- **In the Organizer.** You can rotate a photo almost anytime by pressing Ctrl/⌘ plus the left or right arrow key. Another option is to choose Edit→Rotate 90° Left (or Rotate 90° Right). Also, in Full Screen view (page 51), there are Rotate buttons at the top of the Quick Edit panel. Finally, there's a Rotate button at the bottom of the Media view window. (If you want to rotate the other way, click the tiny arrow to the right of this button, and then click the pop-out button that appears.)

- **In the Editor.** Click the Rotate button at the bottom of the screen to turn your image counterclockwise. (If you want to turn your photo clockwise instead, click the tiny arrow next to this button, and then click the button that appears.) You can also right-click/Control-click a thumbnail in the Photo Bin and choose Rotate 90° Left (or Rotate 90° Right). Finally, you can go to Image→Rotate→90° Left (or 90° Right)

- **In the Raw Converter.** Click the left or right arrow above the preview area. (Flip to page 272 to learn about the Raw Converter.)

Those commands all get you one-click, 90-degree changes. But Elements has all sorts of other rotational tricks up its sleeve, as the next section explains.

Rotating and Flipping Options

Elements gives you several ways to change a photo's orientation. To see what's available, in the Editor, go to Image→Rotate. You'll notice two groups of rotate commands in this menu; for now, it's the first group you want to focus on. (The second group of commands works on layers, which are explained in Chapter 6.) The first group of commands includes:

- **90° Left/Right**. Use these commands to fix digital photos that arrive in Elements on their sides.

- **180°**. This turns your photo upside down and backward.

- **Custom**. Selecting this command brings up a dialog box where, if you're mathematically inclined, you can type in the precise number of degrees you want to rotate the photo.

- **Flip Horizontal**. Flipping a photo horizontally means that if your subject was gazing soulfully off to the left, she's now gazing soulfully off to the right.

- **Flip Vertical**. This command turns your photo upside down *without* changing the left/right orientation the way Rotate 180° does.

> **TIP** When you flip photos, remember that you're making a mirror image of *everything* in the photo. So someone who's writing right-handed becomes a lefty, any text in the photo will be backward, and so on.

Figure 3-3 shows these commands in action.

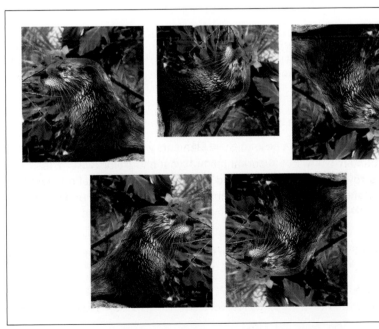

FIGURE 3-3

You can use the rotate commands to send this otter tumbling.

Top row (left to right): The original, the photo rotated 90 degrees to the right, and the photo rotated 180 degrees.

Bottom row: The photo flipped horizontally (left) and vertically (right).

If you want to position a photo at an angle (as you might in a scrapbook), use the Free Rotate Layer command described on page 87.

Straightening the Contents of an Image

What about all those photos you've taken where the main subject (a person or a building, say) isn't *quite* straight? You can flip those pictures around forever, but if your camera was off-kilter when you snapped the shot, your subjects will still lean like a certain tower in Pisa.

Elements can help with this problem, too. It includes a nifty Straighten tool that makes adjusting the horizon as easy as drawing a line. It can even automatically create material to fill in any empty spaces left along the edges after you straighten, something like the way Elements can fill empty edges in panoramas (page 368). This section explains the details.

> **TIP** Most of the time, the Straighten tool does the trick. But if you find this tool too fiddly or you encounter one of the few cases where it can't get things looking perfect, use the old-school method: the Free Rotate Layer command, described on page 87.

The Straighten Tool

If you can never seem to hold a camera perfectly level, you'll love this tool. Here's how to straighten a crooked photo:

1. **Open a photo, and then activate the Straighten tool.**

   You'll find it at the lower right of the Modify section of the Tools panel; its icon is a carpenter's level. Or just press the P key.

2. **Make any necessary changes to the Tool Options settings.**

   Your choices are described after this list.

3. **Tell Elements where the image's horizon is.**

   Drag to draw a line in the photo to show Elements where horizontal *should* be. Figure 3-4 shows how—by drawing a line that traces the boundary between the ocean and the sky. The line appears at an angle when you draw it. That's fine, because Elements is going to level out the photo, making your line the horizontal plane.

> **TIP** If you have a photo of trees, sailing ships, skyscrapers, or any other subject where you'd rather straighten vertically than horizontally, just hold down Ctrl/⌘ while you drag. That way, the line you draw determines the *vertical* axis of the photo. (It's important to press the mouse button *before* you press the Ctrl/⌘ key, or this trick won't work.)

FIGURE 3-4

Left: To correct the crooked horizon in this photo, simply draw a line along the part that should be level. It's easiest to do this by choosing a clearly marked boundary like the horizon here, but you can draw a line across anything you want to make level.

Right: Elements automatically rotates the photo to straighten its contents.

4. **Elements automatically straightens your photo (and crops it, if you chose that setting in the Tool Options area, as explained in a sec).**

   If you don't like what Elements did, press Ctrl+Z/⌘-Z to undo it and draw another line. If you're happy, you're all done, except for saving the file (Ctrl+S/⌘-S).

The Tool Options settings give you some control over how Elements handles the edges of your newly straightened photo. Once the picture is straightened, the edges are going to be a bit ragged, so you can choose what Elements should do about that:

- **Grow or Shrink** makes Elements add extra space (blank canvas or an autofill, explained below) around the edges of the photo so that every bit of the original is still there. It's up to you to crop the image afterward (see page 89).

- **Remove Background** tells Elements to chop off the ragged edges to give you a nice, rectangular image. The downside to this setting is that you lose some of the perimeter of your photo—though just a bit, so it's not usually a big deal.

- **Original Size** makes Elements keep the photo's dimensions exactly the same— even if that means including some blank space along the perimeter or autofilling the blank space, as explained next. You may also lose some of the edges of the original image, particularly the corners.

The "Autofill edges" checkbox makes edge control easier than ever. Turn on this setting and Elements analyzes the contents of your photo and invents *new* material to fill in the empty spaces along the edges. It doesn't always do a perfect job, but it's absolutely amazing when it works. Definitely give this setting a try.

If your photo has layers (see Chapter 6), you can use the Straighten tool to straighten just the active layer (page 188) by going to the Tool Options area and turning off Rotate All Layers. If you want Elements to straighten your whole photo, then leave this checkbox turned on.

The Straighten tool is best for photos where you were holding the camera crooked. If you try this tool and it makes things in your photo look odd, then perhaps straightening isn't what it needs. Architectural photos, for instance, may look a bit crooked before you use this tool—but a lot worse afterward. If that house is *still* leaning even though you're sure the ground has been leveled correctly, then most likely your real problem is *perspective distortion* (a visual warping effect). To fix that, use the Correct Camera Distortion filter instead (see page 382).

> **TIP** You can also straighten photos in the Raw Converter. There's a Straighten tool in its toolbox, and you use it just like the Editor's Straighten tool. Page 277 tells you more.

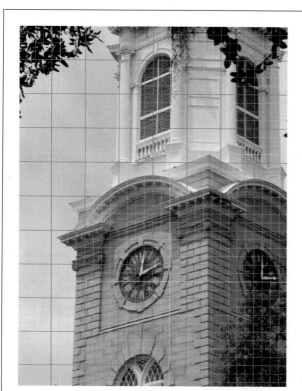

FIGURE 3-5

If you need help figuring out where straight is, add a grid or guidelines in the Editor.

The bright aqua lines shown here are guides; the others are the grid. (Neither will show up when you print your photos.)

Use the grid to help straighten an image.

Guides are especially useful when you're adding items to a photo, since you can make things like text blocks (page 484) automatically line up by making them snap to the guidelines, as explained in the box on page 87.

Grids, Guides, and Rulers

Elements gives you plenty of help when it comes to getting things straightened and aligned. In the Editor, you can turn on several features that make it really easy to create all kinds of projects:

- **Grid**. This option puts your entire image under a network of gridlines, as in Figure 3-5, which is really helpful when you're doing a free rotation (explained below) and aren't sure where straight is. Just go to View→Grid to toggle the grid on and off. You can adjust the grid's spacing in Edit→Preferences→Guides & Grid/Photoshop Elements Editor→Preferences→Guides & Grid. That's also where you can change the grid's color to make it show up better; in the Preferences window, simply click the color square, and then choose a color from the Color Picker (page 255).

- **Rulers**. If you want to measure something in an image, go to View→Rulers, and rulers appear along the sides of the image. You can change the unit of measurement—if you'd like to see, say, pixels or percentages rather than inches—by right-clicking/Control-clicking the ruler and choosing from the pop-out menu, or by going to Edit→Preferences→Units & Rulers/Photoshop Elements Editor→Preferences→Units & Rulers.

- **Guides**. Guides are a great way to get things lined up. You can create as many guides as you want in an image. Just go to View→New Guide and choose a horizontal or vertical line (you can't change the orientation of a guideline once you create it). You can specify a position in your image, or just create the guide anywhere by clicking OK, and then use the Move tool to drag it where you want it. (If the rulers are visible, you can just drag from the ruler to create a guide without going to the View menu.) Once you

get your guidelines set up, you can keep yourself from accidentally moving them by going to View→Lock Guides. To remove guides, go to View→Clear Guides.

If you save a photo with guides in it and send it to someone else using Photoshop or a version of Elements that can display guides (versions 6–13; Elements 6 and 7 can *see* guides, they just can't create them), that person will see your guides. If someone sends you a file with guides in it, you can see the guides if you turn them on in the View menu (View→Guides).

Guides are really handy, particularly for projects like scrapbooking, because you can make anything you add to a file *snap* (jump) right to the guide's location by choosing View→Snap To→Guides. If you decide you'd rather move objects freely, just select the same menu option again to toggle snapping off. (You can also have objects snap to the grid, but you can change this setting only when the grid is visible.) You can temporarily disable snapping when it's turned on in the menu by holding down the Ctrl/⌘ key as you drag.

You can also choose to snap to layers by choosing View→Snap To→Layers (layers are explained in Chapter 6), in which case anything you add to a layered file will automatically line up with the contents of the layer below the one that's currently active. Snapping to document bounds (View→Snap To→Document Bounds) gives you the option of not being terribly precise near the edge of a document. If you drag a crop or a selection in your photo anywhere near the edge, when this feature is turned on, the crop or selection edge will jump to the edge of your photo. You can disable either or both of these features in the View→Snap To menu, just like Guides and Grid.

Free Rotate Layer

You can also use the rotate commands to straighten photos, or to turn them at angles for use in scrapbook pages or album layouts. The command that's best for this is Free Rotate Layer, which lets you grab a photo and spin it to your heart's desire. (If you aren't sure where straight is, Elements can help you figure it out, as the box above explains.)

TIP You can use all the rotate commands on individual layers. Chapter 6 explains layers, but you don't have to understand them to use the Free Rotate Layer command.

To use Free Rotate Layer:

1. **Go to Image→Rotate→Free Rotate Layer.**

   If your image includes a Background layer, Elements automatically converts it to a regular layer for you. (You'll learn more about this in Chapter 6.)

2. **Drag to adjust your photo, as explained in Figure 3-6.**

   Your picture may look kind of jagged while you're rotating. Don't worry about that—Elements will smooth things out once you're done. As you drag, you'll see a little black pop-up showing how many degrees you've rotated the image; it goes away as soon as you release the mouse button.

FIGURE 3-6

Free Rotate Layer lets you straighten the contents of a photo—or even spin it around in a circle. Just grab either the handle at the bottom center of the photo or one of the square handles around its outside, both circled. (If you're on a Mac, the center handle is just a box like the corner ones.) When you move your cursor near one of the handles, it turns into a curved, two-headed arrow.

When you've gotten hold of a handle, drag to adjust your photo the way you'd straighten a crooked picture on the wall. When you're happy with what you've done, click the green checkmark below the image. Or, if you don't like the results, click the Cancel button—the red No symbol—instead.

3. **When you've got the image positioned where you want it, click the Commit button (the green checkmark) or press Enter. (If you don't like what you did, click the Cancel button to cancel the rotation.)**

If you were straightening the photo (rather than angling it), you've got a nice straight picture, but the edges are probably pretty ragged, since the original had slanted, unrotated sides. You can take care of that by cropping the photo as explained next.

Cropping Pictures

Whether or not you straighten your digital photos, sooner or later you'll probably need to *crop* them—trim them to a certain size. Most people crop photos for one of two reasons: To print on standard-size photo paper, you usually need to cut away part of the image to make it fit the paper. Then there's the "I don't want *that* in my picture" reason. Fortunately, Elements makes it easy to crop away distracting background objects and people you'd rather not see.

A few cameras take photos that are proportioned exactly right for printing on standard-size paper, like 4" × 6" or 8" × 10". (An image's width-to-height ratio is known as its *aspect ratio*.) But most cameras create images that aren't the same proportions as any of the standard photo paper sizes. Figure 3-7 shows an example of cropping to fit on such paper.

FIGURE 3-7

When you print on standard-sized paper, you may have to choose the portion of your digital photo that you want to keep.

Left: The photo as it came from the camera.

Right: After cropping—ready for a 4" × 6" print.

The extra area most cameras include gives you room to crop wherever you like. You can also crop out different areas for different size prints (assuming you save the original photo). If you'd like to experiment with cropping or changing resolution (explained on page 105), download *river.jpg*—the image used in Figure 3-7—from this book's Missing CD page at *www.missingmanuals.com/cds*.

> **TIP** If your photo isn't in the Organizer or another image-management program that automatically protects the original, it's best to crop a *copy* of the image, since cropping throws away the pixels outside the area you choose to keep. And you never know—you may want those pixels back someday.

If you're not sure how to crop an image, or if you need to meet some common requirements for photo contests, Elements offers some special crop overlays that can help crop photos to pleasing proportions. The next section teaches you how to use them.

The Crop Tool

You can use the Crop tool in either Expert mode or the Quick Fix window. This tool got a major makeover in Elements 13, so it may take some getting used to. It still includes a helpful list of preset sizes to make your job easier (page 93 explains how to use them), but now it also makes suggestions on how to best crop your image. (You can also crop to an exact size, as explained on page 93.) Here's how to use the revamped Crop tool:

1. **Activate the Crop tool.**

   Click its icon in the Tools panel (it's at the top left of the Modify section) or press C.

   Once you activate the Crop tool, you see a grid (called the *crop overlay*) over your image. That's the tool's first crop suggestion. The grid may cover the whole photo or just a part of it. The part of your photo that will be cropped away at the current settings is masked out with a gray film to help you focus on the area you'll keep if you accept this suggestion.

2. **Decide how to crop your image.**

   You can drag the crop overlay around, or you can resize it by dragging a corner of the box or one of its edges. Also, if you move your mouse down over the four thumbnails in the Tool Options area's Crop Suggestions section, Elements offers you a suggested crop for each one. If you find a suggestion you like, click its thumbnail. You can then adjust it by scooting it around in your photo with your mouse.

TIP It's important to understand that the suggestions Elements offers are pretty generic. They aren't based on a sophisticated analysis of the contents of your photo, so don't just randomly accept one. Take charge and make your own decision about the best crop. You can do a much better job of deciding what looks good than Elements can.

As you drag the crop box, a small black pop-up appears, showing the size your photo would be if you cropped it using the current settings. If you drag the right or left edge of the box, you see the changing numbers for the width of the photo. Drag the top or bottom edge instead, and you see the changing height dimension. Drag a corner and you see both the width and height numbers.

TIP You may sometimes find the Crop tool a little crotchety. For example, if the tool won't let you drag where you want and keeps insisting on creating a particular-sized crop, you need to reset it. Simply click the little four-line square at the far right of the Tool Options area and choose Reset Tool. If you want *all* your tools to go back to their original settings, choose Reset All Tools instead.

You can also rotate the crop box to any angle (a handy way to straighten *and* crop in one go). To do so, put your cursor near one of the box's handles (the cursor turns into the curved, double-headed arrow circled in Figure 3-8), and then drag. For example, if your image is crooked, turn the bounding box so that its outline is parallel to where straight should be in the photo; Elements will then straighten out your photo when you crop. As with Free Rotate Layer, when you drag, a black pop-up shows you how many degrees you've rotated the photo.

TIP You can even add blank space (called *canvas*) on one or more sides of your image with the Crop tool. To do that, just drag the crop box so that it's outside the boundaries of the image. When you accept the crop, the extra space appears.

You can also choose a different *crop overlay* (explained in a sec) to help you create a more appealing image, or turn the overlay off altogether if it bugs you. In the Tool Options area, just choose the one you want.

3. **When you're sure you've got the crop you want, press Enter/Return, click the green Commit checkmark, or double-click inside the area you're going to keep, and you're done.**

    If you change your mind, click the red Cancel button or press Esc, and Elements undoes the selection so you can start over.

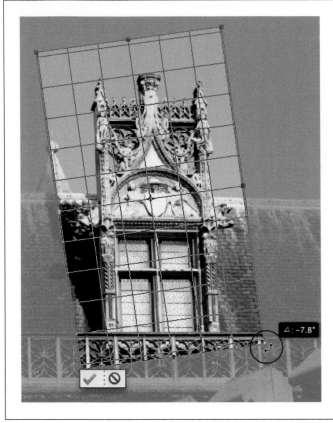

FIGURE 3-8

To change your selection from horizontal to vertical or vice versa, just move your cursor outside the crop box and it turns into the rotation arrows circled here. Then drag to rotate the crop box the same way you would rotate a whole image (see Figure 3-6).

Rotating your selection doesn't rotate the photo—just the crop box.

When you're done adjusting the crop box, press Enter/Return or click the green Commit checkmark to tell Elements you're satisfied. The red Cancel button cancels your crop.

The Crop tool's various overlays can help you crop photos in the most visually pleasing way. Choose an option by clicking one of the Grid Overlay icons in the Tool Options area, either before or after you've clicked a Crop Suggestion thumbnail or dragged in your image with the Crop tool (but before you *accept* the crop), and you'll see guidelines that help you decide where to crop. Here are your options:

- **None**. This option gives you no visible overlay, just the empty crop box.

- **Rule of Thirds**. This is the option Elements chooses automatically the first time you use the Crop tool; it divides the crop area into thirds, both vertically and horizontally. Figure 3-9 explains how to use this overlay.

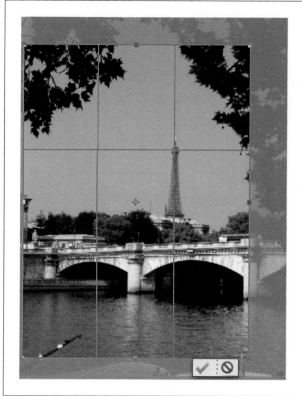

FIGURE 3-9

The basic idea behind the Rule of Thirds is simple: Most people find images more pleasing to the eye if the main point of interest isn't placed squarely in the center. Instead, if you think of dividing a photo into thirds both horizontally and vertically (as this grid does), your subject will have more impact if it falls along one of those dividing lines or—even better—where two lines intersect.

Here, the crop places the Eiffel Tower on a vertical line, the bridge on a horizontal one, and the place where those two points of interest meet falls where the two lines intersect, making the cropped version better composed than the original, uncropped photo.

- **Grid**. This puts a smaller grid over your image. You always see this smaller grid when you rotate the crop box, as shown in Figure 3-8, but if you haven't clicked this thumbnail, the overlay should return to the one you've chosen as soon as you release the mouse button.

■ CROPPING TO AN EXACT SIZE

You don't have to eyeball things when using the Crop tool. You can enter any dimensions you want in the Tool Options area's W (width) and H (height) boxes, or choose one of the presets from the unlabeled Aspect Ratio menu above those boxes. This menu includes several standard photo sizes, like 4" × 6" and 8" × 10". It starts off set to No Restriction, which means you can drag freely. The Use Photo Ratio option lets you crop your image by using the same width/height proportions (the *aspect ratio*) as the original. Figure 3-10 teaches you a timesaver: how to quickly swap the width and height numbers.

FIGURE 3-10

To swap the crop box's width and height settings, just click these little arrows. If you click them while there's a crop overlay visible in your image, then Elements swaps the overlay's dimensions, too.

WARNING If you enter a number in the Tool Options area's Resolution box that's different from your image's current resolution, the Crop tool *resamples* your image to match the new resolution. (Resolution is explained starting on page 105.) Page 111 explains what resampling is and why it's not always a good thing.

Cropping with the Marquee Tool

The Crop tool is handy, but you may find that all the suggestions it makes drive you nuts. Fortunately, you can also crop with the Rectangular Marquee tool, which is no harder to use than the Crop tool, but you get to make all the decisions yourself. And there's one other big difference between the two: With the Crop tool, all you can do to the selected area is crop it; the Rectangular Marquee tool, in contrast, lets you make lots of other changes to the selected area, like adjust its color, which you may want to do before you crop.

To make a basic crop with the Marquee tool:

1. **Open a photo and then activate the Marquee tool.**

   Click the little dotted rectangle near the top of the Tools panel or press M. Figure 3-11 shows you the shape choices you get in the Tool Options area for the Marquee tools. For cropping, choose the Rectangular Marquee tool.

FIGURE 3-11

Once you've activated the Marquee tools, you can use these buttons in the Tool Options area to choose a shape—rectangle or ellipse. The Tools panel icon reflects the shape you select here.

2. **Drag across the part of the photo you want to keep.**

As you drag, you'll see the same little pop-up with the dimensions of the selected area that you see when you use the Crop tool.

When you let go of the mouse button, the dimensions pop-up disappears and Elements puts dotted lines like the ones shown in Figure 3-12 around the selected area. (Chapter 5 has more about making selections.) These dotted lines are sometimes called "marching ants." (Get it? The dashes look like ants marching around your picture.) The area inside the marching ants is the part that you're keeping. If you make a mistake, press Esc or Ctrl+D/⌘-D to get rid of the selection and start over. As with the Crop tool, if you want to be sure you get everything at the edge of a photo, you can start dragging a little outside the image, and the marching ants will snap to the photo's edge.

FIGURE 3-12

When you let go after making your Marquee selection, you see the "marching ants" around the selection's edge.

You can reposition the marquee by dragging it—just put your cursor anywhere inside the dotted outline and then drag.

Marching Ants

3. **Crop the photo.**

Go to Image→Crop. The area outside your selection disappears, and Elements keeps only the area you selected in step 2.

If you want to crop a photo to a particular *aspect ratio* (proportion), you can do that easily. Once the Rectangular Marquee tool is active but *before* you drag to make a selection, go to the Tool Options area. From the Aspect menu, choose Fixed Ratio, and then enter the proportions you want in the W (width) and H (height) boxes. Finally, drag and crop as described in the previous list, and the photo will end up with the exact proportions you entered.

You can also crop to an exact *size* with the Rectangular Marquee tool:

1. **If you plan to print the cropped image, start by checking the resolution of your photo. (If you don't plan to print the image, only its size matters, not its resolution, so skip to step 2.)**

   To find the current resolution, go to Image→Resize→Image Size (or press Alt+Ctrl+I/Option-⌘-I) and make sure the Resolution number (ppi) is somewhere between 150 and 300 (300 is best, for reasons explained on page 109). If the number looks good, click OK and go to step 2.

   If the resolution is too low, change the number in the Resolution box to what you want. Make sure that the Resample Image checkbox is turned off, and then click OK.

2. **Activate the Rectangular Marquee tool.**

   Click the Rectangular Marquee tool's icon (the dotted rectangle) in the Tools panel or press M. Check the Tool Options area to make sure you've got the Rectangular Marquee tool, not the Elliptical Marquee tool (see Figure 3-11).

3. **Enter your Tool Options settings.**

   First, set the Aspect menu to Fixed Size. Next, enter the dimensions you want in the W and H boxes. (You can also change the unit of measurement from pixels to inches, percentages, or centimeters; just replace "px" to "in," "%," or "cm.")

4. **Drag or click anywhere in your image.**

   Elements creates a selection the exact size you entered in the Tool Options. You can reposition it by dragging or using the arrow keys.

5. **Crop the image.**

   Go to Image→Crop.

> **TIP** If you're doing your own printing, there's no reason to restrict yourself to standard photo sizes like 4" × 6"—unless, of course, you need the image to fit a frame of that size. But most of the time, your images could just as well be square, or long and skinny, or whatever proportions you want. You can be especially inventive when sizing images for the Web. So don't feel that every photo you take has to be straitjacketed into a standard size.

The Cookie Cutter tool, which shares the same Tools panel slot as the Crop tool, also gives you a way to create really interesting crops, as shown in Figure 3-13.

FIGURE 3-13

With the Cookie Cutter tool, you don't have to be square. It lets you crop images to various shapes, from the kind of abstract border you see here to heart- or star-shaped outlines.

To learn how to use this tool, see page 429 in Chapter 12.

Zooming and Repositioning Your View

Sometimes, rather than changing the size of a photo, all you want to do is change your view of it in Elements so you can get a better look at it. For example, you may want to zoom in on a particular area, or zoom out so you can see how edits you've made have affected the photo's overall look.

This section is about how to adjust your view of images. Nothing you do with the tools and commands covered in this section changes anything about the actual photo—just the way you see it onscreen. Elements gives you lots of tools and keyboard shortcuts to help with these views; soon you'll probably find yourself changing perspective without even thinking about it.

Image Views

Before you start changing your view of photos, it's good to get familiar with the different ways you can position images. Back in Chapter 1, you learned how to manage panels and bins. This section covers your options for image windows, which behave a little differently.

You can choose between viewing images as tabs or in their own floating windows. Elements automatically starts out using tabs, but sometimes you may prefer to work with windows. For instance, if you want to use the Transform commands (page 387), putting the image into a tab gives you plenty of room to pull the handles that command places around the image, but you may find it easier to work with *multiple* images if each one is in its own window. There are a bunch of options for either kind of view, and even if you're an Elements veteran but haven't quite gotten the hang of this system, you should read this section in case you accidentally wind up in a view you didn't want. Figure 3-14 shows the difference between tabs and windows.

FIGURE 3-14

Top: Three floating windows in Cascade view.

Bottom: The same three images as tabs. Notice that you see only one image—the others are tucked away out of sight. To see one of the other images, click its tab near the top of the screen (circled). The tab's background will fill every part of the main Elements window that isn't occupied by bins, however large that area may be. The active image is easy to spot because its tab is lighter gray than the other images' tabs.

To give yourself maximum viewing flexibility, go to Edit→Preferences→General/Photoshop Elements Editor→Preferences→General, turn on "Allow Floating Documents in Expert Mode," and then click OK. When this setting is turned off, you're stuck with tabs no matter what you choose in the Editor's menus. When it's on, you can quickly switch back and forth between windows, tabs, or even a combination of the two.

> **NOTE** You can also choose to let your images combine as tabs (just like image tabs in the main Editor window) within floating windows, so that you can have two or more photos in one floating window. This can help keep you organized when, for example, you're working on a project that involves a lot of photos; you can use this trick to group together the ones you want to use until it's time to work on them. To give yourself this option, go to Edit→Preferences→General/Photoshop Elements Editor→Preferences→General and make sure that "Enable Floating Document Window Docking" is turned on. On the other hand, if this feature drives you crazy, you'll be pleased to know you can turn it *off* here.

Since accurate image viewing is crucial in Elements, the Editor's Window, View, and Layout menus all include options that let you control how the program displays images. The Window and View menus are up at the top of your screen, and the Layout menu is one of the buttons at the bottom left of the Editor's main window. When you go to Window→Images, you get several options for displaying images (a couple of them are available in only the Mac version of Elements, as noted below):

- **Tile**. Your image windows or tabs appear edge to edge so they fill the available desktop space. For example, with two photos open, each one gets half the workspace; with four photos, each one gets a quarter of it, and so on. With tabs, you have a lot of additional options when you use the Layout menu, described in Figure 3-15.

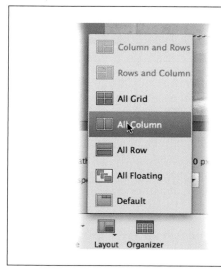

FIGURE 3-15

To arrange tabs to work with multiple images, click the Layout button at the bottom of the Editor's Expert mode window, and then choose the arrangement you want.

Default is the way tabs normally look, with only one visible and just the header tabs of the other images in view. If you have only one image file open, all the other options in this menu are grayed out. If you have only two images open, then the top three options (which are for three or more photos) are grayed out.

If you're using floating windows, clicking a layout's thumbnail consolidates them all into tabs in the layout you choose here.

- **Cascade**. Your image windows appear in overlapping stacks. Most people find cascading windows (Figure 3-14, top) the most practical view when they want to compare or work with two images. (This option is grayed out if you're working with tabs.)

- **Float in Window**. To make a single image's tab into a window, click the image's tab to make it the active one, and then choose this option.

- **Float All in Windows**. If you have a bunch of tabs, choose this option to turn them all into floating windows.

- **Consolidate All to Tabs**. Got a lot of windows that you want to turn back into tabs? Choosing this option does the trick.

- **New Window**. Choose this command and you get a separate, duplicate window for your active image. This view is a terrific help when you're working on fine details. You can zoom way in on one view while keeping the other window in a regular view so you don't lose track of where you are in the photo. (Don't worry about version control or remembering which window you're working in—both windows just show different views of the *same* image; you're not creating a separate file.) If you haven't turned on floating windows, this command creates a new tab instead, although that's not as useful.

- **Minimize (Mac only)**. If you want to send the active image window to the Dock, choose this option or press ⌘-M. Click the image in the Dock to bring it back to Elements. (If you're working with tabs, then the whole Elements window gets minimized when you choose this command.)

- **Bring All to Front (Mac only)**. Use this command to bring all your open Elements image windows to the foreground (handy if documents from several programs are covering them up).

- **Match Zoom**. Makes Elements display all your windows at the same magnification level as the active window (the one you're currently working in).

- **Match Location**. Elements makes the display in all your image windows match the active window so you see the same *part* of each image, like the upper-right corner or the bottom-left edge.

The Editor's View menu also gives you some handy commands for adjusting the view of your active image window or tab:

- **Zoom In/Out**. Zooming is explained on page 102. These menu commands are an alternative to using the Zoom tool.

TIP Keyboard shortcuts are the fastest way to zoom: Press Ctrl-+/⌘-+ to zoom in and Ctrl--/⌘-- to zoom out. The next section explains the Zoom tool in detail.

- **Fit on Screen**. This command makes your image as large as it can be while still keeping the whole thing visible. You can also press Ctrl+0/⌘-0 to get this view (that's the number zero, not the letter O), or double-click the Hand tool's icon in the Tools panel (unsurprisingly, the icon is a hand).

- **Actual Pixels**. For the most accurate look at the onscreen size of your photo, choose this option. If you're creating graphics for the Web, this view shows how big your image will be in a web browser. Keyboard shortcut: Ctrl+1/⌘-1. Or double-click the Zoom tool's icon (the magnifying glass) in the Tools panel.

- **Print Size**. This view is really just a guess by Elements, because it doesn't know exactly how big a pixel is on your monitor. But it's a rough approximation of the size the image would be if you printed it at its current resolution. (Resolution is explained on page 105.)

While you may find the whole tab vs. window business a little confusing at first, it gives you lots of ways to stay organized while working. The box below has some additional tips for keeping things under control.

Elements gives you three useful tools to adjust your view of a particular image: the Zoom tool, the Hand tool, and the Navigator panel, all of which are explained in the following sections.

ORGANIZATION STATION

Managing Image Windows

In addition to the various menu commands discussed in this section, there's another way to control whether you have tabs or windows without trekking up to the menu bar: dragging. (You need to turn on floating windows *and* floating window docking before these tricks will work; page 99 tells you how.) Here are a few shortcuts:

- **Turn a tab into a window**. Just grab the tab's title bar and drag down. The tab pops off and turns into a floating window.

- **Turn a window into a tab**. Drag the window up toward the top of the Elements workspace until you see a blue outline. This outline is Elements' way of telling you that, if you let go of the mouse button, it'll consolidate the window with the outlined area, just like it consolidates panels (see Figure 1-10 on page 16).

- **Create tabs in a floating window**. Say you're working on combining elements from many different images, and it's getting hard to know which is where. To put two images in one floating window, just drag one window's title bar

onto another window's title bar; when you see the blue outline, let go of your mouse. You now have a floating window with two tabs. (Repeat this trick as many times as you want for a multitabbed window.)

- **Avoid making tabs**. When you're working with floating windows, if the tops of the windows move too close together, Elements wants to combine them. If you're dragging windows around and you see the telltale blue outline, just keep dragging till it disappears.

- **Undo accidental tabs**. If you create a tab you didn't mean to, grab the top of the image you want to turn back into a floating window, and then drag it loose from the tab group.

Just remember that in Elements, anytime you're dragging something and a blue outline appears, what you're dragging is going to get consolidated with something if you let go of the mouse. If you don't want that to happen, keep dragging until the outline disappears.

The Zoom Tool

Some of Elements' tools require you to get a really close look at your image to see what's going on. Sometimes you even need to see individual *pixels* as you work, as shown in Figure 3-16. The Zoom tool makes it easy to zoom your view in and out.

FIGURE 3-16

There will be times when you want to zoom way, way in on an image.

You may even need to go pixel by pixel in tricky spots, as shown here.

The Zoom tool lives at the very top of the Tools panel; its icon is a magnifying glass. Click it or press Z to activate the tool. Once you do that, two magnifying glass buttons appear at the left end of the Tool Options area. To zoom in, click the one with the + sign on it, and then click the spot in your photo where you want the zoom to focus. The point you click becomes the center of your view, and the view size increases again each time you click. To zoom out, in the Tool Options area, click the magnifying glass with the – sign on it instead.

> **TIP** Holding Alt/Option while you click makes the Zoom tool do the opposite of what it's currently set to do. For instance, if the tool is set to zoom in, then pressing this key makes it zoom out.

The Zoom tool has several other Tool Options settings:

- **Zoom**. You can either drag this slider or click the number to its right and then type what you want, and the view immediately jumps to that percentage. The maximum is 3200 percent, and the minimum is 1 percent.

- **Resize Windows To Fit**. Turn on this checkbox and the image windows get larger or smaller as you zoom, according to your current view. The image always fills the whole window with no gray space around it. (At least that's how it's *supposed* to work; sometimes it's a bit buggy.)

- **Zoom All Windows**. If you have more than one image window, turn on this checkbox and the zoom level of all the windows changes simultaneously when you zoom in one window. (This option works with tabs, too, so be careful—you may unintentionally zoom an image that's hidden behind the one you're working on.)

> **TIP** Holding down the Shift key while zooming makes all your windows zoom together, just as if you'd turned on the Zoom All Windows checkbox.

- **1:1**. This button has the same effect as choosing Actual Pixels from the View menu. It's explained on page 101.

- **Fit Screen**. This button does the same thing as the View menu's "Fit on Screen" command—see page 101.

- **Fill Screen**. This makes your photo fill Elements' whole viewing area, even if the image doesn't all fit onscreen at once.

- **Print Size**. This is a duplicate of the View menu command of the same name. See page 101 for the lowdown.

> **TIP** You don't need to bother with the Zoom tool at all—you can use your keyboard instead. Press Ctrl-+/⌘-+ to zoom in and Ctrl--/⌘-- to zoom out. Just hold down Ctrl/⌘ and keep tapping the + or – key until you see what you want. (You can zoom to 100 percent by double-clicking the Zoom tool's icon in the Tools panel.) It doesn't matter which tool you're using—you can always zoom in or out this way. Because you'll do a lot of zooming in Elements, these keyboard shortcuts are ones to remember.
>
> And if you have a mouse with a scroll wheel, you can use that to zoom, too. Go to Edit→Preferences→General/ Photoshop Elements Editor→Preferences→General and turn on "Zoom with Scroll Wheel." (If you only want to use the scroll wheel occasionally, you can zoom by holding down Alt/Option and scrolling, even when that preference *isn't* turned on.)

The Hand Tool and Navigator Panel

With all that zooming, sometimes you can't see your whole image at once. Fortunately, the Hand tool lets you change which part of an image appears onscreen. It's super easy to use: Just click the hand icon at the top of the Tools panel or press H to activate it. When you do, your cursor turns into the little icon shown in Figure 3-17. Simply drag your photo to move it around in the window. This tool is really helpful when you're zoomed way in or working on a large image.

FIGURE 3-17

The easiest way to activate the Hand tool is to press and hold the space bar on your keyboard. (You can tell when the Hand tool is active because you see this white-gloved cursor.) No matter what you're doing in Elements, pressing the space bar calls up the Hand tool (unless you're using one of the type tools, of course—see Chapter 14). When you let go of the space bar, Elements switches back to the tool you were previously using.

If you find that you can't back out of the Hand tool, just give your space bar a whack—it may be sticking.

The Hand tool gives you the same All Windows option you get with the Zoom tool, but you don't have to adjust the Tool Options settings to activate it. Just hold down Shift while using the Hand tool, and all your windows scroll in sync. The Hand tool also gives you the same four buttons as the Zoom tool (1:1, Fit Screen, Fill Screen, and Print Size); they're described on page 103.

Figure 3-18 shows the Navigator panel—a somewhat more sophisticated alternative to the Hand tool—which is really useful for working on big photos or when you want to have a slider handy for micromanaging the zoom level. To call it up, go to Window→Navigator. (It appears as part of the grouped floating panel [page 11], but if you're in the Custom Workspace [page 12] you can drag it out and close the rest of the group to get it out of your way.)

FIGURE 3-18

Meet the Navigator, which is perfect for keeping track of where you are in a large image.

You can travel around the image by dragging the little red rectangle shown here, which marks the area of the photo that's currently displayed onscreen. And you can adjust your zoom level by dragging the slider, clicking the percentage and either typing a new number or pressing Alt/Option plus the up or down arrow key, or clicking the + and – buttons on either end of the slider.

Changing the Size of an Image

The previous section explained how to resize your *view* of an image—how it appears on your monitor. But sometimes you need to change the *actual* size of an image, and that's what this section is about.

Resizing photos brings you up against a pretty tough concept in digital imaging: *resolution*, which measures, in pixels, the amount of detail your image can show. What's confusing is that resolution for printing and for onscreen use (like email and the Web) are quite different.

You need many more pixels to create a good-looking print of an image than you do to view the image clearly onscreen. A photo that's going to print well almost always has too many pixels in it to display easily on many monitors, and as a result, its file is usually pretty hefty for emailing. So you often need two copies of a photo for the two different uses. (If you want to know more about the nitty-gritty of resolution, a good place to start is *www.scantips.com*.)

This section gives you a brief introduction to both onscreen and print resolution, especially in terms of what decisions you'll need to make when using the Resize Image dialog box. You'll also learn how to add more canvas (blank space) around photos, which you'd do to make room for a caption below an image, for instance, or when you want to combine two photos.

To get started, open a photo you want to resize and then go to Image→Resize→Image Size or press Alt+Ctrl+I/Option-⌘-I. Either way, you see the Image Size dialog box (Figure 3-19).

FIGURE 3-19

This dialog box gives you two different ways to change a photo's size. Use the settings shown here when preparing a photo for onscreen viewing. (The number next to Pixel Dimensions—here, 28.6M—tells you the current size of your file in megabytes or kilobytes.) Before you can make any changes here, you have to turn on the Resample Image checkbox at the bottom of the dialog box (not shown), since changing pixel dimensions always involves resampling (see page 111).

Resizing Images for Email and the Web

It's important to learn how to size photos so that they show up easily and clearly onscreen. Have you ever gotten an emailed photo that was so huge you could see only a tiny bit of it on your monitor at once? That happens when someone sends an image that isn't optimized for onscreen viewing. Happily, it's easy to avoid that problem once you know how to correctly size photos for onscreen use.

The Image Size dialog box is divided into two main sections: Pixel Dimensions (visible in Figure 3-19) and Document Size. You'll use the Pixel Dimensions settings when you know the image is going to be viewed only onscreen. (The Document Size settings relate to printing, which is covered on page 109.)

Monitors are concerned only with the size of a photo as measured in pixels, known as the *pixel dimensions*. On a monitor, a pixel is always the same size (unlike a printer, which can change the size of the pixels it prints). Your monitor doesn't know anything about pixels per inch (ppi), and it can't change the way it displays a photo even if you change the photo's ppi settings, as shown in Figure 3-20. (Graphics programs like Elements can change the size of your onscreen view by, say, zooming in, but most programs can't.) All you have to decide is how many pixels long and how many pixels wide you want the photo to be. You control those measurements in the Pixel Dimensions section of the Image Size dialog box.

FIGURE 3-20

One of these apple photos was saved at 3000 ppi, another at 300 ppi, and one at 3 ppi. Can you tell which is which?

Nope.

They all look exactly the same on your monitor because they all have exactly the same pixel dimensions, which is the only resolution setting your monitor understands. In other words, monitors don't care about images' ppi settings.

What dimensions should you use? That depends on who's going to see your photos, but as a general rule, small monitors today are usually 1024 pixels wide by 768 pixels high, although netbook screens can be quite a bit smaller than that. And some monitors, like the largest Dell and Apple models, have many more pixels than that, while smartphone screens are all over the place in terms of pixel dimensions.

Still, if you want to be sure that people who view your photo onscreen won't have to scroll to see the whole thing, a good rule of thumb is to make the longest side of the photo no more than 650 pixels (it doesn't matter whether that's the width or the height). And if you want people to be able to see more than one image at a time, you may want to make your photos smaller than that. Also, some people still set their monitors to display only 800 pixels wide by 600 pixels high, so you may want to create even smaller images to send to them.

On the other hand, if you send really small pictures to people with deluxe, high-resolution monitors or high-end smartphones where the individual pixels are minuscule, they're likely to complain that the photos are too tiny to see in detail. So if you send to a varied group of folks, you may need to make different copies for different audiences. On the whole, it's better to err on the side of caution—nobody will have trouble receiving and opening an image that's too small, but an overly large attachment can cause problems for people with small mailboxes and low-resolution monitors.

TIP   To get the most accurate look at how your photo displays on a monitor, go to View→Actual Pixels.

Also, although a photo always has the same pixel dimensions, you can't control the exact physical dimensions at which those pixels display on other people's monitors. A pixel is always the same size on any given monitor (as long as you don't change the monitor's screen resolution), but different monitors have different-sized pixels. Figure 3-21 may help clarify this concept.

FIGURE 3-21

Both these screens are running at 1280 × 800 pixels, but as you can see, the monitor in the back is physically much larger. Because of that, each pixel on that screen is much bigger than on the laptop in front.

NOTE In the following sections, you'll learn what to do when you want to *reduce* the size of an image. It's much easier to get good results when making a photo smaller than when making it larger. Elements *can* increase the size of an image using a technique called upsampling, but you often get mediocre results; page 111 explains why.

To resize a photo for emailing or posting online, start by making extra sure you're not resizing the original. You're going to be shedding pixels that you can't get back, so if your photo isn't already in the Organizer, resize a copy of it (File→Duplicate) rather than the original. Then, here's what you do:

1. **Call up the Image Size dialog box.**

   Go to Image→Resize→Image Size or press Alt+Ctrl+I/Option-⌘-I.

2. **At the bottom of the dialog box, turn on the Resample Image checkbox.**

   You won't be able to make any changes to the photo's pixel dimensions until you do this.

3. **In the Pixel Dimensions section, enter the dimension you want for the longer side of the photo.**

   As explained earlier, you usually want 650 pixels or fewer, unless you know for sure that your recipients have up-to-date equipment and broadband Internet connections. Be sure to choose pixels as the unit of measurement. You just need to enter a number for *one* dimension; Elements automatically figures out the other dimension as long as the Constrain Proportions checkbox is turned on (it's near the bottom of the dialog box).

4. **Check the settings at the bottom of the dialog box.**

   The Scale Styles checkbox doesn't matter, so leave it off. Constrain Proportions and Resample Image should be turned on. (*Resampling* means changing the number of pixels in an image.) The Resample Image menu lists the different resampling methods you can choose from. Adobe recommends Bicubic Sharper when you're making an image smaller, but you may want to experiment with the other options if you don't like the results Bicubic Sharper gives you. (The menu includes the suggested use for most of the methods in parentheses after their names.) Just try one option, and then undo it and go back and try again with a different setting to see which you prefer.

5. **Click OK.**

   Elements resizes the photo, although you may not immediately see a difference onscreen. (To see the difference, go to View→Actual Pixels before and after you resize.) To make your changes permanent, save the resized photo.

Sometimes Elements resizes an image automatically—for example, when you use the Organizer's E-Mail command (see page 565). But the method described here gives you more control than letting Elements make all the decisions for you.

TIP If you're also concerned about the file's size in megabytes or kilobytes, use the Save For Web dialog box (see page 557) instead, which helps you create smaller files.

Resizing for Printing

If you want great prints, you need to think about a photo's resolution quite differently than you do for onscreen images. As a general rule, when it comes to printing, the more pixels the photo has, the better. That's the reason camera manufacturers keep packing more megapixels into their new models—the more pixels you have, the larger you can print a photo and still have it look terrific.

TIP Even before you take photos, you can do a lot toward making them print well if you always choose the largest size and the highest quality setting on your camera (typically Extra Fine, Superfine, or Fine).

When you print, you need to consider two things: the photo's size in inches (or whatever your preferred unit of measurement is) and its resolution in pixels per inch (ppi). These settings work together to determine the quality of your print.

Your printer is a virtuoso that plays pixels like an accordion: It can squeeze the pixels together and make them smaller or spread them out and make them larger. Generally speaking, the denser the pixels (the higher the ppi), the higher the photo's resolution and the better it looks. If your photo doesn't have enough pixels, the print will look *pixelated*—jagged and blurry. The goal is to have enough pixels so that they'll be packed fairly densely—ideally at about 300 ppi.

You usually don't get a visibly better result if you go over 300 ppi—you just have a larger file. And depending on your tastes, you may be content with your results at a lower ppi. For instance, some photos taken with Canon cameras come into Elements at 180 ppi, and you may be happy with how they print. But 200 ppi is usually considered about the lowest density for an acceptable print at a size you can hold in your hand. The larger the image, the farther away you'll view it, so you can often get by with a lower pixel density for huge prints (like the kind you'd frame and hang on a wall) if necessary. Figure 3-22 shows why it's so important to have a high ppi setting.

To set the size of an image for printing:

1. **Call up the Image Size dialog box.**

   Go to Image→Resize→Image Size, or press Alt+Ctrl+I/Option-⌘-I.

2. **Check the image's resolution.**

   Take a look at the Document Size section of the dialog box (Figure 3-23). Start by checking the Resolution (pixels/inch, a.k.a. ppi) setting. If it's too low, like 72 ppi, go to the bottom of the dialog box and turn off the Resample Image checkbox. Then enter the ppi you want in the Resolution field.

   When you increase the ppi setting, Elements should automatically lower the values in the Width and Height fields, making the document smaller because of the greater density of the pixels. If it doesn't, click OK, and then reopen the Image Size dialog box.

FIGURE 3-22

Different resolution settings can dramatically alter print quality. These photos have been printed and then scanned so you can see the results of printing them.

Top: A photo with a resolution of 300 ppi. Notice that the image looks pretty smooth—you can't see individual pixels.

Bottom: The same photo with a resolution of 72 ppi. Too few pixels stretched too far causes this kind of blocky, blurry print. When you can see individual pixels (as you can here), a photo is said to be "pixelated."

FIGURE 3-23

Crop your image to the shape you want (see page 89), and then use this section of the Image Size dialog box to set its size for printing.

3. **Check the physical size of the photo.**

In the Document Size area, look at the Width and Height numbers. Are they what you want? If so, you're all done, so click OK. If they're not what you want, continue with the next step.

4. **If the size numbers aren't right, resize the photo.**

If the proportions aren't what you want, click Cancel, crop the photo (page 89), and then come back to the Image Size dialog box. (Don't try to reshape an image using this dialog box.)

Once you've cropped the image and opened the dialog box again, turn on the Resample Image checkbox and, if you're making the photo *larger*, choose Bicubic Smoother from the drop-down menu at the bottom of the dialog box; if you're making the photo *smaller*, choose Bicubic Sharper instead. (These settings are Adobe's recommendation, but you may find that you prefer one of the other resampling choices.) Be sure to read the next section to understand how you're affecting the photo when you do this.

Make sure that Constrain Proportions is turned on, and then, in the dialog box's Document Size section, enter the size you want for the width or height (Elements calculates the other dimension for you). Scale Styles doesn't matter, so leave it off.

5. **Click OK.**

Elements resizes the photo so it's ready for printing.

■ RESAMPLING

Resampling is an image-editing term for changing the number of pixels in an image. The results of resampling are permanent, so you want to avoid resampling an original photo if you can help it. As a rule, it's easier to get good results when you *downsample* (make a photo smaller) than when you *upsample* (make a photo larger).

When you upsample, you're *adding* pixels to the image. Elements has to get them from somewhere, so it makes them up. It's pretty good at doing this, but these pixels are never as good as the ones that were in the photo to begin with, as you can see in Figure 3-24.

When you enlarge an image to bigger than its original size, you'll definitely lose some quality. So, for example, if you try to stretch a photo that's 3 inches wide at 180 ppi to an 8 × 10-inch print, don't be surprised if the results look pretty bad.

The Image Size dialog box's Resample Image menu offers several resampling methods, and they do a really good job when you find the right one for your situation. Adobe recommends choosing Bicubic Smoother when you're upsampling (enlarging) images and Bicubic Sharper when you're downsampling (reducing) them, but you may prefer one of the others. It's worth experimenting with them all to see which you like.

FIGURE 3-24

Here's a closeup look at what happens to a photo when you resample it.

If you'd like to try this yourself, download the file russian_box.jpg from this book's Missing CD page at www.missingmanuals. com/cds. Zoom in really close so you can see the pixels.

The photo as it came from the camera.

Downsampled to 72 ppi.

Upsampled back to the original resolution. See how soft the pixels look compared to the original?

Adding Canvas

Just like the works of Monet and Matisse, your photos appear in Elements on digital "canvases." Sometimes you'll want to add more canvas to make room for text or to combine photos into a collage.

You add canvas by going to Image→Resize→Canvas Size. You can change the canvas size using a variety of measurements. If you don't know exactly how *much* more canvas you want, then choose "percent" from the Width or Height drop-down menu (the other one changes automatically). Then you can guesstimate that you want, say, 2 percent more canvas or 50 percent more. Figure 3-25 shows how to get your photo into the right place on the new canvas.

TIP If you just want to add canvas to the bottom of your image for a caption, check out page 454 to learn about the Captions action.

Changing the size of the canvas doesn't change the size of your picture any more than pasting a postcard onto a full-size sheet of paper changes the size of the post-card. In both cases, all you get is more empty space around the picture. The "Canvas extension color" menu lets you make the new canvas whatever color you like. You can choose your current foreground or background color, or white, black, gray, or "Other," which brings up the Color Picker. (Actually, if you want a custom color, you don't need to use this menu. Just click the color square to the right of the menu to bring up the Color Picker, and when you click OK, Elements chooses Other for you. This works even if you have the menu open and have already chosen something else from it.) You can see these options only if your image has a Background layer (see page 189); if not, the "Canvas extension color" menu is grayed out, and Elements automatically makes the added canvas transparent.

FIGURE 3-25

The Canvas Size dialog box isn't as complicated as it looks.

The strange Anchor grid with arrows pointing everywhere lets you decide exactly where to add canvas. The Anchor box represents your photo's current position, and the arrows surrounding it show where Elements will add canvas. Click any of the arrows to tell Elements where to position your photo on the new canvas.

In the top pair of images here, the canvas was added equally around all sides of the image. In the bottom pair, the new canvas was added below and to the right of the image. Setting the "Canvas extension color" to Background makes it easy to see where the added canvas is (here, it's blue).

The Relative checkbox is useful when you know, for instance, that you want your canvas to be 10 percent larger than it is now; in that example, you'd enter 10 percent in the Width and Height boxes. If this checkbox is turned off, you have to work with absolute numbers, so you'd enter 110 percent in those fields to do the same thing.

TIP You can also add canvas with the Crop tool by dragging a crop so that the boundaries of the crop overlay are outside the edges of the image, as explained on page 91.

Elemental Elements

CHAPTER 4:

The Quick Fix

CHAPTER 5:

Making Selections

CHAPTER 6:

Layers: The Heart of Elements

The Quick Fix

With Elements' Quick Fix tools, you can dramatically improve a photo's appearance with just a click or two. The Quick Fix window includes easy-to-use tools that help you adjust the brightness and color of your photos and make them look sharper. You don't even need to understand much about what you're doing—just click a button or move a slider, and then decide whether you like how your image looks.

You can also frame photos here and apply some fancy special effects (think Instagram filters) and textures with just a click. For example, you can make your photo look like it's printed on metal or was painted long ago on a wall where the paint is now cracking and flaking off. Elements 13 includes lots of new effects that are really fun and incredibly easy to use.

> **TIP** You can also share your photos right to Facebook, Twitter, Revel, and a few other popular sites right from Quick Fix. Just click the Share button at the upper right of the window. (There's more about sharing photos on page 576.) If you want to use your photos in a Create project (Chapter 15), just click the Create button (also in the window's upper right) and choose a project. When you finish in Create, you'll be in Expert mode. If you want to get back to the Quick Fix, just click the word "Quick" at the top of your screen.

Even if you *do* know what you're doing, you may still find yourself using the Quick Fix window to tweak things like shadows and highlights because it gives you a handy before-and-after view as you work. Also, the window's Vibrance, Temperature, and Tint sliders can come in handy for advanced color tweaking, like finessing the overall color of an otherwise finished photo. You also get two tools—the Selection Brush and the Quick Selection tool—that let you easily change specific areas of photos.

Besides letting you make general fixes, the Quick Fix window also makes it a snap to whiten teeth and fix blemishes in a photo. You can even add text or crop your photo. And Adobe has made it super easy to decide just what to do to an image by adding a number of *presets* to the adjustments; you'll learn about them on page 123. These presets are great if you need extra help—just pick one of them as a starting point and work from there.

In this chapter, you'll learn how (and in which order) to use the Quick Fix tools. If you have a newish digital camera, you may find that the Quick Fix window gives you everything you need to take your photos from pretty darn good to dazzling.

> **TIP** If a whole chapter on Quick Fix is frustratingly slow, you can start off by trying out the ultrafast Auto Smart Fix—a quick-fix tool for the truly impatient; page 27 explains how to use it. Also, Guided Edit may give you enough help to accomplish what you want to do; page 23 has the full story.

■ The Quick Fix Window

It's easy to get to the Quick Fix window, as long as you're in the Editor: Just click the word "Quick" near the top of your screen.

The Editor remembers which component you were last using (Quick, Guided, or Expert). So if you're working in the Organizer and want to send photos over to the Editor, if you right-click/Control-click a photo in the Organizer and choose "Edit with Photoshop Elements Editor," your photo will go right to the Quick Fix window if that's where you were the last time you used the Editor. If not, just click the Quick tab near the top of the screen.

You can also get to Quick Fix from some of the projects in Create mode: Just right-click/Control-click the photo you want to fix, and then choose Edit Quick; you get sent to Quick Fix with the photo ready for your adjustments. When you come into Quick Fix this way, you see a button at the left of the screen that says "Return to Creations." When you finish editing the image, click this button to go back to where you left off in your project.

> **TIP** You can also apply many quick fixes right from the Organizer, even in Full Screen view. See the box on page 121 for details.

The Quick Fix window looks like a stripped-down version of the Expert mode window (see Figure 4-1). Your tools are neatly arranged on both sides of the image: On the left, there's a nine-item toolbox; on the right, the Adjustments panel, which includes six sections for different adjustments you can make (see Figure 4-2).

At the bottom left of the Quick Fix window is the same group of buttons you have in Expert mode: Photo Bin, Tool Options, Undo, Redo, Rotate, Layout, and Organizer. They work the same way in Quick Fix as they do elsewhere in the Editor.

FIGURE 4-1

The Quick Fix window. If you have several photos open when you launch this window, you can use the Photo Bin at the bottom to choose the image you want to edit. Just click the Photo Bin button at the bottom of your screen to make the bin's contents visible, and then double-click an image's thumbnail to make that photo the active image—the one that's displayed front and center in the Quick Fix preview area.

See Figure 4-2 for a closeup view of the Adjustments panel on the right side of this window.

At the bottom right of the window is a new set of buttons:

- **Adjustments**. Click this button to see the Adjustments panel shown in Figure 4-1 and Figure 4-2, where you work on improving your photo.

- **Effects**. Click this button, and the panel on the right side of the window switches to show you thumbnails of the special effects that you can apply with just a single click, like aging a photo or making it look like a pencil sketch. Page 143 has more on these effects.

- **Textures**. Click this button to do things such as make your photo look like it's printed on canvas, like it had a color wash applied to it long ago, or like it's on a bumpy chrome surface.

- **Frames**. If you want to give your photo a border that looks like a frame or makes your photo look like an old film print that's lying on the page, click this button.

> **NOTE** There's more about using effects, textures, and frames on page 143.

FIGURE 4-2

Each section name here is actually a big button. When you click one (such as Exposure, as shown here), that section expands so that you can use the commands it contains. Click another section and the previously open one closes.

The following sections give you a quick overview of the tools Quick Fix offers and then explain how to use them.

> **TIP** If you need extra help, check out Guided Edit (page 23), which walks you through each step of basic editing projects.

The Quick Fix Toolbox

In the Editor, the Quick Fix window's toolbox holds an easy-to-navigate subset of the tools available in Expert mode. All the tools work the same in both modes, and you can use the same keystrokes to switch tools. And just as in Expert mode, when you click a tool, its Tool Options replace the Photo Bin. (To bring the Photo Bin back into view, click the Photo Bin button at the bottom of the screen.) From top to bottom, here's what you get:

- **The Zoom tool** lets you telescope in and out on your image—perfect for getting a good, close look at details or pulling back to see the whole photo. (See page 102 for more on this tool.) You can also zoom by using the Zoom slider in the upper-right corner of the image preview area.

Quick Fixes in the Organizer

The Organizer gives you several ways to apply Quick Fix's auto corrections without launching the Editor. The Organizer's Photo Fix Options panel has buttons that let you apply Auto Smart Fix, Auto Color, Auto Levels, Auto Contrast, or Auto Sharpen; fix red eye; and crop photos. For more selective editing, you'll still want the Editor, but if Auto is your thing, you'll be very happy staying in the Organizer. And if you use the Organizer, you get the added benefit of having your fixes automatically made on a copy of your image, which Elements saves in a *version set* (page 71) with the original.

There are two ways to get to the Organizer's auto fixes:

- **Just click it.** In the main Organizer window, click the Media tab near the top of the screen (if it's not already selected), and then click the Instant Fix button at the bottom right of the window to see a panel of editing options. When you're done editing, just click the Instant Fix button again to close the panel.

- **Use a different view.** In the Organizer, you can press F11/⌘-F11 for Full Screen view or F12/⌘-F12 for a side-by-side comparison (on a Mac, depending on your keyboard, you may need to add the fn key to these keyboard shortcuts). Once you do that, click the arrow at the right end of the control strip that appears to show its hidden controls, and then click Fix; a Quick Edit panel appears on the left side of your screen. (The panel tends to be shy and collapse against the left edge of the screen, so you may need to click it to pop it open). Each of the panel's icons is a button for one of the auto fixes. Just click one to apply that fix while you've got a large view of your photo—handy for tweaking images as you preview a newly imported batch of photos, for example. When you're done tweaking your images, press Esc to return to the standard Organizer view.

Read on for more about what these fixes do. They work the same way in the Organizer as they do in the Editor.

- **The Hand tool** helps move your photo around in the image window—just like grabbing it and moving it with your own five fingers. There's more about this tool on page 103.

- **The Quick Selection tool** lets you apply Quick Fix commands to specific portions of the image. Once you make a selection with this tool, the commands you use will change only the selected area, not the entire photo. You can also use the regular Selection Brush in Quick Fix; just activate the Quick Selection tool and then click the Selection Brush icon in the Tool Options area (the brush that's pointed down, like it's painting).

What's the difference between the two tools? The Selection Brush lets you paint a selection *exactly* where you want it (or mask out part of your photo to keep it from changing), while the Quick Selection tool figures out the boundaries of your selection based on marks you make on the image (which don't have to be precise). Also, the Quick Selection tool is far more automatic than the regular Selection Brush. You can read more about these tools beginning on page 154. (To get the most out of them, you need to understand the concept of selections; Chapter 5 tells you everything you need to know.)

- **The Red Eye Removal tool** lets you darken those red, demonic-looking flash reflections in people's eyes. This tool works on the green reflections in pets' eyes, too. Generally, if you need to fix red eyes on people or glowing eyes on pets, you should use this tool first, before doing any other edits to your photo. See page 126 to learn how to use it.

- **The Whiten Teeth tool** makes it super simple to brighten your subject's pearly whites. Page 136 explains how to use it.

- **The Type Tool**. To add text to an image, just click it with this tool and start typing. The Tool Options at the bottom of the window make it easy to choose a different font and change the size and color of the text. In the Quick Fix window, you can do anything that doesn't require access to the Layers panel, including bending and warping text (see page 488). Chapter 14 is all about the many things you can do with text in Elements.

- **The Healing Brushes**. The Spot Healing Brush lets you make truly invisible corrections to fix blemishes in a snap. Page 312 explains all about using this helpful tool. For now, if you're a beginner, first zoom in so you can see what you're doing, activate this tool, and then use the slider in the Tool Options area to choose a brush size that just barely covers the spot you want to fix. Then click that spot, and Elements fixes it right up so it blends with the surrounding area.

   You can also use the regular Healing Brush in Quick Fix—just click its icon in the Tool Options area (it looks like a Band-Aid *without* a dotted semicircle next to it). Page 315 explains how to use this tool.

- **The Crop tool** lets you change the size and shape of a photo by cutting off areas you don't want (see page 90).

> **TIP** If the contents of your photo need straightening (see page 84), it's usually easier to straighten in Expert mode before switching to Quick Fix, since the Quick Fix toolbox doesn't include the Straighten tool. However, there's a sneaky way to straighten with the Crop tool that you can use in Quick Fix, too—see page 91 for details.

- **The Move tool** lets you rearrange items in your photos, but in the Quick Fix window it's most useful when you're working with the frames in the Frames panel. Page 182 has more about the Move tool in general, and page 144 explains how to use the frames.

The Adjustments Panel

When you switch to Quick Fix mode, the Adjustments panel appears on the right side of your screen, as you saw back in Figure 4-1. This is where you make the majority of your adjustments. Elements helpfully arranges the panel into six sections—Smart Fix, Exposure, Levels, Color, Balance, and Sharpen. (If you see something else in the panel, click the Adjustments button at the bottom right of your screen). In most cases, it makes sense to start with the panel's top section and work your way down until you get the results you want. (See page 137 for more suggestions on what order to work in.)

TIP If the Adjustments panel is in your way, you can make it disappear by clicking the Adjustments button at the bottom right of the window; click this button again to bring the panel back. (This same technique works on the other Quick Fix panels, too.)

You can expand and collapse sections within the panel as you work, as explained in Figure 4-3.

FIGURE 4-3

Clicking the name of a section in the Adjustments panel collapses or expands that section. When you click another section, the previous one closes, so you can see the tools and commands for only one section at a time.

In sections like this one that offer multiple editing options, click the tabs at the top of the section to see what's available. Here, for example, if you click Highlights, you'll see the previews and thumbnails for adjusting the brightest areas of the photo.

Besides these handy fixes, you can also use most of the Expert mode menu commands if you need something that's not included in the Adjustments panel.

■ USING PRESETS

Elements has a handy feature to help the undecided: *presets*. When you click a section in the Adjustments panel, a grid of nine tiny thumbnails appears below that section's slider (see Figure 4-4). Each thumbnail represents a different preset for that slider.

FIGURE 4-4

Put your cursor over any of the thumbnails to see its effect applied to your photo.

If you decide not to make any changes, just click the thumbnail with the curved arrow over a line on it (the center image here) to return your photo to how it looked when you opened that section of the Adjustments panel.

If you don't have super-micro vision, these thumbnails are probably too darn small for you to be able to tell the difference—but not to worry: Place your cursor over a thumbnail (without clicking) and Elements previews that setting on your image itself so you can get a good view. If you like what you see, click the thumbnail to apply that change to your photo.

To reset your image back to what it looked like when you began using the current group of presets, click the thumbnail with the curved arrow on it. (If you've already moved on to another preset group, you can use the Undo button at the bottom of the window, or just use the standard Undo command [Ctrl+Z/⌘-Z] instead.) If you want to undo *all* the changes you've made in Quick Fix, click the blue Reset icon at the panel's top right.

> **TIP** As you make changes with the Adjustments panel's sliders and presets, Elements displays a numeric value to the right of each slider. If you have several similar photos to fix, when you get the first photo how you like it, jot down these numbers. Then, when you open the next photo, just click the number next to each slider (it turns into a text box) and type in the value you want.

Different Views: After vs. Before and After

When you open an image in Quick Fix, your picture appears by itself in the main window with the word "After" above it to let you know that you're in After Only view. Elements keeps the Before view—your original photo—tucked out of sight. But you have three other layout options, which you can choose anytime: Before Only, "Before & After - Horizontal," and "Before & After - Vertical." You switch between views by picking from the View drop-down menu at the top left of the image area (circled in Figure 4-5). Both of the before-and-after views are helpful when you're trying to figure out whether you're improving a photo.

■ Editing Your Photos

The Quick Fix window's tools are pretty easy to use. You can try one or all of them—it's up to you. And whenever you're happy with how your photo looks, you can leave Quick Fix and go back to Expert mode or the Organizer.

> **TIP** If you just want to rotate a photo, simply click the Rotate button below the image area. To rotate in the *opposite* direction, click the tiny arrow to the right of the Rotate button, and then click the button that appears. (See page 82 for more about rotating photos.)

FIGURE 4-5

*The Quick Fix window's
before-and-after views
make it easy to see how
you're changing a photo.
This is "Before & After -
Horizontal" view, which
displays the two versions
side by side. To see them
one above the other,
choose "Before & After -
Vertical" instead.*

*If you want a more de-
tailed view, use the Zoom
tool or the Zoom slider at
the top of the window to
focus on just a portion of
the image.*

In Quick Fix, Elements automatically applies any changes you make—you don't have
to do anything to accept them. If you're tweaking an image and decide you don't like
how it's turning out, click the blue Reset icon at the top of the Adjustments panel
to return your photo to the way it looked *before* you started working in Quick Fix.
(The Reset icon is a blue arrow arching over a straight line, and it's just below the
word "Share.") Keep in mind that clicking this button undoes *all* Quick Fix edits, so
don't use it if you want to undo only a single action. For that, just click the Undo
button at the bottom of the window, or use the regular Undo command: Choose
Edit→Undo, or press Ctrl+Z/⌘-Z.

When you make a change and then close a section of the Adjustments panel, your
image remains changed, so remember to undo that edit or reset the photo (or undo
that change) if you're just experimenting and don't want to *keep* that change.

Fixing Red Eye

Anyone who's ever taken a flash photo has run into the dreaded problem of *red
eye*—those glowing, demonic pupils that make your little cherub look like a character
from an Anne Rice novel.

Red eye is even more of a problem with digital cameras than with film cameras, but luckily Elements has a simple and terrific tool for fixing it. All you need to do is click the red spots with the Red Eye Removal tool, and your problems are solved. You can also use this tool to fix *pet eye*, a.k.a. *green eye*, the animal equivalent. Fixing pet eye is explained later in this section.

This tool works the same in both Quick Fix and Expert mode. Here's what you do:

1. **Open a photo and zoom in so you can see where you're clicking.**

   Use the Zoom tool to magnify the problem eyes. (Switch to the Hand tool if you need to drag the photo around so the eyes are front and center.)

2. **Activate the Red Eye Removal tool by clicking the red-eye icon in the tool-box or pressing Y.**

3. **Click the red part of the pupil (see Figure 4-6).**

   That's it! Just one click should fix the problem. If it doesn't, press Ctrl+Z/⌘-Z to undo the edit, and then try *dragging* over the pupil instead. Sometimes one method works better than the other. You can also try adjusting this tool's two settings, Darken Amount and Pupil Size, which are explained in a moment.

4. **Repeat the process on the other eye, and you're done.**

FIGURE 4-6

When using the Red Eye Removal tool, zoom in so you get a good look at the pupils. Don't worry if your photo is so magnified that it loses definition—just make the red area large enough so you can click right in its center.

The eye on the left here has already been fixed. Notice what a good job this tool does of keeping the highlights (called catch lights) in the eye that's been treated.

TIP You can also apply the Organizer's Auto Red Eye Fix in Quick Fix and Expert mode. In either window, just press Ctrl+R/⌘-R or go to Enhance→Auto Red Eye Fix. (Alternatively, you can activate the Red Eye Removal tool and then, in the Tool Options area, click Auto Correct.) The only tradeoff to using Auto Red Eye Fix in the Editor is that you don't *automatically* get a version set like you do when using the tool in the Organizer, but you can create a version set when you save your changes, as explained on page 71.

If you need to adjust how the Red Eye Removal tool works, the Tool Options area gives you two controls, although 99 percent of the time you can ignore them:

• **Pupil Radius**. Drag this slider to tell Elements how large an area to consider part of the pupil.

• **Darken**. If the result is too light, drag this slider to the right.

If you can't get a good result by using the existing settings, undo your red-eye correction, move these sliders, and then try again.

The Tool Options area also includes a checkbox for Pet Eye, in case Fluffy or Fido needs a fix. The different structure of animals' eyes makes them reflect green instead of red, so this setting tells Elements to look for the right color. (In older versions of Elements, the Red Eye Removal tool couldn't cope with animals at all.) Turn this checkbox on before starting to correct your pet's glaring retinas. The results you'll get with this setting are rather mixed. In Figure 4-7, you can see how well it works when conditions are right, though it doesn't always work this well. It's certainly worth a try, though.

FIGURE 4-7

Top: A classic case of pet eye makes this kitty look not merely annoyed, but rather alarming.

Bottom: Two clicks with the Red Eye Removal tool using the Pet Eye setting make him look just a bit grumpy instead of murderous, but if you look very closely you can still see a few glowing green pixels it missed along the upper edges of his eyes.

TIP If you're dealing with raw files, you can fix red eye right in the Raw Converter (page 277), although the Raw Converter's tool doesn't have a Pet Eye setting.

Another Red-Eye Fix

The Red Eye Removal tool does a great job most of the time, but it doesn't always work, especially on animals' eyes. Expert mode gives you a couple of other ways to fix red eye (and pet eye) that work in almost any situation. Here's one:

1. **Zoom way, way in on the problem eye.** You want to be able to see the individual pixels.

2. **Use the Eyedropper tool (page 257) to sample the color from a good area of the eye, or from another photo.** Check the Tools panel's foreground color square (page 253) to make sure you've got the color you want.

3. **Activate the Pencil tool (page 407) and set its size to 1 pixel.**

4. **Click the bad or empty pixels of the eye to replace their color with the shade you sampled in step 2.** Remember to leave a couple of white pixels for a catch light (the pupil's glinting highlight).

This process works even if the eye is *blown out* (that is, all white with no color info left).

If you're a layers fan, you can also fix red eye by selecting the bad area, creating a Hue/Saturation Adjustment layer (page 218), and then desaturating the red area. However, this method doesn't work too well if the eye is blown out.

Smart Fix

The Quick Fix window's secret weapon is the Smart Fix command, which automatically adjusts a picture's lighting, color, and contrast, all with one click. You don't have to figure anything out—Elements does it all for you. This command generally works better on photos that are underexposed (too dark) than overexposed (too bright), but it doesn't hurt to give it a try even on overexposed shots.

You'll find the Smart Fix command in the aptly named Smart Fix section of the Adjustments panel, and it's about as easy to use as hitting the speed-dial button on your phone: Click the Auto button at the bottom of the Smart Fix section and, if the stars are aligned, your picture will immediately look better. Figure 4-8 gives you a glimpse of its capabilities.

TIP You'll find Auto buttons scattered throughout Elements. When you click one, the program makes a best-guess attempt to apply whatever change the Auto button is next to (Smart Fix, Levels, Contrast, and so on). It never hurts to at least *try* clicking these buttons; if you don't like the result, you can always perform the magical undo: Edit→Undo or Ctrl+Z/⌘-Z.

FIGURE 4-8

Left: This photo, taken in a dim interior, is pretty dark.

Right: The Auto Smart Fix button improved it significantly with just one click. You may then want to use the tools in the Adjustments panel's Balance section (page 134) to really fine-tune the color.

To try this fix for yourself, download leaset.jpg from this book's Missing CD page at www.missing-manuals.com/cds.

If you're happy with Auto Smart Fix's changes, you can move on to another photo, or try sharpening the same photo a little if the focus appears a bit soft (see page 134). You don't need to do anything to accept the Smart Fix changes, but if you're not thrilled with the results, take a good look at your picture. If you like what Auto Smart Fix did but the effect is too strong or too weak, press Ctrl+Z/⌘-Z to undo it, and then try one of the Smart Fix section's presets or play with its slider instead. This slider does the same thing as the Auto Smart Fix button, only *you* control the degree of change. Watch the image as you drag the slider to the right. (If your computer is slow, there will be a certain amount of lag, so go slowly to give Elements a chance to catch up.) If you overdo it, click the Undo button at the bottom of the Editor window and start again.

> **TIP**   You'll usually get better results by moving the Smart Fix slider in several small increments rather than in one big, sweeping movement.

Incidentally, these are the same Smart Fix commands you see in the Editor's Enhance menu: Enhance→Auto Smart Fix (Alt+Ctrl+M/Option-⌘-M) has the same effect as clicking the Auto button in the Smart Fix section of the Adjustments panel, and Enhance→Adjust Smart Fix (Shift+Ctrl+M/Shift-⌘-M) displays a Smart Fix slider you can tweak.

Sometimes Smart Fix just isn't smart enough to do everything you want, and sometimes it does things you *don't* want. Fortunately, you still have several other editing options that are covered in the following sections. (If you don't like what Smart Fix has done to your photo, remember to undo its effect before making other changes.)

> **TIP** Auto Smart Fix is one of the commands you can also apply from within the Organizer, so there's no need to launch the Editor if all you want to do is run this command. See the box on page 121 for more about making fixes in the Organizer.

Adjusting Exposure

You can use the presets or the slider in the Adjustments panel's Exposure section to make adjustments to your photo's overall exposure. You may want to use this section first, if you think your image needs it. But if the image's exposure looks fine, you can skip this section and move on to the Levels section.

> **TIP** There's another way to adjust the exposure and tone of your photos: Auto Smart Tone. It's described on page 142.

Adjusting Lighting and Contrast

The Levels section of the Adjustments panel lets you make sophisticated adjustments to photos' brightness and contrast. You may be surprised: Sometimes problems you *thought* stemmed from exposure or even focus can be fixed with these commands.

■ LEVELS

If you want to understand how Levels works, you're in for a long, technical ride. But if you just want to know what it can do for your photos, the short answer is that it adjusts their brightness by redistributing their color information. Levels changes (and hopefully fixes!) both brightness and color at the same time.

If you've never used a photo-editing program before, this may sound rather mysterious, but photo pros will tell you that Levels is one of the most powerful commands for fixing and polishing pictures. To find out if its magic works for you, click the Auto Levels button at the bottom of the Levels section. Figure 4-9 shows what a big difference it can make.

What Levels does is complex. Chapter 7 has loads more details about what's going on behind the scenes and how you can apply this command more precisely.

> **NOTE** Although the Auto Levels and Auto Contrast buttons appear at the bottom of each tab in the Levels section (Shadows, Midtones, and Highlights), they always work on your *entire* image, so you get the same result no matter which tab is displayed when you click these buttons.

FIGURE 4-9

A quick click of the Auto Levels button can make a dramatic difference.

Left: This original photo isn't bad, and you may not realize that the colors could be better.

Right: Here you can see how much more effective the photo is once Auto Levels has balanced the colors.

To try this yourself, download ocean. jpg *from this book's Missing CD page at* www.missingmanuals.com/cds.

■ CONTRAST

In Quick Fix, the main alternative to Auto Levels is Auto Contrast. Most people find that their images tend to benefit from one or the other of these options. Contrast adjusts the relative darkness and lightness of an image without changing its color, so if clicking Auto Levels in the Adjustments panel's Levels section made the colors in your image go all goofy, try clicking the Auto Contrast button instead (remember to undo Auto Levels first).

> **TIP** After you apply Auto Contrast, look closely at the edges of the objects in your photo. If your camera's contrast was already high, you may see a halo or a sharp line around the objects. In that case, the contrast is too high; undo Auto Contrast (Ctrl+Z/⌘-Z) and try another fix instead.

FREQUENTLY ASKED QUESTION

Calibrating Your Monitor

Why do my photos look awful in Elements?

You may find that your images look really terrible when you open them in Elements even though they look decent in other programs. For example, they may look all washed out, or reddish or greenish, or even black and white. If that's the case, you need to calibrate your monitor, as explained on page 239. It's easy to do, and it makes a big difference.

The reason for this is that Elements is what's known as a *color-managed* program. You can read all about color management on page 237. For now, you just need to know that color-managed programs pay much more attention to the settings for your monitor than other programs (like word processors) do. Color-managed programs are a little more trouble to set up initially, but the advantage is that you can get truly wonderful results if you invest a little time and effort.

■ SHADOWS, MIDTONES, AND HIGHLIGHTS

The other fixes in the Levels section of the Adjustments panel do an amazing job of bringing out details that are lost in the shadows or bright areas of your photo. Figure 4-10 shows what a difference they can make.

FIGURE 4-10

Left: This image has overly bright highlights and shadows that are much too dark.

Right: After adjusting the shadows and highlights, you can see there's plenty of detail here. (Use the Adjustments panel's color sliders—described in the next section—to get rid of the orange tone.)

To use these fixes, click the appropriate tab in the Adjustments panel's Levels section. Although there are presets for each of these fixes, you'll probably find you have more control by using the sliders. Here's what each one controls:

- **Shadows**. Nudge this slider to the right, and you'll see details emerge from murky black shadows as Elements lightens the dark areas of your photo.

- **Midtones**. Use this fix *after* you've adjusted the photo's shadows and highlights, which can make an image look flat—like it doesn't have enough contrast between dark and light areas. This slider can help bring back a more realistic look.

- **Highlights**. Use this slider to dim the brightness of overexposed areas.

> **TIP** You may think you need only lighten shadows in a photo, but sometimes just a smidgen of Highlights may help, too. Don't be afraid to experiment with this slider even if you've got a relatively dark photo.

Go easy: Getting overenthusiastic with these sliders can give your photos a flat, washed-out look.

Adjusting Color

The Color section of the Adjustments panel lets you—surprise, surprise—play around with the colors in your images. In many cases, if you've been successful with Auto Levels or Auto Contrast, you won't need to use this section.

■ AUTO COLOR

The Color section's Auto button is another one-click fix. In some ways, it seems like Auto Color should be up in the Levels section because, like Levels, it simultaneously adjusts color and brightness, but it looks at different information in photos to decide what to do.

When you're first learning to use Quick Fix, you may want to try Auto Levels, Auto Contrast, and Auto Color to see which generally works best for your photos. Undo the changes after you use each one and compare your results. Most people find they prefer one of the three most of the time.

Auto Color may be just the ticket for your photos, but you may also find that it shifts colors in strange ways. Try it and see what you think. If it makes your photo look worse, just click the Reset icon at the top of the Adjustments panel or press Ctrl+Z/⌘-Z to undo it, and go back to Auto Levels or Auto Contrast. If they *all* make your colors look a little wrong, or if you want to tweak the colors in your photo, move on to the Color sliders and presets instead.

■ THE COLOR SLIDERS

If you want to adjust the colors in your photo without changing its brightness, try the Color section's sliders. For instance, your digital camera may produce colors that don't quite match what you saw when you took the picture; you may have scanned an old print that's faded or discolored; or you may just want to change the colors in a photo for the heck of it.

Whatever the case, the sliders in the Color section are for you (you can click preset thumbnails, too). Just click the appropriate tab near the top of the section:

- **Saturation** controls the intensity of the image's color. For example, you can turn a color photo to black and white by moving this slider all the way to the left. Move it *too* far to the right and everything glows with so much color that your photo looks radioactive.

- **Hue** changes the color in an image from, say, red to blue or green. If you aren't aiming for realism, you can have fun using this slider to create funky color changes.

- **Vibrance** used to be available only in the Raw Converter (see Chapter 8), but it's such a useful tool that Adobe added it to Quick Fix, too. While Saturation adjusts all colors equally, the Vibrance slider is much smarter: It increases the intensity of the duller colors while holding back on colors that are already so vivid they may oversaturate. If you want to make colors pop, try this slider.

You probably won't use all three sliders on a single photo, but you can if you like. To fine-tune the color, you may want to move on to the next panel: Balance. In fact, in many cases you'll need *only* the Balance fixes.

Balancing Color

Photos often have the right amount of saturation, but suppose there's something about the color balance that just isn't right, and moving the Color section's Hue slider (described above) makes everything look funky. Fortunately, the Adjustments panel's Balance section contains two very useful tabs for adjusting the overall colors in an image:

- **Temperature** lets you adjust colors from cool (bluish) to warm (orangeish). Use this slider for things like toning down the warm glow you see in photos taken in tungsten lighting, or just for fine-tuning color balance.

- **Tint** adjusts the green/magenta balance of a photo, as shown in Figure 4-11.

FIGURE 4-11

Left: This kind of greenish tint is a common problem with many digital cameras, especially cellphone cameras.

Right: A little adjustment of the Tint slider clears it up in a jiffy.

It's not always as obvious as it is here that you need a tint adjustment. If you aren't sure, the sky can be a dead giveaway: Is it robin's egg blue like the left photo here? If so, tint is what you need.

There are presets for these adjustments, too, but if you're after realistic color, you may find that they're all much too exaggerated, so you're probably better off using the sliders.

> **TIP** In early versions of Elements, these sliders were grouped with the Color sliders, since you'll often use a combination of adjustments from both groups. Chapter 7 has lots more about how to use Expert mode to really fine-tune your image's colors.

Sharpening

Now that you've finished your other corrections, it's time to sharpen your photo, so move down the Adjustments panel to the Sharpen section. Sharpening creates the effect of better focus by improving the edge contrast of objects in photos. Once again, an Auto button is at your service; click it to get things started. Figure 4-12 shows what you can expect.

FIGURE 4-12

Left: The original image. Like many digital photos, it could stand a little sharpening.

Middle: What you get by clicking the Sharpen section's Auto button.

Right: The results of using the Sharpen slider to apply stronger sharpening than Auto Sharpen does.

The sad truth is that there really isn't any way to improve the focus of a photo once you click the shutter. Photo-editing programs like Elements sharpen by increasing the contrast where they perceive edges of objects, which is why it's best to make sharpening your last editing step. Sharpening *first* can have strange effects on other editing tools you apply afterward.

TIP If you see funny halos around objects in your photos or strange flaky spots (making your photo look like it has eczema), those are sure signs of oversharpening; reduce the Sharpen setting until they go away. In fact, many modern cameras apply a pretty hefty dose of sharpening right in the camera, so you may decide you like your photo best with no extra sharpening at all.

Always look at the image's actual pixels (View→Actual Pixels) when sharpening, because that gives you the clearest sense of what you're doing to your picture. If you don't like what Auto Sharpen does (a distinct possibility), you can undo it (click the Undo button or press Ctrl+Z/⌘-Z) and try the Sharpen slider instead. Zero sharpening is all the way to the left; dragging the slider to the right increases the amount of sharpening Elements applies. You can also click the preset thumbnails, but it's probably easier to use the slider. As a general rule, you want to sharpen photos you plan to print more than images destined for use online. Page 260 has lots more about sharpening.

NOTE If you've used photo-editing programs before, you may be interested to know that the Auto Sharpen button applies Adjust Sharpness (page 263) to photos. But unlike when you apply Adjust Sharpness from the Enhance menu, Auto Sharpen doesn't give you any control over the settings. The good news is that if you want to use Adjust Sharpness—or even if you prefer to use Unsharp Mask (page 260)—you can get that control from within Quick Fix. Just go to the Enhance menu and choose the sharpener of your choice.

At this point, all that's left to do is crop your photo; page 89 tells you everything you need to know. And if you like, you can give your photo a bit more punch by using the Touch Up tools explained in the next section.

> **TIP** If you have a Mac, OS X has some pretty sophisticated sharpening tools built right in. Preview lets you apply Luminance Channel sharpening, a complex technique you might like better than Elements' sharpening options. Open a photo in Preview and give it a try (choose Tools→Adjust Color→Sharpness) to see whether you prefer it to what Quick Fix can do.

Whitening Teeth

The Quick Fix toolbox contains a special tool to help whiten dull or discolored teeth. It's very easy to use—just drag over the area you want to change, and Elements makes a detailed selection of the area and applies the change for you. Here are the details:

1. **Open a photo and make your other corrections first.**

> **NOTE** If you're an old hand at using Elements, use Whiten Teeth *before* sharpening. But if you're a beginner and not comfortable with layers (see Chapter 6), sharpen first. (See page 137 for more about why.)

2. **Click the Whiten Teeth tool's icon (the toothbrush) or press F.**

   Either way, your cursor turns into a circle with crosshairs in it.

3. **Drag across the area you want to whiten.**

   Just drag over the teeth in your photo, and Elements automatically creates a selection that includes the entire object it thinks you want. (It works just like the Quick Selection tool [page 154], only it also whitens the selected area.) You'll see marching ants appear (page 95) around the area Elements is changing (see Figure 4-13).

FIGURE 4-13

Just a quick swipe across these teeth selected and whitened them while keeping them looking realistic.

4. **If Elements selected too much or too little, tweak the selection's size.**

   The Tool Options area contains three little brush icons. Click the top icon to create a new selection, click the middle one and then drag to add to the existing selection, or click the bottom one and then drag over an area you want to remove from the existing selection. (You don't *have* to use the Tool Options settings: You can just drag to extend your selection, or Alt-drag/Option-drag to remove some of it.)

5. **Once you're happy with the change, you're done.**

   You can back up by clicking the Undo button or pressing Ctrl+Z/⌘-Z to undo your changes step by step. Just keep going to eliminate the whitening completely if you don't like it.

> **NOTE**   Quick Edit's Whiten Teeth and Type tools create a layered file (see Chapter 6). If you understand layers, you can go back to Expert mode and make changes after you use these tools to do things like adjust the opacity or blend mode of the new layer. You can always discard your changes by discarding the layer they're on. And for the Whiten Teeth tool, you can even edit the area affected by the changes by editing the layer mask it creates (page 213) or using the Smart Brush tool (page 233) in Expert mode.

As mentioned above, after you work with this tool, Elements leaves you with a layered file. Normally that isn't a problem, even if you don't know anything about layers, but once in a while you may find that nothing happens when you try to make further changes to your photo. In that case, click the Expert tab near the top of the screen to switch to Expert mode. In the Layers panel (if you don't see it, display it by going to Window→Layers), look for the word "Background" and click it. Once you do, that part of the panel should turn blue (if it doesn't, click it again). Now you can go back to the Quick Fix window (by clicking the Quick tab near the top of the screen) and do whatever you want to your photo. However, the whitened teeth may behave differently from the rest of the photo. If that happens and you haven't closed the photo since using Whiten Teeth, use the History panel (page 25) to back up to before you used it.

> **NOTE**   If you've used a previous version of Elements and you're looking for the Make Dull Skies Blue and Black and White—High Contrast tools, you'll find them in Expert mode as options for the Smart Brush (page 233). The Smart Brush also has a Whiten Teeth option, so there's no need to switch to Quick Fix just for that.

Quick Fix Suggested Workflow

There are no hard-and-fast rules for what order you need to use the Quick Fix tools. As mentioned earlier, Elements lays out the tools in the Adjustments panel in the order that usually makes sense. But you can pick and choose whichever tools you want, depending on what your photo needs.

If you're the type of person who likes a set plan for fixing photos, here's one order in which to apply the commands:

1. **Rotate your photo (if necessary) by using the buttons below the image preview.**

2. **Fix red eye (if necessary) as explained on page 126.**

3. **Fix any blemishes with the Spot Healing Brush (page 312).**

4. **Crop the image.**

   If you know you want to crop your photo, now's the time. Doing so gets rid of any problem areas before they affect other adjustments. For example, say your photo has a lot of overexposed sky that you want to crop out. If you leave it in, that area may skew the effects that the Levels and Color fixes have on your image. So if you already know where you want to crop, do so before making other adjustments for more accurate results. (If you aren't yet sure what you want to trim, it's OK to wait until later to crop.)

5. **Fix exposure (if necessary).**

   If your photo's overall exposure is way out of whack, try using the Adjustments panel's Exposure section to adjust it. If the exposure is only bad in spots, skip this step.

6. **Try Auto Smart Fix and/or the Smart Fix slider; use the Undo command if you don't like the results.**

   Pretty soon, you'll get a good idea of how likely it is that this fix will do a good job on your photos. Some people love it; others think it makes their pictures too grainy.

7. **If Smart Fix didn't do the trick, work your way down through the Adjustments panel's Levels, Color, and Balance sections until you like the way your photo looks.**

   Read the sections earlier in this chapter to understand what each fix does to your photo.

8. **Sharpen your image.**

   Try to make sharpening your last adjustment, because other commands can cause funky results on photos you've already sharpened. But if you're a beginner and not comfortable with layers, you can sharpen *before* using the Whiten Teeth tool. (See page 137 for more about why you'd wait to use it.)

To close your photo from the Quick Fix window, click the X at the top right of the preview area, choose File→Close, or press Ctrl+W/⌘-W.

TIP When you're in Quick Fix mode, you can switch to Expert mode at any point if you want tools that aren't available in Quick Fix.

■ Other Fast Fixes

As if all of the options described above weren't enough, Adobe gives you two *more* ways to fix photos fast. Both of these features are only available from the menus at the top of your screen. The first one, "Adjust Color for Skin Tone," is available in both Quick Fix and Expert modes, but for some reason you have to switch over to Expert mode for the second one, Auto Smart Tone—it's not available in Quick Fix.

Adjusting Skin Tones

If you're like most amateur photographers, your most important photos are of people: family members, friends, or even just fascinating strangers. Elements has a feature designed especially for correcting photos with people in them: the "Adjust Color for Skin Tone" command, available from the Enhance menu in both Quick Fix and Expert modes.

This command's name is a bit confusing. What it actually does is adjust your *whole* image based on the skin tone of someone in the photo. The idea is that you're likely much more interested in the way the people in your photos look than in how the background looks, so "Adjust Color for Skin Tone" makes good skin color its top priority. This is another automatic fix, but there's a dialog box where you can tweak the results once you've previewed Elements' suggested adjustments.

Generally, you want to use this command *after* making any overall changes to your photo, but *before* you sharpen the image. Here's how to use this command:

1. **Call up the "Adjust Color for Skin Tone" dialog box (Figure 4-14).**

   In either Quick Fix or Expert mode, go to Enhance→Adjust Color→"Adjust Color for Skin Tone." Once the dialog box appears, you may need to move it out of the way so you can see what's happening in your photo.

FIGURE 4-14

While this dialog box is open, your cursor turns into a little eyedropper when you move it over your photo. Just click the best-looking area of skin you can find. Clicking different spots gives different results, so you may want to experiment by clicking various places.

You can't drag the dialog box's sliders until after you click. Once Elements adjusts the photo based on your click, use the sliders to fine-tune the results.

TIP If you understand layers (Chapter 6), you may want to make a duplicate layer and apply this command to the duplicate. That way you can adjust the intensity of the result by changing the layer's opacity (see page 196). You can also apply a layer mask (page 210) to protect areas you don't want Elements to change.

2. **Tell Elements which patch of skin to use for calculating color adjustments.**

   Find a portion of your photo where your subject's skin has relatively good color, and click it.

3. **Tweak the results.**

   Elements is often a bit overenthusiastic in its adjustments, so you may need to use the sliders in the dialog box to get more pleasing, realistic color. You can get an idea of which way to move them by looking at the colors in their tracks:

   - The Tan slider increases or decreases the browns and oranges in the skin tones.

   - The Blush slider increases the rosiness of the skin as you move the slider right and decreases it as you move it left.

   - The Ambient Light slider works just like the Temperature slider in the Adjustments panel (page 134).

   You may get swell results with your first click or have to use all the sliders to get a truly realistic result—it depends on the photo. As you work, Elements previews the changes right in your photo. If you mess up and want to start again, click the dialog box's Reset button. If you decide you'd rather use another tool instead, click Cancel.

4. **When you like what you see, click OK.**

   Elements applies your changes. If you want to undo them, press Ctrl+Z/⌘-Z.

"Adjust Color for Skin Tone" seems to work better on fair skin than on darker skin tones, and it's better at making fairly subtle adjustments than dramatic ones. Also, notice that skin tones aren't the only colors that change—Elements adjusts *all* the colors in the photo (Figure 4-15). By the time you've got the skin looking just right, you may find that your image has acquired quite a color cast. If this bothers you, try a different tool. On the other hand, you can create some very nice late-afternoon light effects with this command.

While "Adjust Color for Skin Tone" is really meant as a kind of alternative fast fix, you may find it's most useful for making small, final adjustments to photos you've already edited using other tools.

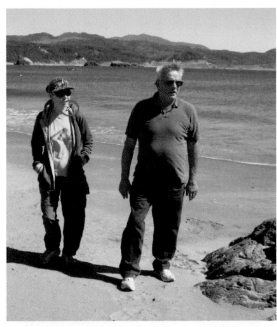

FIGURE 4-15

Top: This photo has a slight blue cast to it. The cursor (circled) is ready to fix this with a single click on the woman's neck.

Bottom: After clicking with "Adjust Color for Skin Tone," the entire image is much warmer, especially the sand.

Auto Smart Tone

Elements includes yet another kind of auto correction, but you have to go up to the Enhance menu at the top of your screen to find it. When you use Auto Smart Tone, Elements automatically corrects the tonality of your photo (its brightness, contrast, exposure, and so on) and then presents you with a way to make further adjustments. The interesting thing about Auto Smart Tone is that it can watch what you do to your photos, learn how you like to adjust them, and remember and reapply similar corrections to future images.

It's quite easy to use this command:

1. **In either Quick Fix or Expert mode, open a photo and then go to Enhance→ Auto Smart Tone.**

   Elements makes its best guess about the best adjustments to make to your image and applies them, but you don't have to accept what it does—you can easily tweak the results.

2. **In the Auto Smart Tone window that appears, adjust the changes Elements applied.**

   The window displays your already-corrected image in the middle, surrounded by four thumbnails of other corrections, one in each corner (Figure 4-16). In the middle of your image is a black dot with four arrows radiating from it; Adobe calls this the *joystick*. Just grab the joystick and drag it toward the thumbnail that looks closest to how you want your photo to look. As you drag, a grid appears over the center of your image. Just keep dragging until you like what you see.

FIGURE 4-16

Learning from previous fixes has helped Auto Smart Tone improve this underexposed photo a little as soon as the window opens. But you can help it do much better by grabbing the joystick (circled) and moving it toward the corner thumbnail that looks best to you.

3. **Click OK to accept the corrections.**

   Click Cancel if you decide the process isn't helping your photo any.

Click the four-line square at the bottom of the window to see a pop-out menu with two options: "Learn from this correction," which tells Elements to remember what settings you liked for this image and to use them as a basis for future adjustments, and "Show corner thumbnails," which toggles the corner thumbnails on and off.

You may find this command really helpful or you may not like what it does at all. Generally speaking, for adjusting a single photo, your may find that one of the other auto fixes (described beginning on page 128) works just fine. But if you have a bunch of similar photos to correct, the "Learn from this correction" setting can shorten the amount of time you need to spend on each one.

The corrections that Auto Smart Tone makes are pretty sophisticated, and you may find it worth spending some time to get comfortable with it. If you use Elements in conjunction with Adobe's Lightroom, you may find that Auto Smart Tone does an even better job with your photos than Lightroom's Auto Tone, for example.

TIP   You can tell Auto Smart Tone to start over with its remembering. Say you've been fixing a bunch of photos that are too dark and now you've got a batch that are too *light*. You don't want Auto Smart Tone to make the same changes it learned to make to the dark photos, so go to Edit→Preferences→General/Photoshop Elements Editor→Preferences→General and click Reset Auto Smart Tone Learning. That tells Elements to forget everything it's remembered so far about how to adjust your images and start learning what you do from now on.

■ Getting Fancy: Effects, Textures, and Frames

In addition to making basic corrections to your images, Elements' Quick Fix window also lets you gussy them up by using the panels that are hidden when you first start the Quick Fix: Effects, Textures, and Frames. One of the best new features in Elements 13 is all the new effects that Adobe added, which let you give your photos lots of the artistic and filtered looks that are so popular right now.

They couldn't be easier to use: Just head to the bottom right of the Quick Fix window and click the button for the panel that contains what you want to add to your photo. If you click Effects, you may have to wait a bit, since Elements is busy creating a thumbnail for each effect that shows it applied to *your* image. Once the thumbnails appear, just scroll through them and click the one you want to try. There are even more choices than you can see at first, as Figure 4-17 explains.

FIGURE 4-17

Elements includes even more effects than you can see when you first bring up the Effects pane. Each effect has four hidden alternative versions. When you click any effect, its section expands to show you four more *thumbnails, offering you a variety of versions, so you can get several different looks from the same effect depending on which thumbnail you click. You may need to wait a few seconds while Elements figures out how to apply the effect to your photo, since most of them are pretty complex and your computer has to do a lot of work behind the scenes before you see the final result.*

When you move on and click a different effect, the previous effect's section closes back up so you're not overwhelmed by all the available options.

Figure 4-18 shows an example of the types of things you can do with these fun features. If you don't like the result, use Ctrl+Z/⌘-Z to undo it and try another one, or click the Reset button at the panel's upper right to undo *everything* you've done in the Quick Fix window. If you like what you did, all you need to do is save your changes.

NOTE When you click the Effects button, you may have to wait a moment to see the thumbnails in the Effects panel. That's because Elements is busy creating a thumbnail of what *your* photo will look like with each effect added to it. (The Textures and Frames panels just use generic thumbnails.)

There's no special order in which you need to apply effects or textures—you can switch back and forth and stack them up by applying more than one to your photo. But you should wait to apply a *frame* after you're through with the effects and textures, because effects and textures may not have a visible impact on your image once you've added a frame. That's because all three panels add *layers* to your file (see Chapter 6)—some of the frames add *several* layers—and Elements may not target the correct layer for other changes once you've added a frame; page 137 explains why. A good rule of thumb is to use the Quick Fix panels from left to right:

first make any adjustments to your image, then add a special effect, then a texture, and finally a frame (if you want to use them all on one image, that is).

FIGURE 4-18

Top: Here's a photo straight from the camera.

Bottom: After a few clicks in the Quick Fix window's Effects, Textures, and Frames panels, the image is all ready for you to use in a project or on a scrapbook page.

NOTE The Effects and Textures panels are unique to Quick Fix—this is the only place you can find them in Elements (although you can apply different effects in Expert mode, as explained in Chapter 13). The options in the Frames panel are a subset of the frames available in the Graphics panel in Expert and Create modes, and they work the same way.

Once your photo is framed, Elements should automatically activate the Move tool (if it doesn't and you want to make adjustments to the frame, simply click the tool's icon in the toolbox). With this tool active, you can right-click/Control-click your photo for a menu that gives you many ways to adjust the frame, and adjust the size of your photo or the part that's visible in the frame by dragging one of the handles on the image. (You'll also see the Tool Options settings explained on page 20.) The Move tool is explained in detail on page 182.

If you apply effects, textures, or a frame to your photo in the Quick Fix window and later change your mind, in Expert mode, just click over to the Layers panel and delete the layer(s) that Elements added when you applied those changes.

TIP If you understand layer masks (page 210), you can control which parts of your photos are affected by the effects and textures by editing the layer masks that Elements adds when it applies them.

Making Selections

One of Elements' most impressive talents is its ability to let you select part of an image and make changes to only that area. Selecting something tells Elements, "*This* is what I want to work on—don't touch the rest of my image."

You can select a whole image or any part of it. Using selections, you can fine-tune images in very sophisticated ways: Change the color of just one rose in a bouquet, for instance, or change your nephew's festive purple hair back to something his grandparents would appreciate. Graphics pros will tell you that good selections make the difference between shoddy, amateurish work and a slick, professional job.

Elements includes a bunch of different Selection tools. You can draw a rectangular or circular selection with the Marquee tools; paint to create a selection with the Selection Brush; or just drag in your photo with the Quick Selection tool and let Elements figure out the exact boundaries of your selection. The Transform Selection command lets you resize selections in a snap, and the Refine Edge dialog box is a great help with difficult selections like hair and fur. The Content-Aware Move tool lets you move an object to a different location in your photo, while it analyzes the image to create plausible new material to fill in the hole where the object was originally. And Elements 13 gives you an interesting new tool for adjusting your selections after you've made them: the Refine Selection Brush, which lets you easily reshape any selection; it's explained on page 177.

> **NOTE** If you've used older versions of Elements and you're looking for the Magic Extractor, unfortunately it's gone now. You'll find some workarounds on page 171.

For most selection jobs, there's no right or wrong tool. With experience, you may find that you prefer working with certain tools more than others, and you'll often use more than one tool to create a perfect selection. Once you've read this chapter, you'll understand all of Elements' Selection tools and how to use them.

> **TIP** It's much easier to select an object that's been photographed against a plain, contrasting background. So if you know you're going to want to select a bicycle, for example, shoot it in front of a blank wall rather than, say, a hedge.

Selecting Everything

Sometimes you want to select a whole photo, like when you need to copy and paste it. Elements gives you some useful commands that help you make basic selections:

- **Select All** (Select→All or Ctrl+A/⌘-A) tells Elements to select your whole image. You'll see "marching ants" (Figure 5-1) around the outer edge of the picture. If you want to copy your image into another picture or program, Select All is the fastest way to go.

> **NOTE** If the photo contains layers—which you will learn about in Chapter 6—you may not be able to get everything you want with the Select All command. In that case, use Edit→Copy Merged, or press Shift+Ctrl+C/ Shift-⌘-C instead.

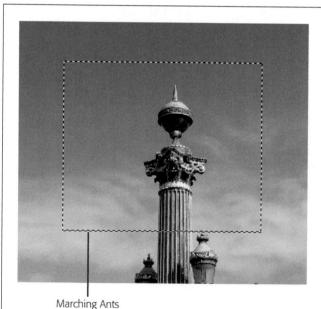

FIGURE 5-1

The popular name for these dotted lines is "marching ants" because they march around your selections to show you where the edges lie.

The ants let you know that your selection is active, meaning that whatever you do next will apply only to the selected area.

Marching Ants

- **Deselect Everything** (Select→Deselect, Esc, or Ctrl+D/⌘-D) removes any current selection. Remember this keystroke combination, because you'll probably use it a lot.

- **Reselect** (Select→Reselect or Shift+Ctrl+D/Shift-⌘-D) tells Elements to reactivate the selection you just canceled. Use Reselect if you realize you still need a selection you just got rid of (Ctrl+Z/⌘-Z works, too).

- **Hide/View a Selection** (Ctrl+H/⌘-H) keeps your selection active while hiding its outline. This is handy because sometimes the marching ants can be distracting or make it hard to see what you're doing. To bring back the ants, just press Ctrl+H/⌘-H again.

> **TIP** If a tool acts goofy or won't do anything, start your troubleshooting by pressing Ctrl+H/⌘-H to make sure you don't have a hidden selection you forgot about.

Selecting Rectangular and Elliptical Areas

Selecting a whole photo is all well and good, but many times your reason for making a selection is precisely because you *don't* want to make changes to the whole image. So how do you select just part of a picture?

The easiest way is to use the Marquee tools. You already met the Rectangular Marquee tool back in Chapter 3 in the section on cropping (page 89). If you want to select a block, circle, or oval in an image, the Marquee tools are the way to go. As the winners of the Most Frequently Used Selection Tools award, they get top spot in the Select section of the Editor's Tools panel in Expert mode. You can modify how they work, like telling them to create a square instead of a rectangle, as Figure 5-2 explains. Here's how to use them:

1. **Press M or click the Marquee tools' icon in the Tools panel.**

   The Rectangular Marquee tool is the dotted rectangle at the upper right of the Tools panel's Select section. (If you used the Elliptical Marquee tool last, you see a dotted oval instead.)

2. **Choose the shape you want to draw: a rectangle or an ellipse.**

   At the left end of the Tool Options area, click the rectangle or the ellipse to pick a shape, or just tap the M key again to switch between the two shapes.

3. **If you want Elements to soften the selection's outline, in the Tool Options area, adjust the Feather slider.**

   Feathering makes the edges of a selection softer or fuzzier for better blending (when you're trying, say, to replace Brad Pitt's face with yours). The box on page 152 explains how feathering works.

FIGURE 5-2

To make a perfectly circular or square selection with the Marquee tools—rather than an elliptical or rectangular one, respectively—hold down the Shift key while you drag.

After you draw a selection, you can reposition it by dragging it or tapping the arrow keys on your keyboard. You can also adjust it with Elements' Transform Selection command, which is explained on page 173.

4. **Drag within your image to make a selection.**

   Wherever you initially click becomes one of the corners of your rectangular selection or a point just beyond the outer edge of your ellipse (you can also draw perfectly circular or square selections, as Figure 5-2 explains). The selection's outline expands as you drag.

   If you make a mistake, just press Esc. You can also press either Ctrl+D/⌘-D to get rid of *all* current selections or Ctrl+Z/⌘-Z to remove the most recent one.

The items in the Tool Options area's Aspect drop-down menu give you three ways to control the size of your selection: Normal lets you manually control it; Fixed Ratio lets you enter proportions in the W (width) and H (height) boxes; and Fixed Size lets you enter specific dimensions in the W and H boxes. The Anti-aliasing checkbox is explained in the box on page 152.

Once you've made a selection, you can move it around in the photo by dragging it or using the arrow keys on your keyboard to nudge it. And the Transform Selection command lets you drag a selection larger or smaller, or change its shape; page 173 tells you how.

Paste vs. Paste Into Selection

Newcomers to Elements are often confused by the fact that the program has two Paste commands, Paste and Paste Into Selection. Knowing what each one does will help you avoid problems:

- Ninety-nine percent of the time, **Paste** is the one you want. This command simply places your copied object wherever you paste it. Once you've pasted the object, you can move it by moving the selected area.

- **Paste Into Selection** is a special command for pasting a selection into *another* selection. Your pasted object appears only *within* the bounds of the selection you paste it into. When you use this command, you can still move what you paste, but it won't be visible anywhere outside the edges of the selection you pasted it into.

For example, say you want to put a beautiful mountain view outside a window: First, select and copy the mountain (Ctrl+C/⌘-C). Next, select the window, and then choose Edit→Paste Into Selection to add the view. After that, you can maneuver the mountain photo around until it's properly centered. But if you move it outside the boundary of your window selection, it just disappears. And, once you deselect, your material is permanently in place; you can't move it again.

If you understand layers (see Chapter 6), here's another way to think about the difference: Paste creates a new layer, while Paste Into Selection puts what you paste on the existing layer.

Selecting Irregularly Sized Areas

It would be nice if you could get away with making only simple rectangular and elliptical selections, but life is never that neat. If you want to change the color of one fish in your aquarium picture, for example, selecting a rectangle or an oval just isn't going to cut it.

Thankfully, Elements gives you other tools that make it easy to create very precise selections—no matter their size or shape. In this section, you'll learn how to use the rest of the Selection tools. But first you need to understand the basic controls that they (almost) all share.

Feathering and Anti-Aliasing

If you're old enough to remember what supermarket tabloid covers looked like before Photoshop, you probably had a good laugh at the obviously faked photos. Anyone could see where the art department had physically glued a piece cut from one photo onto another picture.

Nowadays, the pictures of Brangelina's vampire baby from Mars look *much* more believable because Photoshop (and Elements) let you add *anti-aliasing* and *feathering* when you make selections.

Anti-aliasing is a way of smoothing the edges of a digital image so they don't look jagged. When you make selections, the Lasso tools and the Magic Wand let you decide whether to use anti-aliasing. It's best to leave anti-aliasing on unless you want a really hard-looking edge on your selection.

Feathering, on the other hand, blurs the edges of a selection. When you make a selection that you plan to move to a different photo, a tiny bit of feathering can do a lot to make it look like it's always been part of the new photo. Some Selection tools, like the Marquee tools, let you set a feather value before you use them. And you can feather *existing* selections by choosing Select→Feather or pressing Alt+Ctrl+D/Option-⌘-F.

Generally, a 1- or 2-pixel feather gives your selection a natural-looking edge without visible blurring. A larger feather creates soft edges, as you can see in Figure 5-3. If you apply a feather value that's too high for the size of your selection, you see a warning that reads, "No pixels are more than 50% selected"; reduce the feather number to placate Elements.

FIGURE 5-3

Old-fashioned vignettes like this one are classic examples of when you'd want a fairly large feather. In this image, the feather is 15 pixels wide. The higher the feather value, the softer the edge.

(Incidentally, there's also a Vignette Effect in Guided Edit if you need more help.)

Controlling the Selection Tools

If you never make mistakes or change your mind, you can skip this section. If, on the other hand, you're human, you need to know about the mysterious little icons that appear in the Tool Options area when one of the Selection tools is active (see Figure 5-4).

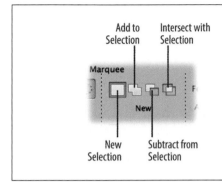

FIGURE 5-4

These cryptic icons can save you hours once you understand how to use them to control the Selection tools.

These icons don't look like much, but they tell the Selection tools how to do their jobs: whether to start a new selection with each click, to add to what you've already selected, or to remove things from the current selection. They're available for all the Selection tools except the Selection Brush, the Quick Selection tool, and the Refine Selection Brush, which have their own sets of options. From left to right, here's what they do:

- **New** is the standard selection mode that you'll probably use most of the time. When you click this icon and start a new selection, your previous selection disappears.

- **Add** tells Elements to add what you select to whatever you've *already* selected. Unless you have an incredibly steady mouse hand, this option is a godsend because it's not easy to get a perfect selection on the first try. (Holding down the Shift key while you use any Selection tool temporarily switches you to this mode.)

- **Subtract** removes what you select next from any existing selection. (Holding down Alt/Option while selecting the area you want to remove does the same thing.)

- **Intersect** is a bit confusing. This mode lets you take a selected area, make a new selection, and wind up with only the area where the selections overlap, as Figure 5-5 shows. (The keyboard equivalent is Shift+Alt/Shift-Option.) Most people don't need this one much, but it can be useful for things like creating special shapes. If you need a selection shaped like a quarter of a pie, for instance, create a circular selection, and then switch to "Intersect with Selection" and drag a rectangular selection from the circle's center point. You'll wind up with just the arc-shaped area where they intersect.

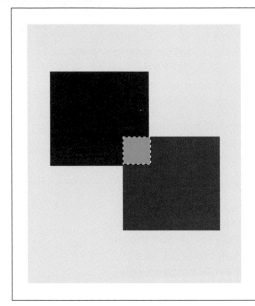

FIGURE 5-5

Intersect mode lets you take two separate selections and select only the area where they intersect. If you have an existing selection, then when you select again, your new selection includes only the overlapping area.

Here, the top blue square was the first selection, and the bottom fuchsia square was the second. The bright green area is the final selection.

■ Selecting with a Brush

Elements gives you two very special brushes for making selections. The Selection Brush has been around since Elements 2, so if you've used the program before, you probably know how handy it is. But these days it often takes a backseat to the Quick Selection tool, which makes even the trickiest selections as easy as doodling. The Quick Selection tool automatically finds the bounds of the objects you drag it over, while the Selection Brush selects only the area directly under your cursor. Using the Quick Selection tool in combination with the Refine Edge dialog box makes it incredibly simple to create the kinds of selections that would have driven you half crazy trying to get right in old versions of Elements.

These two brushes are grouped together in the Tools panel, and they're available in both Expert and Quick Fix modes because they're so useful. You may well find that with these two brushes, you rarely need the other Selection tools.

It couldn't be easier to use the Quick Selection tool:

1. **Activate the Quick Selection tool.**

   It shares a slot in the Tools panel's Select section with the Selection Brush, the Magic Wand, and the Refine Selection Brush. Click this slot or press A, and then—if one of the other tools is active instead—click the Quick Selection tool's icon in the Tool Options area or tap the A key until you see its icon.

NOTE Make sure you have the right tool active. All these similar icons can be a little confusing at first. The simplest way is just to look at the tool's name at the upper left of the Tool Options area.

2. **Drag within your photo.**

   As you move the cursor, Elements calculates where it thinks the selection's edges should be, and the selection outline (the marching ants) jumps out to surround that area. It's an amazingly good guesser. You don't even need to cover the entire area or go around the edges of the object—Elements does that for you.

   This tool has a few Tool Options settings, which are explained below, but you mostly won't need to think about them—at least, not till you've finished making your selection. Then you'll probably want to try using the Refine Edge dialog box (explained in the next section).

3. **Adjust the selection.**

   Odds are that, on the first try, you won't get a perfect selection that includes everything you wanted. To increase the selection's area, drag over the additional area you want to add to the selection. A small move usually does it, and the selection jumps outward to include the area that Elements thinks you want, as shown in Figure 5-6.

FIGURE 5-6

Left: It would be tough to select this water lily by hand because of the pointy petals. One drag with the Quick Selection tool produced this result. Notice how well the tool found the petals' edges.

Right: Another drag across the lily selected the whole blossom. Creating this selection took less than 5 seconds. (Elements missed a little bit on the edges in a couple of spots. Reduce the brush size and drag again to add those, or switch to the regular Selection Brush to finish up.)

To remove an area from the selection, hold Alt/Option while dragging over or clicking that area.

2. **Use the options in the dialog box's Edge Detection and Adjust Edge sections to refine your selection's edges.**

These tools and sliders, which are explained after this list, let you tweak and polish the selection's edges. It may take Refine Edge a few seconds to catch up to you when you adjust one of these settings, so go slowly and watch to see just how you're changing the edges. It usually doesn't take much to get any soft edges you're trying to select. If you go too far, you may see more of the background color bleeding through, or Elements may even decide to omit some flyaway hairs or other fine details.

> **TIP** If you just want to adjust the edges of an easy-to-select object like a kayak or a toaster, you can skip right to the dialog box's Adjust Edge section, tweak those sliders, and then click OK. But for tricky selections, you'll need the help of the Edge Detection settings, too.

3. **In the Output section, choose what kind of selection you want and where you want it to appear (in the current document or a new one) once you're done with Refine Edge.**

The Output To drop-down menu gives you six choices that are all explained below. You can even save your extracted selection to a brand-new file, if you want.

4. **When you like what you've done, click OK.**

If you decide not to refine your selection's edges after all, click Cancel. To undo all the changes you've made in this dialog box and start over, Alt-click/Option-click the Cancel button (it turns into a Reset button).

The Refine Edge dialog box is packed with options. It may look a bit confusing at first, but like most things in Elements, it's logically arranged. The dialog box is divided into four main sections: View Mode, Edge Detection, Adjust Edge, and Output. As in the Quick Fix window, you don't need to use all the adjustments (only the ones you want), and generally your best bet is to start at the top and work down.

The first section, View Mode, is full of useful ways to get the best possible look at your selection. As mentioned above, you have the Hand and Zoom tools on the left, and the View menu, which gives you seven different ways to see your selection; click the View thumbnail to see your options. Each view has a keyboard shortcut that makes it easy to switch among them without using your mouse, or you can keep tapping the F key to cycle through them all:

- **Marching Ants (keyboard shortcut: M)** shows the regular selection outline that you normally see.

- **Overlay (V)** displays the red mask overlay you get when using the Selection Brush in Mask mode (page 162). The red area is the *unselected* part of your image. This view is a good way to check for holes and jagged edges.

- **On Black (B)** shows just the selected area against a black background.

- **On White (W)** displays your selection against a white background. In most cases, this view works well. Elements usually starts you off in this view the first time you use Refine Edge. (After that, Elements remembers which view you used last time and automatically selects it.)

- **Black and White (K)** shows only the outline of the selection in white against a black background so you aren't distracted by the details in your image.

- **On Layers (L)** shows your selection against the transparency checkerboard (see page 43).

- **Reveal Layer (R)** shows the current layer (or the whole image if you aren't working with layers yet) with the selection outline hidden. In other words, this view shows what you would see with no selection at all.

This section also includes two checkboxes to give you even more help:

- **Show Radius (keyboard shortcut: J)**. Turn this on and you see only the outline of your selection, the part you're adjusting with the Refine Edge dialog box. It's helpful to turn on this setting after you've used the Radius slider in the Edge Detection section; doing so lets you see exactly the area that Elements is analyzing for Smart Radius (explained below).

- **Show Original (P)**. When you turn on this setting, Elements displays your original image without a visible selection. If the image isn't layered, you'll see the same thing you'd see in Reveal Layer view described above. This is a great way to go back and see where you started to make sure you like the effect your Refine Edge edits are having.

The next section is Edge Detection. If your selection is fine except for needing a little feathering or smoothing, you can skip this section, but for tricky selections, this is where the magic starts:

- **Smart Radius**. Turn on this checkbox and Elements goes to work analyzing the edges of your selection to see whether they're hard or soft, and figuring out what it needs to do to improve them. You can control the results (to some extent) by using the Radius setting below this checkbox. Figure 5-8 shows Smart Radius at work. (This setting may be turned on when you open the Refine Edge dialog box, but it doesn't affect anything until you move the Radius slider, described next.)

- **Radius**. This slider tells Elements how far from your original marching ants to search for potential edges. You can adjust this setting either by dragging the slider or clicking where it says 0.0 and typing a number of pixels. Increasing this setting softens the edges of your selection to some extent. So if you selected the edge of a roof or other hard object, for instance, you'd want to leave this set to 0.0 (unless the roof is thatched, maybe). The fuzzier the object you selected, the farther to the right you'll probably want to move this slider.

FIGURE 5-8

Left: Here's what the edge of this rough selection looks like when you first launch Refine Edge.

Right: As you can see, turning on Smart Radius and adjusting the Radius setting makes Elements think a lot harder about where the edges of the selection should be.

There are also two special tools to the left of the Edge Detection section that can help you fine-tune your selection even more; press the E key to toggle between them:

- **Refine Radius**. If Elements isn't quite finding everything you want to select, then run this tool over the spots on the edge of your selection where you want the program to pay more attention. This forces Elements to refine its calculations for that region, making the selection more precise. Brushing over soft edges like hair or fur, for example, increases the amount of detail in the selection's edges.

- **Erase Refinements**. If, on the other hand, Elements starts taking in too *much* of the surrounding area when you use the Refine Radius tool, this tool acts like an eraser to tell Elements to ignore the area where you drag.

> **TIP** While the Refine Edge window is onscreen, you can use the Zoom tool and the keystrokes for zooming in and out (page 102) to get as large a view as you need to see just how you're changing the edges of your selection.

As if all those features weren't enough, the dialog box's Adjust Edge section gives you even *more* ways to tweak your selection's outline. This section's first two settings, Smooth and Feather, are most helpful for hard-edged selections where you don't need the other Refine Edge tools so much. To adjust the following settings, you can either drag the slider or type a number in pixels (for Smooth and Feather) or a percentage (for Contrast and Shift Edge).

- **Smooth**. This setting gets rid of jagged edges in your selection. Be careful: A little smoothing goes a long way. If you've increased the Smart Radius setting, you probably don't want to use this option, too.

- **Feather**. Feathering (which also softens edges) is explained in the box on page 152.

- **Contrast**. Use this slider if you find that everything you've done to your selection has melted away all the edge differentiation between your subject and the background, and you want to increase the contrast between your selection and the surrounding area. Usually, though, you're better off going back to the dialog box's Edge Detection section and adjusting your selection there.

- **Shift Edge**. This setting adjusts the *size* of your selection. Move the slider left to contract the selection or right to expand it. The main use for this setting is to help when you've included too much of the contrasting background in your selection, although the Decontaminate Colors setting (explained next) may be able to fix that better than this slider. However, sometimes shifting the selection's edges a bit helps the Smart Radius feature do its job better.

Finally, the Output section gives you another immensely helpful tool for tweaking the coloration of your selection's edges: the Decontaminate Colors checkbox. After all that edge adjusting, your final selection may still include some of the background color you don't want, like the blue shirt of the person who was holding the fuzzy duckling in your original photo. Turn on this checkbox and then use the Amount slider below it to tell Elements how much to try to replace any color fringes with nearby colors (not necessarily the colors of your selection). Move the slider right and Elements changes more pixels; move it left and Elements changes fewer. Using the View menu to switch back and forth between your current view and Reveal Layer view is a good way to monitor how the Amount slider is affecting the colors in your photo.

The Output section also lets you send your perfected selection out for use in many different ways. After all that work refining it, you'll want to get the most use out of your exquisite selection, so the Output To menu lets you tell Elements what to do when you click OK in the Refine Edge dialog box:

- **Selection.** If you simply want a plain ol' selection, only a much-improved one, choose this option.

- **Layer Mask**. If you understand layers and masks (see Chapter 6, especially page 210), then select this option and Elements will turn your selection into a mask for your original layer.

- **New Layer**. Select this option if you want to save your selected object on its own layer in your original image. Elements cuts the selection out and puts it on a transparent background in your image.

- **New Layer with Layer Mask**. Choose this and you get a duplicate layer in your image that includes a layer mask based on the selection.

- **New Document**. If you want to cut out your selected object to use on its own, this option creates a brand-new file containing nothing but your selection on a transparent background.

- **New Document with Layer Mask**. Choose this option and Elements copies the entire original layer (the one that was the basis for your selection) into a new document that includes a layer mask based on the selection.

> **NOTE** If you used Decontaminate Colors, you can't choose Selection or Layer Mask from the Output To menu—you have to choose one of the New Layer or New Document options instead. That's because Decontaminate Colors changes the color of pixels in your image, so it does more than just change the edges of a selection. Adobe imposes this restriction to help preserve your original image.

There aren't any particular Refine Edge settings that apply to every selection. Most of the time you'll need to play around with several of its sliders to get the best result. But if you want the Refine Edge dialog box to always open with the same settings (you always want Smart Radius turned on, say), turn on the Remember Settings checkbox at the bottom of the dialog box. After that, the next time you launch Refine Edge, all the settings should be just the way you left them.

The Selection Brush

The Selection Brush is great for creating complex selections when you want to be totally in charge (without the help you get from the Quick Selection tool), and for cleaning up selections made with other tools, especially if you're trying to fix holes within such a selection. You can use it on its own or as a complement to the Quick Selection tool.

The Quick Selection tool doesn't always put the edges of your selection exactly where you want them. In contrast, the Selection Brush gives you total control because it selects only the area you drag your cursor over. You can even let go of the mouse button, and each time you drag again, Elements automatically adds to your selection; you don't need to change modes in the Tool Options area or to hold down the Shift key, as you do with other Selection tools.

The Selection Brush also has a Mask mode, where Elements highlights what *isn't* part of your selection, which is great for finding tiny spots you've missed and for checking the accuracy of your selection's outline. In Mask mode, anything you paint over gets *masked* out; in other words, it's protected from being selected. Masking is a little confusing at first, but you'll soon see how useful it is. Figure 5-9 shows the same selection made with and without Mask mode.

The Selection Brush is pretty simple to use:

1. **Click the Selection Brush's icon in the Tools panel or press A.**

   You may not see the Selection Brush at first because it shares a Tools panel slot with the Quick Selection tool, the Magic Wand, and the Refine Selection Brush. If you see one of those tools' icons instead, just click it, and then click the Selection Brush's icon in the Tool Options area; it's the brush that looks like it's painting—its tip points down.

FIGURE 5-9

*Left: This flower was selected by
painting with the Selection Brush
in Selection mode. It looks just
like the selections you can make
using any of the Selection tools.*

*Right: The same selection in Mask
mode. The red covers everything
that's not part of the selection.*

2. **In the Tool Options area, choose either Selection mode or Mask mode and
the brush size and hardness you want.**

   All these settings are explained after this list.

3. **Drag over the area you want to select.**

   If you're in Selection mode, the area you drag over becomes part of your selection, and Elements puts marching ants around it. If you're in Mask mode,
   the area you drag over is *excluded* from becoming part of your selection, and
   Elements puts a red film over it.

The Selection Brush gives you several Tool Options choices:

- **Mode**. This unlabeled drop-down menu is where you tell Elements whether
  you want to create a selection (Selection) or exclude an area from being part
  of a selection (Mask).

- **Brush thumbnail**. Click the triangle to the right of this squiggly line to choose
  from lots of different brushes. (For more about brushes, see page 396.)

- **Size**. To change the brush cursor's size, drag this slider or click the pixel value
  and then type in a new one. Or you can press the close bracket key (]) to enlarge
  the cursor (keep tapping it until you get the size you want) or the open bracket
  key ([) to shrink it. You can also put your cursor over the word "Size" and scrub
  to the left or right to make the brush smaller or larger, respectively. (Don't know
  how to scrub? For more on this nifty feature, see page 197.)

TIP The bracket-key shortcuts work with any brush, not just the Selection Brush.

- **Refine Edge.** You can use Refine Edge to adjust the edges of your selection as explained in the previous section.

- **Hardness**. This setting controls the sharpness of the brush cursor's edge, which affects your selection (see Figure 5-10).

FIGURE 5-10

These two brushstrokes show the way the Hardness setting affects the edges of a selection.

Two different selections were made in this green rectangle. The top selection was made at 100 percent hardness, and the bottom one at 50 percent hardness. (The selected area was then deleted to show the outlines more clearly.)

Switching between Selection and Mask mode is a good way to see how well you've done when you finish making a selection. In Mask mode, the areas of your image that *aren't* part of the selection have a red film over them, so you can clearly see the selected area.

> **TIP** You don't have to live with a red mask. To change the mask's color, in the Tool Options area, click the color square below the Overlay slider (the Selection Brush has to be active and in Mask mode for this setting to appear). In the window that pops up, either click a color swatch or click the multicolored circle in the window's bottom right, and then use the Color Picker to choose a different hue. You can also tweak the Overlay setting in the Tool Options area to adjust how well your image shows through the mask.

To temporarily make the Selection Brush do the opposite of what it's been doing, hold down Alt/Option while you drag. This can save a lot of time when you're making a tricky selection, since you don't have to keep hopping down to the Tool Options area to change modes, and you can keep the view (either your selection or the mask) the same. For example, if you're in Selection mode and you've selected too large an area, Alt-drag/Option-drag over the excess to remove it. If you're masking out an area, Alt-drag/Option-drag to *add* to the selection. This may sound confusing, but it'll make sense once you try it. Some things are easier to learn by doing.

> **TIP** The Selection Brush is useful for fine-tuning selections you've made with the other Selection tools. Quickly switching to the Selection Brush in Mask mode is a great way to check for spots you've missed—the overlay makes them really easy to spot.

The Magic Wand

The Magic Wand is a slightly temperamental—and occasionally highly effective—tool for selecting irregularly shaped but uniformly colored (or nearly so) regions. If there's a big area of a particular color, the Magic Wand can find its edges with one click.

This tool isn't actually all that magical: All it does is search for pixels with similar color values. But if it works for you, you may decide Adobe should keep "magic" in this tool's name because, when it cooperates, it's a great timesaver, as Figure 5-11 shows.

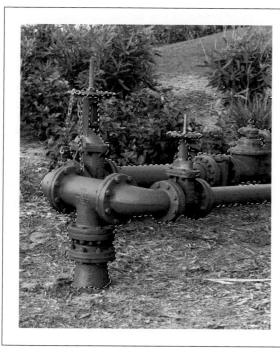

FIGURE 5-11

Just one click with the Magic Wand created this nearly perfect selection of this blue pipeline.

If there isn't a big difference between the color of the area you want to select and the colors of neighboring areas, this tool won't be as effective as it was here.

You'll find the Magic Wand in the same Tools panel slot as the Quick Selection tool, the Selection Brush, and the Refine Selection Brush. Its icon is an upward-pointing wand with a yellow starburst tip. To activate it, either press the A key repeatedly or, in the Tools panel, click the icon for whichever tool from the group is visible, and then head to the Tool Options area and click the Magic Wand's icon.

Using the Magic Wand is pretty straightforward: Just click anywhere in the area you want to select. Depending on the Wand's *tolerance* setting (explained in the following list), you may nail the selection right away, or it may take several clicks to get everything. If you need to click more than once, remember to hold down Shift so that each click adds to your selection—otherwise, each click simply creates a new selection.

As mentioned above, the Magic Wand does best when you offer it a good, solid block of color that's clearly defined and doesn't have a lot of different shades in it. It doesn't work well for selecting colored areas that have any shading or tonal gradations—you have to click and click and click.

Elements includes some special Tool Options settings that can help the Wand do a better job:

- **Tolerance** controls how many shades the tool selects. A higher setting includes more shades (resulting in a larger selected area), while a lower setting gets you fewer shades (and a more precise selection). If you set the tolerance *too* high, you'll probably select a lot more of your image than you want.

- **Sample All Layers** works if you have a layered file (you'll learn about layers in the next chapter). Turn on this checkbox to make the Magic Wand select the color in *all* the image's layers. If you want it to select the color only in the active layer, then leave this setting turned off.

- **Contiguous** makes the Magic Wand select only similarly colored areas touching one another. This checkbox is on by default, but sometimes you can save a lot of time by turning it off, as Figure 5-12 explains.

- **Anti-aliasing** is explained in the box on page 152.

The Tool Options for the Magic Wand also give you access to the Refine Edge dialog box so you can fix up the edges of your selection, as explained on page 156.

The big disadvantage of the Magic Wand is that it tends to leave unselected, contrasting areas around the edge of your selection that are a bit of a pain to clean up. So you may want to give the Quick Selection tool (page 154) a spin before trying the Magic Wand, especially if your goal is to select a range of colors. However, if you put a Magic Wand selection on its own layer (see Chapter 6), you can use Refine Edge or the Defringe command (page 171) to help clean up the edges.

The Lasso Tools

The Magic Wand is pretty handy, but it works well only when your image has clearly defined areas of color. If you want to select something from a cluttered background, the Magic Wand just won't cut it. In cases like that, the easiest option is to draw around the object you want to select.

Enter the Lasso tool. Elements actually has *three* lasso tools: the Lasso, the Polygonal Lasso, and the Magnetic Lasso. Each one lets you select an object by tracing around it.

You activate the lasso tools by clicking their icon in the Tools panel's Select section (just below the Move tool), and then selecting the particular variation you want in the Tool Options area, or by repeatedly pressing the L key till you see the right tool. Then simply drag around the outline of an object to make your selection.

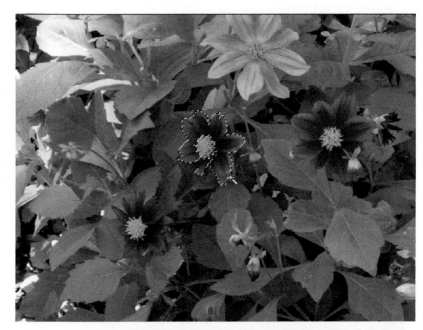

FIGURE 5-12

Top: With the Contiguous checkbox turned on, the Magic Wand only selects the red part of the flower you click with it.

Bottom: By turning this setting off, you can select all the areas that are that shade of red with just one click. Then you can use the Selection Brush (page 162) to quickly clean up the selection.

The following sections cover each lasso tool in detail. All three let you apply feathering and anti-aliasing as you make a selection (see the box on page 152), and the basic Lasso and Polygonal Lasso give you access to Refine Edge (page 156) right in their Tool Options settings.

■ THE BASIC LASSO TOOL

The basic Lasso tool is useful for making rough selections that you plan to clean up later. For instance, use the Lasso to drag quickly around what you want to select, and then use the Refine Selection Brush (page 177) to create a more refined selection.

To use this tool, simply activate it (your cursor changes to the lasso shape shown in Figure 5-13), and then click your photo and drag around the outline of what you want to select. When the end of your outline gets back around and joins up with the beginning, you've got a selection. (If the start and end points don't meet up, then when you let go of your mouse, Elements connects them with a straight line.) The only settings for this tool are Feather and Anti-Aliasing, explained in the box on page 152.

FIGURE 5-13

The end of the cursor's "rope," not the lasso's loop, is the selection-drawing part of the basic Lasso tool.

If this cursor shape bothers you, then press the Caps Lock key to change it to crosshairs instead.

It's not always easy to make an accurate selection with the Lasso, especially if you're using a mouse. A graphics tablet (page 583) is a big advantage when using this tool, since tablets let you draw with a pen-shaped stylus. But even if you don't have a graphics tablet, you can make all of Elements' tools work just fine with your mouse once you get used to their quirks.

It helps to zoom way in and go very slowly when using the Lasso. Many people use this tool to quickly select an area that roughly surrounds an object (as in Figure 5-13), and then go back with other Selection tools—like the Selection Brush or the Magnetic Lasso—to clean things up.

TIP If you need to draw a straight line for part of your selection, hold down Alt/Option and click the points where you want the line to start and end. So if you're selecting an arched Palladian window, for instance, once you get around the curve at the top and reach the straight side, press Alt/Option and click at the bottom of the side to get the whole side all in one go. You need to have already clicked in your image with the tool at least once before you press this key, though, or this trick won't work.

Once you've created a selection, you can click the Refine Edge button in the Tool Options area to adjust and feather the edges. If you decide you don't want your selection anymore, press Esc or Ctrl+D/⌘-D to get rid of it.

■ THE MAGNETIC LASSO

The Magnetic Lasso is a very handy tool, especially if you were the kind of kid who could never color inside the lines or neatly cut out paper chains. This tool snaps to the outline of any clearly defined object you're trying to select, so you don't have to follow the edge exactly.

As you might guess, the Magnetic Lasso works best on objects with well-defined edges, so you won't get much out of it if your subject is a furry animal, for instance. This tool also likes a good, strong contrast between the object and the background.

To use this tool, click to start a selection, and then move your cursor around the perimeter of what you want to select. (Just as with the basic Lasso tool, you can change the cursor's shape by pressing the Caps Lock key.) Then double-click back where you began to finish your selection. The Tool Options settings let you adjust how many *anchor points* the Magnetic Lasso puts down as you move your mouse and how sensitive it is to the edge you're tracing, as shown in Figure 5-14.

> **TIP** You can Ctrl-click/⌘-click at any point, and the Magnetic Lasso will immediately close up whatever area you've surrounded by drawing a straight line from the last anchor point to where you started.

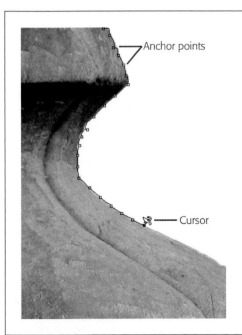
Anchor points

Cursor

FIGURE 5-14

One nice thing about the Magnetic Lasso is that it's easy to back up as you're creating a selection.

As you move your mouse, this tool lays down tiny boxes called anchor points, as shown here. If you make a mistake, pressing Backspace/ Delete takes you back one point each time you press the key. (To completely get rid of a Magnetic Lasso selection you've begun but not completed, press Esc.)

If the Magnetic Lasso skips a spot or won't grab onto a spot you want it to, you can force it to put down an anchor point by clicking once where you want the point to go.

In addition to Feather and Anti-aliasing (explained in the box on page 152), the Magnetic Lasso has four other Tool Options settings:

- **Width** tells the tool how far to look when it's trying to find an edge. This value is in pixels; you can set it as high as 256.

- **Contrast** controls how sharp a difference the Magnetic Lasso should look for between the object's outline and its background. A higher number makes Elements look for sharper contrasts, and a lower number makes it look for softer ones.

- **Frequency** controls how often Elements puts down anchor points (Figure 5-14).

- **Use tablet pressure to change pen width**—the little icon of a pen tip to the right of the other Tool Options settings—works only if you have a graphics tablet (page 583). When you turn this setting on, how hard you press with the stylus controls how Elements searches for the edge of objects you're trying to select: When you bear down harder, it's more precise (in other words, it doesn't look as far); when you press more lightly, you can be a bit sloppier, and Elements will still find the edge.

Many people live full and satisfying lives paying no attention whatsoever to these settings, so don't feel that you have to fuss with them. You can usually ignore them unless the Magnetic Lasso misbehaves.

> **TIP** You get better results with the Magnetic Lasso if you go more slowly than if you speed around an object. Like most people, the Magnetic Lasso does better work if you give it time to be sure where it's going.

■ THE POLYGONAL LASSO

At first, this may seem like a totally useless tool. It works something like the Magnetic Lasso in that it puts down anchor points (though you have to click each time you want it to add one and you don't see the boxes for each point like you do with the Magnetic lasso [see Figure 5-14]), but it creates only perfectly straight line segments. So you may think, "That's great if I want to select a stop sign, but otherwise, what's the point?"

Actually, if you're one of those people who just plain *can't* draw, and you even have a hard time following the edge of an object onscreen, this is the tool for you. The trick is to move your cursor very short distances between clicks. Figure 5-15 shows the Polygonal Lasso in action.

The big advantage of this tool over the Magnetic Lasso is that it's much easier to keep it from getting into a snarl. Your only Tool Options settings for this tool are Feather and Anti-aliasing (which are explained in the box on page 152), as well as Refine Edge (page 156).

The selection path drawn
by the Polygonal Lasso

Polygonal Lasso cursor

FIGURE 5-15

If you have limited dexterity, the Polygonal Lasso tool and a lot of clicks eventually get you a nice, accurate selection. You just need to zoom way, way in to use this tool to select an object that doesn't have totally straight sides.

Here, the Polygonal Lasso easily made it around the curve of this stone by clicking to make extremely short segments.

Extracting Objects

Ever feel the urge to pluck an object out of a photo so you can use it on its own or somewhere else? For example, say you want to take an amazing shot you got of the moon and stick it in another photo. How do you do that?

For several versions, Elements included the Magic Extractor to help you with this task, but that feature disappeared in Elements 12. But you still have plenty of options for extracting objects, beginning with the traditional method: In the Layers panel, double-click your Background layer to make it a regular layer (or you won't get transparent areas around the object; page 189 has more on this), make your selection, invert it (page 172), and then delete the rest of the image.

You can also use the handy Defringe Layer command, explained in Figure 5-16, to clean up any messy contrasting pixels around the edge of the object. The new Photomerge Compose command (page 379) lets you do this, too.

Another option is to give the Refine Edge dialog box (page 156) first crack at extracting your object, especially if it's got tricky edges. Refine Edge can do fancy extracting, including saving your extracted object to a masked layer or a new document, so this can also substitute for the Magic Extractor.

If you plan to use the object in another image, you can simply select it, press Ctrl+C/⌘-C to copy it, click the image where you want to put it, press Ctrl+V/⌘-V to paste it in, and then use the Move tool (page 182) to precisely position the object.

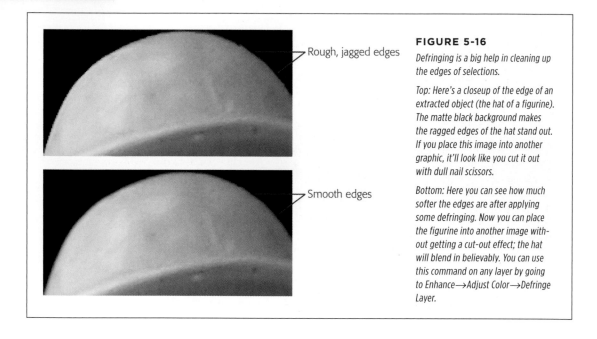

FIGURE 5-16

Defringing is a big help in cleaning up the edges of selections.

Top: Here's a closeup of the edge of an extracted object (the hat of a figurine). The matte black background makes the ragged edges of the hat stand out. If you place this image into another graphic, it'll look like you cut it out with dull nail scissors.

Bottom: Here you can see how much softer the edges are after applying some defringing. Now you can place the figurine into another image with-out getting a cut-out effect; the hat will blend in believably. You can use this command on any layer by going to Enhance→Adjust Color→Defringe Layer.

Labels in figure: Rough, jagged edges / Smooth edges

Changing and Moving Selections

Now that you know all about making selections, it's time to learn some of the finer points of using and manipulating them. Elements gives you several options for changing the areas you've selected and for moving objects around after you select them. You can even save a tough selection so that, if you need it again later, you don't have to go to all the trouble of recreating it. This section has the lowdown.

Inverting Selections

One thing you often want to do with a selection is *invert* it. That means telling Elements, "You know the area I've selected? I want you to select everything *except* that area." Why would you want to do that? Because sometimes it's easier to select what you *don't* want.

For example, suppose you have an object with a complicated outline, like the building in Figure 5-17. If you want to use just the building in a scrapbook of your trip to Europe, it's going to be difficult to select. But the sky is just one big block of color, so it's easy to select with the Magic Wand.

To invert a selection, simply make a selection with any tool that suits your fancy, and then go to Select→Inverse or press Shift+Ctrl+I/Shift-⌘-I. Now the part of your image that you *didn't* select is selected. Easy, huh?

FIGURE 5-17

Say you want to make some adjustments to this building. You could spend half an hour meticulously selecting all that Gothic detail, or just select the sky with a couple of clicks of the Magic Wand, and then invert your selection to get the building.

Top: Here, the marching ants around the sky show that it's the active selection—but that's not what you want.

Bottom: Inverting the selection (Select→Inverse) puts the ants around the building instead, without your going to the trouble of tracing over all the elaborate, lacy details of the roofline.

Resizing Selections

What if you want to tweak the size of your selection? For example, say you want to move the outline of your selection outward a few pixels to expand it. Elements gives you a really handy way to do that: the Transform Selection command.

With Transform Selection, you can easily drag any selection larger or smaller, rotate it, squish it narrower or shorter, or pull it out longer or wider (imagine smooshing a circular selection into an oval, for instance). This is really handy, as you can see in Figure 5-18.

NOTE As its name implies, Transform Selection does all these things to the *selection*, not to the object you've selected. If you want to distort an *object*, you can do that with the Move tool (page 182) or the Transform commands (page 387). And if you want to make freehand changes to the shape of your selection, use the Refine Selection Brush, described in the next section.

FIGURE 5-18

Left: Sometimes it's tough to draw exactly the selection you want. Here, attempting to avoid the sign and the palm fronds led to cutting off part of the rope bumper on the boat's bow.

Right: After you've decided that it would be easier to clone out any unwanted fronds (page 318 explains how), Transform Selection makes it easy to resize the selection to include the whole rope.

To use Transform Selection:

1. **Make a selection.**

   Use the Selection tool(s) of your choice. Transform Selection is especially handy when you've used one of the Marquee tools and didn't get the selection quite right.

2. **Go to Select→Transform Selection, or right-click/Control-click inside your selection and then choose Transform Selection from the shortcut menu.**

   Either way, a bounding box with little square handles appears around your selection, as shown in Figure 5-18. (The bounding box is rectangular even if your selection is some other shape.) The Tool Options area changes to show the settings for this feature, which are the same as those for the Transform tools (page 387). Most of the time, you won't need to worry about these settings.

3. **Drag the bounding box's square handles and adjust the area covered by your selection.**

   The different ways you can adjust a selection are explained after this list.

4. **When you get everything just right, click the green checkmark or press Enter/Return to accept your changes.**

   If you mess up or change your mind about the whole thing, click Cancel (the red No symbol) or press Esc to revert to your original selection.

You can change your selection in most of the same ways you learned about back in the section on cropping (page 89):

- **To make the selection wider or narrower**, drag one of the side handles.

- **To make the selection taller or shorter**, drag a top or bottom handle.

- **To make the selection larger or smaller**, drag a corner handle. Before you start, take a quick look at the Tool Options: If you want the selection's shape to stay exactly the same, then make sure the Constrain Proportions checkbox is turned on; if you want the shape to change (get smooshed or stretched), then turn this checkbox off.

- **To rotate the selection**, move your cursor near a corner handle till you see the curved arrows, and then drag to spin the selection's outline to the angle you want.

Transform Selection is a great feature, but it only expands or contracts your selection in the same ways the Transform tools can change things. In other words, you can change the selection's width, height, and proportions, but you can't change a star-shaped selection into a dog-shaped one, for example. (In that situation, you should simply start a new selection from scratch.) Elements gives you a number of other ways to adjust a selection's size, which may work better for you in certain situations, although in most cases Transform Selection is probably the easiest.

But what do you do if you just want to enlarge the selection to include surrounding areas of the same color? Elements has you covered. Figuring out which of the following commands to use can be confusing because the two ways to enlarge a selection sound really similar: Grow and Expand. You may think they do the same thing, but there's a slight, important difference between them, as Figure 5-19 shows:

- **Grow** (Select→Grow) moves your selection outward to include more similar, contiguous colors, no matter what shape your original selection was. This command doesn't care about shape; it just finds more matching contiguous pixels.

- **Expand** (Select→Modify→Expand) preserves the shape of your selection and just enlarges it by the number of pixels you specify.

- **Similar** (Select→Similar) does the same thing as Grow but looks at *all* the pixels in your image, not just ones adjacent to the current selection.

- **Contract** (Select→Modify→Contract) shrinks a selection by the number of pixels you specify.

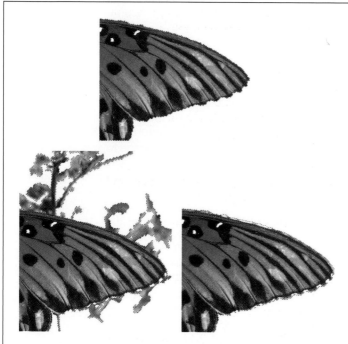

FIGURE 5-19

Top: Here's the original selection of this butterfly wing. Elements missed some small areas on the edge. (The area outside the selection was deleted to make it easier to see what's selected.)

Bottom left: If you use Grow to enlarge the selection, you also get parts of the background that are similar in tone. As a result, your selection isn't wing-shaped anymore.

Bottom right: If you use Expand instead, the selection still is still shaped like the wing, but the edges of the selection have moved outward to include the dark border area you missed the first time. Here the selection moved out more than you'd want—it took in some of the background—but Elements preserved the shape of the original selection.

POWER USERS' CLINIC

Smoothing and Bordering

Most of the time, you'll probably use Refine Edge to fine-tune your selections, but Elements gives you two other ways to tweak selection outlines:

- **Smoothing** (Select→Modify→Smooth) is a not-always-dependable way to clean up ragged spots in a color-based selection (the kind you'd make with the Magic Wand, for instance). You enter a pixel value in the Smooth Selection dialog box, and Elements evens out your selection based on that number by searching for similarly colored pixels. For example, if you enter *5*, Elements looks at a 5-pixel radius around each pixel in your selection. In areas where most of the pixels are already selected, it adds in the others. In areas where most pixels *aren't* selected, it deselects the ones that were selected to get rid of jagged edges and holes in the selection. This command

is handy, but smoothing is sometimes hard to control. Usually it's easier to clean up your selection by hand with the Selection Brush.

- **Bordering** (Select→Modify→Border) adds an anti-aliased, transparent border to your selection. You can think of this command as selecting the selection's outline. You might use it when your selection's edges are too hard and you want to soften them, although you're probably better off using Refine Edge instead. But if you go this route, enter a border width in the Border Selection dialog box, and then click OK. Elements then selects only the border of your selection, so you can also apply a slight Gaussian blur (see page 446) to soften that part of the photo.

Reshaping Selections

Transform Selection is a useful feature, but it has some limitations. For example, you can't use it to completely change the shape of your selection: If you started with a rectangular selection, you can't curve one side of the selection. Not to worry, though. Elements 13 includes a new tool just for adjusting and cleaning up selections after you've made them: the Refine Selection Brush.

If you've ever tried to make a difficult selection, you know how time consuming it can be. The Refine Selection Brush is intended to simplify the process by making it easy to refine rough selections. This brush analyzes your photo and looks for edges within the area you brush over so that it can snap your selection to the bounds of objects in your photo. It's a bit fiddly, but here's how to use it:

1. **Make a selection.**

   It doesn't have to be great. Even just drawing roughly around the object you want to select with the Lasso tool may be good enough.

2. **Activate the Refine Selection Brush and choose an editing mode for it.**

   It shares a Tools panel slot with the Quick Selection tool, the Selection Brush, and the Magic Wand, so click whichever of those is currently visible, or tap the A key till you see the Refine Selection Brush. Its icon is a down-pointing brush pushing a dotted line ahead of it. (Don't confuse this with the Selection Brush, whose icon includes a dotted line arcing up from the brush.)

   Next, in the Tool Options area, choose an editing mode by clicking one of the four icons to the right of the various tool icons. Each mode is explained after this list.

3. **Use the brush to push your selection's edges to where they should be.**

   The Refine Selection Brush has a unique cursor, shown in Figure 5-20, and it's important to choose an appropriate brush size for the area you're working in. So use the Tool Options area's Size slider to get the size you need.

   You want a brush size that's large enough for the cursor's dark center to cover a good part of what you want to change, while keeping the lighter gray part of the cursor over an edge that Elements can use for reference. In situations like the area between the spokes of the wagon wheel in Figure 5-20, you may need to adjust the brush size as you go.

   Once you've got the right brush size, just drag over the part of your selection that you want to change. The Refine Selection Brush has a few settings (described after this list) that you can adjust to the tool do a good job.

4. **When you're happy with your new selection outline, you're done.**

   You don't need to do anything more except use your improved selection.

FIGURE 5-20

This cursor is unique to the Refine Selection Brush. When you drag with this tool, Elements automatically changes the area that's under the dark center circle (the actual brush cursor); Elements also analyzes the area under the lighter outer rim for edges to snap (make the selection's edge jump) the selection to.

It's important to choose a brush size that's large enough to allow the tool to get a good analysis of the selection's edges while not letting the dark area get so large that it takes in more of your photo than you want.

The Refine Selection Brush has four little mode icons like the other Selection tools, but these are a bit different:

- **Add to selection.** If you choose this mode, then no matter where your cursor is in your image when you drag with this tool—whether inside your existing selection or outside it—Elements adds the material you drag over to your selection.

- **Subtract from selection.** In this mode, even if your cursor is inside the existing selection, dragging makes the Refine Selection Brush remove whatever you drag over. For instance, if you've selected a water tower, you can use this mode to remove the background area visible between the tower's legs, even though that area is within your original selection.

- **Push.** This is the mode you'll normally use with this tool. Push mode makes the Refine Selection Brush automatically find and analyze the edges of the objects you drag over. If you move the cursor within a selected area, that area gets removed from your selection. If you drag over an area outside your selection, Elements adds that area to your selection. The Refine Selection Brush is smart enough to know where you are: Although it can be hard to see, there's a tiny plus or minus sign in the center of the brush, depending on whether you're adding to or subtracting from your selection.

- **Smooth.** If your selection contains bumpy edges, this mode can smooth them out. Simply drag over the lumpy edges to make them smoother.

The most useful aspect of this brush is the way it automatically searches for edges to *snap* the selection to (see page 87 for more about snapping). You can control how vigorously the Refine Selection Brush does this by adjusting the Snap Strength setting. Move the slider to the right to make the tool snap your selection only short distances, or to the left if you'd rather it snap farther. (This setting isn't available when using the brush in Smooth mode.)

Moving Selected Areas

So far you've learned how to move and reshape selections themselves (the marching ants), but often you make selections because you want to move selected *objects* around—like putting that dreamboat who wouldn't give you the time of day next to you in a class photo.

There are several ways to do this, even without using any special tool, but you'll probably want to try out the Content-Aware Move tool described on page 180. For now, here's the simplest, tool-free way to move something from one image to another:

1. **Select the object you want to move.**

   Make sure you've selected everything you want—it's really annoying when you paste a selection from one image to another and then find that you missed a spot.

2. **Press Ctrl+C/⌘-C to copy it.**

   You can use Ctrl+X/⌘-X if you want to *cut* it out of your original; just remember that, if you do that, you leave a hole behind.

3. **Put the selected object into its new home.**

   If you want to dump the object into its very own document, choose File→New→"Image from Clipboard." Doing so creates a new document with just your selection in it.

   If you want to place the object into an existing photo, then use Ctrl+V/⌘-V to paste it into another image in Elements, or even into a document in another program.

> **TIP** You can also use Refine Edge to select, cut out, and paste your object into a new file, all in one go. Flip back to page 156 to learn how.

Once the object is where you want it, you can use the Move tool (page 182) to position it, rotate it, or scale it to fit the rest of the photo.

> **TIP** If you copy and paste a selection and then notice that it's got partially transparent areas in it, back up and go over your selection with the Selection Brush using a hard brush cursor. Then copy and paste again.

■ THE CONTENT-AWARE MOVE TOOL

Elements includes two Move tools that you can use to arrange things in your photos. The traditional Move tool has been at the top of the Elements toolbox as long as the program has existed, and you'll still prefer that tool in some situations, especially when working with layers, which are explained in the next chapter. But if you want to move an object from one place in your photo to another, or to duplicate objects, you definitely want to try the Content-Aware Move tool first, since it makes it super easy to get seamless, plausible results most of the time. Here's how to use it:

1. **Activate the Content-Aware Move tool.**

   Press Q or click this tool's icon in the Tools panel (the crossed arrows in the Modify section).

> **TIP** Use this tool when you want to move something within a single image. If you want to move an object from one image to another, try the new Photomerge Compose feature described on page 379.

2. **Decide whether you want to move the object or copy it.**

   If you want to move it from its original location, then in the Tool Options area, click the Move radio button. If you want to move a *copy* of the object instead, then click the Extend radio button. Figure 5-21 shows the difference.

FIGURE 5-21

Top: Let's say you need to use the dessert on this sideboard as an illustration. This photo is OK, but everything is pretty spread out.

Bottom: With the help of the Content-Aware Move tool, you can bring the oranges and plates much closer to the cake.

As you can see, this tool did a pretty good job, but the area to the left of the oranges still needs a bit of cleanup help. Moving the tool's Healing slider to the left may help get rid of this problem spot. (Do this while your Content-Aware Move tool selection is still active.) If that doesn't work, try the Clone Stamp (page 318).

3. **Click in the photo and drag to make a selection around the object you want to move.**

   This selection doesn't have to be very precise, but if there's a nearby detail you really don't want to include, try to avoid it when making your selection. For instance, if you're moving or duplicating a flag from one spot on a roof to another, including some of the sky is no big deal, but you want to be careful around the roofline, since if you drag a piece of the roof along with the flag, it may not match the roofline in the flag's new home.

   The Tool Options area includes the usual squares for adding to and subtracting from selections (page 152), but you probably won't need to use them much. Be aware, however, that if you create a selection with this tool and then click in your photo *outside* the selection, you lose the selection you had and start a new one. (Press Ctrl+Z/⌘-Z if you do this by mistake.)

4. **Once you see the marching ants around your object, drag it to its new home.**

   It may take a minute to see the final result because Elements has some work to do: it analyzes the area where the object *was* and does its best to seamlessly blend the moved object into the new area. If you aren't satisfied with the location, you can keep dragging the selection around as long as you see the marching ants.

   If you selected the Move option in step 2 above, Elements also creates new material to fill in the area where the object used to be.

5. **If necessary, use the Healing slider to adjust Elements' handiwork.**

   The Tool Option area's Healing slider tells Elements how much area to consider when blending the object into its new home and filling the spot where it was originally. If Elements picks up too much detail from around the object, move this slider to the left. If Elements doesn't include enough detail from the surrounding material, move this slider to the right.

   If you're using the tool's Move mode, as you move this slider, be sure to watch both the area around the moved object *and* the area where it came from. (With Extend mode, pay more attention to the object you're moving.)

The one disadvantage to this tool is that, once you drag the object, as soon as you let go of your mouse button, your moved object merges into the photo. You don't get an opportunity to resize it or flip the object if, for instance, you need to duplicate an eye in a damaged photo. However, there is a workaround, if you understand layers (which are explained in the next chapter): put the moved object on its own layer.

To do that, before you start using the Content-Aware Move tool, create a new layer (choose Layer→New Layer or press Shift+Ctrl+N/Shift-⌘-N). Then, activate the tool and make sure that Sample All Layers is turned on in the Tool Options area. That setting tells Elements to put the moved object on a separate layer, making it easy to grab with the regular Move tool (explained next) so that you can flip it, rotate it to a better angle, resize it, and so on. If you don't create a new layer, once you move your object, it immediately becomes part of the existing layer, so there's no opportunity to do anything like, say, flipping a table leg so you can replace one that's missing.

> **NOTE** If you use this layer trick with the tool's Extend radio button turned on, then only the moved area appears on the new layer and it's very easy to choose that layer and make changes to it. However, if the *Move* radio button is turned on, then your new layer will get material from both the moved object *and* the stuff that Elements creates to fill the hole where the object was, so you need to be careful to select only the moved object if that's all you want to change. Turning off the Background layer's visibility (page 196) can help you see what you're doing.

■ THE MOVE TOOL

You can also move things around within a photo by using the Move tool, which lets you cut or copy selected areas. Unlike the Content-Aware Move tool, if you move an object without copying it, this tool doesn't do anything about the hole left behind. The big advantage of the Move tool is that you can resize the object you're moving or adjust it by using the Transform tools (page 387). Figure 5-22 shows how to use the Move tool to conceal distracting details.

FIGURE 5-22

Left: To get rid of the meter-access hatch in this photo and keep it from drawing attention away from the lovely flowerboxes, select a piece of the sidewalk, and then activate the Move tool and hold down the Alt/Option key while dragging to copy the selected area. (If you use the Move tool without *holding down Alt/Option, Elements cuts the selected object instead, leaving a hole in your photo.)*

Right: After using the Clone Stamp (page 318) to blend in the new piece, you'd never know that slab of sidewalk wasn't solid.

The Move tool lives at the top left of the Tools panel's Select section. To use it to relocate an object, first select the object, and then:

1. **Activate the Move tool.**

   Click the Move tool's icon or press V. Your selection stays active but is now surrounded by a rectangle with square handles on it.

2. **Move the selection as described after this list and then, when you're satisfied with its position, press Enter/Return.**

As long as the selection is active, you can work on your photo in other ways and then come back and reactivate the Move tool. (If you're worried about losing a complex selection, save it as described in the next section.)

If you're not happy with what you've done, just press Ctrl+Z/⌘-Z as many times as needed to back up and start over again.

You can move a selection in several different ways:

- **Move it**. If you simply move a selection by dragging it, you leave a hole in the image where the selection was, because the Move tool *truly* moves the selection. So unless you have something under it that you want to show through, this probably isn't what you want to do.

- **Move a copy**. If you press the Alt/Option key as you drag with the Move tool, you'll copy the selection so the original stays where it is. But now you have a duplicate to move around and play with, as shown in Figure 5-22, left.

- **Resize it**. You can drag the square handles that the Move tool puts around your selection to resize or distort the selected material, which is great when you need to change the size of your selection. The Move tool lets you do the same things as Free Transform (see page 392).

- **Rotate it**. You can also rotate a selection the same way you can rotate a picture by using Free Rotate (page 87): Just grab a corner handle and turn it.

TIP   You can save yourself a trip to the Tools panel and move selections without activating the Move tool. To move a selection without copying it, just place your cursor in the selection, hold down Ctrl/⌘, and then drag the selection. To move a copy of a selection so you don't damage the original, do the same thing, but hold down Ctrl+Alt/⌘ Alt instead; to move *multiple* copies, simply repeat this process.

The Move tool is also a great way to manage and move objects that you've put on their own layers (Chapter 6), which is what the Tool Options area's Arrange, Align, and Distribute sections are for. Page 200 explains how to use the Move tool to arrange layered objects.

Saving Selections

You can tell Elements to remember the outline of a selection so that you can reuse it again later on. This is a wonderful, easy timesaver for particularly intricate selections. It's also handy if the "Text on Selection" tool (page 500) misbehaves, forcing you to restart Elements to get it working again; just save the selection before you quit Elements, and then reload it to pick up where you left off.

NOTE   Elements' saved selections are the equivalent of Photoshop's *alpha channels*. Keep that in mind if you decide to try tutorials written for Photoshop. Incidentally, alpha channels saved in Photoshop show up in Elements as saved selections, and vice versa. You can save a selection, load it again, and then save the file with the selection active to have it appear as an alpha channel in other programs that understand alpha channels, like Microsoft Word or Apple's Pages.

To save the current selection, choose Select→Save Selection, name the selection, and then click OK. When you want to use that selection again, simply go to Select→Load Selection, and there it is waiting for you.

> **TIP** When you save a feathered selection and then change your mind about how much feather you want, use the Refine Edge dialog box to adjust it. You can also save a hard-edged selection, load it, and then go to Select→Feather to add a feather to it. That way, you can change the feather amount each time you use the selection, as long as you remember not to save your *change* to the selection.

■ EDITING A SAVED SELECTION

If you need to tweak a saved selection, it's probably just as easy to start your selection over, but you can edit saved selections if you want. This can save you time if the original selection was really tricky to create.

Say you've got a full-length photo of somebody, and you've created and saved a selection of the person's face (and named it, naturally enough, Face). Now, imagine that after applying a filter to that selection, you decide it would look silly to change only the person's face and not his hands, too. So you want to add the hands to your saved selection.

You can do this in a couple of ways. The simplest is to load the Face selection, activate your Selection tool of choice, put the tool in "Add to Selection" mode, select the hands, and then save the selection again with the same name.

But what if you already have the hands selected and you want to add them to the existing, saved Face selection? Here's what you'd do:

1. **Go to Select→Save Selection.**

   In the Save Selection dialog box, choose Face from the Selection drop-down menu. When you do, all the radio buttons in the dialog box become active.

2. **In the dialog box's Operation section, choose "Add to Selection," and then click OK.**

   Elements adds your current selection (the hands) to the saved Face selection and saves the whole shebang, so now the saved Face selection includes the hands, too. (Unfortunately, you can't rename a saved selection. If it bothers you to keep the old name, just load the selection again by going to Select→Load Selection, and then save it as a *new* selection with a new name.)

> **TIP** If you find yourself frequently making changes to saved selections, you may want to consider using layer masks (page 210) instead, as they're much quicker to modify than selections.

Layers: The Heart of Elements

If you've been working mostly in the Quick Fix window so far, you've probably noticed that, once you close a file, the changes you've made to it are permanent. In other words, you can undo stuff while the file is still open, but once you close it, you're stuck with what you've done.

Fortunately, there's a better way to work. In Elements, you can keep your changes (most kinds, anyway) and still revert to the original image if you use *layers*, a nifty system of transparent sheets that keeps each component of the image on a separate sliver that you can edit. Layers are one of the greatest image-editing inventions ever: By putting each change on its own layer, you can rearrange an image's composition and add or subtract changes whenever you want.

If you use layers, then you can save a file and quit Elements, come back days or weeks later, and *still* undo what you did or change things around some more. There's no statute of limitations for the edits you make using layers.

Some people resist learning about layers because they fear layers are too complicated. But they're actually really easy to use once you understand how they work. And once you get started with layers, you'll realize that using Elements without them is like driving a Ferrari in first gear. This chapter gives you the info you need to get comfortable working with layers.

Understanding Layers

Imagine that you want to figure out the various ways you can redecorate a room in your house. The first thing you do is create a bare-bones drawing of the room. Now imagine you've also got a bunch of transparent plastic sheets that each contain an image that changes the room's look: a couch, different colors of carpeting, a standing lamp, and so on. Your decorating work is now pretty easy, since you can add, remove, and mix and match the transparencies with ease.

Layers in Elements work pretty much the same way: They let you add and remove objects, and make changes to the way the image looks. And you can modify or discard any of these changes later on.

Figure 6-1 shows an Elements file that includes layers. Each object in the flyer is on a different layer, so it's a breeze to remove or rearrange things. (If you want to follow along and work with a layers-heavy file, download *gardenparty.psd* from this book's Missing CD page at *www.missingmanuals.com/cds*.)

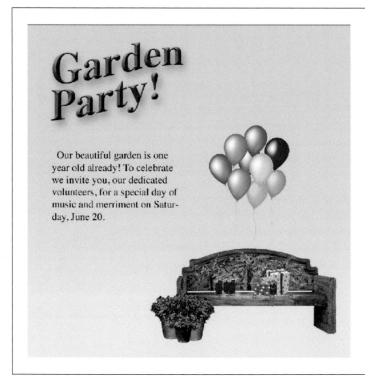

FIGURE 6-1

Every object in this flyer—the background, the bench, the balloons, each block of text—is on its own layer, which makes changing things a snap.

Want to try a new background, get rid of the balloons, or pick a different date? No problem!

NOTE   It's important to understand that photos from your camera start out with just one layer. That means if you've got a photo like the one in Figure 6-2 left, all the objects in it—the people, the ground they're standing on, and so on—are on the same layer. (Until you select an object and place it on its own layer, that is.)

That said, Elements often generates layers *for* you when you need them. For example, Elements automatically creates layers when you do things like move an object from one photo to another or use the Smart Brush tool (page 233), which thoughtfully puts its changes on their own layer.

You can also use layers for many adjustments to your photos, which lets you tweak or eliminate those changes later on. For instance, say you used Quick Fix's Hue slider to adjust the colors in your image, but the next day decide you don't like what you did—you're stuck (unless you can dig out a copy of your original image). But if you'd used a *Hue/Saturation Adjustment layer* (page 217) to make the change instead, you could just throw out that layer and keep all your other edits. Pretty neat, huh? You can also use layers to combine parts of different photos, as shown in Figure 6-2.

FIGURE 6-2

Layers make it easy to combine elements from different images. Maybe you can't afford to send your grandparents on a real trip to China, but once you understand layers, you can give them a virtual vacation.

When you copy part of one photo into another image, as was done here, Elements automatically places the pasted-in material on its own layer. You don't have to do anything to create the layer—it just appears when you paste. (Page 219 has more about combining elements from different photos.)

Once you understand how to use layers, you'll feel much more comfortable making radical changes to images, since any mistakes will be simple to fix. Not only that, but by using layers, you also can easily make lots of sophisticated edits that are otherwise very difficult and time-consuming. But the main reason to use layers is for creative freedom: They let you easily add lots of special effects that would be tough to create any other way.

The Layers Panel

The Layers panel is your control center for any layer-related action you want to perform, like adding, deleting, or duplicating layers. Figure 6-3 shows the Layers panel for an image with lots of layers. It includes each layer's name and little thumbnails of the layers' contents. You can adjust the size of the thumbnails or even turn them off altogether, as explained in Figure 6-4.

The Layers panel usually contains one layer that's *active*, meaning that anything you do, like painting, will affect only that layer. You can tell which layer is active by looking at the Layers panel, where the active layer is highlighted in blue (see Figure 6-3).

FIGURE 6-3

Here's the Layers panel for the flyer in Figure 6-1.

Each row represents a separate layer.

An eye icon means that a layer is visible. To hide a layer—helpful if you want to see what you're doing while working on other layers—click its eye icon. Elements puts a red slash across the icon to indicate that the layer is hidden. To make the layer visible again, simply click the eye icon again.

It helps to keep the Layers panel handy whenever you work with layers, not only for the info it gives you, but also because you can usually manipulate layers more easily in the panel than directly in the image. And many changes, like renaming layers, you can make only in the panel.

Labels in figure:
- Layer mode
- Layer opacity
- Layer has style applied
- Active Layer
- Eye icon = layer visibility
- Layer name
- Layer mask
- Layer thumbnail
- Layer is partially locked

NOTE If you use the layer-selection tricks described on page 206, then you can wind up with multiple active layers or none, but you generally want to have only one active layer.

FIGURE 6-4

To change the size of the thumbnails in the Layers panel, open the panel's pop-out menu by clicking the little square in the panel's upper-right corner that's made up of horizontal lines. (If you're using the Custom Workspace [page 12], the square is above the trashcan icon.). At the bottom of the menu, choose Panel Options, and this dialog box appears. Here, medium-sized icons are selected.

If you change the Thumbnail Contents setting from Entire Document to Layer Bounds, you get a larger view of any objects surrounded by transparency: Elements enlarges the object as much as it can within the Layers panel's thumbnail without showing all the empty space around it. This is helpful for keeping track of objects in a file with lots of layers.

When you look at a layered image, you're looking down on the stack of layers from the top, just as if you were looking at overlays on a drawing. The layers appear in the same order as in the Layers panel—the top layer of your image is at the top of the panel. Layer order is important because what's on top can obscure what's beneath it.

Elements lets you perform lots of slick maneuvers in the Layers panel: You can make a layer's contents invisible and then visible again, change the order in which layers are stacked, link layers together, change layers' opacity, add and delete layers—the list goes on and on. The rest of this chapter covers all these options and more.

TIP The Layers panel is really important, so most people like to keep it around. In the Basic Workspace (page 10), doing so is easy: It's so important that it's the first of the panel buttons at the lower right of the Editor's main window. In the Custom Workspace (page 12), you can use any of the panel-management techniques described on page 17 to put the Layers panel where it's easy to get to while you work.

The Background

The bottom layer of any image is a special kind of layer called the *Background*. When you first open an image or photo in Elements, its one existing layer is named Background (assuming nobody has already edited the file in Elements and changed things, that is). The name Background is logical because whatever else you do will happen on top of this layer.

NOTE There are two exceptions to the first-layer-is-always-the-Background rule. First, if you create a new image by copying something from another picture, then you just have a layer named Layer 0. Second, Background layers can't be transparent, so if you choose the Transparency option when creating a file from scratch, then you have a Layer 0 instead of a Background layer.

As far as content, the Background can be totally plain or busy, busy, busy. A Background layer doesn't literally contain only the background of your photograph—your whole photo can be on a Background layer. It's entirely up to you what's on this layer, and what you place on other layers you add. With photographs, people often keep the original photo on the Background layer, and then perform adjustments and embellishments on other layers above it.

You can do a lot to Background layers, but there are a few things you *can't* do: change their blending modes (see page 198), opacity (page 196), or position in the layer stack. If you want to do any of those things, then you need to convert it into a regular layer first. To do so, double-click the Background layer in the Layers panel (or single-click its padlock icon), or go to Layer→New→Layer From Background. Or, if you try to make certain kinds of changes to the Background layer (like applying a layer style [page 461]), then Elements prompts you to change it into a regular layer. Don't be confused by the little lock icon on a Background layer in the Layers panel—you can still make almost any edit to it.

TIP When you click a Background layer with them, the Background Eraser and Magic Eraser tools automatically turn a Background layer into a regular layer. For example, say you have a picture of an object on a solid background and you want transparency around the object. One click with the Magic Eraser turns the Background layer into a regular layer, eliminates the solid-colored background, and replaces it with transparency. (There's more on the Eraser tools on page 416.)

You can also transform a regular layer into a Background layer if you want, but you need to start with an image that has no Background layer. It's unlikely that you'll ever need to do this in Elements, but, if you want to try it, here's how:

1. **In the Layers panel, click the layer you want to convert to a Background layer.**

2. **Select Layer→New→Background From Layer.**

   It may take a few seconds for Elements to finish calculating and respond. When it's done thinking, in the Layers panel, Elements moves the layer you changed down to the bottom of the layer stack and renames it Background.

NOTE If you create a Background layer from a masked layer (page 190), Elements permanently applies the layer mask to the image, since Background layers can't be masked.

Which File Types Can Use Layers?

You can add layers to any file you can open in Elements, but not every file format lets you *save* layers.

For instance, if your camera shoots JPEGs, you can open those JPEGs in Elements and add layers to them. But when you try to save these files, Elements presents you with the Save As dialog box instead of just saving. If you turn off the dialog box's Save Layers checkbox, a warning tells you that you have to save as a copy. That's Elements' way of telling you that you can't have layers in a JPEG file, so you need to save the image in another format to keep the layers.

You usually want to choose either Photoshop (.psd) or TIFF as your format when saving a layered image because they both let you keep layers. (PDF files can also have layers, but not PDFs you create in Elements.) But if you don't need the layers, then just save your JPEG as a copy, close the original file, and say No when Elements asks if you want to save your changes.

If someone using the full-featured Photoshop sends you a layered image, then you'll see the layers in the Layers panel when you open the file in Elements. Likewise, Photoshop folks can see layers you create in Elements.

If you open a Photoshop file with a layer that says "indicates a set" when you move your cursor over it in the Layers panel, that's what Photoshop calls a *layer group* or *layer set* (a way of grouping layers into what are essentially folders in the Layers panel), depending on which version of Photoshop created the file. Elements doesn't understand layer sets, so ask the sender to expand the sets and then send you the file again. Alternatively, you can use the Layer→Simplify command to convert the set to a single layer, which may or may not be editable. Or you can search the Internet for add-on toolsets (page 586) or look for scripts that will let you expand the set in Elements. Elements+ (page 586) is one option.

Creating Layers

As you learned earlier in this chapter, your image files don't automatically have multiple layers. Lots of newcomers to Elements expect the program to be smart enough to put each object in a photo onto its own layer, which is a lovely dream, but Elements isn't *that* brainy. To experience the joy of layers, you first need to add at least one layer to your image; you'll learn how in the next few sections.

> **TIP** It may help you to follow along through the next few sections, so open a photo of your own or create a new file to use for practice. (See page 39 for details on how to create a new file; if you go that route, choose a white background.) Or download either *gardenparty.psd* or *daisies.jpg* from this book's Missing CD page at *www.missingmanuals.com/cds*.

Adding Layers

Elements gives you several ways to add a new layer:

- Choose Layer→New→Layer.
- Press Shift+Ctrl+N/Shift-⌘-N.
- In the Layers panel, click the "Create a new layer" icon labeled in Figure 6-5.

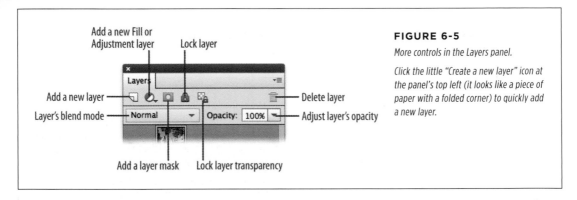

FIGURE 6-5

More controls in the Layers panel.

Click the little "Create a new layer" icon at the panel's top left (it looks like a piece of paper with a folded corner) to quickly add a new layer.

Add a new Fill or Adjustment layer

Lock layer

Add a new layer

Layer's blend mode

Delete layer

Adjust layer's opacity

Add a layer mask   Lock layer transparency

When you create a new layer by using any of these methods, the layer starts out empty. In other words, nothing in your image changes until you *use* the new layer for something (you paint on it, for example). In the Layers panel, the new layer appears just above the layer that was active when you added the new one. Elements always puts new layers directly above the active layer, so if you want a new layer at the top of the stack, click the current top layer to make it active before creating the new layer.

TIP The only practical limit to the number of layers you can have in a single document is your computer's processing power. But if you find yourself regularly creating projects with upward of 100 layers, you may want to upgrade to Photoshop, which has tools that make it easier to manage lots of layers.

As mentioned earlier, some things you do create new layers automatically. For instance, if you copy and paste an object from another photo (see page 219 for instructions) or add artwork from the Content panel, then the object automatically arrives on its own layer. That's really handy because it lets you put the new item right where you want it without disturbing the rest of your composition.

So why would you want to manually create new layers? One example is when you want to clone something (page 318). If you don't add a separate layer to clone on, then your changes go right onto your existing layer and become part of it; once you save and close the file, you can't undo any of that cloning. But if you put your changes on a separate layer, you can always go back and discard that layer if you change your mind. Elements doesn't automatically create a layer when you clone, so you have to add one yourself.

Deleting Layers

If you decide you don't want a particular layer anymore, you can easily delete it. Figure 6-6 shows the simplest method, although Elements also gives you a few other options:

- Select Layer→Delete Layer.

- Right-click/Control-click the layer in the Layers panel, and then choose Delete Layer.

- Click the button at the upper right of the Layers panel (the square made of horizontal lines), and then choose Delete Layer.

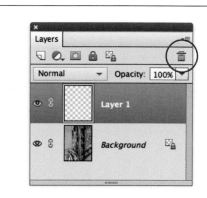

FIGURE 6-6

To get rid of a layer, either drag it onto the Layers panel's trashcan icon (circled) or activate the layer and then click the trashcan. If you use the latter technique, Elements asks whether you want to delete the active layer; click Yes and it's history.

After you delete a layer, as long as you haven't closed the file, you can get that layer back by using the Undo command (page 25). But once you close the file, the layer is gone forever.

Duplicating Layers

Creating a copy of a layer can be really useful. Many Elements features, like filters and color-modification tools, don't work on brand-new, *empty* layers. But if you apply such changes to your original photo layer, they alter it in ways you can't undo later. The workaround is to create a *duplicate* of the image layer and then make your changes on the copy. That way, you can ditch the duplicate later if you change your mind, and your original layer remains unchanged. If you use layer masks (page 210), you'll often duplicate existing layers while working with them.

If all this seems annoyingly theoretical, try activating a new, blank layer and then going to Enhance→Adjust Color→Adjust Hue/Saturation, for example. When you do that, you see the stern dialog box shown in Figure 6-7.

FIGURE 6-7

Elements is usually pretty helpful when you try to do something that just won't work, like applying a Hue/Saturation adjustment to an empty layer.

The solution here is just to switch the Layers panel's focus to a layer that has something in it.

TIP Very rarely, you may encounter the dreaded "no pixels are more than 50% selected" warning. Several things can cause this, but the most common are too large a feather value on a selection (see the box on page 152) or trying to work in the empty part of a layer that contains objects surrounded by transparency.

Elements gives you several ways to duplicate a layer and its content. In the Layers panel, click the layer you want to copy to make it active, and then do one of the following:

- Press Ctrl+J/⌘-J. (Be sure you don't have any active selections when you do this, or Elements copies only the *selection* to the new layer.)

- Choose Layer→Duplicate Layer.

- In the Layers panel, drag the layer you want to copy onto the "Create a new layer" icon.

- In the Layers panel, right-click the layer and, from the shortcut menu, choose Duplicate Layer.

- Click the little four-line square at the upper right of the Layers panel, and then choose Duplicate Layer.

All these methods copy everything in the active layer into the new layer. You can then mess with the duplicate as much as you want without damaging the original. Also, all of these methods except the keyboard shortcut and dragging onto the New Layer icon bring up a dialog box where you can name the new layer and even choose to use it in a new file or in another image (if you have more than one image open).

Copying and Cutting from Layers

You can also create a new layer that consists of only a *piece* of an existing layer. This is helpful when you want to do things like apply a layer style to one object on the layer. But first you need to decide whether you want to *copy* your selection or *cut* it out and place it on the new layer.

What's the difference? It's pretty much the same as copying versus cutting in your word-processing program. When you use the "New Layer via Copy" command (you'll learn where to find this command in a sec), the area you select appears in the new layer and remains in the old layer, too. "New Layer via Cut," on the other hand, removes the selection from the old layer and places it on the new layer, leaving a corresponding hole in the old layer. Figure 6-8 shows the difference.

FIGURE 6-8

The difference between cutting and copying is obvious when you move the new layer to see what's beneath it.

Left: With "New Layer via Copy," the original bird is still in place in the underlying layer.

Right: When you use "New Layer via Cut," the excised bird leaves a hole behind.

Naming Layers

You may have noticed that Elements isn't terribly creative when it comes to naming layers: You get Layer 1, Layer 2, and so on. Fortunately, you don't have to live with those names.

Renaming layers may sound like a job for people with way too much time on their hands, but if you're working on a project that has lots of layers, you may find it easier to pick out the layers you want if you give them descriptive names. (Incidentally, you can't rename a Background layer; you have to change it into a *regular* layer first. Also, Elements helps you out with Text layers by naming them using the first few words of text they contain.)

To rename a layer:

1. **Double-click its name in the Layers panel.** The name becomes an active text box.

2. **Type the new name.** You don't even need to highlight the text—Elements does that for you automatically.

As with any other change, you then have to save the image to keep the new layer name.

Once you've used one of the techniques described in Chapter 5 to select what you want to copy or cut, your new layer is only a couple of keystrokes away:

- **New Layer via Copy**. To copy your selection to a new layer, press Ctrl+J/⌘-J or go to Layer→New→"Layer via Copy." (If you don't select anything beforehand, then Elements copies your *whole* layer, making this a good shortcut for creating a duplicate layer.)

- **New Layer via Cut**. To cut your selection out of your old layer and put it on a new layer by itself, press Shift+Ctrl+J/Shift-⌘-J or go to Layer→New→"Layer via Cut." Just remember that this command leaves a hole in the original layer. (If you cut something from a Background layer, the hole is filled with your current background color.) If you want to cut and move *everything* on a layer, press Ctrl+A/⌘-A before you cut, although usually it's easier just to move the layer instead. To do that, drag the layer up or down the stack in the Layers panel until it's where you want it.

> **TIP** Elements gives you a quick way to use a layer as the basis for a new document. Instead of copying and pasting, you can create a new document by going to Layer→Duplicate Layer or by clicking the four-line square in the upper right of the Layers panel and choosing Duplicate Layer. Either way, you get a dialog box with a Document drop-down menu that lets you place the duplicate layer into the file you're currently working on, into any image currently open in the Editor, or into a new document of its own. You can also create a new document based on only *part* of a layer by selecting the area you want, pressing Ctrl+C/⌘-C to copy it, and then going to File→New→"Image from Clipboard."

◼ Managing Layers

The Layers panel lets you manipulate layers in all kinds of ways, but you need to understand a few more of the panel's cryptic icons. Some of the things you can do with layers may seem obscure when you first read about them, but once you actually use layers, you'll quickly see why these options exist. The next few sections explain how to manipulate layers in several different ways: Hide them, group them, change how they look, and combine them.

Hiding Layers

You can turn layers' visibility off and on at will, which is tremendously useful. For example, if the image you're working on has a busy background, it can be hard to see what you're doing when working on a particular layer. Hiding the Background layer can help you focus on the layer you're interested in. To turn off a layer's visibility, head over to the Layers panel and click the eye icon to the layer's left; the red slash through the icon tells you that a layer is hidden. To make the layer visible again, just click the eye icon again.

> **TIP** If you have a bunch of hidden layers and decide you don't want them anymore, click the Layers panel's upper-right button (the little four-line square) and choose Delete Hidden Layers to get rid of all of them at once.

Adjusting Layer Opacity

Your choices for layer visibility aren't limited to on and off. You can create immensely cool effects by adjusting the *opacity* of your layers. In other words, you can make a layer partially transparent so that what's underneath it shows through.

To adjust a layer's opacity, click the layer in the Layers panel, and then click the Layers panel's Opacity box and type the percentage you want. Alternatively, click the triangle to the right of the Opacity box and then drag the pop-out slider, or put your cursor on the word "Opacity" and *scrub* (drag) left for less opacity or right for more. (Figure 6-9 explains the advantage of scrubbing.) If you'd like to experiment with creating Fill and Adjustment layers (page 215) and changing their modes and opacity, download *daisies.jpg* from this book's Missing CD page at *www.missing manuals.com/cds*.

FIGURE 6-9

You can watch the opacity of your layer change on the fly if you drag your cursor back and forth over the word "Opacity."

You'll often get the best effect with blend modes (page 198) if you adjust the opacity of their layers.

In addition to letting you change the opacity of existing layers, Elements also lets you set the opacity of a layer when you create it (though you can change it later using the methods described above). When you create a layer by pressing Shift+Ctrl+N/ Shift+⌘+N or choosing Layer→New→Layer, you can set the new layer's opacity in the New Layer dialog box that appears. Alternatively, you can Alt-click/Option-click the Layers panel's New Layer icon to bring up the New Layer dialog box so you can set the opacity.

> **NOTE** You can't change a Background layer's opacity. If you want to do that, you first have to convert it to a regular layer; page 190 explains how.

Locking Layers

If you've gotten a layer just perfect and don't want to accidentally change it, you can *lock* it to protect you from yourself. Locking keeps you from changing a layer's contents.

To lock *everything* on a layer so you can't make any changes to it, make sure the layer is active, and then click the blue padlock at the top of the Layers panel. When you do, a matching blue padlock appears in the panel to the right of the layer's name, and Elements puts a dark-gray outline around the padlock icon at the top of the panel. Now if you try to paint on that layer or use any other tools on it, your cursor turns into a No symbol (a circle with a diagonal line through it) to remind you that you can't edit that layer. To unlock the layer, just activate it, and then click the blue padlock icon at the top of the panel again.

> **NOTE** Locking a layer only keeps you from *editing* that layer. It doesn't stop you from flattening it or merging it into another layer, or from cropping your image.

You can also lock only the *transparent* parts of a layer—helpful when you want to modify an object that sits atop a transparent layer, like the seashell in Figure 6-10. When you do that, the transparent parts of your layer stay transparent no matter what you do to the rest of it.

FIGURE 6-10

After isolating an object on its own layer, you may want to paint only on the object, for example, and not on the transparent part of the layer.

Left: On a regular layer, paint goes wherever your brush does.

Right: With the layer's transparency locked, the brushstroke stops at the edge of the seashell, even though the brush cursor (the circle) is on the transparent part of the layer.

To lock the transparent parts of a layer, activate the layer, and then, at the top of the Layers panel, click the "Lock transparent pixels" icon—the smaller blue padlock with a checkerboard next to it. (It's grayed out if the active layer doesn't have any transparent parts.) When you do, the same icon appears in the panel to the right of the layer's name, and Elements puts a gray border around the icon at the top of the panel. To unlock the layer, activate it in the Layers panel, and then click the padlock-and-checkerboard icon at the top of the panel again.

Blend Modes

At the top of the Layers panel is an unlabeled drop-down menu that's usually set to Normal (and, in the New Layer dialog box, there's a Mode menu that's usually set to Normal). This is your *blend mode* setting. When used with layers, blend modes control how the objects on a layer combine, or *blend*, with the objects on the layer(s) beneath them. By using different blend modes, you can make an image lighter or darker, or even make it look like a poster with just a few bold colors in it. Blend modes can also control how some tools—those with blend mode settings—change your image. Tweaking a tool's blend mode can sometimes dramatically change your results.

Blend modes are an awful lot of fun once you understand how to use them. They can help you fix under- or overexposed photos and create all kinds of special visual effects. You can also use some tools, like the Brush tool, in different blend modes to achieve different effects. The most common blend mode is Normal, in which everything you do behaves just the way you'd expect: An object shows its regular colors, and paint acts just like real-world paint.

Page 411 has lots more about how to use blend modes. For now, take a look at Figure 6-11, which shows how you can totally change the way a layer looks just by changing its blend mode.

FIGURE 6-11

This photo of cassia flowers has a Pattern Fill layer over it. (Page 215 has more about Fill layers.)

Here you see the effect of changing the pattern layer's blend mode. In Normal blend mode at 100 percent opacity, the pattern would completely hide the leaves, but by changing the blend mode and opacity of the pattern layer, you can create very different looks.

The modes shown here are Normal (top), "Linear Dodge (Add)" (bottom left), and Hard Mix (bottom right). Notice how "Linear Dodge (Add)" makes everything much lighter and Hard Mix produces a vivid, posterized effect.

Not every blend mode makes a visible change to every image; some of them may seem to do nothing. That's to be expected. It just means that you don't have a condition in your image that responds to that particular mode change. See page 267 for one example of a situation where a mode change makes an *enormous* difference.

Fading in Elements

One great thing you get in the full-featured Photoshop that Elements lacks is the ability to *fade* special effects and filters. Fading gives you fine control over how much these features change an image. For example, filters often generate harsh-looking results, so Photoshop's Fade command lets you adjust a filter's effect until it's what you intended.

Happily, you can approximate the Fade command in Elements: First, apply filters, effects, or layer styles to a duplicate of your original layer. Then, reduce the duplicate layer's opacity till it blends in with what's below (and change its blend mode, if necessary) to get exactly the result you want.

■ REARRANGING LAYERS

One of the truly amazing things you can do with Elements is move layers around. Changing the stacking order of layers lets you make different objects appear in front of or behind each other. For example, if you've got two objects and each is on its own layer, you can position one object behind the other. To do so, in the Layers panel, just grab a layer and drag it to where you want it.

> **TIP** Remember, you're always looking down onto the layer stack when you view your image, so moving something up in the Layers panel's list moves it toward the front of the picture.

Figure 6-12 shows the early stages of the garden party invitation from Figure 6-1. The potted plants are already in place, and the bench was brought in from another image. But the bench came in at the top of the layer stack, in front of the flowers. To put the bench behind the plants, simply drag the bench layer below the plants layer in the Layers panel.

> **NOTE** Background layers are the only kind of layer you can't move. If you want to put a Background layer in another spot in the layer stack, first convert it to a regular layer (page 190), and *then* move it.

You can also move layers by going to Layer→Arrange and choosing one of these commands:

- **Bring to Front** (Shift+Ctrl+]/Shift-⌘-]) sends the active layer to the top of the stack so the layer's contents appear in your image's foreground.

- **Bring Forward** (Ctrl+]/⌘-]) moves the layer up one level in the Layers panel so it appears one step closer to the front of your image.

- **Send Backward** (Ctrl+[/⌘-[) moves the layer down one level so it's one step farther back in the image.

FIGURE 6-12

Top: When you bring a new element into an image, it comes in on top of the active layer. In this case, that made the bench the front object.

Bottom: Move the new layer down in the Layers panel, and it appears behind the objects on layers above it. In this example, the bench moves behind the plants.

- **Send to Back** (Shift+Ctrl+[/Shift-⌘-[) puts the layer directly above the Background layer so it appears as far back as possible.

- **Reverse** (no keyboard shortcut) switches two layers' locations in the stack. You have to activate two layers (by Ctrl-clicking/⌘-clicking them in the Layers panel, for example—see the box on page 206) before using this command.

> **TIP** These commands (except Reverse) are also available from the Move tool's Tool Options or by right-clicking/Control-clicking in your photo when the Move tool is active. As a matter of fact, using the Move tool is a great way to rearrange layers, as the next section explains.

■ ARRANGING LAYERS WITH THE MOVE TOOL

You can use the Move tool to select and arrange layers right in the image window, without trekking over to the Layers panel. (If you need a refresher on Move tool basics, flip to page 182.)

Say you've got an image that has several different objects in it, and each object is on its own layer. To arrange layers with the Move tool:

1. **Activate the Move tool by clicking its icon in the Tools panel or pressing V.**

    You want the *regular* Move Tool, the one at the top left of the Tools panel's Select section, not the Content Aware Move tool.

2. **Choose the layer(s) you want to move.**

    As soon as you activate the Move tool, you see a bounding box (dotted lines with square handles) around the contents of the active layer in your image. As you move your cursor over the image, you see a blue outline around the object the cursor is over (if it's not on the active layer)—no matter how far down the layer stack the object's layer is (see the baseball in Figure 6-13). When you click an object to select the layer you want to move, a bounding box with square handles on it appears around the contents of that layer. (If there's more than one object on the layer, they all get included.) Shift-click to select objects on multiple layers, and the bounding box expands to include everything you've selected. You can also drag to create a selection around multiple objects and choose them that way. (For instance, in Figure 6-13, you could drag over both the balls and the mitt to move them as a group.)

3. **Move the layer(s).**

    You can do this by clicking the Tool Options area's Arrange icon, choosing Layer→Arrange, or right-clicking inside the bounding box in the image. Whichever method you use, you see all the choices described in the previous section ("Bring to Front," Bring Forward, and so on) except for Reverse, which is available only from the Layer menu. You can also use keyboard shortcuts (again, except for Reverse).

> **NOTE** If you select multiple layers, you may find that some of the arrange commands are grayed out (meaning you can't choose them). If that's a problem, just click elsewhere in the image to deselect the layers, and then move the layers one at a time instead of as a group.

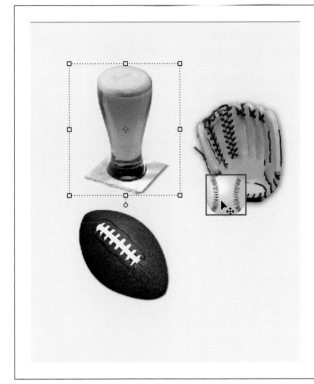

FIGURE 6-13

The Move tool lets you select objects that are on any layer, not just the active one.

When you move the cursor over an object, you see a blue outline around its layer. Here, the compass layer is active (you can tell by the bounding box around it), but the Move tool is ready to select the baseball (as indicated by the blue box around it), even though it's not on the active layer.

If all these outlines annoy you, you can get rid of them by heading to the Tool Options area and turning off the Show Bounding Box and "Show Highlight on Rollover" checkboxes. If you want to force the Move tool to concentrate only on the active layer, then turn off the Auto Select Layer checkbox, too.

Aligning and Distributing Layers

You can also use the Move tool to arrange objects in an image. The tool's *aligning* feature can arrange the items on each layer so that they line up straight along their top, bottom, left, or right edges, or through their centers. For example, if you align the top edges, then Elements makes sure that the top of each object is exactly in line with the tops of all the others.

TIP   Don't forget that you can add guidelines (page 87) to help position objects just so in an image. Also, the options in the View→Snap To submenu (Layers and Document Bounds) are very helpful for precise positioning; see the box on page 87 for details.

You'll also find it a breeze to evenly distribute the *spacing* between multiple objects. The Move tool's *distribute* feature spaces out objects based on their edges or centers. If you distribute the top edges, for example, Elements makes sure there's an even amount of space from the top edge of one object to another. Figure 6-14 shows examples of aligned and distributed guitars.

FIGURE 6-14

Top: Each of these guitars is on its own layer, but they need to be tidied up if you want them in a neat stack.

Bottom left: Here's the result of selecting the guitars with the Move tool and then picking Align→Center. As you can see, the guitars' centers are aligned, but they're not evenly distributed.

Bottom right: The same guitars after a trip to Distribute→Middle. Note that they're evenly spaced but still overlapping. That's because Distribute doesn't add any additional space between the outermost objects. If you want wider spacing between objects, then make sure they're farther apart before you distribute them.

NOTE Distributing objects is especially handy when you're creating projects like those described in Chapter 15.

Aligning and distributing layers with the Move tool works much like rearranging layers:

1. **Activate the Move tool by clicking its icon in the Tools panel or pressing V.**

   Like arranging layers, aligning and distributing work only with the regular Move tool, not with the Content Aware Move tool.

2. **Select the objects you want to align.**

   This maneuver works only if each object is on its own layer. So if you have multiple objects on one layer, move them to their own layers one at a time by selecting each object and then pressing Shift+Ctrl+J/Shift-⌘-J.

Once all the objects are on their own layers, Shift-click inside the blue outline that appears around each object when you put your cursor over it to activate each layer you want to work with, or Shift-click or Ctrl-click/⌘-click in the Layers panel to activate the layers you want.

3. **Choose how you want to align or distribute the objects by clicking the option you want in the Tool Options area.**

   The Align and Distribute sections both offer the same choices: Top, Center, Bottom, Left, Middle, and Right. The little thumbnails (each of which is actually a button) show you how your objects will line up. Just click the one that matches what you're going for. (You need to select at least three objects in order to use the Distribute commands.)

NOTE   You can apply as many different align and distribute commands as you like, as long as the layers you're working with are still active.

Linking and Clipping Layers

What if you want to move several layers at once? For instance, in the garden party image back on page 186, two layers contain potted plants in terra-cotta pots. If you want to move them both in front of the bench, it's kind of a pain to drag each plant layer individually. Fortunately, Elements gives you a way to keep your layers united, as this section explains.

■ LINKING LAYERS

Sometimes, you want to move a couple of layers as a group, while still keeping the layers separate. In that case, you can *link* two or more layers together so they travel as a unit, as shown in Figure 6-15.

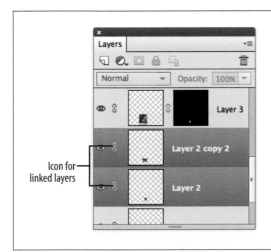

Icon for
linked layers

FIGURE 6-15

In the Layers panel, Shift-click or Ctrl-click/⌘-click to select the layers you want to link, and then click the little chain icon next to one of the layers' thumbnails to link them together. The chain icon turns orange on each of the linked layers to let you know they're connected.

To unlink them, simply click one of the linked layers in the Layers panel, and then click the chain icon again.

You can also merge layers (as explained in the next section) into one layer. Or you can use the layer-activation commands described in the box below and skip linking altogether; as long as the layers all stay selected, they travel as a group. But the advantage of linking is that the linked layers stay associated until you unlink them—you don't need to worry about accidentally clicking somewhere else in the panel and losing your layer grouping.

ORGANIZATION STATION

Activating Layers

You can quickly choose multiple layers when you want to do things like link, move, or delete layers. For your quick-activation pleasure, Elements gives you a whole group of layer-activation commands, which you'll find in the Select menu. Here's what they do:

- **All Layers**. Choose this command and Elements activates every layer *except* the Background layer. Even if you've turned off a layer's visibility (page 196), it still gets activated.

- **Deselect Layers**. When you're done working with layers as a group, pick this command and you won't have any layers activated until you click one.

- **Similar Layers**. This command is the most useful in the group. Choose it and Elements activates every layer

that's the same type as the currently active one, no matter where it is in the stack. For example, if you have a Text layer active when you choose Similar Layers, then Elements activates *all* the Text layers in the file you're working on. Or if you have an Adjustment layer active, it activates all the Adjustment layers. You can use this command to quickly activate a stack of Adjustment layers you want to drag to another image, for instance, using the technique described on page 219.

You can also Shift-click to activate multiple layers that are next to one another in the Layers panel, or Ctrl-click/⌘-click to activate layers that are separated. That way, you can avoid the Select menu altogether. Once you're done working with the layers you activated, you can either use the Deselect Layers command or just click another layer to make it the active one.

■ CLIPPING LAYERS TOGETHER

An even more powerful way to combine layers is to group them together using a *clipping mask*. This technique sounds complex, but it's actually quite easy and very powerful. With this kind of grouping, one layer (the clipping mask layer) influences the other layers it's grouped with.

> **NOTE** This technique used to be called "grouping," but starting with Elements 8, Adobe changed it to "clipping," which is what it's called in Photoshop. The behavior is exactly the same as the old grouped layers—only the name is different.

Clipping layers isn't anything like linking them. You can probably understand the process most easily by looking at Figure 6-16, which shows how to crop the image on one layer by using the shape of an object on another layer.

> **NOTE** If you clip two layers together, Elements applies the *bottom* layer's Opacity setting to both layers.

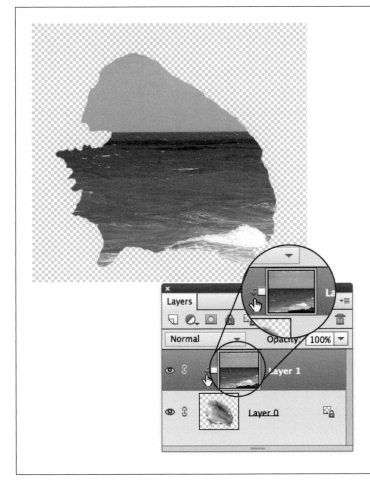

FIGURE 6-16

This image began life as a picture of a seashell on one layer and an ocean scene on the layer above it. Because the ocean layer was above the shell layer in the Layers panel, the ocean image totally hid the shell. But interesting things happen when you clip these layers together: The ocean layer automatically gets cropped to the shape of the seashell layer below it. The fancy way to say that is the shell now acts as the clipping mask for the ocean image.

In the Layers panel shown here, the tiny downward-bent arrow with the white square next to it (just above the cursor) indicates that the ocean layer is clipped.

Once the layers are clipped together, you can still slide the top layer around with the Move tool to reposition it so that you see exactly the part of it that you want. In Figure 6-16, for example, the ocean layer was positioned so the breaking wave appears at the bottom of the shell shape.

To clip two layers together, position them next to each other in the Layers panel by dragging. (Put the one you want to act as the mask *below* the other image.) Then make the top layer (of the two you want to clip) the active layer. Finally, choose Layer→Create Clipping Mask or press Ctrl+G/⌘-G.

NOTE You can clip more than two layers together at once as long as they're all next to each other in the Layers panel.

Here's another way to clip layers together: Hold down Alt/Option, and then, in the Layers panel, move your cursor over the dividing line between the layers you want to clip. When two linked circles appear by your cursor, click once and Elements clips those layers together with a clipping mask.

If you get tired of the layer grouping or want to delete or change one of the layers, then select one of the clipped layers and go to Layer→Release Clipping Mask or press Ctrl+G/⌘-G again to undo the grouping.

> **TIP** Elements gives you an even easier way to clip layers: The New Layer dialog box has a "Use Previous Layer to Create Clipping Mask" checkbox. Turn it on, and Elements pre-clips your new layer to the layer below it.

Merging and Flattening Layers

By now, you probably have some sense of how useful layers are. But there's a downside to having layers in an image: They take up a lot of storage space, especially if you have a bunch of duplicate layers. (In other words, layers make files bigger.) Fortunately, you don't have to keep layers in your files forever. You can reduce a file's size quite a bit—and sometimes also make things easier to manage—by merging layers and flattening images.

◼ MERGING LAYERS

You may sometimes have two or more separate layers that really could be treated as one layer, like the plants in Figure 6-1. Fortunately, you aren't limited to just linking those layers together; once you've got everything arranged just right, you can *merge* them together into a single layer, as shown in Figure 6-17. Also, if you want to copy and paste your image, standard Copy and Paste commands typically copy only the top active layer (if you have more than one layer active), so it helps to get everything into one layer—at least temporarily—by merging layers. You'll probably merge layers quite often when you're working with multilayer files; for example, when you've got multiple objects that you want to edit simultaneously.

You have a couple of different ways to merge layers, depending on what's active in your image. You can run either of the following commands by heading up to the Layer menu, clicking the Layers panel's upper-right button (the four-line square), or by using keyboard shortcuts:

- **Merge Down** (Ctrl+E/⌘-E) combines the active layer with the layer immediately beneath it. (If the layer just below the active layer is hidden, then you can't run this command.)

- **Merge Visible** (Shift+Ctrl+E/Shift-⌘-E) combines all the visible layers in the current document into one layer. If you want to combine layers that are far apart, then just temporarily hide the ones in between (and any other layers that you don't want to merge) by clicking their eye icons.

It's important to understand that once you merge layers and then save and close your file, you can't just unmerge them. While your file is still open, you can use any of the Undo commands, but once you exceed your history states limit (page 25), you're stuck with the merged layers.

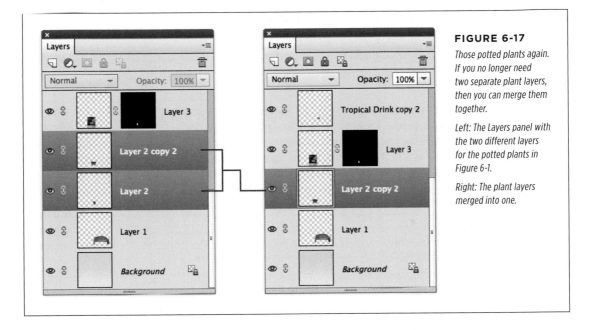

FIGURE 6-17

Those potted plants again. If you no longer need two separate plant layers, then you can merge them together.

Left: The Layers panel with the two different layers for the potted plants in Figure 6-1.

Right: The plant layers merged into one.

TIP The box on page 210 explains how to combine *all* your layers into one while still keeping separate copies of the individual layers.

Sometimes, when a layer contains text or shapes drawn with a shape tool, you can't merge that layer right away; Elements needs to *simplify* the layer first. Simplifying means converting its contents to a *raster object*—a bunch of pixels subject to the same resizing limitations as any photo. For example, after you rasterize a Text layer, you can apply filters to the text or paint on it, but you can't edit the words anymore. (See page 424 for more about simplifying and working with shapes, and Chapter 14 to learn about working with text.) Unlike Elements 10 and earlier, if you try to merge a layer that needs to be simplified first, Elements 13 doesn't ask you if you want to do this—it just *automatically* simplifies the layer and merges it with the others you activated before applying the Merge command.

■ **FLATTENING AN IMAGE**

Layers are simply swell when you're working on an image, but they're a headache when you want to share the file, especially if you're sending it to a photo-printing service (their machines usually don't understand layered files). Even if you're printing at home, the large size of a multilayer file can make it take forever to print. And if you plan to use your image in other programs, very few non-Adobe programs are totally comfortable with layers, so you may get some odd results.

In these cases, you can squash everything in your picture into a single layer. You do this by *flattening* your image: Go to Layer→Flatten Image or, in the Layers panel, click the four-line square and choose Flatten Image. Or, to keep your original intact, go to File→Save As, and in the Save As dialog box, turn *off* the Layers checkbox (which will turn *on* the "As a Copy" checkbox) before clicking the Save button.

> **TIP** Saving your image as a JPEG file automatically gets rid of layers, too.

There's no keyboard shortcut for flattening because it's something you don't want to do by accident. Like merging, flattening is a permanent change. Cautious Elements veterans always do a Save As (instead of a plain Save) before flattening. That way you have a flattened copy *and* a working copy with the layers intact, just in case. Organizer version sets (page 71) can help you here, too, because they let you save an image in different states, so you can have both a layered and a flattened version.

> **NOTE** Flattening creates a Background layer out of the existing layers in an image, which means that you lose transparency, just as with a regular Background layer. If you want to create a single layer *with* transparency, then use the Merge Visible command (page 208) instead.

POWER USERS' CLINIC

Stamp Visible

Sometimes you want to perform an action on all your image's visible layers without permanently merging them together. You can do this quickly and easily—even if your file contains dozens of layers—with the Stamp Visible command, which combines the contents of all your visible layers into a new layer at the top of the layer stack. Stamp Visible is great because it creates a new, combined layer that you can work on while leaving your existing layers untouched, in case you want them back later.

To use this command, make sure the top layer in your image is active, and then press Shift+Alt+Ctrl+E/Shift-Option-⌘-E or hold down Alt/Option while selecting the Merge Visible command from either the Layer menu or the Layers panel's menu (which you open by clicking the square made of four horizontal lines). However you run the command, Elements creates a new layer at the top of the Layers panel and fills it with the combined contents of all your other layers. To keep a layer or two from being included in this new layer, simply hide those layers before running Stamp Visible. You can also use Stamp Visible on only some of your layers. Just make sure the layers you want are all together at the bottom of the layer stack, and then click the top layer that you want included before pressing the shortcut keys mentioned above. When you do that, the Stamp Visible layer appears just above the layer you selected.

Layer Masks

Elements gives you an incredibly powerful tool for getting the most out of layers: *layer masks*.

What are they and why are they such a big deal? As their name implies, layer masks let you hide (or "mask") *parts* of layers. Back in Chapter 5, you learned about selecting parts of photos and using Refine Edge to cut objects out of an image, and earlier in this chapter you learned how to hide whole layers and to cut or copy something to a new layer. Those are all fine techniques, but if next week you change your mind about exactly what you want to include in your image, you have to start all over again. Wouldn't it be cool if you could just make the parts of your photo that you don't want vanish, and then make them reappear later on if you change your mind?

Layer masks let you do exactly that: They're like invisibility cloaks for layers, and it's totally up to you how much they cover. When you mask part of a layer, the visible part looks like an object that's been cut out and surrounded by transparency, but the rest of the layer is all still there—it's just hidden away. Plus, showing or hiding more of what's on the layer is as easy as painting on it, and there's no statute of limitations—you can come back to the layer and adjust things whenever you want. Figure 6-18 helps explain why this is such a great way to work.

 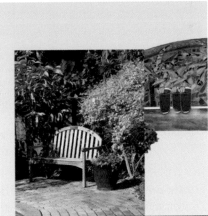

FIGURE 6-18

Left: Here's part of that flyer from Figure 6-1. The blue pot in the front looks right at home, doesn't it?

Right: The blue pot actually came from this photo. To isolate the pot, a layer mask was placed over the rest of the photo, hiding it. (The mask was turned off here to show you the original image.) If you wanted to, you could go back and edit the mask to reveal more of the photo or change what the mask covers if, say, you'd rather use one of the bushes behind the pot in your flyer instead.

In full Photoshop, layer masks have been *de rigueur* for all sorts of changes for years now because they're incredibly powerful and easy to use. The only downside to layer masks is that the extra content makes your file somewhat larger, but that's a small price to pay for so much flexibility.

NOTE   Adjustment and Fill layers (which you'll learn about in the next section) automatically come with layer masks already attached to them; you don't have to do anything to add them.

Layer masks are a tad confusing at first, but you'll quickly get the hang of them and learn how much they can do for you. The easy way to remember what they do is to think of them as Halloween masks for your layers: Whatever is behind the mask is hidden, and you can see everything that's not covered by the mask.

You can add a layer mask to any layer except a Background layer. Here's how:

1. **Make sure the layer you want to mask is active.**

   If it's not, click it in the Layers panel.

2. **Add a layer mask.**

   You have several choices for how the mask should start off:

   - **Empty, showing all the layer's contents.** To create a "blank" layer mask (in other words, one that starts out not covering anything in the layer), just click the "Add layer mask" icon at the top of the Layers panel (it looks like a circle within a square, as shown back in Figure 6-5) or choose Layer→Layer Mask→Reveal All. When you do, a pure white mask thumbnail appears in the Layers panel to the right of the active layer's thumbnail. (You can see an example of such a mask by flipping ahead to Figure 6-20.)

   - **Filled, completely hiding the layer.** To create a "full" layer mask that covers everything in the active layer, Alt-click/Option-click the "Add layer mask" icon in the Layers panel or choose Layer→Layer Mask→Hide All. Elements adds a black mask thumbnail to the Layers panel. You'd use this option if you wanted to hide most of the layer. That way, you can just reveal ("unmask") the areas you want visible, like the eyes and lips of a portrait, for example. That's faster than painting over everything else in the layer. (You'll learn how to edit layer masks in a moment.)

   - **With only a selection visible.** To hide all but certain areas of the active layer, select the parts you want to keep visible, and then click the "Add layer mask" icon or go to Layer→Layer Mask→Reveal Selection. Elements masks everything *but* your selection, leaving only the selected area(s) visible. You only see the selected area, but everything else is *still there*—it's just hidden.

   - **With only a selection hidden.** To hide only a few bits of the layer, select those parts and then Alt-click/Option-click the "Add layer mask" icon or go to Layer→Layer Mask→Hide Selection. Elements hides the selected area(s).

   TIP Remember, you can create masks and masked layers from selections right in the Refine Edge dialog box, too (page 156).

You'll learn how to edit the area covered by a mask in a moment, but first here are a few other useful things you can do with a layer mask:

   - **Disable it.** If you want to see your layer without the mask, in the Layers panel, just right-click/Control-click the mask's thumbnail and choose Disable Layer Mask, or go to Layer→Layer Mask→Disable. Everything that the mask was hiding reappears and Elements puts a big red X over the mask's thumbnail to remind you that it's disabled.

After you disable a layer mask, your menu choice changes to read "Enable" instead. Just choose it to toggle the mask back on.

- **Merge it into the layer**. If you decide that you don't ever need to edit a layer mask again, right-click/Control-click its thumbnail in the Layers panel, and then choose Apply Layer Mask (or go to Layer→Layer Mask→Apply), and the mask becomes a *permanent*, uneditable part of the layer it's attached to. Basically, doing this puts you in the same situation you'd be in if you used the "Layer via Copy" command or if you'd selected something and then deleted the rest of the layer (meaning you lose all the flexibility you get by using a layer mask), so this isn't something you'll do often.

- **Unlink it**. When you add a layer mask, a little chain appears in the Layers panel between the layer's thumbnail and the mask's thumbnail to indicate that they work as a unit. But if you unlink them, you can move the mask separately from the layer itself. This is handy when you've got a mask the size and shape of the area you want to see perfectly masked out, only it's not quite over the right part of the image. In that case, unlink the mask from the layer so you can drag the mask without moving the layer's contents. To do that, just click the chain icon between their thumbnails or go to Layer→Layer Mask→Unlink. The chain disappears and you can now use the Move tool to rearrange things. To relink them, click the spot where the chain icon was or choose Layer→Layer Mask→Link.

- **Delete it**. To get rid of a layer mask and return the layer to its unmasked state, right-click/Control-click the mask's thumbnail in the Layers panel and choose Delete Layer Mask, or go to Layer→Layer Mask→Delete.

■ EDITING A LAYER MASK

Now that you have a mask, it's time to learn how to change the area it covers. You do this by simply painting on it with black or white. Painting with black increases the *masked* area; painting with white increases the *visible* area. "Black conceals and white reveals" is an old Photoshop saw that helps remind you what each color does.

You can work on the mask by painting directly in the main image window, or make the layer mask visible and work in either of two special mask views, which are sometimes helpful when the objects in your image have tricky edges, or if you need to check for missed spots. Here's the simplest way to make changes to the area covered by a layer mask:

1. **Make sure the masked layer is active.**

   If it isn't, click it in the Layers panel. This step is important: If the masked layer isn't active, you'll add paint to the image rather than the mask.

2. **In the Layers panel, click the layer mask's thumbnail.**

   You tell Elements whether you want to work directly on the layer or on the layer *mask* by clicking the thumbnail of the one you want. (You can tell which one is active because Elements puts an extra little outline around its thumbnail.) As soon as you click the mask's thumbnail, your foreground and background color squares change to white and black. Press X to swap the colors, if necessary, or just press D if for some reason you don't see black and white.

3. **Paint directly on your image.**

   Use the Brush tool (page 396; keyboard shortcut: B) to paint on the image. Paint an area black to hide it or white to show it. Remember: Black conceals and white reveals. (An easy way to switch between your foreground and background colors is to press X.)

   You can also use the selection tools the same way you would on any other selection to change the mask's area. (See Chapter 5 if you need help making selections.) If you watch the layer mask's thumbnail in the Layers panel, you'll see that it changes to show where you've painted. This mask thumbnail is the only place where you actually see black or white paint appear. In your image itself, you just see more or less of what's in the photo, depending on which color paint you're using. (If you *do* see black or white paint appearing in your image, press Ctrl+Z/⌘-Z to undo it and go back to step 2 again.)

> **TIP** You can use shades of gray to adjust a layer mask's transparency. Simply paint on the mask with gray to change the opacity of the area revealed on the layer. The darker the gray, the less of what you paint over shows through the mask; the lighter the gray, the more of what you're painting shows through. Paint with dark gray, for example, for a faint, ghosted effect, the sort of thing you might use to create a background for stationery.

To make a layer mask visible in the main image window (rather than just as a thumbnail in the Layers panel), you simply click it in the Layers panel while holding down certain key combinations. Elements gives you a choice of two different ways to see the masked area, as shown in Figure 6-19. If you Alt-click/Option-click the mask's thumbnail, you see the black-and-white layer mask (instead of your photo) in the image window. Add the Shift key when you click to see a red overlay on the photo instead. Press the same keys again while clicking the mask's thumbnail (or just click the thumbnail of the layer the mask is attached to) to get back to a regular view of your image.

The black-and-white mask view shows only the mask itself, not your photo beneath it. This is a good choice when you want to check how clean the edges of your selection are. But if you're adding or subtracting areas of your photo, use the red-overlay view instead so you can see the objects in your photo as you paint over them. You can use the method described earlier to paint in either view.

FIGURE 6-19

Here are two different views of the layer mask from Figure 6-18.

Left: To see the masked area in black and the unmasked area in white, Alt-click/Option-click the layer mask's thumbnail in the Layers panel.

Right: To see a red overlay atop the masked area, Alt+Shift-click/Option-Shift-click the mask's thumbnail instead.

Layer masks are incredibly powerful, and this section covered only the very basics, but there are literally *thousands* of different uses for them. For instance, you can paint the edges of a photo with grunge brushes to create interesting borders, or apply a black-to-white gradient to a layer mask to make the layer fade on one edge. There are entire books written about masking techniques, and once you get started you'll want to explore more ways you can use this powerful feature to help your creativity soar. To learn how to mask a particular object (like hair, say), just Google "mask hair photoshop" and you'll get more tutorials than you could work through in a lifetime. Katrin Eismann's *Photoshop Masking & Compositing* (New Riders Press) is one of the most complete books on the subject, although a fair amount of the book (like the parts about using the Pen tool) pertains only to Photoshop.

TIP　Full Photoshop also has another kind of mask, called the Quick Mask. If you try a tutorial written for Photoshop that calls for Quick Mask, just use Elements' Selection Brush in Mask mode instead.

■ Adjustment and Fill Layers

Adjustment layers and *Fill layers* are special types of layers. Adjustment layers let you manipulate the lighting, color, or exposure of the layers beneath them. If you're mainly interested in using Elements to spruce up photos, then you'll probably use Adjustment layers more than any other kind of layer. They're great because they let you undo or change your edits later on.

You can also use Adjustment layers to take the changes you've made to one photo and apply those same changes to another photo (see the box on page 216). And after you've created an Adjustment layer, you can limit future edits so they change only the area of the photo affected by the Adjustment layer. You'll find out about all the things you can do with Adjustment layers in the next few chapters. This section simply explains how to create and manipulate them.

Fill layers are exactly what they sound like: layers filled with a color, pattern, or *gradient* (a rainbow-like range of colors—see page 465). Fill layers are great when you've cut an object out of its original image and want to put some color behind it, for example.

One cool thing about both Adjustment and Fill layers is that they automatically come with layer masks, as shown in Figure 6-20.

FIGURE 6-20

Adjustment and Fill layers, like the Hue/Saturation Adjustment layer shown here, always display two things in the Layers panel: an icon on the left and a thumbnail on the right. The thumbnail represents the layer's layer mask, which you can use to control the area that's affected by the adjustment. As for the icons, each type of Adjustment layer and Fill layer has its own unique icon.

With Adjustment layers, just click the layer you want to change to make it the active layer, and then go to the Adjustments panel to tweak things. With Fill layers, double-click the layer's icon to bring up a dialog box where you can change the layer's settings.

> **TIP** Digital photographers should check out Photo Filter Adjustment layers, which let you make the sort of adjustments to photos that used to require you to put a colored piece of glass over your camera's lens. See page 299 for more info.

GEM IN THE ROUGH

Adjustment Layers for Batch Processing

Page 306 shows you how to perform *batch* commands—that is, simultaneously applying adjustments to groups of photos using the Process Multiple Files command. The drawback to that command is that it gives you access to only some of Elements' Auto commands, so your editing options are really limited.

So what do you do if you're a fussy photographer who's got 17 shots that are all pretty much the same and you'd like to apply the same fixes to all of them—do you have to edit each

one from scratch? Nope. Simply open the photos you want to fix, and then drag the Adjustment layer you used on the first photo onto each of the other photos. (Page 219 shows you how to drag layers between images.) That way, each photo gets the same adjustments at the same settings. It's not as fast as true batch processing, but it takes a lot less time than editing each photo from scratch.

Adding Fill and Adjustment Layers

Creating an Adjustment or Fill layer is easy: In the Layers panel, click the half-blue/half-white circle to display the menu shown in Figure 6-21. The menu includes all your Adjustment and Fill layer options (the first three items are Fill layers; the rest are Adjustment layers).

FIGURE 6-21

To create a new Adjustment or Fill layer, click the half-blue/half-white circle to see this menu, and then pick the type of layer you want.

If you'd rather work from the menu bar, then go to Layer→New Adjustment Layer (or Layer→New Fill Layer) and choose a type.

■ FILL LAYERS

Elements can create three types of Fill layers: Solid Color, Gradient (a rainbow-like range of colors—see page 468), and Pattern (page 324 has more about patterns). When you create a Fill layer, Elements displays a dialog box where you can tweak the layer's settings. After you make your choices, click OK, and the new layer appears.

You can change a Fill layer's settings later by selecting it in the Layers panel and then going to Layer→Layer Content Options or, in the Layers panel, double-clicking the layer's left-hand icon. Either way, the layer's dialog box reappears so you can tweak its settings.

■ ADJUSTMENT LAYERS

When you create an Adjustment layer, the layer appears in your image, and the Adjustments panel appears so you can tweak the layer's settings (Figure 6-22). (The exception is the Invert Adjustment layer—if you create one of those, you see the Adjustments panel but it doesn't include any settings you can change.) Confusingly, you won't see the word "Adjustments" at the top of this panel; instead, the heading reflects the *type* of Adjustment layer you added: Levels, Hue/Saturation, or whatever. The exact settings in the panel also depend on the type of Adjustment layer you added. In Basic mode, the Adjustments panel is always floating—you can't put it into the Panel Bin.

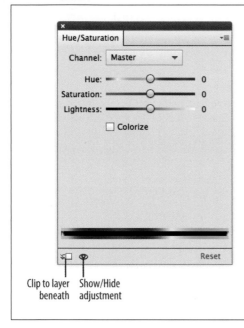

FIGURE 6-22

The Adjustments panel appears when you create a new Adjustment layer. The name at the top of the panel matches the type of layer you added (here, a Hue/Saturation Adjustment layer was added).

The icons at the panel's bottom let you view your image with and without the Adjustment layer, so you can judge how you're changing things. You can also clip the Adjustment layer to the layer beneath it in the Layers panel, or unclip it (see page 208).

Clip to layer beneath   Show/Hide adjustment

The Adjustments panel is really handy because it lets you see the settings for any Adjustment layer anytime. In the Layers panel, just double-click the left-hand icon of the Adjustment layer you want to change, and Elements displays the Adjustments panel showing the settings for that layer.

Elements lets you add the following kinds of Adjustment layers:

- **Levels**. This is a much more sophisticated way to apply levels than using the Auto Levels button in Quick Fix or the Enhance menu's Auto Level command. For most people, Levels is *the* most important type of Adjustment layer. Page 243 has more about using levels.

- **Brightness/Contrast**. This does pretty much the same things as the Quick Fix adjustment (covered on page 131).

- **Hue/Saturation**. Again, this is much like the Quick Fix command (page 133), only with slightly different controls.

- **Gradient Map**. This one is tricky to understand and is explained in detail on page 475. It maps each tone in your image to a new tone based on the gradient you select. That means you can apply a gradient so that the colors aren't just distributed in a straight line across your image.

- **Photo Filter**. Use this type of layer to adjust the color balance of photos by adding warming, cooling, or special-effects filters, just like you might attach to the lens of a film camera. See page 299 for more info.

- **Invert**. This Adjustment layer reverses the colors in your image to their opposite values, for an effect similar to a film negative; page 347 has details.

- **Threshold**. Use this kind of layer to make everything in a photo pure black or white (with no shades of gray). See page 347.

- **Posterize**. This one reduces the number of colors in an image to create a poster-like effect, as explained on page 347.

You can edit an Adjustment layer's layer mask the same way you edit any other layer mask (page 213). The only difference is what happens when you edit the mask: Instead of showing or hiding the objects in your photo, you show and hide the adjustment's *effects*, since this kind of a layer contains an adjustment instead of an image.

You delete Adjustment and Fill layers the way you delete any other layer. Simply drag the layer to the Layers panel's trashcan and it's gone. You can also click the Layer menu, right-click the layer in the Layers panel, or click the Layers panel's upper-right menu button (the square made of four horizontal lines); all these routes give you a Delete Layer option.

Moving Objects Between Images

Layers let you easily combine parts of different photos. If you're using tabs (page 97), the simplest way to do this is by copying and pasting: Select what you want to move (press Ctrl+A/⌘-A if you want to move the whole photo), and then press Ctrl+C/⌘-C to copy it. Next, make the destination image active by double-clicking it in the Photo Bin, and then press Ctrl+V/⌘-V to paste. The pasted material comes in on its own layer, and you can then use the Move tool to rearrange it in its new home.

> **TIP** You can also use the new Photomerge Compose feature to move a person or object from one photo to another. It's a lot more complicated than the method described here, but it gives you the option to adjust the lighting of the two images after combining them. Page 379 explains how to use Photomerge Compose.

You can also move objects between images by dragging. To do this, you need to choose one of the tiled views if you're using tabs (page 97), or Tile or Cascade (Window→Images→Tile or Cascade) if you're using floating windows (page 97). Just put what you want from Photo A into its own layer, and then drag it onto Photo B. You can use the Move tool to move the object from one image to another, or simply drag it. The trick is that you have to drag the layer from Photo A's *Layers panel*. If you try to drop one photo directly onto another photo's window, then you'll just wind up with a lot of windows stacked on top of one another. Figure 6-23 shows how to execute this maneuver.

Photo A   Photo B

Outline shows where
you are going

FIGURE 6-23

The goal here is to get the silverware from Photo A (whose Layers panel is visible) onto the tablecloth in Photo B. When combining parts of different images, you always drag from the Layers panel onto a photo window. (If you try to drag a photo onto a photo, it won't work unless you activate the Move tool first.) When you do this, you may see a shadowy version of what was in the Layers panel for Photo A (as shown here) or just the little clutching hand cursor and no outline at all, depending on your operating system.

Once you've dropped the object onto the other image, use the Move tool to reposition it, if necessary.

TIP You can also drag a photo directly from the Photo Bin onto another image. However, doing so places the dragged layer as a Smart Object, which means you can enlarge or shrink the layer as much as you want, but you'll have to simplify the layer to make certain other edits to it. There's more about Smart Objects on page 517.

But what if, rather than moving a whole layer, you just want to move a particular *object* to another photo? Just follow these steps:

1. **Open both photos in Expert mode.**

   You can pull off this maneuver in a tabbed view, but most people find it easier to use floating windows. To use floating windows, first go to Edit→Preferences→General/Photoshop Elements Editor→Preferences→General and make sure that "Allow Floating Documents in Expert Mode" is turned on. Next, go to Window→Images→"Float All in Windows," and then go back to Window→Images and choose Tile or Cascade.

If you want to use tabs instead, go to the Layout menu below the Photo Bin and choose a layout that gives you a view of all your images.

2. **Prepare both photos for combining.**

Go to Image→Resize→Image Size, and then make sure both photos have the same Resolution (ppi) setting (see page 105 for a refresher on resizing and resolution). Why? If one photo is way bigger than the other, then the moved object could easily blanket the entire target image.

You don't absolutely *have* to do this size balancing, but it'll make your life a lot easier, since it helps avoid having an enormous or tiny pasted object. (Keep reading for more advice about resolution when moving objects and layers.)

3. **Select what you want to move.**

Use the selection tool(s) of your choice (see Chapter 5), and add a 1- or 2-pixel feather to the selection to avoid a hard, cut-out looking edge.

4. **Move the object.**

There are several ways to move what you selected to the other image:

- **Copy and paste.** Press Ctrl+C/⌘-C to copy the object from the first photo. Next, click the second photo to make it active, and then press Ctrl+V/⌘-V to paste what you copied.

- **Use the Move tool.** Press V to activate the regular Move tool, and then drag the selection to the other photo. As you're moving, you may see a hole in the original where the selection was, but as long as you keep your mouse button pressed till you get over the second photo, Elements fills the hole back in after you let go of your mouse. (If seeing this hole bothers you, just Alt-drag/Option-drag to move a *copy* of the selection instead.) It would be nice if you could use the Content Aware Move tool for this technique, but unfortunately you can't.

- **Drag the layer.** If the object you want to move is already on its own layer and surrounded by transparency, then you can just drag the layer from the first photo's Layers panel into the destination photo's main image window or tab.

No matter which method you use, Elements puts whatever you moved on its own layer in the combined image.

5. **If necessary, use the Move tool to position or resize the transported object, as shown in Figure 6-24.**

See page 182 for more about using the Move tool.

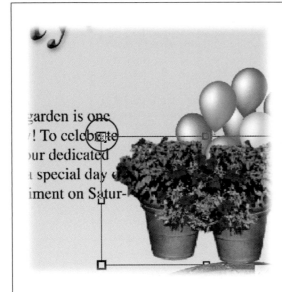

FIGURE 6-24

If you forget to balance out the relative sizes and resolutions of the photos you're combining, then you can wind up with a giant object in your photo, like these flowers.

The solution is simple: Just activate the Move tool and then Shift-drag a corner of the oversized item's resizing box (circled). (You may need to drag the new object around a bit in order to expose a corner.)

Don't forget that you can use all the Move tool's features (page 202) on your new object.

6. **Save your work.**

   If you may want to make further adjustments to the object you moved, then save the combined image as a TIFF or Photoshop (.psd) file to keep the layers. (Remember that if you save it as a JPEG, then you lose the layers and you can't easily change or move the new object anymore.)

Here are a few things to keep in mind when copying from one image to another:

- **Watch out for conflicting resolution settings (see page 105)**. The destination image (that is, the one receiving the moved layer or object) controls the resolution. So if you bring in a layer that's set to 300 pixels per inch (ppi) and place it on an image that's set to 72 ppi, then Elements sets the object you're moving to 72 ppi; its overall apparent size will increase proportionately as the pixels get spread out more.

- **Lighting matters**. Objects that are lit differently stand out if you try to combine them. If possible, plan ahead and use similar lighting for photos you're thinking about combining. You may want to check out the new Photomerge Compose feature, which lets you move objects from one photo to another and then adjusts the lighting for you.

- **Center the moved layer**. If you're dragging a layer and want Elements to center it in the new image, then Shift-drag the layer.

- **Feather with care**. A little feathering (page 152) goes a long way toward creating a realistic combined image.

- **Watch your settings**. When you move an object from one image to another, it keeps the blend mode and opacity it had in the first image. For example, if you drag over an object that was at 40% opacity and in Dissolve mode, it will have those same settings in the new image, so you may need to make adjustments.

TIP If you'd like more practice using layers and moving objects between photos, visit this book's Missing CD page at *www.missingmanuals.com/cds* and download the table tutorial, which walks you through most of Elements' basic layer functions.

Retouching

CHAPTER 7:
Basic Image Retouching

CHAPTER 8:
Elements for Digital Photographers

CHAPTER 9:
Retouching: Fine-Tuning Images

CHAPTER 10:
Removing and Adding Color

CHAPTER 11:
Photomerge: Creating Panoramas, Group Shots, and More

Basic Image Retouching

You may be perfectly happy using Elements only in Quick Fix mode. That's fine, as long as you understand that you've hardly scratched the surface of what the program can do. Sooner or later, you'll probably run across a photo where your best Quick Fix efforts just aren't enough. Or maybe you're simply curious what else Elements has under its hood. That's when you finally get to put all your image-selecting and layering skills to good use.

Elements gives you loads of ways to fix photos beyond the limited options in Quick Fix. This chapter guides you through fixing basic exposure problems, shows you various ways of sharpening photos, and (most importantly) explains how to improve the colors in your images. You'll also learn how to use the amazing Smart Brush tool that lets you apply many common fixes by brushing over the problem area.

To get the most out of Elements, you need to understand a little about how your camera, computer, and printer think about color. Along with resolution (page 105), color is one of the most important concepts in Elements. After all, almost all the adjustments that image-editing programs make involve changing the color of pixels. So quite a bit of this chapter is about understanding how Elements—and by extension, you—can manipulate the color in images.

> **TIP** Most of Elements' advanced-fix dialog boxes have a Preview checkbox that lets you watch what's happening as you adjust the settings. It's a good idea to keep these checkboxes turned on so you can decide whether you're improving things. And for a handy "before" and "after" comparison, simply toggle the checkbox on and off.

▉ Fixing Exposure Problems

Incorrectly exposed photos are *the* number one problem photographers face. No matter how carefully you set up a shot and how many different settings you try on your camera, it always seems like the picture you want to keep is the one that's over- or underexposed.

The Quick Fix commands (page 128) can really help photos, but if you've tried using them to bring back a picture that's badly exposed, you've probably run into the limitations of what Quick Fix can do. Similarly, the Shadows/Highlights command (page 230) can do a lot, but it's not intended to fix a photo whose exposure is totally botched—just ones where the contrast between light and dark areas needs a bit of help. And if you push Smart Fix (page 128) to its limits, the results may be a little strange. In those situations, you need to move on to some of Elements' more powerful tools to help improve the image's exposure.

> **TIP** In this section, you'll learn about the more traditional ways of correcting exposure in Elements, as well as how to use the Smart Brush tool for corrections. But be sure to also check out the Adobe Camera Raw Converter (page 272), which can help with your JPEG and TIFF images, too. Your results with non-raw photos may vary, but the Raw Converter just might turn out to be your best choice.

UP TO SPEED

Understanding Exposure

What exactly *is* exposure, anyway? You almost certainly know a poorly exposed photo when you see one: It's either too light or too dark. But what precisely has gone wrong?

Exposure refers to the amount of light your film (or the sensor in your digital camera) received when you released the shutter. A properly exposed photo shows details in *all* parts of the image—light and dark. Shadows in such images aren't just pits of blackness, and bright areas are more than washed-out splotches of white.

Deciding Which Exposure Fix to Use

When you open a poorly exposed photo in Elements, the first thing to do is figure out what's wrong with it, just like a doctor diagnosing a patient. If the exposure isn't right, what exactly is the problem? Here's a list of common symptoms to help figure out what to do next:

- **Everything is too dark**. If your photo is really dark, try adding a Screen layer, as explained on page 230. If it's just a bit too dark, try using Levels (page 243).

- **Everything is too light**. If the whole photo looks washed out, try adding a Multiply layer (page 230). If it's just a bit too light, try Levels (page 243).

- **The photo is mostly OK, but the subject is too dark or the light parts of the photo are too light**. Try the Shadows/Highlights command (page 230) or the Smart Brush tool (page 233).

- **You just can't decide quite what the problem is**. Try Auto Smart Tone (page 142), which adjusts the overall tone of your photo as you drag around a grid.

If you're lucky (or a really skilled photographer), you may not see any of these problems, in which case, skip to page 243 if you want to make the image's colors pop. And if you're lucky enough to have *bracketed* exposures (multiple exposures of exactly the same image), then check out the Exposure Merge feature (page 292), which makes it simple to blend them into one properly exposed image.

> **NOTE** You may have noticed that Brightness/Contrast (page 131) wasn't mentioned in the preceding list. A lot of people jump for the Brightness/Contrast controls when facing a poorly exposed photo. That's logical—after all, these settings can usually help improve the picture on your TV or monitor. But in Elements, about 99 percent of the time, you've got a whole slew of powerful tools—like Levels and the Shadows/Highlights command—that can do much more than Brightness/Contrast can, but feel free to give Brightness/Contrast a try when you need to make only very subtle changes.

Fixing Major Exposure Problems

If your photo is completely over- or underexposed, you need to add special layers to correct the problem. You follow the same steps to fix either issue; the only difference is the layer blend mode (page 98) you use: *Multiply* darkens an image's exposure while *Screen* lightens it. Figure 7-1 shows Multiply in action and gives you a sense of the limitations of this technique if your photo's exposure is *really* far gone.

FIGURE 7-1

In photography terms, each Multiply layer you add is roughly equivalent to stopping your camera down one f-stop, at least as far as the dark areas are concerned.

Left: This photo is totally overexposed, and it looks like there's no detail there at all.

Right: Multiply layers darken things enough to bring back a lot of the washed-out areas and bring out quite a bit of detail. But as you can see, even Elements can't do much in areas where there's no detail at all, like the sky and the white framing around these windows.

If you'd like to try this exposure fix yourself, download brickwindow.jpg from this book's Missing CD page at www.missingmanuals.com/cds.

Be careful, though: If only part of your photo is out of whack, using a Multiply or Screen layer can ruin the exposure of the parts that were OK to start with, because these layers increase or decrease the exposure of the *whole* photo. So if the exposure problem doesn't affect the entire image, try the Smart Brush (page 233) or Shadows/Highlights command (page 230) instead. Or use a layer mask to restrict the Multiply or Screen layer's changes to only part of the image, as explained in step 4 next.

If the whole photo needs an exposure correction, here's how to use layers to fix it:

1. **Duplicate your image layer.**

   Open your photo and press Ctrl+J/⌘-J or go to Layer→Duplicate Layer. Check to be sure the duplicate layer is the active layer.

2. **In the Layers panel, change the new layer's blend mode.**

   From the drop-down menu in the panel's upper left, choose Multiply if the photo is overexposed or Screen if it's underexposed. (Make sure you change the *duplicate* layer's mode, not the original layer's.)

3. **If needed, adjust the layer's opacity.**

   If the effect of the new layer is too strong, then at the top of the Layers panel, lower its Opacity setting.

4. **If you decide that part of the image was better exposed *before* you added the new layer, mask out the areas where the exposure was OK.**

   Follow the instructions on page 210 to add a mask to the duplicate layer, and then paint with black over the areas where the original image was properly exposed so that the Background layer shows through. Remember that you can also paint on the mask with shades of gray to control how *much* of the original shows through, which can be very helpful in getting the most realistic results from this technique.

5. **Repeat as necessary.**

   You may have to use as many as five or six layers if your photo is in really bad shape. If you need extra layers, you'll probably want them at 100 percent opacity, so you can just keep pressing Ctrl+J/⌘-J to duplicate the current top layer, including its layer mask (if you added one).

   You're more likely to need several more layers to fix overexposure than underexposure. And there are limits to what Elements can do for a blindingly overexposed image. Overexposure is usually tougher to fix than underexposure, especially if the area is blown out (see the box on page 231).

The Shadows/Highlights Command

This command is one of Elements' best features. It's incredibly powerful for adjusting only the dark or light areas of a photo without messing up the rest of it. Figure 7-2 shows what a great help it can be.

Avoiding Blowouts

An area of a photo is *blown out* when it's so overexposed that it appears plain white—in other words, your camera didn't record any data at all for that area. (Elements isn't great with total underexposure—pure black—either, but that doesn't happen quite as often. Most underexposed photos have *some* tonal gradations in them, even if you can't see them very well.)

A blowout is as disastrous in photography as it is when you're driving. Even Elements can't fix blowouts, because there's no data for it to work with. So you're stuck with the fixes discussed in this chapter, which are never as good as a properly exposed original.

When you're taking pictures and choosing camera settings, remember that it's generally easier to correct underexposure than overexposure. So if you live where there's really bright sunlight most of the time, you may want to make a habit of backing your exposure compensation down a hair. Depending on your camera, subject, and the average ambient glare, try starting with the exposure compensation set at –.3 and adjusting from there. (Dig out your camera's manual to find out how to do that.)

You can also try *bracketing* shots—taking multiple photos of exactly the same subject with different exposure settings. Then you can combine several exposures for maximum effect using Elements' Exposure Merge feature (page 292).

FIGURE 7-2

The Shadows/Highlights command can bring back details in photos where you were sure there was no info at all—but sometimes at a cost.

Left: The sky and the grass aren't bad, but you'd never know there were oranges on these trees.

Right: A dose of Shadows/Highlights unearths plenty of details, though the overall effect is a bit flat when you push this command this far. This photo needs more work, but at least now you can see what kind of trees these are.

The Shadows/Highlights command in Expert mode works pretty much the same way it does in Quick Fix (page 132). The single flaw in this great feature is that you can't apply it as an Adjustment layer (page 215), so you may want to apply it to a duplicate layer rather than the original. That way, you can discard the changes later on if you want to take another whack at adjusting the photo. In any case, it's easy to make amazing changes to your photos with Shadows/Highlights. Here's how:

1. **Open a photo and duplicate the image layer (Ctrl+J/⌘-J) if you want to.**

   If you haven't edited the photo before, the image layer is probably the Background layer, but you can use this command on any layer. Duplicating the image layer makes it easier to undo Shadows/Highlights later if you change your mind.

2. **Go to Enhance→Adjust Lighting→Shadows/Highlights.**

   Elements opens the Shadows/Highlights dialog box and makes your photo several shades lighter. (You may need to drag the dialog box out of the way to get a good view of your image.) Don't panic—as soon as you select this command, the Lighten Shadows setting automatically jumps to 35 percent, which is way too much for most photos. Just shove the slider back to 0 to undo this change before you start making corrections.

3. **Adjust the sliders in the Shadows/Highlights dialog box until you like the result.**

   The sliders do exactly what they say: Lighten Shadows makes the dark areas of the photo lighter, and Darken Highlights makes the light areas darker. (Midtone Contrast is discussed in a moment.) Dragging the sliders to the right increases their effect.

4. **When your photo looks good, click OK.**

> **TIP** If you're applying Shadows/Highlights on a duplicate layer, you can use a layer mask (page 210) to restrict your changes to only certain areas of the image.

The Shadows/Highlights dialog box is a cinch to use because you just make decisions based on what you're seeing. When you're using it, keep these tips in mind:

- **You may want to add a smidgen of the opposite tool to balance things out.** For example, if you're lightening shadows, you may get better results by giving the Darken Highlights slider a teeny nudge, too.

- **The Midtone Contrast slider can help keep your photo from looking flat after you adjust the other sliders, especially if you've made big adjustments.** Move the Midtone Contrast slider to the right to increase the photo's contrast. Doing so usually adds a bit of darkening, so you may need to adjust one of the other sliders after you use it.

- **You can overdo the Shadows/Highlights feature.** If you see halos around the objects in your photo, you've pushed the settings too far.

TIP If the Shadows/Highlights feature washes out your photo's colors—making everyone look like they've been through the laundry too many times—adjust the color intensity with one of the Saturation commands, either in Quick Fix or Expert mode (as described on page 133). Watch people's skin tones when increasing the saturation—if the people in your photo start looking like sunless-tanning-lotion disaster victims, you've gone too far. Also, check out the Vibrance slider in Quick Fix (page 133), or try adjusting colors with Color Curves (page 331).

Correcting Part of an Image

The Shadows/Highlights command is great if you want to adjust *all* the light or dark areas of a photo, but what if you want to tweak the exposure in only certain areas? Or what if the photo's background looks fine, but you want to tweak the subject a little? You can use a layer mask on a duplicate layer and make adjustments there, or you can select the area you want to tweak, copy the selection to a new layer, and then make adjustments to that layer. But Elements gives you an even simpler way to apply a correction to just the area you want: the Smart Brush tools.

■ CORRECTING COLOR WITH A BRUSH

The Smart Brush is actually two different tools—the Smart Brush and the Detail Smart Brush—that work just like the Quick Selection tool and the regular Selection Brush, respectively. Only instead of merely selecting part of your photo, they also *edit* it as you brush. So you may be able to make targeted adjustments to different areas of your photo just by drawing a line over them. (The smart brushes don't always work, but when they do, they're truly amazing.) The smart brushes don't alter your original image because they always put the changes they make on new layers, so it's easy to edit the areas they affect.

This section explains how to correct exposure with the Smart Brush, but you have a whole menu of different things you can do with this tool: Change the color of someone's jacket, apply different special effects, put a little lipstick on someone, convert an area to black and white—the list goes on and on. As a matter of fact, if you've been working in the Quick Fix window, you may have already met the Smart Brush, although it doesn't go by that name there: The Whiten Teeth tool (page 136) uses the Smart Brush to apply its effects.

Here's how to put this nifty pair of tools to work:

1. **In Expert mode, open a photo, and then activate the Smart Brush.**

   Click the tool's icon in the Tools panel (it's in the Enhance section: the wide house-painter's brush just below the Red Eye Removal tool) or press F. Check the Tool Options area to be sure you're using the *regular* Smart Brush. It shares its Tools panel slot with the Detail Smart Brush, which works like the Selection Brush in that it changes only the area directly under the cursor instead of automatically expanding your selection to include the whole object you brush over. For now, see if the regular Smart Brush is smart enough to select the area you want.

2. Choose the adjustment you want to apply.

In the Tool Options area, click the thumbnail to the right of brush icons. Then choose a category from the Presets drop-down menu and find an adjustment you like. (Both smart brushes have the same Tool Options settings, discussed on page 236. The important one is explained in Figure 7-3.)

FIGURE 7-3

The things you can do with the Smart Brush are grouped into the categories listed in this drop-down menu. Select different categories to see different presets. Each thumbnail image shows that option applied to a photo.

For exposure issues, start by looking at the Lighting category (choose Lighting from the drop-down menu at the top of the panel). You can choose to make the area you're about to paint darker or brighter, increase or decrease its contrast, or add a spotlight effect to it. Just put your cursor over each thumbnail to find the effect you want, and then click it to select it.

3. Drag over the area you want to change.

This step is just like using the Quick Selection tool (page 154). You don't need to make a careful selection, since Elements figures out which area it *thinks* you want to include and creates the selection for you. A simple line should do it. As you drag, Elements applies the adjustment you chose in step 2 (and an Adjustment layer appears in your Layers panel).

4. If necessary, tweak the selection.

If Elements didn't quite select everything you want, then add to the selection by brushing again. (If you've got the Tool Options area's Inverse checkbox turned on—more on that in a sec—then your selected area looks the same as the rest of the photo. If you're doing an inverse black and white, for example, the colored area becomes black and white like the rest of the photo till you let go of the mouse button.)

If you *still* need to modify the selection, then use the selection-editing tools explained in Figure 7-4. If you're really unhappy with the Smart Brush's selection talents, then head back to the Tool Options area and switch to the Detail Smart Brush instead.

You can invert a selection by turning on the Inverse checkbox in the Tool Options area. Then what you brush over is *excluded* from your selection, and everything else is included. You can turn on the checkbox before or after using the Smart Brush, as long as it's still the active tool. If you come back to the Smart Brush after using another tool, then you need to reactivate your Smart Brush selection by clicking the pin shown in Figure 7-4 before you can invert the selection.

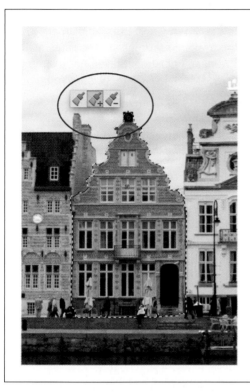

FIGURE 7-4

Once you've used the Smart Brush, Elements puts a little icon called a pin (the red icon in the area circled here) in your photo to let you know that the selected region is now under the power of the Smart Brush. Click the pin to see a trio of icons (circled) that let you edit the selected area. From left to right, the icons are New Selection, "Add to Selection," and "Subtract from Selection."

If you're pressed for time, there's an even quicker way to modify your selection: Just drag again to expand the area affected by the Smart Brush (or to use the same adjustment on another part of your photo). The Smart Brush always adds new areas when you click again; it doesn't start a new selection each time you click the way the regular selection tools do. Alt-drag/Option-drag to remove changes from an area.

You'll see the pin anytime you activate the Smart Brush again, even after you've closed and saved your photo.

5. **Once Elements has selected the right area, adjust the effect (if necessary).**

The Smart Brush gives you several ways to change what it's done:

- **Choose a different adjustment.** Head to the Tool Options area and choose a different adjustment (see step 2). Elements automatically updates your image.

- **Add another adjustment.** If you want to tweak your image in a second way, head to the right end of the Tool Options area, click the little four-line square, and then choose Reset Tool. Then you can drag in your image again and the Smart Brush will put down an *additional* adjustment instead of just changing what you've already done. You can also use this technique to double up an effect—to add Lipstick twice, for instance—if you thought the first pass was too faint. Each Smart Brush adjustment gets its own pin, so if you have two Smart Brush adjustments in your photo, then you'll have two pins, too. (Each pin is a different color.) You can add as many different adjustments as you like.

- **Change the settings for and adjustment you've already applied.** Rather than adding another Adjustment layer to increase the effect, you can adjust the settings for the change you've already made. Double-click the adjustment's pin in your image. Depending on the kind of adjustment you've made, a window or panel pops up showing the current settings so you can tweak the effect you're brushing on. (Not all the Smart Brush adjustments have adjustable settings.) Since the Smart Brush uses Adjustment layers to make most of its changes, the available settings are the same as they would be if you had created a regular Adjustment layer. For example, if you're using the Brighter option, as shown in Figure 7-3, then you get the settings for a Brightness/Contrast Adjustment layer.

NOTE If you're using certain of the Smart Brush's black-and-white adjustments, you may not be able to edit them afterward. If you try, you'll just see a weird message telling you that the layer was created in the full version of Photoshop, even though you know it wasn't. You can delete the Adjustment layer or edit its layer mask, but that's all. Also, if you apply effects (page 456) with the Smart Brush, once you're done, the only edit you can make to them is to adjust the area they cover. (The thumbnails for effects look like a tree instead of the photo thumbnails you normally see—the presets in the Smart Brush's Artistic category are all Effects, for example, although the presets in the Reverse Effects and Special Effects categories aren't.)

6. **When you're happy with how things look, you're done.**

   You can always adjust your Smart Brush edits later. Just activate the Smart Brush (click it in the Tools panel or press F) and the pin(s) reappear so you can easily change what you've done. To delete Smart Brush changes, go to the Layers panel and discard their layers (you can do this anytime, whether the Smart Brush is active or not). You can also edit a Smart Brush adjustment's layer mask the way you'd edit any other layer mask, as described on page 213. But usually it's easier just to click the pin and then adjust your selection.

The Smart Brush is especially handy for projects like creating images that are part color and part black-and-white, or even for silly special effects like making an object look like it's been isolated on a '60s-style psychedelic background.

TIP Check out the textures available for the Smart Brush—they're handy for creating backgrounds for isolated objects. To find them, head to the Tool Options area, click the thumbnail image, and in the panel that appears, choose Textures from the Presets drop-down menu.

The Smart Brush has several Tool Options settings, but you usually don't need to use them:

- **Presets**. Click this thumbnail image for a panel of all the possible Smart Brush adjustments, grouped into categories.

- **Selection brushes**. These three brush icons let you tell Elements how you want to adjust your selection:

— Click the top brush icon to add the same effect elsewhere in your photo. (Just clicking someplace else with the brush does the same thing. Be careful, though: The Smart Brush may think that the new area is a continuation of your previous selection, so it may combine the two. If that happens, try using a smaller brush.)

— Click the middle brush icon to put the Smart Brush in add-to-selection mode (the brush enters this mode automatically even if you don't click this icon).

— Did the Smart Brush take in more area than you wanted? Click the bottom brush icon before brushing away what you don't want, or just Alt-drag/ Option-drag.

- **Size**. If you have trouble getting a good selection, then try adjusting the size of your brush.

- **Brush Settings**. Click this button to change the brush's size, hardness, spacing, angle, or roundness. If you have a graphics tablet, the Size setting in this panel gives you a couple of ways to control brush size on the fly.

- **Inverse**. If you want to apply the adjustment to the area you *didn't* select with the Smart Brush, then turn on this checkbox.

- **Refine Edge**. Click this button if you want to make the edges of your effect sleeker, or to extract the area you've edited for use elsewhere. Page 156 has details.

TIP If you like the *idea* of the Smart Brush but never seem to find exactly the adjustments you want, or if you always want to change the settings you apply, then you can create your own presets, as described in the box on page 238.

Controlling the Colors You See

You want your photos to look as good as possible and to have beautiful, breathtaking color. Heck, that's probably why you bought Elements. But now that you've got the program, you're likely having a little trouble getting things to look the way you want. Does the following situation sound familiar?

- Your photos look great onscreen, but your prints are washed out, too dark, or the colors are all a little wrong.

- Your photos look fine in programs like Word or Windows Explorer, but they look awful in Elements.

Making Smart Brush Presets

While the Smart Brush offers a lot of different presets, you may find it slightly frustrating if Elements doesn't have a setting for a correction you use frequently. No problem—as long as you can use Adjustment layers (page 215) to achieve the effect you want, you can create your own presets, and they'll appear alongside the ones from Adobe.

To get started in Windows, go to *C:\ProgramData\Adobe\Photoshop Elements\13.0\Photo Creations\adjustment layers*. These files are hidden, so you need to turn on hidden files to see them (the Tip on page 588 tells you how). On a Mac, go to *[your hard drive]→Library→Application Support→Adobe→Photoshop Elements→13.0→Photo Creations→adjustment layers* (if you need help finding this folder, see page xxiii). No matter what your operating system, you see three files for each preset:

- **A PSD file** containing the preset's actual settings.

- **A JPEG file**, which you need if you want to have a little preview in the menu.

- **An XML file** that tells Elements what category to include the preset in, like the "Black and White" or Lighting category.

Basically, you need to edit *copies* of these files to make new ones for each preset you want to add. Here's how:

1. **Open one of the PSD files in the Editor.** Pick the one that's the closest to what you want. The PSD file is a 160-pixel square image with an Adjustment layer on it. Save the file with a new name so you don't mess up the original.

2. **Change the file's settings.** In the Layers panel, click the Adjustment layer to select it, and then—in the Adjustments panel—tweak its settings. Then save the file.

3. **Create a new thumbnail.** You can just save the original thumbnail with a new name. (Thumbnails are 74-pixel square JPEGs, in case you want to make a new one from scratch.)

4. **Create a new XML file.** Open the XML file and do a Save As, changing the name to that of the preset you just created. (In Windows, open the file with Notepad, a text editor; in the Save As dialog box, choose All Files in the "Save as type" menu. On a Mac, use TextEdit, but be sure to save the file as plain text [.txt].) Then look through the contents of the file for a line like this:

```
<name value="$$$/content/adjustmentlayers/
ContrastHigh=Contrast High" />
```

In this example, you'd be adapting the Contrast High preset, so you'd find the two instances of its name (note that there's no space in the first instance), and then change them to the name of your new preset. You can also edit the preset's tooltip (the text that appears when you point to its thumbnail) and category (you can use an existing category or create a new one).

When you're finished making changes, save the file. Name it *[my effect].metadata* (replace "[my effect]" with the preset's actual name). Make sure all three files are in the "adjustment layers" folder described above. Next, in Windows, go to *C:\ProgramData\Adobe\Photoshop Elements\13.0\Locale\en_US* (this path is different if you aren't in the United States), and delete *MediaDatabase.db3* to refresh the list of presets. (Note that deleting this file will also delete all items in your Favorites panel [page 527].) In OS X, it's *[your hard drive]→Library→Application Support→Adobe→Photoshop Elements→13.0→Locale→en_US* (or your location). The next time you start Elements, you should see your new preset alongside the ones that came with Elements.

What's going on? The answer has to do with the fact that Elements is a *color-managed* program. That means Elements uses information about your monitor when deciding how to display images. Color management is the science of making sure that the color in an image is always exactly the same, no matter who opens the file or what kind of hardware she's viewing it on or printing it with. If you think of all the different monitor and printer models out there, you get an idea of what a big job this is.

Graphics pros spend their whole lives grappling with color management, and you can find plenty of books about the finer points of it. At its most sophisticated, color management is complicated enough to make you curl up in the fetal position and swear never to create another picture. Luckily, Elements makes color management easy. Most of the time, you have only two things to deal with: monitor calibration and color space. The following pages cover both.

> **NOTE** There are a couple of other color-related settings for printing, but you can deal with those when you're ready to print. Chapter 16 has the details.

Calibrating Your Monitor

Most programs pay no attention to your monitor's color settings, but color-managed ones like Elements rely on the monitor's *profile*—the information your computer stores about your monitor's settings—when deciding how to display a photo onscreen or how to print it. If that profile isn't accurate, the color in Elements won't be either.

So you may need to *calibrate* your monitor, which is a way of adjusting its settings. A properly calibrated monitor makes all the difference in the world in getting great-looking results. If your photos look bad only in Elements or if your printed pictures don't look anything like they do onscreen, then calibrating is a good way to begin fixing the problem.

Calibrating a monitor sounds intimidating, but it's actually not that hard—some people think it's even kind of fun. And it's worth it, because afterward your monitor may look a thousand times better than you thought it could. Calibrating may even make it easier to read text in Word, for instance, because the contrast is better.

Your calibrating options are:

- **Use a colorimeter**. This method may sound disturbingly scientific, but it's actually the easiest and best. A *colorimeter* is a device with special software that does the calibrating *for* you; using such a device is much more accurate than calibrating by eye. For a long time, only pros could afford colorimeters, but these days, if you shop around, you can find something like the Spyder4EXPRESS or ColorMunki Smile for about $100. If you're willing to spend more, you can find professional calibrators like the i1Display Pro or the ColorMunki Display. If you're serious about controlling colors in Elements, using a colorimeter is by far your best option.

> **NOTE** The colorimeter's software will probably ask you to set your monitor's brightness and contrast before you begin calibrating, even though many modern monitors don't have any easy way to adjust these settings. If you're happy with your monitor's current brightness and contrast, you can safely ignore this step. The next steps will ask you to choose a white point and gamma for your monitor. Unless you have a reason to use different settings, you usually want to set the white point to 6500 (Kelvin) and your gamma to 2.2.

- **Use a program**. Whether you have a Windows computer or a Mac, you likely have some kind of software that can help you improve what you see:

    — **Windows**: There's a good chance that the drivers (software) for your computer's graphics card include some kind of calibration tool. Go to Control Panel→"Appearance and Personalization"→Display→Calibrate Color to use the Windows calibrator.

    — **Mac**: If you go to System Preferences→Displays→Color→Calibrate, you can use Apple's Display Calibrator Assistant to calibrate your monitor—sort of (see Figure 7-5). You can also find lots of calibration programs online, but most of them aren't much, if any, better than the Assistant.

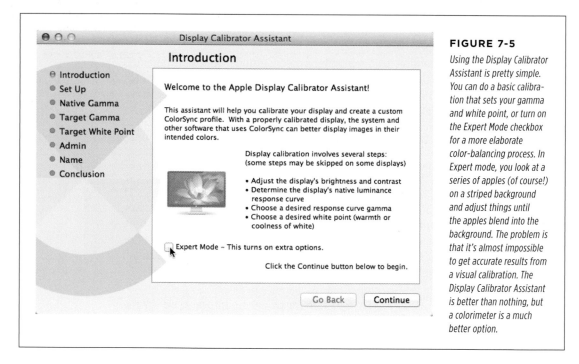

FIGURE 7-5

Using the Display Calibrator Assistant is pretty simple. You can do a basic calibration that sets your gamma and white point, or turn on the Expert Mode checkbox for a more elaborate color-balancing process. In Expert mode, you look at a series of apples (of course!) on a striped background and adjust things until the apples blend into the background. The problem is that it's almost impossible to get accurate results from a visual calibration. The Display Calibrator Assistant is better than nothing, but a colorimeter is a much better option.

If your photos still look a little odd even after you've calibrated your monitor, you may need to turn on the Ignore EXIF setting in the Editor's preferences; Figure 7-6 explains how.

Choosing a Color Space

The other thing you may need to do to get good color from Elements is to check which *color space* the program is using. Color spaces are standards that Elements uses to define colors. That may sound pretty abstruse, but they're simply ways of defining what colors mean.

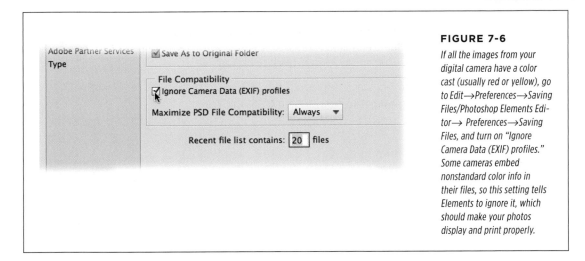

FIGURE 7-6

If all the images from your digital camera have a color cast (usually red or yellow), go to Edit→Preferences→Saving Files/Photoshop Elements Editor→ Preferences→Saving Files, and turn on "Ignore Camera Data (EXIF) profiles." Some cameras embed nonstandard color info in their files, so this setting tells Elements to ignore it, which should make your photos display and print properly.

For example, when someone says "green," what do you envision: a lush emerald color, a deep forest green, a bright lime, or something else? Choosing a color space helps make sure that everything that handles a digital file—Elements, your monitor, your printer, and so on—sees the file's colors the same way. Over the years, the graphics industry has agreed on standards so that everyone has the same understanding of what you mean when you say "red" or "green"—as long as you specify which color space (set of standards) you're using.

Elements gives you two color spaces to pick from: *sRGB* (also called *sRGB IEC61966-2.1* if you want to impress your geek friends) and *Adobe RGB*. When you choose one, you're telling Elements which set of standards you want it to apply to your photos.

If you're happy with the colors you see on your monitor in Elements and you like the prints you're getting, you don't need to make any changes. If, on the other hand, you aren't satisfied with what Elements is showing you, you'll probably want to modify your color space, which you can do in the Color Settings dialog box (Figure 7-7). Go to Edit→Color Settings or press Shift+Ctrl+K/Shift-⌘-K. Here are your choices:

- **No Color Management**. This setting makes Elements ignore any information that your file already contains—like color-space data from your camera—and doesn't attempt to add any color info to the file. (When you do a Save As, the Embed Color Profile checkbox offers you the option of embedding your monitor profile in the file. Don't turn on this checkbox, since your monitor profile is best left for the monitor's own use, and putting the profile into the file might cause trouble if you ever send the file someplace else for printing.)

Color Settings

❓ Learn more about: Color Settings

OK

Cancel

Choose how to manage color in your images:
○ No Color Management
○ Always Optimize Colors for Computer Screens
○ Always Optimize for Printing
◉ Allow Me to Choose

Note: The "No Color Management" setting will ignore and discard embedded color profiles if they exist. The other settings will utilize embedded profiles or convert to sRGB or AdobeRGB, if the embedded profiles cannot be supported.

FIGURE 7-7

If you select "Allow Me to Choose," you see the Missing Profile dialog box each time you open an untagged image.

(You'll learn about color tags in a sec.)

- **Always Optimize Colors for Computer Screens**. This option selects the sRGB color space, which is what most web browsers use; this is a good choice when you're preparing graphics for the Web. Many online printing services also prefer sRGB files. This is the setting that's selected when you first run Elements; you need to change it only if you want to use one of the others.

- **Always Optimize for Printing**. This option uses the Adobe RGB color space, which is wider than sRGB, meaning it allows more color gradations. This is sometimes your best choice for printing—but not always. Don't be afraid to try one of the other settings instead. Many home inkjet printers actually cope better with sRGB or no color management than with Adobe RGB.

- **Allow Me to Choose**. This option assumes that you're using the sRGB color space, but lets you assign either an Adobe RGB tag, an sRGB tag, or no tag at all (color tags are explained in a moment). After you select this option, each time you open a file that isn't sRGB, you see the dialog box shown in Figure 7-7, which you can use to assign a different profile to the photo. Just save the image once without a profile (turn off the Embed Color Profile checkbox in the Save As dialog box), and then reopen it and choose the profile you want from this dialog box. Or, the box on page 244 explains an easier way to convert a color profile if you need to make a change.

So what's your best option? Once again, if everything looks good, leave things alone. Otherwise, for general use, you're probably best off starting with No Color Management and then trying the other options if that doesn't work.

When you save the file, Elements attempts to embed it with a *color tag*, info about the file's color space—either Adobe RGB or sRGB. (This kind of tag isn't related to the Organizer tags you read about in Chapter 2.) If you don't want a color tag—also known as an *ICC profile* (ICC stands for International Color Consortium)—in your file, just turn off the Embed Color Profile checkbox before saving the file. Figure 7-8 shows where to find the profile information in the Save As dialog box, and how to turn the whole process off.

FIGURE 7-8

When you save a file, Elements offers to embed a color tag in it. If you're using No Color Management, you can safely turn off the Embed Color Profile checkbox and leave the file untagged.

Assigning a profile is helpful because then any program that sees the file knows what color standards you're working with. But if you're new to Elements, you'll usually have an easier time if you don't start embedding profiles in files without a good reason.

> **NOTE** When you're working in a given color space (sRGB or Adobe RGB), if you open a file that's tagged with a *different* color space, Elements will open the image in your *current* color space without telling you that it's done so. That means you won't know that there's a mismatch between the file's color tag and the color space you're using. (If, on the other hand, you try to open a file in a color *mode* that Elements can't handle, like CMYK, then Elements offers to convert it to a mode you can use.) For example, if you have an Adobe RGB file and you're working in "Always Optimize Colors for Computer Screens" (which uses the sRGB color space), Elements doesn't warn you about the mismatch the way early versions of the program did—it just opens the file. So if you consistently get strange color shifts when you open your Elements-edited files in other programs, check to see if there's a profile mismatch between your images and Elements.

▌ Using Levels

People who've used Elements for a while will tell you that the Levels command is one of the program's most essential tools. You can fix an amazing array of problems simply by adjusting the level of each *color channel* in your images. Each color displayed on your monitor is composed of three channels: red, green, and blue. In Elements, you can make very precise adjustments by adjusting these channels separately.

Converting Profiles in Elements

If you're a color-management maven, Elements gives you a feature you'll really appreciate—the ability to convert an image's color tag from one color space to another. If you've been working in, say, sRGB and now you want your photo to have the Adobe RGB profile, you can convert it by going to Image→Convert Color Profile→"Convert to Adobe RGB Profile." If you're in Adobe RGB, you'll see "Convert to sRGB Profile" instead; your current color profile choice is grayed out.

This same submenu also lets you *remove* the current image profile, a process that is a *true* conversion: It correctly maps out your image's colors for the new profile, so they don't shift the way they might if you were just to tag a photo with a different profile.

Why would you want to do such a conversion? If, for example, you use Adobe RGB when editing photos, but you're sending them to an online printing service that wants sRGB instead, then you may want to think about converting them.

Just as its name suggests, Levels adjusts the amount, or level, of each color in an image. You can make several different adjustments with Levels, from brightening a photo's overall colors to fixing a color cast (page 250 has more about color casts). Many digital photo enthusiasts treat almost every picture they take to a dose of Levels because there's no better way to spruce up the color.

The way Levels works is fairly complex. Start by thinking of the possible ranges of brightness in any photo on a scale from 0 (black) to 255 (white). Some photos may have pixels in them that fall at both those extremes, but most photos don't. Even the ones that do may not have the full range of brightness in each individual color channel. Most of the time, you'll find some empty space at one or both ends of the scale.

When you use Levels, you tell Elements to consider the range of colors available in your photo as the *total* tonal range it has to work with, and Elements redistributes the image's colors accordingly. Basically, you just get rid of the empty space at the ends of the scale of possibilities. This can dramatically change the color distribution in a photo, as you can see in Figure 7-9.

Fortunately, it's much, much easier to *use* Levels than to understand it, as you know if you've tried Auto Levels in Quick Fix (page 130), a command that's great for, well, quick fixes. But if you *really* need to massage an image, Levels has a lot more under the hood than you can access in Quick Fix. The next section shows you how to get at these settings.

FIGURE 7-9

A simple Levels adjustment can make a huge difference in the way your photos look.

Left: The gray-green cast to this photo makes everything rather dull.

Right: Levels not only removes the color cast, but it also gives the photo better contrast and sharpness.

Understanding the Histogram

Before you get started adjusting Levels, you need to understand the heart, soul, and brain of the Levels dialog box: the *histogram*, visible in Figure 7-10. (You can call up this dialog box by pressing Ctrl+L/⌘-L.)

FIGURE 7-10

One of the scariest sights in Elements, the Levels dialog box is actually your friend. If it frightens you, take comfort in knowing that you can always click the Auto button here, which is the same Auto Levels command as in Quick Fix. But it's worth persevering because the other options here give you much better control over the end results.

The histogram is the black bumpy mound in the middle of the dialog box. It's really nothing more than a bar graph indicating the distribution of the colors in your photo—there's just no space between the bars, which is why it looks like mountains.

From left to right, the histogram shows the brightness range from dark to light (the 0–255 range mentioned earlier in this section). The height of the "mountain" at any given point shows how many pixels in your photo have that particular brightness. You can tell a lot about a photo by where the mound is before you adjust the image, as Figure 7-11 explains.

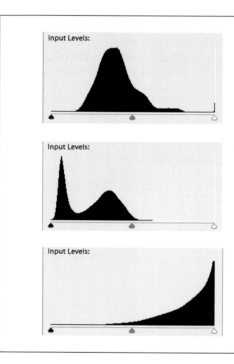

FIGURE 7-11

Top: If the bars in the histogram are all smooshed together like this, your photo doesn't have a lot of tonal range. As long as you like how the photo looks, that's not important. But if you're unhappy with the photo's color, it's usually harder to get it exactly right in this kind of photo than in one that has a wider tonal range.

Middle: If the mound is bunched up on the left side of the histogram, your photo is underexposed.

Bottom: If you just have a big lump on the right side, your photo is overexposed.

Above the Levels dialog box's histogram is the Channel menu. If you click it, you can choose to see a separate histogram for each individual color channel. You can adjust all three channels at once with the RGB setting, or change each channel separately for maximum control.

The histogram contains so much info about your photo that Adobe also makes it available in Expert mode in its own panel (Figure 7-12), so you can always see it and use it to monitor how you're changing the colors in an image. Once you get fluent in reading Histogramese, you'll probably want to keep this panel around.

The histogram is just a graph, and you don't do anything to it directly. When you use Levels, you simply use the histogram as a *guide* to help you tell Elements what to consider the black and white points—that is, the darkest and lightest points—in your photo. (Remember, for these settings, you're thinking in terms of brightness values, not shades of color.)

FIGURE 7-12

If you keep the histogram available by opening the Histogram panel (Window→Histogram), you can always see what effect your changes are having on the photo's color distribution.

To get this nifty Technicolor view, choose Colors from the panel's Channel drop-down menu. To update the histogram to reflect any changes you've made to the image, click the triangle in its upper right as shown here, or the circling arrows above it.

If you're into statistics, there are a bunch of them at the bottom of this panel, but if you're not a pro, you can safely ignore these numbers.

Once you've set these end points (you'll learn how in a moment), you can adjust the image's *midtones*—the tones in between that would appear gray in a black-and-white photo. If that seems complicated, it's not—at least, not when you're actually doing it. Once you've made a Levels adjustment, the next time you open the Levels dialog box, you'll see that your histogram's values now run the whole length of the scale because you've told Elements to redistribute your colors so that they cover the full dark-to-light range.

The next two sections show you—finally!—how to actually adjust an image with Levels.

> **TIP**   Once you learn how to interpret Elements' histograms, you can try your hand with your camera's histogram (if it has one). Your camera's histogram can be a big help in figuring out how well exposed your shot is going to be, or to check how you did after a shot. Alas, you'll need to check your owner's manual to figure out how to display the histogram on your particular camera.

Adjusting Levels: The Eyedropper Method

One way to adjust Levels is to set the image's black, white, and/or gray points by using the eyedroppers in the Levels Adjustments panel. It's quite simple—just follow these steps:

1. **Bring up the Levels Adjustments panel by selecting Layer→New Adjustment Layer→Levels.**

   If you like, you can name the layer in the New Layer dialog box that appears, or just click OK to get on with it and create the layer. If you don't want a separate layer for your Levels adjustment, go to Enhance→Adjust Lighting→Levels or press Ctrl+L/⌘-L instead. (You'll get a dialog box instead of the panel, but it works the same way.) But making the Levels changes on an Adjustment layer gives you more flexibility for making future changes.

2. **If necessary, move the Adjustments panel or the Levels dialog box out of the way so you have a good view of your photo.**

   The dialog box loves to plunk itself down smack in the middle of the most important part of your image. Just grab its top bar and drag it somewhere else.

3. **In the Adjustments panel or Levels dialog box, click the black eyedropper.**

   In the Adjustments panel, from top to bottom, the eyedroppers are black, gray, and white. In the dialog box, they're arranged from left to right instead.

4. **Move your cursor over your photo and click an area that should be black.**

   Should be, not *is*. That's a mistake lots of people make the first time they use the Levels eyedroppers: They click a spot that's the same color as the eyedropper rather than one that ought to be that color. For instance, if your photo includes a wood carving that looks black but that you know is actually dark brown instead, that's a bad place to click. Try clicking a black coffee mug or belt instead. This process is called "setting a black point."

5. **Repeat with the other eyedroppers for their respective colors.**

   Now select the white eyedropper and then click a spot that should be white (like maybe a cloud that's a little off-white now), and then use the gray eyedropper to click one that should be gray; doing so sets your white and gray points. That's the way this process is *supposed* to work, anyway, but you can't always use all the eyedroppers in a given photo. Experiment to see what gives you the best-looking results.

> **TIP** You don't always need to set a gray point. If you try to set it and think your photo looked better without it, just skip that step.

6. **If you're using the dialog box, when you're happy with what you see, click OK.**

   If you're working with the Adjustments panel, you don't have to do anything: Elements has already applied your changes, so you're done.

See, it's not so hard. If you mess up, just click the dialog box's Reset button to start over again. In the Adjustments panel, click the word "Reset" at the panel's bottom right.

Adjusting Levels: The Slider Method

The eyedropper method works fine if your photo has spots that should be black, white, or gray, but sometimes your pictures don't have any of these colors. Fortunately, the Levels sliders give you yet another way to apply Levels. This is by far the most popular method, and it gives you maximum control over your colors.

In the Levels Adjustments panel or dialog box (press Ctrl+L/⌘-L to open it), right below the histogram, are three little triangles called *input sliders*. The left slider sets the black point in your photo, the right slider sets the white point, and the middle slider adjusts the midtones (grays). You just drag them to make changes to the color levels in your photo, as shown in Figure 7-13.

FIGURE 7-13

To use the Levels input sliders, simply drag the left and right sliders from the ends of the track until they're under the outer edges of the color data in the graph.

The red arrows in this figure show where you'd position the left and right sliders for this particular photo, respectively. If there's empty space on the end of the graph (as there is here), just move the slider until it's under the first mound of data.

When you move the left input slider, you tell Levels, "Take all the pixels from this point down and consider them black." With the right slider, you're saying, "Make this pixel and all higher values white." The middle slider adjusts the brightness values that are considered medium gray. All three adjustments improve the contrast of your image.

TIP If there are small amounts of color data (flat lines) at the ends of the histogram, or if all the data is clumped in the middle of the graph, watch your photo as you move the left and right input sliders to decide how far in you should drag them. Moving them *all* the way in may be too drastic. Your own taste should always be the deciding factor when adjusting a photo.

Here's the easiest way to use the Levels sliders:

1. **Bring up the Levels dialog box or the Levels Adjustments panel.**

   Use one of the methods described in step 1 of the eyedropper method (page 247). If necessary, move the dialog box or panel so you've got a clear view of your photo.

2. **Grab the black input slider (the one below the left end of the histogram) and drag it to the right, if necessary.**

   Move it over until it's under the farthest-left part of the histogram that has a mound in it. For the histogram in Figure 7-13, for example, you'd move the left slider just a tiny bit, to where the left red arrow is. (Incidentally, although you're adjusting the image's colors, the Levels histogram is always black and white—you don't see any color in the dialog box itself.)

You may not need to move the black slider at all if there's already a good bit of data at the left end of the histogram. You don't have to adjust all the sliders for every photo.

3. **Grab the white slider (the one on the right) and drag it left, if necessary.**

   Bring it under the farthest-right area of the histogram that has a mound in it.

4. **Now adjust the gray slider.**

   This is the *midtones* slider, and it adjusts—you guessed it—the midtones of your image. Move it back and forth while watching your photo until you like what you see. This slider has the most impact on the overall result, so take some time to play with it.

> **TIP** If you know the numerical value of the pixels you want to designate for any of these settings, you can type that information into the unlabeled input levels boxes below the histogram. You can set the gray value from 0.10 to 9.99 (it's set to 1.00 automatically), and the other two boxes anywhere from 0 to 255.

5. **If you're using the Levels dialog box, click OK to let Elements know you're done.**

You can adjust the whole image at once or each color channel individually. The most accurate method is to open the Levels dialog box and then choose each color channel in turn from the Channel drop-down menu. Adjust the end points for each channel, and then choose RGB from the menu and tweak just the midtones (gray) slider.

The last controls you may want to use in the Levels dialog box or Levels Adjustments panel are the Output Levels sliders, which work roughly the same way as the brightness and contrast controls on your TV. Moving these sliders makes the darkest pixels darker and the lightest pixels lighter. Image pros call this process "adjusting the tonal range of a photo."

Adjusting Levels can improve almost every photo, but if your image has a bad *color cast*—if it's too orange or too blue, say—you may need something else. The next section explains how to get rid of color like that.

Removing Unwanted Color

It's not uncommon for an otherwise good photo to have a *color cast*—that is, to have all its tonal values shifted so it's too blue, like Figure 7-14, or too orange.

Levels Before Curves

I never know where to start adjusting the colors in my photos. Some photo mavens talk about using Levels, others about Curves. Which should I use?

In addition to Levels, Elements includes a much-requested feature from Photoshop—*Color Curves*. Despite the name, the Curves tool isn't some kind of arc-drawing tool; instead, it's a sophisticated way of adjusting the colors in photos. Curves works something like Levels, but with many more points of correction.

In Elements, you get a simplified version of Photoshop's Curves dialog box, with a few preset options. Because this version doesn't have quite as many adjustment points as in Photoshop, you get some of the advanced color control of Curves without all the complexity.

Generally speaking, a quick Levels adjustment is usually all you need to achieve good, realistic color. But if you still aren't satisfied with the contrast in your image or you want to create funky artistic effects, flip to page 331 to learn how to use Color Curves.

FIGURE 7-14

Left: You may wind up with photos like this if you forget to change your camera's white balance— a setting that tells your camera what type of lighting conditions you're shooting in (daylight, incandescent, and so on). This is an outdoor photo taken with the camera set for incandescent indoor lighting. It's not awful, but it definitely lacks the warmth of the fall day.

Right: Elements warms things up in a jiffy with just one click on the gray sand in the foreground (the cursor is circled so you can see where to click). The photo still needs other adjustments, but the color is back in the right ballpark.

Elements gives you several ways to correct color-cast problems:

- **Auto Color Correction** doesn't give you any control over its changes, but it often does a good job. To use it, go to Enhance→Auto Color Correction or press Shift+Ctrl+B/Shift-⌘-B.

- The **Raw Converter** (page 272) may be the easiest way to fix color problems, though it works only on raw, JPEG, and TIFF files. Just run your photo through the Raw Converter and adjust its white balance as described on page 277.

- **Levels** gives you the finest control of all. You can often eliminate a color cast by adjusting the image's individual color channels (as explained in the previous section) till the unwanted color is gone. The drawbacks are that Levels can be very fiddly for this sort of work; sometimes this method doesn't work if the problem is severe; and it can take much longer than the other methods.

- **Remove Color Cast** is a command designed to correct a color cast with one click. The next section explains how to use it.

- The **Photo Filter command** gives you much more control than the Remove Color Cast command, and you can apply Photo Filters as Adjustment layers, too. See page 299 for details.

- The **Average Blur filter**, used with a blend mode, can fix color casts, too. As you'll read on page 452, it's something like creating a custom photo filter.

- The **Adjust Color for Skin Tone** feature makes Elements adjust a photo based on the skin colors of people in the image. In practice, this adjustment is often more likely to *introduce* a color cast than to correct one, but if your photo has a slight bluish cast that's visible in the subject's skin (as explained on page 139), it may do the trick. This option works best for slight, annoying casts that are too subtle for the other techniques in this list.

> **NOTE** If you're a fan of Color Variations from older versions of Elements, sorry, but Adobe removed that feature back in Elements 12.

You can use any of these methods, but a good bet is to start with Levels and then move on to the Remove Color Cast or Photo Filter command. To practice any of the fixes you're about to learn, download the photo *crossover.jpg* from this book's Missing CD page at *www.missingmanuals.com/cds*.

The Remove Color Cast Command

This command uses an eyedropper to adjust the colors in a photo based on the pixels you click. With this method, you show Elements where a neutral color should be. As you saw in Figure 7-14, Remove Color Cast can make a big difference with just one click. To use it:

1. **Go to Enhance→Adjust Color→Remove Color Cast.**

   Your cursor should change to an eyedropper when you move it over your photo. If it doesn't, in the Remove Color Cast dialog box, click the eyedropper icon.

2. **Click an area that should be gray, white, or black.**

   You only have to click once in your photo for this feature to work. As with the Levels eyedropper tool, click an area that *should be* gray, white, or black (as opposed to an area that's *currently* one of these colors). If the image you're trying to fix has several such areas, try clicking different spots in the photo. Just click Reset in the dialog box between each click on the photo until you find the spot that gives you the most natural-looking color.

3. **Click OK in the dialog box.**

Remove Color Cast works pretty well if your image has areas that should be black, white, or gray—even if they're tiny. If your image doesn't have any areas that should be one of those colors, consider using the Photo Filter command instead (page 210).

> **TIP** If you generally like what Auto Levels does for your photos but feel that it leaves behind a slight color cast, a click with Remove Color Cast may be just the right finishing touch.

Choosing Colors

So far, the color corrections you've read about in this chapter have all done most of the color assigning for you. But a lot of the time, you want to *tell* Elements what colors to work with—like when you're selecting the color for a Background or Fill layer, or when you want to paint on an image.

Although you can use any of the millions of colors your screen can display, Elements loads only two colors at a time. You choose these colors by using the foreground and background *color squares* at the bottom of the Tools panel (see Figure 7-15).

FIGURE 7-15

The top square displays your foreground color (here, that's blue); the bottom square displays your background color (pink). To switch to the standard colors—black and white—either click the two tiny squares labeled here or press D. Click the curved double-headed arrow or press X to swap the foreground and background colors.

Foreground and background mean just what they sound like—use the foreground color with tools like the Brush or the Paint Bucket, and the background color to fill in backgrounds. You can include as many colors in your images as you want, of course, but you can only use two at any given time.

The color-picking tools at the bottom of the Tools panel let you control the color you're using in a number of different ways:

- **Reset default colors**. Click the tiny black and white squares below the foreground square to return to the standard settings: black for the foreground color and white for the background color. (Pressing the D key does the same thing.)

- **Swap foreground and background colors**. Click the little curved two-headed arrow above the color squares to make the background color into the foreground color, and vice versa. This is helpful when you've inadvertently made your color selection in the wrong box. Say you set the foreground color to yellow, but you actually meant to make the *background* color yellow; just click these arrows or press X and you're all set.

- **Change either color square to whatever color you want**. Click either square to call up the Color Picker (explained on page 255) to make your new choice. There's no limit on the number of colors you can select in Elements. (Well, technically there is, but it's in the millions, so you should find enough choices for anything you want to do.)

You have a few different ways to select foreground and background colors. The next few sections explain how to use the Color Picker, the Eyedropper tool, and the Color Swatches panel.

When working with some of Elements' tools, like the type tools, you can also choose a color in the tool's Tool Options area. Adobe knows that, given a choice, most people prefer to work with either Color Swatches or the Color Picker, so it's come up with a way to accommodate both camps, as shown in Figure 7-16.

FIGURE 7-16

Whether you prefer using Color Swatches or the Color Picker, for most tools, you can choose your favorite method in the Tool Options area.

Click the color sample in the box to bring up the Color Swatches. If you prefer the Color Picker, click the multicolored circle (circled) to call it up. (This is different from how things worked in old versions of Elements.)

TIP   Adobe gives you other ways to create colors. You can go to *https://kuler.adobe.com/create/color-wheel* and use Adobe Kuler, which also comes in app form for your iOS gadget. And if you have an iPad, you've got yet *another* way to create colors for Elements: Adobe's Color Lava app lets you use your fingers to blend colors and then send them to Elements. Head to *www.photoshop.com/products/mobile/colorlava* for more info. (That web page says you need Photoshop to use Color Lava, but it works with Elements, too.)

The Color Picker

Figure 7-17 shows the Color Picker, which has an intimidating number of options, but most of the time you don't need them all. Choosing a color is as simple as clicking wherever you see the color you want. Here's how:

FIGURE 7-17

For many beginners, the most important parts of Elements' Color Picker are the vertical, rainbow-colored slider in the middle (called, appropriately enough, the Color slider*) and the big square box, called the* Color field*.*

Use the slider to get the general color you want, and then click within the field to pick the exact shade.

1. **In the Tools panel, click the foreground or background color square.**

   Elements launches the Color Picker. Some tools—like the Paint Bucket (page 407) and the Selection Brush's mask color option—also use the Color Picker. It works the same way no matter how you get to it.

2. **Choose the color range you want to select from.**

   Use the vertical Color slider in the middle of the dialog box to slide through the spectrum until you see the color you want in the big, square Color field.

3. **In the Color field, click the spot where you see the exact shade you want.**

   You can keep clicking around and watch the color in the window's "new" box change to reflect what you click. The "current" box shows your original color for comparison.

4. **Click OK.**

   The color you selected now appears in the foreground or background square in the Tools panel (depending on which one you clicked in step 1).

That's the basic way to use the Color Picker. The box below explains how to enter a numeric value for a color (if you know it) and how to change which shades the Color Picker offers you.

> **NOTE** You're not limited to Elements' Color Picker. If you prefer, you can use your operating system's Color Picker instead (maybe you're used to working with the Windows Picker, for example). Here's how:
>
> - **Windows**: In the Elements Editor, go to Edit→Preferences→General. At the top of the dialog box, set the Color Picker menu to Windows. From then on, when you click a color square in Elements, the Windows Color Picker opens up looking pretty feeble, with just a few colored squares and some white ones. But if you click Define Custom Colors, it expands, giving you access to most of the same features as in the Adobe picker. (The plain white squares are like little pigeonholes where you can save your color choices.)
>
> - **Mac**: Go to Photoshop Elements Editor→Preferences→General and, from the Color Picker menu at the top of the dialog box, select Apple. You may prefer Apple's color picker if you like to choose colors from a color wheel. There's even a fun view where you choose from a box of crayons. You can save colors in Apple's color picker by dragging them from the Color field at the top of the window onto the squares at the bottom. Then click a square to choose that color the next time you want it.

POWER USERS' CLINIC

Paint by Number

Elements' Color Picker includes some sophisticated controls that most folks can ignore. But in case you're curious, here's what the rest of the Color Picker does:

- **H, S, and B fields**. These numbers determine the hue, saturation, and brightness of a color, respectively. They control pretty much the same values as the Hue/Saturation adjustment (page 335).

- **R, G, and B fields**. These numbers let you specify the amount of red, green, and blue you want in the color you're picking. Each field can have a numerical value anywhere from 0 to 255; a lower number means less of the color, a higher number means more. For example, 128 R, 128 G, 128 B is neutral gray. By changing the numbers, you change the blend of the color.

- **# (hex number) field**. If you're creating web graphics, this box is where you can enter a special six-character

hexadecimal code that tells web browsers which colors to display. You can click a color in the Color field to see the hex number for that shade.

- **Only Web Colors**. Turning on this checkbox ensures that the colors you see in the Color field are drawn only from the 216 colors that antique web browsers can display. For example, if you're creating a website and you're really worried about color compatibility with Netscape 4.0, this setting is for you. If you see a tiny cube just to the right of the color sample box (as in Figure 7-17), the color you're using isn't deemed web safe. But these days, it's hard to think of a time when you'd want to bother turning on this setting.

The Color Picker/Eyedropper Tool

If you've ever repainted your house, you've probably had the frustrating experience of spotting the *exact* color you want to use, but not having a way to capture that color. That's one problem you'll never run into in Elements thanks to the handy Eyedropper tool, which lets you sample any color on your monitor and make it your foreground color. If you can get a color onto your computer, Elements can grab it.

> **NOTE** Technically, this tool *used* to go by the sensible name of Eyedropper, but for some incomprehensible reason Adobe now calls it the Color Picker tool even though it has nothing to do with the Color Picker described on page 255, at least not directly. To avoid confusion, this book calls this tool by its old name: the Eyedropper tool. If you go looking for it in the Tools panel, just look for the eyedropper icon in the Draw section.

Sampling a color (that is, snagging it for your own use) couldn't be simpler with the Eyedropper: Just move your cursor over the color you want, and then click. It even works on colors that aren't in Elements, as explained in Figure 7-18. Sampling is perfect for projects like scrapbook pages where you want to use, say, the color from an event program cover as a theme color for the project. Just scan the program and then sample the color with the Eyedropper tool.

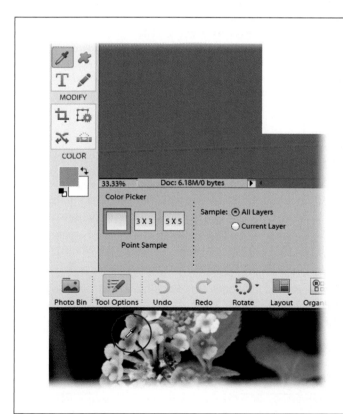

FIGURE 7-18

To use the Eyedropper tool to sample colors outside of Elements, activate the tool, and then click anywhere in your Elements document and keep your mouse button pressed. Then, while still holding down your mouse button, move your cursor to the non-Elements object (a web page, for instance), until it's over the area you want to sample. (Watch your foreground color square as you drag—it changes to reflect the color your cursor is currently over.)

When you let go of your mouse button, the new color appears in Elements' foreground color square. (If you let go before you get to the non-Elements object, this trick won't work.)

Here, the Eyedropper (circled) is sampling the purple color from a photo that's open in Windows Photo Viewer. If you don't have a big monitor, it can take a bit of maneuvering to get the program windows positioned so you can perform this procedure.

The Eyedropper is one of the easiest tools to use:

1. **Click the eyedropper icon in the Tools panel or press I.**

   Your cursor changes into a tiny eyedropper.

2. **Put your cursor over the color you want to sample.**

   If you want to watch the color in the foreground color square change as you move the Eyedropper tool around, hold the mouse button down.

   If you have a layered file, you can use the radio buttons in the Tool Options area to tell Elements whether to sample from *all* the image's layers or just the active layer.

3. **When your cursor is over the color you want, click or let go of your mouse button.**

   Elements loads your color choice as the foreground color so it's ready to use. (To set the background color instead, Alt-click/Option-click the color you want.)

To keep the new color around so you can use it later without having to get the Eyedropper out again, save it in the Swatches panel. The next section teaches you how.

> **TIP** Unless you tell it otherwise, the Eyedropper tool selects the color of the *exact* pixel you click. But since there may be some slight pixel-to-pixel variation in a color, you can set it to sample a little block of pixels instead and then average them. In the Eyedropper's Tool Options area, you can choose between the exact pixel you click (Point Sample), a 3-pixel square average, or a 5-pixel square average; just click the option you want. You can also do this by right-clicking/Control-clicking your image when the Eyedropper tool is active, and then choosing from the pop-up menu. Oddly enough, this setting also applies to the Magic Wand (page 165). Change it here and you change it for the Wand, too.

The Color Swatches Panel

The Color Swatches panel holds several preloaded groups of colors you can choose from. To call it up, go to Window→Color Swatches. You can park it in the Panel Bin just like any other panel or leave it floating on your desktop. When you're ready to choose a color, just head to this panel and click the swatch you want, and it appears in the Tools panel's foreground color square or in the color box of the tool you're using.

The Color Swatches panel is really handy when you want to keep certain colors at your fingertips. For instance, you can put your logo colors into it, and then you always have them available for any graphics or ads you create in Elements.

Elements starts you off with several different *libraries* (groups) of color swatches; click the drop-down menu at the top of the panel to see them all. Any swatch you create using the techniques in the next section appears at the bottom of the current library; you can save it there or create your own swatch libraries.

Using the Color Swatches panel to select your foreground or background color is as easy as using the Eyedropper tool; Figure 7-19 shows you how. And Figure 7-20 explains how to change the way the panel displays swatch info.

FIGURE 7-19

When you move your cursor over the Color Swatches panel, it changes to an eyedropper. Simply click to select a foreground color, or Ctrl-click/⌘-click to pick a background color.

If you're using a preloaded color library, you'll see labels appear as you move your cursor over each square, as shown here.

FIGURE 7-20

To see swatch information displayed like this, click the four-line square at the top right of the panel and select Small List.

Depending on the library you're using, in addition to small thumbnails of each color, you may see the colors' names or hex numbers.

■ SAVING COLORS IN THE SWATCHES PANEL

You can save any colors you've picked using the Color Picker or Eyedropper tool. (If you don't save them, you'll lose them as soon as you select a different swatch library or close the panel.) After sampling a color, you can save it as a swatch in one of two ways: Click the New Swatch icon at the top of the Color Swatches panel (it looks like a piece of paper with a folded corner) or click the four-line square in the panel's upper right, and then choose New Swatch. Either way, a window appears where you can name and save your new swatch.

Your new swatch appears at the bottom of the current swatch library, and its name shows up as a pop-up label when you put your cursor over it in the panel. You can rename the swatch by right-clicking/Control-clicking it, and then choosing Rename

Color Swatch. To delete a swatch that you've saved, Alt-click/Option-click it or drag it to the trashcan icon in the Color Swatches panel.

If you want to keep your swatches separate from the ones that come with Elements, you can create your own swatch libraries. To do that, click the four-line square at the top right of the Color Swatches panel and pick Save Swatches. Then give the new library a name and save it.

You can also find downloadable swatch libraries online (see page 586 for some suggestions of where to look). The best way to load these into Elements is to use the Preset Manager, explained on page 587.

NOTE When you create a new swatch library, its name doesn't show up in the list of libraries until the next time you start Elements.

Sharpening Images

Digital cameras are wonderful, but it's often hard to tell how well-focused your photos are until you download them to a computer. And because of the way cameras' digital sensors process information, most digital image data needs to be *sharpened*.

Sharpening is an image-editing trick that makes pictures look more clearly focused. Elements includes some almost miraculous tools for sharpening images. (It's pretty darned good at blurring them, too, if that's what you want; see page 446.) This section explains your options.

Unsharp Mask

Although this feature sounds like the last thing you'd ever want to use on a photo, Unsharp Mask reigned as the Supreme Sharpener for generations of image correction, despite having the most counterintuitive name in all of Elements.

To be fair, it's not Adobe's fault. "Unsharp mask" is an old darkroom term, and it actually does make sense if you know how our film ancestors used to improve a picture's focus. It refers to a complicated darkroom technique that involved making a blurred copy of the photo at one point in the process.

For several versions of Elements, Unsharp Mask ranked right up there with Levels as a contender for most useful tool in Elements, and some people still think it's the best way to sharpen photos. Figure 7-21 shows how much a little Unsharp Mask can do for pictures.

To use Unsharp Mask, first finish all your other corrections and changes. A good rule of thumb for sharpening is "last and once." That's because Unsharp Mask (or any sharpening tool, for that matter) can undermine other adjustments you make later on, so always make sharpening your last step. And repeatedly applying sharpening can degrade your image's quality.

FIGURE 7-21

Left: The photo as it came from the camera.

Right: The same photo treated with a dose of Unsharp Mask. The change is subtle, but notice how much clearer the individual hairs in the dog's coat are and how much better defined the eyes and mouth are.

TIP An exception to the rule about sharpening only once is when you're converting raw images (page 271): You can usually sharpen them both in the Raw Converter and then again as a last step in the Editor without causing problems.

If you're sharpening an image that has layers, be sure the active layer has something in it. (Applying sharpening to a Levels Adjustment layer, for example, won't do anything.) Also, perform any file-format conversions before sharpening. Finally, you may want to sharpen a duplicate layer just in case you decide to undo your changes later; press Ctrl+J/⌘-J to create the duplicate layer.

NOTE It's helpful to understand just exactly what Elements does when it "sharpens" a photo. It doesn't magically correct the focus. As a matter of fact, it doesn't really sharpen anything. Instead, it increases the contrast where colors meet, giving the *impression* of crisper focus. So while Elements can dramatically improve a shot that's a little soft, it can't fix that old double exposure or a shot where the subject is just a blur of motion.

When you're ready to apply Unsharp Mask:

1. **Go to Enhance→Unsharp Mask.**

   You can use Unsharp Mask in either Expert or Quick Fix mode.

2. **In the Unsharp Mask dialog box, adjust the settings until you like what you see.**

   Move the sliders until you're happy with your photo's sharpness (the following list explains what each one does). In the preview part of the dialog box, you can zoom in and out and grab the photo to adjust which part you see. It's also a good idea to drag the dialog box off to the side so that you can see the changes in your actual image. (You get the most accurate look at how you're affecting the image if you set the view to 100 percent or Actual Pixels.)

3. **When you're satisfied, click OK.**

The Unsharp Mask sliders work much like other tools' sliders:

- **Amount** tells Elements how much to sharpen, in percent terms. A higher number means more sharpening.

- **Radius** lets Elements know how far from an *edge* (a place where two colors meet) it should look when increasing the contrast.

- **Threshold** controls how different a pixel needs to be from the surrounding pixels before Elements considers it an edge and sharpens it. If you leave this setting at zero—which is the standard setting—Elements sharpens *all* the image's pixels.

There are many, many different schools of thought about where to move the sliders or which values to plug into each box. Whatever works for you is fine. The one thing you want to watch out for is *oversharpening*. Figure 7-22 explains how to know if you've gone too far.

FIGURE 7-22

The perils of oversharpening.

This is just a normal pumpkin, not a diseased one, but oversharpening gives it a flaky appearance and makes the straw in the background look sketched in rather than real.

The presence of halos (like those along the edge of the pumpkin) is often your best clue that you've oversharpened an image. The spots and scaly bits are called sharpening artifacts, which you want to keep an eye out for when you sharpen images.

You'll probably need to experiment a bit to find out which settings work best for you. Photos you plan to print usually need to be sharpened to an extent that makes them look slightly oversharpened on your monitor, so you may want to create two separate versions of your photo: one for onscreen viewing and one for printing. The Organizer's version sets (page 71) are great for keeping track of multiple copies like this.

Adjust Sharpness

The Unsharp Mask technique was around long before digital imaging, and a lot of people (including the folks at Adobe) have been thinking that, in the computer age, there's *got* to be a better way to sharpen. Happily, there is. The latest tool in the war on poor focus is Adjust Sharpness. In Elements 13, this feature is completely new under the hood and it gives you even more control over sharpening than you had in previous versions of Elements.

Unsharp Mask (described in the previous section) helps boost a photo's sharpness by using a process something like reducing Gaussian blur (page 446). Problem is, Gaussian blurring is rarely the cause of a picture's poor focus, so there's only so much Unsharp Mask can do. In real life, blurry photos are usually caused by one of two things:

- **Lens blur**. Your camera's prime focal point isn't directly over your subject, or your lens isn't quite as sharp as you'd like it to be.

- **Motion blur**. You moved the camera—or your subject moved—while you pressed the shutter button.

Adjust Sharpness is as easy to use as Unsharp Mask, and it gives you settings to correct all three kinds of blur—Gaussian, lens, and motion. And in Elements 13, you get some new settings to help you sharpen your photos even more accurately.

When you first open the Adjust Sharpness dialog box, its settings are almost identical to those of Unsharp Mask. It's the *extra* things Adjust Sharpness can do that make it a more versatile feature. Here's how to use it:

1. **Make sure the layer you want to sharpen is the active layer.**

   See Chapter 6 if you need a refresher on layers.

2. **Go to Enhance→Adjust Sharpness.**

   You can reach this menu item from either Expert mode or Quick Fix.

3. **In the Adjust Sharpness dialog box, tweak the various settings.**

   As shown in Figure 7-23, the dialog box gives you a decently sized preview. It's usually best to stick with 50 or 100 percent zoom (use the + and – buttons below the preview to zoom) for the most accurate view. The other settings are explained in detail after this list.

4. **When you like the way your photo looks, click OK.**

Adjust Sharpness

☑ Preview

Preset: Custom ▾

Amount: ──○────── 100 %

Radius: ──○────── 1.0 px

Remove: Gaussian Blur ▾ 0 ° ⊙

▼ Shadows

Fade Amount: ──────────○── 100 %

Tonal Width: ─○────────── 8 %

Radius: ○─────────── 1 px

Highlights

Fade Amount: ────────○──── 66 %

Tonal Width: ○──────────── [Enter the amount of correc]

Radius: ○──────────── 1 px

❓ Learn more about: Adjust Sharpness

⊟ 100% ⊞   Cancel   OK

FIGURE 7-23

The Adjust Sharpness dialog box in Elements 13 includes a number of new controls that let you micromanage what happens to sharpening in the dark and very light areas of your photos, both of which can be major problem areas with basic sharpening. Just click the flippy triangle to the left of the words "Shadows / Highlights" to expand the window so you can see these extra controls.

Near the top of the Adjust Sharpness dialog box is the Preset drop-down. You can safely ignore that menu for now, although it can come in handy if you have a bunch of images with similar sharpness problems; page 266 has the details.

The first two sliders in the Adjust Sharpness dialog box, Amount and Radius, work exactly the same way they do in Unsharp Mask (page 262). Here's what the other settings do:

- **Reduce Noise.** Sharpening often brings out hidden noise (graininess) in photos. If sharpening your photo made it noisier, use this setting to bring it back down. Although this setting is supposed to be smart enough to leave the edges of objects in your photos sharp and only go after noise, you should still be careful—if you get too aggressive with this slider, you can melt away all the crispness you just added to your image. Nudge this slider very gently, a little at a time, and keep checking the results in your document window, not just in the dialog box's preview area.

- **Remove**. This is where you choose what kind of fuzziness to fix: Gaussian, lens, or motion blur. If you aren't sure which you want, try all three in turn and see which works best.

- **Angle**. If you're dealing with motion blur, you can improve your results by telling Elements the *angle* of the motion. For example, if your grip on the camera slipped, the direction of motion would be downward. Move the line in the little circle or type a number in degrees to approximate the angle. (It's awfully tricky to get the angle exactly right, so you may find it easier to sharpen without messing with this setting.)

TIP Although the Amount and Radius settings in the Adjust Sharpness dialog box control the same things as they do in Unsharp Mask, that doesn't necessarily mean that you can just plug your favorite Unsharp Mask settings into the Adjust Sharpness dialog box and get the same results. You may prefer very different numbers for these settings for the two features.

Those are the settings you use for most everyday sharpening, but new in Elements 13, the dialog box also gives you a bunch of extra settings to help in more difficult situations.

Sometimes it can be tricky to get consistent sharpening across the whole tonal range of an image, so Adobe added a Shadows/Highlights section to the Adjust Sharpness dialog box. You can now adjust the settings for very dark and very light areas separately. Just click Shadows/Highlights to expand that section, and you'll see two additional sets of sliders, one for shadows and one for highlights. Both sections have the same three settings:

- **Fade Amount** determines how much sharpening Elements applies to either the dark or light areas of your image (depending on whether you're adjusting this setting in the Shadows or Highlights section). It goes from 0% (no different from how the rest of the image is sharpened) to 100%.

- **Tonal Width** tells Elements how wide a range of brightnesses to affect. This slider starts off at 50%. Move it to the left to restrict Elements to a smaller tonal range (darker areas for the Shadows slider, brighter areas for the Highlights slider), or to the right for a larger range of tones. For example, moving the Shadows slider to the left would restrict sharpening to darker tones, while moving it to the right would include brighter areas. In the Highlights section, moving this slider to the left restricts sharpening to lighter tones, while moving it to the right starts including tones more toward the midrange.

- **Radius** tells Elements how large an area around each pixel it should consider when looking for areas to sharpen. If you leave this slider set at 1, that's the narrowest area available. To tell Elements to look farther, move this slider to the right.

Using these sliders lets you get attractive sharpening in the difficult outer tonal ranges, especially dark or shadowed areas, which have been notoriously difficult to work with in the past.

TIP If you're working in the Adjust Sharpness dialog box and don't like the way your changes are affecting your image, click the dialog box's Preset menu and choose Default to return the dialog box to its original settings.

■ CREATING AND SAVING PRESETS

If you have a big batch of images that you know are going to need the same sharpening settings—like a dozen different shots of a model taken using your camera's burst mode or a motor drive—you can speed things up by adjusting one image with the Adjust Sharpness dialog box and then saving those settings as a preset.

The dialog box's Preset drop-down menu makes it easy to work with presets:

- **Create a preset.** Just move the Adjust Sharpness dialog box's sliders to where you want them. When you've got everything sharpened just right, click the Preset menu, and then choose Save Preset. In the window that opens, name your preset and then save it. Don't change the save location Elements suggests or the program won't be able to find your preset. (In Windows, they go in *C:\Users\[user]\ AppData\Roaming\Adobe\Photoshop Elements\13.0\Presets\Smart Sharpen*. In OS X Elements saves presets to *[your hard drive]→Library→Application Support→Adobe→Adobe Photoshop Elements 13→Presets→Smart Sharpen*.) After that, the name of your preset appears in the Preset menu.

- **Use presets created by others.** You aren't limited to your own presets. If someone else creates a preset and sends it to you, just open the Preset drop-down menu, choose Load Preset, and then navigate to the file. (You can also use this option to find your own presets if for some reason they don't appear in the menu.

- **Remove presets.** If you want to get rid of a preset, head to the Preset menu and choose Delete Preset; in the window that opens, choose the doomed preset from the pull-down menu, and then click Delete. If you want to get rid of *all* your custom presets, choose All Presets instead.

Some people who've used Smart Sharpening in the full-featured Photoshop swear they'll never go back to Unsharp Mask. Adjust Sharpness is Elements' version of Smart Sharpening, so give it a try and see if you, too, like it better than Unsharp Mask. To give you an idea of the difference between the two methods, Figure 7-24 shows the dog from Figure 7-21 again, only this time with a dose of Adjust Sharpness instead of Unsharp Mask. Some people consider Adjust Sharpness too darned fiddly to use, so feel free to go back to Unsharp Mask if it works better for you. (And, Mac folks, don't forget that you also have the option of sharpening in Preview [page 136]).

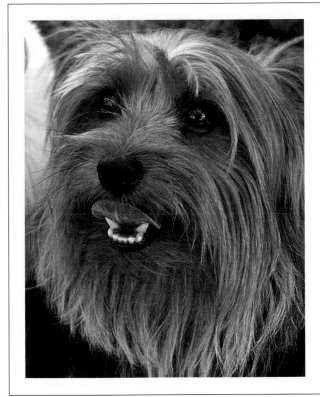

FIGURE 7-24

Here's the terrier from page 261, only this time he's been sharpened using Adjust Sharpness.

Notice how much each hair in his coat stands out, and how much more detail you can see in his nose and mouth.

The High-Pass Filter

Unsharp Mask is definitely the traditional favorite, and Adjust Sharpness is the latest thing in sharpening, but there's an alternative method that many people prefer because you apply it on a dedicated layer, which means you can lessen the effect later by adjusting the layer's opacity. Moreover, you can use this method to punch up the colors in a photo as you sharpen. It's called *high-pass sharpening*.

All sharpening methods have their virtues, and you may find that you choose a technique according to the content of your photo. Try the following procedure by downloading the photo *tiles.jpg* from this book's Missing CD page at *www.missingmanuals.com/cds*:

1. **Open a photo and make sure the layer you want to sharpen is the active layer.**

2. **Duplicate the active layer by pressing Ctrl+J/⌘-J.**

   If you have a multilayered image and you want to sharpen *all* the layers, first flatten the image or use the Stamp Visible command (see the box on page 210) so everything is on one layer.

3. **Go to Filter→Other→High Pass.**

   Your photo now looks like the victim of a mudslide, buried in featureless gray. Don't panic—that's what's supposed to happen. You'll restore the color in step 6.

4. **In the High Pass dialog box, move the slider until you can barely see the outline of your subject.**

   Usually that means picking a setting between roughly 1.5 and 3.5. If you can see colors, your setting is probably too high. (If you can't quite eliminate every trace of color without totally losing the subject's outline, a little bit of color is OK.) Keep in mind that the edges you see through the gray are the ones that will get sharpened the most. Use that as your guide for how much detail to include.

5. **Click OK to close the High Pass dialog box.**

6. **At the top left of the Layers panel, use the unlabeled drop-down menu to set the new layer's blend mode to Overlay.**

   Ta-da! Your subject is back again in glowing, sharper color, as shown in Figure 7-25.

FIGURE 7-25

Left: A closeup look at the original photo.

Right: High-pass sharpening using the Vivid Light blend mode makes the colors stand out more, but it also makes all the tiles a bit coarser and rougher looking than they were in the original. For this technique, you can use any of the blend modes in the group with Overlay except Hard Mix and Pin Light. Vivid Light can make colors pop, but watch out for sharpening artifacts (page 272), since they'll be more vivid, too. Overlay gives you a softer effect.

TIP There's yet another way to create "pop" in photos: the Raw Converter's Clarity setting (page 284), which sharpens *and* enhances contrast. (If you know what "local contrast enhancement" means, this setting does something similar.) You can use it on raw, JPEG, and TIFF files. It's especially useful for clearing haze from shots.

The Sharpen Tool

Elements also gives you a dedicated Sharpen tool for working on specific areas of a photo rather than the entire image. It's a special brush that sharpens just the areas you drag it over; Figure 7-26 shows it in action. To get to it, click the Blur tool's icon in the Tools panel or press R, and then, in the Tool Options area, choose the Sharpen tool (the triangle).

The Sharpen tool has some of the same Tool Options settings as the Brush tool (see page 397 for more about brush settings), as well as a few all its own:

- **Mode** lets you increase the visibility of an object's edge by choosing from several different blend modes; Normal typically gives the most predictable results.

- **Brush**. You can choose a brush style here, but usually the one Elements selects is OK.

- **Size**. You need to be fairly precise about the size of the brush cursor so you can target the details you want to sharpen without affecting the surrounding areas.

FIGURE 7-26

The Sharpen tool isn't meant for sharpening whole photos, but it's great for sharpening details.

Here it's being used to touch up the details in the middle statue. (The red arrow points to the circular cursor.)

Approach this tool with caution: It's super easy to overdo it. One pass too many or too high a setting and you'll start seeing artifacts.

- **Strength** controls how much the tool sharpens what you drag it over. A higher number means more sharpening.

- **Sample All Layers** makes the Sharpen tool work on *all* the image's visible layers. Leave this checkbox off if you want to sharpen only the active layer.

- **Protect Detail**. This setting helps avoid *pixelation* (blockiness)—at least, it's supposed to. In reality, this setting doesn't always have much effect. Adobe suggests leaving it turned on unless you're after an exaggerated sharpening effect.

Elements for Digital Photographers

I f you're a fairly serious digital photographer, you'll be delighted to know that Adobe hasn't just loaded Elements with easy-to-use features. The program also includes a collection of pretty advanced tools pulled straight from the full-featured Photoshop.

Number one on the list is the Adobe Camera Raw Converter, which lets you convert and edit *raw files*—a format some cameras use to give you maximum editing control. In this chapter, you'll learn about the raw format and why you may (or may not) want to use it. But don't skip to the next chapter if your camera shoots only JPEGs: You can use the Raw Converter to edit JPEG and TIFF images, too, which can come in really handy. Working with JPEGs and other image formats in the Raw Converter is explained on page 289.

> **NOTE** Whereas JPEG and TIFF are acronyms for technical photographic terms, the word "raw"—which you may occasionally see in all caps (RAW)—actually refers to the pristine, unprocessed quality of these files.

This chapter also explains Exposure Merge, which lets you combine different versions of a photo to create a single image with a higher dynamic range (a wider range of correctly exposed areas) than you can get from a single shot. You'll also get to know the Photo Filter command, which helps adjust colors by replicating the old-school effect of placing filters over camera lenses. And Elements has some truly useful batch-processing tools that let you do things like rename groups of files, convert them to different formats, and even apply basic retouching to them. Read on to learn about all these features.

■ The Raw Converter

Probably the most useful thing Adobe has done for photography buffs is to include the Adobe Camera Raw Converter in Elements. For many people, this feature alone is worth the price of the program, since you just can't beat the convenience of being able to perform conversions in the same program you use for editing.

If you don't know what raw is, it's just a file format (a group of formats, really, since every camera company has its *own* raw format with its own file extension), but it's a very special one. When your digital camera takes a photo, it doesn't really take a picture. It captures three separate sets of data, one for each of the color channels (red, green, blue). That information then needs to be processed into something that you can recognize as an image, and your digital camera contains a little computer that processes your photos right inside the camera. If you shoot in JPEG format, for instance, your camera makes some decisions about things like sharpness, color saturation, and contrast before it saves the JPEG files to its memory card.

But if your camera lets you shoot raw files, then you get the *unprocessed* data straight from the camera. Shooting in raw lets you make your own decisions about how your photos should look, to a much greater degree than with any other format. It's something like getting a negative from your digital camera—what you do with it in your digital darkroom is up to you.

That's raw's big advantage—total control. The downside is that every camera manufacturer has its own proprietary raw format, and the format varies even among models from the same company. Also, no regular graphics program can edit these files, and very few programs can even open them. Instead, you need special software to convert raw files to a format you can work with. In the past, that usually meant you needed to get software from the camera's manufacturer before you could move your photo into an editing program like Elements.

Enter Adobe Camera Raw, which lets you convert your files right in Elements. Not only that, but the Adobe Camera Raw plug-in that comes with Elements lets you make sophisticated corrections to your photos before you even open them. Many times, you can do everything you need right in the Converter, so that you're done as soon as you open the converted file. (Of course, you can then open the file in the Editor and use any of the program's tools on it.) Using Adobe Camera Raw saves you tons of time, and it's compatible with most cameras' raw files.

> **NOTE** Adobe regularly updates the Raw Converter to work with new proprietary raw formats produced by different camera manufacturers, and to include updated profiles for existing cameras. So if your camera's raw files don't open, check for a newer version of the Converter by going to Help→Updates in the Editor. (When you install Elements, it's set to periodically check for updates automatically, but this is how you check manually.) If you aren't sure which version of the Raw Converter you have (you can't remember whether you've applied the latest update, for instance), go to Help→About Plug-In→Camera Raw/Photoshop Elements Editor→About Plug-In→Camera Raw to check.

Using the Raw Converter

For all the options it gives you, the Raw Converter is really easy to use. Adobe designed it to automatically calculate and apply what it thinks are the correct settings for exposure, shadows, brightness, and contrast. You can accept the Converter's decisions or override them and do everything yourself—it's your call.

While you may find the Converter's various settings, tools, and tabs a little overwhelming at first, it's actually laid out quite logically. Here's an overview of how to use it (you'll get the details in a moment):

1. **Open a file in the Raw Converter (it's shown in Figure 8-1).**

   All you have to do to call up the Raw Converter from either the Organizer or the Editor's Expert mode window is open a raw file.

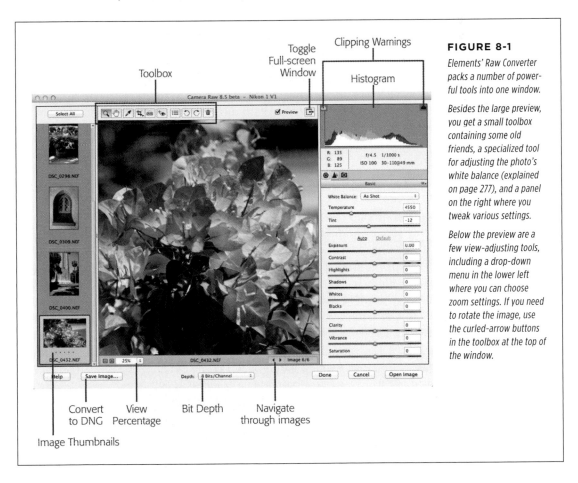

FIGURE 8-1

Elements' Raw Converter packs a number of powerful tools into one window.

Besides the large preview, you get a small toolbox containing some old friends, a specialized tool for adjusting the photo's white balance (explained on page 277), and a panel on the right where you tweak various settings.

Below the preview are a few view-adjusting tools, including a drop-down menu in the lower left where you can choose zoom settings. If you need to rotate the image, use the curled-arrow buttons in the toolbox at the top of the window.

NOTE If you run Elements on a screen that's less than 768 pixels high (like on a netbook, say, or if you've reduced your monitor's resolution to less than that), the Raw Converter window may not appear. Elements just automatically converts your file and then opens it in the Editor without giving you a chance to tweak anything.

2. **Adjust your view and do any necessary rotating, straightening, and cropping.**

   The Raw Converter has its own tools for all these tasks, so you don't need to go into the Editor to perform any of them.

3. **Adjust the image's settings.**

   This is the best part of shooting raw images: You can tweak settings for things like exposure, lighting, and color. The Raw Converter also lets you apply final touchups like noise reduction, sharpening, and so on.

4. **Leave the Raw Converter and go to the Editor.**

   The Raw Converter is a powerhouse for improving your photo's fundamental appearance, but to perform all the other adjustments Elements lets you make—applying filters, adding effects, and so on—you need to move your image to the Editor, which is also where you save the file in the standard graphics format of your choice (like TIFF, PSD, or JPEG).

NOTE To get some practice with the Raw Converter, you can download the sample raw image *Raw_practice. mrw* from this book's Missing CD page at *www.missingmanuals.com/cds*, but be warned: It's a big file.

To start converting a raw file, in the Organizer, right-click/Control-click the file, and then choose "Edit with Photoshop Elements Editor" (or press Ctrl+I/⌘-I) to bring up the Raw Converter window. (If you select multiple raw files and the Converter doesn't open automatically when you run this command, you can find your files in the Editor's Photo Bin by going to the menu above the bin and choosing "Show Files selected in Organizer." Select them all, and then double-click one of their thumbnails to display them in the Converter.) If you're starting from the Editor, just go to File→Open. Figure 8-2 explains how to work with multiple files in the Raw Converter.

NOTE In Windows, you may not be able to open raw files by double-clicking them outside Elements (on the desktop, for instance). If you try that, Windows may open the file in its Photos app, or you may see a message to the effect that your computer has no idea what program to use to open that file. (Windows may also offer to take you to a website where you can download the files necessary to display your raw photos.) To make your computer always use Elements to open raw files, follow the steps on page 37.

On a Mac, you can usually open raw files in Preview. As long as you don't have a very new—or very old—camera (or one of the few models that Apple doesn't have the necessary information for), OS X should understand the raw files your camera creates.

FIGURE 8-2

When you have several files open in the Raw Converter, you get this handy filmstrip view down the left side of the window.

You can select a single image from the group by clicking it, and then your changes apply only to that file. Shift-click or Ctrl-click to select multiple images (or use the Select All button at the top of the filmstrip), and all the selected files get changed along with the one in the main preview area.

When you finish your tweaks and click Open, all the selected files appear in the Editor's Photo Bin. If you want to save a group of them in another format, and then use the Process Multiple Files command (page 301).

One important point to remember about raw files: *Elements never overwrites the original file.* As a matter of fact, Elements *can't* modify the original raw file in any way. So your original is always there if you want to try converting it again later using different settings. It's something like having a negative from which you can always get more prints. This also applies to *any* image you edit in the Raw Converter, not just raw files. You can crop a JPEG file here, for instance, and your original JPEG doesn't get cropped—only the copy you open from the Converter. (Page 289 has more about working with non-raw files in the Converter.)

TIP   If you shoot Raw+JPEG (where your camera takes one photo and saves it as both a raw file and a JPEG file), you may find that the Photo Downloader (page 30) gets very confused by this scenario. If you have problems importing these files into the Organizer, try using another method to get the photos onto your computer, and then use File→"Get Photos and Videos"→"From Files and Folders" to bring them into the Organizer.

■ ADJUSTING YOUR VIEW

When the Raw Converter opens, you see something like Figure 8-1. Before you decide whether to accept the automatic settings that the Converter makes or to do your own tweaking, you need to get a good, close look at the image. The Converter makes it easy to do this by giving you a large preview of the image and a handful of tools to help adjust what you see:

- **Zoom and Hand tools**. These are in the toolbox at the top of the Converter window. You use them here exactly the same way as elsewhere in Elements. (The Zoom tool is covered on page 102; the Hand tool is described on page 103. The keyboard shortcuts for adjusting the view and scrolling also work in the Raw Converter.)

- **View percentage**. Below the lower-left corner of the preview area is a drop-down menu with preset sizes. Simply choose the size you want, or click the + or – button to zoom in or out.

- **Full Screen**. Just above the upper-right corner of the preview area is an icon that looks like a page with a double-headed arrow on it. Click it or press F to put the Raw Converter into full-screen mode. Click it or press F again to toggle back to the normal view.

- **Histogram**. In the upper-right corner of the Converter window is a histogram that helps you keep track of how your changes affect the colors in the photo. Flip back to page 245 for more on the fine art of reading histograms.

> **TIP** Another handy feature in the Raw Converter is the area right below the histogram, where you can see important shooting information about your photo, like the aperture and ISO speed (*ISO* is a digital camera's version of film speed). Put your cursor over a pixel in the image and the pixel's RGB values (page 237) appear here, too.

Once you've gotten a close look at the photo, you have a decision to make: Did Elements do a good enough job of choosing settings for you? (In other words, do you like how your photo looks?) If so, you're done. Just click the Open Image button in the Converter's lower-right corner, and Elements opens the photo in the Editor, ready for any artistic changes or cropping. If you prefer to make adjustments to the photo in the Converter, read on. (If you're happy with Elements' conversion but you want to sharpen the picture, then skip ahead to page 286.)

> **NOTE** Everyone gets confused by the Save Image button in the Converter's lower-left corner. That button is actually the DNG Converter (see page 291), and all you can do when you click it is create a DNG file. To save your edited raw file, click Done if you want to save your changes without actually opening the file, or click Open Image to open it in the Editor and then save it in the format of your choice.

■ ROTATING, STRAIGHTENING, AND CROPPING

Before tweaking the image's other settings, you can make the following basic adjustments to photos right in the Raw Converter:

- **Rotate it**. Click one of the rotation arrows above the image preview.

- **Straighten it**. The Raw Converter has its own Straighten tool, which you use just like the one in the Editor's Tools panel (page 84), although it has a different cursor. (It's just to the right of the Crop tool in the Raw Converter's toolbox; keyboard shortcut: A.) However, you don't see the photo actually straighten out in the Converter—Elements just shows you the outline of where the edges of the straightened photo will be. You have to open the photo in the Editor to make Elements apply the straightening.

- **Crop it**. The Raw Converter has a Crop tool somewhat like the one in the Editor (page 90). To crop to a particular aspect ratio, click the Crop tool's icon (or press C), and then right-click/Control-click in your image. To crop to a particular size, choose Custom from the shortcut menu, and then, in the dialog box that appears, enter the dimensions. (You also need to select inches, centimeters, or pixels, or enter a custom aspect ratio.) Your cropping info gets saved along with the raw file, so the next time you open the file in the Converter, you see the cropped version.

  As with straightening, Elements just draws a mask over the cropped area in the Converter; you can still see the outline of the whole photo. To adjust your crop, make sure the Crop tool is active, and then drag one of the handles that appear around the cropped area. To revert to the uncropped original later, activate the Crop tool, and then right-click/Control-click in the image preview and choose Clear Crop.

> **TIP** You can also fix red eye in the Raw Converter—the Red Eye Removal tool is in the toolbox just to the right of the Straighten tool (keyboard shortcut: E), and it works the same way it does everywhere else in Elements (see page 126). You'll have to open the image into the Editor to use Pet Eye correction, though.

Adjusting White Balance

The pane on the right side of the Raw Converter window gives you lots of ways to tweak and correct photos' color, exposure, sharpness, brightness, and noise level. The pane is divided into three tabs. Start with the one labeled Basic, which contains, well, the *basic* settings for the major adjustments. (The Raw Converter automatically opens to this tab.)

To Shoot in the Raw or Not

Should I shoot all my pictures in raw format?

It depends. Using raw format has pros and cons. You may be surprised to learn that some professional photographers *don't* use raw. For example, many journalists don't, and it's not common with sports photographers, either.

To help you decide whether to get involved with raw, here's a quick look at the advantages and disadvantages. On the plus side, you get:

- **More control**. With raw, you have a lot of extra chances to tweak your photos, and you get to call the shots, instead of your camera making the processing decisions.

- **More fixes**. If you're not a perfect photographer, raw is more forgiving than other formats, so you can fix a lot of mistakes (though even raw can't make a bad photo great).

- **No need to constantly fuss with white balance while shooting**. That said, you'll have better quality data to work with if your camera's white-balance settings are correct.

- **Nondestructive editing**. The edits you make in the Raw Converter don't change your original image one jot. It's always there if you need to make a fresh start.

But raw also has some significant drawbacks. For one thing, you can't just open a raw file and start editing it the way you do with JPEGs. You always have to convert it first, whether you use the Raw Converter or one supplied by the company that made your camera. Other disadvantages include:

- **Larger file size**. Raw files are smaller than TIFFs, but they're usually much bigger than the highest-quality JPEGs. Consequently, you need bigger (or more) memory cards if you regularly shoot raw.

- **Slower speed**. It generally takes cameras longer to save raw files than JPEGs—something to keep in mind when you're taking action shots. Most modern cameras have a buffer that holds several shots and lets you keep shooting while the camera is saving, but you may hit the limit pretty quickly if you're using burst (rapid-advance) mode, especially on a pocket-sized point-and-shoot camera that uses raw. In that case, you just have to wait. (Most digital single-lens reflex cameras are pretty fast with raw these days, but they're generally even faster with JPEGs.)

- **More time consuming**. The JPEG-processing abilities of many cameras have improved significantly in the past few years, and they generally create decent JPEG images. So for a lot of people for casual shooting it's just not worth the extra step of fiddling around with all the Raw Converter's settings. You can almost always get a much better final image by shooting in raw and then tweaking the Converter's settings, but if you're just grabbing a quick snap of, say, a house that's for sale, it may not be worth the extra minute or two to create a masterpiece.

You may want to try a few shots of the same subject in both raw and JPEG to see whether you notice a difference in the results. Generally speaking, raw offers the most leeway if you want to make significant edits, but you need to understand what you're doing. JPEG is easier if you're a beginner.

The bottom line: It's your call. Some excellent photographers wouldn't think of shooting in anything *but* raw, while others think it's too time consuming.

First, check the White Balance setting at the top of the Basic tab. Adjusting white balance is often the most important step in making photos look their best. This setting adjusts all the colors in a photo by creating a neutral white tone. If that sounds a little strange, stop and think about it for a minute: The color you think of as *white* actually changes depending on lighting conditions. At noon there's no warmth (no orange/yellow) to the light because the sun is high in the sky. Later in the day when the sun's rays are lower, whites are warmer. Indoors, tungsten lighting is much warmer than fluorescent lighting, which makes whites rather bluish or greenish. Your eyes and brain easily compensate for these changes, but sometimes your camera may not, or may overcompensate, giving your photos a color cast. The Raw Converter's White Balance setting lets you create more accurate color by neutralizing the image's white tones.

Most digital cameras have their own collections of white-balance settings. Typical choices include Auto, Daylight, Cloudy, Tungsten, Fluorescent, and Custom. When you shoot JPEGs, picking the correct setting really matters, because it's tough to readjust white balance, even in a program like Elements (unless you tweak the JPEG with the Raw Converter as explained in the box on page 289, and even then the results may not be what you want).

With raw photos, you can afford to be a little sloppier about setting your camera's white balance, because you can easily fix things in the Raw Converter. Getting the white balance right can make a huge difference in how your photo looks, as you can see in Figure 8-3.

FIGURE 8-3

Left: The lighting in this shot has a bluish cast that makes it look chilly, but a single click with the White Balance tool (circled) on the gray path can fix that.

Right: As you can see, the correct white balance makes the image much warmer and more vivid.

The Raw Converter gives you several ways to adjust an image's white balance:

• **Drop-down menu**. The White Balance menu at the top of the Basic tab starts out set to As Shot, which means the Converter is showing your camera's settings. You can use this menu to choose from Auto, Daylight, Cloudy, and so on. It's worth giving Auto a try because it picks the correct settings surprisingly often.

- **Temperature**. Use this slider to make the photo warmer (more orange) or cooler (more blue). Dragging the slider right warms the photo; dragging it left cools it. If you're experienced in doing this by the numbers, you can type a temperature in the text box in degrees Kelvin (the official unit of measurement for color temperature) instead. Use this slider and the Tint slider (described next) together for a perfect white balance.

- **Tint**. This slider controls the green/magenta balance of the photo, pretty much the way it does in Quick Fix. Move it left to increase the amount of green in the photo, or right for more magenta.

- **White Balance tool**. The eyedropper icon up in the Converter window's toolbox is actually the White Balance tool (keyboard shortcut: I). Activate it, and then click any white or light-gray spot in your photo, and Elements calculates the white balance based on those pixels. This is the most accurate method in this list, but you may have a hard time finding neutral pixels to click with it. If you choose a blown-out area, Elements will warn you to pick another spot with more information in it.

If you're a good photographer, then much of the time a good white balance and a little sharpening may be all your photo needs before it's ready to go out into the world.

Adjusting Tone

The next group of sliders in the Raw Converter's Basic tab—Exposure through Blacks—helps you improve an image's exposure and lighting (also known as *tone)*. If you want the Converter to make decisions for you, click the word "Auto" above these sliders, and the program selects what it thinks are the best positions for each of the six sliders. If you don't click anything, then the Converter starts you off with the Default settings. Here's the difference between Auto and Default:

- **Auto**. The Converter automatically adjusts the photo by using the same software-powered guesswork behind the other Auto buttons throughout Elements. If you *always* want the Converter to apply auto adjustments, see Figure 8-4.

- **Default**. The Raw Converter has a database of basic tone settings for each camera model. If you choose Default, then you see the baseline settings for your camera, and it's up to you to make further adjustments to the photo. If you want, you can set your own defaults (where the sliders are when your photo opens), too, as explained on page 284. So if you don't like what you got with Auto, for example, then just click the word "Default" to switch the photo back to how it was when you opened it.

After you've clicked Auto or Default (or neither), you can override any tone setting by moving its slider. If you go to the trouble of shooting raw, then you may well want to, as Figure 8-5 demonstrates.

FIGURE 8-4

To make the Raw Converter always open your photos with the Auto settings applied, open the Raw Converter Preferences dialog box by clicking the three-line icon in the Raw Converter's toolbox or pressing Ctrl+K/⌘-K.

In the dialog box, turn on the "Apply auto tone adjustments" checkbox, as shown here, and from then on, the Raw Converter is in Auto mode—at least for the tone settings.

FIGURE 8-5

Left: The Raw Converter's Auto settings make this photo look like a lost cause.

Right: With a little bit of manual adjustment, you can see that the camera actually captured plenty of details for the Raw Converter to bring out.

If you've converted raw files in old versions of Elements, you'll notice that the sliders in the current version of the Raw Converter (version 8.6) are very different from what they were in versions 6 and below. Even the ones that have the same names work differently (and better) than they used to. For one thing, each slider starts out dead in the middle (at 0), giving you more ability to adjust it either up or down. Here's a rundown of what each one does:

- **Exposure**. A properly exposed photo shows the largest possible range of detail—shadows contain enough light to reveal details, and highlights aren't so bright that all you see is white. Move this slider left to decrease exposure or right to increase it. (This setting has the greatest effect on midtones.)

- **Contrast**. This slider also adjusts the image's midtones; move it right for greater contrast in those tones, or left for less. People usually use this slider last of the six sliders in this group because things can shift pretty dramatically if you use other sliders after increasing contrast.

- **Highlights**. This clever slider can bring down overexposed highlights (recovering details that were lost in those areas) without underexposing the rest of the photo, or increase the brightness of highlights that are too dark.

- **Shadows**. This slider adjusts the shadow values in the photo and determines which pixels become black. Increasing this setting may help improve the image's contrast. Drag the slider right to lighten shadows or left to darken them.

- **Whites**. Use this slider to set the photo's white point, more or less the way you do with Levels (page 243).

- **Blacks**. Use this slider to set your black point, again something like the way you do with Levels.

Most of the time, you'll use several of these sliders to get a perfectly exposed photo. However, in a change from the usual "work from the top down" way that most groups of controls in Elements work, you may want to start with Whites and Blacks and *then* go back up to Exposure and the others. It's quite amazing how much more range you can pull out of a photo in the Raw Converter with a little careful adjustment.

One thing to watch for: Although you can make pretty large adjustments, setting the tone sliders too high may still *clip* some of your highlights (meaning they'll be so bright that you won't see any detail in them). Figure 8-6 explains more about clipping.

TIP If you've been fiddling around with a slider and then decide you need to start over, double-click it to return it to 0 (the middle).

Once you have things adjusted the way you want, you can move on to the Basic tab's other sliders, described in the next section. You can also save your current settings for use with other photos, or undo all the changes you've made, as explained on page 284.

NOTE If you're upgrading from version 6 of the Raw Converter or older, the sliders in this group are different from what you're used to seeing. The newer version has greatly improved controls for adjusting your photos, but if you *really* want to see the sliders you're used to using, you can switch back to them; the box on page 286 explains how.

FIGURE 8-6

To help you get the tone settings right, the Raw Converter includes two triangles above the ends of its histogram (they're labeled back in Figure 8-1). Click them to turn on "clipping warnings" that reveal where your image's highlights (in red) or shadows (in blue) lose detail at your current settings. (If the photo isn't clipped, then the triangle for that end of the histogram is dark. If the triangle is white or colored, then you have a problem; click the triangle to turn the mask on to see the clipping.)

As you adjust the Raw Converter's tone settings, the mask changes accordingly. This photo shows that, unless you adjust your settings, the red and blue areas will be clipped when you open the photo in the Editor.

Adjusting Clarity, Vibrance, and Saturation

The final group of settings in the Raw Converter's Basic tab controls the vividness of your image's colors. Most raw files have lower saturation to start with than you'd see in the same photo shot as a JPEG, so people often want to boost the saturation of their raw images. Move the sliders right for more intense color, or left for more muted color. (If you know you'll *always* want to adjust the intensity of the color in your photos, then you can change the Raw Converter's standard setting by moving the sliders until you have the intensity you want, and then creating a new camera default setting as described on page 284.)

Here's what each of these sliders does:

- **Clarity**. This slider is a bit different from the other two. Clarity isn't strictly a color tool, although it's an absolutely amazing feature. If you're an experienced Elements sharpener, you may have heard of a technique called *local contrast enhancement*, where you use the Unsharp Mask with a low Amount setting and a high Radius setting to eliminate haze and bring out details. That's sort of what this slider does: Through some incredibly sophisticated computing, it creates an edge mask for your photo that it uses to increase detail. This setting can do wonderful things for many—maybe even most—photos by improving contrast and adding punch. Give it a try, but be sure you're viewing your photo at 100 percent magnification (or more) so you can see how you're changing things.

- **Vibrance**. This slider works the same way it does in the Quick Fix window: It increases the intensity of dull colors without oversaturating already-vivid ones. If you want to adjust an image's saturation, then try this slider first, before you move the Saturation slider.

- **Saturation**. This slider controls how vivid the image's colors are by changing the intensity of *all* its colors by the same amount.

■ SAVING YOUR SETTINGS

Most of the time, you'll want to use the current Raw Converter settings on only the specific photo(s) you're editing right now. But the Converter gives you a bunch of ways to save time by saving settings for future use. Below the histogram, to the right of the word "Basic," are three tiny lines with a minute arrow at their bottom right. Click that icon to see a drop-down menu. Whatever you choose from this menu determines how the Converter converts your photo. Here are your choices:

- **Image Settings**. This is the "undo all my changes" option. If you've made some changes to your photo in the Converter but want to revert to the settings the Converter originally presented you with, then choose this option.

- **Camera Raw Defaults**. The Raw Converter contains a profile of typical settings for your camera model that it uses as its baseline for the adjustments it makes. That's what you get when you use this option. These are the settings you see when you first open a photo in the Converter.

- **Previous Conversion**. If you've already processed a photo and want to apply the same settings to the photo you're currently working on, then choosing this setting applies the settings from the last raw image you opened (*if* it's from the same camera).

- **Custom Settings**. Once you start changing the Raw Converter's settings, this option becomes active (you see a checkmark next to it). You don't need to select it—the Converter does that automatically as soon as you start making adjustments.

Since individual cameras—even if they're the same model—may vary a bit (as a result of the manufacturing process), the Camera Raw Defaults settings may not be the best ones for your camera. You can override the default settings and create your own set of defaults for any camera. Here's how:

- **To change your camera's settings:** If you know that you *always* want a different setting for one of the sliders—like maybe the Shadows setting should be at 5 instead of the standard setting of 0—move any or all of the sliders to where you want them, and then choose Save New Camera Raw Defaults from the menu discussed above. From now on, the Converter opens photos from that camera with these settings as the starting point.

- **To revert to the original settings for your camera:** If you want to go back to the way things were originally, then choose Reset Camera Raw Defaults from the menu described above.

> **TIP** You can apply the same changes to multiple photos at once. Page 275 explains how.

The Raw Converter's preferences include a couple of special settings that may interest you. (To bring up the Camera Raw Preferences dialog box, in the Raw Converter's toolbox, click the icon with three lines.) These preferences can be really useful, especially if you have more than one camera:

- **Make defaults specific to camera serial number**. Turn on this checkbox if you have more than one of a particular camera model; for instance, if you carry two bodies of the same model with different lenses, or if both you and your spouse have the same camera model. This setting lets you have a different default for each camera body.

- **Make defaults specific to camera ISO setting**. Since you may shoot very differently at different ISO settings (ISO is the digital equivalent of film speed), you can turn on this setting and then create a default that the Converter applies only to photos shot at ISO 100, at ISO 1600, and so on.

> **TIP** If you regularly share photos with other people using Adobe programs, you'll be pleased to know that the Raw Converter's preferences let you choose whether your settings get saved in the Camera Raw database or in a sidecar XMP file that goes along with the image. If you choose the XMP option, then your settings become portable along with your photo—so if you send the image to someone else using Adobe's Raw Converter, the settings come along for the ride (as long as you send the XMP file, too).

You don't have to create default settings to save the changes you make to a particular photo. If you just want to save the settings for the photo or group of photos you're working on right now without having to open them all in the Editor and save them in another format, make your changes and then click the Raw Converter's Done button to update the settings for the image file(s).

TIP   You can also choose a different camera profile for the Raw Converter to use as a basis for adjusting your photos. The box below explains how.

Adjusting Sharpness and Reducing Noise

Once you've got your image's exposure and white balance right, you may be almost done tweaking the photo. But in most cases, you'll want to click over to the Raw Converter's Detail tab to do a little sharpening: On the right side of the Raw Converter, above the word "Basic," click the icon that looks like two triangles.

None of the adjustments on this tab have Auto settings, although you can change the standard settings by moving their sliders where you want them, and then creating a new camera default (page 284).

POWER USERS' CLINIC

Working with Profiles

The Raw Converter has yet *another* trick up its sleeve. (If you're a beginner, you can safely ignore this feature, but it's pretty handy for raw experts.) In addition to the Basic and Detail tabs, the Converter also has a Camera Calibration tab (its icon is a little camera). This tab includes a Process menu that lets you choose which process the Converter uses to convert your raw files, and a Name drop-down menu.

Your choices in the Name menu depend on your particular camera model, but the list typically includes a group of profiles with names like Adobe Standard, Camera Portrait, Camera Neutral, and so on; some numbered profiles that seem to imply you're using an older version of Adobe Camera Raw; or a combination of both kinds of profiles. What's the point of this cryptic list? It lets you choose from the different *profiles* for your camera—basically, sets of parameters that the Raw Converter uses to convert the raw files from cameras into recognizable photos. The Raw Converter can use any profile with any process you choose from this tab's Process menu.

Just click through the profiles in the Name menu to see their effects (watch how the preview of your image changes) and choose the one you like best. (You can edit these profiles in Photoshop, but not in Elements.) If you're wondering why the menu includes older ACR (Adobe Camera Raw) versions like 4.2, that's because it lists the version numbers for when the built-in Adobe Camera Raw profiles were last updated. (Not all camera models list these older profiles.) So if you've been thinking, "You know, I prefer the way my raw files looked a couple of versions ago," no problem. Just pick the older profile from the Name menu to use that instead of the newest one.

The first set of sliders on this tab is labeled Sharpening. Sharpening increases the edge contrast in photos, which makes them appear more crisply focused. The sharpening tools in the Raw Converter are a bit different from those in the Editor, but some of the sliders should look familiar if you've sharpened before, since they're similar to the settings for Unsharp Mask and Adjust Sharpness:

- **Amount** controls how much the Converter sharpens. The scale here goes from 0 (no sharpening) to 150 (usually way too much sharpening).

- **Radius** governs how wide an area the Converter considers an edge. Its scale goes from 0.5 pixels to 3 pixels. Generally, the more fine detail in your photo, the lower you want this setting to be.

- **Detail** controls how the Converter applies sharpening. At 100—the right end of the scale—the effect is similar to Unsharp Mask (in other words, you can overdo it if you aren't careful). At 0, you shouldn't see any sharpening halos at all.

- **Masking** is a very cool feature that reduces the area where sharpening takes place so that only edges get sharpened. With a setting of 0, everything in the photo gets sharpened equally. If you find that the Converter is sharpening more details than you like, then use this slider to create an edge mask that keeps it from sharpening areas inside the edges. The farther right you move this slider, the more area you protect from sharpening. As you adjust this slider, the Converter does some amazing behind-the-scenes calculations, so don't be surprised if there's a little lag in the preview when you move this slider.

The Masking and Detail settings work together to perform really accurate sharpening, which is why their sliders go so high—you won't like the effect from just one of them set all the way up, but by experimenting with both sliders, you can create excellent sharpening in your photos.

TIP As Figure 8-7 explains, you can get an extremely helpful view of your image if you hold the Alt/Option key as you move the sliders.

FIGURE 8-7

If you've tried high-pass sharpening (page 267), then you won't have any trouble understanding this view. Just Alt-drag/Option-drag the Detail tab's Masking slider to see this black-and-white view of your image. The lack of color makes it easy to focus on what you're doing to the photo's edge sharpness, so you get an accurate view of the effect the slider is having.

(The other sliders in the Sharpening section also show different views when you Alt-drag/Option-drag them: Amount displays a black-and-white view, while Radius and Detail are more like what you see when applying the High-Pass filter.)

If you're not planning on making any further edits to your photo when you leave the Raw Converter, then go ahead and sharpen the image here. On the other hand, some people prefer to wait and sharpen only after they finish making additional adjustments in the Editor, so they skip these sliders. But you can usually sharpen here and then sharpen *again* later (in the Editor) without any problems.

The second group of settings on this tab (under Noise Reduction) work together to reduce *noise* (graininess) in your photos. Noise is a big problem in digital photos, especially with 10-plus megapixel cameras that don't have the large sensors found in single-lens reflex cameras, and with cellphone cameras. Here's how these adjustments can help:

- **Luminance**. By moving this slider, you can reduce grayscale noise, which gives photos an overall grainy appearance—something like what you see in old newspaper photos. The slider always starts at 0, since you don't want to use more than necessary—moving it to the right reduces noise but also softens the image's details. The following two sliders become active only if you move this slider:

  — **Luminance Detail**. This slider helps set the threshold for luminance noise reduction. If you set it high, you preserve more details but may have a noisier photo. If you set it low, you have less noise, but maybe less detail, too.

  — **Luminance Contrast**. Set this slider higher to preserve some of the contrast you might lose with the Luminance slider, but *too* high a setting here can produce blotches or mottling. Set this slider low and you get smoother results that preserve more of the image's texture, but you may lose some contrast.

- **Color**. If areas of your photo that should be evenly colored contain obvious clumps of different-colored pixels, this setting can help smooth things out. Drag it to the right to reduce the amount of color noise.

- **Color Detail**. This slider works on color noise the same way the Luminance Detail slider works on luminance noise. If you set this slider high, detailed color edges get preserved, but you might see some color speckling in your photo. Set it low and you'll have less color noise, but you may see some bleeding where colors meet.

In most cases, it may take a fair amount of fiddling with these sliders to come up with the best compromise between sharpness and smoothness. It helps if you zoom in to 100 percent or more when adjusting these settings.

Choosing Bit Depth

Once you've got your photo looking good in the Raw Converter, you have one more important choice to make: Do you want to open it in Elements as an 8-bit file or a 16-bit file? *Bit depth* refers to how many pieces of color data, or *bits*, each pixel in an image can hold. A single pixel of an 8-bit image can have 24 pieces of information in it—8 for each of the three color channels (red, green, and blue). A 16-bit image holds far more color info than an 8-bit photo. How much more? An 8-bit image can hold up to 16 million colors, which may sound like a lot—until you realize that a 16-bit image can hold up to 281 *trillion* colors.

TIP You can adjust 16-bit images with microscopic precision, but your home printer prints only in 8-bit color. If you want to do all your editing (or at least 90 percent of it) in 16-bit color, then consider upgrading to Photoshop.

WORKAROUND WORKSHOP

Non-Raw Files in the Raw Converter

If your camera shoots JPEGs and you've always been curious what this raw business is all about, you can find out for yourself—sort of. You can open and process JPEG, PSD, and TIFF files with the Raw Converter. (If you want to try another kind of file, save it as a TIFF and *then* open it with the Raw Converter. That way you can take advantage of the Converter's special tools, like Vibrance and Clarity, for any photo.)

To do this, in the Editor, just go to File→"Open in Camera Raw" or press Alt+Ctrl+O/Option-⌘-O. (Unfortunately, you have to do this from within the Editor—there's no similar option in the Organizer.)

The image opens in the Converter, and you can work on it just like a real raw file—well, almost. Here's the thing about using other formats in the Converter: When your camera processed the JPEG file that it wrote to its memory card, it tossed out the info it didn't need for the JPEG, so Elements doesn't have the same amount of data to work with as it does for a *true* raw file. The Converter lets you create a DNG—digital negative—file (page 291) from a JPEG, but it can't put back the info that

wasn't included in the JPEG, so this feature isn't very useful for most people.

Because non-raw files don't have as much info as raw files, working with them in the Raw Converter can lead to some iffy results. You may find that the Converter does a bang-up job on your photo, or you may decide you liked it better before you started messing with it. There are so many variables involved that it's really hard to predict the results you'll get, but it's definitely worth a try.

Once you open a non-raw file in the Raw Converter this way, from then on it will *automatically* open in the Converter. If you want it to open in the regular Editor, just hold down the Shift key as you open the file to bypass the Raw Converter.

If you find you like using the Raw Converter for JPEGs, then you may want to experiment with reducing your camera's saturation, contrast, and sharpening settings, if possible. That's because you're more likely to get good results from the Raw Converter if your image is fairly neutral to start with.

Most digital cameras produce raw files with 10 or 12 bits per channel, although a few can shoot 16-bit files. The Raw Converter can save any of these original bit depths as either 8- or 16-bit files. You'd think it would be a good idea to save digital files at the largest possible bit depth, but you'll find quite a few restrictions on what you can do with 16-bit files in Elements. You can open them, make some corrections, and save them, but that's about it. You can't work with layers or apply the more artistic filters to 16-bit files, although you can use many of Elements' Auto commands. If you want to work with layers on 16-bit files, then you need to upgrade to Photoshop.

NOTE Your scanner may *say* it handles 24-bit color, but this is actually the same as what Elements calls 8-bit. Elements goes by the number of bits per color channel, whereas some scanner manufacturers try to impress you by giving you the total for all three channels ($8 \times 3 = 24$). So when you see really high bit numbers on scanners—assuming they're not machines for commercial print shops—you can usually get the Elements equivalent by dividing by three.

Once you've decided between 8- and 16-bit color, make your selection in the Depth drop-down menu at the bottom of the Raw Converter window. This setting is "sticky," so until you change it, all your images open in the color depth you choose here. If you ever forget what bit depth you've chosen, your image's title bar or tab tells you, as Figure 8-8 shows.

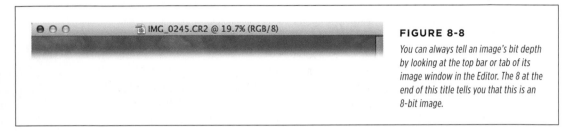

FIGURE 8-8

You can always tell an image's bit depth by looking at the top bar or tab of its image window in the Editor. The 8 at the end of this title tells you that this is an 8-bit image.

> **TIP** If you decide to create a 16-bit image and later become frustrated by your lack of editing options, then you can convert it to 8-bit by choosing Image→Mode→8 Bits/Channel in the Editor. (However, you *can't* convert an 8-bit image to 16 bits.)

If you want to take advantage of any 16-bit files you have, you may want to convert *copies* of them to 8 bits, and then use either the Save As command or the Organizer's version-set option when you save them. That way, you'll still have the 16-bit files for future reference. (Incidentally, your Save options are different for the two bit depths: JPEG, for instance, is available only for 8-bit files, because JPEGs are *always* 8-bit. Because of this, if you try to save a 16-bit file as a JPEG, Elements makes you save it as a copy.)

A popular choice when you're thinking about your order of operations (*workflow*, in photo industry–speak) is to first convert your raw file as a 16-bit image to take advantage of the increased color information and make basic corrections, and then convert to 8-bit for the fancy stuff like adding artistic filters or layers in the Editor.

Finishing Up

Now that you've got your photo all tweaked, sleeked, and groomed to look exactly the way you want, it's time to get it out of the Raw Converter. To do that, click the Open Image button in the Converter's lower-right corner, which sends the image to the Editor, where you can save it in the format of your choice, like TIFF or JPEG. (Why not click the Raw Converter's Save Image button? Adobe should probably rename this button, which confuses everyone. The Save Image button is actually just a link to the DNG Converter discussed in the next section.)

If you just want to save your changes without opening the file, just click Done to close the Converter. The next time you open the raw file, the Raw Converter will remember where you left off.

Converting to DNG

A few years ago, there was a lot of buzz about Adobe's DNG (digital negative) format, and if you shoot raw, you should know what it is. As you learned at the beginning of this chapter, every camera manufacturer uses a different format for raw files. Even the formats for different cameras from the *same* manufacturer differ. It's a recipe for an industry-wide headache.

Adobe's solution is the DNG format, which the company envisions as a more standardized alternative to raw files. Here's how it works: When you convert a raw file to a DNG file, it still behaves like a raw file—you can still tweak its settings in the Raw Converter, and you still have to save it in standard image formats like TIFF or JPEG to use it in a project. But the idea behind DNG is that if you save your raw files in this format, then you don't have to worry about whether Elements 35 can open them. Adobe clearly hopes that all camera manufacturers will adopt this standard, putting an end to the mishmash of different formats that make raw files such a nuisance to deal with. If all cameras used DNG, then when you bought a new camera you wouldn't have to worry about whether your programs could open your images.

You can create DNG files from raw files right in the Raw Converter. At the bottom left of the window, just click the Save Image button, and up pops the DNG Converter shown in Figure 8-9. Choose where you want to save the file, and then select how to name it. You get the same naming options as with Process Multiple Files (page 301), but since you can only use the DNG Converter to convert one file at a time, you may as well keep the photo's current name and just add the .dng extension to the end of it.

FIGURE 8-9

Elements' DNG Converter.

The bottom section of this window lets you tell Elements whether to compress the file, how to handle the image preview, and whether to embed your original raw file in the DNG file. Generally, you're best off leaving the settings in this section the way they are here, unless you need to make DNG files that are compatible with old versions of Elements. In that case, set the Compatibility drop down menu to the version of the Raw Converter where you want to be able to open the DNG file.

Over the years, people have had other good ideas that never really took off, like the JPEG 2000 format (see page 75). DNG hasn't proved to be quite as universal as Adobe had hoped, so a fair number of people are becoming a bit skeptical about the ultimate fate of DNG, and it's not nearly as popular now as it was a few years ago. Whether you create DNG files from your raw files is up to you, but either way, it's probably prudent to hang onto the original raw files as well.

> **TIP** If you want to convert a group of raw files to DNG in one batch, the easiest way is to go to Adobe's website (*www.adobe.com/downloads*), search for "DNG," download the standalone DNG Converter, and then make a shortcut to it on your desktop so it's always available. Then just drop a folder of raw images onto this icon, and the DNG Converter processes the whole folder at once. (You can drop just a single image if that's all you want to convert.) You can also save all the images open in the Raw Converter as DNG files at once by highlighting them in the list on the left side of the window, and then clicking Save Images.

Blending Exposures

If you've been using a digital camera for any length of time, you know what a juggling act it can be to get a photo that's properly exposed from its deepest shadows to its brightest highlights. With most digital cameras, you're likely to hit the clipping point (page 283) in an image much sooner than you want to: If you up the exposure so the shadows are nice and detailed, then about half the time you blow out the highlights. On the other hand, if you adjust the exposure settings down to favor the highlights, then your shadows are murkier than an old Enron annual report. Figure 8-10 shows the problem.

Digital blending is a technique photographers use to get around these limitations. To use it, you *bracket* your shots, meaning you take two or more identical photos of your subject at different settings—one exposed for shadows and one for highlights—and then combine them, choosing the best bits of each one. People who are fanatical about getting their images truly perfect may combine several different exposures.

That technique is great for landscapes, but if you're shooting hummingbirds, roller-skating chimps, or toddlers, you know it's just about impossible to get two identical shots of a moving subject. And if you're like many people, you may not realize you didn't capture what you wanted until you see the shot on your computer at home. But even if you only have one photo of that perfect moment, you can sometimes cheat a bit and get a similar result from processing the photo twice in the Raw Converter (once to favor the shadowy areas, and once for the highlights) so you wind up with two exposures. The problem is figuring out how to combine them into one great image.

> **TIP** The Raw Converter may be able to tease enough exposure range from your photo so that you don't need to blend two exposures, even if it's not a raw file. So try adjusting the image in the Converter before using the techniques described in this section. The box on page 289 explains how to work with non-raw files in the Raw Converter.

FIGURE 8-10

*Here's a classic example
of the kind of image that
can benefit from exposure
merging.*

*This photo of a late-after-
noon balloon launch really
needs to be processed
three different ways: once
for the sky, once for the
gorge and the waterfalls,
and once for the trees atop
the cliffs.*

If you can't make the Raw Converter's settings work, or if the Raw Converter just
makes you nervous, Elements gives you another super simple way to blend images.
It's called Photomerge Exposure, and it's as easy to use as any of the program's other
Photomerge features (see Chapter 11). It can even be a one-click fix, if you want.

Photomerge Exposure offers several ways to blend photos. Your main choice is between an automatic merge, where Elements makes most of the decisions, and a manual merge, which gives you more control but requires a little more effort. The following sections explain your options.

> **NOTE** Exposure merging isn't meant for blending two totally different photos together, like replacing the blown out sky in your photo of the Taj Mahal with a good sky from a photo of your dude-ranch trip. To use Photomerge Exposure, your photos should be pretty much identical except for their exposures. So use images you took with your camera's exposure bracketing feature, or even one shot you've processed twice or more to get one good version with properly exposed highlights, one with good shadows, and so on. Sadly, Elements actually does a better job with a single photo processed two ways than it does with multiple shots, so if you don't like what you get by blending two actual exposures, take the best one, process it two ways, and then use those files as the basis of your merge.

Automatic Merges

It's incredibly easy to combine photos using Photomerge Exposure's Automatic Merge feature because Elements makes most of the decisions for you. (If that's not for you, you can opt for a manual merge, where you call the shots; the next section explains how.) Here's what you do:

1. **Prepare, open, and select your images.**

   You can start with two or more photos where you used exposure bracketing on your camera, or with one image that you've processed in two (or more) different ways in the Raw Converter (page 272)— for example, once favoring the shadows and once the highlights. Elements lets you combine up to 10 photos, so create as many different versions as you need to make sure every part of the image is properly exposed. Then, in the Photo Bin, select the photos you want to work with, and you're ready for the next step.

2. **Call up the Photomerge Exposure window.**

   In either Expert mode or Quick Fix, go to Enhance→Photomerge→Photomerge Exposure. Either way, the Photomerge Exposure window opens. It's a lot like the windows for Group Shot, Faces, and Scene Cleaner, so if you've used any of those features before, it'll feel familiar.

3. **Tell Elements you want to perform an automatic merge.**

   Most of the time, the Exposure Merge window opens with the Automatic tab active and the final, automatically merged image displayed in the preview area in the middle of the window. If it doesn't, simply click that tab on the right side of the window. (It's easy to tell which tab is active without even looking at the right side of the window: In Automatic mode, you see only one image in the preview area, while in Manual mode you see two.)

4. **Select a merge option and make any adjustments you want.**

On the right side of the Exposure Merge window are two radio buttons that let you choose the type of automatic merge:

- **Simple Blending.** Elements does everything—all you have to do is click Done.

- **Smart Blending.** If you pick this option, you can use the three sliders below it to adjust the merge. (The sliders are explained after this list.) Elements uses a different kind of analysis on your photo here than it does if you opt for Simple Blending, so don't be surprised if the appearance of your image shifts a bit when you click this radio button.

You can't use the sliders if you have Simple Blending selected; they become active only when you choose Smart Blending.

5. **When you're happy with what you see, click Done.**

Elements blends the photos in a new file so that your originals are preserved. Don't forget to save the blended image.

That's all there is to it. Elements usually does a pretty good job (depending on your photos, of course), as shown in Figure 8-11. But if you aren't satisfied with what Elements proposes for your image, you can help the program by choosing Smart Blending and then nudging the Smart Blending sliders. Here's what each slider does:

- **Highlight** controls the way Elements blends the bright areas of the images.

- **Shadows** adjusts the blend of the darker areas.

TIP If you've used Shadows/Highlights (page 230), you already know everything you need to about these two sliders.

- **Saturation** adjusts the blended image's color intensity, which is handy if the blend made your photo look a little drab or oversaturated. It's similar to the Saturation slider in Quick Fix (page 133).

Manual Merges

Automatic merges are super easy to do, even for beginners, but sometimes Elements doesn't get it right. Or maybe you just like telling Elements what to do rather than accepting its judgment about your images. Either way, manual merges are what you want.

You begin a manual merge the same way as an automatic one (follow steps 1 and 2 on page 294). Then, once you have the Photomerge Exposure window open, do the following:

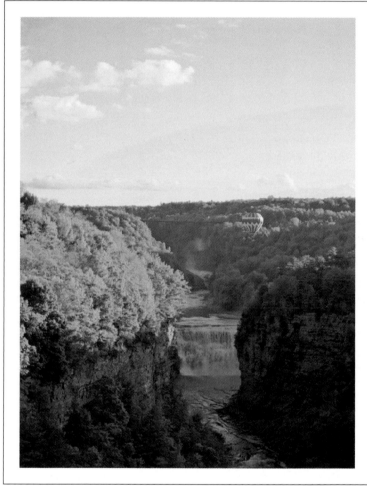

FIGURE 8-11

Here's what Elements proposes as a Simple Blending merge for the photo shown in Figure 8-10. You'd probably want to tweak this image some in the Editor, but overall, Photomerge Exposure did a pretty good job.

You can do even better by making a manual merge instead (see page 295, where you have more control over how the images blend together. For instance, the sky is still a tad light in this version.

1. **Tell Elements you want to make a manual merge.**

   On the right side of the Photomerge Exposure window, click the Manual tab if it's not already active. When you do, Elements changes the preview area to display spaces for two photos. (You can use up to 10 photos in a manual merge, but you work with only two at a time.)

2. **Choose a final photo.**

   This is the photo that's going to be the basis of your merge—the one you'll blend bits of other photos into. Usually, you'll want to pick the photo with the largest area of correct exposure, though the Tip on page 297 describes an exception to this rule. Drag your final photo of choice from the Photo Bin into the right-hand slot (which, conveniently, is labeled "Final").

> **TIP** If you're blending several exposures, you may get the best results if you choose the one with the best midtones as your final photo, even if that's not the one with the largest properly exposed area. That's because, when blending images, Elements likes to start from the middle and work outward (in other words, it does better if you let it figure out the midtones first before making it blend the shadows and highlights).

3. **Choose a source photo.**

   This is the photo you'll copy bits from to put in the final photo. Double-click it in the Photo Bin to tell Elements it's the one you want to use, and it appears in the left-hand slot. (Elements sometimes picks a source image for you, but it's not always a good guesser and you may want to override the choice it made.)

4. **Tell Elements what to copy.**

   Click the Pencil Tool button on the right side of the window, and then drag over the areas in the source photo that you want to move to the final photo. This tool works like the Quick Selection tool in that it automatically expands the selection from the line or dot you make. (It's not like the regular Pencil tool in the Expert mode Tools panel.) If it selects too much or if you drag over something by mistake, use the Eraser tool to remove some of your marks (see Figure 8-12).

FIGURE 8-12

Here's the midpoint of creating a manual merge of the image in Figure 8-10. (The Show Regions checkbox is turned on to make it easier to see what Elements is doing.) The trees on the cliffs are being brought over from the source image, as indicated by the blue mask on the final image. However, the balloon itself is a tad overexposed in spots in the source image, so you may want to go back with the Eraser tool and remove the marks over it so that it doesn't get copied over, or else zoom the view way in to erase only the blown-out white parts.

5. **If you need to, align the photos.**

If your copied material is slightly out of alignment with the final photo (a common problem if you used exposure bracketing for live subjects), in the Manual tab, click Advanced Options, and then scroll down and click the Alignment Tool button. When you do, three little target marks appear in each preview when you move your cursor over the photo. Drag the marks so they're in the same spot in each photo (like over a tiger's eyes and mouth in bracketed wildlife photos), and then click the Align Photos button. Elements figures out the difference in perspective between the two images and corrects for it.

> **NOTE** If you look closely, you'll see that the targets are numbered. Be sure to put the same number target over the same spot in both photos. In other words, don't put target 1 over an eye in one photo and a mouth in the other, for example; put target 1 over the left eye in each photo.

6. **Tweak the blending.**

You may be horrified by how crudely Elements blends the images at first, but that's OK. There are two settings in the Manual tab that you can use to fix things:

- **Opacity.** Use this slider to adjust the source image's transparency for a more realistic effect.

- **Edge Blending.** Turn on this checkbox and Elements automatically refines the edges of the blend to avoid a cut-and-pasted look. Try turning on this checkbox *before* adjusting the Opacity slider.

> **TIP** If you want a large view of your images while you're working, you can temporarily hide the Photomerge Exposure panel by clicking the Hide Panel button at the bottom right of the Elements window. To bring it back, click the button again (it's now labeled "Show Panel").

7. **If you wish, repeat steps 3–6 with other images.**

To add details from another image that you preselected, drag it into the Source slot and repeat the process. You can keep doing this to combine a total of 10 images. Each additional photo gets a different colored marker to help you keep track of what came from which photo.

8. **When you like what you see, click Done.**

As with an automatic merge, Elements creates a new, layered file for the blended image so your originals are untouched.

If you need to adjust the view while you're working on a merge, Elements gives you some help:

- **Zoom and Hand tools**. Your old friends live in the little toolbox to the left of the images. They work the same way here as everywhere else in Elements.

- **Show Strokes**. This checkbox in the Manual tab lets you show or hide the marks you make with the Pencil tool.

- **Show Regions**. Turn this on and Elements displays a yellow mask over the final photo, with blue over the areas where it's blending in material from the source photo, as shown in Figure 8-12. The balloon and top of the cliffs are blue because that's what's coming over from the source photo. (If you add more photos, each gets a colored mask that matches its marker color.)

> **TIP** Photomerge Exposure is fun, but you may want something a bit more powerful. In that case, you should explore *HDR* (high dynamic range) programs and plug-ins. Regardless of whether you have a Windows computer or a Mac, a good place to start is *www.hdrlabs.com*. Mac folks should also check out Bracketeer from Pangeasoft (*www.pangeasoft.net*), an excellent exposure-blending program that produces wonderful results.

WORKAROUND WORKSHOP

Manually Blending Exposures

Elements' Photomerge Exposure tool makes it pretty easy to blend exposures, but you may not care for the final result, no matter how much effort you put into it. In that case, you can just blend the images yourself by stacking them up:

1. **Open both exposures in Expert mode.** You can work with only two images at once when you do it this way.

2. **Pick the photo with the largest amount of properly exposed area.** That's going to be the top layer of your combined image.

3. **Turn that photo into a regular layer.** Double-click its name in the Layers panel to unlock it; you can then give it a name, if you want, or just click OK to accept the one Elements gives it. A faster way is just to click the padlock icon on the layer's thumbnail, which lets you skip having to OK the new layer.

4. **Apply a layer mask to it.** Click the layer mask icon at the top of the Layers panel (the circle within a square).

5. **Combine the images.** From the Layers panel, drag the masked photo's layer thumbnail onto the other image's main image window, or select the masked photo by pressing Ctrl+A/⌘-A, and then copy and paste it into the other image. (See page 219 for more about moving layers from one photo to another.)

6. **Edit the layer mask to combine the images.** On the layer mask, paint out the badly exposed areas of the masked photo to let the well-exposed parts of the other image show through. See page 213 for the details of how to do this.

To add additional exposures, merge the two existing layers first (page 208), and then repeat the process with another image.

◼ Photo Filter

Elements' Photo Filter feature gives you a host of nifty filters to work with. They're the digital equivalent of the lens-mounted filters used in traditional film photography, and they can help you correct problems with an image's white balance and perform a bunch of other fixes from the seriously photographic to the downright silly. For example, you can correct bad skin tone or dig out an old photo of your fifth-grade nemesis and make him green. Figure 8-13 shows the Photo Filter in action.

FIGURE 8-13

You can use the Photo Filter to correct the color casts caused by artificial lighting or reflected light.

Left: This photo had a strong warm cast from nearby incandescent lighting.

Right: The filter named "Cooling Filter (LBB)" took care of it.

Conversely, you'd use one of the warming filters to counteract a blue cast caused by fluorescent lighting.

Elements comes with 20 photo filters, but for most people, the first six in the list (see step 2 below) are the most important: three warming filters and three cooling filters, which you use to get rid of color casts caused by poor white balance (see page 277). These filters sometimes work better than the Color Cast eyedropper (page 252) because you can control their strength using the Density slider (explained in a moment). You can also apply them as Adjustment layers, so you can tweak them later on.

To apply a photo filter:

1. **Open the Photo Filter dialog box, or create a new Adjustment layer.**

   Go to Filter→Adjustments→Photo Filter, or Layer→New Adjustment Layer→ Photo Filter. Either way, you see the Photo Filter adjustment controls. If you're applying the Photo Filter directly to your image, you get a dialog box. If you go the Adjustment-layer route, the controls appear in the Adjustments panel instead (after you click OK to create the layer), but both offer exactly the same controls.

2. **Choose a filter from the drop-down list, or click the Color radio button and choose a color.**

   The drop-down list gives you a choice of filters in preset colors. The numbers following the names of some filters correspond to the numbers of the equivalent glass filters you'd use on a film camera.

To pick your own custom color, click the color square to bring up the "Select filter color" dialog box—which is really just the Color Picker (page 255)—and choose the shade you want. Pick a color for the filter, and Elements applies it to your image so you can decide whether you like it (you may have to drag the dialog box out of the way to see your image). When you've got the color you want, click OK to close the Color Picker.

3. **In the Photo Filter dialog box or Adjustments panel, use the Density slider to adjust the filter's intensity.**

   Moving the slider right increases the filter's effect; moving it left decreases it. If you leave the Preserve Luminosity checkbox turned on, then the filter doesn't darken the image. Turn off this checkbox and your photo gets darker when you apply the filter. Watch your image to see the effect.

4. **When your photo looks good, save it.**

■ Processing Multiple Files

If you're addicted to batch-processing photos, then you'll love Elements' Process Multiple Files feature. In addition to renaming files and changing their formats, you can do a lot of other very useful things with this tool, like add copyright information or captions to multiple files, or even apply some of Quick Fix's Auto commands.

To call up the batch-processing dialog box, in Expert mode, go to File→Process Multiple Files. You see yet another headache-inducing, giant Elements dialog box. Fear not—this one is actually pretty easy to understand. If you look closely, you see that it's divided into sections, each with a different specialty (see Figure 8-14).

> **TIP** Process *Multiple* Files is the name of this command, but if you want, you can run it on just one photo (although you'll usually find it easier to use the Save As command instead; see Chapter 2 for more about saving files). Just open a photo, go to File→Process Multiple Files, and then, in the Process Files From drop-down menu, choose Opened Files. You can even opt to save the new version to the desktop so you don't overwrite the original.

The following sections cover each part of the Process Multiple Files dialog box. You *have* to use the first section (which tells Elements which files to process), but you'll probably want to use only one or two of the other sections at any given time (though you *can* use them all, as Figure 8-14 shows).

> **TIP** If you're working in the Organizer, then you can do some batch-processing without opening the Editor. Select the files you want, and then go to File→Export As New File(s) (or press Ctrl+E). You get a dialog box that lets you change the files' format, pick a new size from a list of presets, set a destination for the new images, and choose a new "common base name" (if you want). If you choose this last option, then your files get the new name plus a sequential number. (By the way, this command is a great way to create a folder of JPEGs to send to a photo-printing service.)

FIGURE 8-14

You could call Process Multiple Files "Computer, Earn Your Keep," because it can make so many changes at once.

Here, the dialog box is set up to apply the following changes:

Rename every file (from things like PICT8983 to basketball_tournament001, basketball_tournament002, and so on), convert the images to PSD format, apply Auto Levels and Auto Sharpening, and add the filename as a caption.

You can make all that happen just by clicking OK.

Choosing Files

The top-left section of the Process Multiple Files dialog box is where you tell Elements which files to convert and where to put them once it processes them. You start by selecting an option from the Process Files From drop-down menu. Choosing Import brings up the same options you get when you select File→Import; use this setting to convert files as you bring them into Elements—from a camera or scanner, for example.

> **TIP** To process files that are scattered around in different locations on your hard drive, speed things up by opening the files first or gathering them into one folder. If you have a couple of folders' worth of photos to convert, put all those folders into one *containing* folder and then use the Include All Subfolders option explained in a moment; that way, Elements converts all the files at once.

Here's a step-by-step tour of the process:

1. **Choose the files you want to convert.**

   Use the Process Files From drop-down menu to select which kind of files you want: ones in a folder (Folder), ones you imported from a camera or scanner (Import), or ones that are currently open (Opened Files).

2. **If you chose Folder, then tell Elements which folder you want.**

   Click the Browse button next to the Source field and, in the dialog box that appears, choose a folder. (Files you want to process have to be in a folder if they aren't already open.) If you have folders *within* a folder and you want to operate on all those files, too, then turn on the Include All Subfolders checkbox. Otherwise, Elements processes only the files in the top-level folder.

3. **Pick a destination.**

   The Destination field tells Elements where to put the files after it processes them. Most of the time, you'll want a new folder for this, so click Browse to the right of this field, and then, in the window that opens, click New Folder. You can choose an existing folder in the Browse window, but a word of warning if you go this route: Be careful about turning on the "Same as Source" setting; Figure 8-15 explains why.

FIGURE 8-15

In the Process Multiple Files dialog box, if you turn on the "Same as Source" checkbox, Elements warns you that it's going to replace your originals with the new versions. That can be a timesaver, but it's dangerous, too—if something goes wrong, then your originals are toast.

Bottom line: Don't turn on "Same as Source" unless you have backup copies stored someplace else.

The following sections explain the various things Process Multiple Files can do to the files you've selected.

Renaming Files

Being able to rename a group of files in one fell swoop is a very cool feature, but it has a few limitations. If you think it means you can give each photo a unique name like "Keisha and Gram at the Park," followed by "Fred's New Newt," and so on, you're going to be disappointed. Instead, what Elements offers is a quick way of applying a similar name to a group of files. That means you can easily transform a folder filled with files named *DSCF001.jpg, DSCF0002.jpg*, and so on, into the slightly friendlier *Keisha and Gram001.jpg*, and *Keisha and Gram002.jpg*.

To rename files, turn on the Process Multiple Files dialog box's Rename Files check-box. Below it are two text boxes with drop-down menus next to them (a + sign separates the menus). You can enter anything you like in these boxes, and Elements will replace every filename in the group with it. Or you can choose any of the options in the menus (both menus are the same).

> **TIP** If you turn on the "Same as Source" checkbox, then Elements grays out the Rename Files option. So if you want to put your renamed files in the same folder as the originals, leave "Same as Source" turned off and select that folder in the Destination field in the top part of the dialog box. That way Elements places your renamed files in the same folder as the originals without *replacing* the originals.

The menus offer you a choice of the document name (in three different capitalization styles), serial numbers, serial letters, dates, extensions, or nothing at all (which gives you just numbers without any kind of prefix). Figure 8-16 shows the many options.

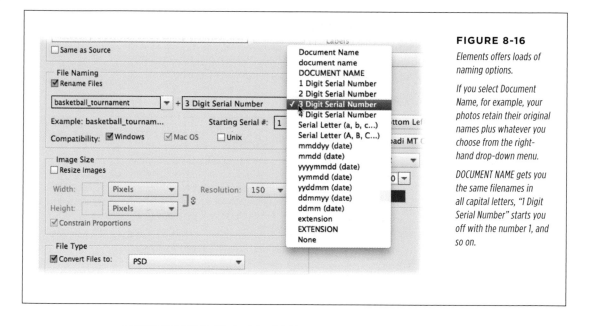

FIGURE 8-16

Elements offers loads of naming options.

If you select Document Name, for example, your photos retain their original names plus whatever you choose from the right-hand drop-down menu.

DOCUMENT NAME gets you the same filenames in all capital letters, "1 Digit Serial Number" starts you off with the number 1, and so on.

> **TIP** If you want to add serial numbers to your filenames, you can designate the starting number in the "Starting serial#" box. Elements always starts out by suggesting 1, but you can type over the 1 to change it to any number you please. Once you make a choice, you see an example of how the filename will look. So if you type *tongue_piercing_day* into the first text box and choose 3 Digit Serial Number in the second, for example, then Elements names your photos *tongue_piercing_day001.jpg, tongue_piercing_day002.jpg,* and so on.

You also get to tell Elements which operating systems' naming conventions it should use when assigning the new names, as explained in Figure 8-17. If you send files to people or servers that run other operating systems, then you know how important this is. Your best bet is to play it safe and turn on all three checkboxes; you never know when you may need to send a photo to your nephew who uses Unix.

FIGURE 8-17

These settings tell Elements to watch out for any characters that would violate the naming conventions of the operating systems you select. This is handy if, say, your website is hosted on a Unix server and you want to be sure your filenames don't create problems for it. The checkbox for your own operating system is always turned on, and you can choose to be compatible with either (or neither) of the other two.

Changing Image Size and File Type

The Image Size and File Type sections of the Process Multiple Files dialog box let you resize photos and change their file formats, respectively. The Image Size settings work best when you're trying to reduce file sizes (say you've got a folder of images that you've converted for web use but found are still too large).

> **NOTE** Before you make any big changes to a group of files, it's important to understand how changes to an image's resolution and file size affect its appearance. See page 105 for a refresher.

To apply image-size changes, turn on the Resize Images checkbox, and then adjust the Width, Height, and Resolution settings, all of which work the same way as those described on page 109. You'll get better results with Process Multiple Files if you make sure all the images you run it on in one batch have the same orientation. In other words, use it on a group of landscape-oriented files and then on a group of portrait-oriented images—don't use it on both types of files at once.

The File Type section lets you convert files from one format to another. This is probably the most popular batch-processing activity. If, for example, your camera creates JPEGs and you want to edit TIFFs, then you can change a whole folder at once. Simply turn on the "Convert Files to" checkbox and then, from the drop-down menu, select the type of files you want to create.

The final setting on the left side of the dialog box is a checkbox that makes Elements log any errors it runs into while processing your files. It's a good idea to turn this checkbox on, as explained in Figure 8-18.

FIGURE 8-18

*If you turn on this checkbox, then Elements lets you know
if it runs into any problems while converting your files.
It creates a little text log file with the extension .txt and
puts it in the folder with your completed images, whether
or not there were any problems. (If nothing went awry,
the file is blank.)*

Applying Quick Fix Commands

In the top-right part of the Process Multiple Files dialog box are some of the same
Quick Fix commands you find in the regular Quick Fix window. If you consistently
get good results with the Auto commands in Quick Fix, then you can use these
checkboxes to run them on a whole folder at once.

You can run Auto Levels, Auto Contrast, Auto Color, Auto Sharpen, or any combination of those commands on all the files you're processing. If you need a refresher on
what each one does, see Chapter 4, beginning on page 130.

Unfortunately, you can't batch-run the Auto *Smart Fix* command from this dialog
box. If that's what you want to do, or if your only reason for opening the Process
Multiple Files dialog box is to use its Quick Fix options (without renaming, resizing,
or using any of the dialog box's other features), then you can save time by selecting
your photos in the Organizer and running those commands right from the Organizer's
Instant Fix pane instead, as explained on page 121.

> **TIP** Don't forget that you can also batch-process corrections in the Raw Converter (see page 375). Then open
> the files in the Editor and use Process Multiple Files to save all the changed files at once.

Attaching Labels

The options in the Process Multiple Files dialog box's Labels section let you add
copyright notices (which Elements calls *watermarks*) and captions to images; see
Figure 8-19. Watermarks and captions both get imprinted right onto the photo itself.
The process is the same for creating both; only the content differs. A watermark
contains any text you choose, while a caption is limited to your choices from a group
of checkboxes.

First, you need to choose between a watermark and a caption (select from the drop-
down menu right below the Labels heading). Unfortunately, you can't do both at
once, so if you want both, add one by running Process Multiple Files, and then run
Process Multiple Files *again* on the resulting images to add the other.

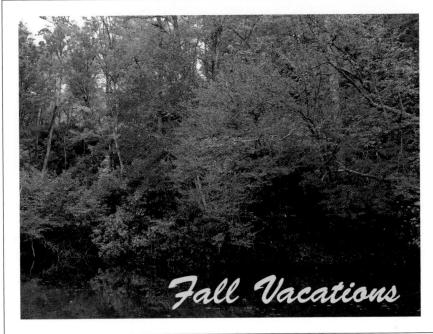

FIGURE 8-19

The text "Fall Vacations" in this image is what Adobe calls a watermark. Elements is very flexible about the fonts and sizes you can choose for a watermark or a caption, but you don't get much say in where it goes on your photo if you use the Process Multiple Files feature.

For maximum flexibility, use a type tool instead, as explained on page 479. The drawback: You can't batch-process using that method.

NOTE You can download *fall.jpg* from this book's Missing CD page at *www.missingmanuals.com/cds* to practice adding your own watermarks and captions.

■ WATERMARKS

To create a watermark, enter some text in the Custom Text box, and then choose where you want the text to go and what it should look like, as explained in a moment. Text you enter here gets applied to every photo in the batch, so this is a great way to add copyright or contact info. (If you want *different* text on each photo, check out the Description option for captions, explained below.)

TIP If you're on a Windows computer and want to include the copyright symbol (©), hold the Alt key while typing *0169* on the number pad (*not* the top row of the keyboard), or use the Character Map (choose Start→All Programs→Accessories→System Tools→Character Map). On a Mac, just press Option-G.

Once you've decided what you want the custom text to say, you need to make some choices about its position and size. These options are the same whether you're adding a watermark or a caption, and if you switch from one to the other before actually running Process Multiple Files, then the settings you chose for one appear for the other:

- **Position** tells Elements where to put the text. Your options are Bottom Left, Bottom Right, or Centered. Careful: Centered doesn't mean "bottom center"—it puts the text smack in the *middle* of your image.

- **Font** lets you choose any font on your computer. (Chapter 14 has tons of info about fonts.)

- **Size** (whose icon is two Ts) determines how big the text is. Click the drop-down menu to choose from several preset sizes, up to 72 points.

- **Opacity** controls how solidly the text prints. Choose 100 percent for maximum readability, or click the down arrow, and then move the slider to the left for watermark text that lets the image underneath it show through.

- **Color** determines—you guessed it—the text's color. Click the box to bring up the Color Picker (page 255) and make your choice.

> **TIP** If you want to use a logo as a watermark, the Process Multiple Files dialog box can't help you. But there *is* a way to apply a logo to a bunch of images in Elements: First, create the logo on a new layer in one of the images, adjust the Layers panel's Opacity setting until you like the results, and then save the file. Now you can drag that layer from the Layers panel onto the image window for each photo where you need it. (If you Shift-drag the layer, then it goes to exactly the same spot on each image, assuming they're all the same size.)
>
> You can also do this with Adjustment layers, which give you a sort of batch-processing capability for applying the same adjustments to multiple files. Another option is to create a custom brush from your logo (page 405) and use that, and then adjust the opacity or apply a layer style (page 461) for a truly custom look.

■ ADDING CAPTIONS

For a caption, you can select any of the following, separately or in combination:

- **File Name**. You can choose to show each file's name as the caption. If you're using the Process Multiple Files dialog box's renaming feature at the same time you're adding captions, then Elements uses the *new* name you're assigning.

- **Description**. Turn this checkbox on to use any text you've entered in the Description section of the File Info dialog box (File→File Info) as your caption. This option is the most flexible one for entering text, and the only way to add different text to each photo you're batch-processing. Just enter text in each photo's Description field *before* you use Process Multiple Files.

- **Date Modified**. This is the date the file was last changed. In practice, that means today's date, because you're modifying your files by running Process Multiple Files on them.

Your choices for how and where the caption will appear are the same as those listed above for watermarks.

Retouching: Fine-Tuning Images

Basic edits like exposure fixes and sharpening are fine if all you want to make are simple adjustments. But Elements also gives you tools for making sophisticated changes that can make the difference between a ho-hum photo and a fabulous one. This chapter introduces you to some advanced editing maneuvers that can help you rescue damaged photos or give good ones a little extra zing.

This chapter shows how to get rid of blemishes—not only those that affect skin, but also dust, scratches, stains, and other photographic imperfections. And you'll find out how to use a new, much-requested feature from Photoshop: Content-Aware Fill, a truly amazing command for fixing problem areas. It lets you patch large areas of a photo with new material that Elements creates by analyzing your image, and it's really easy to use. You'll also learn some powerful color-improving techniques, including how to use the Color Curves tool to enhance an image's contrast and color.

You'll also find out how to use the Recompose tool, which lets you change the size and shape of photos, eliminate empty areas between objects, and even remove unwanted elements from pictures, all without distorting the parts you want to keep. This amazing feature works so well that nobody seeing the results would ever suspect that your photo wasn't originally shot that way.

■ Fixing Blemishes

We live in an imperfect world, but in your photos, it doesn't have to look that way. Elements includes powerful tools for fixing your subjects' flaws: You can erase crow's feet and blemishes from faces, eliminate power lines in an otherwise perfect view, or even hide objects you wish weren't in the photo. Not only that, but these same tools are great for fixing problems in printed photos like tears, folds, and stains—the great foes of photo-scanning veterans. With a little effort, you can bring back photos that seem beyond help.

Two of the most important ways to do this are *cloning* and *healing*. Cloning lets you patch bad areas by hiding them with material from somewhere else. Healing is similar, but when you use this method, Elements evaluates the area *around* the spot you're fixing and blends your repair into what's already there. You'll need to use both techniques to fix badly damaged photos. Figure 9-1 shows the kind of restoration you can accomplish with Elements and a little persistence.

FIGURE 9-1

Top: Here's a section of a water-damaged family portrait. The grandmother's face is almost obliterated.

Bottom: The same image after repairing it with Elements. It took a lot of cloning and healing to get this result, but if you keep at it, you can do the kind of work that would have required professional help before Elements.

If you're working on a photo like this, be sure to check out the Restore Old Photo Guided Edit, which gathers together most of the tools you need for this type of work and suggests an order in which to use them. And if you're really interested in restoring old photos, check out Katrin Eismann's books on the subject (Photoshop Restoration & Retouching [New Riders, 2006] is a good place to start). They cover full-featured Photoshop, but you can adapt most of the techniques for Elements.

Elements gives you five main tools for this kind of work:

- The **Spot Healing Brush** is the easiest way to repair photos. Just drag over the spot you want to fix, and Elements searches the surrounding area and blends that info into the trouble spot, making it indistinguishable from the background. What's more, you get a Content-Aware option, one of the most popular features Elements has borrowed from Photoshop (although Elements' version is much more limited; see page 312). When you use the Content-Aware feature, Elements analyzes your photo so it can create *new* material that looks like part of the original image. This makes the Spot Healing Brush a truly versatile tool for making seamless fixes. Coverage of this tool starts on page 312.

- The **Healing Brush** works much like the Spot Healing Brush, only you get to tell the Healing Brush which part of your photo to use as a source for the material you want to blend in. This tool is usually better at fixing large areas than the Spot Healing Brush, because you don't have to worry about inadvertently dragging in unwanted details (which can happen with the Spot Healing Brush). This tool is described in detail starting on page 315.

- The **Clone Stamp** works like the Healing Brush in that you sample a good area and apply it to the spot you want to fix. But instead of blending in the repair, the Clone Stamp simply covers the bad area with the replacement. This tool, which you'll learn how to use starting on page 318, is best for situations when you want to *completely* hide the underlying area, as opposed to letting any of what's already there blend into your repair (which is how things work with the healing brushes). Depending on the conditions in your photo, the Clone Stamp may also be your best option for creating a realistic copy of details that are elsewhere in a photo. For example, you might use this tool to clone some leaves to fill in a bare spot on a branch, or replace a knothole in a fence board with good wood. But if you want to duplicate larger objects, use the Content-Aware Move tool (described next) instead.

- The **Content-Aware Move tool**, which is explained on page 180, is your go-to tool when you need to duplicate a missing feature. For instance, if you need to replace a damaged table leg, follow the directions on page 180 to duplicate it on a new layer, and then use the Transform commands (page 387) to make it fit perfectly.

- The new **Content-Aware Fill** command lets you replace the contents of a selection with new material that Elements creates based on its analysis of your image. This feature doesn't always work, but when it does, it saves you an incredible amount of time. It's described starting on page 321.

Most of these features work similarly: You drag them over the area you want to change (and then, if you're using the Content-Aware Move tool, drag your selection to the new location). It's as simple as using a paintbrush. In fact, you have to choose a brush like the ones you'll learn about in Chapter 12. Selecting a brush is pretty straightforward; you learn the basics in this chapter. The Content-Aware Fill command is a little different in that you make a selection with any selection tool(s) and then use the command to create your fill.

TIP To smooth out blotchy or blemished skin, check out the Surface Blur filter explained on page 453. It's a good one to try for minor touch-ups that affect large areas. In contrast, the tools described in *this* section are better for fixing individual imperfections, like pimples or scars.

The Spot Healing Brush

The Spot Healing Brush is great at fixing minor blemishes like pimples, lipstick smudges, lint, and so on. Simply paint over the area you want to repair, and Elements searches the surrounding regions and blends them into the spot where you're brushing. Figure 9-2 shows what a great job this tool can do.

FIGURE 9-2

The trick to using the Spot Healing Brush is to work on tiny areas. If you choose too large a brush or drag over too large an area, you're more likely to pick up undesired shades and details from the surrounding area.

Top: Say you want to show off your fine crop of borage, but something's been attacking the leaves. Simply grab a brush that's barely bigger than the blemish, like the one shown here.

Bottom: One click with the Spot Healing Brush and you have a truly invisible fix. It took only a few clicks to repair all the brown spots on this leaf.

If you'd like to experiment with this image, download borage.jpg from this book's Missing CD page at www.missingmanuals.com/cds.

The Spot Healing Brush's ability to borrow information from surrounding areas is great in some situations but a drawback in others. The larger the area you drag the brush over, the wider Elements searches for replacement material. So if there's contrasting material close to the area you're trying to fix, it can get pulled into the repair. For instance, if you're trying to fix a spot on an eyelid, you may wind up with some of the color from the eye itself mixed in with your repair.

You get the best results from this brush when you choose a brush size that barely covers the spot you're trying to fix. If you need to drag to fix an oblong area, for instance, use the smallest brush width that covers the flaw. The Spot Healing Brush also works much better when there's a large surrounding area that looks the way you want your repaired spot to look.

> **TIP** Sometimes you can help Elements out by making a selection before using the Spot Healing Brush, to limit the area where the brush can search for replacement material.

You won't believe how easy it is to fix problem areas with this tool:

1. **Activate the Spot Healing Brush.**

   Click the tool's icon (the Band-Aid) in the Tools panel or press J. Then, on the left side of the Tool Options area, choose the Spot Healing Brush—the one with the dotted selection lines extending from it.

2. **Choose a brush just barely bigger than the flaw you're trying to fix.**

   You can adjust your brush size using the Size slider in the Tool Options area, or by pressing] (the close bracket key) for a larger brush or [(the open bracket key) for a smaller brush.

   The Spot Healing Brush is initially set to Content Aware (explained in a sec), and that's the best setting to try first.

3. **Click—or drag over—the bad spot.**

   If the brush doesn't quite cover the flaw, then drag over the blemished area instead. (You may see a dark-gray area as you drag. Don't worry—it's just there to show you where you're brushing, and it will disappear when you let go.) When you release your mouse button, Elements repairs the blemish.

The Spot Healing Brush has four Tool Options settings:

- **Type**. These radio buttons let you adjust how the brush works:

  — **Proximity Match** tells Elements to search the surrounding area for replacement pixels.

  — **Create Texture** tells it to blend based only on the area you click or drag the cursor over.

  — **Content Aware** tells the program to do some fancy figuring to invent *new* material to blend with the existing photo (see Figure 9-3).

FIGURE 9-3

The Healing Brushes' Content Aware option can produce amazing results with some photos—but it can also result in cases of "so close and yet so far," as in this example.

Top: The only day you could get to the beach with your camera, there were traffic cones everywhere.

Bottom: The Spot Healing Brush's Content Aware option did a great job of zapping the big wooden post, but large areas like all those cones make it confused about what to use as replacement material. You could keep trying the Spot Healing Brush over and over, but at this point it would be faster to use the Clone Stamp (page 318) to fix that area instead.

Your best bet will usually be to try Content Aware first. If it doesn't do a good job, undo what you did and try Proximity Match instead. Generally speaking, if Proximity Match doesn't work well, you'll get better results by switching to the regular Healing Brush (page 315) than by choosing Create Texture, although Adobe suggests that you may get better results from Create Texture if you drag over a spot more than once.

- **Brush**. You can use this drop-down menu to choose a different brush style (see Chapter 12 for more about brushes), but you're usually best off sticking to the standard brush that Elements starts with and just changing its size, if necessary.

- **Size**. This slider controls how big the brush cursor is. You want a brush just barely wide enough to cover the blemish you're healing.

- **Sample All Layers**. Turn on this checkbox if you want the brush to look for replacement material in all your photo's visible layers. If you leave it off, Elements uses material from only the active layer. Be sure to turn this setting on if you created a new, blank layer to heal on so you can blend your work in later by adjusting the healed area's opacity; otherwise, Elements won't have any material to work with.

Sometimes you can get great results with the Spot Healing Brush on a large area *if* it's surrounded by a field that's similar in tone to the spot you're trying to fix, especially if you use the Content-Aware option, but you may find that you need to do extra work to get a perfect result (see Figure 9-3). Sometimes you can switch to Proximity Match and finish up, or you may need the regular Healing Brush (explained next) or the Clone Stamp (page 318) to get things just perfect.

The Healing Brush

The Healing Brush lets you fix much bigger areas than you can usually manage with the Spot Healing Brush. The main difference between the two tools is that, with the Healing Brush, *you* choose the area that Elements blends into the repair. The blending makes the repair look natural, as Figure 9-4 shows.

FIGURE 9-4

Left: After you choose a repair source for the Healing Brush, the source appears inside the brush's cursor. Here, for instance, the cursor contains the part of the waterfall you'll be blending in, rather than the lamppost you'll be covering up. (If this bothers you, see page 400 to learn how to get a regular, empty cursor.)

Right: It took three brushstrokes to eliminate this lamppost (one for where it overlapped the water, one for where it overlapped the grass, and one for where they intersect), but you can see how quickly this tool gets you 99 percent of the way to a natural-looking fix. There's a little bit of haze in the grass along the edge of the cliff that might benefit from a little touching up with the Clone Stamp (page 318), but fixing that takes only another click or two.

TIP   For larger areas, you may want to start by using the Content-Aware Fill command (page 321) instead of the Healing Brush. If that doesn't do it, then give the Spot Healing Brush's Content Aware option a try. If *that* attempt fails, then go with the regular Healing Brush instead. And sometimes you'll want to use both healing brushes. For example, in Figure 9-4, the regular Healing Brush does a good job hiding the lamppost where it was in front of the water and the ground, but you may want to try the Spot Healing Brush's Content-Aware option to get a good transition line between the two.

The basics of using the Healing Brush are similar to that of the Spot Healing Brush: Drag over the flaw you want to fix. The difference is that, with the Healing Brush, you first need to Alt-click/Option-click where you want Elements to look for replacement pixels. The repair material (which Elements calls the *source*) doesn't have to be nearby; in fact, you can sample from a totally different image if you like (to do that, just arrange both images in your workspace so you can easily move the cursor between them). Here are the details:

1. **Activate the Healing Brush.**

   Click the tool's icon (the Band-Aid) in the Tools panel's Enhance section or press J, and then choose it on the left side of the Tool Options area.

2. **Find a good spot to use in the repair and Alt-click/Option-click it.**

   When you Alt-click/Option-click the good spot, your cursor temporarily turns into a circle with crosshairs in it to indicate that Elements will retrieve your repair material from this spot. (If you want to use material from a different photo, the source photo and the one you're repairing have to be in the same *color mode*—see page 41.)

3. **Drag over the area you want to repair.**

   You can see where Elements is sampling the repair material from because it puts a + in that spot. As with the Spot Healing Brush, the area you drag over shows the source material until you release the mouse button.

   When you let go of your mouse, Elements blends the sampled area into the problem area. You often won't know how effective the tool was until Elements is through working its magic (it may take a few seconds for the program to finish its calculations and blend in the repair). If you don't like the result, press Ctrl+Z/⌘-Z to undo it and try again.

The Healing Brush offers quite a few Tool Options settings:

- **Size**. The standard brush generally works well, so you'll probably just need to adjust its size. If you need to change other characteristics of the tool's cursor, you can use the Brush Settings (described next).

- **Brush Settings**. Click this button for a pop-out panel that lets you customize the hardness and shape of your brush cursor (see page 398), as well as the spacing of the marks it makes (page 401). If you have a graphics tablet, you can use this panel's Size menu to tell Elements whether you want to control the brush's size by how hard you press the stylus or by turning the stylus's scroll wheel.

- **Aligned**. If you leave this checkbox turned off, then all the source material Elements uses comes from the spot that you Alt-clicked/Option-clicked—as long as you *click* to make your repair, rather than drag. Turn on this checkbox and Elements keeps sampling new source material as you use the tool; the sampling follows the motion of your brush. If you *drag* in your photo, even if this setting is turned off, the brush behaves as though this setting were turned *on*.

  Generally, for both the Healing Brush and the Clone Stamp (explained next), it's easier to leave this setting turned off. You can still change the source point by Alt-clicking/Option-clicking another spot, but you often get better results if *you* make the decision about when to move to another location rather than letting Elements decide.

- **Source**. If you leave this menu set to Sampled, Elements blends the source material into your image as explained above. If you change this menu to Pattern, Elements blends in a pattern instead. Using the Healing Brush with patterns is explained on page 325.

- **Mode**. This drop-down menu lets you choose from various blend modes (page 98). Most of the time, you want one of the top two options: Normal or Replace. Normal is usually your best choice, but if the replacement pixels give the area you're working on a visibly different texture than the surrounding area, choose Replace instead, which preserves the grain of the photo.

- **Show Overlay**. Click this button for a pop-out panel where you can adjust what you see in the cursor when using this tool. When Show Overlay is turned on, you see a floating, ghostly overlay of the source area where you're sampling, so you can tell exactly how things line up and perform more accurate healing. (If you don't turn on the Clipped option, explained in a sec, this may be a duplicate of your whole photo.) You can use the other settings here to adjust the overlay's opacity or invert it (make the light areas dark and the dark areas light so that you can see details more clearly) for a better view.

  The Clipped option (which is turned on initially) pins the overlay to your brush so you see only a brush-sized piece of overlay rather than one that covers the entire image. Turning on the Auto Hide checkbox makes the overlay disappear when you click so it's not in your way as you work.

  If you want your cursor to be nothing but an empty circle, simply turn off all the settings in this panel.

> **NOTE** The Clone Stamp (explained next) has the same Clone Overlay options as the Healing Brush, and the settings you choose for one tool also apply when you switch to the other tool.

- **Pattern thumbnail**. You won't see this setting unless you've set the Source menu to Pattern. If you did that, click this box to select a pattern.

- **Sample All Layers**. This checkbox tells Elements to sample from all the visible layers in the area where you set your source point. Leave it turned off and Elements samples only from the active layer. Turn this setting on if you want to heal on a new, blank layer. (The advantage of doing so is that, if you find the end result is a little too much—your granny suddenly looks like a Stepford wife, say—you can reduce a healed layer's opacity to let the original show through. Just press Shift+Ctrl+N/Shift-⌘-N to create a new layer and then, in the Tool Options area, turn on Sample All Layers. This is also a good plan when using the Clone Stamp.)

Fixing Dust and Scratches

Scratched, dusty prints can create giant headaches when you scan them. Cleaning your scanner's glass helps, but lots of photos come with dust marks already in the print or—if your digital camera's lens or sensor was dusty—in the file itself.

A similar problem is caused by *artifacts*, blobbish areas of color caused by JPEG compression. If you take a close look at the sky in a JPEG photo, for instance, you may see that, instead of a smooth swath of blue, there are lots of distinct little clumps of each shade of blue.

The Healing Brushes are usually your best tools for fixing these problems, but if the specks are widespread, Elements offers a few other options.

The first is the Reduce Noise filter's JPEG artifacts option (page 443); if you're lucky, that will take care of things.

If it doesn't, another possible solution is the Despeckle filter (Filter→Noise→Despeckle). And if *that* doesn't get everything, undo it and try the Dust & Scratches filter (Filter→Noise→Dust & Scratches) or the Median filter (Filter→Noise→Median) instead. The Radius setting for these last two filters tells Elements how far to search for pixels to use in its calculations; keep that number as low as possible. The downside to using these filters is that they smooth things out in a way that can make images look blurred (Despeckle generally blurs images the least). So before you run them, you'll probably want to create a selection to confine their effects to the areas that need repairing.

One final option: Create a duplicate layer (Layer→Duplicate), run the Surface Blur filter (page 453) on it and then, in the Layers panel, reduce the filtered layer's opacity.

The Clone Stamp

The Clone Stamp is like the Healing Brush in that it adds material from a source point that you select, but the Clone Stamp doesn't *blend in* the new material—it just covers up the underlying area. This makes the Clone Stamp great for when you don't want to leave any trace of what you're repairing. In many cases where you need to repair something in an image, the new Content-Aware Fill command (page 321) will get you 90% of the way to where you need to be, and then you can use the Clone Stamp to fix any little problems around the edges. Figure 9-5 shows an example of when cloning is a better choice than healing.

> **TIP** For duplicating large areas, try the Content-Aware Move tool (page 180). For many kinds of repairs, it's easier to control than the Clone Stamp.

Using the Clone Stamp is much like using the Healing Brush, but you get different results:

1. **Activate the Clone Stamp.**

   Click its icon (the rubber stamp) in the Tools panel's Enhance section or press S, and then choose it in the Tool Options area. The Clone Stamp shares its spot in the Tools panel with the Pattern Stamp, which is explained on page 326. (It's easy to tell which is which because the Pattern Stamp's icon has a little checkerboard to its left.)

FIGURE 9-5

Here's an example of when you'd want to clone rather than heal.

Top: Say you want to get rid of the distracting white part of this banner.

Bottom left: Using Content-Aware healing (page 321) gets you started, but it also heals away part of the drainpipe and duplicates the strap holding it to the building.

Bottom right: By using the Clone Stamp in concert with the Spot Healing Brush, you can remove the white part of the banner and extend the pipe.

TIP   You can clone on a separate layer, just as you can use the Healing Brush on a dedicated layer. It's a good idea to clone on a separate layer, since cloning is so much more opaque than healing, plus doing so lets you adjust the opacity of your repair afterward. So before you start cloning, press Shift+Ctrl+N/Shift-⌘-N to create a new layer, and then turn on Sample All Layers in the Tool Options area.

2. **Zoom in on the spot you want to repair.**

   You may need to zoom way, way in to get a good look at what you're doing. (Page 102 explains how to adjust your view.)

3. **Find a good spot to sample as a replacement for the bad area, and then Alt-click/Option-click that spot.**

   You want an area that has the same tone as the spot you're fixing. The Clone Stamp doesn't do any blending the way the Healing Brush does, so any tone difference will be pretty obvious. When you click a good spot, the cursor turns into a circle with crosshairs in it, indicating the source point for the repair. (When you perform the next step, you'll see a + marking the source point.)

TIP   You can even use source material from a different photo. Just open both images and arrange them so you can see them, and then do your Alt-clicking/Option-clicking in the second image.

4. **Click the spot you want to cover.**

   Elements puts whatever you selected in the previous step on top of what you click, concealing the original. You can drag with the Clone Stamp, but that makes it act like it's in Aligned mode (described after this list), so it's often preferable to click several times for areas that are larger than your sample. (The only difference between real Aligned mode and what you get from dragging with this tool is that with dragging, when you let go of the mouse, your source point snaps back to where it started. If the tool's Aligned checkbox is turned on, your source point stays where you stopped.)

5. **Continue clicking until you've covered the area.**

   With the Clone Stamp, unlike the Healing Brush, what you see as you click is what you get—Elements doesn't do any further blending or smoothing.

The choices you make in the Clone Stamp's Tool Options are important in getting the best results:

- **Brush**. You can click this brushstroke thumbnail for a drop-down menu that lets you select a different brush style (see Chapter 12 for more about brushes), but the standard style usually works pretty well. If the soft edges of the cloned areas bother you, you may be tempted to switch to a harder brush, but that will likely make your photo look like you threw confetti on it, because hard edges won't blend with what's already there.

- **Sample All Layers**. When you turn on this checkbox, Elements samples replacement material from all the visible layers in the area where you set your source point (step 3 above). When it's off, Elements samples only the active layer.

- **Size**. Choose a brush that's just big enough to select your sample without picking up other details that you don't want in your repair. It can be tempting to clone huge chunks to speed things up, but most of the time you'll do better using the smallest brush that gets the sample you want.

- **Opacity**. Elements automatically uses 100 percent opacity for cloning, but you can reduce this setting to let some details of the original show through.

TIP You gain more control by placing your cloned material on another layer (see the Tip in step 1 above) and adjusting *its* opacity setting in the Layers panel than you do by adjusting the *Clone Stamp's* Opacity setting.

- **Mode**. You can choose any blend mode (page 98) for cloning, but Normal is usually your best bet for repairs and corrections. Other modes can create interesting special effects.

- **Aligned**. This setting works exactly the way it does for the Healing Brush (page 316). Turn it on and Elements keeps sampling at a uniform distance from your cursor as you clone; turn it off and it keeps putting down the same source material. Figure 9-6 shows an example of when you'd turn on Aligned. (If you drag the Clone Stamp instead of clicking with it, Elements automatically turns on the Aligned checkbox.)

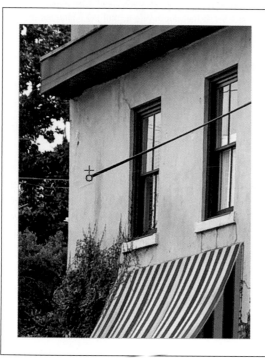

FIGURE 9-6

One way to get rid of the power line in this photo is to use the Clone Stamp's Aligned option.

The thick power line originally entered this photo at the upper left, above the smaller lines you can still see in the background. By choosing a brush barely larger than the thick power line and sampling just above the line, you can replace the entire thing in one long sweep, despite the many changes in the background behind it.

Here, the round cursor is at the left end of what remains of the power line, and the sample point is the + right above the cursor.

- **Clone Overlay**. The Clone Stamp starts out using a clipped overlay, the same way the Healing Brush does. Your options for adjusting the overlay are the same, too (page 317). If you want an empty cursor, just turn off all the options in this panel. The settings you choose here apply when you use the Healing Brush and vice versa.

The Clone Stamp is a powerful tool, but it's crotchety, too. The box on page 321 suggests some ways to make it behave.

Content-Aware Fill

Few things that Adobe has come up with in the past few years have caused as much buzz as Photoshop's Content-Aware Fill command, which makes fixing problem areas in your photos as easy as making a selection. And now it's available in Elements, too.

Keeping the Clone Stamp Under Control

The Clone Stamp is a great tool, but it sometimes has a mind of its own.

If you suddenly see spots of a different shade appearing as you clone, take a look at the Tool Options area's Aligned checkbox, which has a tendency to insist on staying turned on. Even if you turn it off, it can turn itself back on when you aren't looking.

Once in a great while, the Clone Stamp just won't reset itself when you try to select a new sample point. In that case, try clicking the little four-line square at the right end of the Tool Options area and choosing Reset Tool, as shown in Figure 9-7. If that doesn't do it, quit the Editor and then relaunch it and delete Elements' preferences file. Here's how: Go to Edit→Preferences→General/Photoshop Elements Editor→Preferences→General, click the button labeled "Reset Preferences on next launch," and then restart the Editor. This returns all the Editor's settings to where they were the first time you launched the program, and usually cures about 80 percent of the problems you may run into in Elements.

FIGURE 9-7

You can reset the Clone Stamp (or, for that matter, any Elements tool) by clicking the four-line square at the right end of the Tool Options area (circled) and choosing Reset Tool. (If you want to reset the whole *Tools panel, choose Reset All Tools instead.) This trick clears up a lot of the little problems you may have when trying to make a tool behave.*

This command uses the same Content-Aware technology that the Spot Healing Brush and the Content-Aware Move tool (described later in this chapter) use, but it lets you quickly patch large areas of your image. It doesn't always work, but it's so simple and quick to use that it's always worth trying. When it does work, it's pretty impressive, as you can see from Figure 9-8.

Here's how you use this command:

1. **Use any of the selection tools described in Chapter 5 to make a selection of the area you want to fix.**

   You may also want to create a duplicate layer (Ctrl+J/⌘-J) to use for filling.

   TIP It sometimes helps to expand your selection out a couple of pixels before filling, especially if there's a strong contrast between the area you're filling and the surrounding area, as in Figure 9-8. Page 175 explains how to use the Expand command.

FIGURE 9-8

Top: The barn and the surrounding area are fine in this shot, but the photographer was standing on a covered porch and the roof makes a dark shadow across the top of the photo. Here you see the area selected before using Content-Aware Fill to fix this problem.

Bottom: Content-Aware Fill creates a new section of the sky to replace the shadow. If you look closely, you can see that there's still a dark line along the diagonal edge of the selection. You can either use the Spot Healing Brush to fix it or undo the fill and go back, expand your selection a few pixels, and then redo the fill.

2. **Go to Edit→Fill Selection; in the Fill Layer dialog box that appears, choose Content-Aware from the Contents menu, and then click OK.**

That's all there is to it.

In the Fill Layer dialog box, you can also choose a different blend mode for your fill and adjust its opacity, but it's easier to use a duplicate layer and then adjust the layer's settings afterward so you can see what you're doing. You may want to use the Clone Stamp or the Spot Healing Brush to fix any little problems around the edges of the new material.

If Content-Aware Fill didn't do it for you, then undo it and use one of the other methods described in this section.

WORKAROUND WORKSHOP

Repairing Tears and Stains

With Elements, you can do a lot to bring damaged photos back to life. The Content-Aware Fill command, the Healing Brush, and the Clone Stamp are major players when it comes to restoring pictures. It's fiddly work that requires persistence, but you can achieve wonders if you have the patience.

If you're lucky and large parts of your photo are in good shape, you can use the Content-Aware Move tool to copy the good bits into the problem area, as explained on page 180. It helps to create a new layer before using this tool, so that you can easily reposition, rotate, or resize the copy. If you don't, Photoshop merges the new material right into the existing layer as soon as you release your mouse button.

If you need a mirror image of something, you can use the Rotate commands to flip a selection. For example, if the left leg of a chair is fine but the right one is missing, try selecting and Alt-dragging/Option-dragging the left leg with the Move tool. When it's where you want it, go to Image→Rotate→Flip Selection Horizontal to turn the copied left leg into a new right leg.

If you don't need to rotate an object, sometimes you can just increase the Clone Stamp's brush size and then clone the object where you need a duplicate. However, this technique works well only when the background is the same in both areas.

■ Applying Patterns

In addition to solid colors, Elements also lets you add patterns to images. Patterns let you add interesting designs to images or give more realistic textures to certain repairs. Elements comes with several built-in patterns, and you can download more (see page 586) or create your own.

You can apply patterns with the Healing Brush or the Pattern Stamp. As you learned earlier, the Healing Brush has a pattern setting in its Tool Options area. The Pattern Stamp shares a Tools panel slot with the Clone Stamp, and it works much like the Clone Stamp but puts down a preselected pattern instead of a sampled area. The tool you use to apply the pattern makes a big difference, as you can see from Figure 9-9. The next two sections explain how to use them both.

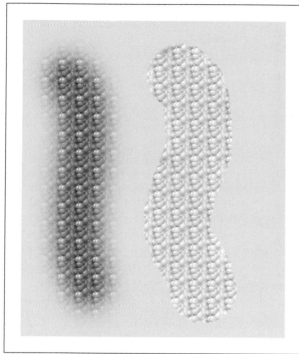

FIGURE 9-9

The same pattern applied with the Pattern Stamp (left) and the Healing Brush (right).

The Pattern Stamp just plunks down the pattern exactly as it appears in the Tool Options area's pop-out panel, whereas the Healing Brush blends the pattern with the underlying color (and texture, when there is any).

To get a softer edge on the Healing Brush's pattern, choose a softer brush in the Tool Options area.

TIP Elements gives you lots of ways to use patterns, including creating a Fill layer (page 216) that's covered with whatever pattern you choose. The Smart Brushes (page 233) also let you apply patterned effects to images, although Adobe officially calls these effects "textures" rather than "patterns." They're particularly nice for creating interest in a flat or empty background area. In the Smart Brushes' Tool Options area, just click the thumbnail image, and then choose Textures from the panel's menu.

The Healing Brush

The Healing Brush's Pattern mode is great for things like improving the texture of someone's skin by applying texture from another photo.

Using patterns with the Healing Brush is just as easy and works the same way as using the tool in normal healing mode: Just drag across the area you want to fix. The only difference is that you don't have to choose a sample point, since the *pattern* is your source. As you drag, Elements blends the pattern you selected into your photo.

After activating the Healing Brush (keyboard shortcut: J), in the Tool Options area's Source menu, choose Pattern; click the pattern thumbnail that appears, and then choose the one you want. You can see more patterns by selecting from the menu at the top of the Pattern panel, or you can create and save your own patterns, as Figure 9-10 explains.

TIP Changing the blend mode (page 98) when using patterns can result in some interesting effects.

FIGURE 9-10

It's easy to create your own patterns. In any image, simply make a rectangular, unfeathered selection, and then choose Edit→"Define Pattern from Selection." Your pattern appears at the bottom of the current Pattern panel, and a dialog box pops up so you can name the new pattern.

To use a whole image as a pattern, don't make a selection—just go to Edit→Define Pattern.

To rename or delete a pattern later, right-click/Control-click it in the Pattern panel. You can also download hundreds of different patterns from various online sources (see page 586), and then use the Preset Manager (page 587) to make them available in Elements.

The Pattern Stamp

This tool is like the Clone Stamp, but instead of copying sampled areas, it puts down a predefined pattern that you select from the Pattern panel. The Pattern Stamp is useful when you want to apply a pattern to an image without mixing the pattern with what's already there. For instance, to see what your patio would look like if it were a garden, you could use the Pattern Stamp to paint a lawn and a flower border on a photo of your patio.

To get started, click the Clone Stamp in the Tools panel or press S, and then choose the Pattern Stamp in the Tool Options area. Then click the pattern thumbnail in the Tool Options area to open the Pattern panel so you can pick one. The other options for this brush (like the size, hardness, and so on) are the same as for the Clone Stamp. The one extra option is the Impressionist checkbox demonstrated in Figure 9-11, which is mostly useful for creating special effects.

Once you've selected a pattern, simply drag in your image where you want Elements to put that pattern.

■ Recomposing Photos

The previous sections taught you how to remove flaws and objects you don't want in photos by manually covering them up bit by bit or by letting Content-Aware Fill do the heavy lifting for you. But Elements gives you another way to get rid of unwanted stuff in your photos: the Recompose tool.

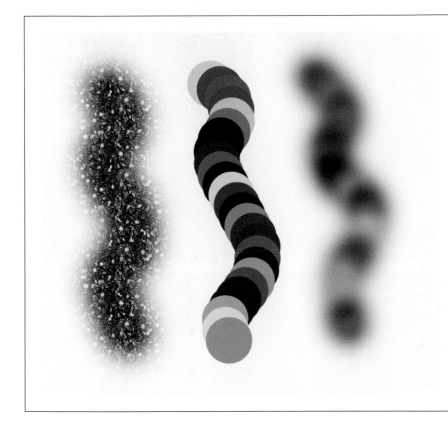

FIGURE 9-11

If you turn on the Pattern Stamp's Impressionist checkbox, Elements blurs the pattern, creating an effect vaguely like an Impressionist painting—but only if you use a soft brush.

Here you see the same pattern put down with the Pattern Stamp using different settings: with the Impressionist setting turned off (left), and with the Impressionist checkbox turned on using a hard brush (center) and a very soft brush (right).

The Recompose tool is one of the coolest features in Elements. It lets you eliminate unwanted objects and people from a photo just by scribbling a line over them and then moving the edges of the photo to reshape it. Amazingly, Elements can keep the rest of the photo undistorted as it makes the unwanted objects vanish. Figure 9-12 shows what this tool can do. Want to get rid of your daughter's ex-boyfriend in that group shot? Just draw a line on him in the photo, push the image's edges closer together, and he's history. Couldn't get your feuding coworkers to stand close together for the holiday party photo? No problem—you can easily remove the empty space between them.

You can also use the Recompose tool to alter the shape of a photo without cropping it. Have a landscape-oriented photo that you wish were portrait-oriented instead? Recompose can fix that. There are limits to what it can do, but with a suitable photo, you can just shove it into the proportions you want, and Elements will keep everything looking perfectly normal and not distorted.

So when do you use Recompose and when do you use Content-Aware Fill? The box on page 329 can help you decide which tool to use.

FIGURE 9-12

Top: Say you only have a wide photo of your great-grandparents, but you want to put it in a narrow frame. You could shrink it down till it fits, but then the image would be too small. Instead, just make a few marks on it with the Recompose tool (the green marks mean "Keep this").

To use the tool's Quick Highlight setting—which makes the tool automatically mark the whole area you drag over, the way the Quick Selection tool's selection expands to encompass whole objects—right-click/Control-click your photo, and then choose Use Quick Highlight from the shortcut menu. The Normal Highlight setting (which this tool uses unless you change it) usually produces fairly similar results, but Quick Highlight makes it easier to see exactly what you're choosing. To recompose the image after adding these marks, just drag one of its edges toward the middle of the photo.

Bottom: The end result. Your ancestors will now fit nicely in their new frame.

Elements has to do an awesome amount of calculating to make this tool work, but it's actually one of the easier tools to use:

1. **Open a photo and activate the Recompose tool.**

   The Recompose tool is at the top right of the Tools panel's Modify section. Its keyboard shortcut is W.

Recomposing vs. Content-Aware Filling and Moving

Elements always gives you many ways to tackle a problem. You may feel a little confused about how to choose between the Recompose tool, the Content-Aware Fill command, and the Content-Aware Move tool. Every photo is different, but here are some rough guidelines:

- Choose the **Recompose tool** when you need to move objects closer together or farther apart, but only in a vertical or horizontal plane, since this tool makes changes only in a straight line. In other words, if you want to move Phillip from Rosalie's left side to her right, this isn't the best choice—although it's great if Rosalie is standing between Phillip and Amelia and you want to remove Rosalie from the photo entirely. Also, remember that when you use this tool, you'll change the shape of the image, so choose Recompose only when that's not a problem (See Figure 9-12, for example).

- The **Content-Aware Fill command** is your best choice when your goal is to preserve the image's overall dimensions or proportions and get rid of an unwanted object. This command is great for, say, removing an ugly electrical transformer from the yard in front of your house. And it *may* do a good job of filling the space between two people, but you're equally likely to find that they've grown extra limbs in the filled area.

- Use the **Content-Aware Move tool** if you need to move a person or object at an angle from its original location, or if there are things in your photo between an object's original location and destination that you don't want to lose. For example, this tool can do a great job of moving Phillip from Rosalie's left side to her right.

2. **Tell Elements which parts of the photo you *don't* want to change.**

   You use the Recompose tool's Protection Brush to indicate which areas you want preserved. To select this brush, head to the Tool Option area's Recompose section and make sure the blue brush with the + sign beside it is selected; then drag over the areas you want to keep. This is kind of like using the Quick Selection tool in that you don't have to select *everything*; just make enough marks so that Elements knows which objects you want to preserve. However, this tool is more literal-minded than the Quick Selection tool, so you may need more marks when using it.

   If you make a mistake, in the Tool Options area, click the eraser icon just to the right of the Protection Brush's icon (it also has a + sign beside it) to remove the marks you don't want.

TIP The Recompose tool has a hidden menu to speed things up: When the tool is active, right-click/Control-click your photo and you can choose Use Quick Highlight (shown in Figure 9-12), which makes the process of telling Elements what to keep and what to eliminate much faster. This setting also tends to produce better results.

   To automatically select the people in your photo, in the Tool Options area, click the "Highlight Skin tones" icon (the little green man to the right of the No Restriction button). This feature works only on full-color images, not on sepia images like the one in Figure 9-12.

3. **Optionally, tell Elements what you want to get rid of.**

To delete specific objects or areas, drag over them with the Removal Brush (in the Tool Options, click the blue brush icon with the – sign next to it). Like the Protection Brush, the Removal Brush has its own eraser to its right (also with a – sign next to it) that you can use to correct any mistakes you make with the brush.

TIP You don't always need to use both of the Recompose tool's brushes. You can even try not marking anything at all before recomposing your photo, but you'll likely get better results if you give Elements *some* guidance. If you make a mistake with either brush, use the corresponding eraser to remove the stray marks.

---

4. **Recompose the photo.**

Once you're through marking up your photo, use the bounding box around the image to resize it. It works just like the Move tool's bounding box: Grab a square handle or a corner and then drag to change the image's shape. There are also several Tool Options settings that you can use to make the photo a specific size; they're explained after this list.

Watch the unwanted areas disappear as you drag the edges closer together.

TIP If you want to make your image wider or taller than it is now (to make a portrait-oriented photo into a landscape-oriented one, for example), you first need to add canvas (page 112) to give the new width or height someplace to go. Just keep in mind that Elements isn't as good at removing objects when you're making the image *larger* as it is when you're shrinking the image.

---

5. **Finish up.**

When you're happy with how things look, click the Commit button (the green checkmark) or press Enter/Return. If you decide you don't want to recompose after all, or if you need to go back and adjust the marks you made on the picture, click the red Cancel button or press Esc. When you're done, crop off any extra blank space on the edges of the photo (see page 89).

TIP You may find that some remnants of removed objects reappear after you click the checkmark or press Enter/Return. Just use the Clone Stamp or Healing Brush to get rid of them.

The Recompose tool has several Tool Options settings to make your job easier:

- **Brushes and erasers**. There are four icons in the Tool Option area's Recompose section. In the top row are the "Mark for Protection" brush and the "Erase highlights marked for protection" brush (for erasing Protection Brush marks you don't want), and in the bottom row are the "Mark for Removal" brush and "Erase highlights marked for removal" (for erasing Removal Brush marks you made by mistake).

- **Size**. This is just like the size setting for any brush tool. To adjust this setting, drag the slider, click the numeric value and enter a size in pixels, put your cursor over the word "Size" and scrub (page 197), or use the bracket key shortcuts (page 163). Chapter 12 covers brushes in detail.

- **Threshold**. This setting tells Elements how much you want to protect the details from distortion. For best results, leave it set to 100 percent.

- **Preset**. Normally this button is set to No Restriction (which lets you drag the bounding box any which way to resize the image), but if you click it, you can choose an option to recompose the photo's current aspect ratio to one of several popular photo-paper sizes or the 16:9 aspect ratio popular for images used in high-definition videos. If you make a choice here or in the W and H boxes (explained next), Elements recomposes your photo to that size.

- **W (width) and H (height)**. If you want your final image to be a custom size, enter it here. Click the arrows between these boxes to swap the numbers.

- **Highlight Skin tones**. Click this icon (the little green man) and, if you're lucky, Elements selects the people in your photo. It's kind of dicey, though—you may find Elements prefers other objects to the folks in your pictures, but it's worth a click, since you can always undo Elements' selection.

What's most amazing about this tool is the way your background still looks real when you're done. Someone seeing your recomposed photo would never guess that it didn't start out looking like it does now. Recomposing doesn't work for every photo, but when it does, the results are almost magical.

Color Curves: Enhancing Tone and Contrast

If you hang around photo-editing veterans, you'll hear how useful Photoshop's Curves tool is. Contrary to what you might think based on its name, Curves isn't a drawing tool. Instead, it works much like Levels (page 243), but with many more points of correction. Adobe includes a simplified version of this tool in Elements and calls it *Color Curves* to remind you what it's for.

Unlike Levels, which let you adjust an entire photo's white point, black point, and midtone settings, the Color Curves tool lets you target specific tonal regions. For instance, it lets you make only the shadows lighter or only the highlights darker. Maybe that's why some pros say that Color Curves is Levels on steroids. (The box on page 251 has advice on when to use Levels and when to use Color Curves.)

Curves, in its original-strength Photoshop version, is a pretty complicated tool, so Adobe makes it easier to use in Elements. You start with a group of preset adjustments to choose from (see Figure 9-13). These presets are shortcuts to the types of basic enhancements you'll use most often; just click one to try it. If you like what it does, you're done. If you aren't satisfied with any of the presets, you can easily make changes using the Adjust Color Curves dialog box's sliders.

Here's how to improve a photo's appearance with Color Curves:

1. **Open a photo and make a duplicate layer.**

   Press Ctrl+J/⌘-J or go to Layer→Duplicate Layer. Elements doesn't let you use Color Curves as an Adjustment layer, so you're safer applying it to a duplicate layer in case you want to change something later.

TIP If you decide you'd like to restrict your adjustment to a particular area, you can apply a layer mask (page 210) to the duplicate layer and edit the mask so your adjustment changes only part of the photo. For instance, if you're happy with everything in your shot of Junior's Little League game *except* the catcher in the foreground, do a Color Curves adjustment on a duplicate layer, and then mask out everything but him.

---

2. **Go to Enhance→Adjust Color→Adjust Color Curves.**

   Elements opens the Adjust Color Curves dialog box (Figure 9-13), which shows your original image on the left.

3. **Choose a Color Curves preset.**

   Scroll through the "Select a Style" list and click the preset that seems closest to what you want. Feel free to experiment by clicking different presets. (As long as you're just clicking in the list, you don't need to click Reset between each one; Elements starts from the original image each time you click.)

The dialog box gives you a decent-sized look at how you're changing things, but for important photos, you can also preview the effect right in the image. To do that, drag the dialog box out of the way and check the actual photo to see how you're changing things before you commit.

4. **Decide whether you like the changes.**

    If you're satisfied, click OK and you're done. If not, continue on to the next step.

5. **Make any further adjustments.**

    If you think your photo still doesn't look quite right, use the sliders shown in Figure 9-14 to tweak the photo. (These sliders are explained in a moment.) Click Reset if you want to undo the changes you've made with the sliders. Notice how subtle the preset curves are—a tiny nudge makes a big difference, so be gentle.

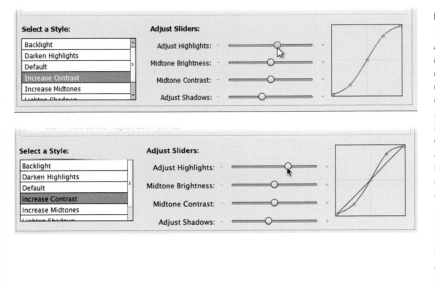

FIGURE 9-14

When you first open the Adjust Color Curves dialog box, the graph on the right shows a straight, diagonal line. Any changes you make cause the points on the graph to move, resulting in a curve. To go back to the straight line, click Reset (not shown) or choose Default in the "Select a Style" list.

Top: The Windows version of Adjust Color Curves. The straight line disappears after you start adjusting things and you only see the resulting curve.

Bottom: The Mac version continues to show the straight diagonal line in addition to the curved one after you adjust your settings.

6. **When you're happy with the photo's new look, click OK.**

Don't forget to save your changes. If you used a duplicate layer, you can always change your mind later on and start over with a fresh layer.

TIP If you've used Curves add-ons in an old version of Elements—like those from Richard Lynch or Grant Dixon, for example—or if you've used Photoshop's Curves Adjustment layers (you power user, you!), the Color Curves tool may take a bit of getting used to, since you can't adjust the curve by dragging it. If not being able to drag drives you nuts, SmartCurve (*http://tinyurl.com/mccrrb9*) is a popular, free, Windows-only add-on that lets you drag to your heart's content (unfortunately, there's no Mac equivalent). Also, some of the add-on toolsets for Elements let you make corrections on a graph rather than with the sliders. (See page 586 for more about add-ons.)

Once you have some Color Curves experience under your belt, you probably won't be satisfied with the presets, so don't hesitate to use the dialog box's sliders to adjust different tonal regions in your photo:

- **Adjust Highlights**. Drag this slider left to darken the photo's highlights, or right to lighten them.

- **Midtone Brightness**. If you'd like the middle range of colors to be darker, move this slider left. Move it right to make the midtones brighter.

- **Midtone Contrast**. This slider works just like the one in Elements' Shadows/Highlights feature (page 230): Move it right to increase the photo's contrast or left to decrease it.

- **Adjust Shadows**. If you want to lighten shadowy areas, move this slider right. To darken them, move it left.

As you drag the sliders, you can see the point you're adjusting move on the graph and watch the curve change shape. Although it's fun to watch the graph, pay more attention to what's happening in your photo.

Color Curves is such a potent tool that it can change a photo in ways you don't intend. So rather than using Color Curves to make huge adjustments, try another tool first, and then use Color Curves for the final, subtle tweaks. But if you *want* to create wild special effects, then Color Curves may be just the ticket; see Figure 9-15 for an example.

■ Making Colors More Vibrant

Do you drool over the luscious photos in travel magazines, the ones of vivid destinations that make real life seem drab by comparison? What *is* it about those photos that makes them so dramatic? Often the answer is the *saturation*, or intensity, of the colors. Supersaturated color makes for darned appealing landscape and object photos, regardless of how the real thing may rate on the vividness scale.

FIGURE 9-15

Many people prefer to use Color Curves for artwork and special effects rather than adjusting photos. Jimi Hendrix fans may like the Adjust Color Curves dialog box's Solarize preset, which Adobe includes to give you a starting point for funky pictures like this one. (Others say this preset should serve as a warning about going overboard with this tool.)

You can also apply the Solarize adjustment to part of a photo with the Smart Brush tool (page 233). But if you use the brush method, you can't edit the settings afterward, so you may prefer to apply Solarize using Color Curves on a duplicate layer.

There are various ways to adjust a photo's saturation. Some cameras have features that help control it, but Elements lets you do even more. For example, by increasing or decreasing a photo's saturation, you can shift the image's perceived focal point, change its mood, or just make it more eye-catching.

By increasing your subject's saturation and decreasing saturation in the rest of the photo, you can focus viewers' attention, even in a crowded photo. Figure 9-16 shows an example of this technique.

It's easy to change saturation. You might want to start with the Quick Fix Vibrance slider (see page 133). If that doesn't work well, try using either of the more traditional methods—the Hue/Saturation dialog box or the Sponge tool—which are explained in the following sections. For big areas or when you want a lot of control, go with the Hue/Saturation dialog box. If you just want to quickly paint a different saturation level (either higher or lower) on a small spot in your photo, the Sponge tool is faster.

The Hue/Saturation Dialog Box

Hue/Saturation is one of the most popular commands in Elements. If you aren't satisfied with the results of a simple Levels adjustment (page 243), you may want to work on the image's hue or saturation as the next step toward getting eye-catching color.

FIGURE 9-16

Top: All the yellow flowers in this image are equally bright, including those in the background, so you might miss the insect on the front blossom.

Bottom: To make the insect and its flower stand out from the crowd, desaturate the rest of the image.

Download the photo skipper.jpg from this book's Missing CD page at www.missingmanuals.com/cds to try this technique yourself.

Hue simply means the color of your image—whether it's blue or brown or purple or green. Most people use Elements' saturation adjustments more than the hue controls, but both hue and saturation are controlled by the aptly named Hue/Saturation dialog box (Figure 9-17). You can use the dialog box's Hue slider to change the color of objects in photos, but you'll probably want to adjust saturation far more often.

> **TIP** Many consumer-grade digital cameras and smartphone cameras automatically crank the saturation of JPEG photos into the stratosphere. That's great if you love all the color, but if you prefer not to live in a Technicolor universe, you can move the Saturation slider (in the Hue/Saturation dialog box or the Adjustments panel) to the left to desaturate photos and remove some of the excess color.

FIGURE 9-17

The Hue/Saturation controls include a drop-down menu that lets you adjust specific color channels.

For example, if only the reds are excessive (a common problem with some brands of digital cameras), you can lower the saturation of just the reds without changing the other channels.

When you use Hue/Saturation, it's a good idea to make most of your other corrections first—like Levels or exposure changes. Then follow these steps:

1. **If you want to adjust only part of the photo, select the area you want to change.**

   Use whatever selection tool(s) you prefer. (See Chapter 5 for a refresher.)

2. **Call up the Hue/Saturation dialog box.**

   Go to Enhance→Adjust Color→Adjust Hue/Saturation, or to Layer→New Adjustment Layer→Hue/Saturation. As always, if you want to make changes that are easy to undo, use an Adjustment layer instead of working directly on the photo. (If you go the Adjustment layer route, you'll make your changes in the Adjustments panel rather than a dialog box, but your options are exactly the same.)

TIP   Using an Adjustment layer gives you more flexibility because you can always come back and edit the layer's mask later on if you change your mind about what you want to modify. See page 215 for more info.

---

3. **In the dialog box or panel, move the sliders until you like what you see.**

   To adjust only saturation, ignore the Hue slider. Drag the Saturation slider right to increase the amount of color or left to decrease it. If necessary, move the Lightness slider left to make the image's color darker, or right to make it lighter.

   If you're using an Adjustment layer, you're done. If you're using the dialog box, click OK when you're satisfied.

Incidentally, you don't have to change *all* the colors in your photo equally; Figure 9-17 explains how to focus on individual color channels.

> **TIP** Generally speaking, if you want to change a pastel to a more intense color, you'll need to increase the color's saturation *and* reduce its lightness (by moving the Lightness slider left) if you don't want the color to look radioactive.

Adjusting Saturation with the Sponge Tool

The Sponge tool gives you another way to adjust saturation. Even though it's called a "sponge," this tool works like any other brush tool in Elements; the process of choosing the size and hardness is the same as choosing them for a brush (see page 398). Figure 9-18 shows the kind of effect the Sponge has.

> **TIP** Although the Sponge tool is handy for working on small areas, all the dragging it requires gets old when you're working on a large chunk of an image. For those situations, use Hue/Saturation (page 334) instead.

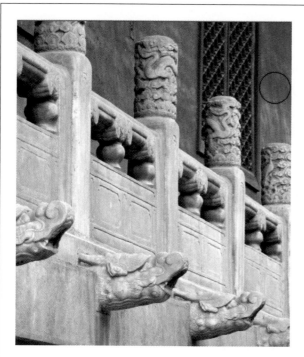

FIGURE 9-18

The Sponge tool was applied to the upper-right part of this wall, increasing its color saturation and making the paint redder.

Approach the Sponge tool with caution: It can quickly start to degrade your image's quality, especially if you've made lots of other adjustments to it. So if you start to see noise (graininess), undo your sponging and try again at a reduced Flow setting.

If you have a hard time coloring (or decoloring) inside the lines, select the area you want before sponging. That way the tool won't have any effect outside the selection, so you can be as sloppy as you like.

You may want to press Ctrl+J/⌘-J to create a duplicate layer before using the Sponge. That way you can throw out the duplicate layer later if you don't like the changes, or add a layer mask to restrict the area they affect (page 210). Here's how to use this tool:

1. **Activate the Sponge tool.**

   Press O (that's the letter, not the number) or click its icon in the Tools panel (it's in the Enhance section, just below the Clone Stamp), and then choose the Sponge in the Tool Options area. Then select the brush size and settings you want (they're explained after this list).

2. **Drag over the area you want to change.**

   If you aren't seeing enough of a difference, increase the tool's Flow setting (explained in a moment) a little. If the effect is too strong, reduce the Flow setting.

The Sponge tool's Tool Options offer a couple of unique settings:

- **Mode**. Here's where you tell the Sponge whether to saturate (add color) or desaturate (remove color).

- **Flow**. This setting governs how intense the tool's effect is; a higher number means more intensity.

■ Changing an Object's Color

In Chapter 4, you saw one way to change the color of an object: Select it and then use Quick Fix's Hue and Saturation sliders. Elements also gives you other ways to achieve the same result: You can use an Adjustment layer, the Replace Color command, or the Color Replacement tool. (The Smart Brush tools offer a whole menu of color changes, too; see the Tip below for the lowdown.)

Which method you should choose depends on your photo and personal preference. Using an Adjustment layer gives you the most flexibility if you want to make changes later. Replace Color is the fastest way to change a color that's widely scattered throughout your image. And the Color Replacement tool lets you quickly brush a replacement color over the one you want to change. Figure 9-19 shows the kind of complex color change you can make in a jiffy using any of these methods.

TIP The Smart Brush (page 233) lets you target an area and make a quick color adjustment, so you might think that sounds like a good tool for changing color. It *can* be, but its color presets are pretty limited (and pretty ugly). Also, the Smart Brush doesn't just apply a single color—it uses gradient maps (page 475) instead. If you can get the effect you like using the Smart Brush, go for it. But it's tough to adjust color with this tool, since you have to either pick a different gradient or edit the one the Smart Brush used (page 236 tells you how). On the whole, the methods described in the following pages are much easier to control.

FIGURE 9-19

What if you have a green-and-white vase but you really want a red-and-white one?

Elements can make it so!

Using an Adjustment Layer

You can use a Hue/Saturation Adjustment layer to make the kind of color changes you saw in Figure 9-19. The advantage of this method is that you can go back later and change your settings or the area affected by the layer (as opposed to changing the whole image). The process is the same as the one described on page 336, only this time you start by making a selection:

1. **Select the object whose color you want to change.**

   Use any of the selection tools (see Chapter 5). If you don't make a selection before creating the Adjustment layer, it'll change your whole photo.

2. **Create a new Hue/Saturation Adjustment layer.**

   Go to Layer→New Adjustment Layer→Hue/Saturation. The new layer affects only the area you selected.

3. **Use the Adjustments panel's sliders to tweak the color until it looks good, and then click OK.**

   Use the Hue slider first to pick the color you want. Next, use the Saturation slider to adjust the color's vividness, and then the Lightness slider to adjust its darkness.

This method is fine if it's easy to select the area you want to change. But what if there are a bunch of widely scattered areas of color that need changing, or you want to change one shade everywhere it appears in a photo? For that, Elements offers the Replace Color command, explained next.

Replacing Specific Colors

Take a look at the green-and-white vase in Figure 9-19 again. Do you have to tediously select each green area if you want to make it a red-and-white vase? You *could* do it that way, but it's far easier to use the Replace Color command, which changes every instance of the color you select, no matter where it appears in the image. When you run this command, you'll see one of those Elements dialog boxes that looks a bit intimidating, but it's a snap to use once you understand how it works.

You don't need to start by making a selection when you use this command but, as usual, you should run it on a duplicate layer (Ctrl+J/⌘-J) if you want to keep your options open for future changes. And before you start, be sure the active layer *isn't* an Adjustment layer, or Replace Color won't work. Then:

1. **Open the Replace Color dialog box.**

   Go to Enhance→Adjust Color→Replace Color. The Replace Color dialog box in Figure 9-20 appears. You may need to drag it out of the way so you can see your whole photo.

2. **Move your cursor over your photo.**

   The cursor changes to an eyedropper. Make sure that the leftmost eyedropper in the Replace Color dialog box (the one *without* a + or – sign next to it) is the active one, as in Figure 9-20.

3. **Click an area of the color you want to replace.**

   Elements selects all the areas that match the particular shade you selected, but you won't see marching ants in your image the way you do with the selection tools. If you click more than once, you *change* your selection instead of adding to it. To add to your selection (that is, to select additional shades), Shift-click in your photo instead, or select the middle eyedropper (the one with the + sign next to it) and then click in your photo again. To remove a color, Alt-click/Option-click your image instead, or select the rightmost eyedropper (the one with the – sign) and then click. To undo your selecting and start over, Alt-click/Option-click the Cancel button to turn it into a Reset button.

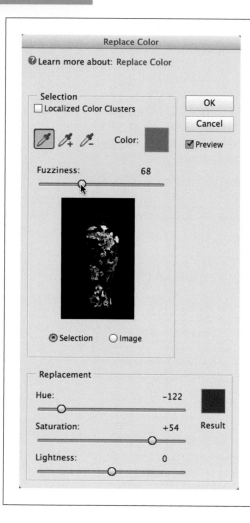

FIGURE 9-20

The preview image that looks like a negative shows where the sliders will affect the image's color. The lighter areas are where Elements plans to substitute your new color.

Use the Hue and Saturation sliders to adjust the replacement color (shown in the Result box here). The Fuzziness setting (explained in Figure 9-21) works a little like the Magic Wand's Tolerance setting, and the Localized Color Clusters checkbox is something like the Magic Wand's Contiguous setting—it restricts the selection to colors near where you click.

To protect a particular area of your chosen color from being changed, paint a mask on it by using the Selection Brush in Mask mode before *you run the Replace Color command.*

4. **When you've selected everything you want to change, move the dialog box's sliders to change the color.**

   The Hue, Saturation, and Lightness sliders work exactly the way they do in the Hue/Saturation dialog box (page 336). Move them and watch the Result box to their right to see what color you're concocting. You can also click the Result box to bring up the Color Picker and choose a shade there. If you need to tweak the area you're changing, use the Fuzziness slider to adjust the range of colors that Color Replacement affects, as Figure 9-21 explains.

FIGURE 9-21

Fuzziness is similar to the Magic Wand's Tolerance setting (page 166).

Take a close look at the red parts of this vase—there's still a lot of green in the center of some of them. To change more pixels, set the Replace Color dialog box's Fuzziness higher by dragging it right (in this image, that change would make all the green spots turn red).

If Elements is changing areas you don't want to, move the Fuzziness slider left instead.

After choosing a replacement color, look closely at your photo. If the replacement color isn't showing up in all the areas you want, click the missing spots with the dialog box's middle eyedropper to fix them.

5. **Click OK to close the Replace Color dialog box.**

The Color Replacement Tool

You can also brush on a color change with the Color Replacement tool, which lets you brush a different color onto an area without changing any colors besides the one you target. Figure 9-22 shows how it works.

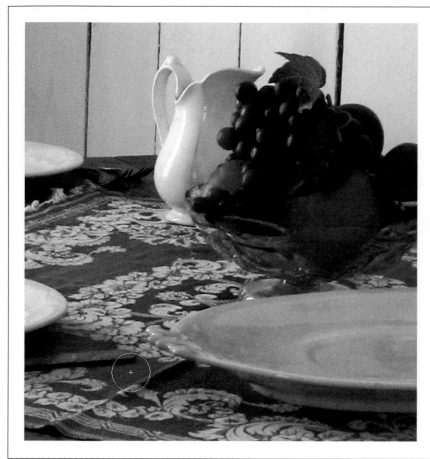

FIGURE 9-22

Here's an example of when the Color Replacement tool comes in handy.

Say you have a red-and-white tablecloth but you think this photo would look better if it were blue and white. In this particular photo, the Replace Color command (page 341) and the Magic Wand (page 165) would be hard to use, since the fruit is fairly similar in color to the tablecloth. But with the Color Replacement tool, you can drag over the tablecloth's intricate pattern without getting blue anywhere else.

In this example, the tool's mode is set to Hue, so that the blue matches the dullness of the original red.

Using the Color Replacement tool is straightforward:

1. **Set your foreground color square to the color you want to use as a replacement.**

   To change colors, click the foreground color square in the Tools panel, and then choose a new hue from the Color Picker.

2. **Activate the Color Replacement tool and pick a brush size.**

   Click the Brush tool in the Tools panel or press B and then, in the Tool Options area, choose the Color Replacement tool. Its icon is a brush with a color square next to it. For this tool, you usually want a fairly large brush, as shown in Figure 9-22. (See Chapter 12 to learn all about brushes.)

3. **Click or drag in your photo to change the color.**

   Elements targets the color that's under the *crosshairs* in the center of the brush cursor. So in Figure 9-22, for example, keeping the crosshairs over the tablecloth ensures that only the tablecloth changes.

> **TIP** You may want to use the Color Replacement tool on a duplicate layer (Ctrl+J/⌘-J) so you can adjust the layer's opacity to control the effect.

The Tool Options settings make a big difference in the way this tool works:

- **Brush Thumbnail**. You can't choose a different brush here; this thumbnail just gives you a preview of the brush's size.

- **Size**. Use this slider to adjust how big the brush is.

- **Tolerance**. This is like the Magic Wand's Tolerance setting: The higher the number, the more shades of color Elements changes. This setting is the key to getting good results with this tool.

- **Mode**. This controls the tool's blend mode (page 98). Generally you'll want to choose Color or Hue, although you can get some funky special effects with Saturation. Luminosity is the one you'll probably use least, since it just changes the brightness of the original color to the brightness of the new color; the hue and saturation of the original color remain.

- **Limits**. This setting tells Elements where to look when it searches for color. Discontiguous means the tool changes only instances of the color immediately beneath the brush's center. Contiguous means it also changes similar-colored areas that are touching areas of that color that are under the cursor.

- **Brush Settings**. Most of the settings you see when you click this button (Hardness, Spacing, and Roundness) are the same as for any brush (see Chapter 12 for more about brushes). In addition, if you're using a graphics tablet, you can choose to control the size of the brush or its Tolerance setting with your stylus's scrollwheel (if it has one) or how hard you press the stylus (page 584).

- **Sampling**. These three eyedroppers are the secret to making this a useful tool. They tell the Color Replacement tool *how* to look for colors to replace. Here's what they do, from left to right:

  — **Continuous** tells the brush to keep replacing every color you drag over.

  — **Once** tells it to replace the color where you first click and ignore other colors it passes over. At least that's how this eyedropper *should* work. In reality, it usually makes the brush behave more like the Clone stamp (page 318) in unaligned mode: you apply color by clicking repeatedly instead of dragging.

— **Background Swatch** tells the tool to look for the color that's currently in your background color square and replace that color—and *only* that color— whenever you brush over it. If you use this setting, be sure your background color is set to the one you want to change; use the Eyedropper tool (page 257) to sample the color before you switch to the Color Replacement Brush.

- **Anti-aliasing**. This setting smooths the edges of the replacement color; it's best to leave it turned on.

Special Effects

Elements gives you some other useful ways of drastically changing the look of an image. You can apply these effects as Adjustment layers (by choosing Layer→New Adjustment Layer) or as filters (by going to Filter→Adjustments; there's much more about filters in Chapter 13). Either route gives you the same options (except for Equalize, which is available only as a filter). Figure 9-23 shows them in action

FIGURE 9-23

You can get some interest-ing special effects with the Adjustment commands, whether you apply them as filters or Adjustment layers. (If you want to run them as filters, it's not a bad idea to do so on a duplicate layer.)

Top row (left to right): The original photo, Invert, Equalize.

Bottom row (left to right): Posterize and Threshold.

In most cases, you use these adjustments as steps along the way in a more complex treatment of a photo, but they're effective by themselves, too. Here's what each one does (listed in the order they appear in the Filter menu):

- **Equalize** makes the darkest pixel in the photo black and the lightest one white, and then redistributes the brightness values of all the colors in the photo to give them all equal weight. If you have an active selection when you run this filter, Elements brings up a dialog box that lets you choose whether you want it to equalize the whole photo or equalize it based on your selection. For example, say you have an image of dark woods and a bright sky and you've selected part of the sky. If you tell Elements to equalize based on the selection, the program brightens the whole image to the level of the pixels in the sky selection without including the dark, wooded areas in its calculations. So the resulting equalized photo is much brighter than it would have been if you'd told Elements to base its calculations on the *whole* photo. Equalize doesn't always work, but sometimes it does a great job of increasing the brightness of a dim photo.

- **Gradient Map** is pretty complicated. According to Adobe, it "maps the gray-scale range of an image to the colors of a specified gradient fill." (If you want to know what the heck *that* means, turn to page 475.) Basically, it lets you apply a gradient based on the light and dark areas of the photo; the gradient's colors replace the existing colors. Give it a shot and see whether you like the result.

- **Invert** makes your image look like a negative. It's so useful in doing artistic things to photos that Elements lets you invert images anytime by pressing Ctrl+I/⌘-I. To invert just part of an image, check out the Smart Brush tools (page 233), which have some interesting variations on inversion in their Special Effects menus, or use a duplicate layer with a layer mask (page 210) and edit the area that's covered by the mask.

> **NOTE** If you think choosing the Invert option sounds like a great way to turn negatives you scanned in with a basic flatbed scanner into positive images, that works only if your negatives are black and white. Color negatives have an orange mask on them that Elements can't easily undo, so you're best off using a dedicated film scanner that's designed to cope with negatives, or at least a scanner that has software for dealing with the mask.

- **Posterize** reduces the total number of colors in the photo, creating a less detailed, more poster-like image. The lower the number you enter in the Posterize dialog box or Adjustments panel, the fewer colors you get and the more extreme the result. If you want blocky, poster-like edges in a photo, try Filter→Artistic→Poster Edges instead of—or in addition to—this adjustment.

- **Threshold** turns every pixel in the photo pure white or pure black—you won't find any shades of gray here. Figure 9-24 explains how to tweak this adjustment's settings.

- **Photo Filter** lets you make color corrections, like removing color casts. Page 299 explains this filter in detail.

FIGURE 9-24

This graph is a histogram (page 245) showing the light-to-dark distribution of the pixels in the image.

The slider controls the dividing point between black and white pixels in a Threshold adjustment. Slide it left if you want more white pixels, or right for more black ones.

Removing and Adding Color

A stunning black-and-white image is so much more than just a color photo without color. If you love classic black-and-white photography or yearn to be the next Ansel Adams, you'll be over the moon with the high-quality black-and-white conversions Elements can do.

If, on the other hand, you can't imagine why anyone would willingly abandon color, consider that, in a world crammed with eye-popping colors, black and white really stands out. Or say you need to have something printed where you *can't* use color illustrations. And for artistic photography, there's nothing like black and white, where tone and contrast make or break the photo, without colors to distract you from its underlying structure.

In this chapter, you'll learn how to turn a color photo black and white, and how to create images that are only partly in color. You'll also learn how to reverse the process and colorize black-and-white images.

> **TIP** In addition to the methods described in this chapter, Elements 13 includes some excellent guided edits that make it easy to create popular black-and-white and single-color effects. Just click the word "Guided" at the top of the Editor's window and then look in the Photo Effects section. Click the name of the edit you want to try, and Elements walks you through each step.

■ Making Color Photos Black and White

Generally, just removing the color from a photo produces an image that's flat and uninteresting. A good black-and-white photo usually needs more contrast than you'll get if you simply zap the color. And you can create different effects and moods in a photo depending on what you emphasize in the black-and-white version.

Converting images to black and white has traditionally been a pretty complicated process. If you do a Google search, you'll find dozens of recipes for doing so. Fortunately for you, Elements makes it easy to perform this task, and even to do sophisticated tweaking of the different color channels. Just follow these steps:

1. **Open a photo and make sure it's ready to convert.**

    If the file has multiple layers, either flatten it by choosing Layer→Flatten Image (see page 209) or make sure the layer you want to convert is active by clicking it in the Layers panel.

    To convert only part of the photo, either select the area you want to make black and white or create a duplicate layer (Ctrl+J/⌘-J) and then, after you do the conversion, use a layer mask to control which areas are black and white (see page 210).

    NOTE As always, it's best to perform this technique on a copy of your photo, not the original.

2. **Go to Enhance→"Convert to Black and White," or press Alt+Ctrl+B/Option-⌘-B.**

    The "Convert to Black and White" dialog box appears. It includes helpful before and after previews of the image, and the controls shown in Figure 10-1.

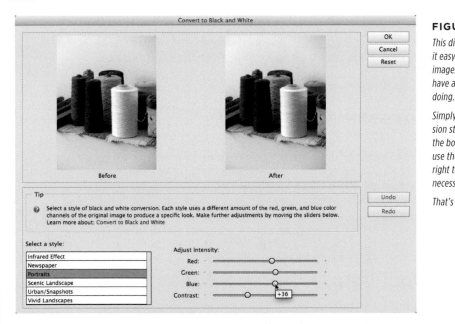

FIGURE 10-1

This dialog box makes it easy to transform images—even if you don't have any idea what you're doing.

Simply choose a conversion style from the list at the bottom left, and then use the sliders on the right to tweak the result, if necessary.

That's it!

3. **Choose a conversion style.**

In the dialog box's bottom left, Elements lists various conversion-style presets. Click a style in the list to apply it to your photo. Try each one to find your favorite. (There's more info about these styles after this list.)

4. **Tweak the conversion, if necessary.**

Use the dialog box's sliders (Red, Green, Blue, and Contrast) to increase or decrease the prominence of each color channel (the box on page 352 has more info about how color channels relate to black-and-white images). You don't need to understand color channels to do this; just move the sliders around and see what they do; the After image shows how you're changing things. Go gently—it doesn't take much to make a big difference.

Once you move a slider, the Undo and Redo buttons on the right side of the dialog box become clickable. Use them to step backward and forward through your changes. To start from scratch, click Reset.

5. **When you're satisfied with how the photo looks, click OK.**

Be sure to carefully examine your actual image before clicking OK. Don't just rely on the smallish preview window—move the dialog box around your screen so you can see the whole photo before accepting the conversion. (If you decide against creating a black-and-white image, click Cancel.)

If you performed the conversion on a duplicate layer and decide you want only a *partially* black-and-white image, then after you click OK, apply a layer mask (page 210) and paint away the areas you want to leave in color (page 213 explains how to edit the mask). Just remember: "Black conceals and white reveals."

> **TIP** You may want to emphasize certain details in the photo without making additional changes to its overall tonality. To do that, use the Dodge and Burn tools (page 410) once you've completed the conversion.

The different conversion styles have descriptive names, like Portraits and Scenic Landscape, but don't put too much stock in those names. They're simply less intimidating ways of describing preset color-channel settings. Be sure to test out the various styles to see which works best on your photo. For instance, you may prefer the way Uncle Julio looks when you choose Newspaper style instead of Portraits style.

> **TIP** There's a helpful Black and White edit in Guided Edit→Photo Effects, which lets you adjust the photo's contrast and add a soft glow, if you like.

Elements also gives you an even *easier* way to convert a photo to black and white (but it's an all-or-nothing scenario—you can't adjust the tones in the image): the Effects panel's black-and-white tint effect. Open the Effects panel (Window→Effects), and then click the Effects tab at the top of the panel (if it's not already selected). From the panel's drop-down menu, choose Monotone Color, and then double-click the black-and-white tree to apply the effect.

Also, some frames in the Graphics panel's Frames section (page 526)—like a few of the Color Tint frames—automatically convert a photo to black and white when you place it in the frame. Page 514 explains how to use frames.

Color Channels and B&W

Why should I make changes to a photo's color channels when I'm creating a black-and-white image?

Back in Chapter 7, you read about how photos consist of three separate color channels: red, green, and blue. In your camera's original file, each of these channels is recorded as variations of light and dark tones—in other words, as a black-and-white image. This image file tells your computer or printer to render a particular channel as all red, blue, or green, and then blend these three monotone channels to make all the colors you see.

When you convert a photo back to black and white, each of these channels contains varying amounts of details from your photo, depending on the color of your original subject. So the green channel might have more detail from your subject's eyelashes, while the red channel may have more detail from the bark on the tree she's standing under. (Remember, the color channels themselves don't necessarily correspond to the color of the objects you see in the final photo. Or, put another way: Your camera uses a mixture of red, green, and

blue to create what look like eyelashes, bark, and so on to us humans.) And there's often more *noise* (graininess) in one channel than the others.

The "Convert to Black and White" dialog box's Red, Green, and Blue sliders let you increase or decrease the presence of each color channel so you can adjust how prominent various details are in the photo. These adjustments can greatly change the appearance of the final black-and-white image. (The Contrast slider, not surprisingly, adjusts the contrast—page 131—of the combined channels.)

That's the theory behind those color-channel sliders, but fortunately, you don't have to understand it to use them effectively. Just be sure you have a good view of your photo (zoom in and, if necessary, move the dialog box), and then move the sliders till you're happy with what you see. If you plan to print your converted photo, the Tip on page 354 has some info on how to get a good black-and-white print from a color inkjet printer.

■ Removing Color from Photos

Because one size never fits all, Elements gives you a few other, totally different ways to remove color from images. The instructions in the preceding section are usually your best bet when converting a whole photo to black and white. But if you're in a hurry or you're looking to do something artistic, like change a color photo into a drawing or a painting, try one of these three methods:

- **Switch color modes**. You may remember from page 41 that you need to choose a color mode for your photos: RGB, Bitmap, or Grayscale. You can remove the color from a photo simply by changing its mode to Grayscale: Go to Image→Mode→Grayscale. This method is quick, but it's also a bit destructive, since you can't apply it to a layer: The whole photo is either grayscale or not, and once you save and close the photo, its color info is gone for good. So be sure to perform this technique on a *copy* of your photo, not the original.

- **Remove Color**. You can keep a photo in RGB mode and drain its color by going to Enhance→Adjust Color→Remove Color, or by pressing Shift+Ctrl+U/Shift-⌘-U. This command removes the color from only the active layer, so if the file has more than one layer, you need to flatten it first (choose Layer→Flatten Image) or the other layers will keep their colors.

The Remove Color command is really just a way of completely desaturating a photo—like you might do when using the Hue/Saturation command (described next). Remove Color is faster but doesn't give you as much control as the Hue/Saturation command. Figure 10-2 shows the difference between applying the Remove Color command and converting an entire image to grayscale as explained in the previous bullet.

FIGURE 10-2

Depending on which method you use, uncoloring a photo can generate very different results.

Top: Each of these rabbits has a pure color value of 255. In other words, you're looking at rabbits that are 100 percent blue, green, and red, with zero as the value for the other two color channels.

Middle: The same images with their color modes converted to grayscale (Image→Mode→Grayscale).

Bottom: Using the Remove Color command gives you quite different results.

- **Hue/Saturation**. Call up the Hue/Saturation dialog box (page 335) by going to Enhance→Adjust Color→Adjust Hue/Saturation, and then move the Saturation slider all the way to the left or type *–100* into the Saturation box. The advantage of this method is that, if you don't care for the shade of gray you get, you can desaturate each color channel separately by using the dialog box's drop-down menu.

TIP If you're planning to print your newly black-and-white photo, the paper you use can make a *big* difference in the results. If you don't like the gray tones you get with your usual paper, try a different weight or brand. You'll need to experiment, because the inks for various printer models interact differently with various brands of paper. And if you plan on printing lots of black-and-white photos, you may want to look into buying a photo printer that lets you substitute several shades of gray ink for your color cartridges.

Creating Spot Color

Removing *almost* all the color from a photo but leaving one or two objects in vivid tones—called *spot color*—is an effective artistic device that's long been popular in the print industry. (In the commercial printing business, the term "spot color" means something else—it refers to the use of special inks for a particular color in a multicolor image.) Figure 10-3 shows an example.

TIP Check your camera's special effects settings for a spot or accent color option. Many cameras can create black-and-white images with only one shade left in color.

FIGURE 10-3

In Elements, you can easily remove color from part of an image.

Left: The original, full-color photo.

Right: Now the color is gone from everything except the caboose.

This section explains four easy ways to create this effect.

This section walks you through four of the easiest methods for creating spot color. (To practice the maneuvers you're about to learn, download the practice file *caboose. jpg* from this book's Missing CD page at *www.missingmanuals.com/cds*.)

NOTE In addition to the methods described here, Elements 13 has two new guided edits for this: "Selective Black and White" (which is essentially the same method described in the next section) and the interesting B&W Color Pop effect, which lets you create the kind of gritty image with a single color in it that's so popular in advertising right now. To use any of these, just go to Guided Edit (click the word "Guided" at the top of the Elements window, and then click Photo Effects), and then click the effect for which you want to see step-by-step instructions.

Brushing Away Color

Creating black-and-white areas in a color photo is super easy in Elements. One way is to use the Smart Brush to convert an area to black and white while making a selection (see Figure 10-4). In other words, you paint the object you want to make black and white, and Elements selects and converts it—all while preserving the color in the rest of your photo. If you want to keep most of the image in color and convert only small portions of it to black and white, or vice versa, definitely try this method first.

FIGURE 10-4

With the Smart Brush, converting part of a photo to black and white is as simple as making a selection.

Top: The puppy is really cute, but the bright blue shirt draws your eye away from him.

Bottom: Drag over the puppy with the Smart Brush with the Inverse option turned on, and he stays in color while the rest of the photo turns black and white.

To paint away color with the Smart Brush:

1. **Open a photo in Expert mode, and then activate the Smart Brush.**

   Press F or click its icon (the housepainter's brush) in the Tools panel. Check the Tool Options to be sure you have the *regular* Smart Brush activated and not the Detail Smart Brush (the pointier brush icon).

   Happily, the Smart Brush puts its changes on their own layer, so you don't need to create a duplicate layer before using it.

2. **Choose the style of black-and-white conversion you want.**

   The thumbnail in the Tool Options area is actually the pop-out menu for the Smart Brush's presets. Click the thumbnail and then, in the panel that appears, click the drop-down menu and choose "Black and White."

   Elements offers a number of different conversion styles, and the names don't mean much, so it's best to go by the thumbnail preview when choosing one. To make the thumbnails a little easier to see, click the four-line square in the panel's upper right and choose Large Thumbnail. Then click the thumbnail that looks most like what you want (if you don't like it once it's applied, you can change it as explained in a sec).

3. **In your photo, drag over the object that you want to make black and white.**

   The Smart Brush should select the object and convert it, all in one go. If you have a hard time getting a good selection, go back to the Tool Options area and switch to the Detail Smart Brush (page 233) instead. It works like the regular Selection Brush, changing only the area directly under the cursor, so you'll have more work to do, but you'll get a more accurate selection.

That's all there is to it. If you don't like the conversion style you chose or want to change the area the brush affects, click the pin icon that appears in your photo anytime the Smart Brush is active, and then make your changes, like selecting a different thumbnail. (See page 235 for more about how to fine-tune Smart Brush edits.) You can also adjust the affected area by editing the Smart Brush's layer mask, as explained on page 235.

The Smart Brush is great when you want a photo that's mostly in color with only a small area of black and white. If you want the opposite—a photo that's mostly black and white with only a small area of color, like the puppy in Figure 10-4—then turn on the Tool Options area's Inverse checkbox (which reverses the area changed by the effect), and then brush over the area you want to keep in color. That way, the part you brush over stays in color, while the rest of the photo turns black and white. You can also use one of the methods described in the following sections.

TIP The Smart Brush's black-and-white conversion settings aren't always editable. Depending on which conversion style you chose, you may see a confusing message that claims that the Adjustment layer was created in Photoshop, even though you just created it in Elements. That's because Adobe uses the Smart Brush to make some Photoshop-only conversion styles available in Elements, so you can *apply* them, but not tweak them once you're done. The Blue lens filter is one example of a style where all you can change is how much of your photo it affects, not the settings for the conversion style itself.

Erasing Colors from a Duplicate Layer

You can also easily remove colors from parts of an image with the Eraser tool. With this method, you place a color-free layer over the colored original, and then erase bits of the top layer to let the color below show through. Here's how:

1. **Open a photo and then create a duplicate layer.**

   Press Ctrl+J/⌘-J or go to Layer→Duplicate Layer. This new layer will become the black-and-white version.

2. **Remove the color from the new layer.**

   Make sure the top layer (the new one you just created) is the active layer, and then go to Enhance→"Convert to Black and White" or to Enhance→Adjust Color→Remove Color. You should now see a black-and-white version of your image.

3. **Erase the areas of the top layer where you want to see color.**

   Use the Eraser tool (page 416) to remove parts of the top layer so the colored layer underneath it shows through. Usually you'll get the best results with a fairly soft brush.

If you want an image that's mostly colored with only a few black-and-white areas, reverse this technique: Remove the color from the bottom layer and leave the top layer in color; then erase as described above.

When you're finished, you can flatten the layers, if you want. But by keeping them separate, you have the option of going back and erasing more of the top layer later on, or starting over by trashing the layer you erased.

Removing Color from Selections

If you don't want your image to have multiple layers, you can make a selection and then use the "Convert to Black and White" or Remove Color command. Just make sure you perform this technique on a copy, *not* the original image—you don't want to risk wrecking the original photo.

While the Smart Brush is the handiest tool for uncoloring small areas, as explained above, the method described here is best if you don't like any of the Smart Brush's presets or if you're dead set against adding a new layer. Here's what you do:

1. **Mask out the area of the image where you want to keep the color.**

   Use the Selection Brush in Mask mode (see page 162) to paint over the area where you want to *keep* the color, to protect it from being changed in step 2. In other words, you'll make everything black and white *except* where you paint with the Selection Brush.

   If you want to keep the color in most of your photo and remove it from only one or two objects, then paint over them with the Selection Brush in Selection mode instead, or use the Quick Selection tool.

2. **Remove the color from the selected area.**

   Go to Enhance→"Convert to Black and White," or to Enhance→Adjust Color→ Remove Color. Either way, Elements removes the color from the areas not protected by the mask but leaves the part under the mask untouched. (You can also do this by going to Enhance→Adjust Color→Adjust Hue/Saturation, and then moving the Saturation slider all the way to the left.)

   If you have trouble seeing what you've done, temporarily switch from Mask mode to Selection mode, or just click another tool and then click back to the Selection Brush to make any changes.

You should now see color only in the areas you didn't select. This method is the least flexible of all the ones described in this chapter because, once you close your image, the change is permanent. That's why you definitely don't want to use this method on the original photo.

Using an Adjustment Layer and the Saturation Slider

Finally, you can remove color using a Hue/Saturation Adjustment layer. This method doesn't offer you the tone adjustments you can make when using the Enhance menu's "Convert to Black and White" option, but using an Adjustment layer lets you both add and subtract areas of color later on. Here's what you do:

1. **Select the area you want to make black and white.**

   Use any selection tool you like (see Chapter 5 for a refresher). If it's easier to select the area where you want to *keep* the color instead, do that, and then press Shift+Ctrl+I/Shift-⌘-I to invert your selection so the area that will lose its color is selected instead.

2. **Create a Hue/Saturation Adjustment layer.**

   Go to Layer→New Adjustment Layer→Hue/Saturation, or click the Layers panel's New Adjustment Layer icon (the half-black, half-white circle) and choose Hue/ Saturation.

3. **In the Adjustments panel, move the Saturation slider all the way to the left to get rid of the color.**

With this method, you can go back and edit the Hue/Saturation Adjustment layer's layer mask to change the amount of colored area, including letting only partial color show, as you can see in Figure 10-5. But most of the time you'll get a better-looking black-and-white conversion with the duplicate-layer technique described on page 350.

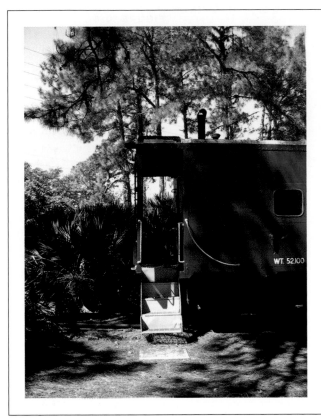

FIGURE 10-5

By painting on the layer mask with different shades of gray, you can make the adjustment's effect partially transparent.

Here, a fairly light gray was used to paint over the trees and ground on the left side of the image so that a little green and brown show through, but it's not the bright, saturated color of the original photo.

(Only part of the left side of the image was painted so you can see the contrast with what was there before.)

▉ Colorizing Black-and-White Photos

So far, you've read about ways to make color photos black and white. But what about when you want to add color to a black-and-white image? Elements lets you do that, too. For instance, you can give an old photo the sort of hand-tinted effect you sometimes see in antique prints, as shown in Figure 10-6.

You can easily color things in Elements. But before you start tinting a photo, first make any needed repairs. (See page 309 for repair strategies, or page 228 for exposure fixes.) When the image is in good shape, here's how to color it:

1. **Make sure the photo is in RGB mode.**

   Go to Image→Mode→RGB Color. If your photo is in any other mode, you won't be able to color it.

FIGURE 10-6

Left: If you decide to color an old black-and-white or sepia photo, put each color you add on its own layer. That way you can adjust the transparency or change the hue or saturation of one color without changing the other colors, too.

Right: A very low opacity is enough for old photos like this one if you want to give the impression of a print that was hand-colored.

See the box on page 361 for more tips on colorizing old photos.

2. **Create a new layer in Color blend mode.**

   Go to Layer→New→Layer and then, in the New Layer dialog box, select Color from the Mode menu. With this blend mode, you can paint on the layer and the image's details will still show through. Click OK to create the layer.

3. **Paint on the new layer.**

   Press B to activate the Brush tool (page 396), set the Tools panel's foreground color square to whatever color you want to add to the image, and then paint on your image. If the color goes on too heavy, undo what you did, reduce the brush's opacity using the slider in the Tool Options area, and then redo your painting.

4. **Repeat steps 2 and 3 for each additional color you want to add.**

   As Figure 10-6 explains, it's a good idea to add a new layer for each color. So when you're done with one color, change your foreground color, add a new layer in Color blend mode, and then paint away. This makes it easier to go back later and fix just one thing without risking the rest of your hard work.

You can also paint directly on the original layer (if you do, try switching the Brush tool's blend mode to Color). But if you do that, you'll find it far more difficult to fix things if you make a mistake. Working on the original layer also doesn't give you much of an out if you decide later that, say, the lip color you painted on doesn't look so great with the skin color you chose.

Hints for Coloring Old Photographs

If you want to add some color to an antique black-and-white image, it's easier to create a separate layer for each part of a face you're going to color—lips, eyes, cheeks, skin—than to try to control different shades on one layer. That way, you can easily change just one color later on. Then, when you're done working on the photo, you can merge the layers by choosing Layer→Merge Visible or Layer→Merge Down (see page 298).

Here are some other tips for when you're aiming for that 19th-century look:

- To create a photo that looks like it was hand-colored a century ago, paint at less than 100 percent opacity—the tinting on old photos is very transparent.

- If you select an area before painting, you don't have to worry about getting color where you don't want it, because the paint is confined to your selection.

- Skin colors are really hard to create in the Color Picker. Instead, try sampling skin tones from another photo. If it's a family photo, the odds are good that the current generation's skin tones are reasonably close to Great-Granddad's. (If you're comfortable using Elements' more advanced features, a gradient map [page 475] can be an excellent way to create realistic skin shading, although it usually takes lots of gradient editing to get things just right. The face in Figure 10-6 was colored using a low-opacity gradient map based on the Copper gradient that comes with Elements.)

The steps just described are handy when you want to use many different colors on a photo, but if you want to add only a *single* color to part of the photo, the easiest way is to use the Smart Brush:

1. **Be sure the photo is in RGB mode.**

   Go to Image→Mode→RGB Color. If the image isn't in RGB mode, the Smart Brush will paint only in shades of gray rather than in the color you select.

2. **Activate the Smart Brush, and then choose a color to paint with.**

   Press F or click the Smart Brush's icon in the Tools panel. Then head to the Tool Options area and click the thumbnail to the right of the Smart Brush icon. On the panel that appears, choose Color from the drop-down menu, and then click one of the thumbnails to select the color you want.

3. **In your image, drag over what you want to color.**

   The Smart Brush automatically creates a selection and colors it.

> **TIP** If you don't get a good selection with the regular Smart Brush, try the Detail Smart Brush instead.

4. **Tweak the effect.**

The brush tends to apply color pretty heavily, so you may want to go to the Layers panel and reduce the Smart Brush layer's opacity (see page 196 for more about layer opacity).

The Smart Brush works well if you happen to like one of its available color choices. But if you don't, use the new-layer method described earlier in this section, which lets you choose any color you want.

Tinting a Whole Photo

You can give an entire photo an overall tint, even if the original is a grayscale photo. Tinting is a great way to create a variety of different moods.

Elements gives you three basic ways to tint photos. (There are a lot more than that, but these should get you started.) The first two methods described in this section (layer style and frames from the Graphics panel) are faster, but the last (Colorize) lets you tweak the settings more. Figure 10-7 shows the results of using the layer-style method on a color photo.

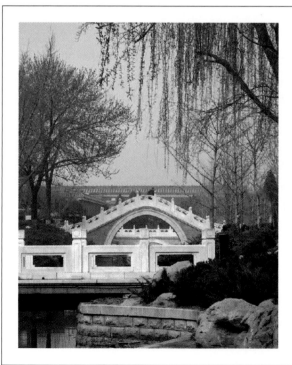

FIGURE 10-7

The easiest way to create a monochrome color scheme is to use the Photographic Effects layer styles, which are explained in Chapter 13.

This image had the Red Tone style applied to the original color photo. Elements removed the existing color and recolored the image in one click.

The downside to this method is that you can't edit the color once you're done if you later decide you'd rather have, say, blue.

TIP For a more subtle effect, you can use Photo Filters, described on page 299. The Effects section of the Effects panel (page 457) also has some terrific monotone tint effects.

For either method, if you want to keep the original color (or lack thereof) in part of the photo, then before you tint the image, use the Selection Brush in Mask mode to mask out the area you don't want to change.

> **NOTE** Some of the Graphics panel's frame effects (page 526) automatically add tints to photos when you apply them.

■ USING A LAYER STYLE

Although many people never dig down far enough to find them, Elements includes Photographic Effects layer styles that make tinting a photo as easy as double-clicking. You'll learn more about layer styles on page 461, but this section tells you all you need to know to use the Photographic styles. It's a simple process:

1. **Create a duplicate layer.**

   Go to Layer→Duplicate Layer or press Ctrl+J/⌘-J. (If you don't create a duplicate layer and your original has only a Background layer, Elements will ask if you want to convert it to a layer when you apply the style in step 3; when it does, click OK.)

2. **If necessary, change the image's mode to RGB.**

   Go to Image→Mode→RGB Color. It doesn't matter whether the original image is in color; the layer style will get rid of the original color and tint the photo all at the same time.

3. **Choose a layer style.**

   Go to the Effects panel (choose Window→Effects to open it) and, at the top of the panel, click the Styles tab. Then, from the panel's drop-down menu, choose Photographic Effects. Double-click the color square you like or drag it onto the photo.

   You can click around and try different colors to see which you prefer. Undo (Ctrl+Z/⌘-Z) after each style you try, since sometimes an existing layer style can change the way a new one affects your photo.

4. **When you like what you see, you're done.**

The drawback to this method is that you can't easily go back and edit the layer style's color. Even if you call up the Style Settings dialog box (page 462), you don't get any active checkboxes, because these styles don't use those settings. Instead, you need to use a Hue/Saturation adjustment (see page 335) to go back later and change the layer style's tint color.

■ THE GRAPHICS PANEL'S TINT EFFECTS

The Graphics panel includes some frames that automatically apply tints to photos, as shown in Figure 10-8. (To display this panel, go to Window→Graphics.) These range from simple all-over colors like sepia to fading gradients. (See page 465 for more about gradients.)

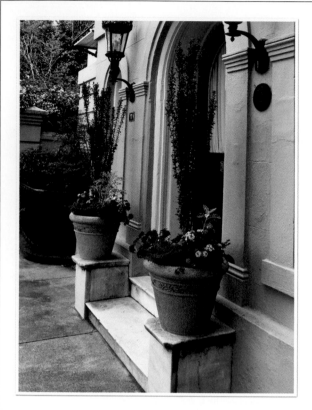

FIGURE 10-8

Using the Graphics panel, you can apply elaborate effects—like this fading gradient, drop shadow, and frame—just by dropping your photo into a frame.

The effect used here is the Color Tint Blue Fadeout 20px.

You can read more about the Graphics panel's frames on page 514. To tint a photo, choose By Type from the panel's left drop-down menu and Frames from its right one, and then scroll down the list of thumbnails. If there's a color other than gray inside a frame (like blue, red, or sepia), that means Elements will tint your photo when you apply that frame to it. To apply a frame, simply double-click its thumbnail or drag the thumbnail onto your photo.

TIP The Effects panel's Photo Effects section also has some very effective color tints. Page 456 explains how to apply effects.

■ USING COLORIZE

To add a color tint to a grayscale photo or to change the color of a photo that already has color in it, you can use the Colorize checkbox in either the Hue/Saturation dialog box or the Adjustments panel. With this method, you can choose any color you like, as opposed to the limited choices of the layer styles and frames explained in the previous sections. And once you've selected a color, you can adjust its intensity with the Saturation slider. Figure 10-9 explains how the Colorize setting changes the way the Hue/Saturation command works.

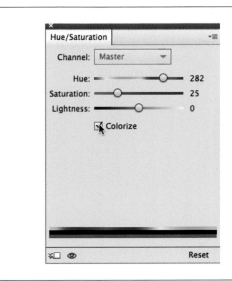

FIGURE 10-9

To color something that doesn't have any color info in it, like a white shirt or a grayscale image, in the Adjustments panel, turn on the Colorize checkbox. (If you don't use an Adjustment layer, you get the same checkbox in the Hue/Saturation dialog box.)

If you don't turn on this checkbox, you can adjust the hue, saturation, and lightness of white all day long, but all it'll do is go from white to gray to black because there's no color info there for Elements to work with.

Also, if something is pure white (meaning it contains no color data at all), you may need to darken it by moving the Lightness slider to the left before any color shows up.

Here's how to work with the Colorize checkbox:

1. **Make sure your photo is in RGB mode.**

   Go to Image→Mode→RGB Color.

2. **Add a new layer for colorizing the photo.**

   You don't *have* to perform this step, but it gives you more flexibility for making changes later. Go to Layer→New Adjustment Layer→Hue/Saturation, and then click OK.

   If you prefer not to use an Adjustment layer, just go to Enhance→Adjust Color→Adjust Hue/Saturation. Then, in the Adjustments panel or the Hue/Saturation dialog box, turn on the Colorize checkbox. If you don't like the color Elements chose, that's OK—you're going to change it in the next step.

3. **Adjust the color until it looks the way you want it to.**

   In either the Adjustments panel or the Hue/Saturation dialog box, move the Hue, Saturation, and Lightness sliders until you get the look you want. Figure 10-10 shows the results. (If you selected and masked an area before starting this process, that part should still show the original color.)

TIP Want to turn a full-color photo to a monotone image in a hurry? Just turn on the Colorize checkbox—you don't need to remove the photo's color first—and Elements reduces the image to just one color. The advantage to using this method rather than a layer style is that you can use the sliders to select any color you want.

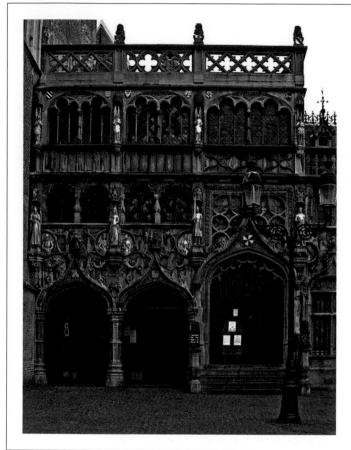

FIGURE 10-10

This photo was tinted purple by turning on the Colorize checkbox in the Hue/Saturation dialog box. (The Colorize checkbox in the Adjustments panel works exactly the same way.)

The gold ornaments were masked out so they stayed in full color.

If you used an Adjustment layer and you change your mind about the colorizing, head to the Layers panel and double-click the Hue/Saturation layer's left icon (the sliders). Doing so brings up the controls for the Hue/Saturation adjustment again so you can change the settings. You can also edit the layer mask, as described on page 213, if you want to change the area that's affected by the Adjustment layer. When everything looks good, you can merge all the image's layers (or press Shift+Alt+Ctrl+E/ Shift-Option-⌘-E to produce a new merged layer above the existing layers). You can then use Levels and Elements' other color-editing tools to tweak the tint effect.

If you *didn't* use an Adjustment layer, you don't have these editing options. If you don't like the colorizing, your only option is to undo it by pressing Ctrl+Z/⌘-Z, which you can do as long as the image is still open on your screen; once you close the image, the change is permanent.

Photomerge: Creating Panoramas, Group Shots, and More

Everyone's had the frustrating experience of trying to photograph an awesome view—like a city skyline or a mountain range—only to find that it's too wide to fit into one picture. Elements comes to the rescue once again: the Photomerge command lets you stitch together a group of photos you shot while panning across the horizon to create a panorama that's much larger than any single photo your camera can take. Panoramas can become addictive once you've tried them, and they're a great way to get those wide, wide shots that are beyond the capability of your camera lens.

Elements includes the same great Photomerge feature that's part of Photoshop, which makes it incredibly easy to create super panoramas. Not only that, but Adobe also gives you a few fun twists on Photomerge that are unique to Elements: Faces, which lets you easily move features from one face to another; Group Shot, which lets you replace folks in group photos; and Scene Cleaner, for those times when your almost-perfect vacation shot is spoiled by strangers walking into the frame. There's also a new merge in Elements 13: Photomerge Compose, which steps you through moving an object from one image to another, and then adjusts the lighting between the two images to make a more realistic blend.

> **NOTE** Elements includes one more kind of merge: Photomerge Exposure, which lets you blend differently exposed versions of the same scene (like photos taken using your camera's exposure bracketing feature) to create one image that's perfectly exposed from its deepest shadows to its brightest highlights. You can learn all about it on page 292.

Finally, if you're into photographing buildings (especially tall ones), you know that structures in your photographs can appear to lean backward or sideways as a result of distortion caused by your camera's lens. This chapter shows you how to use the Correct Camera Distortion filter to straighten things back up. You'll also learn how to use the Transform commands to adjust or warp images.

Creating Panoramas

It's incredibly simple to make panoramas in Elements. You just tell the program which photos to use, and Elements automatically stitches them together. Figure 11-1 shows what a great job it does. (If you'd like to try creating this panorama yourself, you'll find *mountainA.jpg*, *mountainB.jpg*, *mountainC.jpg*, and *mountainD.jpg* on this book's Missing CD page at *www.missingmanuals.com/cds*.)

FIGURE 11-1

Here's a four-photo panorama made with Photomerge. The photos had big variations in exposure and were taken without a tripod, but Elements still managed to take them straight from the camera with no adjusting and blend them seamlessly.

Elements can merge as many photos as you want to include in a panorama. The real size limitation comes when you want to *print* your compositions. If you create a five-photo horizontal panorama but your paper is letter size, for example, your printout will only be a couple of inches high, even if you rotate the panorama to print lengthwise. However, if you're a panorama addict, you can buy a special printer with attachments that let you print on rolls of paper, so that there's no limit to the image's longest dimension. You can also use an online printing service, like Shutterfly, to get larger prints than you can make at home. (See page 530 for more about ordering prints online.)

You'll get the best panoramas if you plan ahead when shooting photos. The pictures should be side by side, of course, and they should overlap one another by at least 30 percent. Also, you'll minimize the biggest panorama problem—matching the color between photos—if you make sure they all have identical exposures. While Elements can do a lot to blend exposures that don't match well, for the best results, adjust your photos *before* you start creating a panorama (see Chapter 7). It helps to keep them side by side so you can compare them as you work. (See page 97 to learn how to arrange photos in Elements.) The box on page 372 has more tips for taking merge-ready shots. However, Elements has gotten pretty good at blending photos together even if they have somewhat different exposures, as Figure 11-2 shows.

FIGURE 11-2

*Top: Here's what you get
with all the checkboxes
in the Photomerge dialog
box turned off. Not bad,
but clearly stitched
together.*

*Bottom: With the Blend
Images Together setting
turned on, Elements does
a fine job of smoothing the
transitions between the
photos. This image also
shows what happens to
your image's perspective
if you turn on Geometric
Distortion Correction (page
371).*

When the photos you want to combine look good, you're ready to create a panorama. Just follow these steps:

1. **Go to Enhance→Photomerge→Photomerge Panorama.**

    The Photomerge dialog box opens.

2. **Tell Elements which photos to merge.**

    If the images you want to include are already open, simply click the Add Open Files button. Otherwise, from the Use drop-down menu, choose Files or Folder, and then click the Browse button to navigate to the photos you want. After you select them in the window that appears and click OK, Elements adds them to the list in the Photomerge dialog box. Add more files by clicking Browse again. To remove a file, click it in the dialog box's list, and then click Remove.

    TIP You can select raw files in the Photomerge dialog box, although you don't get any controls for adjusting how the raw files are converted (but you may get a pretty good merge anyway). Photomerge works only with 8-bit files (page 288), so you need to set the Raw Converter to 8 bits before you start.

3. **From the Layout list on the left side of the Photomerge dialog box, choose a merge style.**

    Ninety-nine percent of the time, you'll want to choose Auto, which works great in most cases; Elements takes care of everything and usually produces a nice panorama. The other styles are for special situations:

- **Perspective.** When you select this option, Elements adjusts the rest of the images to match the middle one (Elements automatically figures out which image this is; you don't need to do anything to indicate it) by using skewing and other Transform commands to create a realistic view.

- **Cylindrical.** Sometimes when you adjust perspective, you create a panorama shaped like a giant bow tie (as in Figure 11-2, top). Cylindrical *mapping* (the method Elements uses to plan out the panorama) corrects this distortion. (It's called "cylindrical" because it's like looking at the label on a bottle: the middle part seems the largest, and the image gets smaller as it fades into the distance, like a label wrapping around the sides of a bottle.) You may want to use this style for really wide panoramas.

> **NOTE** If you choose Auto, Elements may use either Perspective or Cylindrical mapping when it creates your panorama, depending on what it thinks will work best for your photos.

- **Spherical.** This option aligns and transforms your images as if you were standing inside a globe and pasting them on the wall. This is a good choice if your source images cover more than 180 degrees along the horizon. It's similar to Cylindrical but also corrects distortion on the vertical axis, not just side to side.

- **Collage.** If you choose this option, Elements rotates your photos, if needed, to align them perfectly, but it doesn't make any perspective changes to them. If you want to combine your photos exactly as they are, this is your best bet. Elements usually crops the completed panorama, though.

- **Reposition.** Elements overlaps your photos and blends their exposures, but it doesn't make any changes to their perspectives.

> **NOTE** If you've used Elements before and you're looking for the old Interactive Layout merge style that let you manually adjust your images, that's gone now.

4. **Tell Elements how to combine the images.**

   At the bottom of the Photomerge dialog box are three checkboxes that can make a big difference in the final panorama:

   - **Blend Images Together.** This option tells Elements to smooth the transitions between your photos and blend the colors in the images. Leave this setting on unless you have a good reason to turn it off.

   - **Vignette Removal.** If you're merging photos that have some *vignetting* (shadowy corners caused by things like your camera's lens hood or the lens itself), turn on this setting and Elements will fix that while it merges the photos.

- **Geometric Distortion Correction.** The top image in Figure 11-2 is shaped like a big bow tie, a common outcome when stitching lots of images together. Turn this setting on and Elements squares things up a bit, as you can see in the bottom image in Figure 11-2. However, you may not like the result; it's totally up to you whether to turn this checkbox on.

> **NOTE** You can't turn on Vignette Removal or Geometric Distortion Correction if you choose the Collage or Reposition merge style.

5. **Click OK to create your panorama.**

   Elements whirls into action, combining, adjusting, and looking for the most invisible places to put the seams. Once it's done, it displays your completed panorama.

> **NOTE** Elements makes a lot of complex calculations when creating a panorama, especially if you're combining lots of images or if there are big exposure differences between the photos, so this step may take awhile. Don't assume that Elements is stuck; it may just need a few minutes to finish working.

6. **Tell Elements whether to fill in any empty edges in the panorama.**

   When Elements finishes combining the images, you see a dialog box asking if you'd like the program to automatically fill in the edges of the panorama to make it rectangular. Elements uses Content-Aware Fill (page 321) to do this, and sometimes you can get pretty amazing results.

   However, this requires Elements to do a lot of serious thinking, and if there's a lot of empty space in the panorama, you can expect your computer to slow to a crawl while Elements works. If the panorama is large, Elements may take *minutes* to ponder it—and then announce that your computer doesn't have enough memory (although this shouldn't happen in Elements 13 unless your computer is seriously deficient in RAM). If it does happen, there are a couple of things to try. First, go to Edit→Preferences→Performance/Photoshop Elements Editor→Preferences→Performance and increase the amount of RAM available for Elements to use. Second, click Cancel and try starting your Photomerge over, this time with Geometric Distortion Correction turned on or using the Collage merge style so there's less empty space to fill.

> **NOTE** If you have Elements fill in the edges, it creates a merged layer of all the photos in your panorama and works on that, so your file size will be much larger.

You'll probably want to crop the panorama, but otherwise, you're all done (except for saving the completed file). You can do anything to the panorama that you can do to any other photo. The Recompose tool (page 326) is especially useful for adjusting proportions in panoramas, if you need to do that.

TIP   Elements creates layered panoramas, and if you look at the Layers panel you can see layer masks that show how much of each photo it used. Since you know how to edit layer masks (page 210), you can manually make changes, if you want.

IN THE FIELD

Shooting Tips for Good Merges

The most important part of creating a great panorama starts before you even launch Elements. You can save yourself a lot of grief by planning ahead when shooting photos.

Most of the time, you know *before* you shoot that you'll want to merge the photos. You don't often say, "Wow, I have seven photos of the Captain Jack Sparrow balloon at the Thanksgiving Day parade that just happen to be exactly in line and have a 30 percent overlap between each one. Guess I'll try a merge!"

Before you take pictures for a panorama, set your camera to be as much in manual mode as possible. The biggest headache in panorama making is trying to get the exposure, color, brightness, and so on to blend seamlessly (but Elements is darned good at blending the outlines of the physical objects in photos). So lock your camera's settings so that the exposure of each image is as identical as possible. Even small digital cameras that don't have much in the way of manual controls may have some kind of panorama setting—like Canon's Stitch Assist mode—that does the same thing.

(Your camera may actually be able to make merges that are at least as good as what Elements can do, because the camera does the image-blending internally. Check whether your model has a panorama feature.)

The more your photos overlap, the better. Elements does what it can with what you give it, but it's really happy if about a third of each image overlaps with the next.

Use a tripod if you have one, and *pan heads* (tripod heads that let you swivel the camera in an absolutely straight line). As long as your shots aren't wildly out of line, Elements can usually cope. But if you don't use a tripod, you may have to do quite a bit of cropping to get even edges on the finished result.

Regardless of whether you use a tripod, keep the camera—rather than the horizon—level to avoid distortion. In other words, focus your attention more on leveling the body of the camera than on what you see through the viewfinder. Use the same focal length for each image, and try not to use the zoom, unless it's manual, so you can keep it exactly the same for every image.

TIP   Before you send your panorama out for printing, flatten it (Layer→Flatten Image), since most commercial printers don't accept layered files. Also, if you zoom way in on your layered panorama and look at the seams, you may occasionally see what look like hairline cracks. Merging or flattening the layers gets rid of these cracks.

■ Merging Different Faces

Merging isn't just for making panoramas. One of the Elements-only tools that Adobe includes is Faces, a fun (OK, let's be honest—silly) feature that lets you merge parts of one person's face with another person's face. You can use it to create caricature-like photos, or to paste your new sweetie's face over your old sweetie's face in last year's holiday photo. Figure 11-3 shows an example of what Faces can do.

FIGURE 11-3

Faces is really just for fun.

You can create composite images like this one, and then use Elements' other tools to make the photo even sillier, if you like.

Although you'd be hard put to think of a serious use for Faces (it *may* work for something like copying a smile from one photo to another image of the same person with a more serious expression, but the result may not be top quality), it's fun to play with and simple to use:

1. **Choose the photos you want to combine.**

   You need to have at least two photos open in the Photo Bin before you start. You can Ctrl-click/⌘-click to preselect the photos you want to use.

2. **Call up the Faces window.**

   Go to Enhance→Photomerge→Photomerge Faces (you need to be in Expert mode or this command is grayed out).

   If you didn't preselect images, a dialog box asks you to choose the photos you want to include. You can either click Cancel—and then, in the Photo Bin, Ctrl-click/⌘-click the photos you want to use and then choose the Photomerge Faces command again—or click Open All to include all the images in the Photo Bin. Elements then opens the Faces window, which has a preview area on the left and an instruction pane on the right.

3. **Pick a final photo.**

   This is the photo into which you'll paste parts of a face from one or more other photos. Drag a photo from the Photo Bin into the Final area (the right-hand preview).

4. **If you don't like the source photo Elements selected, choose another one.**

This is the photo from which you'll copy part of a face to move to the final image. Click an image in the Photo Bin, and it appears in the left-hand preview area. You can copy from many different photos, but you can work with only one source photo at a time. (When you're done working with a source photo, just click the next one you want. That way, you can use the ears from one photo, the nose from another, and so on.)

5. **Tell Elements how to align your photos.**

This step is really important, because otherwise Elements can't adjust for any size or angle differences between the two shots. In the Photomerge Faces pane, click the Alignment Tool button, and the three crosshairs shown in Figure 11-4 appear in each image (Adobe calls them targets). You may need to move your cursor over a photo to see them.

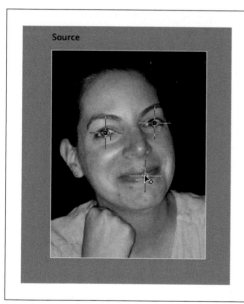

Source

FIGURE 11-4

To tell Elements how to align your photos, drag one of these three crosshairs over each eye and the mouth in each photo. (You need to move your mouse over the photo to make the crosshairs appear.)

If you look closely at the crosshairs, you'll see that each one is numbered. Be sure to get the ones with the same numbers over the same features in both photos. For instance, don't put Target 1 over the left eye in one photo and the right eye in the other; put it over the left eye in both images.

Position the crosshairs over the eyes and mouth in each photo. (If you need help seeing what you're doing, there's a little toolbox on the left with your old friends the Zoom and Hand tools, so you can reposition the photo for the best view.) Then click the Align Photos button, and Elements adjusts the images so they're the same size and sit at the same angle.

6. **Tell Elements what features to move from the source image to the final image.**

In the Photomerge Faces pan, click the Pencil tool and then, in the source photo, draw over the area you want to move. In a few seconds, you should see the selected area appear in the final photo. You only need to draw a quick line—

don't try to color over all the material you want to move. In the Photomerge Faces pane, you can adjust the size of the Pencil tool's cursor if it's hard to see what you're doing, or if the tool is grabbing too much of the surrounding area.

If Elements moves too much stuff from the source photo, in the Photomerge Faces pane, click the Eraser tool, and then remove part of your line. Watch the preview in the final image to see how you're changing the selection. To start over, click the Reset icon (the arching blue arrow over a line) at the top of the pane.

7. **When you're happy, click Done.**

   Elements creates your merge as a layered file. You can edit it using any tool to do things like clean up the edges or manually clone (page 318) a little more material than Elements moved. And you can make your image even sillier using the Transform commands (page 383), the Liquify filter (page 493), and so on.

The Photomerge Faces pane includes two settings you can adjust:

- **Show Strokes**. If you want to see what you're selecting with the Pencil tool, leave this checkbox on.

- **Show Regions**. Turn this on to see a translucent overlay on the final image, which makes it easier to tell which parts you're copying over from your source photo. This is just like the regions options for Exposure Merge (page 297).

It would be nice if you could use this feature to merge things besides faces, but it doesn't do a very good job of that. Even for faces, if you're doing something important, like repairing an old photo with parts from another picture of the same person, you may prefer to create your own selections and then manually move and adjust things (see page 219). But the Faces feature's alignment tools can simplify the process enough that it's worth giving it a try to see if it can do what you want.

Arranging a Group Shot

Have you ever tried taking photos of a bunch of people? Almost every time, you get a photo where everything is perfect—except for that one guy with his eyes shut. In another shot, that guy is fine, but other people are yawning or looking away from the camera. You probably thought, "Dang, I wish I could move Ed from that photo to this one. Then I'd have a perfect shot." Adobe heard you, and Group Shot is the result. It's designed for moving one person in a group from one photo to another, similar photo.

You launch Group Shot by going to Enhance→Photomerge→Photomerge Group Shot in either Quick Fix or Expert mode. The steps for using Group Shot are the same as for Faces, except that you don't normally need to align the photos, since Group Shot is intended for situations where you were saying, "Just one more, everybody!" as opposed to moving people from photos taken at different times with different angles and lighting.

If you *do* need to align your photos, you can do that by clicking the Advanced Options button in the Photomerge Group Shot pane. Then just place the markers the same way you do in Faces (see Figure 11-4), and then click Align Photos. Another advanced option is Pixel Blending, which adjusts the moved material to make it closer in tone to the rest of the final image.

> **NOTE**   It would be great if you could use Group Shot for things like creating a photo showing several generations of your family by combining parts of photos taken over many years. But Group Shot moves someone from the source photo and pastes that person into the *same spot* in the final photo, and then creates a composite layer in the completed merge. That means Elements merges the relocated person into the Background image rather than leaving him as an extracted object, so you can't put that person in a different spot. So you need to tackle your generational-photo project the old-fashioned way: by moving each person onto a separate layer and then repositioning everybody where you want them.

Tidying Up with Scene Cleaner

You've probably had this experience when showing your vacation photos: "Here's a shot of Jodi and Taylor at the rim of the Grand Canyon. Those other people? No idea who they are; they just walked into the shot." Scene Cleaner was made to fix photos like that. It lets you eliminate unwanted people or elements in images to create photos like the ones you see in travel magazines that show famous sights in their lonely glory, without any tourists cluttering up the scene.

> **TIP**   Scene Cleaner is great if you have two photos you can use, but if not, try selecting the unwanted person(s) or objects and then using Content-Aware Fill (page 321).

Scene Cleaner is easy to use, but you'll get better results if you can plan ahead when taking your photos. In order to get a people-less landscape (or one with only people you know), you need to shoot multiple photos from nearly the same angle, and all the areas you want to feature should be uninhabited in at least one photo. So, for instance, if you can get one shot of the Statue of Liberty where all the tourists are on the left side of her crown and one where they're on the right side, you're all set. Then you can use Scene Cleaner to create a more perfect world:

1. **Open the photos you want to combine.**

   You can work with from two to ten images in Scene Cleaner, but only two at a time. If you have more photos open than you want to use, just select the ones you want in the Photo Bin. If you want to use *all* your open images, you can wait for the window that prompts you to select some photos, and then click Open All.

   In addition to being taken from nearly the same vantage point, the images should have similar exposures. For instance, if a cloud was passing overhead so that one photo is bright and one is shadowy, you'll have to do some fancy touch-ups afterward to blend the tones. In fact, it's usually easier to fix this kind of problem beforehand. See Chapter 7 for the full story on correcting exposures.

2. **Go to Enhance→Photomerge→Photomerge Scene Cleaner.**

   Elements automatically aligns the first two photos you chose in step 1, so there may be a slight delay before you see the Scene Cleaner window.

3. **Choose a final image.**

   This is the base image into which you'll put parts of the other photo(s). Most of the time, you'll want to choose the overall best image you have of your subject—the one you're happiest with except for the intruders. Drag the photo you want from the Photo Bin into the Final preview area (the right-hand slot).

4. **If you don't like the source image Elements picked, choose a different one.**

   Look through your photos to find one that's "clean" (meaning people- or object-free) in the area where the people or objects you want to remove from the final photo are. For example, if your final image is a photo of the Statue of Liberty with tourists on the left side of her crown, you'd want the source photo to show the Statue of Liberty with *no* tourists on the left side of her crown. Click that photo in the Photo Bin, and it appears in the Source preview area (the left-hand slot).

   NOTE As with Faces, you can use many source images, but you work with only one at a time; just click the next source photo in the Photo Bin when you're ready for it.

   ---

5. **If necessary, align the photos manually.**

   Usually you don't need to do this, but if Elements didn't do a good job of automatically aligning the photos, then in the Photomerge Scene Cleaner pane, click the Advanced Options button and you'll see the three markers described in the section on Faces (page 372). This time, instead of the eyes and mouth, place them over three similar locations in each photo. Each target has a tiny number next to it, so try to get the crosshairs with the same numbers in the same place in each photo. (In other words, you don't want target 2 at the bottom of one photo and the top of the other.) Then click the Align Photos button.

6. **Tell Elements what you want to move.**

   If the Pencil tool isn't active, click it in the Photomerge Scene Cleaner pane. Then, in the source image, draw over the area you want to move to the final photo. Just draw a quick line—Elements figures out exactly what to move. (Alternatively, you can go to the Final preview area and draw over the area you want to *cover*—Elements can figure it out either way.)

7. **If needed, adjust the areas.**

   Use the Pencil tool again to add more areas, or the Eraser tool to remove bits if Elements moved too much. You can use the Eraser in either preview area, Source or Final. If you have more than two photos to work with, in the Photo Bin, click another photo to display it in the Source slot, and then select the area(s) you want. If you need to see the edges of the areas that Elements is moving, turn on the Show Regions checkbox, explained in Figure 11-5. If the exposures don't blend well, click the Advanced Options button and turn on Pixel Blending for a smoother merge.

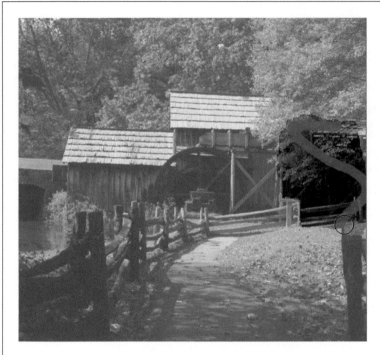

FIGURE 11-5

When you turn on Show Regions, Elements covers your photo with this mask. Here the yellow shows the original area from the final photo, and the lighter blue shows the section (without the passerby) brought over from the source photo. The brighter blue is the actual stroke. (You can turn off Show Strokes if this bothers you, but normally you see the stroke line only when your cursor is over the photo.) If you look closely, it would be a good idea to use the Eraser tool to remove a little of the grass that's interfering with the top of the fence post on the right.

This mask is helpful if you have a hard time getting exactly the amount of source material you want, because the overlay gives you a better idea of where to erase or add material.

8. **When you're happy, click Done.**

   Don't forget to save your work. If you want to start over, click Reset (the blue arrow-and-line icon at the top of the panel). If you decide to give up on the merge, click Cancel.

Most of the time, you need to use only Scene Cleaner's Pencil and Eraser tools, but Adobe gives you some additional options to help you out when necessary:

- **Show Strokes**. Leave this checkbox turned on or you can't see where you're drawing with the tools.

- **Show Regions**. If you turn this checkbox on, you see a blue-and-yellow overlay showing the exact material you're moving (see Figure 11-5).

To see the following two choices, click the Advanced Options button:

- **Alignment Tool**. Click this button to manually set the comparison points if you don't like Elements' automatic choices. Step 5 above explains how to do so.

- **Pixel Blending**. Just as with Faces, you can turn on this setting when there's a discrepancy in the color or exposure of the photos so that they combine more seamlessly.

It's not always easy to get enough clear areas to blend, even with multiple photos. But if you have the right kind of source photos, you can create the impression that you and your pals had a private tour of your favorite places.

Combining Photos with Photomerge Compose

If you understand layers, it's pretty easy to move a person or object from one photo to another. But if you're a beginner and would like a little more help doing this, Elements 13 includes the new Photomerge Compose command, which is designed to help you with projects like moving Great-Grandpa from his wedding photo into a multigenerational photo taken years after his death. Figure 11-6 shows what it can do.

Elements walks you through each step of the process, including fixing the lighting for you if there's a big discrepancy between the photos:

1. **Open the photos you want to work with, select two of them in the Editor's Photo Bin, and then go to Enhance→Photomerge→Photomerge Compose.**

   If you don't select any photos first, you'll see a dialog box where you can click Open All to open the first two photos in the bin. (You can work with only two photos at a time when using Photomerge Compose.)

   Elements makes copies of your photos as it goes, so this process won't alter your original images.

2. **In the Photomerge Compose window, drag the image containing the object you want to move into the preview area.**

   Elements will open a copy of the other image, the one where you're going to place the object, when the time comes. You don't have to do anything about that photo.

3. **Select the object you want to move.**

   The pane on the right side of the window offers you two familiar selection tools: Quick Select and Selection Edit (both explained in Chapter 5), and one that's unique to this window: Outline Select, which works something like the Lasso tool. You draw a line around what you want to select and, when you come back to the beginning and connect up to where you started, Elements selects everything inside the line you drew. Elements puts a red mask over the unselected part of the image so you can see your selection better (just like using the Selection Brush in mask mode).

There's a zoom slider at the upper right of the preview area to help you focus in on what you're doing.

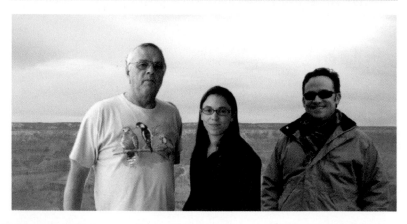

FIGURE 11-6

If some people couldn't get to the Grand Canyon with you on your trip, that's no reason they can't join you in your vacation photo via Photomerge Compose.

Top: These two couldn't make it to the Grand Canyon...

Middle: ...so this guy went by himself.

Bottom: With a little Elements magic, you can create a group shot of everyone together at the Grand Canyon.

4. **Refine the edges of your selection, and then click Next.**

The Photomerge Compose pane gives you the usual Add and Subtract controls and a brush-size slider to help you get a good selection. Once you have the object selected to your satisfaction, you can click the Advance Edge Refinement button to make sure you have a perfect selection. Once you click this button, you see the Set Background As menu, which lets you see the area you selected either as part of the original image (Source Image); against a transparent, black, or white background; or with the red mask over the unselected area (Overlay). Click the Refine Edge button to bring up the regular Refine Edge window, explained on page 156.

TIP Adding some smoothing in the Refine Edge dialog box can go a long way toward creating a more plausible combined image. A few of its settings aren't available in Photomerge Compose.

Once your selection is just as you want it, click Next, and Elements extracts the object and places it into the background photo.

5. **Position the object in the background photo and resize it, if necessary.**

There's a button in the Photomerge Compose pane for the Move tool, but you don't need to click it, since the Move tool is active as soon as you start this step. Once you have the object positioned, if you notice that you skipped a spot or included too much in your selection, you can adjust how much of the object you see by clicking the Hide brush (need to conceal something you didn't mean to include) or the Reveal brush (missed a spot), and then painting over the area you need to fix.

NOTE When you're resizing the moved object, it may look horribly pixelated, but as soon as you click the green Commit checkmark, everything should smooth right out.

You can adjust the size, opacity, and hardness of either brush using the sliders in the pane, and you can zoom in or out using the slider above the right side of the preview area.

If you find you need to make bigger changes than you can easily make here, click the Back button to go back to the previous pane and start your selection again.

6. **Once everything is adjusted perfectly, click Next to see the combined image.**

The Photomerge Compose pane changes to display buttons and sliders to help you tweak the lighting of your combined photo. You may need to resize the pasted image quite a bit, and you can use the Move tool for that. Your selected object is added to the background photo as a Smart Object, which means you can resize it all you want without worrying about it pixelating, but you'll need to simplify the layer to perform many kinds of additional edits on it, like painting on it or running filters. There's more about Smart Objects on page 517.

7. **Make any necessary lighting adjustments.**

Click the Auto Match Color Tone button to make the moved object's lighting and color look like that of the background image. If you don't care for the result, you can manually tweak the luminance (brightness), contrast, temperature, and saturation by moving the sliders. If the result is really bad, you can click the Reset button and just use the sliders without using Auto Match Color Tone at all.

If you decide you're making things worse, click the pane's Reset button to return the image to where it was when you launched Photomerge Compose. If you just want to adjust the outline of your selected object, click the Back button instead.

TIP When you're finished, Elements presents you with a layered file with a layer mask on the layer that contains the moved object. Sometimes it's simpler to just edit this layer mask (page 213) than to try to fix the outline within Photomerge Compose.

---

8. **When you're finished, click Done.**

If you decide you'd rather forget the whole thing, click Cancel instead.

■ Correcting Lens Distortion

If you ever photograph buildings, you know that it can be tough getting good shots with a fixed-lens digital camera. When you get too close to the building, the lens causes distortion, as shown in Figure 11-7. You can buy special perspective-correcting lenses, but they're expensive (and if you have a pocket camera, they aren't even an option). Fortunately, you can use Elements' Correct Camera Distortion filter to fix photos after you take them. This is another popular Photoshop tool that Adobe transferred over to Elements, minus a couple of advanced options.

Correct Camera Distortion is a terrifically helpful filter, and not just for buildings. You can also use it to correct the slight balloon effect you sometimes see in closeups of people's faces (especially in shots taken with a wide-angle setting). You can even deploy the filter for creative purposes, like producing the effect of a fish-eye lens by pushing the filter's settings to their extremes.

Here are some telltale signs that it's time to summon Correct Camera Distortion:

- You've used the Straighten tool on your image but things still don't look right.

- The image's horizon is straight, but the photo has no true right angles. In other words, the objects in the photo lean in misleading ways. For instance, buildings lean in from the edges of the frame or lean away from you.

- Every time you straighten to a new reference line, something else gets out of whack. For example, say you keep choosing different lines in the photo that ought to be level, but no matter which one you choose, something else in the photo goes out of plumb.

FIGURE 11-7

Here's a classic candidate for Elements' Correct Camera Distortion filter. See how the buildings appear to lean back and to the right?

This type of distortion is common when you're using a point-and-shoot camera in a narrow space that doesn't let you get far enough away from your subject. Fortunately, this filter can fix such problems in a jiffy.

- Your image has a dark, shadowy effect in its corners (called *vignetting*). You can also use this filter to *create* vignetting for special effects.

Adobe has made this filter extremely easy to use:

1. **Open a photo, and then go to Filter→Correct Camera Distortion.**

   The dialog box shown in Figure 11-8 appears. You'll probably find it helpful to turn on the Show Grid checkbox below the preview area, which places a grid over the image to help you align things.

NOTE Even though Correct Camera Distortion is in the Filter menu, you *can't* reapply it using the Ctrl+F/⌘-F keyboard shortcut the way you can with most other filters—you always have to select it from the Filter menu.

---

2. **If necessary, use the Hand tool to adjust your photo in the dialog box.**

You want a clear view of a *reference line*—something you know you want to correct, like the edge of a building. If the distortion is really bad, finding a true reference line may be impossible, but try to find at least one line that's pretty closely aligned to the grid, so you can use it as a reference for changing the photo.

If your photo is too big or too small for a good view, you can also use the view controls (including + and – buttons) in the dialog box's lower-left corner. The Hand tool adjusts both your photo and the grid, so you can't use it to position your photo *relative* to the grid. However, the Hand tool doesn't do anything unless you can't see your whole image in the dialog box at once.

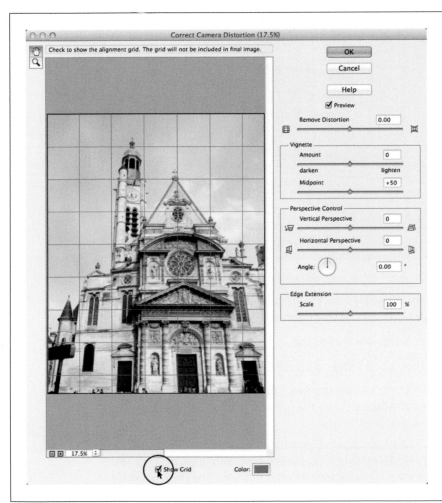

FIGURE 11-8

Use the sliders on the right side of the window to correct the different kinds of distortion in your photo.

It helps to display the grid shown here by turning on the Show Grid checkbox below the preview area (circled) so that you have straight lines for reference. To change the grid's color, click the Color box.

3. **Make your adjustments.**

   This filter lets you fix three different kinds of problems: barrel/pincushion distortion, vignetting, and perspective problems. These errors are the ones you're most likely to run into, and correcting them is as easy as dragging sliders around. You may need to make only one adjustment, or you may need many (the upcoming bulleted list helps you decide which controls to use).

   As you tweak these settings, watch the grid carefully to see how things are lining up. When everything is straightened to your satisfaction, you're done. To start over, Alt-click/Option-click the Cancel button (it changes to a Reset button) and return your photo to the state it was in when you summoned this filter.

4. **If you wish, scale the photo.**

   As you make adjustments, you'll probably notice some empty space appearing on either side of the canvas (the background area of your file). This often happens when Elements pinches and stretches a photo to correct distortion. To make things right, you have two options: Click OK and then crop the photo yourself using any of the methods you learned about starting on page 89, or use the Correct Camera Distortion dialog box's Edge Extension slider to enlarge the photo so it fills the image window. If you use the second method, Elements crops some of the photo, and you have little control over what it chops off. After all the effort you've put into using this filter, you may as well do your own cropping to get the best possible results, so you may not want to bother with the Edge Extension slider.

5. **Click OK to apply the changes.**

   If you don't like the way things turned out, then reset your photo by Alt-clicking/Option-clicking the Cancel button. If you just want a quick look at where you started (without undoing your work), toggle the Preview checkbox on and off.

The Correct Camera Distortion filter gives you a few different ways to adjust images. Your choices are divided into sections according to the kinds of distortion they fix:

- **Remove Distortion**. Use this slider to fix *barrel distortion* (objects in your photo ballooning out, like the sides of a barrel, as shown in Figure 11-9) and its opposite, *pincushion distortion* (your photo has a pinched look, with the edges of objects pushing in toward the center). Move the slider right to fix barrel distortion or left to fix pincushion distortion.

TIP   Barrel distortion is usually worst when you use wide-angle lens settings, while pincushion distortion generally happens when you use a telephoto lens that's fully extended. Barreling is more common than pincushioning, especially when you use a small point-and-shoot camera. You can often reduce barrel distortion in a small camera simply by avoiding your lens's widest setting. For instance, if you change the aperture setting from f2.8 to f5.6 (consult your owner's manual to learn how) or just zoom in a tad, you may see significantly less distortion.

- **Vignette**. If the photo has dark corners (usually caused by shadows from the camera's lens or a lens hood), you need to spend time with these sliders. Vignetting typically afflicts owners of digital single-lens reflex cameras, or people who use add-on lenses with fixed-lens cameras. Move the Amount slider right to lighten the corners or left to darken them. The Midpoint slider controls how much of the photo is affected by the Amount slider. Move it left to increase the area (to bring it toward the center of the photo), or right to keep the vignette correction near the corners. Consider turning off the Show Grid checkbox while you're working with these sliders so you have an unobstructed view of how you're changing the lightness values in the photo. (Turn it back on again if you have other adjustments to make afterward.)

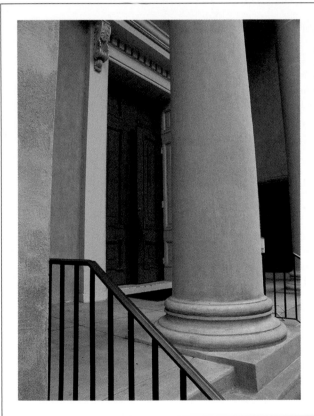

FIGURE 11-9

A classic case of barrel distortion. This photo has already been straightened with the Straighten tool, but things are still out of plumb; notice how the columns and walls lean in toward the top of the photo. You can even see a bit of a curve in the pillar on the far right.

Barrel distortion is the most common kind of lens distortion, and you can easily fix it with the Correct Camera Distortion filter.

> **TIP** Each of the adjustment sliders is accompanied by a box where you can type a number instead of moving the slider. If you want to make the same adjustments to several photos, take note of the numbers you used to fix the first photo, and then plug those numbers into the boxes for the other photos.

- **Perspective Control**. Use these sliders to correct objects like buildings that appear to be tilting or leaning forward or backward. It's easiest to understand these sliders by looking at the icons at their ends, which show the effect you'll get by moving the slider in that direction. The Vertical Perspective slider spreads the top of your photo wider if you move the slider left and makes the bottom wider if you move it right. (If buildings seem like they're leaning backward, move this slider left.) The Horizontal Perspective slider is for when your subject doesn't seem to be straight on in relation to the lens (for example, if it appears rotated a few degrees right or left). Move the slider left to bring the left side of the photo toward you, or right to bring the right side closer.

You can rotate the entire photo by moving the line in the Angle circle to the position you want, or by typing a number in the text box next to it. A small change here has a huge effect. Here's how it works: There are 360 degrees in a circle, and your photo's starting point is 0.00 degrees. To rotate the photo counterclockwise, start from 0.01 and then go up in small increments to increase the rotation. To go clockwise, start with 359.99 and then reduce that number.

- **Edge Extension**. As explained in step 4 above, when you're done fixing a photo with the Correct Camera Distortion filter, you're likely to end up with some blank areas along the edge of the canvas. Move the Scale slider right to enlarge your photo and get rid of those blank areas. (Moving the slider left shrinks your photo and enlarges the blank areas, but you'll rarely want to do that.)

One important thing to keep in mind: Unlike the Zoom tool, the Scale slider changes the *actual* photo, not just your view of it: After you use this slider and then click the Correct Camera Distortion dialog box's OK, Elements resizes and crops your photo. So if you want the objects in your photo to stay the same size, don't use this slider. Instead, just click OK, and then crop using any of the methods discussed in Chapter 3.

The most important thing to remember when using Correct Camera Distortion is that a little goes a long way. For most photos, the best method is to start small and work in tiny increments. These distortions can be subtle, and you often need to make only minor adjustments to correct them.

TIP The Correct Camera Distortion filter isn't just for corrections. For example, you can use it to make your sour-tempered boss look truly prune-y by pincushioning him. (Just make sure you do it at home, not on your work computer!) Or you can add vignettes to photos for special effects, and use the filter on shapes (simplify them first; see page 424), artwork, or anything else that strikes your fancy.

■ Transforming Images

You'll probably end up using the Correct Camera Distortion filter for most of your straightening and warp-correcting. But Elements also includes a set of Transform commands, demonstrated in Figure 11-10, that come in handy when you want to make a change to just *one* side of a photo, or make final tweaks to a correction you made with Correct Camera Distortion. You can also apply these commands just for fun to create wacky photos or text effects. The following pages explain all your options.

FIGURE 11-10

Left: While you could use Correct Camera Distortion to straighten a slanting building like this one, sometimes it's easier to make straightforward corrections like this by switching to the Transform commands and just giving the object a yank to pull it where you want it.

Right: It took only a dose of Skew and a bit of Distort to pull the building straight and make it tall again.

Skew, Distort, and Perspective

Elements gives you four Transform commands, including three specialized ones—Skew, Distort, and Perspective—to help straighten out objects in photos. They all move objects in different directions, but the way you use them is the same. When you choose a Transform command (you'll learn how in a sec), the same box-like handles appear around your photo that appear when the Move tool is active. Just drag a handle in the direction you want the photo to move. Figure 11-11 shows how to use these commands.

To see the list of Transform commands, go to Image→Transform. Here's what they do:

- **Free Transform** (keyboard shortcut: Ctrl+T/⌘-T) is the most powerful Transform command because it includes all the others—you'll learn about it in the next section. Although Free Transform is the most capable command, it can also be the trickiest to use. You may find it easier to use one of the other Transform commands so you don't have to worry about inadvertently moving a photo in an unwanted direction.

- **Skew** slants an image. If a building in your photo looks like it's leaning to one side, for example, you can use this command to straighten it back up.

> **NOTE** Transform commands work only on layers or active selections. So if you have only a Background layer, Elements automatically turns it into a regular layer when you use Transform commands.

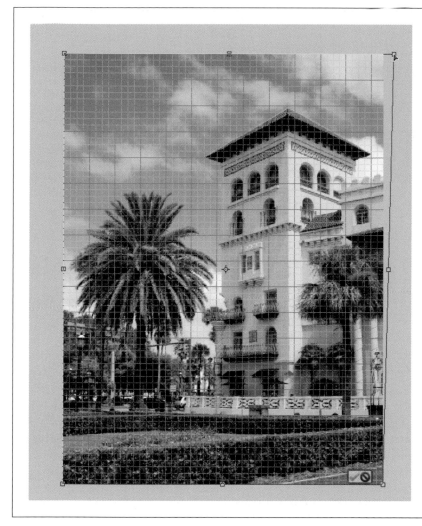

FIGURE 11-11

Here's an example of how you'd use the Skew command to pull a building upright.

To apply the Transform commands, make sure you can reach the handles on the image's corners. If you're using tabbed windows (page 97), you're all set because you already have plenty of space around the image. But if you're working with floating windows (page 97), just drag the window's lower-right corner to enlarge it beyond the size of the image to give yourself room to pull.

- **Distort** stretches a photo in the direction you pull it. Use it to make buildings (or people) taller and skinnier, or shorter and squatter.

- **Perspective** stretches a photo to make it look like parts are nearer or farther away. For example, if a building in a photo looks like it's leaning away from you, you can use this command to pull the top back toward you.

TIP If you have an active selection, then you can apply the Transform commands to just that selection.

All the Transform commands—including Free Transform—have the same Tool Options settings, shown in Figure 11-12.

FIGURE 11-12

The Tool Option for the Transform commands. The W and H boxes let you specify dimensions when you're resizing an image. To scale by dragging instead, click the Scale icon, and then drag any of the square scaling handles that appear on the bounding box around your image.

From left to right, here's what the Tool Options settings control:

- **Transform.** These three buttons let you choose the type of transformation you want to perform without making a trek up to the Image→Transform submenu:

  — **Rotate**. Grab a corner of the image to make a free rotation (see page 87), or use the Angle setting (explained below) instead.

> **TIP** If you Shift-drag while rotating an image, it turns in 15-degree increments.

  — **Scale**. Click here to resize the image by dragging it.

  — **Skew**. Click this icon, and then pull a corner of the image to the left or right.

- **Reference point**. This strange little doodad (shown in Figure 11-13) lets you tell Elements where you want the fixed point to be when you transform something; it's a miniature cousin of the Canvas Size dialog box's placement grid (page 113). The reference point starts out in the image's center, but you can tell Elements to move everything using the image's upper-left corner or the bottom-right corner as the reference point instead. To do that, click the circle that you want it to use as the reference.

FIGURE 11-13

This nine-circle icon in the Tool Options area is where you set the reference point for transformations, which tells Elements the central point to rotate around. (The dark circle is the current reference point.) For example, if you want the photo to spin around its upper-left corner instead of its center, click the upper-left circle, as shown here.

- **W and H**. You can resize the image by dragging, or by entering a percentage in one of these boxes.

- **Constrain Proportions**. Turn on this checkbox to preserve the image's original proportions.

- **Angle**. To rotate the image by degrees, click the number here and then type what you want. You can also drag the line in the circle to rotate the photo.

In most cases, you can transform an object without paying much attention to these settings—just grab a handle and drag. Here's what you do:

1. **Position the image to give yourself room to work.**

   Position a photo so that you'll have room to drag the Transform handles far beyond its edges (Figure 11-13 explains how). If you're using tabbed windows, you probably have plenty of room.

2. **Choose how you want to transform the image.**

   Go to Image→Transform, and then select a command. It's not always easy to tell which one will work best for a given photo, so you may want to try all three in turn. You can always change your mind and undo your changes by pressing Esc before you accept a change, or by pressing Ctrl+Z/⌘-Z after you've accepted it.

   You can use Transform commands only on regular layers, so if your image just has a Background layer, the first thing Elements does when you select one of these commands is convert the Background layer to a regular layer. (However, you can apply Transform commands to a *selection* on a Background layer without converting it to a regular layer.)

   Once the Transform command is active, handles appear around your image.

3. **Transform the image.**

   Grab a handle and pull in the direction you want the image to move. You can switch to another handle to pull in a different direction. If you make a mistake, press Esc to return to the original photo.

4. **When you're happy with how the photo looks, accept the change.**

   Click the Commit button (the green checkmark) below your photo or press Return. If you decide not to apply the transformation after all, click the Cancel button (the red No symbol) or press Esc.

TIP Before clicking the Commit button, you can switch to another Transform command and add that transformation to the image, too.

Free Transform

Free Transform combines all the other Transform commands into one and lets you warp images in many different ways. If you aren't sure what you need to do, Free Transform is a good choice.

You use Free Transform exactly the way you use the other Transform commands, following the steps in the previous section. The difference is that with Free Transform, you can pull in *any* direction, using keystroke-drag combinations to tell Elements which kind of transformation you want to apply. Each of the following transformations does exactly the same thing it would if you selected it from the Image→Transform menu:

- **Distort**. To make the photo taller or shorter, Ctrl-drag/⌘-drag any handle. Your cursor turns into a gray arrowhead when you move it over a handle.

- **Skew**. To make the photo lean to the left or right, Shift+Ctrl-drag/Shift-⌘-drag a handle in the middle of a side. Your cursor turns into a gray arrowhead with a tiny double-headed arrow next to it. (The double-headed arrow's orientation shows you which way you can pull: if it's vertical, you want to drag mostly up or down; if it's horizontal, pull that handle horizontally. Move to a different handle and the cursor's orientation may change.)

- **Perspective**. To correct an object that appears to lean away from or toward you, press Shift+Alt+Ctrl/Shift-Option-⌘ while dragging a corner handle. You see the same gray arrowhead cursor as when you're distorting.

Free Transform is the most powerful of all the Transform commands, but when you're pulling in several different directions, it's easy to distort the photo. That's why some people prefer to use the simpler Transform commands and apply multiple transformations instead.

> **TIP** To transform only the *shape* of a selection (not its contents), try the Transform Selection command (page 173), which lets you make any of these changes to a selection's outline without calling up Free Transform. To change the *contents* of a selection, use the tools covered in this chapter instead.

Artistic Elements

CHAPTER 12:
Drawing with Brushes, Shapes, and Other Tools

CHAPTER 13:
Adding Fun and Useful Effects

CHAPTER 14:
Text Elements

Drawing with Brushes, Shapes, and Other Tools

I f you're not artistically inclined, you may feel tempted to skip this chapter. After all, you probably just want to fix and enhance your photos—why should you care about brush techniques? Surprisingly enough, you should care quite a lot.

In Elements, brushes aren't just for painting a moustache and horns on a picture of someone you don't like, or for blackening your sister's teeth in an old school photo. Lots of Elements' tools use brushes to apply their effects. So far, you've already run into the Selection Brush, the Clone Stamp, and the Color Replacement Brush, to name just a few. And even with the basic Brush tool, you can paint with lots of things besides color, such as light or shadows. In Elements, when you want to apply an effect in a precise manner, you often use some sort of brush to do it.

If you're used to working with real brushes, their digital cousins can take some getting used to, but there are many serious artists who now paint primarily in Photoshop. With Elements, you get most of the same tools as in the full Photoshop, if not quite all the settings for each tool. Figure 12-1 shows an example of the detailed work you can do with Elements and some artistic ability.

This chapter explains how to use the Brush tool and some of the other brush-like tools (such as the Erasers), as well as how to draw shapes even if you can't hold a pencil steady. You'll also learn some practical applications for your new skills (like dodging and burning photos to enhance them), and a super easy method of cropping photos in sophisticated, artistic ways—a technique scrapbookers love.

> **TIP** If you have an iPad and like to finger paint, you can create drawings on your iPad in Adobe's Eazel app, and then send them to Elements to use in your projects. To learn more, head to *www.photoshop.com/products/mobile/eazel*, or look for Eazel in the App Store.

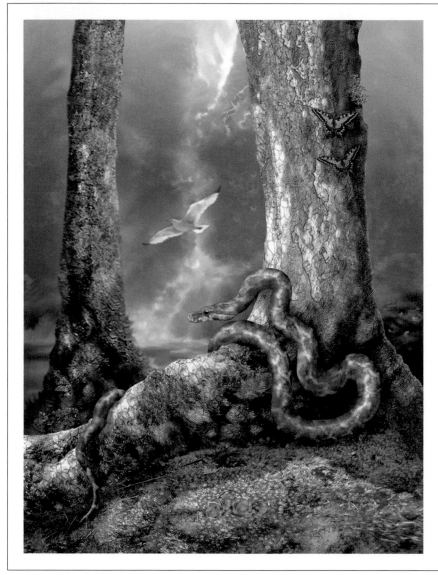

FIGURE 12-1

If you learn to wield all of Elements' drawing power, you can create amazingly detailed artwork. This complex drawing by artist Jodi Frye was done entirely in Elements.

You can see more of Jodi's work at her website, http://jodifrye.weebly.com.

■ Picking and Using a Basic Brush

In Expert mode, if you look at the Tools panel, you'll see the Brush tool at the upper left of the Draw section. To activate it, click its icon or press B.

The Brush tool shares its Tools panel slot with the Impressionist Brush and the Color Replacement tool. You can switch among them by clicking their icons in the Tool Options area or tapping the B key. You can read about the Impressionist Brush later in this chapter (page 406) and about the Color Replacement tool on page 343. This section is about the regular ol' Brush tool.

The Tool Options area gives you lots of ways to customize the Brush tool (Figure 12-2). Here's a quick rundown of these settings from left to right:

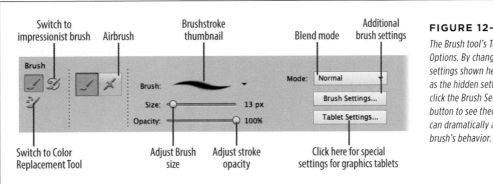

FIGURE 12-2

The Brush tool's Tool Options. By changing the settings shown here as well as the hidden settings—click the Brush Settings button to see them—you can dramatically alter any brush's behavior.

- **Airbrush**. This pair of icons lets you toggle the Brush tool so it behaves like an airbrush. Click the pen-like airbrush icon on the right to use the Brush as an airbrush, and then click the normal brush icon on the left to switch back to a regular brush mode. Figure 12-3 shows how this works.

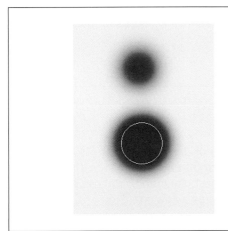

FIGURE 12-3

As with real airbrushes, Elements' airbrush continues to "spray" paint as long as you hold down the mouse button, regardless of whether the mouse is moving.

Top: Here's what you get with one click with the Brush tool in regular, non-airbrush mode.

Bottom: Here's the effect of one click with the same brush in Airbrush mode. See how far the color spread beyond the cursor (the circle)? Not every brush tool offers an airbrush option, but it can be handy for the ones that do.

- **Brushstroke thumbnail**. This squiggle shows the stroke you'd get with the current settings. Click it to display the Brush panel, where you can view and select Elements' brush *libraries*, which are basic brush collections. You can also download many more libraries from various websites (see page 586).

If you click the panel's drop-down menu (which is initially set to Default Brushes), you'll see that you get more than just hard and soft brushes of various sizes (see Figure 12-4). You also get special brushes for drop shadows, brushes that are sensitive to pen pressure if you're using a graphics tablet—which you can also use with a mouse, but you won't have as many options—and brushes that paint shapes and designs.

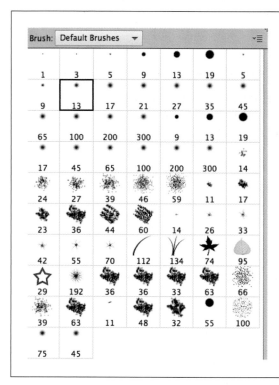

FIGURE 12-4

Elements gives you a pretty good list of brushes to choose from, and you can add your own. (Page 405 explains how to create brushes.) Here you see just one of the many built-in brush libraries, Default Brushes.

To see this view of your brushes, go to the upper right of the Brush panel, click the four-line square, and then choose Small Thumbnail from the menu. You can also drag the upper-right corner of the panel to resize it so you can see more brushes at once.

NOTE One very cool feature of Elements' brushes is that any changes you make to a brush are reflected in the little brushstroke thumbnail in the Tool Options area.

- **Size**. This slider lets you adjust the size of the brush cursor—anywhere from 1 pixel up to sizes that may be too big to fit on your monitor (the maximum is 2500 pixels in diameter or in the longest dimension). You can also click the pixel value next to this slider and then type a new size. Figure 12-5 shows yet another way to adjust settings like brush size using your mouse. Or, as you're working, you can press the close bracket key (]) to quickly increase brush size, or the open bracket key ([) to decrease it.

FIGURE 12-5

You don't need to grab a slider to adjust its setting. Just put your cursor over the word "Size," and the cursor changes into a pointing hand with a double-headed arrow. That's your cue that you can scrub (click and drag) back and forth right on the setting to make changes—left for smaller or less, right for larger or more. This trick works anywhere you see a slider.

- **Opacity**. This setting lets you control how thoroughly the brushstrokes cover what's beneath them. You can use the slider, type in any percentage you like (from 1 to 100), or scrub as shown in Figure 12-5. The maximum—100 percent—gets you total coverage (at least in Normal mode—see the next bullet).

- **Mode**. Here's where you choose the brush's *blend mode* (you'll learn more about the various modes later in this chapter). What you choose here determines how the brush's color interacts with what's in your image.

- **Brush Settings**. Clicking this button brings up the Brush Settings panel, which offers oodles of ways to customize your brush, all of which are covered in the next section. If you're using the Brush tool for artistic purposes, it pays to familiarize yourself with these settings, since this is where you can set a chiseled stroke or a fade, for example.

- **Tablet Settings**. One of the biggest differences between drawing with a mouse and drawing with a real brush is that, on a computer, it doesn't matter how hard you press the mouse. But if you've got a *graphics tablet*, an electronic pad that causes your pen movements to appear onscreen instantly, you can replicate real-world brushing, including pressure effects. Click this button to see settings that let you tell Elements which brush characteristics should respond to the pressure of your stroke. Page 583 tells you all about using a tablet.

TIP If you ever want to return a brush to its original settings, click the four-line square in the upper-right corner of the Tool Options area, and then choose Reset Tool.

To actually *use* the Brush tool, adjust the Tool Options settings, make sure the color you want to paint is the foreground color (page 253), and then simply drag across the image wherever you want to paint.

TIP If you're used to painting with long, sweeping strokes, that technique can be frustrating in Elements. That's because when you undo a mistake (by pressing Ctrl+Z/⌘-Z), Elements undoes *everything* you've done while you've been holding down the mouse button. In tricky spots, you can save yourself some aggravation by using shorter strokes so you don't have to lose that whole long curve you painstakingly worked on just because you wobbled a bit at the end. (In these situations, the Eraser tool [page 416] is also handy for tidying up.)

To draw or paint a straight line, simply click where you want the line to start, press and hold Shift, and then click where you want the line to end; Elements draws a straight line between those two points. (Remember to click the first point and *then* press Shift, or you may draw lines where you don't want them.)

FREQUENTLY ASKED QUESTION

What Happened to My Cursor?

One thing that drives newcomers to Elements nuts is having the Brush cursor change from a circle to little crosshairs, seemingly spontaneously. This is one of those "It's not a bug, it's a feature" situations. Many tools in Elements offer the option of what's called a *precise cursor*, shown in Figure 12-6. There are situations where you may prefer to see those little crosshairs so you can tell *exactly* where you're working.

You toggle between the precise cursor and the circular cursor by pressing the Caps Lock key. So if you press that key by accident, you may find yourself in precise-cursor mode with no idea how you got there. Just press Caps Lock again to switch back to the regular cursor.

There's one other way you may wind up with the precise cursor, and in this situation you have no choice in the matter: when your image is so small in proportion to the cursor that

Elements *has to* display the crosshairs to show the brush in the right scale for your image. Zooming in usually gets your regular cursor back, unless you're working with a 1-pixel brush, which always uses crosshairs.

If you want, you can elect to always see the crosshairs *within* the regular, circular cursor. In the Preferences dialog box (Edit→Preferences→Display & Cursors/Photoshop Elements Editor→Preferences→Display & Cursors), in the Painting Cursors section, turn on "Show Crosshair in Brush Tip" and you'll always have a mark at the exact center of your brush. If you'd like to see a brush icon instead of a circle, choose Standard, and if you'd like the circle to always be as big as the entire brushstroke (as opposed to say, in the airbrush where the stroke normally extends beyond the actual circle), choose Full Size Brush Tip.

FIGURE 12-6

Adobe calls these crosshairs the precise cursor. Elements sometimes makes your cursor look like this when you're zoomed way out on an image.

To get the normal cursor back, try zooming in, and read the box above for further advice.

Modifying Your Brush

When you click the Brush Settings button in the Tool Options area, Elements displays a panel that lets you customize the brush in a number of sophisticated and fun ways.

(You'll run into a version of this panel for some of the other brush-like tools, too, like the Healing Brush.) Mastering these settings goes a long way toward getting artistic results in Elements:

- **Fade** controls how fast the brushstroke fades out—just the way a real brush does when it runs out of paint. A lower number means it fades out quickly (very few marks—see the Spacing bullet below), while a higher one means the fade happens slowly (more marks). Counterintuitively, leaving this setting at 0 means no fading at all—the stroke is the same at the end as it is at the beginning.

  You can pick any number up to 9,999, so with a little fiddling, you should be able to get just the effect you want. If the brush isn't fading fast enough, decrease this setting; if it fades too fast, increase it. A smaller brush usually needs a higher setting than a larger brush does. And you may find that you need to set the brush spacing (explained in a sec) in the 20s or higher to make fading show any visible effect.

> **TIP** As you tweak the brush settings, the brush thumbnail in the Tool Options area changes to reflect the new settings.

- **Hue Jitter**. Some brushes, especially the ones you can use to paint objects like leaves, automatically vary the color of their brushstrokes for a more interesting or realistic effect. In other words, brushes that use hue jitter don't put down only the two colors, but a *range* of hues in between. This setting controls how fast the brush switches between the background and foreground colors. The higher the number (percentage) here, the faster the color varies; a lower number makes the brush take longer to get from one color to the other. Not all brushes respond to this setting, but for the ones that do, it's a pretty cool feature. Figure 12-7 shows how it works.

> **TIP** If you're a by-the-numbers kind of person, you can click any of the numbers at the right ends of the sliders in the Brush Settings panel to turn them into text boxes where you can type in a number instead of using the slider.

- **Scatter** means just what it sounds like: how far apart the marks get distributed in your brushstroke, including how far the marks appear above and below the stroke itself. When you paint with a brush in Elements, you're actually putting down many repetitions of the brush shape rather than a simple line. So if you set scatter to a low percentage, you get a dense, line-like stroke, whereas a higher value creates an effect more like random spots.

- **Spacing** controls how far apart Elements lays down the brush marks when you paint—in other words, how frequently the brush makes a mark along the path of the stroke. A lower number makes them close together, a higher number farther apart, as shown in Figure 12-8.

FIGURE 12-7

Top: A brushstroke with no hue jitter. (Some brushes, like this one, automatically do a little color shading even without hue jitter turned on, as you can see here.)

Middle: The same brushstroke with a medium hue jitter value. The colors used here are red and blue.

Bottom: The same brushstroke with a high hue jitter value. It takes a fairly high number to get all the way from red to blue in a stroke this short.

FIGURE 12-8

From top to bottom, this image shows the same brushstroke with the spacing set at 5 percent, 75 percent, and 150 percent.

You may have wondered why some of the brushstroke thumbnails look like long caterpillars, when the brush should paint an object, like a star or a leaf. The reason? Cramped spacing. The thumbnail shows the spacing as Elements originally sets it. Widen the spacing to see separate objects instead of a clump.

- **Hardness** controls whether the brush's edge is sharp or fuzzy. This setting isn't available for all brushes, but when it is, you can choose any value between zero (the fuzziest) and 100 percent (the most defined edge).

- **Roundness** and **Angle**. Painters don't use only round brushes, and you don't have to in Elements, either. If you've ever painted with a real brush, you'll understand these settings right away. They let you create a more chiseled brush edge and rotate it so that the edge isn't always facing the same direction.

Some of the brushes in Elements' libraries, like the calligraphic and faux-finish brushes, aren't round. But you can adjust the roundness of *any* brush to make it more suitable for chiseled strokes, as shown in Figure 12-9. For rectangular brushes, lowering the Roundness setting just squishes the cursor into a flatter rectangle rather than making it less round.

FIGURE 12-9

Here's the bottom of the Brush Settings panel. To adjust a brush's angle and roundness, drag the white dots to make the brush rounder or narrower, and then grab the arrow and spin it to the angle you want. You can also click the current Angle or Roundness setting and type a new number.

The Brush Settings panel also includes a checkbox labeled "Set this as a default." Turn it on if you want to make all your brushes behave exactly the same way. Not all of the panel's settings are available for all brushes, though; some won't change and some will be grayed out for certain brushes.

Saving Modified Brush Settings

If you modify a brush and like your creation, you can save it as a custom brush. Elements lets you alter any existing brush and save the result—a great feature if you're working on a project that's going to last awhile and you don't want to keep modifying the settings. (Don't worry: When you modify an existing brush, Elements preserves a copy of the original.)

To create a custom brush:

1. **Choose a brush to modify.**

   Select any brush in the Brush panel (Figure 12-4).

2. **Make the changes you want.**

   Change the brush's settings until you get what you're after. The brush thumbnail in the Tool Options area reflects your new settings.

3. **Tell Elements you want to keep the new brush.**

   In the Tool Options area, click the brush thumbnail to open the Brush panel and then, in the panel's upper right, click the four-line square and choose Save Brush. Elements asks you to name your brush; you don't *have* to, but named brushes are easier to keep track of. The name will appear as pop-up text when you put your cursor over the brush's thumbnail in the Brush panel.

4. Click OK.

The brush shows up in the Brush panel at the bottom of the current list of brushes. If you make lots of custom brushes, you may want to create a special set for them using the Preset Manager (see page 587).

Deleting a brush is pretty straightforward: Select it in the Brush panel and then, in the panel's upper right, click the four-line square and choose Delete Brush. Or you can Alt-click/Option-click the brush's thumbnail in the panel. (When you hold down the Alt/Option key, the cursor turns into a pair of scissors; simply click with the scissors to delete the brush.)

You can also select something in an image and save it as a brush, as the next section explains.

Special Brushes

So far you've learned about brushes that behave pretty much as brushes do in the real world—they paint a stripe of something, whether that's color, light, or even transparency. But in the digital world, a brush doesn't have to be just a brush. With some of Elements' brushes, you can paint stars, flowers, disembodied eyeballs, gravel, or even rubber ducks with just one stroke, as shown in Figure 12-10.

FIGURE 12-10

Even if you can't draw a straight line, you can digitally doodle using Elements' brushes.

Everything in this lovely drawing was done with brushes that come with Elements. The leaves were painted with a brush that paints leaves, the yellow ducks come from a brush that paints ducks, and so on.

If you click the brush thumbnail in the Tool Options area, you'll see the list of brushes in the current category and a drop-down menu that lets you investigate Elements' other *brush libraries* (sets of brushes). The brushes used in Figure 12-10, for example, came from several different categories. Many of them are in the Special Effects brush library, but some are scattered around in the other libraries.

These special brushes respond readily to changes in the Brush Settings panel (covered earlier in this chapter on page 400). Your choices there can make a huge difference in the effect you get, like whether the brush paints swaths of smooth grass like a lawn, or scattered sprigs of dune grass, for instance. And if you're using a graphics tablet (page 583), many brushes are sensitive to pen pressure.

> **TIP** If you've tried some of the Special Effects brushes and found the results rather anemic, you can always go back once you've painted with them and punch up their color using a Multiply layer, just as you would with an overexposed photo (see page 229).

Making a Custom Brush

You can turn any picture, or selection within a picture, into a brush that paints the shape you've selected. Figure 12-11 shows what a cluster of flowers looks—and behaves—like when it's been turned into a brush.

> **NOTE** Remember that, by definition, brushes aren't any specific color, so when you create a brush from a selection, you save only the *shape* of the selection, not the color of it. The color you get when you use the brush is whichever color you choose to apply. If you want to save a *colored* sample, try saving your selection as a pattern (page 326) instead, or using the Clone Stamp (page 518).

It's surprisingly easy to create a custom brush from any object in an image:

FIGURE 12-11

Left: To make a brush that draws poinsettias, just select one in a photo and then save it as a brush.

Right: You can paint better than you thought! And with this brush, your poinsettias can be any color you like.

1. **Open the image that includes what you want to use as a brush.**

   You can choose an area as large as 2500 pixels square. (You can resize your selection once it's a brush, just the way you can resize any other brush, so don't worry if it's a big area. That said, if you use a super-detailed brush at a tiny size setting, it may lose some definition.)

2. **Select the object or region you want.**

   Use any of Elements' selection tools to do this. It's a good idea to inspect your selection with the Selection Brush in Mask mode (page 162), because any stray areas you include by mistake will get painted with each stroke.

3. **Create your brush.**

   Go to Edit→"Define Brush from Selection." A dialog box appears showing the selection's shape and asking you to name the new brush. Check the thumbnail to be sure it's exactly what you had in mind. If it is, click OK; if not, click Cancel and try again.

The new brush shows up at the bottom of your current list of brushes. If you want to get rid of it, simply Alt-click/Option-click its thumbnail, or highlight the thumbnail, click the four-line square in the upper-right corner of the Brush panel, and then choose Delete Brush.

The Impressionist Brush

When you paint with the Impressionist Brush, Elements blurs and blends the edges of the objects in your photo, like in an Impressionist painting. At least that's what's *supposed* to happen. This brush is very tricky to control, but you can get some really interesting effects with it, especially if you paint on a duplicate layer and play with that layer's Opacity setting. Usually, you'll want a really low opacity with this brush, or some of the curlier Style settings (explained in a sec) will make your image look like it's made from poodle hair. Changing the brush's Mode setting (page 411) can also help control the effect.

To activate the Impressionist Brush, press B or click the Brush tool's Tools panel icon, and then click this tool's icon in the Tool Options area (it's the one with the curlicue). This brush has most of the same Tool Options settings as the regular Brush, but if you click the Advanced button, you'll see three additional settings:

- **Style** determines what kind of brushstroke effect the brush will create.

- **Area** tells Elements the diameter of the painting area, meaning how much area the actual stroke should cover. This is usually much larger than the size of the cursor itself.

- **Tolerance** controls how similar in color the pixels the brush passes over have to be before they're affected by the brush.

The Impressionist Brush isn't really the best tool for creating true Impressionist effects, although its blurring qualities can sometimes be useful because it covers large areas faster than the Blur tool. If your goal is to create a hand-painted look, you may prefer the brushstroke filters (Filter→Brush Strokes); page 435 explains how to use them. The Smudge tool (page 414) is another excellent—though time-consuming—way to create a painted effect.

The Pencil Tool

Basically just another brush, the Pencil tool lives at the lower-right corner of the Tools panel's Draw section. Click its icon (a pencil, of course) or press N to activate it.

The Pencil tool has many of the same settings as the Brush tool—like size, mode, and opacity—but it offers only hard-edged brushes. In other words, you can't draw fuzzy lines with this tool, not even the kind of lines you can sketch with a soft pencil in real life; the Pencil tool's lines are *always* well defined. This tool is handy when you want to work on a pixel-by-pixel basis.

You use the Pencil tool the same way as any other brush. The big difference is the Auto Erase checkbox in the Tool Options area. Turning it on makes the Pencil tool paint with the background color over areas that contain the foreground color. But if you start dragging in an area that doesn't include the foreground color, it paints with the foreground color instead. This is really confusing until you try it. Take a look at Figure 12-12 for some help understanding this setting, or better yet, create a blank file and try it yourself.

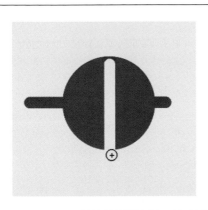

FIGURE 12-12

The Pencil tool's slightly confusing Auto Erase option was used to create two lines here: a horizontal one of the foreground color (purple) and a vertical one of the background color (light green).

The horizontal line was drawn by starting with the cursor outside the purple circle (so the Pencil erased the green, leaving a purple line across the circle). The vertical line was drawn by starting inside the purple circle, causing Elements to expose the background color.

The Paint Bucket

When you want to quickly fill a large area with color, the Paint Bucket is the tool for you. It's in the Tools panel's Draw section, right below the Brush tool. Simply activate the Paint Bucket by clicking its icon or pressing its keyboard shortcut (K), adjust its Tool Options settings (described below), and then click in your image; Elements floods all the available area (either the whole image or the current selection) with your foreground color. It works something like the Magic Wand: Just as the Magic Wand *selects* only the color you click, the Paint Bucket *fills* only the color you click.

Most of the Paint Bucket's Tool Options settings are probably familiar:

- **Pattern**. Normally, the Paint Bucket fills the affected area with your current foreground color, but click the square with diagonal lines on it to make this tool use a pattern instead. Click the pattern thumbnail in the Tool Options area, and then choose an existing pattern or create your own, just as you would with the Pattern Stamp (page 326).

> **NOTE** Adjust the Paint Bucket's Tool Options settings *before* clicking in your photo.

- **Opacity**. One hundred percent opacity gives you total coverage: Nothing shows through the paint you put down. Lower this percentage for a more transparent effect.

- **Tolerance**. This setting works the same way it does for the Magic Wand (page 165): The higher the number, the more shades the paint fills.

- **Mode**. You can use the Paint Bucket in any blend mode, as explained later in this chapter (page 411).

- **All Layers**. Turn on this checkbox and the paint fills *any* pixels that meet your criteria (determined by the tool's other Tool Options settings), no matter what layer they're on. (The Paint Bucket actually *paints* on the active layer, but with this setting turned on, it looks for pixels to change based on all the layers in your image. If it's turned off, the Paint Bucket only works on the active layer.) To exclude a particular layer when All Layers is turned on, click that layer's eye icon in the Layers panel to hide it. Don't forget that you can lock the transparent and translucent parts of layers in the Layers panel (see page 198).

- **Contiguous**. This is another setting that should be familiar from the Magic Wand (page 166). If you leave this checkbox on, you change only areas of the chosen color that touch one another. Turn it off, and Elements changes *all* areas of the color you click, whether they're contiguous or not.

- **Anti-aliasing**. This setting smooths the edges of the paint. Leave it turned on unless you have a specific reason not to.

You can undo a Paint Bucket fill with the usual Ctrl+Z/⌘-Z.

> **TIP** You can sometimes improve blown-out skies by using the Eyedropper to select an appropriate shade of blue from another photo, and then using the Paint Bucket at a very low opacity to fill the blown-out areas of the sky in the problem photo.

■ Dodging and Burning

Like Unsharp Mask, dodging and burning are old darkroom techniques used to enhance photos and emphasize particular areas. Dodging *lightens* images and brings out hidden details in the range you specify (midtones, shadows, or highlights), and burning *darkens* photos and brings out details in a given range. Both tools live with the Sponge tool in the Tools panel's Enhance section.

You may think that, given the Shadows/Highlights command, you don't need these tools. But they're useful because, unlike Shadows/Highlights, they let you make *selective* changes, rather than affecting the whole image or requiring tedious selections. To dodge or burn, you just paint your changes. Figure 12-13 shows an example of when you might need to work on a particular area. Of course, you can also make a selection and then use Shadows/Highlights on just that, which you may want to try in addition to dodging and burning.

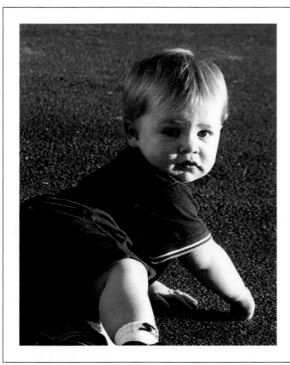

FIGURE 12-13

The overall shadow/highlight balance of this photo is about right, but the strong sideways lighting creates quite an imbalance over this little guy's face.

Careful dodging and burning can help fix problems like this, as Figure 12-14 shows.

Skillful use of dodging and burning can greatly improve photos, although it helps to have an artistic eye to spot what to emphasize and what to downplay. You can use these tools alongside Elements' black-and-white conversion feature (page 349) to emphasize certain areas of your photos. Masters of black-and-white photography, like Ansel Adams, relied heavily on dodging and burning (in the darkroom, in those days) to create their greatest images.

Both the Dodge and Burn tools are really just variants of the Brush tool, except they don't apply color—they just *affect* the colors and tones that are already present in your photo. Adobe refers to them as the "toning tools."

One word of warning about these tools: Unless you use them on a duplicate layer, you can't undo their effects once you close the file, so be careful how you use them. In fact, unless they're working on black-and-white photos, many people prefer the results they get dodging and burning using the method described in the box on page 413 to those of the *actual* Dodge and Burn tools.

> **TIP** If you need to make selective adjustments to just part of a photo, you may also want to try some of the Smart Brush's lighting settings (page 233). A little experimenting will give you a sense of which tools you prefer in different situations. You may also want to see what the Auto Smart Tone feature can do for your photo (page 142).

Dodging

You can use the Dodge tool to lighten parts of an image and to bring out details hidden in shadows. It's a good idea to create a separate layer when using this tool (Layer→Duplicate Layer or Ctrl+J/⌘-J) to preserve the original image in case you go overboard. (Be sure you apply the Dodge tool to a layer that has something on it, or nothing will happen.) Here's how to use it:

1. **Activate the Dodge tool.**

   Click the Sponge tool's icon at the lower right of the Tools panel's Enhance section or press O, and then, in the Tool Options area, click the Dodge tool's icon (the lollipop-like paddle). You'll see some of the usual brush settings, but with two differences: a Range setting that determines whether the tool works on highlights, midtones, or shadows; and an Exposure setting that determines the strength of the tool's effect.

2. **Adjust the tool's settings and then drag over the area you want to change.**

   For a more realistic result, choose a low Exposure setting and then drag repeatedly over the area you want to change, as shown in Figure 12-14 (that's true for the Burn tool, as well). After you're done, if you think the tool's effect is too strong, you can always reduce the layer's opacity (as long as you're working on a duplicate layer).

Burning

The Burn tool works just like the Dodge tool but does exactly the opposite: It darkens. Use the Burn tool to uncover details in images' highlights. Of course, there have to be *some* details there for the tool to work with; if a photo's highlights are blown out, you won't get any results, no matter how much you apply the tool. The Burn tool is grouped with the Sponge and Dodge tools in the Tools panel; its icon is a curled hand.

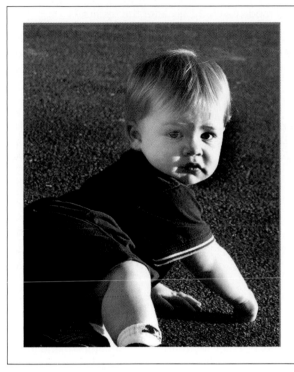

FIGURE 12-14

Here's the boy from Figure 12-13 after a dose of the Dodge and Burn tools. The shadowed side of his face is easier to see, but the contrast there is pretty flat, while it's much too dramatic on the sunny side of his face. (The effects are deliberately too strong here to show you the perils of getting overzealous with either tool.)

See page 413 to learn a different method for selectively adjusting highlights and shadows. Both methods have advantages and disadvantages.

Most of the time, you'll probably want to use the Dodge and Burn tools in combination. They can help draw attention to specific parts of a photo, but they work best for subtle changes. Applying them too vigorously—especially on color photos—creates an obviously faked look. Black-and-white photos (or color images converted to black and white) can generally stand much stronger contrasts.

Blending and Smudging

You can control how Elements blends colors you add to an image with the colors that are already there. This section takes a look at two different blending methods: using *blend modes* to determine how the colors you paint change what's already in the image, and using the Smudge tool to mix parts of an image together.

Blend Modes

Blend modes are almost limitless in the ways they can manipulate images. They control how the color you add when painting interacts with the existing pixels in an image—whether you just add color (Normal mode), make the existing color darker (Multiply mode), or change the color saturation (Saturation mode).

Image-editing experts have found plenty of clever ways to use blend modes for some really sophisticated techniques. Thorough coverage of these techniques would make this book the size of the Yellow Pages, but Figure 12-15 shows a few examples of how simply changing a brush's blend mode can radically alter the results.

FIGURE 12-15

This photo shows the effect of some of the different blend modes when used with the Brush tool.

The same color paint (pink) was used for each of the vertical stripes, but each one used a different blend mode—and you can see how different the results are.

From left to right, the modes are Normal, Color Burn, Color Dodge, Vivid Light, Difference, and Saturation.

Elements' various blend mode menus (such as the Brush tool's Mode menu in the Tool Options area), group blend modes according to the effects they have. You won't always see every group or all the choices, but in Elements' menus, the top group typically includes what you might call "painting modes," followed by modes for darkening, lightening, adjusting light, applying special effects, and adjusting color.

Keep in mind that the modes sometimes work quite differently with layers than with tools. In other words, painting with a brush in Dissolve mode may produce an effect quite different from creating a layer in Dissolve mode and painting on it.

There are so many ways to combine blend modes that even Elements pros can't always predict the results, so experimenting is the best way to learn about them. They're really cool and useful once you get used to them, but if you're just starting out in Elements, there's no need to worry about them right away.

> **TIP** If you'd like to learn more about each mode, you can find a lot of useful tutorials on the Web. A good place to start is *www.photoshopgurus.com/tutorials/t010.html*. (Ignore the section "Additional blend mode information"—that's only for Photoshop folks.)

Blend Modes Instead of Dodge and Burn

You can do a lot in Elements without ever touching blend modes. But if you take time to familiarize yourself with them, you might find they become a regular part of your image-editing toolkit. For instance, you may prefer the effect you get using a layer in Overlay mode to that of the Dodge and Burn tools.

To adjust a photo using a layer in Overlay blend mode, first make basic adjustments like Levels or Shadows/Highlights. Then, when you're ready to fine-tune the photo by enhancing details, here's what you do:

1. **Create a new layer.** Go to Layer→New→Layer or press Shift+Ctrl+N/Shift-⌘-N.

2. **In the New Layer dialog box, choose Overlay from the Mode menu, turn on the "Fill with Overlay-neutral color (50% gray)" checkbox, and then click OK.** You won't see anything happen to your photo just yet.

3. **Set your foreground and background colors to black and white, respectively.** Press D to set the foreground and background squares to black and white.

4. **Activate the Brush tool.** Choose a brush (set to Normal mode) and set its opacity very low, maybe 17 percent or less. (You'll need to experiment a bit to see how low a setting is low enough.)

5. **Paint over the areas you want to adjust.** Paint with white to bring up the detail in dark areas and with black to darken overly light areas. (Remember that you can switch from one color to the other by pressing X.) The details in your photo magically become clearer.

Figure 12-16 shows the results of using Overlay mode on the image from Figure 12-13 so you can compare the results. This method has the added advantage of being adjustable—simply change the opacity of the Overlay layer to tweak the results. You can carry this technique to extremes for really interesting effects when you want an artistic (rather than realistic) result.

FIGURE 12-16

Here's the little boy from Figure 12-13 again, this time after a dose of Overlay blending, as described in the box above.

Unlike the results of using the Dodge and Burn tools (Figure 12-14), the color isn't grayish, which is good. But the contrast where shadowed areas meet bright ones still needs some work.

The Smudge Tool

The Smudge tool does just what you'd think: smears the colors in an image as if you were rubbing them with your finger. You can even "finger paint" with it, if you feel the call of your inner preschooler. Adobe describes the effect of the Smudge tool as being "like a finger dragged through wet paint." It's sort of like a cousin to the Liquify filter (page 493), but with fewer options.

> **TIP** Another great way to create drawn or painted effects in your photos is to try the Comic, Graphic Novel, and "Pen and Ink" filters, especially on a duplicate layer at a reduced opacity or in different blend modes.

If you want to turn photos into paintings (as in Figure 12-17), the humble Smudge tool is your most valuable resource. For really artistic smudging, you need a graphics tablet so you can vary the stroke pressure. (You can use this tool without a tablet, but the effect won't be nearly as good.) To learn more about this kind of smudging, you can find some excellent tutorials online; search for *beagle smudge tutorial* and *Renaissance man smudge tutorial*. These first appeared in the Retouching forum at Digital Photography Review (*www.dpreview.com*), and you can still find many excellent examples of smudging there. The forums at *www.retouchpro.com* are another favorite hangout of expert smudgers.

FIGURE 12-17

In effect, the Smudge tool lets you turn a photo into a painting. With the help of a graphics tablet, you can join the ranks of the many skilled smudgers who create amazing effects using only this tool.

The bottom three petals of this hibiscus blossom show preliminary smudging. The brushes you use determine whether the effect is smooth, as you see here, or more heavily stroked. To blend in other colors, use the tool's Finger Painting option.

A word of warning: If you have a slow computer, there will be quite a lag between when you apply the Smudge tool and when you see its effect onscreen. This delay makes the tool tricky to control, because you have to resist the temptation to keep going over an area until you see results.

You'll find the Smudge tool hidden under the Blur tool in the Tools panel. Click the Blur tool's icon (the water drop) or press R and then, in the Tool Options area, choose the Smudge tool (its icon, not surprisingly, is a finger that looks like it's painting).

The Smudge tool has mostly the same Tool Options settings as other brush tools, but it also includes the Sample All Layers checkbox, just like the Healing Brush and the Clone Stamp (page 317 describes this option), as well as two additional settings:

- **Strength**. This setting does just what it says—controls how much the tool smudges colors together. A higher number results in more blending.

- **Finger Painting**. Turning on this checkbox makes the Smudge tool smear in the current foreground color at the start of each stroke. When this setting is turned off, the tool uses the color that's under the cursor at the start of each stroke. (Figure 12-18 shows the difference.) This option is useful for creating artistic smudges, like adding a contrasting color to help your strokes stand out more.

FIGURE 12-18

The strokes on the left were done with the Smudge tool's Finger Painting checkbox turned on, which introduced a bit of the foreground color (orange, in this case) into the beginning of each stroke. This technique is really useful for shading and when you need to mix in just a touch of another color.

The smudging on the right was done with the Finger Painting setting turned off, so it uses only the colors that are already in the image.

Once you've chosen your settings, smudge away.

NOTE When using the Smudge tool, you see results only where two colors come together because it blends together the pixel colors where edges meet. So if you use Smudge in the middle of an area of solid color, nothing happens unless you've turned on the Finger Painting setting.

■ The Eraser Tools

Everyone makes mistakes. That's why Adobe has thoughtfully included three different mistake-fixers in Elements. The Eraser, the Magic Eraser, and the Background Eraser share a slot at the upper right of the Tools panel's Draw section; their keyboard shortcut is E. You'll probably use all three tools at one time or another. This section explains what each one does.

Using the Basic Eraser

The standard Eraser tool is basically just another kind of brush tool, only it *removes* color instead of adding it. How it works varies depending on where you use it. If you use it on a regular layer, it replaces the color with transparency. If you use it on a Background layer or one in which transparency is locked, it replaces whatever color is there with your current background color (see Chapter 6 for more about how layers work).

The Eraser's Tool Options settings are pretty much the same as for any other brush—including brush style, size, and opacity—with a couple of different twists:

- **Opacity** determines how much color gets removed; at 100 percent, it's all gone (or all replaced with the background color).

- **Type**. This setting tells Elements what shape eraser you want to work with: Brush, Pencil, or Block. You can see the difference in how the Eraser is going to work by watching the brush-style preview in the Tool Options area as you change modes. Picking Brush or Pencil mode lets you choose any brush cursor you like. The Brush option lets you make soft-edged erasures, while Pencil mode makes only hard-edged erasures. Choosing Block mode changes the cursor to a square so you can use it like an artist's erasing block—sort of.

Here's how to use this handy tool:

1. **Activate the Eraser tool.**

   Press E or click the tool's icon in the Tools panel (it's a pink eraser, so it's easy to spot).

2. **Choose your settings.**

   In the Tool Options area, select a size, type, and opacity. (As noted earlier, the opacity setting works differently here than it does for regular brushes.)

3. **Drag anywhere in the image to remove what you don't want.**

You may need to change the Eraser's Size setting a few times. It's usually easiest to use a small cursor (or the Background Eraser tool—page 418) to accurately clear around the edges of an object you want to keep, as shown in Figure 12-19. Then you can use a larger brush to get rid of the remaining chunks once you don't have to worry about accidentally going into the area you want to keep.

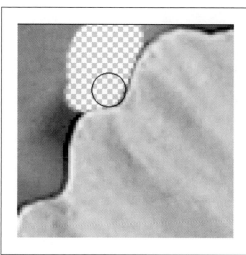

FIGURE 12-19

Accurately erasing around an object usually means zooming way, way in so you can see which pixels the Eraser is changing.

You can use a selection to limit where the Eraser operates. Just select the area where you want your erasing to happen and the Eraser will stop erasing when it reaches the edge of your selection. It's usually easiest to select what you want to keep*, and then press Shift+Ctrl+I/ Shift-⌘-I to invert the selection so that the area you want to erase is selected.*

It's tedious to erase around a long outline or to remove entire backgrounds with the Eraser tool. Fortunately, Elements has two *other* kinds of erasers for those situations.

The Magic Eraser

Once you try the Magic Eraser, you're likely to wonder why the heck Adobe gave this pedestrian tool such an intriguing name. What's so magic about it? Not much, really. It's called "magic" because it works a lot like the Magic Wand tool in that you can use it to select pixels in a particular color or range (which you control with the Tolerance setting). Its icon even has the same little starburst as the Magic Wand's icon to remind you of the relationship.

The problem, as Figure 12-20 shows, is that the Magic Eraser doesn't do as clean a job as the other erasers. Still, it can be a big help in eliminating large chunks of solid color. Moreover, if you're lucky, you may be able to clean up any ragged edges with the Refine Edge dialog box (page 156) or the Defringe Layer command (page 171). (To use Refine Edge, you'll need to select the layer's contents, or click in the empty background area with the Magic Wand, and then choose Select→Inverse.)

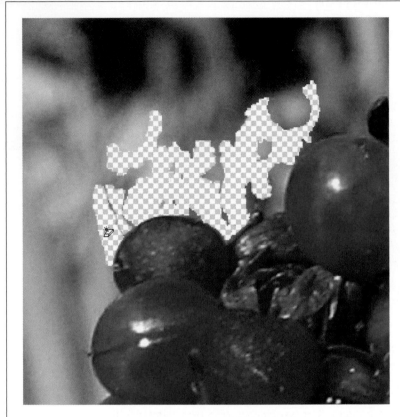

FIGURE 12-20

Here's a closeup look at the Magic Eraser at work on the background behind a cluster of berries. A couple of clicks with this tool got rid of a chunk of the background, and setting the tolerance higher would've gotten even more. But if you look closely, you can see the disadvantage of this tool: The edges of the berries are fringed with dark, ragged areas it didn't eliminate.

You may be able to clean up the edges with the Defringe Layer command (page 171) or Refine Edge dialog box (page 156), but those methods aren't always 100 percent successful.

If you're looking to achieve really clean results, it's typically best to use the Magic Eraser in combination with at least one of the other erasers. One sometimes-useful side effect of the Magic Eraser is that, when you click a photo with it, Elements automatically turns the image's Background layer into a regular layer, just the way the Background Eraser (explained next) does. So if you want to do something to the remaining object that requires a regular layer—like applying a layer style (page 461)—this tool saves you a step.

The Background Eraser

Lots of people think *this* eraser deserves the name "Magic" much more than the Magic Eraser tool. This tool—as you can guess from its name—is a tremendous help when you want to remove all the background around an object.

The Background Eraser deletes all the pixels under your cursor (but outside the edges of the object) and renders the area it's used on transparent, even if that area is on a Background layer. (If you activate this tool and then click a Background layer, your computer may hesitate for a sec because it's busy transforming the Background into a regular layer.) Here's how to use it:

1. **Activate the Background Eraser.**

   Press E or, in the Tools panel, click the Eraser icon, and then choose the Background Eraser in the Tool Options area. (Its icon is an eraser with a pair of scissors next to it.)

2. **Choose a brush size.**

   When you activated the Background Eraser, your cursor turned into a circle with crosshairs in its center. These crosshairs are important: They're the Background Eraser's "hot spot." Elements turns any color that you drag them over into transparency.

   The size of the cursor (the circle) changes depending on how large a brush you choose in the Tool Options area, but the crosshairs stay the same size. As you can see in Figure 12-21, with a large brush, there may be a lot of space around the crosshairs. That makes it easy to remove big chunks of the background at once, since everything within the cursor's circle gets eliminated.

   > **NOTE** If *all* your brush tools start using crosshairs as their cursors (not just the Background Eraser), the box on page 400 tells you how to get back to the regular, circular cursor.

3. **Drag in your photo.**

   Move around the edge of the object you want to keep, being careful not to let the crosshairs touch the object itself, or else you'll start erasing it, too. If you make a mistake, just press Ctrl+Z/⌘-Z.

The Background Eraser has three Tool Options settings to help you refine how it works (though you may not need to change any of these settings to get the results you want):

- **Tolerance**. This setting tells the Background Eraser how similar colors have to be for it to remove them. It's just like the Magic Wand's Tolerance setting (page 166).

- **Brush Settings**. If you want to use a different brush style, click this button and then choose your settings (they're explained on page 400).

- **Limits**. Do you want the Background Eraser to remove only contiguous color or *all* the patches of a certain color, no matter where they are in your image? This works exactly like the Magic Wand's Contiguous setting (page 166).

If you want to remove the background around an object, you may find it most effective to start by using the Background Eraser around the object's edges, and then switch to the other Erasers to clean up. The advantage of this method is that you don't have to clean up junk left over from the Magic Eraser. Plus it's easier to maneuver the Background Eraser than the regular Eraser, especially if you don't have a graphics tablet.

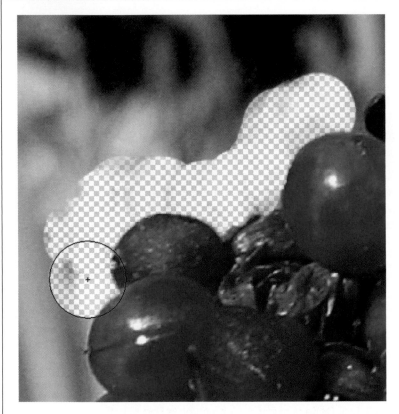

FIGURE 12-21

The Background Eraser does a very careful job of separating these berries from their background. Just be sure to keep the little crosshairs away from the color you want to keep.

Here, because the crosshairs are outside the red area, only the greenish background is getting removed. But if you moved the crosshairs over a berry, the Background Eraser would bite chunks out of it.

Drawing with Shapes

So many brush options and Adobe still isn't done—there's yet *another* way to draw things in Elements. The program's shape tools (which share a slot in the Tools panel) let you draw geometrically perfect shapes, regardless of your artistic ability. And not just simple shapes like circles and rectangles: You can draw animals, plants, starbursts, picture frames—all sorts of things, as shown in Figure 12-22. This tool should appeal to anyone whose grade-school "masterpieces" always got put up on the wall...behind the piano.

NOTE When you draw a shape with one of the shape tools, Elements automatically fills it with color. If you're looking to add a simple, *empty* rectangle, square, circle, or ellipse rather than one filled with color, see the box on page 428.

FIGURE 12-22

Here are just a few of the shapes you can draw with Elements' shape tools, even if you flunked elementary school art class.

These objects look even more impressive once you gussy them up with layer styles (page 461).

> **NOTE** If you want to create text that follows the outline of a shape—to put words around the outside of a trombone, say—see the Tip on page 504.

Turning yourself into an artist by using Elements' shape tools is easy. Just follow these steps:

1. **Open an image or create a new file.**

   You can add shapes to any file you can open in Elements.

2. **Activate the Shape tool.**

   Click the shape tools in the Tools panel (they're in the Draw section right above the Pencil tool) or press U. The shape tools are sometimes a little confusing to Elements newcomers because their Tools panel icon reflects the shape that's currently active—so it may be a rectangle, a polygon, or a line, for instance. (You'll see an irregular blue blob if you haven't used these tools before.)

3. **Select the shape you want to draw.**

   Use the icons on the left side of the Tool Options area to choose a custom shape, a rectangle, a rounded rectangle, an ellipse, a polygon, a star, or a line. (If you select the custom shape, you have *lots* of shapes to choose from; click the black-and-white shape currently displayed in the Tool Options area to pick one.) All the shapes, and their accompanying options, are described in the following sections.

4. **Adjust your Tool Options settings.**

   When you switch to the shape tools, your foreground color automatically appears in the Tool Options area to indicate that Elements will use that color when you use the tool. If you want a different color, click the color box in the Tool Options area to bring up the Color Swatches panel. If you click the rainbow-colored circle on the lower-right corner of the Color Swatches panel, you get the Color Picker instead (page 255).

   If you have special requirements, like a rectangle that's exactly 1″ × 2″, click the Tool Options area's Unconstrained menu, choose Fixed Size, and then enter a size for your shape in the boxes below the button. The menu usually offers a couple of other choices, too, but they vary depending on which shape tool you're using.

   There's also a Tool Options setting that lets you apply a layer style (see page 461) as you draw the shape. To use it, just to the right of the shape thumbnail, click the white rectangle with a red slash through it, and then choose the style you want from the Styles panel. To go back to drawing without applying a style, choose the square with the diagonal red line through it. (Sometimes you may need to reset the Shape tool to stop using a chosen style. To do that, click the four-line square at the top right of the Tool Options area and choose Reset Tool.)

5. **Drag in your image to draw the shape.**

   Notice that *how* you drag affects the final appearance of the shape. For example, the direction you drag determines its proportions. If you're drawing a fish, say, you can drag so that it's long and skinny or short and fat. Even with practice, it can take a couple of tries to get exactly the proportions you want.

The shape tools automatically put each shape on its own layer. If you don't want them to do that, or need to control how shapes interact, use the square icons in the middle of the Tool Options area. They're the same as the ones for managing selections (page 153). They let you add more than one shape to a layer, subtract one shape from another, keep only the area where shapes intersect, or exclude the areas where they intersect. If you want to draw multiple shapes on one layer, for example, click the "Add to shape area (+)" button, which looks just like the "Add to Selection" button (see Figure 5-4 on page 153). That way, all the shapes you add end up on the same layer. (Shapes don't have to touch or overlap to use this option.)

Clicking the Tool Options area's Simplify button turns any shape from a vector image (which is infinitely resizable) into a raster image (one that's drawn pixel by pixel). The box on page 424 tells you everything you need to know about the difference between these types of images, including why and when you'd want to make this change.

The following sections describe all the main shape categories and their special settings.

The Custom Shape Tool

This tool lets you draw a huge variety of different objects, as you can see in Figure 12-23. Its icon is an irregular blue blob. Click it in the Tool Options area or keep pressing U until it appears in the Tools panel.

FIGURE 12-23

Here are some of the shapes available when you use the Custom Shape tool.

To expand this panel so you can see more shapes at once, drag its upper-right corner.

Once the Custom Shape tool is active, the Tool Options displays a black-and-white thumbnail labeled with the name of the current shape; click this thumbnail to display the Shape Picker. Various shapes automatically appear, but if you use the drop-down menu at the top of the Shape Picker, you get a lot more choices. To scroll through them all, choose All Elements Shapes.

> **TIP** The Shape Picker includes a copyright symbol you can use if you want something official-looking that's easy to enlarge and use as a watermark on your photos.

Click Unconstrained in the Tool Options area to see a menu with these options:

- **Unconstrained**. This setting lets you control the proportions of the shape by dragging.

- **Defined Proportions**. Makes the shape keep its original proportions.

- **Defined Size**. The shape is always the size it was originally created to be—dragging won't make it bigger or smaller. Elements just plunks it down at a fixed size you can't control (except by resizing it after the fact).

- **Fixed Size**. Select this option and then, in the W and H boxes, enter the dimensions you want the shape to be. You can use inches, pixels, or centimeters as the unit.

In addition, the From Center checkbox lets you draw the object from its center rather than an edge.

> **NOTE** You can add more shapes to Elements, although you can't *create* shapes in Elements (you need Photoshop to do that). You can find thousands of custom shapes online. Just search for *custom shapes Photoshop*, or check the sources suggested on page 586. The names of shape files end in *.csh*. In Windows, put your downloaded shape files in *C:\Program Files\Adobe\Photoshop Elements 13\Presets\Custom Shapes*. On a Mac, it's *Applications→Adobe Photoshop Elements 13→Support files→Presets→Custom Shapes*. After that, the next time you start the Editor, the shapes will appear in the Shape Picker in their own category with the same names as the .csh files.

Rasterizing Vector Shapes

Back in Chapter 3, you read about how the majority of images (definitely your photos) are just a bunch of pixels to Elements. These types of images are known as *raster* images. The shapes you draw with the shape tools work a little differently; they're what's called *vector* images.

A vector image is made up of a set of directions specifying what kind of geometric shapes your computer should draw. The advantage of vector images is that you can enlarge or shrink them without producing the kind of pixelation (blockiness) you get when you resize a raster image too much.

Shapes keep their vector characteristics until you *simplify* the layers they're on. Simplifying (which is also called *rasterizing*) just means that Elements turns the shape into regular pixels—in other words, into a raster image. Once you simplify vector images, they have the same resizing limitations as regular photos. For example, you can make a raster image smaller without running into trouble, but you can't make it larger than 100 percent without losing quality, just as with a photo.

Sooner or later, you may want to transform a vector image into a raster image so you can do certain things to it, like apply filters or effects. If you try to do something to a vector image that requires simplifying (rasterizing) a layer, Elements generally asks you to do so via a dialog box. To rasterize the shape, click OK, or click the Simplify button in the Tool Options area. Just remember that, once you rasterize a shape, if you try to resize it, you won't get the clean, unpixelated results that you could when it was a vector image. If you need to resize a simplified shape, it's easiest to start over with a new shape—if that's feasible. (This kind of situation is yet another good reason to use layers!)

Also, before you simplified the layer, you could change the shape's color by clicking the Tool Options area's color box, and the active shape would automatically change to the new color. After you simplify the layer, the shape totally ignores what you do with the Tool Options settings. That's because simplifying affects the *whole* layer—everything on it gets simplified. So once you simplify a shape, you have to select it and change its color the way you would with an object in a photo.

The Graphics panel brings yet another wrinkle to the raster/vector situation: Smart Objects (page 517). The items in the Graphics panel (frames, backgrounds, and other doodads) act as vector objects, with the special additional quality that they may also seek out a particular place in the layer stack. Choose a background from this panel, for instance, and it knows to zip down and replace your former Background layer.

Rectangle and Rounded Rectangle

The Rectangle and Rounded Rectangle tools work pretty much the same way as the Custom Shape tool, and they're both really popular for creating web page buttons. To activate either tool, click the current shape tool in the Tools panel and then click the one you want in the Tool Options area, or press U repeatedly until one of their icons appears in the Tools panel.

On the left side of the Tool Options area, you see the same color box and layer-style button that appear for the other shape tools. In addition, you can click the Unconstrained menu to see the following settings:

- **Unconstrained**. Elements selects this option automatically unless you change it. It lets you draw a rectangle with whatever dimensions you want; how you drag determines the proportions.

- **Square**. To draw a square instead of a rectangle, select this option before you start, or just hold down the Shift key as you drag.

- **Fixed Size**. This setting makes Elements draw a shape that's exactly the size you specify. Just enter the dimensions you want in the boxes below this menu in inches, pixels, or centimeters.

- **Proportional**. Use this setting if you know the proportions you want the rectangle to have, but not the exact size. For example, if you select this option and then enter a width of 2 and a height of 1, then no matter where you drag, the shape will always be twice as long as it is high.

The Tool Options area also includes two checkboxes that help you further refine the rectangle.

- **From Center**. This setting lets you draw the shape from its center instead of from a corner. It's useful when you know where you want the shape to go but aren't sure how big it needs to be.

- **Snap**. This checkbox tells Elements to make sure that the edges of the rectangle fall exactly on the edge of a pixel to help create crisper-looking edges. It's available only for the Rectangle and Rounded Rectangle tools.

Most of the shape tools have similar options, though the Rounded Rectangle has one Tool Options setting of its own: *radius*, which is the amount (in pixels) that the corners are rounded off; a higher number means more rounding.

Ellipse

The Ellipse tool has the same Tool Options settings as the Rectangle tool. The only difference is that you can opt for a circle instead of a square. You can also draw a circle by pressing the Shift key while you drag with this tool.

Polygon and Star Tools

You can draw many kinds of regular polygons with these tools. Figure 12-24 explains the difference between them. With both tools, you use the Tool Options area's

Sides setting to control how many sides the shape has. And both these tools have a Smooth Corners checkbox, which you can turn on if you don't want sharp edges at the shape's corners.

The Star tool also has a couple options of its own:

- **Indent**. Enter a percentage here to set how much the sides should be indented.

- **Smooth Indents**. Turn this checkbox on if you don't want sharp interior angles on your star.

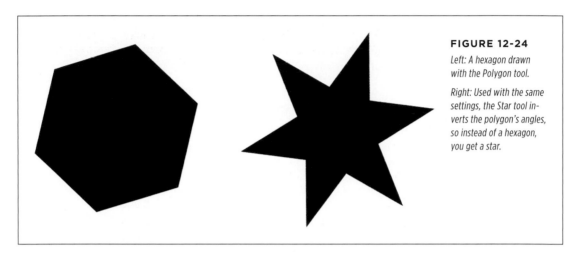

FIGURE 12-24

Left: A hexagon drawn with the Polygon tool.

Right: Used with the same settings, the Star tool inverts the polygon's angles, so instead of a hexagon, you get a star.

Line Tool

Not surprisingly, you use this tool to draw straight lines and arrows. Specify the width of the line in pixels in the Tool Options area. The "Arrow head" menu lets you choose whether Elements puts an arrowhead on the line at its beginning, end, or both. If you choose to add an arrowhead, these additional settings appear to help you control what it looks like:

- **W (Width) and L (Length)**. These settings determine how wide and long the arrowhead is. The unit of measurement here is the percentage of the line's width, so if you enter a number lower than 100, the arrowhead will be narrower than the line it's attached to. You can pick values between 10 and 5,000 percent. If your length setting is too low, you'll get a shape that looks more like a T than an arrow.

- **C (Concavity)**. Use this setting if you want Elements to indent the side of the arrowhead where it meets the line. This number determines the amount of curvature on the widest part of the arrowhead (see Figure 12-25). You can pick a number between –50 percent and +50 percent.

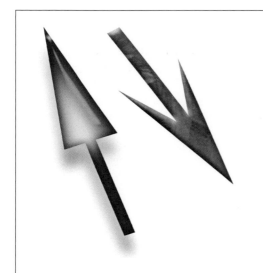

FIGURE 12-25

Two arrows drawn with the Line tool. (Both arrows have layer styles applied to them so they don't look flat. You'll learn more about layer styles in the next chapter.)

Left: An arrow with no concavity.

Right: An arrow with concavity set to +50 percent.

If you prefer fancier arrows, you'll find some in the Custom Shape tool's settings. In the Shape Picker's drop-down menu, choose the Arrows category (see page 423).

The Shape Selection Tool

The gray arrow icon you see in the Tool Options area when you have any of the shape tools active is the Shape Selection tool. This is a special kind of Move tool that works only on shapes that haven't been simplified yet (page 424), as explained in Figure 12-26.

NOTE You can always use the Move tool, even on shapes that haven't been simplified, where you could use the Shape Selection tool instead.

The Shape Selection tool works just like the Move tool: Drag a shape to move it, hold down Alt/Option while you drag to copy (instead of move) the original shape, drag the handles that appear around the shape to resize it, and so on. (Unfortunately, you can't align and distribute shapes with this tool the way you can with the Move tool. So if you need to line things up, use the regular Move tool instead.)

You can also use the Shape Selection tool to combine multiple shapes into one by clicking the Tool Options area's Combine icon. The Tool Options also include the same choices you have when using any of the shape tools: add, subtract, intersect, and exclude.

FIGURE 12-26

The Shape Selection tool gives you the same kind of bounding box as the Move tool, and it works the same way, but only on shapes that haven't been simplified.

When the Shape Selection tool is active, you can also apply transformations like skewing and rotating (page 387). The Transform settings appear in the Tool Options area when you start rotating or pulling at the shape to change it.

Once you simplify a shape's layer, you have to use the regular Move tool to move it around.

Drawing Outlines and Borders

If you've played around with the shape tools, you may have noticed that you can't draw shapes that are just outlines (that is, ones that aren't filled with color). No matter what you do, the shapes you draw are always solid. Even if you haven't ever touched a shape tool, you may be wondering how the heck to get a simple, plain-colored border around a photo.

The easiest way to create an outline is to make a selection using the Rectangular Marquee tool or another selection tool, and then select Edit→Stroke (Outline) Selection. The Stroke dialog box pops up so you can enter a width for the line in pixels and choose a color. You'll also see these settings:

• **Location** tells Elements where you want the line: around the inside edge of the selection, centered on the edge of the selection, or around the outside. (If you're bordering an entire photo, don't choose Outside; if you do, the

border won't show up because it'll be off the edge of the image.)

• **Mode** lets you choose a blend mode (page 411) for the outline and set its opacity. Using a mode can create a more subtle edge than a normal stroke does.

• **Preserve Transparency** ensures that any transparent areas in the active layer *stay* transparent.

When you're finished adjusting the dialog box's settings, click OK and then deselect (press Ctrl+D/⌘-D or just click someplace else in the image) to get rid of the marching ants, and you've got yourself an outlined shape.

Be sure to also check out some of the simple frame designs in the Graphics panel (page 526), which let you apply a border with just a few clicks.

■ The Cookie Cutter Tool

At first glance, you may think the Cookie Cutter is a pretty silly tool. But actually, it's so handy that you may use it all the time once you understand it. The Cookie Cutter creates the same shapes as the Custom Shape tool, but you use it to crop a photo to the shape you choose. Want a heart-shaped portrait of your sweetie? The Cookie Cutter is the tool for you. If you're a scrapbooker, just a couple of clicks can get you results that would take *ages* (and a bunch of special scissors) to create with paper.

If you're not into that sort of thing, don't go away, because hidden in Elements' built-in shapes library are some of the most sophisticated, artistic crop shapes around. You can use them to get the kinds of effects that people pay commercial artists big bucks to create—like abstract crops that give a photo a jagged or worn edge (great for contemporary effects). You can also combine the result with a stroked edge, as explained in the box on page 428, and maybe a layer style (page 461), too. Even without any additional frills, your photo's shape will be more interesting, as shown in Figure 12-27.

FIGURE 12-27

A quick drag with the Cookie Cutter tool is all it took to create the bottom graphic from the top photo.

If you want to create custom album or scrapbook pages, you can rotate or skew the crops before you commit them. (Page 387 explains how to rotate and skew images.)

TIP Elements also gives you a couple of other ways to create cutouts and fancy edge effects. If you're on a Windows PC and plan to print a cropped photo for use in a scrapbooking project, for example, check out the Picture Package feature (page 548); the frames there include some shape crops, and you can do everything right in the Organizer's Print dialog box, if those shapes work for you. (Despite the name, you can make a Picture Package with only one photo.) This doesn't work on Macs, though.

On both Macs and Windows computers, the Graphics panel's Frames section (page 526) includes a bunch of crops, ranging from simple shapes like stars to elaborate edges that make a photo look like a worn-out billboard.

And for an ultra-fancy effect, check out the Out of Bounds action in Guided Edit (page 460), which makes your subject look like it's stepping or flying out of the edges of the photo; the Picture Stack Guided Edit, which makes a photo look like it's made from many photos piled together; or the Puzzle Effect Guided Edit, which makes your photo look like a partly completed jigsaw puzzle. (There are also a few puzzle frames in the Graphics panel for a similar effect with less customization.)

You use the Cookie Cutter just like the Custom Shape tool, but it *cuts* a shape from a photo instead of drawing a shape:

1. **Activate the Cookie Cutter tool.**

   Click the Crop Tool in the Tools panel (it's at the upper left of the Modify section) and then choose the Cookie Cutter in the Tool Options, or press C.

2. **Select the shape you want your photo to be.**

   In the Tool Options area, choose a shape from the Shape Picker by clicking the black-and-white shape thumbnail. Use the drop-down menu at the top of the Shape Picker to select a specific category of shapes, or choose All Elements Shapes. You have access to all of Elements' custom shapes, but pay special attention to the Crop Shapes category.

3. **If necessary, adjust the other Tool Options settings.**

   You have the same shape-drawing options as for the Custom Shape tool (page 423), so you can set a fixed size or constrain proportions, if you want. Click the Unconstrained button to see your choices.

   You can also feather the shape's edges. Just drag the Feather slider, or click the number to the right of the slider and then enter an amount (in pixels). See page 152 for more about feathering.

   Turn on the Crop checkbox to crop the edges of your photo so they're just large enough to contain the shape.

4. **Drag in your photo.**

   Elements puts a mask over the photo, and you see only the area that will still be there once you crop, surrounded by transparency. As you drag, you see a pop-up displaying the size of the cropped area in inches or whatever measurement you've chosen in Elements' Units & Rulers preferences (the box on page 87 explains how to change this unit). This pop-up is new in Elements 13.

5. **If necessary, adjust the crop.**

   You can reposition the shape mask or drag its corners to resize it. Although the cropped areas disappear, they'll reappear as you reposition the mask if you move it so that they're included again.

   Once you've created the shape but before you've committed it (which you'll do in the next step), you'll see the Transform options (page 387) in the Tool Options area, which means that you can skew or distort the shape, if you want. You can drag the mask around to reposition it, or Shift-drag a corner to resize it without altering its proportions. It may take a little maneuvering to get exactly the parts of the photo you want inside the shape.

6. **When you've got things lined up just right, click the Commit button (the green checkmark) below the shape or press Enter/Return.**

   If you don't like the results, click the Cancel button (the red circle) or press Esc instead.

   Once you've committed your crop, you can use Ctrl+Z/⌘-Z to undo it and try something else.

TIP The Cookie Cutter tool replaces the areas it removes with transparency. If the transparency checkerboard makes it too hard for you to get a clear look at what you've done, temporarily add a white or colored Fill layer beneath the cropped layer. Then when you're happy with the crop, simply delete the extra layer.

Adding Fun and Useful Effects

There's a common saying among artistic types who use software in their studios: *Tools don't equal talent*. And it's true: No computer program is going to turn a klutz into a Klimt. But Elements has some special tools—*filters, actions,* and *layer styles*—that can sure help you fool a lot of people. It's amazing what a difference these features can make in the appearance of an image with only a couple of clicks.

Filters are a jaw-droppingly easy way to change how photos look. You can use certain filters for enhancing and correcting images, but Elements also gives you a bunch of other filters that are great for unleashing all your artistic impulses, as shown in Figure 13-1.

Most filters have settings that let you control how they change your photo. Elements comes with more than *100* different filters, so there isn't room in this chapter to cover each one individually, but you'll learn the basics of applying filters and get in-depth coverage of some of the ones you're most likely to use.

Actions, on the other hand, are like little macros or scripts designed to make elaborate changes to your image, such as creating a three-dimensional frame around it or making it look like a pencil sketch or an oil pastel. One of the most popular features in recent versions of Elements is the Actions panel, which makes it easy to add and use actions. (You can find a few actions in the Effects panel, too, which are also easy to apply—you just double-click a button—but you can't tweak their settings as easily as you can with filters, since effects are programmed to make specific changes.)

> **NOTE** Full-featured Photoshop lets you record and save your own actions and install actions created by others. You can use certain Photoshop actions in Elements, but you can't *create* actions in Elements.

FIGURE 13-1

Filters let you add all sorts of artistic effects to photos. Here you see two plain photos on the left, and two examples of how you can transform them with filters on the right. In both cases, several filters were applied to build up the effect.

Top: These images show how you can make a photo resemble a colored-steel engraving.

Bottom: These images show how you can create a watercolor look.

If you want to try this yourself, you can find the original photos—rooftops.jpg and bauhinia.jpg—on this book's Missing CD page at www.missingmanuals.com/cds.

Elements also gives you some spiffy special effects in Guided Edit. If you've used older versions of Elements for a while, you may think Guided Edit is just for beginners, but now there's plenty there even if you're an old pro. You can use it to create elaborate effects like the popular high-key and low-key looks for portraits, make an image look like it's made from a pile of separate photos, make a photo of a full-sized object or landscape look like a photo of a miniature version, or make a pop-art image à la Warhol. Page 458 has the lowdown.

Layer styles change the appearance of only one layer of an image. They're great for creating impressive-looking text, but you also can apply them to objects and shapes. And most layer styles include settings you can modify.

If you want to get really creative, you can combine filters, actions, and layer styles in the same image. You may end up spending hours trying different groupings, because it's addicting to watch the often-unpredictable results you get when mixing them up.

The last section of this chapter focuses on *gradients*. A gradient is a rainbow-like range of color that you can use to color in an object or background. You can also use gradients and *gradient maps*—gradients that are distributed according to the brightness values in a photo—to do precise retouching.

Using Filters

Filters let you change the look of photos in complex ways, but applying them is as easy as double-clicking. Elements gives you tons of filters, grouped into categories to help you choose one that does what you want. This section offers a quick tour through these categories and some info about using a few of the most popular filters.

Applying Filters

Elements lets you apply filters from three different places: the Filter menu, the Effects panel, and the Filter Gallery, a great feature that helps you get an idea of how your photo will look when you apply the artistic filters. (The Filter menu is the only place where you can see *every* filter.)

Elements' filters do the same thing no matter which way you apply them. The following sections explain your options in detail.

TIP You can easily apply the same filter repeatedly: Press Ctrl+F/⌘-F and Elements applies the last filter you used with whatever settings you last used. The top item in the Filter menu also lists your last-used filter; selecting its name there has the same effect as the keyboard shortcut.

■ THE FILTER MENU

In the Filter menu, you choose a filter from the list by category and then by name. The menu groups your filters into categories; they're listed on page 440. There's a divider below the bottom category (Other). When you first install Elements, the Digimarc filter is the only filter below this line, but other filters you download or purchase will appear here, too.

When you choose a filter from this menu, one of three things happens:

- **Elements applies the filter**. This happens if the filter's name *doesn't* have an ellipsis (...) after it. Just look at the result in your photo, and if you don't like its effect, press Ctrl+Z/⌘-Z to undo it. If you do like it, you're done.

- **Elements opens a dialog box**. In the Filter menu, filters that have adjustable settings have an ellipsis (...) after their names. When you select one of these filters (mostly corrective ones like Dust & Scratches), Elements opens a dialog box so you can tweak their settings. Adjust the settings while watching the dialog box's preview area, and then click OK.

- **Elements opens the Filter Gallery**. Some of the more artistic, adjustable filters call up the Filter Gallery so you can see a large preview of what you're doing and rearrange the order of multiple filters before applying them. Page 437 explains how to use this feature.

Regardless of how you apply a filter, if you're not happy with its effect, you can undo it by pressing Ctrl+Z/⌘-Z. If you like it, just save your image.

> **TIP** Since you can't undo filters after you've closed your image, many people apply them to duplicate layers. Press Ctrl+J/⌘-J to duplicate the active layer.

■ EFFECTS PANEL

If you're more comfortable with visual clues when choosing a filter, you can find most filters in the Effects panel (Figure 13-2), which, logically enough, is also where you apply effects (page 456).

FIGURE 13-2

The Effects panel shows you what the filters look like when applied to this picture of a tree.

Click the panel's Filters tab, and then, from the drop-down menu (the one that says "Artistic" here), choose a category. Put your cursor over a filter's thumbnail (without clicking) to see a tooltip of the filter's name. If you know what you want a filter to do but don't know what it's called, scrolling through these thumbnail images can help you find the one you want.

To apply a filter from this panel, double-click the appropriate thumbnail or drag the filter's thumbnail from the panel onto your image.

To call up the Effects panel, go to Window→Effects or click the Effects button at the bottom right of your screen, and then click the Filters tab (if it's not already selected). To find a filter, select a category from the panel's drop-down menu or choose Show All. The categories are the same as the ones in the Filter menu, except that the Adjustments category is available only through the Filter menu, and the Sharpen category appears in the panel but *not* the Filter menu. To apply a filter from the panel, double-click its thumbnail or drag its thumbnail onto your image.

One drawback to applying filters from this panel is that you don't get a chance to adjust their settings. Even if the filter is one that has a dialog box or settings in the Filter Gallery, you won't see it here—Elements just applies the filter to your photo using the filter's current settings.

■ THE FILTER GALLERY

The Filter Gallery (Figure 13-3) takes things one step further by showing you a preview of what a filter looks like when applied to *your* image. It gives you a large preview window, sailboat thumbnails so you can tell what each filter does, and (most importantly) it lets you apply filters as if they were layers: You can stack them up and change the order in which Elements applies them to the image.

Some filters automatically open the Filter Gallery when you choose them from the Filter menu or Effects panel, though you can also call up the Gallery without first choosing a filter by going to Filter→Filter Gallery. The biggest drawback to the Gallery is that you can't apply *every* Elements filter from it—only some of the ones with adjustable settings.

Image Preview

Click to Collapse/Expand Thumbnail Area

Settings for Current Filter

Adjust Preview

Filter Thumbnails

Visibility

Create New Effect Layer

Active Layer

Delete Layer

FIGURE 13-3

Elements' Filter Gallery.

For an even larger preview area, click the triangle button in the window's upper right (labeled) to collapse the thumbnail area and regain that section for preview space.

To resize the Filter Gallery window, just drag one of its corners.

Changing the order of filters can make a big impact on how they affect images. For example, you get very different results if you apply Ink Outlines *after* the Sprayed Strokes filter rather than vice versa. The Gallery makes it easy to play around and see which order gives you the look you want. This layer-like behavior of the filters in the Gallery is only for previewing, though—your document doesn't include any new layers after you apply the filter(s).

The Gallery is more for artistic filters than for corrective ones. You can't apply filters in the Adjustments and Noise categories from here, for instance. All the Gallery filters are in the artistic, brushstroke, distort, sketch, stylize, and texture categories. (The next section includes an overview of all the filter categories.)

The Filter Gallery window is divided into three panes. On the left is a preview of what your image will look like when you apply the filter(s). The center pane holds thumbnails of the different filters, and the right side contains the settings for the current filter. Your *filter layers* (which, technically, Adobe calls "Effects layers") are at the bottom of the settings pane, where you can see what filters you've applied, add or subtract filters, and change their order.

> **NOTE** As noted above, you don't create any new, permanent layers when you use the Filter Gallery. Filter layers work something like regular layers (see Chapter 6), but they're just what you might call "working layers": They're only to help you figure out which order to apply filters in; they don't actually become new layers in your image. In other words, you have separate filter layers only until you click OK in the Filter Gallery; then all your chosen filters get applied to the image in the order you specified. You can't apply various filters via the Filter Gallery, close your photo, come back later, and still see the filters as individual, changeable layers in the Gallery. And most important, the filters become part of the regular layer to which you apply them.
>
> Also, if you've used a recent version of the full-featured Photoshop, be aware that Elements doesn't create editable smart filters the way Photoshop does—it handles filters the way *early* versions of Photoshop (CS2 and below) did. Keep this in mind if you're trying to do something based on instructions written for Photoshop (directions you found online, say).

In addition to letting you adjust the settings for a given filter, the Filter Gallery lets you perform a few other tricks:

- **Adjust your view of the image**. In the Gallery's lower-left corner, click the percentage or the up/down triangles (you see only one triangle in Windows) next to it to bring up a list of preset views to choose from. You can also click the + and – buttons to zoom in or out. Easier still, use the Ctrl-+/⌘-+ and Ctrl- –/⌘-– keyboard shortcuts to zoom in and out, respectively.

- **Choose a new filter**. Click a filter's thumbnail once, and Elements displays that filter's settings and updates the image preview to reflect how your image would look with that filter applied—usually. (See the box on page 439 for details.)

- **Add a new filter layer**. Each time you click the New Filter Layer icon (see Figure 13-4), Elements adds another filter layer.

Filter Performance Hints

If Elements could speak and you asked it about filters and effects, it would say, "Easy for *you*." Although you don't have to do much to use these features, the program has a huge amount of work to do. Elements is pretty fast, but if your computer is slow or memory-challenged, it can take a long time to apply filters or update the image preview. (Filters that have their own dialog boxes—as opposed to the Filter Gallery—show their progress by displaying a flashing line under the size percentage below the preview area.)

You can speed things up by applying filters to a selection for previewing. Simply select part of your image before applying a filter, and Elements applies it to just that area. Here are a few other filter-related tips worth remembering:

- Filters don't do anything if they don't have pixels to work on, so be sure you're targeting a layer with something in it, not an Adjustment layer.

- If you apply a filter to a selection, you'll usually want to feather (page 152) or refine (page 156) the selection's edges to help them blend into the rest of the image.

- In the Filter Gallery or in any filter dialog box, Alt-click/Option-click the Cancel button to turn it into a Reset button. Clicking Cancel closes the window, while clicking Reset lets you start over without having to call up the filter again.

- If filters are grayed out in the Filter menu, check to be sure you're not in 16-bit mode (page 288) or in grayscale, bitmap, or indexed color mode (all explained on page 41).

FIGURE 13-4

If you've used layers before (see Chapter 6), these circled icons should look familiar. In the Filter Gallery, the one on the left adds a new filter layer to your image instead of a regular layer. Click the trashcan icon to delete a filter layer.

The eye icons next to each filter layer turn visibility on and off just as they do in the Layers panel. Remember, filter layers don't show up as real layers in the Layers panel—only in the Filter Gallery.

- **Change the position of filter layers**. Drag them up and down in the stack shown in Figure 13-4 to change the order in which Elements will apply them to your image.

- **Hide filter layers**. Click the eye icon next to a filter layer in the filter-layer panel to turn off its visibility, as in the regular Layers panel. If a filter layer is hidden, you won't see its effect after you click OK to apply the filters.

- **Delete filter layers**. Select any filter layer by clicking it, and then click the trashcan icon to delete it.

- **Change a filter layer's content**. You can change what kind of filter is in a particular layer. For instance, if you applied several filters and wish you could change the Smudge Stick filter to the Glass filter, you don't have to delete the Smudge Stick layer; just select it and then click the Glass filter's thumbnail in the middle pane to change that layer's contents.

Filter Categories

Elements divides filters into categories to help you track down the one you want. Some categories, like Distort, contain filters that vary hugely in what they do to photos. Other categories, like Brush Strokes, contain filters that are obviously related to one another. Here's a breakdown of the categories:

- **Correct Camera Distortion**. This isn't actually a category, but rather a single filter that lets you correct perspective distortion (think tall buildings) as well as vignetting (shadows) caused by your camera's lens. It's explained in detail on page 382.

- **Adjustments**. These filters apply photographic, stylistic, and artistic changes to photos. Most of them are explained on page 146; the Photo Filters are covered on page 299.

- **Artistic**. This huge group of filters can do everything from giving a photo a cut-from-paper look (Cutout) to making it resemble a quick sketch (Rough Pastels). You generally get the best results with these filters by using several of them or applying the same one several times.

- **Blur**. These filters let you soften focus and add artistic effects. They're explained on page 443.

- **Brush Strokes**. The filters in this category apply brushstroke effects and create a hand-painted look.

- **Distort**. These filters warp images in a variety of ways. The Liquify filter (page 493) is the most powerful.

- **Noise**. Use these filters to add or remove grain. They're explained on page 442.

- **Pixelate**. These filters break up an image in different ways, making it show the dot pattern of a magazine or newspaper's printed image (Halftone), or giving it the fragmented look you see on television when a show conceals someone's identity (Mosaic).

> **NOTE** The Color Halftone filter makes images look like they're made of many dots of color, like a magazine photo or other printed illustration, or comic-style pop art. But it's not the same as *true* halftone screening, which Elements can't do. So if the print shop you're working with needs a halftone, you need to either use the full-featured Photoshop or ask the printer to create the halftone for you.

- **Render**. This group includes a diverse bunch of filters that let you do things like create a lens flare effect and make an image look like fibers or clouds.

- **Sharpen**. This category, which contains only the Unsharp Mask filter (page 260), appears in the Effects panel but not in the Filter menu. (The sharpening commands are in the Enhance menu instead.)

- **Sketch**. These filters can make a photo look like it was drawn with charcoal, chalk, crayon, or some other material, or like it was embossed in wet plaster, photocopied, or created with a rubber stamp.

> **TIP** If you want to make your photos look like illustrations, check out the Comic and Graphic Novel filters. You can create some really interesting graphics by using these filters on a duplicate layer and then playing around with the blend mode, as shown in Figure 13-5. These filters aren't included in the Filter Gallery or the Effects panel, just the Filters menu (they're in the Sketch category), and they're very processor-intensive. Even a fast, new computer with plenty of memory may take quite a while to apply these filters, but the end result is worth it.

FIGURE 13-5

Here's an example of how you can use the Comic and Graphic Novel filters to jazz up photos.

Top: A boring shot of an old cabin.

Bottom left: The same photo with the Comic filter's Sunny Day setting applied to a duplicate layer in Vivid Light blend mode.

Bottom right: This time the duplicate layer got the Graphic Novel filter's Twisted Plot setting on a layer in Overlay blend mode.

- **Stylize**. These filters create special effects by increasing the contrast in a photo and displacing pixels. They can make a photo look radioactive, like the objects in it are moving quickly, or reduce it to outlines.

- **Texture**. These filters change the surface of a photo to look like it was made from another material. Use them to create a cracked finish, a stained-glass look, or a mosaic effect.

- **Other**. This is a group of technical, customizable filters. The High-Pass filter is explained on page 267. You can use Offset to shift an image or a layer a bit, or to position tiled image layers.

- **Digimarc**. Digimarc is a company that lets subscribers enter their contact info into a database so that anyone who gets one of their photos can find out who holds the copyright. You can use this filter to check for Digimarc watermarks in photos.

You can find a number of filter plug-ins online, ranging from free to very expensive; page 586 suggests some places to look. When you install new filters, they appear at the bottom of the Filter menu.

NOTE Filters are platform specific, which means you can't use plug-ins written for the Windows version of Elements if you're on a Mac and vice versa. And for Elements 13, plug-ins need to be compatible with 64-bit programs. If you aren't sure about whether a plug-in will work with your version of Elements, ask its developer.

Practical Uses for Filters

Filters aren't only for creating fancy artistic effects. They're also great for fixing common image problems. This section covers how to use some of Elements' most popular and useful filters to correct photos and create a few special effects. For instance, you'll learn how to modify graininess to create an aged effect or to smooth out a repair job. And you'll find out how to blur photos to create a soft-focus effect or make objects look like they're moving.

■ REMOVING NOISE: GETTING RID OF GRAININESS

Noise—undesired graininess in an image—is a big problem with many digital cameras, especially ones that have small sensors and high megapixel counts, like most recent point-and-shoot models. It's rare to find a fixed-lens camera with more than 5 megapixels that doesn't have some trouble with noise, especially in underexposed areas.

If you shoot using the raw format, you can correct a fair amount of noise right in the Raw Converter (page 272). But the Converter may give you unpredictable results if you use it on JPEGs. And even raw files may need further noise reduction once you've converted and then edited them.

Elements' Reduce Noise filter is (not surprisingly) designed to help get rid of noise. To run this filter, go to Filter→Noise→Reduce Noise, and Elements opens a dialog box with a preview area on the left and settings on the right. To apply the filter, first use the controls below the preview to set the zoom level to 100 percent or higher.

(You need to see the individual pixels in the photo so you can tell how the filter is changing them as you tweak its settings.) Then adjust the filter's three sliders:

- **Strength**. This controls the overall impact of the filter, which reduces the same kind of noise as the Luminance Smoothing setting in the Raw Converter (page 288). The higher this setting, the greater the risk of softening your photo.

- **Preserve Details**. Using noise reduction can soften a photo and make it look blurry. This setting tells Elements how much care to take to preserve details.

- **Reduce Color Noise**. This control adjusts uneven color distribution in the image. You can set this slider pretty high without harming your photo.

The Remove JPEG Artifact checkbox tells Elements to minimize *JPEG artifacts*—the uneven areas of color caused by JPEG compression (see page 73). A mottled pattern in what should be a clear blue sky is a classic example of JPEG artifacting. Turn on this checkbox to help smooth things out.

For each setting, move the slider right if you want it to have more of an impact or left if you want less. Watch the effect in the preview area to see the changes. (You may notice a little lag time before the preview updates.) When you like what you see, click OK to apply the filter.

The Reduce Noise filter does an OK job on areas with a small amount of noise, like the sky in many JPEG photos, but it's not one of Elements' best tools. If your camera has major noise problems, you may need special noise-reduction software to tackle it. Some of the most popular programs are Neat Image (*www.neatimage.com*), Topaz (*www.topazlabs.com*), and Noiseware (*www.imagenomic.com*), which all have demo versions you can download to try them out. If you do a Google search for "noise reduction software," you'll get a variety of other options as well, including several free programs.

■ ADDING NOISE: SMOOTHING OUT REPAIR JOBS

Elements also gives you a filter for *creating* noise. Why do that when most of the time you try to get rid of noise? One reason is when you're trying to age a photo: To make it look like it came from an old newspaper, for instance, you'd add some noise.

Another common use for noise is to help make repaired spots blend in with the rest of an image. If you've altered part of a photo in Elements, especially by painting on it, odds are good that the repaired area looks perfectly smooth. That's great if the rest of the photo is noise free, but if the photo is a little grainy, that smooth patch will stand out like a sore thumb. Adding a bit of noise makes it blend in better, as shown in Figure 13-6. Also, if you see color banding when you print, adding a little noise to the photo may help fix that.

FIGURE 13-6

Top: If you use the Average Blur filter on a repair in this noisy photo, the blended area stands out, making the repair obvious.

Bottom: Introducing some noise makes the change much less noticeable.

To add noise to a photo, start by selecting the area you want to make noisier. (Using a duplicate layer [Ctrl+J/⌘-J] for the noise is a good idea, since you can always undo changes if they're on their own layer.) Then, here's what you do:

1. **Call up the Add Noise filter.**

   Go to Filter→Noise→Add Noise to bring up the filter's dialog box.

2. **Adjust the filter's settings.**

   The settings are explained after this list. Use the dialog box's preview area to check how the changes are affecting your photo.

3. **When you're satisfied, click OK.**

The Add Noise dialog box has three settings:

- **Amount** controls how heavy the noise will be. Drag the slider right for more noise or left for less. You can also type in a number; a higher percentage means more noise.

- **Distribution** controls how Elements distributes the noise in the image. The Uniform option does just what you'd expect—distributes the noise the same all over. Gaussian produces a more speckled effect. If you're adding noise to duplicate existing noise in a grainy photo, you probably want Gaussian distribution. For an old-newspaper-photo look, try Uniform.

- **Monochromatic** limits you to grayscale noise. Take a look at the bottom-left image in Figure 13-7, and notice how many more colors you can see in the noise than in the solid red of the original (top). The bottom-left apple's noise was applied with the Monochromatic setting turned off.

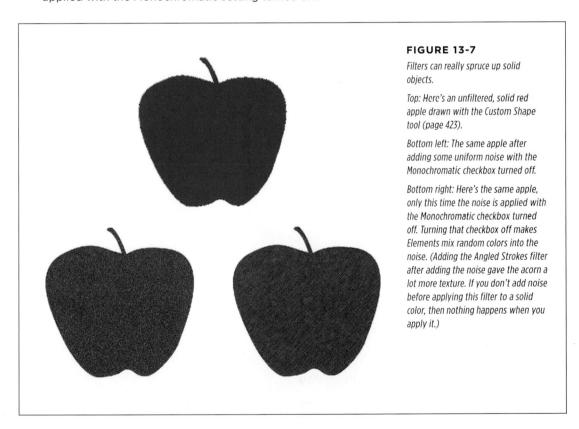

FIGURE 13-7

Filters can really spruce up solid objects.

Top: Here's an unfiltered, solid red apple drawn with the Custom Shape tool (page 423).

Bottom left: The same apple after adding some uniform noise with the Monochromatic checkbox turned off.

Bottom right: Here's the same apple, only this time the noise is applied with the Monochromatic checkbox turned off. Turning that checkbox off makes Elements mix random colors into the noise. (Adding the Angled Strokes filter after adding the noise gave the acorn a lot more texture. If you don't add noise before applying this filter to a solid color, then nothing happens when you apply it.)

Noise can also help when you want to apply special effects to blocks of solid color, as shown in Figure 13-7, bottom right. If you try to apply the Angled Strokes filter to a solid color, for example, you don't see the strokes; adding noise first gives the filter something to work on. To make an abstract background for a project, you can create a blank file, add noise, and then run various filters on it.

■ GAUSSIAN BLUR: DRAWING ATTENTION TO AN OBJECT

Probably the most frequently used of the Blur filters, Gaussian Blur (Filter→ Blur→Gaussian Blur) lets you control how much an image is blurred. Besides using it on large areas, like the background in Figure 13-8, bottom, you can apply this filter at a very low setting to soften lines—useful when you're going for a sketched effect. To try out the different blurs, download *yellowbeak.jpg* from this book's Missing CD page at *www.missingmanuals.com/cds*.

FIGURE 13-8

Top: This little guy felt hidden enough to let the camera get pretty close, and he was almost right: It's hard to focus on him with all the stuff in the background. Blurring the background will center the focus on the bird rather than the distracting details.

Bottom: Applying the Gaussian Blur filter to the background makes the bird the clear focal point. To do this, select the bird, and then choose Select→Inverse before applying the blur.

When using the Gaussian Blur filter, you have to set its *radius*, which controls how much the filter blurs things; a higher radius produces more blurring. Use the filter's preview window to see what you're doing.

Gaussian blur is the classic way to isolate a subject from its background, but Elements gives you an even better way to artistically blur a background: the Lens Blur filter, described next.

■ LENS BLUR: CREATING DEPTH OF FIELD

If you have a point-and-shoot camera, you know how hard it is to get your subject sharp and the background artistically blurred the way you can with larger DSLR (digital single-lens reflex) cameras. To create that effect after the fact, you could add a Gaussian blur as explained in the previous section, but the Gaussian Blur filter applies the exact same blur over the whole area you apply it to. If you look at a photo taken with a DSLR and a good lens, you'll notice that the amount of blurring (called the *bokeh* by those in the know) varies a bit. For example, the far distance is completely blurred, while you may still be able to distinguish objects immediately in front of and behind the focus area.

Elements' Lens Blur filter helps to simulate a real bokeh a little better than a simple Gaussian Blur can. Using the Lens Blur filter is tricky, but with a little fiddling you can often get results that are closer to what you could do with a DSLR camera than you can get with Gaussian Blur. To get the best results, though, you need to be comfortable with layer masking (page 210) and gradients (page 465). If you're just starting out with Elements, try the Depth Of Field effect in Guided Edit's Photo Effects category; it's not in the same class as this filter, but the Lens Blur filter isn't for the faint of heart.

If you just go straight to the Lens Blur filter without doing anything to prepare your image for it, Elements blurs your entire image, so first you need to figure out the area you want to keep in focus. (If your goal is to create a soft-focus effect, then use a tiny amount of Lens Blur on the whole photo.) The simplest way is to select what you want to keep in focus, go to Select→Inverse to select everything *but* that area, and then apply the Lens Blur filter. But if you do that, you'll just have a uniform blur all over, without the graduated effect you'd get in a fancy camera. To achieve that effect, here's what you need to do:

1. **Duplicate the layer you want to apply the blur to.**

   Go to Layer→Duplicate or press Ctrl+J/⌘-J.

2. **On the new layer, select the area you want to keep in focus, and then delete it.**

   Use the selection tool(s) of your choice, and then press Backspace/Delete to remove the selected area. By doing this, the original, sharp version of your subject will show through the blurred layer in the final image.

   At this point, you *could* go straight to the Lens Blur window (step 5), but if you want a really polished effect, you've still got a little more work to do.

3. **Create a layer mask for the new layer.**

   Make sure the new layer is active, and then click the Add Layer Mask icon in the Layers panel (the circle within a square).

4. **Fill the mask with a gradient.**

   Check to be sure the layer mask is active by clicking its icon in the Layers panel, press G to activate the Gradient tool (page 465), and then choose a black-and-white gradient. Next, drag in the image so that the area you want in focus is in the black part of the gradient. (If you mess up, as long as the area you want is in a completely white area, you may be able to fix it with the Invert button as explained in the list of settings below.) You can turn off your Background layer to see if you've got the right area masked out. Once you've got the gradient set up to your liking, disable the layer mask by right-clicking/Control-clicking its thumbnail in the Layers panel and choosing Disable Layer Mask. Then click the left thumbnail for the layer you applied the mask to (the duplicate layer you created in step 1) to make sure it's active.

5. **Call up the Lens Blur filter's window.**

   Go to Filter→Blur→Lens Blur. Your whole image now looks blurry despite your masking, but you'll fix that shortly.

6. **Adjust the filter's settings.**

   There are a lot of them, and they're explained after this list. For now, the most important one is the Source setting in the window's Depth Map section. In the drop-down menu there, choose Layer Mask to get your subject back in focus. Now you can adjust the other settings.

7. **When you're happy with what you see, click OK.**

   You can turn the Background layer back on now, if you like, especially if you want to lower the opacity of the blur layer to reduce its effect. Figure 13-9 gives you a sense of what this filter can do.

This filter's many settings can be a bit intimidating, but you really don't need to understand what many of their names mean. Just move the sliders till you like what you see. Here's what each section of the Lens Blur window does:

- **Preview**. Use the checkbox to toggle the preview off and on for a better look at how you're changing the photo. This filter uses plenty of processing power, so normally you'll want to leave the radio buttons here set to Faster while you're working, and then switch to More Accurate for a last check when you think you're done moving the window's sliders.

FIGURE 13-9

Here's the bird from Figure 13-8 with the Lens Blur filter applied instead of a Gaussian Blur.

In this instance, a radial blur was applied to help blur out the foreground as well as the background area. You can see that it would be a good idea to go back and edit the layer mask so that more of the deck is affected by the blur, but this gives you a rough idea of how it works.

- **Depth Map**. This is where you tell Elements what to use as the source point for the blur. You can choose None (everything's blurred), Transparency, or Layer Mask. The Blur Focal Distance slider is probably the most important setting in this window, because it tells the filter where to center the in-focus part of the photo. Remember, your layer mask is in shades of black and white. You can use the Blur Focal Distance slider to tell Elements which part of the masked area should be in focus. Black is 0 and white is 255, so if you chose 100, for example, you'd be selecting an area covered by the medium-gray part of the mask. It's often easier just to click in the preview area to tell Elements where you want the most focused part to be; when you do that, the focus shifts to the spot you clicked. The Invert checkbox swaps the effect so that what was in focus becomes blurred, and what was blurred becomes focused.

- **Iris**. This section may seem a bit confusing at first if you've never paid much attention to how a camera's lens operates. And, really, the most important setting here is the Radius slider, which sets the maximum amount of blur in the image. So unless you know what you're doing, just focus on the Radius slider and ignore the other settings in this section (leave them at their original settings). But, if you're interested, here's what they do:

Think of a camera lens as working something like an eye. The iris area of an eye controls the size and (in some animals) the shape of the pupil. In the same way, the aperture of your camera is controlled by a mechanism also called an iris (*iris diaphragm*, actually). The overlapping blades that open and close so that light can reach the camera's sensor may be in many different patterns. This setting gives you some choice in just what kind of iris you want Elements to simulate. The Shape menu lets you choose what shape the iris should be. The Radius slider sets the maximum amount of blur in the image, Blade Curvature determines how round the iris is, and Rotation controls how much the iris is rotated, since an iris is rarely a perfect circle, because of the blade configuration. Think of the iris in a cat's eye in bright light where the pupil is more like a slit than a circle—Rotation would tell Elements how much to rotate that slit from perpendicular.

- **Specular Highlights**. These settings sound awfully complicated, but they're actually pretty simple. If you look at photos with a good bokeh, there tends to be a certain amount of *light bloom*—a kind of overbrightness in the very bright highlights. (If you look back at Figure 13-9, you can see examples on the deck and in a couple of the leaves.) To mimic that, use the Brightness slider to determine how bright your out-of-focus highlights are, and the Threshold slider to determine how bright pixels must be in order for them to be affected by the Brightness slider.

- **Noise**. The Lens Blur filter creates a perfectly smooth effect wherever you apply it. In order to make the blurred area match the rest of your image, you'll probably want to add a little bit of noise back into the filtered area. The controls in this section are the same as those for the Add Noise filter you read about on page 443.

While it's possible to get a nice blur with this filter, it's still not going to make a shot from your cellphone fool people into thinking you were using a DSLR with a top-quality lens. So don't feel bad if you prefer the simplicity of using the Gaussian Blur filter.

NOTE In addition to all the blurs discussed here, Elements gives you three other ways to blur photos, all found in Guided Edit→Photo Effects. The first is the Zoom Burst Effect, which is something like a radial blur (see below) with the selected area kept in focus. Adobe describes the effect as similar to what you'd get by zooming your lens with the shutter open. (If you're familiar with the effects you can create in-camera by using a Lensbaby lens, this is very similar.) You may want to give this one a try before using the Radial Blur filter, described next. Another is the Orton Effect, named after the photographer who popularized this otherworldly, dreamy effect; if you've looked at any wedding photos recently, you'll recognize it. The third is the Tilt-Shift effect, which uses blurs to make your photos of full-sized objects look like pictures of miniatures.

■ RADIAL BLUR: PRODUCING A SENSE OF MOTION

As you can see in Figure 13-10, the Radial Blur filter creates a sense of motion. It has two styles: Zoom, which is designed to create the effect of a camera zooming in, and Spin, which produces a circular effect around a center point you designate, as in Figure 13-10.

FIGURE 13-10

A Radial Blur applied in Spin mode.

As you can see, this filter can produce an almost vertiginous sense of motion. If you don't want to give people motion sickness, go easy on the Amount setting. A setting of 5 was used here, but unless you're looking for a psychedelic '60s effect, 1 or 2 is usually plenty.

> **TIP** Before using the Radial Blur filter, check out the Zoom Burst Effect in Guided Edit→Photo Effects. It may be just what you want.

The Radial Blur dialog box looks complicated, but it's really not. (Call it up by going to Filter→Blur→Radial Blur.) Unfortunately, Elements doesn't give you a preview with this filter because applying it requires so much processing power. But the dialog box gives you a choice between Draft, Good, and Best quality for the final results. You can choose Draft and then click OK for a quick look at roughly what you'll get. Then undo it and choose Good for the final version. (Good and Best aren't very different except on large images, so don't feel you have to choose Best for the final version. However, with a reasonably up-to-date computer, you don't need to bother with Draft because your machine can whip up a final version a lot faster than computers could when this filter was first created.)

After choosing a blur method (Zoom or Spin), adjust the Amount slider, which controls how intense the blur will be. Next, click in the Blur Center box to tell Elements where you want the blur centered, as shown in Figure 13-11. Click OK when you're finished, and Elements blurs your image.

FIGURE 13-11

The Blur Center box lets you pick a center point for the Radial Blur filter's effect. Drag the ripple drawing inside the box in any direction.

Here, the center point was moved just to the left and down from its original position in the center of the box.

■ COLOR CORRECTING WITH THE AVERAGE BLUR FILTER

If you've already given the Average Blur filter a whirl, you may be wondering what on earth the folks at Adobe were thinking when they created it. If you use it on a whole photo, the image disappears under a monochromatic soup, something like what you'd get by pureeing all the colors in the photo together.

Oddly enough, this effect makes this filter a great tool for getting rid of color casts (page 250). You can use the Average Blur filter to create a sort of custom Photo Filter (page 299) toned specially for the image you use it on. The secret is using blend modes (page 411). Here's how:

1. **Open an image and make a duplicate of your image layer.**

   Press Ctrl+J/⌘-J or go to Layer→Duplicate Layer.

2. **Apply the Average Blur filter.**

   Make sure the duplicate layer is active (click it in the Layers panel), and then go to Filter→Blur→Average. Your photo disappears under a layer of (probably) unpleasing solid color, but you'll fix that in the next step.

3. **Change the blur layer's blend mode.**

   At the top of the Layers panel, set the unlabeled drop-down menu to Color. Already, things are starting to look better.

4. **Invert the blur layer.**

   Press Ctrl+I/⌘-I to invert the layer's colors.

5. **Reduce the blur layer's opacity and do any other necessary tweaking.**

   Lower the Layers panel's Opacity setting to 50 percent or so. By now, the color should look right—no more color cast. Tweak if necessary, and then save your work.

TIP If you find that, no matter how you adjust the blur layer's Opacity setting, the photo still looks a little flat, you may want to add a Hue/Saturation Adjustment layer (page 218).

The Average Blur filter is a particularly good way to color-correct underwater photos, where it's hard to get a realistic white balance using your camera's built-in settings.

■ IMPROVING SKIN TEXTURE WITH SURFACE BLUR

The Surface Blur filter is yet another way to blur images. At this point you may be thinking that you already have enough ways to eliminate details in your photos, but Surface Blur is actually really handy, especially on pictures of people. This filter is smart enough to avoid blurring details and areas of high contrast, which makes it great for fixing skin. If you want to eliminate pores, for instance, or reduce the visibility of freckles, reach for this filter. It's simple to use, too:

1. **Open an image and make a duplicate layer.**

   Press Ctrl+J/⌘-J or go to Layer→Duplicate Layer.

TIP For best results, start by selecting the area you want to blur (see Chapter 5 for help with selections). Then make your duplicate layer from the selection so you can keep the details in the areas you *aren't* trying to fix. For example, select only the skin of your subject's face, leaving out his mouth and eyes so they won't be affected by the blur. Or, better yet, adjust the whole duplicate layer, and then use a layer mask (page 210) to mask out the areas where you want to keep the details, or just erase those areas.

2. **Apply the Surface Blur filter.**

   Make sure your duplicate layer is active (click it in the Layers panel), and then go to Filter→Blur→Surface Blur; the filter's dialog box appears. If necessary, move the dialog box out of the way so you can watch what you're doing in the main image window and in the dialog box's preview area.

3. **Tweak the filter's settings till you like the effect.**

   The dialog box's sliders are explained after this list. Be cautious—it doesn't take much to make your photo look like a painting. Click OK when the flaws are concealed as much as possible without losing important details like eyelashes.

4. **If you want, change the duplicate layer's blend mode and/or opacity.**

   Use the controls near the top of the Layers panel for this step. If you want to eliminate blemishes, for example, try the Lighten blend mode.

The Surface Blur filter isn't hard to understand, but you usually have to do a fair amount of fiddling with its sliders to get the best balance between softening and preserving detail for a natural-looking effect. Here's what the sliders do:

- **Radius.** As with other filters, this setting controls the size of the area Elements samples for the blur. Move this slider left for a smaller blur or right for a wider blur.

- **Threshold**. This slider controls how different in tone the pixels have to be for Elements to blur them. A low setting means less blurring (fewer tones will be blurred); a higher setting means more blurring.

If you want to do a lot of experimenting, instead of dragging the sliders, try highlighting the number in each setting's box and then using the up and down arrow keys to adjust the effect.

> **NOTE** Elements includes a whole tutorial especially for fixing portrait photos (although it uses the Smart Blur filter rather than Surface Blur). To try it out, go to Guided→Touchups→Perfect Portrait.

Applying Actions and Effects

If you hang around people who use Photoshop, you'll hear them talk about *actions* and how useful they are. An action is a little script—similar to a macro in a program like Word—that automates the steps for doing something, which can save you tons of time. For example, imagine an action that applies your favorite filter and crops a photo to a certain size, or one that creates a complicated artistic effect, like a colorful watercolor look that would take many steps to do manually. Wouldn't it be great if you could use actions in Elements?

Fortunately, you can. The program has always included what Adobe calls *effects* and, under the hood, effects are really actions. And you've always been able to add some Photoshop actions to Elements, although the process was awfully complicated for many versions of Elements. But these days, Elements includes the Actions panel, which makes it just as simple to run actions in Elements as it is in Photoshop. The following pages explain everything you need to know.

Using Actions

Elements comes with a few useful actions to get you started, and you can add your own, as explained later in this section. Here's how to run an action:

1. **Open a photo and then go to the Actions panel (Window→Actions).**

2. **Choose the action you want to run.**

   In the Actions panel, each little yellow folder is an *action set*, a group of related actions. Elements comes with sets that let you add captions (and canvas to display the captions), trim weight from your subjects, resize and crop photos, and apply special effects to them. Choose the specific action you want from a set by clicking its name. Figure 13-12 explains how.

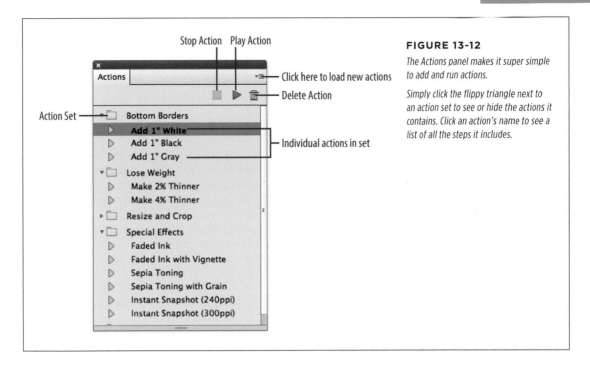

FIGURE 13-12

The Actions panel makes it super simple to add and run actions.

Simply click the flippy triangle next to an action set to see or hide the actions it contains. Click an action's name to see a list of all the steps it includes.

3. **Run the action.**

   Click the triangular Play icon in the panel's upper right, and Elements does its thing. The built-in actions happen pretty much instantly, but if you add actions from other sources, you may see dialog boxes that let you adjust settings for some steps. Just make any changes, click OK, and the action resumes and finishes up. If you want to stop an action while it's running, click the panel's square Stop icon. (You might do that if you prefer the look you get by using only *part* of an action, for example.)

   If you don't like the results, use the History panel to back up to before you started, or keep clicking the Undo button or pressing Ctrl+Z/⌘-Z to step backward through the action, and then try another one instead. (You can't step backward in the Actions panel.)

   That's all there is to it, except to save your file.

One of the best things about the Actions panel is that you can easily add more actions to it. You can't create actions in Elements—you need Photoshop for that—but there are thousands of free actions on the Internet that you can download and add to Elements.

To add actions, just click the four-line square at the upper right of the panel and choose Load Actions. In the dialog box that appears, find the action where it's saved on your computer, and then click Load. If you'd like to try installing an action, Red Steel is the action used to create the building image in Figure 13-1; you can download it from this book's Missing CD page at *www.missingmanuals.com/cds*. It works best on photos with lots of details. On images with large blocks of color, the effect is more like pop art than a colored-steel engraving.

If you're tired of an action or a set, click its name in the Actions panel, and then click the Delete icon (the little trashcan).

NOTE   It's important to understand a few differences between actions in Photoshop and in Elements. Photoshop can run an action on a whole folder of images at once. In Elements, you're restricted to running them on one photo at a time. Also, Elements can't fully perform actions that invoke Photoshop-only commands. For example, if you run an action that includes creating a history snapshot, you'll see a dialog box warning you that that command isn't available. (If you see that warning, you can click Continue to run the rest of the action, but be aware that you won't get the same results as you would in Photoshop.) If you like to play it safe, find actions written specifically for Elements. Page 586 tells you where to look for them.

Effects

Like filters, Elements' effects give you loads of ways to modify a photo's appearance, from adding lizard-skin textures to creating a pencil-sketch effect. Although you apply effects with a simple double-click, these clicks trigger a series of changes. Some effects involve many complex steps, but Elements works so quickly you might not notice all the changes it makes.

NOTE   You usually can't customize or change an effect's settings—they're all or nothing.

You'll find effects in a few different spots in Elements:

- **The Effects panel** is home to some photo effects—like tinting—and some vintage-photo looks. In Elements 13, this panel got a serious makeover, with new categories and some fun new effects, like the elaborate Panels effect shown in Figure 13-13. You'll learn how to use this panel in a sec.

- **The Graphics panel** houses some effects, but they work only on text. This panel is also where all the frames have gone, if you're looking for one you used to apply from the Effects panel in older versions of Elements; page 526 has the scoop.

- **Guided Edit** includes plenty of special effects. If you're looking for an effect you've used in older versions of Elements, check Guided Edit; you may find it there. Page 458 tells you more about using this let-us-show-you-how feature.

- **Quick Fix** includes a bunch of new effects that you can apply only from Quick Fix. If you like the kind of photo filters and effects you can use on your cellphone with apps like Instagram, be sure to check these out.

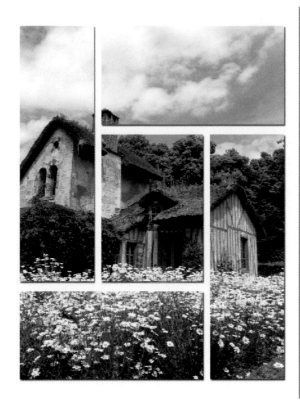

FIGURE 13-13

The Effects panel lets you create this fancy paneled effect with just a double-click.

This is the Pathway effect, and you could customize it by cropping out one of the panels to make space for some text, for example.

To apply an effect from the Effects panel, either click the Effects button at the bottom right of the Editor window or choose Window→Effects, and then click the Effects tab at the top of the panel. Just as with filters, use the panel's drop-down menu to see all your choices or pick from only one category. The thumbnail images give you a preview of how each effect will change your image. To apply an effect, double-click its thumbnail in the panel or drag the thumbnail onto your photo. That's all there is to it. If you don't like the result, press Ctrl+Z/⌘-Z to undo it, since you can't do much to tweak it.

Here are a couple of effects-related tips to help you get the most out of these nifty-but-quirky features:

- A few effects flatten or simplify your image, so it's usually best to make a copy of your image, or wait until you're done making all your other edits, before applying an effect.

- Many effects create new layers; check the Layers panel once you're done applying them. If Elements added a layer for the effect, you may want to flatten your image to reduce its file size before printing or storing it.

It's easy to add effects you've downloaded (see Chapter 19 for tips on where to find effects online). Simply click the four-line square at the Effects panel's upper right, choose Load Effects, find the file on your computer, and then click Load. The effect appears in a category called My Effects. To get rid of an effect added this way, right-click/Control-click its thumbnail in the panel and choose Delete Content. You can only add and delete effects one at a time using these techniques, though, not a whole set of effects.

Actually, most of the time you'll probably want to install actions and effects in the Actions panel instead of the Effects panel, since you have more control there. (Remember, effects are actually actions.) For example, if the action is written to allow it, you can stop an action in the Actions panel and adjust a setting before continuing to the next step, as opposed to the Effects panel, where the action would simply run from start to finish.

> **TIP** If you want to apply an effect to only part of an image, check out the Smart Brush tool (page 233). Some of its presets are quite different under the hood from effects, but the end result may be just what you're after.

Special Effects in Guided Edit

In addition to the options in the Actions Panel's Special Effects category, Elements includes two categories in Guided Edit that contain lots of interesting special effects. Elements carefully walks you through some fairly complex photo work in these edits, which can create pretty impressive results (see Figure 13-14).

FIGURE 13-14

Both of these images began with a simple color photo.

Two clicks created this distinctive Lomo-style image (left), and creating the pop art portrait (right) was only a tad more complicated.

To get started, click the Guided tab near the top of the Editor window, and then, in the panel on the right side of your screen, click the Photo Effects category to display these options:

- **B&W Color Pop.** Use this edit to create the popular look of a black-and-white image with just one color left in it. Additional settings let you create a slightly gritty, atmospheric look.

- **B&W Selection.** This edit walks you through using the Smart Brush to create a black-and-white photo with one object left in color (as opposed to B&W Color Pop, described below, which leaves one *color* wherever it appears in the photo).

- **Black and White.** This edit lets you turn a photo black and white *and* add a soft glow to create the look often seen in classic black-and-white portrait photography.

- **High Key**. This edit helps you to create the look, especially popular for portraits, where the exposure is very bright, with low contrast and very few shadows. High-key images generally seem happy and upbeat.

- **Line Drawing**. If you've tried the Pencil Sketch filter and weren't happy with the results, this guided edit gives you some help with additional tweaks to get a (somewhat) more realistic looking drawn effect.

- **Low Key**. The opposite of a high-key photo, a low-key image is very dark and shadowy with lots of contrast. The emotions they convey are also darker and more thoughtful.

- **Old Fashioned Photo**. Use this guided edit to create a sepia-toned photo with an aged texture.

- **Saturated Slide Film Effect**. You may be old enough to remember the ultra-saturated colors you could get by shooting with certain types of slide film. This guided edit walks you through creating a similar look digitally.

If none of those effects strike your fancy, click the Camera Effects category, which includes the following:

- **Depth Of Field**. If you have a point-and-shoot or cellphone camera that takes photos where the entire image tends to be in focus, you can use this guided edit to simulate the kind of *selective* focus that's possible with a large-sensor camera like a DSLR (where your subject is in sharp focus and extraneous details aren't). You can use the Lens Blur filter (page 447) to achieve the same effect, but this Guided Edit is simpler.

- **Lomo Camera Effect**. The name of this effect may not mean anything to you, but if you click it in the Guided Edit panel, the example image's style should be familiar. Lomo was a brand of camera that produced photos that, technically speaking, weren't the greatest: They were oversaturated, had shadowy vignetted corners, and the registration (alignment) of the color channels was sometimes off, to name a few flaws. But people loved the strong personality of these images, and in recent years, making a photo look like it was taken with a Lomo has become popular. Figure 13-14 (left) shows an example of what Elements creates with this effect.

- **Orton Effect**. As explained on page 450, this edit uses a very soft focus to create a dreamlike mood.

- **Tilt-Shift**. This is a fun effect that you see quite often, where the photo's focus zones are manipulated to make the subject look miniature (a car looks like a toy car, a house looks like a doll's house, and so on).

- **Vignette Effect**. Lets you create soft, shadowy corners in your photos. You can create either a dark or light vignette around your subject.

- **Zoom Burst Effect**. This guided edit applies a radial blur that makes your image look like you're zooming in on the area you choose to keep in focus. The overall effect is something like what you can create by using a Lensbaby lens on your camera.

In addition to those options, there are several fun effects in the Guided Edit panel's Photo Play section. Some of them are a bit complex, but once you've been through the process once or twice, it becomes very easy to create any of them:

- **Out Of Bounds**. This effect makes part of your subject look like it's moving out of the framed image, giving the photo a sort of 3-D look.

> **TIP** Good candidates for the Out Of Bounds effect are photos where there's a fairly strong color contrast between your subject and the background. For example, your daughter will be easier to select if she's playing soccer on a grass field than if she's running on a track amidst her classmates.

- **Picture Stack**. This makes a photo look like you took several shots of different bits of the subject and then arranged them on a table so you could see the whole thing at once. You can choose whether there should be four, eight, or 12 pictures in the stack; adjust the size of the photos' borders; and change the background color, although you really don't see very much of it.

- **Pop Art**. This guided edit helps you create that '60s Andy Warhol look (like the one in Figure 13-14, right) with just a couple of clicks. It works best on photos of people or objects with fairly simple lines rather than super-detailed subjects.

- **Puzzle Effect**. Choose this option to make your photo look like a partially completed jigsaw puzzle.

- **Recompose**. This edit walks you through using the Elements Recompose tool described on page 326.

- **Reflection**. If you've seen any advertising in the past couple of years, you know this look, originally popularized by Apple. Start with a photo of an object with a simple background (or no background at all), and then follow the steps here to create a reflection beneath it, like it's standing on a shiny surface. This is especially great for gussying up photos for places like eBay.

> **TIP** While working on any of these guided edits, you can keep clicking the buttons that change the look of your image (by increasing its saturation, say) to build up a much stronger effect than you get with just one click.

Adding Layer Styles

Like filters and effects, *layer styles* let you transform objects by giving them new characteristics such as drop shadows. Layer styles are especially useful for modifying individual objects, like text and buttons, because you can edit the text and change the button's shape even *after* you've applied the style.

Layer styles, as their name suggests, work on the contents of one layer rather than on a whole image. That's important: A layer style affects *everything* on a given layer. So if you want to apply a layer style to just one object in your picture, select the object, and then put it on its own layer by pressing Ctrl+J/⌘-J (or going to Layer→New→"Layer via Copy") or Shift+Ctrl+J/Shift-⌘-J (or going to New→"Layer via Cut"). You can also mask out part of a layer (page 210) so that, when you apply a layer style to it, it affects only the visible part of the layer. Figure 13-15 shows what you can do with layer styles.

FIGURE 13-15

A few seconds ago, this was just plain black text. It took only a double-click to create this funky, retro-styled effect.

(If you want to channel your inner hippie, the Toy style was applied here.)

You apply layer styles from the Effects panel (choose Window→Effects or click the Effects button at the bottom right of the Editor's window). Click the Styles tab at the top of the panel and then—from the drop-down menu—choose a category or select Show All, and then find a style you like. Next, select the layer you want to modify by clicking its thumbnail in the Layers panel. Finally, back in the Effects panel, double-click the style's thumbnail or drag the thumbnail onto your image. (The box below explains how to modify a style's settings once you've applied it.)

TIP   Some tools, like the type tools, have Tool Options settings that let you choose a layer style.

POWER USERS' CLINIC

Editing Layer Styles

Elements lets you customize layer styles, which can be a lot of fun. Start by applying a layer style to your image, and then either click the Style Settings icon in the Effects panel (the gear), double-click the Layer Style's icon in the Layers panel (the *fx* to the right of the layer's thumbnail), or select Layer→Layer Style→Style Settings. In the Style Settings dialog box that appears (Figure 13-16), you can edit the following:

- **Lighting Angle**. Not surprisingly, this setting controls the direction the light comes from, which determines things like where shadows fall. Think about how shadows move around depending on the sun's location at different times of day; changing the angle here has the same effect on layer styles. (If you drag a shadow, as explained in the next bullet, this setting changes accordingly, but you can also type a number here or drag the line in the circle if you'd rather adjust the angle that way.)

- **Drop Shadow**. If your layer style doesn't include a drop shadow, you can add one by turning on this checkbox.

You can then change the shadow's size, distance, opacity, and even its color. And when the Style Settings dialog box is open, you can drag the shadow around in your image window until it's positioned where you want it.

- **Glow**. This section lets you add or remove inner and outer glows, and set their color, size, and opacity.

- **Bevel**. This lets you change the size or direction of the layer style's bevel.

- **Stroke**. A *stroke* is a border around the edge of the style (most folks simply call these "outlines"). You can change the stroke's color, size, and opacity here, or add a stroke to a style that doesn't have one.

Elements lets you customize styles in so many ways that you can practically make your own style from an existing one. There's just one hitch: You can't change the standard settings for each style or save your custom style, so any changes you make affect the style only as you're currently applying it.

NOTE   You can apply layer styles only to regular layers. If you try to apply one to a Background layer, Elements asks you to convert it to a regular layer first.

Here's a rundown of the choices available in each of the Effects panel's layer-style categories:

- **Bevels** give objects a 3-D look by making them appear raised from the page or embossed into it. Figure 13-17 shows how just adding a drop shadow can add dimension to a simple shape.

- **Drop Shadows** add shadow effects that make an object look like it's floating above the page.

NOTE   To add a drop shadow to an *entire* photo, you have to also add canvas (see page 112) to give the shadow someplace to fall.

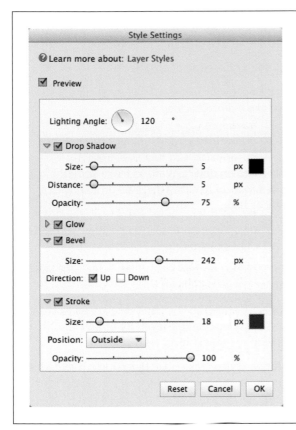

FIGURE 13-16

The Style Settings dialog box gives you lots of choices.

Click the flippy triangles on the left to see the settings for a particular characteristic or to collapse the ones you don't care about to get them out of your way.

To apply a new characteristic to a style (like adding a glow to a style that doesn't already have one), turn on its checkbox.

If there's a color square to the right of a slider, you can click the square to bring up the Color Picker and choose a new color for that setting.

FIGURE 13-17

Here's the apple image from earlier in this chapter.

Just adding a bevel gives it much more dimension and depth.

Complex includes a variety of elaborate styles that can make objects look like they're made from metal, cactus, or several other materials. These styles are particularly useful for applying to text.

- **Glass Buttons** are supposed to make objects look like, well, glass buttons, but many people think they look more like plastic. They're useful for creating web page buttons.

- **Image Effects** give you tons of ways to transform photos, including fading them and making them look like the pieces of a puzzle or a tile mosaic.

- **Inner Glows** add light around the inside edge of an object.

- **Inner Shadows** give an object a hollow or recessed look by casting a shadow within it, rather than outside it like a drop shadow.

- **Outer Glows** create the same kind of light effects as inner glows, only around the *outer* edge of the object.

- **Patterns** apply an overall pattern to an object. Want to make something look like it's made from metal or dried mud, or to fill in a dull background with a vivid pattern? You'll find lots of choices here.

- **Photographic Effects** include traditional photographic techniques. You can add a variety of monochrome effects, like good old-fashioned sepia.

- **Strokes** let you put a black or colored border around the edge of a layer or object. These styles are great for creating outlined text.

- **Visibility** changes a layer's opacity and visibility. Use these styles to create a ghosted effect, or when you're applying multiple layer styles and want to use an object's outline without having the object itself visible.

- **Wow Chrome, Neon**, and **Plastic** styles make objects look like they're made of shiny chrome, outlined in neon, or made of plastic.

If someone sends you a file made using layer styles that you don't have, you can snag those styles for your own use by highlighting the layer that has the styles applied to it and then going to Layer→Layer Style→Copy Layer Style. To use these styles in your own image, click the layer you want to modify, and then choose Layer→Layer Style→Paste Layer Style (this command applies all the styles used in the original image to the active layer in your document).

If you want to duplicate the layer styles from one layer to another within a single image, the process is simpler. In the Layers panel, just Alt-click/Option-click the little *fx* icon for the layer whose style you want to duplicate, and drag it onto the layer you want to apply that style to. (If you drag the *fx* without pressing Alt or Option, you'll *move* the layer style from one layer to the other rather than duplicating it.)

To remove a layer style, in the Layers panel, right-click/Control-click the layer it's applied to, and then choose Clear Layer Style. Alternatively, make sure the layer with the style is the active layer (if not, click it in the Layers panel), and then go to Layer→Layer Style→Clear Layer Style. Either way, this command is all or nothing: If your layer has multiple styles, they *all* go away. To remove one style at a time, use the History panel (page 25) instead.

TIP To see what your image looks like without the styles you've applied to it, go to Layer→Layer Style→Hide All Effects.

You can download hundreds of layer styles from the Web (see page 586 for tips on where to look). To add them, just click the little four-line square at the Effects panel's upper-right corner and choose Load Styles; find the downloaded file on your hard drive; and then click Load. You delete styles using this same menu, but you have to delete the whole set (most layer styles you can download are actually sets including multiple styles)—you can't just delete individual styles within it.

It's easy to get addicted to collecting layer styles because they're so much fun to use. You've been warned!

TIP Styles, effects, and actions you add via the appropriate panel's four-line-square menu are automatically copied into Elements. That means you can move the original files wherever you like, so it's a good idea to keep a special folder with the originals for all your extra content. That way, you'll always know where they are so you can back them up and easily find them if you need to reinstall them. (If you reinstall Elements, you'll need to reinstall all these extras, too.)

Applying Gradients

You may have noticed that a few of Elements' layer styles and effects apply a color tint that fades away at the edges of your layer or image. You can fade and blend colors in almost any way imaginable using *gradients*, which let you create anything from a multicolored rainbow extravaganza to a single color that fades to transparency. Figure 13-18 shows a few examples of gradients.

You can apply gradients directly to your image using the Gradient tool, or create *Gradient Fill layers*, which are whole layers filled with—you guessed it—gradients. You can even edit gradients and create new ones using the Gradient Editor. Finally, there's a special kind of gradient called a *gradient map* that lets you replace the colors in your image with the colors from a gradient. This section covers the basics of all these features.

The Gradient Tool

If you want to apply a gradient to an object in your image, the Gradient tool is the fastest way to go. This tool seems complicated at first, but it's actually easy to use. Figure 13-19 shows its Tool Options settings.

Using the Gradient tool is as easy as dragging: Click where you want the gradient to begin, and then drag to the point where you want it to stop (you'll see a line connecting the beginning and ending points). When you release the mouse button, the gradient covers the available space. (You'll get a more detailed tutorial on using this tool in a moment.)

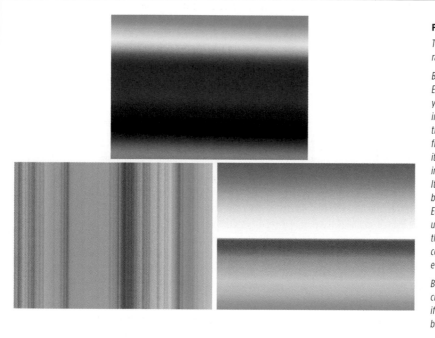

FIGURE 13-18

Top: This gradient creates a rainbow effect.

Bottom left: The Gradient Editor (page 470) lets you create all sorts of interesting effects. Here's the gradient from the top figure again, only this time it's applied left to right instead of top to bottom. Its colors are different because the Gradient Editor's noise option was used (see page 473). Click the Randomize button a couple of times to get this effect.

Bottom right: You can create this kind of gradient if you want a landscape background for artwork.

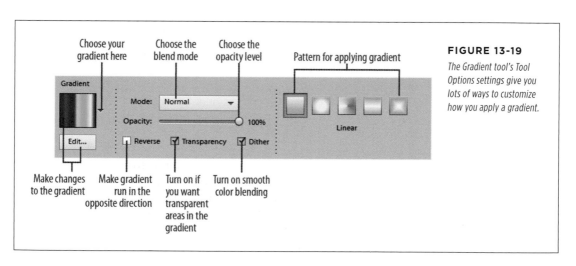

FIGURE 13-19

The Gradient tool's Tool Options settings give you lots of ways to customize how you apply a gradient.

For example, say you're using a yellow-to-white gradient. If you click to end the gradient one-third of the way into your photo, the yellow stops transitioning at that point, since you told Elements to stop the gradient there, and the remaining two-thirds of your photo get covered with white. In other words, a gradient put down by this tool covers the *entire* available space—your whole photo, in this case. Clicking stops the color *transition*—no more yellow beyond that point—but the gradient's end color fills in everyplace else. (Don't worry: This is much easier to understand once you try it.) So if you don't want your whole image affected by the gradient's colors, create a selection first and then drag the gradient within the selection to confine it to that area.

> **TIP** The Gradient tool puts the gradient on the same layer as the image you apply it to, which means that it's hard to change anything about a gradient after you apply it. If you think you might want to alter a gradient, use a Gradient Fill layer instead.

Some of Elements' gradients use your current foreground and background colors, or you can choose from a number of preset gradients with different color schemes. When the Gradient tool is active, in the Tool Options area, click the triangle to the right of the gradient thumbnail to see a palette of different gradients, grouped into categories; use the palette's drop-down menu to choose one and see what it contains. (You can work with the gradients in only one category at a time.)

You can download gradients from the Web and add them to your library using the Preset Manager (page 587); page 586 has suggestions of where to look. You can also create your own gradients from scratch. Creating and editing gradients is explained starting on page 470.

To apply a gradient with the Gradient tool, first make a selection if you don't want Elements to apply the gradient to your whole image. Then follow these steps:

1. **Choose the colors you want to use for your gradient.**

   In the Tools panel, click the foreground and background color squares to choose colors. (Remember, some gradients ignore these colors and use their own preset colors instead.)

2. **Activate the Gradient tool.**

   Click its icon in the Tools panel (the black-and-white rectangle) or press G.

3. **Select a gradient.**

   Go to the Tool Options area, click the tiny triangle to the right of the gradient thumbnail, and then choose the one you want. (If you see the Gradient Editor window, you clicked the thumbnail itself; close the Gradient Editor and try again.) Then make any other necessary changes to the Tool Options settings, which are explained in a moment.

4. **Apply the gradient.**

   Drag in your image to show Elements where the gradient should run. If you're using a linear gradient, you can make it run vertically by dragging up or down, or make it go horizontally by dragging sideways. For Radial, Reflection, and Diamond gradients, try dragging from the center of your image to an edge.

(To drag in a straight line horizontally, vertically, or at a 45-degree angle, press Shift as you drag.) You can drag at an angle, too.

If you don't like the result, press Ctrl+Z/⌘-Z to undo it and try again. Once you like the way the gradient looks, you don't need to do anything special to accept it; just save your image before you close it.

When the Gradient tool is active, the Tool Options area offers the following settings:

- **Gradient**. Click the arrow to the right of this thumbnail to choose a different gradient.

- **Edit**. Click this button or the gradient thumbnail to bring up the Gradient Editor (page 470).

- **Mode**. You can apply a gradient in any blend mode (see page 98).

- **Opacity**. If you want your image to be visible through the gradient, reduce this setting.

- **Reverse**. This setting changes the direction in which Elements applies the colors so that, for example, instead of yellow to blue (from left to right, say), you get blue to yellow.

- **Transparency**. If you want to fade to transparency anywhere in your gradient, turn on this checkbox. Otherwise, the gradient can't include transparent regions.

- **Dither**. Turn on this checkbox and Elements uses fewer colors but *simulates* the full color range using a noise pattern. This can help prevent the gradient's colors from *banding* (having hard-edged transitions), creating smoother transitions between them.

- **Gradient types**. These five buttons determine the way the gradient's colors flow. From left to right, your choices are Linear (in a straight line), Radial (a sunburst effect), Angle (a counterclockwise sweep around the starting point), Reflected (from the center out to each edge in a mirror image), and Diamond. Figure 13-20 shows an example of each type.

Gradient Fill Layers

You can also apply a gradient using a special kind of Fill layer (page 217). Most of the time, this method is better than using the Gradient tool, especially if you want to be able to make changes to the gradient *after* you apply it.

To create a Gradient Fill layer, go to Layer→New Fill Layer→Gradient. The New Layer dialog box appears so you can set the layer's blend mode (page 98) and opacity. When you click OK, Elements fills the new layer with a gradient, and the dialog box shown in Figure 13-21 pops up. You may not like the gradient Elements chose, but don't fret—you can easily change many of the gradient's settings here, or choose a different gradient altogether. Here's what each setting does:

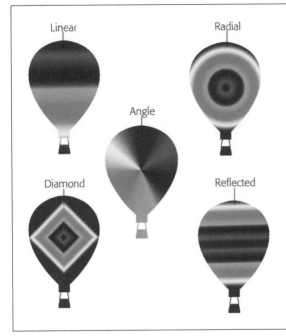

FIGURE 13-20

The same gradient applied using the different gradient types: Linear, Radial, Angle, Diamond, and Reflected.

FIGURE 13-21

This dialog box gives you access to most of the same settings you find in the Gradient tool's Tool Options area. The major difference is that with a Fill layer, you set the gradient's direction by adjusting the Angle setting shown. You don't get a chance to set the direction by dragging directly in your image as you do with the Gradient tool, but while this dialog box is open, you can drag the gradient in your image to change where it transitions.

- **Gradient**. To choose a different gradient, click the arrow next to this thumbnail to see the Gradient panel. Use the panel's drop-down menu to choose a different gradient category.

- **Style**. You have the same choices here as for the Gradient tool (Linear, Radial, and so on). Choose a different style and Elements previews it in your image.

- **Angle**. This setting controls the direction the colors run. To change the direction of the flow, enter a number in degrees or drag the line in the circle.

- **Scale**. This setting determines how large the gradient is relative to the layer. At 100 percent, they're the same size; at 150 percent, the gradient is bigger than the layer, so you see only a *portion* of the gradient in the layer. (For example, if you had a black-to-white gradient, you might see only shades of gray in your image.) If you turn off the "Align with layer" checkbox (explained in a sec), you can adjust the location of the gradient relative to your image by dragging the gradient.

- **Reverse**. Turn on this checkbox to make colors flow in the opposite direction.

- **Dither**. Use this setting to avoid banding and create smooth color transitions.

- **Align with layer**. This setting keeps the gradient in line with the layer. Turn it off and you can pull the gradient around in your image to place it exactly where you want it. At least, that's how it's *supposed* to work; you can usually drag while the dialog box is visible, even if this setting is turned on, but not after you click OK.

When the gradient looks good, click OK to create the layer. You can edit it later by heading to the Layers panel and double-clicking the layer's leftmost icon (the gradient thumbnail). Doing so opens the Gradient Fill dialog box so you can change its settings or choose a different gradient.

Editing Gradients

Elements' Gradient Editor lets you create gradients that include any color you like. You can even make ones in which the color fades to transparency, or modify existing gradient presets. Alas, the Gradient Editor isn't the easiest tool in the world to use. This section tells you the basics you need to get started. Then, as is the case with so many of Elements' features, playing around with the Gradient Editor is the best way to understand how it works.

You need to have the Gradient tool active (simply press G) to launch the Gradient Editor. After you activate the tool, in the Tool Options area, click the Edit button to summon the Gradient Editor (Figure 13-22), which displays the current gradient. You can choose a different gradient by picking from the thumbnails at the top of the Gradient Editor window, or by clicking the Preset menu at the upper left of the window and choosing a category.

To get started using the Gradient Editor, first choose your gradient's type and smoothness settings using the controls below the gradient previews:

- **Type**. Your choices are Solid and Noise. Solid gradients are the most common; they let you create transitions between solid blocks of color. Noise gradients, which are covered later in this section, produce bands of color, as you might see in a spectrometer.

- **Smoothness**. This setting controls how even the transitions between colors are.

FIGURE 13-22

The powerful and complex Gradient Editor.

Here, the aqua stop (where the cursor is) was clicked to make it active. (The dark triangle above the stop is Elements' way of telling you it's the active stop.) The two tiny diamonds on either side of the active stop mark the midpoints of the transitions between the selected color and its neighbors. You can move these diamonds to change the midpoints.

You do most of your work in the Gradient Editor's *Gradient bar*, the long colored bar where Elements displays the current gradient (in Figure 13-22, this bar is rainbow colored). The little boxes (called *stops*) and diamonds surrounding the Gradient bar let you control the gradient's color and transparency.

> **NOTE** The directions in this section are for editing *solid* gradients. Noise gradients work a little differently, as explained on page 473.

For now, you care about only the stops *below* the Gradient bar (the ones above it are explained in the next section). Each one is a *color stop*; it represents where a particular color falls in the gradient. (You need at least two color stops in a gradient.) If you click a stop, its pointed end turns black to let you know that it's the active stop. Anything you do at this point will affect the area governed by that stop.

The color stops let you customize the gradient in lots of different ways:

- **Change where the color transitions**. Click a color stop and you see a tiny diamond appear under the Gradient bar. (If the stop isn't at an end of the gradient, you get *two* diamonds, one on either side of the stop.) The diamond is the midpoint of the color change. Diamonds always appear between two color stops. You can drag the diamond in either direction to skew the color range between two color stops so that your gradient includes more of one color than another. Wherever you place the diamond tells Elements that that's where the color change should be half completed.

TIP To precisely position a stop, activate it and then enter a number (indicating percentage) in the Location box below the Gradient bar; for example, entering *50* positions the stop at the bar's midpoint.

- **Change one of the colors in the gradient**. Click any color stop, and then click the Color rectangle at the bottom of the Gradient Editor to bring up the Color Picker. Clicking the down arrow on the corner of the Color rectangle brings up the Color Swatches panel instead. Either way, choose a new color, and the gradient automatically reflects your change. You can also pick a new color by moving your cursor over the Gradient bar; the cursor turns into an eyedropper that lets you sample a color.

- **Add a color to the gradient**. Click a blank spot beneath the bar to indicate where you want the new color to appear, and Elements adds a new color stop where you clicked. Then you can click the Color rectangle to choose a different color for the new stop. Repeat as many times as you want. To duplicate an existing color in your gradient, click its stop, and then click a blank spot below the bar where you want to use that color again.

- **Remove a color from a gradient**. If a gradient is *almost* what you want but you don't like one of its colors, you don't have to live with it. You can remove a color by clicking its stop to make it active. Then either click the Delete icon (the trashcan) at the bottom right of the Gradient Editor, or just drag the stop downward off the bar. (The Delete icon is grayed out if no color stop is active.)

▇ TRANSPARENCY IN GRADIENTS

You can also use the Gradient Editor to adjust the transparency in a gradient. Elements gives you nearly unlimited control over transparency in gradients, and over the opacity of the color at any point in a gradient. Adjusting opacity in the Gradient Editor is much like using the color stops to edit the colors, but instead of color stops you use *opacity stops*.

NOTE Transparency is particularly nice in images you're creating to use online, but remember that you need to save in a format that preserves transparency, like PNG or GIF, or you lose the transparency. (If you save the file as a JPEG, for example, the transparent areas become opaque white.) See page 555 for more about file formats for the Web.

The opacity stops are the little boxes *above* the Gradient bar. You can move an opacity stop to wherever you want and then adjust it using the Gradient Editor's settings. Click above the Gradient bar wherever you want to add an opacity stop. The more opacity stops in the Gradient bar, the more points where you can adjust your gradient's opacity.

Here's how to add an opacity stop and adjust its opacity setting:

1. **Optionally, click one of the existing opacity stops.**

   The new stop you're about to create will have the same opacity as the stop you click in this step, but you can adjust the new stop once you create it. (You can actually skip this step, but it lets you predetermine the opacity of your new stop.)

2. **Add an opacity stop.**

   Click a blank spot just above the Gradient bar where you want to add a stop. Then, if you want the new stop to be precisely positioned, enter numbers (indicating percentage) in the Location box below the Gradient bar. For example, entering *50* positions a stop at the bar's midpoint.

3. **Adjust the new stop's opacity.**

   Go to the Opacity box below the Gradient bar and either enter a percentage or click the arrow to the right of the number and then move the slider.

   To get rid of a stop, click it and then click Delete (the trashcan) or drag the stop upward, away from the bar.

By adding opacity stops, you can make a gradient fade in and out, as shown in the background of Figure 13-23.

FIGURE 13-23

You can make a gradient fade in and out like this background by adding opacity stops and reducing the opacity of each stop. Here, the white background of the page shows through the transparent areas of the linear gradient.

■ CREATING NOISE GRADIENTS

Elements also lets you create what Adobe calls *noise gradients*, which aren't speckled as you might expect if you're thinking of camera noise. Instead, noise gradients randomly distribute their colors within the range you specify, giving them a banded or spectrometer-like look. The effect is interesting, but noise gradients can be unpredictable. The noisier a gradient is, the more stripes of color it contains, and the greater the number of random colors.

With the Gradient tool active, you can create a noise gradient by tweaking one of the sample ones that comes with Elements. First, go to the Tool Options area and click the down arrow to the right of the gradient thumbnail; this opens the Gradient panel. Next, at the top of the panel, click the drop-down menu and select Noise Samples. Look through the thumbnails that appear and click to select one you like. You can then edit it by clicking the Edit button in the Tool Options area to bring up the Gradient Editor.

TIP If you want to create a noise gradient that's *not* based on one of Elements' Noise Sample presets, click the Tool Options area's Edit button to bring up the Gradient Editor, and then choose Noise from the Type menu.

Noise gradients have some special Gradient Editor settings of their own:

- **Roughness** controls how gradually the gradient transitions from color to color (see Figure 13-24 for details). A higher number not only means less-smooth transitions, but also more shades of color in the gradient.

FIGURE 13-24

The amount of roughness in a noise gradient can make quite a difference in the effect you get.

Top: A solid purple-to-blue gradient.

Middle: A noise gradient with the same colors and 50 percent roughness.

Bottom: A noise gradient with the same colors and 90 percent roughness.

- **Randomize** adds random colors to your gradient (and transparency, too, if you've turned on the Add Transparency checkbox, described in a sec). Keep clicking this button until you get the effect you like.

- **Color Model** determines which color mode you work in—RGB or HSB. RGB gives you red, green, and blue color sliders, while HSB lets you set hue, saturation, and brightness (see page 256 for more about these settings).

- **Restrict Colors** keeps the gradient's colors from getting too saturated.

- **Add Transparency** puts random amounts of transparency into the gradient.

Saving Gradients

After all that work, you probably want to save your custom gradient so you can use it again. You have two ways to save a gradient from the Gradient Editor:

- **Add it as a preset**. If you've made any changes to one of the preset gradients, then Elements has already set the Gradient Editor's Name box to "Custom." You can change this to a more descriptive name by highlighting the text and typing over it. Then click the Add To Preset button. Elements adds your gradient to the current category, and adds a thumbnail of it to the Gradient panel.

TIP   If you forget and click the Add To Preset button *before* naming your custom gradient (or if you just want to change the name you gave it), in the Gradient Editor, right-click/Control-click the gradient's thumbnail, and then choose Rename Gradient.

- **Save the gradient**. In the upper right of the Gradient Editor, click the little floppy-disk icon to open the Save dialog box so you can name the set of gradients you're creating (called a *library*). This method resaves the *entire* library that's visible when you save your gradient, so you'll want to rename it so you don't save over the originals. You'll save it in a special Gradients folder, which Elements automatically takes you to in the Save dialog box. When you want to use the gradient again, click the Gradient Editor's Load icon (the green +), and then select it from the list that appears. The new library appears at the bottom of the Preset menu's list.

TIP   You can also save and load gradients by calling up the Gradient panel (in the Tool Options area, click the arrow to the right of the gradient thumbnail), and then clicking the four-line square in the panel's upper right.

■ Gradient Maps

Gradient maps let you use gradients in nonlinear ways. So instead of a rainbow that shades from one direction to another, with a gradient map, Elements substitutes the gradient's colors for the image's existing colors. You can use gradient maps for funky special effects as well as serious photo corrections.

When you create a gradient map, Elements plots out the brightness values in your image and applies those values to a gradient (light to dark). Then Elements replaces the existing colors with the gradient you chose, using the lightness values as a guide to determine which color goes where. That sounds complicated, and it is (fortunately, Elements does all the work); but if you try it, you'll quickly see what's going on. Take a look at Figure 13-25, where applying a gradient map dramatically livens up a dull photo. But that's not all gradient maps are good for. They're also valuable tools for retouching. See the box on page 478 to learn how to use gradients to fix the color in photos.

FIGURE 13-25

Left: An ordinary shot of a lighthouse.

Right: The image becomes altogether different when you apply a gradient map adjustment to it.

You can apply a gradient map directly to an image by going to Filter→Adjustments →Gradient Map or using the Smart Brush [page 233] (in the Tool Options area, click the thumbnail image, and then choose Special Effects→Rainbow Map). But most times, you'll want to use a Gradient Map Adjustment layer, because it's easier to edit. Here's how:

1. **Create a Gradient Map Adjustment layer.**

   Go to Layer→New Adjustment Layer→Gradient Map. The New Layer dialog box appears so you can choose the layer's blend mode and opacity, and name it if you want. Click OK, and Elements adds a gradient map to your photo, but don't worry if it's not what you had in mind. You can modify it using the Adjustments panel, shown in Figure 13-26.

2. **Select a gradient.**

   In the Adjustments panel, you see a gradient whose colors are based on your current foreground and background colors. That gradient is the map that Elements made of the lightness/darkness values in your image. Click the triangle to the right of the gradient thumbnail, and then choose a gradient. (If you want your image to include color, pick a colored gradient rather than a black- or gray-to-white one.) Elements automatically replaces the colors in your image with the equivalent values from the gradient you chose, so you can click around in the gradient libraries and watch your image change.

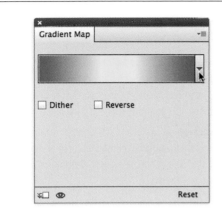

FIGURE 13-26

The Gradient Map Adjustments panel.

Click the tiny arrow to the right of the thumbnail (where the cursor is here) to see a drop-down menu of available gradient patterns.

If you want to make changes to the gradient you chose, click in the thumbnail itself to bring up the Gradient Editor (page 470).

The panel's Dither checkbox adds a little random noise to make the gradient's transitions smoother. The Reverse checkbox switches the direction in which Elements applies the gradient to the map. For example, if you chose a red-to-green gradient, reversing it would put green where it would have previously been red, and vice versa. It's worth giving this setting a try—you can get some interesting effects.

3. **Keep editing until you're satisfied with the result.**

   When you like what you see, save the image. You can always go back and edit the gradient-map layer (as explained in Figure 13-26) by heading to the Layers panel and double-clicking the leftmost icon for this layer.

Remember that you can use gradient maps in any layer blend mode. You can spend hours playing around with gradient maps; try adding other filters and adjustments to produce all sorts of strange results.

TIP Try equalizing your image (Filter→Adjustments→Equalize) after applying a gradient map adjustment—the colors can shift dramatically. Equalizing is a good thing to try if your gradient map makes your image look dull or dingy. You may need to merge the image's layers to get this command to work, since you can't equalize an Adjustment layer. (See page 347 for more about this command.)

Color-Correcting with Gradients

If you just want to use Elements to enhance and correct photos, you may think all this gradient business is a big waste of time. But gradients and gradient maps aren't just for introducing lurid colors into photos—they're also powerful tools for correcting images.

For instance, say you have a photo where one side is darker than the other and you want to apply an Adjustment layer so it affects only the dark side of the image. You can pull this off by bringing up the Adjustment layer's layer mask (see page 210), and then applying a gradient to the mask.

You can also use Gradient Map Adjustment layers in different blend modes to help balance out the colors in photos, although to get the best effect, you may need to use the Gradient Editor to play with the distribution of light and dark values.

Gradient maps are also useful for colorizing skin in black-and-white photos. Set up a gradient based on three or more skin tones, and you can get a more realistic distribution of color than you can by painting

Text in Elements

E lements makes it easy to add text to images. You can quickly create all kinds of fancy text to use in greeting cards, as newsletter headlines, or as graphics for web pages.

Elements also gives you lots of ways to jazz up text: You can apply layer styles, effects, and gradients to it, or warp it into psychedelic shapes. And the Type Mask tools let you fill individual letters with the contents of a photo. Best of all, most of Elements' type tools let you change text with just a few clicks (see Figure 14-1).

And that's not all. You also get three special tools for making artistic text: Text on Selection, Text on Shape, and Text on Custom Path, which let you create text that swoops and turns, or make text run around the edge of an object. You can create very dramatic text effects with these tools, which are covered beginning on page 500. By the time you finish this chapter, you'll know all the ways Elements can add pizzazz to text.

■ Adding Text to an Image

It's a cinch to add text to an image in Elements. Just activate a type tool, choose a font in the Tool Options area, and then type away. The type tools' icon in the Tools panel is easy to recognize: It's a capital T. (It lives at the bottom left of the Draw section.) You can also activate it by pressing T.

Elements actually gives you *seven* different type tools, all of which you can see in the type tools' Tool Options area: the Horizontal Type tool, the Vertical Type tool, the Horizontal Type Mask tool, the Vertical Type Mask tool, the Text on Selection tool, the Text on Shape tool, and the Text on Custom Path tool. You'll learn about the Type Mask and "Text on…" tools later in this chapter; this section focuses on the regular Horizontal and Vertical Type tools. As their names imply, the Horizontal Type tool lets you enter text that runs left to right, while the Vertical Type tool is for creating text that runs down the page.

When you use the type tools, Elements automatically puts the text you create on its own layer, which makes it easy to throw out what you've typed and start over. When a type tool is active, Elements creates a new Text layer each time you click your image.

**Happy
Anniversary**

*Happy
Anniversary*

FIGURE 14-1

With Elements, you can take basic text and turn it into the kind of snazzy headlines you see on greeting cards and magazine covers.

It took only a couple of clicks—a couple of layer styles (Angled Spectrum and a bevel) and some warping—to turn these plain black letters (top) into an extravaganza (bottom).

TROUBLESHOOTING MOMENT

Why Does the Type Tool Turn My Photo Red?

If your image gets covered with an ugly reddish film every time you click it with a type tool, that means you've activated one of the Type *Mask* tools rather than one of the regular type tools. (Type masks, covered later in this chapter, are useful when you want to create text that's cut from an image.) To switch to the regular type tools, just head to the left side of the Tool Options area and click either of the first two icons.

The red mask may also appear if you try to add type to an image that's in Indexed Color mode, like a GIF. If you want to add text to a GIF, first go to Image→Mode→RGB, and then type away. If you still need a GIF when you're done, then use "Save for Web" (page 557) to save your finished file.

Text Options

Activate either the Horizontal or Vertical Type tool, and then take a look at the many Tool Options settings (Figure 14-2), which let you control pretty much every aspect of your text, including its font, color, and alignment. Here are your options:

FIGURE 14-2

The type tools' Tool Options let you control lots of different settings, most of which are pretty standard, like the font and the size of the letters.

The choices on the right side—like Warp Text and Add Layer Style—are where the fun begins.

- **Font Family**. This unlabeled menu lists all the fonts installed on your computer. You can either click the arrow at the right end of this field to display a pop-out menu or, if you know the font you want, just click the name of the current font or start typing the name of the one you want to use instead; Elements automatically completes the name for you.

> **TIP** The Font Family menu displays the word "Sample" in the actual fonts to make it easier for you to find one you like. You can adjust the size of these previews by going to Edit→Preferences→Type/Photoshop Elements Editor→Preferences→Type.
>
> Power users can pay attention to the abbreviations to the left of each font's name: An O indicates an OpenType font, and TT indicates a TrueType font, in case you ever need to know.

- **Font Style**. Here's where you select from the styles available for your font, like bold or italic.

- **Size**. This is where you choose how big the text should be. Text is traditionally measured in *points*—that's what the "pt" here stands for. (The box on page 485 explains the relationship between points and actual size in Elements.) You can click the arrow here and choose a preset size from this drop-down menu, or just type the size you want into this field. And you aren't limited to the sizes shown in the menu—you can enter any number you want, up to 1,296 pts.

TIP If points make you nervous, you can change the type tools' units of measurement to millimeters or pixels by going to Edit→Preferences→Units & Rulers/Photoshop Elements Editor→Preferences→Units & Rulers.

- **Color**. Click this rectangle to bring up the color swatches. You can click a swatch to set the color of your text, or click the rainbow-colored circle at the bottom right of the Swatches panel to open the full Color Picker. When you make a selection, the rectangle in the Tool Options area and your foreground color square both change to reflect your choice.

NOTE When a type tool's cursor is active in your image (so you see a blinking line showing where letters will appear if you type), you can't use the standard keyboard commands to reset your foreground and background colors to black and white (D) or to switch them (X). If you try to use the shortcuts, you'll simply type those letters in your image, so you have to click the relevant buttons in the Tools panel (page 253) instead.

- **Leading**. This setting (whose name rhymes with "bedding") controls the spacing between the lines of text as measured in points. For horizontal text, leading is the difference between the *baselines* (the bottom of the letters) of each line. For vertical text, leading is the distance from the center of one column to the center of the column next to it.

    Figure 14-3 shows what a difference leading can make. Elements automatically sets the leading to Auto, which is the program's guess as to what looks best. You can change the leading by choosing a number from the list or by entering the amount you want (in points, unless you changed the measurement unit in Elements' preferences).

- **Faux Styles**. Yup, faux as in "fake." If your chosen font doesn't have a bold, italic, underline, or strikethrough version, you can tell Elements to simulate that style by clicking the appropriate icon here. (These options aren't available for some fonts.)

- **Alignment**. These buttons tell Elements how to align the text, just like in a word-processing program. If you enter multiple lines of text with the Horizontal Type tool, this is where you tell Elements whether you want it lined up left, right, or centered (for horizontal text). If you use the Vertical Type tool, you can align the columns along the top, bottom, or middle instead.

TIP If you're using the Vertical Type tool, each time you start a new column, Elements puts it to the left of the previous one, so your columns run from right to left. If you want vertical text columns that run left to right instead, you need to put each column on its own layer and position them manually. You can then use the Move tool's Distribute option to space them evenly (page 203).

- Heliskiing
- Parasailing
- Cave Diving
- On-Site Medical Facility

- Heliskiing

- Parasailing

- Cave Diving

- On-Site Medical Facility

FIGURE 14-3

Leading is the space between lines of text.

Top: A list of four items with Auto leading.

Bottom: The same list with the leading set to a higher number to make more space between the rows.

If you adjust the leading of vertical text (which runs top to bottom), you change the space between the columns, rather than between letters within each column. The box on page 488 explains how to tighten up the space between letters that are stacked vertically.

- **Style**. You can use this unlabeled button (which is grayed out until you commit some text) to add funky visual effects to text with layer styles (page 461). After you commit text, this button displays a white square with a red slash through it. To apply styles, first add some text to your image, and then click the Commit button (the green checkmark) below the text. Elements switches you over to the Move tool, so you need to click the type tool again to switch back to it so you can add a style.

> **TIP**   If it drives you nuts to have the Move tool popping up all the time, go to Edit→Preferences→General/ Photoshop Elements Editor→Preferences→General, and turn off "Select Move Tool after committing text."

Next, click the Style button and choose a layer style from the Styles panel. It's important that the text layer is active, but the letters shouldn't be highlighted. (If you still see the Cancel and Commit buttons, Elements won't apply the style, so click the green checkmark to commit the text first.) If you want to remove a style that you've just applied, click the four-line square in the panel's upper-right corner and choose Remove Style, or go to Layer→Layer Style→Clear Layer Style.

- **Orientation**. This button, which has a T with a down-pointing arrow next to it, changes text from horizontal to vertical, or vice versa. (You can't change the orientation of text that doesn't exist yet, so this setting is grayed out until you add some.) You can also change text's orientation by going to Layer→Type→Horizontal or Vertical.

- **Warp**. The little T-above-a-curved-line icon hides a bunch of options for distorting text in lots of interesting ways. There's more about this option on page 488. (The Warp Text command is also available from Layer→Type→Warp Text.) This button is grayed out until you actually type something.

- **Anti-aliasing**. This setting smooths the edges of the text, and you'll usually want it turned on. See page 487 for an explanation of anti-aliasing.

These final two controls don't show up until you've typed something, and they appear in your image rather than the Tool Options area:

- **Commit**. Click this green checkmark after you type some text to tell Elements that, yes, you want the text to stay the way it is.

- **Cancel**. When you add text to an image, Elements automatically places the text on its own layer. Click this button (the red circle with a slash) to delete this newly created Text layer. This button works only if you click it *before* you click the green Commit checkmark. To delete text *after* you've committed it, head to the Layers panel and drag the Text layer onto the trashcan icon.

If you see either of these buttons in your image, that means you haven't committed your text, and many menu options and other tools won't be available until you do. When you see these buttons, you're in what Elements calls *Edit mode*, where you can make changes to the text, but most of the rest of Elements' features aren't available to you. Just click Commit or Cancel to get the rest of the program's options back.

Creating Text

Now that you're familiar with the choices in the Tool Options area, you're ready to start creating text. You can add text to an existing image or start with a new, blank file (if you want to create text to use as a graphic by itself, say). To use either the Horizontal or Vertical Type tool, just follow these steps:

1. **Activate a type tool.**

   Click the T icon in the Tools panel or press the T key on your keyboard and then, in the Tool Options area, select the Horizontal Type tool or the Vertical Type tool.

2. **Modify any Tool Options settings you want to change.**

   See the previous section for a rundown of your choices. You can make changes after you enter the text, too, so your choices aren't set in stone yet. Elements lets you edit text until you simplify the Text layer. (Page 424 explains what simplifying is.)

How Resolution Affects Font Size

It's easy enough to pick a font size in the Text tool's Tool Options area. But you may find that what you thought would be big, bold, headline-size text is so tiny in your image that you can hardly see it. What gives?

In Elements, the actual size of text in an image is tied to the image's resolution. If you thought that choosing 72-point text would give you a headline that's an inch high, it will—but only if the *resolution* of your file is 72 pixels per inch (ppi). The higher the resolution, the smaller that same text is going to be. For example, if the image's resolution is 144 ppi, your 72-point text will print half an inch high; in a 216 ppi image, it'll be a third of an inch high; and so on.

If you're working with high-resolution images, you have to increase the size of your text to allow for the extra pixel packing that comes with increased resolution. It's not uncommon to have to choose sizes that are *much* higher than anything

listed in the Tool Options area's Size menu. Don't be afraid of using really big sizes if you need them—just keep entering larger numbers in the size box until the text looks right in proportion to your image.

Another confusing thing about text in Elements is that the program creates text based on the *actual* size of an image, not your view size. So if you're zoomed way in on an image and you add some text that looks like it's a reasonable size, it may be much smaller when you print the image or see it at actual size. People often try to put very small text on a very big image and wonder why it's so hard to read. If you aren't sure about the actual size of your document, try going to View→Print Size before typing. This view offers only an approximation, but it helps you get a better idea of what the text will look like in the final version of the image.

3. **Enter some text.**

   Click in the image where you'd like the text to go, and then start typing (Elements automatically creates a new Text layer). Type the way you would in a word processor, pressing Enter/Return to create new lines. If you're using the Horizontal Type tool, the horizontal line you see is the baseline the letters sit on. If you're typing vertically, the vertical part of the cursor is the centerline of the characters.

   TIP If you need to change the size of the text after you've typed it, you don't have to keep guessing about the font size. Just head to the Tool Options area, put your cursor over the word "Size," and then scrub left or right to make the text smaller or larger (page 197 explains scrubbing).

   If you want Elements to *wrap* the text (adjust it to fit a given space), before you start typing, *drag* in the image with a type tool to create a text box. Otherwise, you need to insert returns manually. If you create a text box, you can resize it to adjust the text's flow by dragging the box's handles after you finish typing. (You won't be able to do this anymore after you simplify the Text layer.)

   As noted earlier, if you use the Vertical Type tool, you can't make the columns of text run left to right. So if you need several vertical columns of English text, enter one column and then click the Commit button. Then start over again for the next column, so that each column is on its own layer.

TIP Be careful about clicking when a type tool is active—each click creates a new Text layer. That's great if you're creating lots of separate text boxes to position individually, but it's easy to create a layer without meaning to. If you accidentally make a new layer, just delete it in the Layers panel, or merge it with an existing Text layer.

4. **When you like what you see, click the green checkmark below the text (or click anywhere else in your image) to commit what you typed.**

    When you *commit* text, you're telling Elements that you accept what you've created. Once you commit, the type tool's cursor is no longer active in your photo.

    If you don't like what you typed, click the Cancel icon (the red circle and slash) below the text instead, and the whole Text layer goes away.

Once you've entered text, you can modify it using most of Elements' editing tools. You can add layer styles to it (page 461), move it with the Move tool, rotate it, change its color, and so on.

NOTE If you try to paste text into Elements by copying it from a word-processing program, the results can be unpredictable. Sometimes it works fine, but you may find the text comes in as one endlessly long line of words. If that happens, it's often easier to type text into Elements from scratch than to reformat it.

Editing Text

In Elements, you can edit text after you enter it, just like in a word processor. Elements lets you change not only the letters, but the font and size, too, even if you've applied lots of layer styles. You modify text by highlighting it and then making the correction, or by changing the settings in the Tool Options area while the text is highlighted. Figure 14-4 shows the easy way to highlight text for editing.

FIGURE 14-4

If you change your mind about what you typed, no problem. This text is highlighted so that the words can be edited. The best part is that you can change the text to say anything, and Elements preserves all the formatting. (You can't do this after you simplify a Text layer, though.) If you find it hard to highlight text by dragging, go to the Layers panel and double-click the layer's T icon to make Elements highlight all the text on that layer so you can make changes.

TIP As mentioned earlier, the font family menu (page 481) displays the word "Sample" in the fonts themselves. Even better, Elements gives you a quick way to preview what your particular text will look like in various fonts. First, highlight the text, and then click the name of the current font in the Tool Options area. Then use the up and down arrow keys to move around in the font list. Elements changes the highlighted words in your image so they appear in each font you choose as you go through the list.

You can make all these changes as long as you don't *simplify* the text. Simplifying is the process of changing text from a vector shape that's easy to edit to a rasterized graphic (see the box on page 424 for details). In this respect, text works just like the shapes you learned about in Chapter 12: Once you simplify text, Elements doesn't see it as text anymore, just as a bunch of regular pixels.

You can either simplify text yourself by choosing Layer→Simplify Layer, or wait for Elements to prompt you to simplify, which it'll do when you try to do things to the text like apply a filter or add an effect. It's usually best not to simplify until you must.

TIP While the text effects that come with Elements don't simplify text, if you download effects, they may *automatically* simplify text without asking first. So make sure you've made all your edits to the text before using any effects you've downloaded.

■ ANTI-ALIASING: SMOOTHING TEXT

You read about anti-aliasing graphics in Chapter 5 (page 152). Anti-aliasing has a similar effect on text: It gets rid of any jaggedness by blending the edge pixels on letters to make their outlines look smooth, as shown in Figure 14-5.

FIGURE 14-5

An extremely close look at two versions of the same A. The left one has anti-aliasing turned on, making its edges smooth (well, smoother). The edges on the right one are much more jagged and rough looking.

Elements always starts you off with text anti-aliasing turned on, and 99 percent of the time you'll want to keep it on. The main reason to turn it off is to avoid *fringing*—a line of unwanted pixels that make text look like it was cut out of an image with a colored background.

TIP If your text looks really jagged even with anti-aliasing turned on, check your image's resolution: Text often looks poor at low resolution settings, just as photos do. (See page 105 for more about resolution.)

You turn anti-aliasing on and off with the Tool Options area's Anti-aliasing check-box. You can also adjust this setting by going to Layer→Type→Anti-Alias Off (or Anti-Alias On).

NOTE Once you simplify text, you can't change its anti-aliasing setting.

Using Asian Text Options to Control Spacing

When you're using the Vertical Type tool, it can be tough to space letters correctly. Elements lets you adjust the leading (page 492), but with vertical text, that setting affects the spacing between *columns* of letters, not between the letters within a column. Also, sometimes you may want to adjust the spacing between letters written in horizontal text. Elements lets you make either of these fixes, but you need to enlist the help of the program's Asian Text Options—even if you're writing in English.

To get started, go to Edit→Preferences→Type/Photoshop Elements Editor→Preferences→Type, turn on the Show Asian Text Options checkbox, and then click OK. Now, the next time you click in an image with a type tool, you'll see the Asian Text options menu in the Tool Options area, just below the alignment buttons. Click the Asian character or the down-pointing arrow next to it to see a pop-out panel with three options: *Tate-ChuuYoko*, *Mojikumi*, and a drop-down menu with percentages on it. You want the drop-down menu, which is for *Tsume*, a setting that reduces the amount of space around the characters you apply it to.

To apply Tsume, just highlight the characters you want to change in your image, and then select a percentage from this drop-down menu. (The higher the percentage, the tighter the spacing.) You can select a single letter or a whole word when using Tsume. Since it reduces the space all the way around each letter you apply it to, you can use it for either vertical or horizontal text, although for horizontal text, you'll probably use it to tidy up the spacing of just one or two letters. For vertical text, Tsume is a great way to tighten up the spacing of all the characters.

■ Warping Text

Elements lets you warp text in all sorts of fun ways. You can make it wave like a flag, bulge out, twist like a fish, or arc up or down, among other things. These complex effects are really easy to apply, and best of all, you can still edit the text once you've applied them. Figure 14-6 shows just a few examples of what you can do. If you add a layer style, too (page 461), warping is even more effective.

NOTE Warping text is easy to do, but it's also a bit limited. You can control the amount of warp for the style you choose, but you can't just create a free-form style of your own. The section starting on page 500 has information about the special Elements text tools that give you much more flexibility than warping does.

To warp text, follow these steps:

1. **Enter some text.**

   When you're done, use the Move tool to reposition the text, if necessary.

2. **Highlight the text you want to warp.**

   Make sure the Text layer is active, or you won't be able to select what you typed. If it's not active, click it in the Layers panel. To select *all* the text on the layer, double-click its T icon in the Layers panel.

FIGURE 14-6

Elements gives you oodles of ways to warp text. Here are some of the basic warps, applied using their standard settings. Clockwise from upper left, they are Inflate, Fish, Rise, and Flag.

You can tweak these effects endlessly using the sliders in the Warp dialog box. (These examples also have layer styles applied to them.)

3. **In the Tool Options area, click the Create Warped Text button.**

   Make sure a type tool is active or you won't see this button (the T with a curved line under it—it's labeled back in Figure 14-2). When you click it, the Warp Text dialog box shown in Figure 14-7 appears.

FIGURE 14-7

As you can see, Elements gives you lots of ways to warp text.

The sliders in this dialog box are grayed out until you select an option from the Style menu. After that, you can use the sliders to customize the warp effect.

4. **In the Warp Text dialog box, tell Elements how to warp the text.**

Select a warp from the Style menu, like Arc, Flag, or whatever. (To help you pick, Elements includes icons in the list that show the general shape of each warp.) Then make any changes you want to the sliders or the horizontal/vertical orientation of the warp (your options are described in a moment). Tweaking these settings can radically alter the warp's effect. Drag the sliders around to experiment, and watch your image to see the results. (You may have to drag the dialog box out of the way to get a good view.)

5. **When you come up with something you like, click OK.**

NOTE You can't warp text that has the Faux Bold style applied to it (you can warp all the *other* styles to your heart's content). If you forget and try to do so, Elements politely reminds you. The program even offers to remove the style and continue with your warp.

Whatever warp style you choose, you can customize it with the Warp Text dialog box's settings:

- **Horizontal/Vertical**. These radio buttons control the warp's orientation. Most of the time, you'll want to leave this setting the same as the text's orientation, but you can get interesting effects by warping the opposite way. A vertical warp on horizontal text gives more of a perspective effect, like the text is moving toward you or away from you. And you can get some really funky effects by putting a horizontal warp on vertical text.

- **Bend**. This is where you tell Elements how much of an arc you want, if you'd like to change it from Element's standard setting. Just type a percentage (click the existing number to type over it) or drag the slider.

- **Horizontal/Vertical Distortion**. These sliders control how much the text warps in the horizontal and vertical planes. They give you precise control over just how and where the text warps. They work pretty much the same way as the Bend setting: Type in a negative or positive percentage or drag the sliders.

The best way to find the look you want is to experiment. Warping text is lots of fun, especially if you apply a layer style first to give the text a 3-D look.

TIP Many of the warps look best on two lines of text, so that the lines bend in opposite directions. However, you can also get really interesting effects by putting two lines of text on separate layers and applying different warps to each one.

To edit a warp after you apply it, double-click the Text layer's Warp icon in the Layers panel (it's a T with a curved line under it). Doing so automatically makes the Text layer active *and* highlights the text on it. Then, in the Tool Options area, click the Create Warped Text button to open the Warp Text dialog box showing your current settings. Make any changes you want or—to unwarp the text—set the Style menu to None.

■ Adding Special Effects

Besides warping text, you can apply all kinds of layer styles, filters, and special *text effects* to make your words look more elaborate. You can change the text's color, make the letters look 3-D, add brushstrokes for a painted effect, and so on. (There's more about layer styles, filters, and effects in Chapter 13.)

Elements gives you lots of different ways to add special effects to text. The following sections explain three of the most interesting: applying text effects, using a gradient to create rainbow-colored text, and using the Liquify filter to warp text in truly odd ways.

Text Effects

The Graphics panel (page 526) has a whole category dedicated to effects for text (Figure 14-8). You apply these effects the same way you apply any other effect: In the Layers panel, select the Text layer and then, in the Graphics panel, double-click the effect you want. If you don't like the way it looks, press Ctrl+Z/⌘-Z to undo it.

FIGURE 14-8

The Graphics panel includes a whole section of text effects.

Most of these effects—like Animal Fur Zebra and Denim—are unique to this section. Others, like Bevel, are just shortcuts for effects you could also achieve using layer styles, gradients, or other Elements features.

If you've already applied layer styles to your text, it's hard to predict how much these effects will respect the existing layer styles. Some effects build on the changes you've previously made with layer styles, but most undo anything you've done before. Experimenting is the best way to find out what happens when you combine layer styles and effects.

Text Gradients

As you learned in Chapter 13, gradients fill text with a spectrum of color. The simplest way to get these rainbow effects is to apply one of the layer styles or text effects that include a gradient. But those methods don't give you any control over the gradient's colors or direction, so if you have a specific look in mind, you may have to start from scratch and do it yourself. The easiest way is to start with a type mask, as explained on page 496. But if you've already added some text to your image, as long as you haven't simplified the text, you can easily fill it with a gradient.

> **TIP** Heavier, chunkier fonts show off gradients better than thin, spidery ones. Fonts with names that end in Extended, Black, or Extra Bold are good choices, like Arial Black or Rockwell Extra Bold.

First, make sure you've got some text in your image, and then follow these steps:

1. **Create a new layer for the gradient directly above the Text layer.**

   You're going to clip these two layers together (page 206), which is why they need to be next to each other. Click the Text layer to make it the active layer, if it isn't already. Then, to create the new layer, press Shift+Ctrl+N/Shift-⌘-N or go to Layer→New→Layer. In the New Layer dialog box, turn on the "Use Previous Layer to Create Clipping Mask" checkbox to clip this new layer to the Text layer below it, and then click OK.

   Look at the Layers panel to be sure the new layer is the active layer and that it's right above the Text layer. If it isn't active, give it a click in the Layers panel.

2. **Activate the Gradient tool.**

   Click the Gradient tool in the Tools panel (or press G), and then choose a gradient in the Tool Options area. (See page 465 for more about how to select, modify, and apply gradients.)

3. **Drag across your image in the direction you want the gradient to run.**

   Because this layer is clipped to the Text layer, the gradient appears only in the text. If you don't like the result, press Ctrl+Z/⌘-Z and drag again until you like what you see.

That's all you have to do, except of course save your work if you want to keep it. If you like, you can also activate the Move tool and drag the gradient layer around till your text shows the color range you want. You won't see the gradient layer itself as you move it, but the text's colors will change.

> **NOTE** You may have noticed that the Smart Brush tool (page 233) includes Rainbow Map as one of the adjustments you can brush onto an image. Sounds like it might be just the ticket for avoiding all this layer-creation business, doesn't it? Unfortunately, it applies a gradient *map* (see page 475) to an image, not a regular gradient. Because text is all the same tonal level, if you brush the Smart Brush's Rainbow Map onto some text, you'll just get a solid, one-color result, not a rainbow or a gradient at all.

If you just want a single color that fades away, there are a couple of monochromatic gradients in the Graphics panel's text effects category, so you might want to check those out before trying the steps above.

Liquifying Text

Elements' Create Warped Text button (explained on page 488) gives you lots of ways to reshape text. But there's an even more powerful way to warp text: the Liquify filter (see Figure 14-9).

FIGURE 14-9

The Liquify filter can reshape text in many different ways, including bloating letters to give them a freehand appearance (as shown here), making letters twirl around on themselves, or adding a flame-like effect.

Top: Plain text.

Right: After applying the Liquify filter's Bloat tool to each letter separately, you get this more casual, hand-painted effect.

> **TIP**   You can use the Liquify filter to warp *anything* in an image—not just text. Use it to alter objects in photographs and drawings—for example, fix someone's nose, make your brother look like E.T., give a scene a watery reflection, and so on.

To use the Liquify filter on text, you first need to simplify the Text layer by going to Layer→Simplify Layer (or, you can wait and click OK when the Liquify filter asks if you want to simplify); just remember that you can't edit text once you simplify it.

Next, call up the Liquify dialog box by going to Filter→Distort→Liquify or double-clicking the Liquify filter's thumbnail in the Effects panel's Filters→Distort category. Either way, up pops yet another large Elements dialog box. Like most of them, it's fairly straightforward once you learn your way around it. In the upper-left corner is a little toolbox with some very special tools in it (see Figure 14-10). Each tool has its own keyboard shortcut (listed here in parentheses after the tool's name) that works only in this dialog box. Here they are, from top to bottom:

Warp tool
Twirl clockwise tool
Twirl counterclockwise tool
Pucker tool
Bloat tool
Shift Pixels tool
Reconstruct tool
Zoom tool
Hand tool

FIGURE 14-10

The Liquify dialog box's toolbox.

Along with the standard Hand and Zoom tools to help you adjust the view as you work, you get highly specialized tools found nowhere else in Elements.

- **Warp tool (W)**. Lets you push the image's pixels in any direction, although it may take a fair amount of coaxing to create much of an effect.

- **Twirl Clockwise tool (C)**. If you activate this tool and then click your image and hold down the mouse button, the pixels under your cursor spin clockwise. The longer you apply this tool, the more extreme its effect.

- **Twirl Counterclockwise tool (L)**. The opposite of the Twirl Clockwise tool, this one makes the pixels under your cursor spin counterclockwise.

- **Pucker tool (P)**. This tool makes the pixels under your cursor move toward the cursor's center.

- **Bloat tool (B)**. The opposite of the Pucker tool, this one makes pixels move *away* from the cursor's center.

- **Shift Pixels tool (S)**. The pixels you drag this tool over move perpendicularly in relation to the direction of your stroke. For example, if you drag from the top of an image straight down, the pixels you pass over move to the right. Alt-drag/Option-drag to make them shift the opposite way.

- **Reconstruct tool (E)**. Pass this wonderful tool over areas where you've done too much liquifying, and they return to their original condition without undoing the rest of your changes.

- **Zoom (Z)** and **Hand (H) tools**. These are the same Zoom and Hand tools you find elsewhere in Elements.

Your image appears in the preview window in the center of the dialog box. You can adjust the view with the Zoom tool or by using the magnification menu in the dialog box's lower-left corner.

> **TIP** It often helps to zoom in really close when using the Liquify filter. If you've added text to a large image, select the text with the Rectangular Marquee tool before activating this filter. That way, you'll see only the selected area in the filter's dialog box, which makes it easier to get a high zoom level.

On the right side of the dialog box are the filter's Tool Options settings:

- **Brush Size**. You can enter a number as low as 1 pixel or as high as 600 to change the size of your cursor.

- **Brush Pressure**. This controls how much the brush cursor affects the pixels you drag over. The range is from 1 to 100; the higher the number, the stronger the effect. If you're using a graphics tablet, turn on the Stylus Pressure checkbox so that the harder you press, the more effect you get.

- **Stylus Pressure**. Turn this on if you're using a graphics tablet and want the tool to be sensitive to how hard you press.

To use the Liquify filter, just pick a tool from the dialog box's toolbox, adjust the Tool Options settings (if you want), and then drag across your image. This is a processor-intense filter, so there may be a fair amount of lag time before you see results, especially if your computer is slow.

If you like what you see in the dialog box's preview, click OK and wait a few seconds while Elements applies your transformations; then you're done. If you *don't* like what you see, you can always have another go at it. Simply click the Liquify dialog box's Revert button to return your image to the condition it was in before you started using this filter.

The next time you use the Liquify filter, it remembers the tool settings you used last time. You can Ctrl-click/⌘-click the Cancel button (it turns into a Default button) to return your tools to the way they were the very first time you used the Liquify filter. You can also Alt-click/Option-click the Cancel button to turn it into a Reset button. Doing so doesn't reset your image, but rather tells Elements that you want to go back to whatever tool was active when you started the Liquify filter this time. So for instance, if you opened the Liquify filter with the Bloat tool and a 128-pixel brush, then switched to the Pucker tool with a 64-pixel brush, clicking Reset takes you back to the Bloat tool, while clicking Default takes you to the Warp tool (which is the tool that's active the first time anyone opens the Liquify filter). Neither of these buttons changes anything you've done in your image.

◼ Type Masks: Setting an Image in Text

So far in this chapter, you've learned how to create regular text and glam it up by applying layer styles and effects. But you can also create text by filling letters with the contents of a photo, as shown in Figure 14-11.

The Type Mask tools work by making a selection in the shape of your letters. Essentially, they create a kind of stencil that you can then place on top of an image.

Once you've used these tools to create text-shaped selections, you can perform all sorts of neat tricks: emboss the text into an image (so that it looks like it's been stamped there); apply a stroke to the text's outline (useful if the font doesn't have a built-in outline option); or copy the text and move it to another document entirely.

FIGURE 14-11

Using the Type Mask tools, you can create text that's made from an image. These tools also let you emboss text into a photo (see Figure 14-13).

If you'd like to follow along, you can download sunset.jpg—*the photo used as the basis for this image and Figure 14-12—from this book's Missing CD page at* www.missingmanuals.com/cds.

Using the Type Mask Tools

Here's how to create a type mask and lay it over an image so that the letters are filled with whatever is in the image:

1. **Open the image you want to appear inside the text.**

2. **Activate one of the Type Mask tools.**

   Click the type tool in the Tools panel or press T. Then, in the Tool Options area, select the Type Mask tool you want—horizontal or vertical. The Type Mask tools behave just like the regular type tools: A horizontal mask goes across the page, a vertical mask goes up and down. The Type Mask tools also have the same Tool Options settings as the regular type tools, except for Color (the color box is still there, it just doesn't do anything). It's important to choose a really blocky font for the type mask, since you can't see much of the image if you use thin text.

3. **Click your image and start typing.**

   When you click, a red film covers the image. The red indicates the area that *won't* appear in the letters. By typing, you cut a selection through the red area (see Chapter 5 if you need a refresher on selections). In other words, instead of creating regular text, you're creating a text-shaped *selection*. You can see the shape of the selection as you type.

It's hard to reposition the words once you've committed them, so take a good look at what you've got. While the mask is active, you can move it by dragging it, as explained in Figure 14-12.

FIGURE 14-12

Once you've activated the Type Mask tool and clicked in the image, you'll see this red mask appear over the picture. As you type, the text appears, as shown here.

As long as you haven't committed the text yet, you can easily move it around by dragging it (you may need to grab a spot a little ways away from the text itself). You can rotate or resize the letters by pressing Ctrl/⌘ and then grabbing a corner of the bounding box that appears. When you click the Commit icon (the green checkmark—not shown), Elements turns the text into a text-shaped selection.

4. **Adjust the Tools Options settings until you like how the text looks.**

   Once you click the Commit icon (the green checkmark below the text) in the next step, you won't be able to alter the text as easily as you can with the regular type tools. That's because the regular tools create their own layers, while the Type Mask tools just create selections. Once you commit it, the text is just like any other selection—Elements doesn't see it as text anymore, so you can no longer change its size by highlighting it and picking a different size in the Tool Options, for example.

5. **When you're happy with the selection, click the Commit checkmark.**

   When you click this icon, Elements turns the outline of the text into an active selection. You can move the selection's outline by nudging it with the arrow keys, and use the Transform Selection command (page 173) to scoot it around in your image or to resize, transform, or rotate it. (This can make the letters look a little strange, though, so watch the effects carefully.)

6. **Remove the non-text portion of the image.**

   Go to Select→Inverse and then press Backspace/Delete to remove the rest of the image and create letters filled with the image. (If you don't perform this step, you'll just have a text-shaped selection to admire.) Or you can copy and paste the selection into another document.

If you want a transparent background, double-click the Background layer in the Layers panel to turn it into a regular layer *before* you perform this step. Otherwise, the area outside the letters will be filled with the current background color.

Figure 14-13 shows the effect of pressing Ctrl+J/⌘-J to place a type mask selection onto a duplicate layer of its own, and then adding layer styles to the new layer.

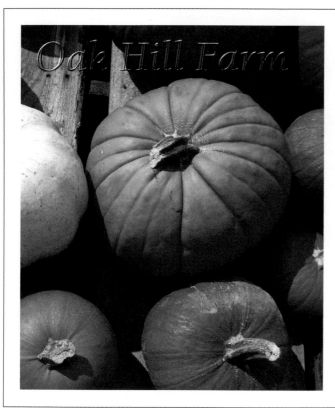

FIGURE 14-13

By copying text to another layer, you can bevel or emboss it into your photo.

This image shows something you need to watch out for—text that's kind of hard to see because it blends into the image. You may need to place your text a few times before it's positioned so that it's legible, or you can add a colored outline (as described in the next section) to make it stand out more.

Creating Outlined Text

If the font you're using doesn't come with a built-in outline style (if it had one, it would appear in the Tool Options area's Style menu—page 481—but very few font families have such a style), Elements gives you three ways to create outlined text. The Graphics panel's text effects (page 491) include an outline effect that you can apply with just a double-click. If you don't like what you get with that, you can also use the Stroke layer styles or the Type Mask tools to outline text. Both of these methods (which are explained in this section) are easy, but they're a bit more time-consuming than using the Graphics panel. On the plus side, they give you more control over the result. Use the layer-styles method if you want the text's outline to be filled in; the type-mask method gives you an empty outline.

To add an outline to text with the Stroke layer style:

1. **Open an Image or create a new one, and then activate a type tool.**

   Click the tool's icon in the Tools panel or press T until you get either the Horizontal or Vertical Type tool (not the Type *Mask* tool).

2. **Adjust the Tool Options settings.**

   Select a font, size, style, and so on.

3. **Enter some text and commit it.**

   After you type the text, click the green checkmark below it.

4. **Apply a Stroke layer style.**

   Open the Effects panel (choose Window→Effects), click the word "Styles" at the top of the panel, choose Strokes from the panel's drop-down menu, and then double-click the style you want. Even if you don't like any of the Stroke styles, go ahead and pick one; you can edit the results in the next step.

5. **Edit the outline, if you wish.**

   In the Layers panel, double-click the Text layer's layer style icon (the little *fx* to the right of the layer's name) to bring up the Style Settings dialog box, where you can change the outline's width and color (see page 462).

Your other option is to use the Type Mask tool to create a text outline like the one shown in Figure 14-14. Here's how:

FIGURE 14-14

The Type Mask tools let you create outlined text almost as quickly as ordinary text.

1. **Open an image or create a new one (if you just want the text to be all by itself), and then activate the Type Mask tool of your choice.**

   Click the type tool's icon in the Tools panel or press T, and then select either of the Type *Mask* tools.

2. **Choose a font and size.**

Use the Tool Options settings to pick a font you like, adjust its size, and so on. Outlined text works better with a fairly heavy font rather than a slender one, and bold fonts work better than regular ones.

3. **Enter some text.**

Click in the image where you want the text to go, and then type away. If you want to warp the text (page 488), do that now, before you commit it.

4. **Make sure you like how your text looks, and then click the Commit icon (the green checkmark).**

Once you commit the text, it changes into a selection that's hard to edit. If you'd rather start over, click the Cancel icon (the red circle with a slash) instead.

5. **Add an outline to the text.**

Be sure the text selection is active, and then go to Edit→Stroke (Outline) Selection. In the Stroke dialog box, choose a line width in pixels and the color you want, and then click OK. (Page 428 has details about your other choices in this dialog box.) Your selection turns into an outline of the text you typed.

> **TIP** You can also create a hollow outline using the Stroke layer styles: Type some text, commit it, and then simplify the Text layer (Layer→Simplify). Next, go to the Effects panel and choose a stroke layer style in a contrasting color. After that, select the color of the text itself (as opposed to the outline) with the Magic Wand (page 165; be sure to turn off the tool's Contiguous setting), and then delete that color. The downside to this approach is that you can't edit the text once you simplify it.

■ Artistic Text

Elements offers three tools for adding really fancy text to images: Text on Selection, Text on Shape, and Text on Custom Path. With these tools, you can make text curve, swoop, and turn, or even run around a circle. They really bump things up when it comes to adding text to images.

All three tools use a concept that used to exist only in full Photoshop: *paths*. A path is just what it sounds like: In the same way that your feet follow a path in the park, a path in Elements is a guideline for where text should go. The path is visible when you're creating it, adding text to it, or editing the Text layer, but it won't appear in the finished image. All folks will see is the cool way you've made the text snake around.

Adding Text to a Selection

The Text on Selection tool is pretty simple to use: Just select the object where you want the text to appear and then type away. Here's how to get started:

1. **Open a photo in the Editor.**

   This tool doesn't work well on blank or solid-colored files. If you want to start with one of those, use the Text on Custom Path tool (explained on page 504) instead, or create a selection before activating this tool (see Chapter 5).

   You don't need to create a separate layer for this maneuver; the tool will automatically put the text on its own layer.

2. **Activate the Text on Selection tool.**

   Press T and then click this tool's icon in the Tool Options area, which is a T with a dotted-line square around it.

3. **Select the object where you want the text to appear.**

   When you first click the photo, you see a cursor that looks like the Quick Selection tool's—a circle with a crosshair inside it—and it works the same way. Drag over the area you want to select, and Elements finds the object's edges for you. Keep dragging to add to the area, or Alt-drag/Option-drag to remove part of the selection.

4. **Adjust the size of the selection and accept it.**

   You can use the Tool Options area's Offset slider to make the selection larger or smaller: Drag it left to reduce the size or right to increase it. (This slider makes a visible difference only if your image is fairly small; on large, high-resolution images, it has no effect.) When you like the selection, click the green Commit checkmark in your image or press Enter/Return to accept the selection. If you want to start over, click the red Cancel icon instead or press Esc.

5. **Choose your Tool Options settings.**

   Pick a font, style (regular, bold, or whatever), size, and color, just as you would with the regular type tools.

6. **Tell Elements where you want the text to appear, and then enter some text.**

   When you committed your selection in step 3, the outline changed from marching ants to a solid line. That's the path for your text, and it's visible only when this tool is active; click over to another tool and the line disappears. It's just a working guideline, and it won't print, either.

   When you move your cursor close to the path, it changes to the text-insertion I-beam shown in Figure 14-15 to let you know that you can start typing. You can click anywhere on the path and type as much or as little as you want. Just be careful not to overrun the starting point if you type all the way around the selection, or you may lose some of the text.

7. **When you're through typing, click the green Commit checkmark.**

   As with the regular type tools, you can't use Enter/Return to commit the text; you have to click the checkmark. If you don't like the way the text looks, click the Cancel icon (the red circle) instead.

> **TIP** Watch out that you don't overrun the beginning of your text when you're typing your way around the selection. If you do that, parts of the text will disappear. You may be able to backspace your way out of it, but if that doesn't work, you'll have to start over.

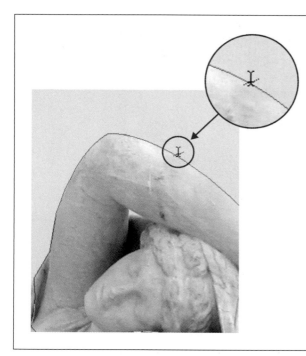

FIGURE 14-15

When your cursor changes to this shape, you're ready to click and then start typing.

If you don't like where the text is going (say it's inside the selection and you want it outside, or vice versa), press and hold Ctrl/⌘ so that a little black arrow appears next to the cursor. Then drag so that it's inside or outside the path and your text will follow it.

It's pretty tricky to see what you're doing sometimes because you also see the Move tool bounding box for the selection itself, but you want to be sure you see the I-beam cursor with the tiny arrow next to it before you start dragging.

That's the basic way to use Text on Selection, but there are a few tricks that make this tool much more useful than it first appears:

- **Use any kind of selection**. Although this tool uses the same selection-making smarts as the Quick Selection tool, you can actually create a selection with any tool, which is handy if your image doesn't give this tool much to work with. Just make a selection *before* you use this tool; that way, when you activate the Text on Selection tool, you should see the Commit and Cancel icons in the image. (If you don't, click once inside the selection to make them appear.) Click the Commit checkmark and you've got yourself a path.

- **Move the text inside or outside the path**. Figure 14-15 explains how to change where the text appears.

- **Move the text's starting point**. If you start typing and then wish you'd started someplace *else* on the path, go ahead and commit the text anyway. Then make sure Text on Selection is still selected in the Tool Options and that the Text layer is active (if it isn't, click it in the Layers panel), and you should see a circle at the beginning of the text's baseline. Grab that and drag it to move the text where you want it. (If you have trouble doing this, you can also click over to the Shape Selection tool [page 427] and grab the text with that tool instead.)

- **Resize the text**. If you wish you'd made the text larger or smaller or that you'd used a different font, that's easy to fix. With any of the text tools active, head over to the Layers panel and double-click the Text layer's T icon to select all the text on it. Then, in the Tool Options area, change the text's font or size till you like what you see. (You can also use the Move and Transform tools on the text, but if you want to change only the letters and not the overall size of the selection, this is the best way to do it.)

- **Resize your selection**. Anytime after you create a selection with this tool but before you commit the text, you can hold down Ctrl/⌘ and you'll see the Move tool's handles appear in your image. Drag one, and the text will follow the new shape. Or, after you commit the text, you can use the Move tool to drag a handle. Both methods resize the selection as well as the letters. Just don't try to make the text a *lot* bigger this way, or it may start to look pixelated.

The one thing you can't do is adjust the spacing of individual letters, unfortunately. Despite this limitation, the Text on Selection tool is great for adding text to your images in ways that are much more interesting than boring straight lines.

Making Text Outline a Shape

You can also make text outline the shape of a heart or butterfly, for example. This is very popular for scrapbooking and projects like greeting cards. It works pretty much the same way as the Text on Selection tool, except you can start with a blank file, if you want. Figure 14-16 shows an example of what you can create.

To get started, activate the Text on Shape tool by pressing T until you see its icon in the Tools panel, which is a capital T with a squiggly square around it. Then:

1. **In the Tool Options area, choose the shape you want.**

   You don't get to choose from *all* of Elements' shapes: Your only options are rectangle, rounded rectangle, ellipse, polygon, heart, speech bubble, and butterfly. However, the Tip at the end of this section explains how to put text around other shapes.

2. **Drag in your image to draw the shape.**

   Once you let go of your mouse, the shape turns into a path, meaning it won't be visible as a shape in the finished image—it's only a guideline for entering text.

FIGURE 14-16

Here's a basic example of what you can do with the Text on Shape tool.

With a pointy shape like this, when you reach the tricky spots, adding a few extra spaces can help keep the letters from piling up.

3. **In the Tool Options area, make your font choices; then click the path where you want the text to start and type away.**

   The Tool Options settings let you adjust the font, style, size, and color of the text.

4. **When you're done, click the green Commit checkmark.**

   If you decide to forget the whole thing, click the red Cancel icon instead.

Some of the shapes put the text inside their paths and some put it outside, but you can use the technique explained back in Figure 14-15 to override this and put the text wherever you want it.

TIP   You can put text around *any* shape, not just the ones available in the Tool Options area when the Text on Shape tool is active. Simply use the Custom Shape tool (page 423) to draw a shape. Next, create a new layer, get out the Magic Wand, turn on the Sample All Layers checkbox, and then use the Wand to select the shape. Once you have a selection, switch to the Text on Selection tool and use it as explained in the previous section. If you don't want the Shape layer to appear in your completed image, simply delete it.

Creating Your Own Path

There's yet *another* way to make text loop and curve, and it's the most flexible of all: creating a custom path for the text to follow. You can draw a path that's any shape you like, and this technique works just as well on a blank file as on an image file. This is a great tool for adding dramatic text effects to images. Here's how to use it:

1. **Activate the Text on Custom Path tool.**

   Press T and then click this tool's icon, which is at the bottom left of the Tool Options area and looks like a T with a squiggle below it.

2. **Draw a path.**

   When you activate this tool, your cursor changes to an old-fashioned fountain pen nib. (If it doesn't, head to the Tool Options area and click the pencil icon.) Simply drag to draw a path for the text. You can follow the outline of an object in a photo, or just draw freehand. Like the paths you can create with the Text on Selection and Text on Shape tools, what you draw here is a non-printing guideline for entering text. As soon as you release your mouse button, you'll see the Commit and Cancel icons.

   If you like the path you draw, click the green Commit checkmark and skip to step 4. If you think your path is imperfect but salvageable, continue with step 3. And if you want to start your path over from scratch, click the red Cancel icon and try again.

3. **Refine the path.**

   If you aren't thrilled with how your path looks, that's OK, because it's easy to fix. In the Tool Options area, click the Modify button (the gray arrow). Figure 14-17 explains how it works. Once you've got the path's anchor points adjusted to your liking, click the green Commit checkmark. If you decide it would be easier to start over, click the red Cancel icon instead.

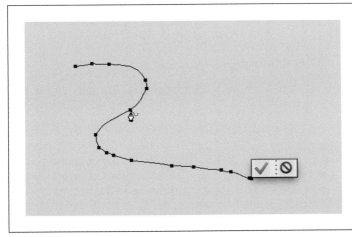

FIGURE 14-17

When you click the Modify button, you see these little square anchor points, which are something like the ones for the Magnetic Lasso tool (page 169).

Drag an anchor point to move it; Alt-click/Option-click a point to remove it; or Shift-click to add a new one. By manipulating the anchor points, you can smooth out a rather bumpy line like this one.

4. **Add some text.**

   After you commit the path, the anchor points disappear and it seems like there's nothing else you can do, but if you move the cursor near the path, you see the I-shaped text-entry cursor appear. But before you start typing, go to the Tool

Options and choose a font, style, size, and color. Then click the path where you want the text to start and type away.

5. **Commit the text.**

When you're through typing, click the green Commit checkmark. (To make the text go away, click the red Cancel icon instead.)

One of the really great things about the Text on Custom Path tool is that you can go back anytime and edit any aspect of your work, as long as you don't simplify it (page 424). Just make sure the Text layer is active and then, in the Tool Options area, click this tool's Modify button; then you can drag the path all over the place. To edit the text, double-click the Text layer's T icon in the Layers panel to select it. You can also use all the techniques for moving and resizing listed in the "Adding Text to a Selection" section (page 500).

> **TIP** When the Modify button is active, you see a circle and an X on the baseline for your text. The X marks the start of the text, and there's a tiny, almost invisible circle that marks the end of it. If you type so much that the text circles back past your starting point, or if you drag the beginning of the text so it's past the circle, some of the letters you typed will disappear or the text will bunch up in weird places on the path. To fix that, find the circle and drag it farther away from the starting point.

Sharing Images

CHAPTER 15:
Creating Projects

CHAPTER 16:
Printing Photos

CHAPTER 17:
Email and the Web

CHAPTER 18:
Creating Slideshows

Creating Projects

I f you're into making scrapbooks, greeting cards, or other photo concoctions, Elements is the perfect tool for you. The program is crammed with add-on graphics, frames, and other special effects; it even lets you create multipage documents. You can dress up pictures in all sorts of creative ways without any other software.

This chapter kicks off with an in-depth look at how to create photo collages. Once you've got those steps under your belt, all the other projects (summarized starting on page 519) use the same basic method.

You'll also learn how to create photo books and calendars using Shutterfly, Adobe's online photo-printing partner. (If you aren't in the U.S. or Canada, you may see Photoworld, Service Photo Online, or Online Photo Service as your options for ordering photo books and calendars.) To learn how to create slideshows with Elements, flip to Chapter 18.

> **NOTE** Most of the templates you use for these projects are actually stored online, so you'll need an Internet connection the first time you choose a new template. After that, Elements stores the template on your hard drive so you don't have to be online to use it, just like the artwork in the Graphics panel (page 526).

Photo Collages

The Create button (at the upper right of your screen in both the Editor and the Organizer) helps you make fancy pages featuring your photos, which you can then share as either printouts or digital files. Although Elements gives you lots of preset layouts to start from, you can customize every aspect of them to create projects that are totally your own.

> **NOTE** This chapter starts by explaining how to create a collage, since that's the most generic of Elements' Create projects, and the others (photo book, calendar, and so on) work like the collage, but with particular limitations and variations for each one. However, in Elements 13, the collage is also the one project you probably *don't* want to make in Create, for the simple reason that you can create one without a special template (unlike, say, a DVD label [page 523]).
>
> In some previous versions of Elements, the Create feature offered options that weren't available elsewhere in the Editor, but that's no longer the case. So, honestly, if you want to create a collage, you're probably better off just starting with a blank file in Expert mode (File→New→Blank File) that's the size you want and then making your project there, since you can save it in any format you like, rotate the page (if you want), and then add everything from the Graphics panel without the limitations that Create imposes.

One type of page you can make in Create is a *photo collage*, which displays one or more photos, with or without a themed background. (Figure 15-1 gives you a glimpse of what you can do.) Elements starts you off with one basic template crammed with suggested photo placeholders, but you can add or remove photos, as well as change the background, frame styles, and other details.

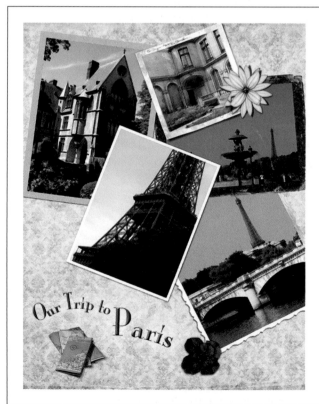

FIGURE 15-1

Except for the photos, all the artwork in this composition came from the Graphics part of the Create panel.

The photos were added first, their layers merged together, and then several filters were applied to give this collage a painted effect (see Chapter 13 for more about filters). The curvy text was created using the Text on Custom Path tool (page 504), and layer styles were applied to it.

Finally, the remaining graphics (the flowers and the maps) were added to make them look like they're lying on a painted page.

To create a photo collage:

1. **Open some photos in the Editor or select them in the Organizer.**

   This step is optional, but if you preselect photos, Elements can automatically place them into the collage for you.

2. **Go to Create→Photo Collage.**

   If you start from the Organizer, Elements bounces you over to the Editor to create the collage. Don't be dismayed by the relatively small size of the Photo Collage window that opens—once you make choices here and then click OK, you'll be working in the main Editor window.

3. **On the left side of the Photo Collage window, choose a page size.**

   If you're confused about the "Print locally" option above the size choices, it's there to indicate that this is a project designed for you to print at home. (Some of the other projects, like photo books [page 519], offer online printing, and for those projects you'll see "Shutterfly" above the list of items you can order from them.)

TIP You can't easily rotate the collage sizes to change them from portrait orientation to landscape or vice versa, so if you start a collage and don't like the orientation for the size you chose, you may find it simpler just to create your collage by starting with a blank file in Expert mode. You can do everything there that you can here—you just don't start out with a pre-designed project, so you have to add all the items you want to include instead of modifying things that are already there.

4. **In the middle of the Photo Collage window, select a theme.**

   Themes add coordinated backgrounds and frames for your photos, and in some cases, coordinated text styles as well. Click a theme's thumbnail to select it, and the right side of the window gives you a closer look at your choice. If you don't like any of the existing themes, it doesn't really matter, since you can change every detail once you get to the main Create window. So just pick the theme you dislike the least.

NOTE When you start your first collage, you may not see any choices other than the cluttered Basic theme, but that doesn't matter. You can quickly get rid of any extra frames in step 7 below.

5. **Tell Elements whether to automatically place your images in the collage.**

   If you leave the "Autofill with Selected Images" checkbox at the bottom of the Photo Collage window turned on, the pictures you chose in the Organizer or

Photo Bin in step 1 automatically appear in the collage when Elements creates it. (If you didn't preselect any photos, the currently active photo in the Editor gets added, if you have any photos open there.) If *you* want to determine which photos go into which slots, turn this checkbox off.

> **NOTE** Unlike some earlier versions of Elements, the Create projects in Elements 13 start with a fixed number of pages. So if you've selected more photos than will fit in your current layout choice, Elements just doesn't place them (rather than automatically increasing the page count to accommodate the extra photos the way, say, Elements 8 did). Nowadays, a collage can be only one page long. So if you want more pages, create a separate file for each one.

6. **When you've made your choices, click OK.**

   Elements sends you back to the main Create window and gets to work creating the collage. When it's done thinking, it displays the collage in the editing area.

   If you preselected photos and left the Autofill checkbox turned on, Elements puts the photos into frames for you. (It puts each image in the collage on its own layer.) If you didn't select any photos (or if you didn't select enough to fill all the slots), you see the text "Click here to add photo or Drag photo here" inside each empty frame. That's fine, because you can add photos in step 8.

   At this point, you're working in what Adobe calls Basic mode, explained in Figure 15-2.

FIGURE 15-2

When you first return to the main Create workspace after choosing a project, Elements puts you in Basic mode. That means that the Artwork panel on the right shows only a limited number of choices that are meant to go well together. You can add graphics and text here, but if you want access to all of Elements' graphics, you need to click the button circled here to switch to Advanced mode.

7. **Choose a layout.**

After Elements creates the collage, the program displays some new options. Below the Create panel is an icon labeled Pages. A collage has only one page, so when you click this icon, your page's thumbnail is displayed in its lonely glory. (For projects that have multiple pages—like photo books—this is where you'd navigate among thumbnails of the project's different pages.)

If you like the preview that Elements shows you, there's no need to change anything. But if you click the Layouts icon below the Create panel, you see a bunch of alternative designs, grouped by the number of photos. To audition a different layout, either double-click its thumbnail or drag it onto the collage in the preview area. If you don't like it, undo it (Ctrl+Z/⌘-Z) and try another one.

TIP   If you plan to use only a couple of photos, one fast way to get rid of the extra photo frames in the Basic layout is to scroll down the Create panel till you see a layout with only one or two photos. Double-click the layout you want and the extra frames go away.

---

8. **Adjust the photos.**

If you haven't already picked photos for this project, drag a photo from the Photo Bin into a frame. (If you don't see the Photo Bin, click the Photo Bin button below the preview area to display it.) Or click the placeholder text in an empty frame in the collage, and then choose a photo using the dialog box that appears.

Regardless of how you get photos into the collage, you can make a number of adjustments to them once they're there. The next section (page 514) explains everything you can do with photos and frames in a Create project, but for now, here are a couple of quick changes you can make:

- Once you click a frame, you should see the Move tool's bounding box around it. (If you want to see the Move Tool's Tool Options, just click the Tool Options button below the preview area.) Use the Move tool to stack your photos in the right order, and align or distribute them, if you want.

- You can change a frame's style by selecting that frame in the collage and then clicking the Graphics button below the Create panel. Then, double-click the frame you want in the panel or drag it onto the photo.

9. **Customize the collage.**

This is the fun part. Click a photo in your collage and drag it into a different position. Or click the Graphics button below the Create panel, and then drag art from the panel onto your collage (these graphics are vector images [page 424], so they'll look great no matter how big or small you make them). You can also add text to the collage by clicking the T on the left side of the preview area and then clicking where you want to add text.

If you switch to Advanced mode (page 518), you can even flatten your image and use filters on the entire page. Figure 15-1 shows an example of the kind of page you can create with a photo collage.

10. **Finish up your collage.**

When you're done, you have a couple of choices of what to do next:

- **Click Save** at the bottom of the Create workspace to bring up the Save As window so you can name the project and save it. You have to save it as a PSE file—a special format just for Create projects (see the box on page 515 for details)—or a PDF file. (If you decide you don't like your collage, click Close at the bottom of the Create workspace instead and then tell Elements not to save your file when it asks.) If you want to create a collage in a regular image format like TIFF or JPEG, then export your collage as explained below.

> **TIP** While you can wait till you're done to save your collage, you might want to click the Save button regularly as you work so you don't risk losing anything in case of a crash.

- **Print your collage** right from Create, the way you would any other file (see Chapter 16). Just click the Print button at the bottom of the Elements window, or press Ctrl+P/⌘-P.

- **Export your collage** so you can share it with people who can't open PSE files, or so you can send it out for printing to a service that accepts only JPEG files, say. Go to File→Export Creations to bring up a window where you can save your collage as a JPEG, TIFF, or PDF file. Just choose the format you want in the drop-down menu, and then click the Browse button and choose where to save it.

> **NOTE** Once you save a Create project, it always opens back up in the Create workspace. That means you can't open it in Expert mode, so just switch over to Advanced mode (page 518) for maximum editing flexibility.

Customizing Your Project

There are lots of ways to personalize your collage. Most of what you've read in the other chapters in this book works here, too. Plus you can do a few special things with photos in a collage. This section explains your options.

■ ADJUSTING PHOTOS AND FRAMES

Elements gives you a ton of ways to tweak the photos in a collage:

- **Rotate a photo in its frame**. Right-click/Control-click a photo and then choose Rotate 90 Right or Rotate 90 Left to turn the photo 90 degrees clockwise or counterclockwise.

- **Adjust the way a photo appears in its frame**. Right-click/Control-click a photo and choose "Position Photo in Frame" (or just double-click it) to bring up the controls explained in Figure 15-3.

About PSE Files

When it comes time to save a Create project in Elements, you get only one editable file-format choice: PSE. (If you save your project as a PDF instead, you won't be able to go back and edit it later.) This special format has both advantages and disadvantages.

When you create a PSE file, you actually create a *folder* containing a separate .psd file for each page (or for each double-page spread, if you're creating a photo book), and a PSE *project file* that contains all the info Elements needs to reassemble the document the next time you open it. That's handy when you're working in Elements, but the drawback is that hardly any other program can read these files.

PSE files work just fine if you print at home or use Shutterfly for online printing; you can send them to Shutterfly as easily as you send JPEGs. The rub comes when you want to use a *different* printing service. If you make, say, a book that you want to print at Lulu.com or MyPublisher.com, they don't accept PSE files—at least not as of this writing. Most printing services require PDF files instead.

Fortunately, Elements can save your multipage PSE file as a multipage PDF that you can upload to your printing service of choice. (Be aware, though, that Elements creates *huge* PDF files.) Usually, you'll want to wait till you're through editing your project to create a PDF. So keep the file in PSE format as long as you still have work to do, and then when you're ready to send it out to a printer other than Shutterfly, save it as a PDF. (Be sure to save the PSE file, too, if you think you might want to edit it again.) There's also an Export Creations command in the File menu; select it and Elements saves all the pages of your photo book as separate JPEGs or TIFFs, or as a single PDF file.

FIGURE 15-3

Double-click a photo in a Create project to see these controls. (If you have trouble bringing them up, try clicking the Move tool in the Create workspace's toolbox before double-clicking the photo.) You can resize the picture with the slider, rotate the photo by clicking the blue rectangles, or search for a new photo by clicking the yellow folder icon. You can also drag a handle of the photo's bounding box to resize the photo or rotate it, just the way you'd use the Move tool. When it looks good, click the green checkmark to accept your changes.

- **Remove a photo from the collage**. Right-click/Control-click the photo, and then choose Clear Photo. To remove the photo's placeholder and frame as well, click the photo to select it, and then press Backspace/Delete.

- **Remove a frame from a photo**. Right-click/Control-click the photo, and then choose Clear Frame.

- **Resize a frame**. You can resize a frame either before or after you put a photo into it. Single-click a blank area within the frame (not the placeholder text) to bring up resizing handles, and then drag a corner handle to make the frame larger or smaller. These handles also let you rotate frames.

- **Resize a frame to fit a photo**. If you want to make a frame fit a photo instead of the other way around, right-click/Control-click the photo and then choose Fit Frame To Photo.

- **Edit a photo**. Right-click/Control-click the photo and choose Edit Quick, and Elements whisks your photo off to Quick Fix so you can make last-minute changes. (For some reason, this command is grayed out in certain types of projects. So it works for photo books but usually not for collages.) When you're finished editing, click the "Back to Creations" button at the top left of the preview area.

- **Add another photo**. Just drag a frame from the Create panel's Graphics section (you may need to click Graphics below the panel to see it) to a blank area of the collage, and then click within the frame to add a photo. (If you get too close to an existing frame, the new frame may replace the existing one. If that happens, just press Ctrl+Z/⌘-Z to undo it and then drag again, more carefully, to the blank spot.) You can also drag a photo into the collage from the Photo Bin.

- **Edit a frame's layer style**. Most of the Create panel's frames have layer styles applied to them. Right-click/Control-click a frame in the collage, and then choose Edit Layer Style to change things like the size of the frame's drop shadow. If you switch to Advanced mode (page 518), you can also edit the styles via the Layers the same way you'd edit any layer style (page 462).

- **Add a filter to a photo**. If you click over to Advanced mode (page 518), you get access to all of Elements' filters (page 435) so you can quickly create a brushed look or a rubber-stamp effect, for example. However, you have to simplify the photo's layer before you can use filters on it (page 209 explains simplifying).

■ ADDING GRAPHICS AND TEXT

It's easy to add all sorts of embellishments to a collage. Click the Graphics button below the Create panel to see a long list of stuff designed to harmonize with your current theme. The list is divided into three categories:

- **Backgrounds**. If you don't like the look of the page's background, just drag in a new one. Drop it anywhere in the preview area (or just double-click it in the Create panel), and Elements replaces the existing background with it. (Backgrounds are *Smart Objects*, which are explained in the box on page 517.)

NOTE If you're in Basic mode, you may not see some of the options described here. To see *all* the artwork the Create panel has to offer, switch to Advanced mode by clicking the button at the top left of the preview area. (Both modes are described in the next section.)

- **Frames**. Elements includes some super fancy frames. Some of them even tint your photo; you can tell which ones will do this by looking at the part of a frame's thumbnail where the picture will go—if it's colored red or blue, for example, then the photo will get tinted that color. Others cut your photo into various shapes. These options give you all kinds of interesting ways to frame your photos, so try a few to see which ones you like. Just double-click one or drag it onto a photo.

- **Graphics**. You can add all sorts of clip art to Create projects. The great thing about these graphics is that they're vector objects (page 424), so you can resize them as much as you want without having them go all pixely—as long as you don't simplify them (page 209). The thumbnails in the Graphics section may look a little funny, and so may the graphics after you drag their handles to make them bigger, but once you press Enter/Return, they should settle down into perfect detail.

TIP If you don't like scrolling all around the Create panel, click the arrow to the right of a category's name to collapse that section and bring the next one into view.

POWER USERS' CLINIC

Smart Objects

Smart Objects are one of the ways Adobe makes Elements' Create projects so fun and easy. Like their big-shot cousins in the full version of Photoshop, these objects seem to know where they are and what you're trying to do—and behave accordingly. Here are a few examples of Smart Objects and what makes them so smart:

- When you apply a new background from the Graphics panel or the Graphics section of the Create panel, it automatically zooms down to the bottom of the layer stack to replace the existing background.

- The frames from the Graphics and Create panels automatically target your photos. Want to frame an image? Just go to the Graphics panel and double-click a frame. It automatically appears in your project, though you may need to adjust its size or the area that it frames.

- You can resize, transform, and distort objects from the Graphics panel's Graphics section as much as you want without affecting their quality. This behavior is something like how vector art works, but what's going on under the hood is quite different. (The preview may appear pixelated, but the actual object should be OK once you click the Commit icon [the green checkmark].)

Anything you put into an Elements file in Expert mode by choosing File→Place becomes a Smart Object, so you can do things like resize the object to any size. Also, anything you drag into one of the Create projects (photos, graphics, whatever) becomes a Smart Object. However, there are a few things you *can't* do to Smart Objects unless you simplify them (page 209). For example, if you try to paint on a Smart Object, you see the message shown in Figure 15-4.

FIGURE 15-4

You can enlarge, shrink, transform, and distort Smart Objects no problem, but if you try to paint on them or apply filters or effects to them, you get this message. It's fine to click OK, but once you do that, your formerly smart object will behave like any other object. For instance, you won't be able to enlarge it to more than 100 percent or it'll go all pixely on you.

■ CREATE MODES: BASIC AND ADVANCED

When you first start working on a Create project in the main Elements window, you're automatically in Basic mode (Figure 15-2 shows what this mode looks like). That means the Create panel shows you only options (like frames and graphics) that Adobe thinks would work well in your particular project. And the only tools available to you on the left side of the screen are the Move, Zoom, Hand, and type tools (Figure 15-5 explains how to add text to your collage). You can also zoom the view by using the slider above the right side of the preview area.

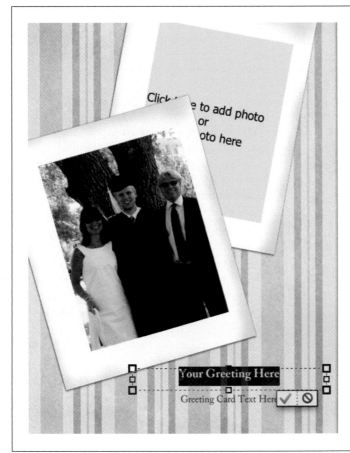

FIGURE 15-5

To add text to a Create project, click the T on the left side of the preview area, and then head to the Tool Options area and adjust the settings for the font, size, and so on (see Chapter 14 to learn about these settings).

Then, if the project has placeholder text, just drag over it, and then type the words you want.

If there's no placeholder text or if you want to add additional text, just click where you want the text to go and start typing.

You can put together a pretty impressive project working in Basic mode, but the folks at Adobe know you may want to do a lot more with your projects, so they created Advanced mode. To use this mode, click the Advanced Mode button above the left side of the preview area (circled in Figure 15-2). When you do that, you get a whole different set of options: The regular Elements Tools panel appears on the left side of the screen, and the button for the Layers panel appears on the lower right, so that you can see your layers. And when you click the Graphics button below the Create panel, you see *all* of Elements' graphics options, not just its suggested choices. You can also bring up other Elements panels, like the Effects panel, by selecting them in the Window menu.

You can toggle back and forth between the two modes as much as you like. Simply click the button above the main preview area to change modes. As a general rule, there's not much point in sticking with Basic mode for collages, since your choices are limited and a bit random, but for projects like photo books, Basic mode offers handy groupings of coordinated content.

NOTE In Elements 13, photo books and calendars are the only kind of Create projects that let you create a file with more than one page. You can't add pages to any kind of project except a photo book, and there's also no way to add extra pages to a file in the Editor anymore, like you could in old versions of Elements.

Photo Books

Elements lets you create several sizes of pages to use in bound photo books, which make great gifts. To get started, go to Create→Photo Book, and you'll see several different sizes to choose from. When you click a size on the left side of the Photo Book window, the right side changes to show details about it, as shown in Figure 15-6. Most photo books are meant to be ordered online, but there's an 8.5″ × 11″ size (well, technically 11″ × 8.5″) that you can print at home. In fact, you can actually print *any* Create project on your home printer, if you like.

FIGURE 15-6

When you choose a size from the list on the left, the right side of the window changes to show what you'll get if you order that kind of book and how much it costs.

Put your cursor over the thumbnails (circled) to see a larger view or get an animated look at sample pages.

At the bottom of the Photo Book window is a box where you can enter the number of pages you want, if you know how long you want the book to be. However, the photo books from Shutterfly automatically start out with 20 pages, since that's the minimum number you need to order from it (Shutterfly's maximum is 100 pages plus the title page), so you can't delete pages to bring the total below 20. If you want to make a 4- or 10-page book, then choose the 11" × 8.5" "print locally" option.

> **NOTE** Shutterfly could change the minimum number of pages it requires for photo books, so don't be surprised if one day you see a different number in the box at the bottom of the Photo Book window.

Creating a photo book is almost exactly like creating a collage (page 511). The only difference is that you have pages to navigate through in the Create workspace's Pages panel (click the Pages button below the Create panel to see it). Just click a different two-page spread to work on those pages. (Elements shows you the double-page spreads you'll see when the book is open.) You can also use the controls above the preview area to step through pages.

> **NOTE** Photo books usually have a cutout front cover, so the first page is the title page.

To add pages to a photo book, in the Pages panel, click the thumbnail of the double-page spread you want to duplicate, and then click the Add Page icon at the top of the panel, as explained in Figure 15-7. To remove a double-page spread (you can't remove just one page), click its thumbnail and then click the trashcan icon. (Keep in mind that Elements won't let you go below the minimum number of pages for Shutterfly-printed books.) You can rearrange pages by dragging their thumbnails in the panel.

FIGURE 15-7

To add a double-page spread to a photo book, click the thumbnail of the existing spread that uses the layout you want (or close to it), and then click the Add Page icon shown here. (Photo books are the only type of file where you can add pages this way.) You can then drag the new page thumbnail to where you want it.

To delete pages, click their thumbnails, and then click the trashcan.

When you finish creating the book, you can click Save or Print at the bottom of the Elements window, as with a collage. And, if you chose one of the Shutterfly options in the Photo Book window, there's also an Order button below the preview area that zips you over to Shutterfly so you can order the book. To order the book from *another* company, just save the file in PDF format, which is accepted almost everywhere.

To save a photo book, click the Save button. If you want to edit the book again later, choose the Photo Project Format (PSE) option (see the box on page 515). If you're already done editing, you can also save it as a PDF file. Or you can use the Export command as explained in the box on page 515. Photo book files have a special icon in the Photo Bin and Organizer that looks like a little stack of pages, but you can't expand it in the bin to see individual pages the way you could in some earlier versions of Elements.

> **TIP** You can create a book of photos without using Elements' Photo Book feature at all. Just open a web browser and head to the Shutterfly website, upload your photos, and then have the company print them in its own style of photo book. This method works with other photo-printing websites, too, like Lulu.com and MyPublisher.com; Mac folks can also order books through iPhoto (and most likely through the new Photos application when it comes out).

Greeting Cards

For greeting cards, Elements lets you choose from several different layouts: some single-page options and several folded styles. (Your actual options depend to some extent on where you are. If you're in England, for instance, you may not see any folded-card templates.) And although they're all templates for cards from Shutterfly, you can also print them at home. The process for creating a card is the same as for a collage (page 509) or photo book. To get started, choose Create→Greeting Card.

> **TIP** You can also create folded cards in the Editor. Just create a blank file that's the size of the paper you'll print it on, and then set a guide (page 87) to help you know where the fold will be. For a single-fold card, create one file for the outside of the card and a second one for the inside. For a card that's folded twice, you need only a single file, but you'll want a second guide for the second fold.

Photo Calendars

You can make very nice wall calendars in Elements. To get started, go to Create→Photo Calendar. In the Photo Calendar window, pick a month and year for the calendar's starting point, and then choose a theme. As with the other Create projects, you get a nice animated preview of each theme.

After you click OK, you can customize each month (add or remove photos, change the background, add artwork, and so on) using the methods explained earlier in this chapter (page 514). There's also a special way to customize specific dates, as Figure 15-8 explains.

> **TIP** Elements' calendars are designed to use a different photo (or group of photos) for each month, but if you want to see the *same* photo of your honey every month, say, you can do that. Just keep dragging it into the layout for each month where you want it to appear.

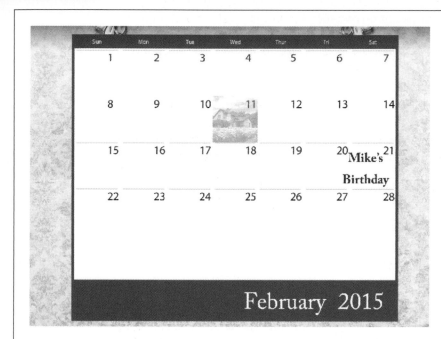

FIGURE 15-8

You can add a photo to any date on the calendar. Just drag an image in from the Photo Bin and then resize it to fit the slot for that date.

You can then jump over to Advanced mode and reduce the photo layer's opacity, as was done here, so you can see what you write on that date square.

And if you like, you can add text to mark your red-letter days (see the box below).

WORKAROUND WORKSHOP

Solving Text Problems in Calendars

You can add text to calendar projects the same way you add text to any other Elements document. Just click the T to the left of the preview area to activate the type tool, and then type away (see Chapter 14 for details).

But adding text to calendar projects can be a little frustrating. Sometimes, when you click to add text to your calendar, the text appears on a layer far down in the layer stack, next to the layer for the number for that day. So if you type in some text and you see only a blank box as you're typing, first check the Tool Options area to be sure that the text's color is set to something that should be visible against the background. If it is, commit your text, and then click over to Advanced mode (page 518), click the Layers button at the bottom of the Editor window, and then drag the text layer up to the top of the layer stack.

◼ CD/DVD Jackets

Elements lets you create CD jewel case inserts and DVD inserts, which appear on the front and back of the case. To make a CD insert in either the Editor or the Organizer, just go to Create→CD Jacket.

The steps for creating a CD jacket are the same as for a photo collage (page 511) except that the layout choices are, of course, different. There's only one template, but after you click OK to close the CD Jacket window and create your project, you can see several layout options by clicking the Layouts button at the bottom of the Create workspace. Pay special attention to photo placement when choosing a layout; remember that the right side of the layout is the front cover. Turn the "Autofill with Selected Images" checkbox off or on to suit you.

Unfortunately, only the "2 Centered" layout even approximately marks out the general spine area, where most CDs display their titles. (To see the names of the various layouts, in the Layouts pane, put your cursor over the various thumbnails—without clicking.) If you decide to enter text that you want to appear on the spine, add a text block, and then either rotate it into position with the Move tool or switch to Advanced mode (page 518) and use the Rotate commands (page 514).

The process for creating a DVD Jacket (Create→DVD Jacket) is identical except for the layout choices.

◼ CD/DVD Labels

You can create stick-on labels for CDs and DVDs with Elements and print them on blank label sheets from any office supply store. To get started, go to Create→CD/DVD Label. As with CD/DVD *jackets*, Elements gives you just one template, but you have various choices in the Layouts pane (each layout creates a single label). When you're done creating your label, go to File→Export [type of project], save your work as a TIFF or JPEG file, and then place it into the template that goes with your specific brand of labels. (Most CD or DVD labels print two to a page.) The major brands, like Avery (*www.avery.com*) and Neato (*www.neato.com*), have free templates you can download from their websites to help you position the labels properly on the page.

TIP   While labels make your discs look great, it's risky to put a stick-on label on any disc you'll use in a computer because, if the label gets stuck in the disk drive, you may have to replace the drive. Consider using a marker to label discs instead, or buying printable discs if your printer can print on them.

◼ Facebook Cover

If you have a Facebook account (and who doesn't?), you know what a hassle it can be to change your profile photo or the large banner image at the top of your Facebook page (which Facebook calls your "cover" photo).

You may have noticed that people do all sorts of creative things to make these two images relate to each other in clever and original ways, and Elements 13 makes it easy for you to do that, too. Then, when you're satisfied with your artistic efforts, you can upload your work right from Elements. Unfortunately, Facebook's rules mean that the uploading process is a bit more complex than you'd probably like it to be, but Elements walks you through all the steps and makes it pretty easy.

In many ways, creating a Facebook cover is like making a collage. Here's what you do:

1. **In either the Editor or the Organizer, go to Create→Facebook Cover.**

   You can start with images already open or selected in the Organizer, or wait till step 3 to add them. (If you select a photo stored in your Revel account, you need to wait while Elements downloads it to your computer.) If you start from the Organizer, you get bounced over to the Editor to actually create your cover.

2. **In the Facebook Cover window, choose a theme, and then click OK.**

   The themes are divided into categories according to how many photos they use (one or multiple). There's a large preview on the right side of the window to help you pick one. You may not care for some of the added doodads (like fancy text blocks) in some of the themes, but don't worry about that stuff. Just focus on the number of photographs a theme uses, since you can customize it later. If you have open photos, turn on the "Autofill with Selected Photos" checkbox to make Elements place your open photos for you (or at least as many of them as the template has room for). If you choose a single-photo template, Elements uses the same photo for both the background banner and the smaller profile image.

   Once you click OK and Elements generates your cover, you may not like the result at all, but that's OK because you can adjust everything in the next step. On the other hand, if you're perfectly happy with how things look at this point, skip ahead to step 4.

3. **Customize your cover.**

   You can adjust each image by double-clicking it to bring up the controls shown back on page 515. Use them to resize your photo, rotate it, or even choose a different photo. If you click the Graphics button at the bottom right of your screen, you see some alternative ways to gussy up your cover image.

   TIP In a single-photo template, the smaller profile image (the one that drops down below the background image's bottom left) is just part of the main image. By moving the large image around and resizing it, you can adjust the part that appears in the profile image, but you can't use a completely different image there.

   If you click the Advanced Mode button, you can then access the Layers panel, which makes it easier to delete frames or ornaments you don't like or to add your own text and graphics. You can also add additional frames from the Graphics panel, just the way you do for a collage (page 513).

   You can delete items from your cover without going to Advanced Mode. If you dislike a graphic or text block, just click it to select it, and then press Delete to get rid of it.

4. **When your cover looks good, upload it to Facebook.**

Click the Upload button at the bottom of your screen. The first time you do this, you'll see a window asking you to authorize Elements to upload media to your Facebook account, then the Facebook sign-in page, and finally another window asking you to complete the authorization. As Elements prepares your cover for uploading, it slices your small profile image apart from the larger cover image. In the preview window that shows you what Elements is planning to upload, there are separate checkboxes for the profile photo and the cover photo. If you want to upload everything, leave them both checked. Click Next to continue.

FIGURE 15-9

You can customize the templates that Adobe provides. Don't like this text block? Just switch to the Move tool, select it, and then delete it. But keep a close eye on exactly what you're deleting. In some cases, other parts of the template may be on the same layer (like the border around the profile image), so it's helpful to make edits like this in Advanced mode (shown here), so you can keep track of the layers.

If you chose to upload both the profile image and the cover image, the window tells you that the cover image has been successfully updated. Click Continue and Elements launches your web browser and takes you to your Facebook page. You can drag your photo to reposition it if you want, but unless you've changed your mind since you started uploading, all you really need to do is click Save Changes.

If you decide you want to work on your project some more instead of uploading it, just click the Save button at the bottom of the screen; then name your file and Elements saves it as a layered PSE file so you can go back to it again later.

If you decide you don't want to save your work *or* upload it, click the Close button and tell Elements not to save your project.

5. **Switch back to Elements and click Continue to update your profile image.**

Elements takes you back to your web browser and your Facebook page. Click Done Cropping to finish up.

◼ Working with the Graphics and Favorites Panels

If you like all the graphics, frames, and other artistic goodies you can use in Create projects, you'll be happy to know you have access to all that stuff for *any* image in Elements. It all lives in the Graphics panel, which you can call up anytime in Expert mode. You also get the Favorites panel, where you can keep the items from the Graphics and Effects panels that you use most often. This section gives you a guided tour of both these panels.

The Graphics Panel

It's easy to navigate through all the goodies the Graphics panel contains (see Figure 15-10). Here's how to use it to glam up your images:

1. **In Expert mode, make sure the panel is visible.**

   If it's not, go to Window→Graphics, or if you're in the Editor's Basic mode (as opposed to Create's Basic mode), click the Graphics button below the Panel Bin.

2. **Choose how you want to search for fun additions to your image.**

   At the top of the Graphics panel are two drop-down menus. In the left-hand menu, choose what you want to search by (like activity, word, or mood), or choose Show All to see everything in the panel.

3. **Refine your search.**

   In the panel's right-hand menu, specify what you want. The items in this menu change depending on what you selected in the left-hand menu. For example, if you choose By Type on the left, then this menu includes Backgrounds, Frames, Graphics, and so on. If you choose By Mood on the left instead, the right-hand menu offers you choices like Active, Adventurous, Fun, Romantic, and Thoughtful.

   > **NOTE** If you know exactly what you're looking for, you can also search by name. Choose By Word in the left menu and the panel displays a text box where you can type in the name or a keyword for what you want. (To see the keywords associated with a particular item in the panel, right-click/Control-click it and choose Details.)

4. **Add the goody to your image.**

   To use anything in the Graphics panel, double-click its thumbnail or drag it onto your image. Every item you add comes in on its own layer. Be careful with backgrounds: they'll replace your existing image if you choose one of those and you only have a Background layer in your photo. If you want to *add* a background, first double click your existing Background layer to change it to a regular layer.

   To remove something you've added, press Ctrl+Z/⌘-Z (if you just added it), or click the object with the Move tool, and then press Delete. If you use the Delete key, Elements asks if you want to "Delete the Layer"—you do, so click OK.

FIGURE 15-10

Using the Graphics panel is super simple. Just use the left-hand menu to choose how you want to search, and then use the right-hand menu to refine your choice. Here you see the results of choosing By Type and Graphics, respectively. Notice that most of the thumbnails pictured here have a tiny blue banner at their upper-right corner. The first time you use a graphic marked with that banner, Elements has to download it, so you'll need an Internet connection. Happily, after Elements has downloaded that object once, it stores it on your computer so it's always available, whether you're online or not.

If you hate a particular item in the panel and want it gone forever, right-click/Control-click it and choose Delete Graphics. (Logically enough, this option is grayed out for online items that you haven't yet downloaded.)

If that method seems like it requires a lot of navigation to find what you want, check out the Favorites panel (described next) for a faster way to reach Graphics panel items you use a lot.

NOTE The full Graphics panel isn't available in the Create workspace's Basic mode. Just switch to Advanced mode (page 518) to see (and use) everything it contains.

The Favorites Panel

If you use the same effects, graphics, and styles over and over, you may find it tedious to keep navigating to them in the Graphics or Effects panels. Simplify things by saving your Graphics and Effects standbys in the Favorites panel so you can get to them with just a click or two. To see the Favorites panel, go to Window→Favorites, or click the Favorites button (the star) at the bottom right of the Editor window.

NOTE The first time you open the Favorites panel, you may be surprised to see that it's not empty. Adobe has chosen a few favorites *for* you; if you're not thrilled with its choices, simply delete them before adding your own.

To add an item to this panel, right-click/Control-click its thumbnail in the Graphics or Effects panel, and then choose "Add to Favorites," or just drag its thumbnail to the Favorites panel. If you forget what one of your favorites is for, you can see a description of it by right-clicking its thumbnail and choosing Details.

To delete a favorite, right-click/Control-click its thumbnail in the Favorites panel and then choose "Remove from Favorites," or click its thumbnail and then click the trashcan icon at the top of the panel. (Unlike in the Graphics panel, trashing something here just removes it from the Favorites panel, not from Elements altogether.)

Printing Photos

Now that you've gone to so much trouble to make your photos look terrific, you no doubt want to share your masterpieces with other people. This chapter and the next two look at the many different options Elements gives you for sharing photos with the world at large.

This chapter covers the traditional method: printing photos. You can print them at home on an inkjet printer, take them to a kiosk at a local store, or order prints online. Elements makes it especially simple to use Shutterfly, Adobe's online printing partner. The best thing about ordering photos online is that you're not limited to just ordinary prints: You can create hardcover books, calendars, embarrassing t-shirts—you name it.

It's worth noting that while the basics of printing are the same whether you're using a Windows computer or a Mac, some things are a bit different between the two platforms. This chapter notes the differences as they come up.

Getting Ready to Print

Whether you're printing at home or sending photos to a printing service, you need to make sure your image files are set up to create good-looking prints.

The first thing to check is the resolution, which controls the number of pixels per inch (ppi) in the image. If the photo doesn't have enough pixels, then the print will look grainy and pixelated. Most photo aficionados consider 300 ppi ideal; a quality print needs a resolution of at least 150 ppi to avoid the grainy look you see in low-resolution photos. See page 105 to learn how to check and—if necessary—tweak a photo's resolution.

> **TIP** Be sure to set the resolution to a whole number—using decimals may make some printers print black lines on your photos. For example, 247 ppi is fine, but 247.35 ppi may cause problems. (Older printers are most likely to have trouble with decimals.)

If you're printing on photo paper or sending photos out for printing, make sure the images are cropped to fit a standard photo paper size. (Cropping is covered starting on page 89.) And if you're printing at home, the paper and ink you use make a big difference in the color and quality of the prints. It may seem like just a marketing scam, but you really *will* get the best results by using the paper and ink your printer manufacturer recommends.

◼ Ordering Prints

You don't need to own a printer to print photos—there's no shortage of companies hoping you'll give *them* the privilege of doing it for you. You can order prints online or use a print kiosk at a local store. Elements makes it really easy to prepare photos for printing either way. Just save the photos in a compatible file format (see page 72 for more about picking a format). JPEG is usually your best bet, but always check with the service you plan to use to see if it has any special requirements.

If you're going to physically take your photos somewhere for printing (as opposed to ordering them online), you can copy the photos to a removable drive or burn them to a CD. To start the process, use the Organizer to export the photos to your desktop. First, in the Organizer, select the photos. Then choose File→Export As New File(s) to call up the window shown in Figure 16-1. If necessary, in the window's File Type section, pick a format (say you have TIFFs and the store needs JPEGs, for example). In the "Size and Quality" section, leave the Photo Size menu set to Original and use the Quality slider to choose maximum quality (11 or 12—this slider becomes active when you choose JPEG as the file type). In the Location section, click the Browse button and choose your desktop. If you want to rename the files, in the Filenames section, select Common Base Name, and then type something in the text field; Elements will give each exported file that new name followed by -1, -2, -3, and so on. When everything looks good, click Export, and Elements sends the files to your desktop. Then use your computer's CD-creation program to burn the exported photos to a disc, or just copy them to a memory card or a portable USB drive.

Adobe has partnered with the popular online photo-printing service Shutterfly to make it simple to upload photos from Elements to its site. You can order prints, books, or any of the other photo-bearing items that it would love to sell you. Of course, you're free to use any *other* online printing service, but ordering from them isn't integrated right into Elements the way it is with Shutterfly. (Outside North America, you may see CeWe or PhotoWorld as your option for ordering prints online.)

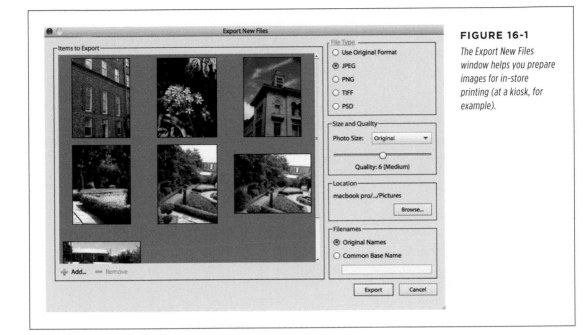

FIGURE 16-1

The Export New Files window helps you prepare images for in-store printing (at a kiosk, for example).

Once you've edited some photos and are ready to place an order, just follow these steps (they're the same for both Macs and PCs):

1. **Select the photos you want to have printed.**

   Open them in the Editor, or select them in the Organizer. (If you start from the Editor, your photos don't have to be in the Organizer.)

2. **Connect to Shutterfly and sign in.**

   You can order prints from Shutterfly from either the Editor or the Organizer:

   • **File menu.** Go to File→Order Prints→Order Shutterfly Prints.

   • **Create menu.** Go to Create→Photo Prints, and then choose Shutterfly from the list of options that appears.

   Regardless of where you start, Elements prepares your photos, connects to Shutterfly, and opens the Shutterfly window. You need to sign into Shutterfly or (if this is your first time using Shutterfly) create an account before you can order. An easy-to-follow series of guided question screens appears to help you set up an account and complete your order (see Figure 16-2).

FIGURE 16-2

You can choose from several different print sizes and order as many of each photo as you like.

As you can see here, you can even add the name of the image or a text message to the back of each print.

3. **Order your prints.**

   Shutterfly lets you add or subtract photos from the batch you're ordering, choose how many of each and which size, pick the finish you want, and so on. Then you enter info about the recipients (their names and addresses); Shutterfly remembers whom you've sent photos to with previous orders, so you don't have to reenter Aunt Suzie's address each time. When your order is all set, enter your payment info, and in a few days you—or your lucky recipients—will receive an envelope of prints in the mail.

   > **TIP** Elements automatically checks for updates to Adobe's partner companies and automatically notifies you about special promotions. You can stop it from doing either by heading to the Organizer and choosing Edit→Preferences→Adobe Partner Services/Elements Organizer→Preferences→Adobe Partner Services and, in the "Check for Services" section, turning off the appropriate checkboxes.

   Even though Elements makes ordering prints from Shutterfly really convenient, you can also use Shutterfly without going through Elements (just go to Shutterfly.com in any web browser), or use other online print services like Snapfish (*www.snapfish.com*). The real advantage of ordering from Elements is convenience.

TIP You can start an order right from the Organizer's Full Screen view (page 572): The Fix panel's Actions section has a "Mark for Printing" button that looks like a printer. Click it when you see photos you want to print. Then, when you return to the Media Browser from Full Screen view, a pop-up window offers you the choice of printing the photos at home or ordering prints. Click Order Prints and Elements prepares your photos and opens the Shutterfly window.

Printing at Home

If you prefer to print photos at home, Elements has you covered. It's quite easy to print from Elements, but this is one of the areas where your operating system makes a little bit of a difference. In Windows, you can print from either the Editor or the Organizer, and the process is pretty much the same from either, although if you want to print groups of photos on a single page, you have to do that from the Organizer. On a Mac, all printing takes place via the Editor, no matter where you start.

NOTE If you're in the wrong place for what you want to print (the Organizer instead of the Editor, say), Elements will either *automatically* take you to the right place or ask if you want to go there.

Before you print, it's really important to be sure the resolution (ppi) of your photo(s) is what you want (see page 105 for more about resolution). It's also a good idea to do any cropping (page 89) before you call up the Print window. You can start from either the Editor or the Organizer, and (in Windows) once you're in the Print window, you can choose to create individual prints, a contact sheet of small thumbnails of all your photos, or a picture package of several sizes of prints. (On a Mac, if you want to create a contact sheet or picture package, you do so from the Editor's File menu; see page 548.) The following sections explain all your options.

Making Individual Prints

The basic process of printing from Elements is the same no matter where you start or what you're printing. If you're printing contact sheets or picture packages (which are covered later in this chapter), there are a few differences between PCs and Macs, and there are a couple of minor ones between how Windows and OS X handle *all* printing projects.

This section is about printing one photo per page from the Editor, since that method offers the most options. (To learn about the minor differences between printing from the Editor and from the *Windows* Organizer, see the box on page 539.) Once you understand how to make single prints from the Editor, you won't have any trouble with other kinds of printing.

■ **PRINTING IN WINDOWS**

1. **In the Editor, choose the photo(s) you want to print.**

   In the Photo Bin, select the photo(s) you want to print. If you don't select any, then Elements will print all your open photos. (You can add or remove photos once you're in the Print window, too [you'll open this window in the next step].)

2. **Go to File→Print or press Ctrl+P.**

   The Print window appears. It's divided into three main sections: On the left is a filmstrip-like view where you can add or remove photos you want to print (Figure 16-3). In the middle is a preview area where you see the image(s) you're going to print and some controls for rotating and adjusting them; there's a blue outline around the area that's going to print. And on the right is a group of numbered settings, listed in the order you need to adjust them.

FIGURE 16-3

On the left side of the Print window (shown here), you can add more photos to print—if they're already in the Organizer.

Click the green + button, and a window opens that lets you browse through all your Organizer photos to choose ones to add. If you want to print photos that aren't in the Organizer, open them in the Editor, and then select them in the Photo Bin before you start the print process.

If you decide not to print one of the photos in the Print window, click its thumbnail, and then click the red – button. (This button is grayed out here because no photos are selected.)

3. **Choose the printer you want to use.**

Select it from the drop-down menu on the right side of the window (Step 1 listed there).

4. **Choose your printer settings.**

On the right side of the Print window under Step 2 (Printer Settings), check to see what Elements proposes for the type of paper and the print quality.

If you don't like its choices, click Change Settings. In the Change Settings window, adjust the settings to your liking. The window includes a setting to change the paper size, but you don't need to use it—you'll choose a size in the main Print window in the next step. Depending on your printer, you may have additional options here, like which paper tray you want the printer to use. When everything looks good, click OK to close the Change Settings window.

5. **Select a paper size and orientation.**

Click the Select Paper Size menu (Step 3 in Elements' Print window) for a list of the sizes available for your printer. What's in this list is determined by the printer you chose in Step 1. If you have a printer that allows borderless printing, you should see several sizes in the list with "(borderless)" after the size. Just choose the one you want. If you know your printer can print borderless but you don't see any borderless options, click the Page Setup button beneath the preview area and make any necessary changes there. (Some printers that allow borderless printing require you to make certain choices in the the print quality or paper sections. You may not be able to print borderless on plain paper, for instance, but only on premium photo paper.) To change the page's orientation, click the icon that shows the orientation you want.

6. **Choose what kind of prints you want to make.**

In the Print window's Step 4 section, choose whether to make individual prints, a contact sheet, or a picture package. In this example, you're making individual prints (one photo per page), so choose that. (If you want to make a contact sheet or a picture package, flip to page 546.)

7. **Select a print size and tell Elements whether to crop the image(s).**

Choose an option from the aptly named Select Print Size menu (Step 5). If you don't want any of the preset sizes, choose Actual Size or Custom. (If you choose the latter, the More Options dialog box appears showing the Custom Print Size settings, which are explained on page 541. Enter your choices, and then click OK.)

With the Print window's "Crop to Fit" checkbox turned off, Elements prints your whole image as large as it can be within the print size you chose, even if that means leaving empty space on some of the edges. If, on the other hand, you want to make your image fill the available space, leave "Crop to Fit" turned on and Elements trims the image to fit the print size you picked. Figure 16-4 shows the difference this setting makes.

8. **Choose how many copies of each page you want to print.**

If you want to make more than one copy of each print, enter a number in the Print field below the "Crop to Fit" checkbox. (Keep in mind that Elements prints this many copies of *every* print in this batch—you can't make three copies of one photo and two of another, for example.)

9. **Print your photo(s).**

Click Print and Elements prints the photo(s). If you change your mind, click Cancel or close the Print window.

FIGURE 16-4

Left: Here's how this photo will print with "Crop to Fit" turned off. Notice the white space at the top and bottom of the blue bounding box.

Right: Leave "Crop to Fit" turned on, and Elements enlarges the photo enough to fill all the space and then crops off any excess (here, it cropped the right and left edges).

■ **PRINTING IN OS X**

1. **In the Editor, choose the photo(s) you want to print.**

In the Photo Bin, select the photos you want to print. (If you don't select any, Elements prints *all* your open photos.) As Figure 16-3 explains, you can add photos once you open the Print window, but they have to be in the Organizer.

2. **Go to File→Print or press ⌘-P.**

The Print window appears. It's divided into three main sections: On the left is a filmstrip-like view where you can add or remove photos you want to print (Figure 16-3). In the middle is a preview area where you see the image(s) you're going to print and some controls for rotating and adjusting them; there's a blue outline around the area that's going to print. And on the right is a group of numbered settings, listed in the order you need to adjust them.

3. **Choose the printer you want to use.**

   Select it from the drop-down menu on the right side of the window (this step is labeled "1").

4. **Select a paper size and orientation.**

   In Step 2 in Elements' Print window, click the Select Paper Size menu for a list of the sizes available for your printer (what's listed is determined by the printer you chose in the previous step). If you want to change the page's orientation, click the icon that shows the orientation you want.

5. **Select a print size and tell Elements whether to crop your image.**

   Choose an option from the aptly named Select Print Size menu (Step 3). If you don't want any of the preset print sizes, choose Actual Size or Custom. If you choose the latter, the More Options dialog box appears showing the Custom Print Size options, which are explained on page 541. Enter your choices and then click OK.

   When the Print window's "Crop to Fit" checkbox is turned off, Elements prints your whole image as large as it can be within the print size you chose, even if that means leaving empty space on some of the edges. So if you want to make your image fill the available space, make sure that "Crop to Fit" is turned on so that Elements will enlarge your photo to completely fill the available space, if necessary, and then trim the image to fit the print size you chose. Figure 16-4 shows the difference this setting makes.

6. **Choose how many copies of each page you want to print.**

   To make more than one copy of each print, enter a number in the Print box below the "Crop to Fit" checkbox. (Keep in mind that Elements prints this many copies of *every* image in this batch—you can't make three copies of one photo and two of another, for example.)

7. **Print your photos.**

   After you click the Print button in Elements' Print window, you see *OS X's* Print dialog box, where you make your final print setting choices—like paper profile (more on that in a minute) and color management. Figure 16-5 explains how it works.

   First, choose the printer you want to use from the dialog box's Printer menu. Next, click Show Details to expand the dialog box (see Figure 16-5), and then choose paper and color options from the unlabeled pull-down menu that starts out set to Layout (it's the one that's open in Figure 16-5, bottom).

   Your paper and color options vary depending on the kind of printer you have. Selecting a paper profile may sound complicated, but it's usually as simple as selecting the kind of paper you plan to use (Photo Paper Plus Glossy, say) from a list of choices. Setting color options can be as easy as choosing "high-quality photo" from a list of quality settings, and usually you'll have someplace to specify Printer Color Management, although probably not in the same menu item. (There's a bit more about color management when printing on page 542.)

When everything is set, click Print and Elements prints your photo(s).

FIGURE 16-5

Use the OS X Print dialog box to choose paper and print-quality settings.

Top: Click the Show Details button circled here to expand the window so you can see all your options.

Bottom: In any version of OS X, you then use the various menus in this expanded dialog box to make your choices.

That's the basic process for printing from Elements. If you're in a hurry or not fussy, you can use it to get a handful of prints in short order. But odds are that you're using Elements precisely because you *are* fussy about your photos, and you may want to tweak several other settings. The next few sections cover all the ways you can customize things like how the photo sits on the page, its color management, and so forth.

> **NOTE**   Elements' Print window isn't *color managed* (page 542), which means that what you see in the window isn't necessarily the same as the colors you'll get when you print. The window's preview is just meant to show you where on the page the photo is going to print (which is the subject of the next section).

Printing from the Windows Organizer

In Windows, if you want to make individual prints from the Organizer, start by selecting the photo(s) in the Organizer's Media Browser rather than in the Editor's Photo Bin. Other than that, the process for printing individual images is exactly the same whether you start in the Editor or the Organizer except for three details, which all involve clicking the More Options button at the bottom of the Prints window:

- **Image positioning**. The Editor always prints one photo per page, regardless of the relative sizes of the photos and your paper, while the Organizer may place more than one photo on a page if there's room. If you want to restrict the Organizer to placing only one image on a sheet, then click the Prints window's More Options button, make sure Printing Choices is selected on the left side of the window, and then turn on the One Photo Per Page checkbox. (There's no Organizer equivalent of the Center Image checkbox in the Editor's Print window—Elements is totally in charge of positioning your photos when you print from the Organizer.)

- **Max Print Resolution**. When you're in the Organizer's Prints window, if you go to More Options→Custom Print Size, you'll see a box labeled "Max Print Resolution." If you don't make a change here, anything you print from the Organizer will print at 350 ppi or less (see page 105 for more about resolution and why this may—or may not—matter to you).

- **Color Management**. Unlike the color-management choices available in the Editor (page 542), when you start in the Organizer and go to More Options→Color Management, the dialog box just lists your current *color space* (see page 240) for your image and a drop-down menu set to "Same as Source." Leave that setting as is—you don't need to change it.

Another handy Organizer feature is that you can mark photos for printing in Full Screen view (page 572). Then, when you return to Media view, a pop-up window gives you the option of printing your photos or ordering prints online (page 530).

Positioning Your Image

In both the Windows and Mac versions of Elements, there are two main ways to adjust the relationship between an image and the paper you print it on. Elements' Print window has some controls for rotating and sizing the image, which are normally all you'll need. If you don't want to print the whole image, you can even scoot the photo around within the preview area to determine which *part* of it will print. And if you like, you can also call up the Page Setup dialog box, which is the same for all programs on your computer. The following sections explain your options.

NOTE Quick reminder: In Windows, you can position your image for printing only if you start from the Editor; if you print from the Organizer, *Elements* decides where to put the image. This section assumes that you're printing from the Editor.

■ PRINT WINDOW SETTINGS

When you open the Editor's Print window, you see your photo in a white preview area surrounded by a blue outline (called a *bounding box*). The white area represents the paper, and the blue box shows the printing boundaries of the photo. The blue outline doesn't get printed. (Incidentally, Adobe's official name for the area inside the blue outline is the Print Well, in case you run into that term in any tutorials.)

Your first impulse may be to grab the photo and try to adjust its placement on the page. But if you do that, rather than moving the blue box, you just move your image *within* the box. You need to pay attention to your cursor to see just what you're going to move, as Figure 16-6 explains.

 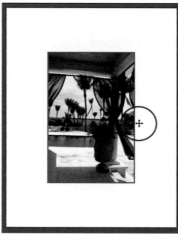

FIGURE 16-6

It's easy to move a photo around on the paper, but you have to be a little careful.

Left: If you drag the photo itself, you get the hand cursor (circled) and you'll simply move the image within the blue box and change what part of the image will print.

Right: To move the photo to another spot on the page, move the cursor close to the edge of the photo till it turns into crossed arrows (circled). These arrows indicate that you can drag the photo to wherever you want it.

To reposition a photo on the page (to print a small photo on the upper-left corner of a large piece of paper, for example), just drag an edge of the blue box wherever you want it. Or, in the window's Position section below the preview area, enter the amount of distance from the top and left edges of the page in inches, centimeters, millimeters, points, or picas.

In addition to moving the blue box itself, there are several ways to change how your image appears *within* it. Here's what you can do:

- **Rotate the photo**. Below the preview area are the same curled-arrow rotation icons you see elsewhere in Elements. Click one to rotate the photo *and* the blue box. If you want to rotate the photo but not the blue box, turn on the Image Only checkbox; that way, the box stays put and the image rotates within it.

- **Resize the photo**. If you don't want to print the whole image, zoom in on part of it using the slider below the preview. (If you need to move the image around to focus on the area you want, drag the image as explained in Figure 16-6.) Be careful with this feature: You can easily enlarge the image beyond a reasonable pixel density. (When you click Print, Elements will warn you if the image is going to print at less than 220 ppi, but as a general rule it's best to take care of any resizing *before* you open the Print window.)

- **Reposition the photo in the box**. As mentioned above, you can drag the image around in the preview area to determine which part of it will print. You can also accidentally drag the image almost out of view; if that happens, just turn on the Center Image checkbox; if doing that doesn't properly recenter the image, cancel your print and start again.

TIP If you turn on the "Crop to Fit" checkbox on the right side of the Print window, Elements crops the image based on its *original* position; it doesn't take into account any dragging that you do. In other words, if you use "Crop to Fit," you can't control which part of your photo Elements prints.

- **Make the image and print size the same**. If you decide to make a 4 × 6-inch print of an image that's the right aspect ratio (shape) for a 5 × 7-inch print, you'll end up with some empty space on the edges because the print size and the aspect ratio aren't equivalent. There are two ways around this. You can turn on "Crop to Fit," and Elements will chop off the edges of the photo. Or, if you've already cropped the image to a photo-paper size, head to the Select Print Size drop-down menu and choose Actual Size. You can also use a custom size, as explained next.

- **Pick a custom print size**. Either choose Custom from the Print window's Select Print Size menu, or click the More Options button and then click Custom Print Size. Either way, you see the More Options dialog box's Custom Print Size settings, where you can type the exact height and width you want to print in inches, centimeters, millimeters, points, or picas.

- **Make the image fill the paper**. If you click the Print Window's More Options button and then click Custom Print Size, you can turn on the "Scale to Fit Media" checkbox, and Elements makes your image larger or smaller so that all of it fits into your desired page size. (After choosing this option, you may need to use your operating system's Page Setup dialog box—described next—to change the page's orientation.)

■ THE PAGE SETUP DIALOG BOX

In the lower-left corner of the Editor's Print window is the Page Setup button. Click it to bring up your operating system's Page Setup dialog box. Normally, you don't need to use this dialog box—choosing your printer in the Print window's Step 1 area takes care of things. But once you've got everything set up in Elements' Print window, you can use the Page Setup dialog box to *override* Elements' settings. You can also select a printer here, but normally choosing a printer in Elements' Print window changes the Page Setup dialog box to match.

Additional Print Options

Elements includes a number of other useful ways to tweak a photo for printing, like putting a border around it, printing crop marks as guides for trimming the printed version, or even flipping it for printing as an iron-on transfer. You'll find the following settings by clicking the Print window's More Options button and then, on the left side of the dialog box that appears, clicking Printing Choices:

- **Photo Details.** You can print the image's shot or creation date, caption, and/or filename on the page with the photo by turning on the relevant checkbox(es) here. Caption text is what you entered in the Organizer; or you can enter it in the Editor by going to File→File Info and typing something in the Description field.

- **Border.** If you want to add a border to the photo, turn on the Thickness checkbox, and then enter a size for the border (in inches, millimeters, or points). Elements shrinks the photo to accommodate the border, even if there's plenty of empty space around the picture, so you may need to enlarge the photo a bit before printing to get the size you originally chose. Click the white square next to the unit-of-measurement menu to bring up the Color Picker so you can choose a border color.

  If the page has empty space you want to fill with a background color, then turn on the Background checkbox and click *its* color square to bring up the Color Picker.

- **Iron-on Transfer.** Turn on the Flip Image checkbox to reverse your image horizontally. You'd do this when printing transfers for projects like t-shirts.

- **Trim Guidelines.** The Print Crop Marks checkbox lets you print guidelines in the margins of the photo to make it easier to trim. These marks are useful mainly for trimming bordered photos so that the borders are perfectly even.

When you've got the various settings how you want them, click Apply at the bottom of the dialog box. When you do that, the Print window's image preview changes to show the options you selected, so if the More Options dialog box is in the way, move it over so you can see the effect of your settings. If you don't like what you see, adjust the dialog box's settings and click Apply again. When you're happy, click OK to close the dialog box and return to the Print window.

Color Management

When you print from the Editor, you can find several advanced color-related settings if you click the Print window's More Options button and then click Color Management on the left side of the More Options dialog box. If you're content with the way your prints look without adjusting these settings, just be happy and ignore them. But if you don't like the color you're getting from Elements, then use these advanced controls to make adjustments.

> **TIP** Color management is a dauntingly complicated subject. The advice in the following pages should be enough to get you started, but if you want to learn more, a good place to start is *Real World Color Management* by Bruce Fraser, Chris Murphy, and Fred Bunting (Peachpit Press). It's geared toward Photoshop, but it's the standard reference on the subject, and much of it applies to Elements.

You may remember from Chapter 7 that Elements is a *color-managed* program, which means it tries to coordinate the color settings used by various devices and programs: your image file (which may retain color settings applied by your camera), your monitor, Elements, and your printer. Sometimes you need to step in and help Elements decide which settings are best, since different devices and programs can have different interpretations of what certain colors look like.

Color management may sound intimidating, but you already did some when you chose a paper type and print quality. Now your most important decision is whether you want Elements or your printer to manage the photo's color settings. You can let Elements *and* your printer have a say in color management, but that almost always mucks things up. The good news is that Elements does its best to keep you from double-managing color, and it tries to make managing the color in your prints as painless as possible.

In the More Options dialog box, you have four main color-management choices to make:

- **Color Handling**. Here's where you decide who's going to be in charge: your printer (Printer Manages Colors) or Elements (Photoshop Elements Manages Colors). The choice you make here determines your options in the rest of these settings. Elements also gives you some hints about your printer settings, as you can see in Figure 16-7.

FIGURE 16-7

When you choose Printer Manages Colors, Elements reminds you to turn on your printer's color-management feature.

In Windows, click Printer Preferences as shown here to adjust your printer's settings. (Macs don't have this button, since you change these settings in the OS X Print dialog box [page 538], although the text in the Elements Print window also refers to "Printer Preferences" for Macs.)

- **Image Space**. This setting shows you which, if any, color space your file is tagged with (for example, sRGB or Adobe RGB). You don't actually choose anything here—this line is purely informative. (See page 240 for more about color spaces.)
- **Printer Profile**. This setting is grayed out unless you chose Photoshop Elements Manages Color from the Color Handling menu. If Elements *is* managing the color,

then you can choose the profile you want from this list, which includes all the profiles Elements can find on your computer.

- **Rendering Intent**. Use this setting to tell Elements what to do if your photo contains colors that fall outside the range of the color space you're using; your choices are explained in the box below.

What's Your Intent?

For most people, the Rendering Intent setting in Elements' More Options dialog box is the most confusing of the color-management options. Here are the basics you need to know to choose a setting.

Sometimes photos contain colors that fall outside the color boundaries of the printing color space you're using; in other words, the print space can't properly display those colors. The Rendering Intent setting tells Elements what to do if it runs into colors like that. You have four choices:

- **Perceptual** tells Elements to preserve the relationship between the colors in your image—even if that means it has to visibly shift some colors to make them all fit.

- **Saturation** makes colors very vivid—but not necessarily very accurate. This setting is more for special effects than for regular photo printing.

- **Relative Colorimetric** tries to preserve the colors in both the image's and printer's color spaces by shifting things to the closest matching color in the printer profile's space. This is Elements' standard setting, and it's usually what you want because it keeps colors as close as possible to what you see onscreen.

- **Absolute Colorimetric** lets you simulate another printer and paper. This setting is for specialized proofing situations.

The easiest way to set up color management, and a good way to start, is to choose Printer Manages Colors. This means that Elements hands the photo over to your printer and lets the printer take care of the color-management duties. Then all you need to do is select the proper paper profile and settings for your printer. Selecting a paper profile may sound kind of technical but actually, you've probably already done it.

In Windows, you picked a paper profile back in Printer Settings→Change Settings (step 4 on page 535). It's usually as simple as choosing, say, Photo Paper Plus Glossy from the list of options there. If you already chose a paper type and print quality in Elements' Print window, your printer preferences should have changed to reflect them. However, your printer may offer some additional choices that are worth exploring. In the More Options dialog box's Color Management section, click the Printer Preferences button (or, in Elements' Change Settings window [page 535], click the Advanced Settings button) to view these settings. The exact wording in the dialog box that appears differs depending on what kind of printer you have, but Figure 16-8 shows a typical printer's settings.

FIGURE 16-8

Setting up color management in your printer's settings is easy. Here, just leaving this particular HP printer's menu set to ColorSmart/sRGB is all it takes. If you plan to let Elements manage color, you'd choose Application Managed Colors instead. Different brands of printers have different names for their color-management systems, so you'll have to hunt around in the window a bit, but it's usually pretty simple to figure out which option you want.

On a Mac, you make your paper profile choices in the OS X Print dialog box, as explained back on page 538. Your options are similar to the ones in Windows; they're just in a different location.

> **TIP**   If your camera takes photos in sRGB and you've been editing them using Elements' No Color Management or "Always Optimize Colors for Computer Screens" settings (Fdit→Color Settings), then don't choose Adobe RGB for the printer profile, as the colors in your images may shift drastically. If for some reason you want to change the color space for the printer, first go to Image→Convert Color Profile, and then apply the Adobe RGB profile to the photo. If you aren't absolutely sure that your printer understands Adobe RGB (many inkjets don't) and you don't have a compelling reason for changing the color setting, then it's best to leave them alone.

You can configure Elements' color settings in a zillion different ways, and you may need to experiment a bit to find what works best. (See the box on page 546 for advice on how to cheaply test out a bunch of different print settings.) If you go looking around for more info, you'll find that this subject is controversial—everyone has a different approach that's the "right" one. But in fact, many different options can lead to good results.

Economical Print Experiments

If you've just bought some top-quality photo paper, you may be suffering from a bit of sticker shock and perhaps are even thinking, "Oh, great. Now I'm supposed to use this stuff up *experimenting*? At that price?"

The good news is that, while you have to bite the bullet and sacrifice a sheet or two, you don't need to waste a whole box of paper. Try this: Make a small selection somewhere in a photo you want to print, press Ctrl+C/⌘-C, and then go to File→New→"Image from Clipboard." You get a new file with only that small piece of the photo in it; this is your test print. Next, go to File→Print, and then drag the partial photo to the page's upper-left corner. Then try printing the page using Elements' standard settings.

If the print looks good, then you're ready to print the whole photo. If, on the other hand, you don't like the result, then press Ctrl+P/⌘-P to bring up the Print window again. This time, drag the test print over to the right a little bit. Adjust your settings (keeping track of the changes you make), and then print again on the *same* piece of paper. Your new test prints out beside the first one. Keep moving the test area around on the page, and you can try out quite a few different combinations of settings, all on one sheet of paper.

■ Printing Multiple Images (Windows)

Elements also lets you print from the Windows Organizer, which gives you many more output options than the Editor, including the ability to print several photos on one page. You can create contact sheets of thumbnails and picture packages (like you'd order from a professional photographer), and easily add all kinds of fancy borders to the photos (by choosing a frame in the Print window's settings). (You can *begin* creating a contact sheet or a picture package in the Editor, but Elements bounces you over to the Organizer for the actual printing.)

NOTE To learn how to print a bunch of images on a Mac, skip to page 548.

Contact Sheets

Contact sheets show thumbnail views of multiple images on a single page. They're great for things like creating a visual reference guide to the photos you've archived on a CD. Or you may want to print a contact sheet of all the photos on a memory card as soon as you download the photos to your computer, even before you edit them (see Figure 16-9).

FIGURE 16-9

Here's how you create a contact sheet on a Windows computer.

In the "Select a Layout" section (circled), the Columns menu lets you decide how many columns of images the contact sheet has. Turn on the Show Print Options checkbox to display the other choices shown here, like Date and Caption.

To print a contact sheet, select the photos you want to print, and then choose File→Print. In Elements' Prints window, go to the "Select Type of Print" menu and choose Contact Sheet. (If you start from the Editor, Elements asks if you want to go to the Organizer, which is where you print contact sheets; click OK.) The window changes to include the "Select a Layout" section visible in Figure 16-9, and you can use the following settings to customize your contact sheet:

- **Columns**. Here's where you decide how many columns of photos to have on a page (up to nine). The more columns, the smaller the thumbnails. Even if you have only one image currently selected, increasing the number of columns shrinks its thumbnail.

- **Show Print Options**. Turn on this checkbox and you can decide whether to have Elements print the image's date, filename, and/or caption (any text in the image's Description field) below each thumbnail. You can also add page numbers if you're printing multiple pages. (If all your selected photos fit on one page, then the Page Numbers checkbox is grayed out.)

You can add and remove images as explained earlier (page 534), and you can click a photo in the layout and then use the slider to zoom, just as with individual prints. When you like the layout, click Print.

> **TIP** You can also start a contact sheet in either the Editor or the Organizer by going to Create→Photo Prints→Contact Sheet. The only advantage to doing it this way is that the Prints window opens with Contact Sheet already selected as the type of print.

Picture Packages

Elements' Picture Package feature lets you print several images on one sheet. You can print a package that's one photo printed repeatedly, or one that includes multiple photos.

To get started, in the Organizer, select the image(s) you want to print, and then press Ctrl+P to call up the Prints window. From the window's "Select Type of Print" menu, choose Picture Package. Next, from the "Select a Layout" menu, pick which composition style you want (choices include four 3" × 5" photos, two 5" × 7" photos, and so on). Then choose a frame, if you want one, from the "Select a Frame" menu. Add photos to your package by clicking the green Add button in the lower-left corner of the window.

> **TIP** You can also start a picture package in either the Editor or the Organizer by going to Create→Photo Prints→Print Picture Package. The only real advantage to going that route is that the Prints window opens with the "Select Type of Print" menu set to Picture Package.

Figure 16-10 shows you how to change the layout of the photos once they're on the page. If you turn on the Fill Page With First Photo checkbox, then you get a whole page dedicated to each photo (with multiple sizes of the image on that page) rather than various photos on each page.

You can select a photo in the layout and then use the rotation buttons and the zoom slider to tweak it. If you turn on the "Crop to Fit" checkbox, Elements crops your photos to fit their slots, but you're probably better off doing any cropping yourself in the Editor instead. When you've got the photos arranged the way you want, click Print.

> **TIP** The box on page 554 has info on creating your own custom picture package.

■ Printing Multiple Images (Mac)

The Mac version of Elements gives you even better options for printing multiple images than the Windows version, because you can *save* your completed projects for future use (you can't do that on a PC). This section explains how to create contact sheets and picture packages.

FIGURE 16-10

Reorganizing a picture package is drag-and-drop easy.

If there's empty space in the layout that you want to fill, or you want to change the photo in a particular slot, just drag a thumbnail from the filmstrip on the left into that slot, or drag a photo from one slot to another.

To remove a photo from the package, click it on the left side of the main window and then click the red Remove button.

Contact Sheets

Contact sheets include a bunch of thumbnails of different photos. You can use them to keep track of the photos on a CD or as a record of all the photos you took in one shooting session, for example. The plug-in that comes with Elements makes it a snap to create a contact sheet that's laid out the way you want. Here's what you do:

1. **Collect your photos.**

   You can make a contact sheet of all your open photos or all the photos in a folder. So decide which photos you want to use and either open them in the Editor or put them in a folder.

2. **Call up the Contact Sheet dialog box (Figure 16-11).**

   Press Option-⌘-P or go to File→Contact Sheet II. (Confusingly, there's no Contact Sheet I option—it was replaced by this one many versions of Elements ago.) You can also go to Create→Photo Prints→Print Contact Sheet in either the Editor or the Organizer, although you'll get bounced over to the Editor to actually create the contact sheet. If you preselect photos in the Organizer, they open in the Editor and you can choose to include them all in step 3.

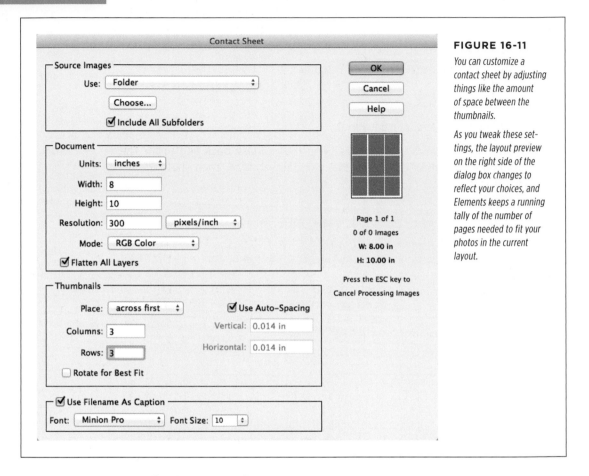

FIGURE 16-11

You can customize a contact sheet by adjusting things like the amount of space between the thumbnails.

As you tweak these settings, the layout preview on the right side of the dialog box changes to reflect your choices, and Elements keeps a running tally of the number of pages needed to fit your photos in the current layout.

3. **Choose your settings.**

   You have lots of options:

   - **Source Images.** This is where you pick which photos to include. You can select the files currently open in the Editor or the files in a certain folder.

   - **Document.** Here's where you select the overall page settings. Set the page size in inches, centimeters, or pixels. Then enter a resolution and choose between RGB and grayscale color mode (see page 41). The Flatten All Layers checkbox doesn't affect your originals—it just creates a contact sheet where text and images are on the same layer—so you can leave it turned on to keep the file smaller.

   - **Thumbnails.** These settings control how the thumbnails are laid out. Choose whether you want the pictures to go across the page or down (as they're being laid out), how many columns and rows you'd like, and whether you want Elements to determine the spacing between images or you want to set the spacing yourself. Turn on the Rotate For Best Fit checkbox to make Elements rotate the thumbnails so they fit on the paper most efficiently. (If you don't like having photos improperly oriented, leave this setting off.)

- **Use Filename As Caption.** Turn on this setting if you want the name of each photo to appear as a caption. Your font choices are Myriad Pro, Minion Pro, or Lucida Grande. Getting a font size you like may take some experimenting.

4. **Click OK to create the contact sheet.**

   Elements goes to work and you see your images flash back and forth. The contact sheet thumbnail in the Photo Bin updates to show each photo as Elements places it.

TIP If you change your mind about making a contact sheet while Elements is working, press the Esc key.

---

5. **Save or print your contact sheet.**

   Your finished contact sheet is just like any other file: You can save it in the format of your choice, print it out, burn it to disc along with the photos it contains—whatever. If you included more photos than could fit on one page, then Elements creates a separate file for each page.

Picture Packages

You can also print a group of pictures on one page. You can make packages that feature one photo at several different sizes, or packages that include more than one photo. Here's how:

1. **In the Editor, go to File→Picture Package.**

   You can also start from either the Editor or the Organizer by going to Create→Photo Prints→Print Picture Package, though you end up in the same Picture Package window in the Editor.

   You don't need to select any photos first, but you may want to open photos in the Editor before starting, since the Picture Package dialog box, like the Contact Sheet dialog box, ignores the Organizer. So it's often simplest to open the photos or collect them into a folder to make them easy to find before you start this process.

2. **Choose your photo(s).**

   The Picture Package dialog box's Use drop-down menu is where you select the pictures you want in the package. If you choose lots of files, Elements adds as many pages as necessary to fit them all in. You can use a single file, a folder of photos, the frontmost open photo, or all open photos. Elements starts by filling the entire layout with copies of one photo, but you can change that in step 4 if you want more than one image per page.

3. **Choose your page size and layout settings.**

Elements gives you lots of options:

- **Document.** This is where you pick the overall settings for the package. You can set the page size (12" × 18", 8" × 10", 10" × 16", or 7.5" × 10.9"), layout (how many photos appear on one page and their sizes), resolution, and whether to use RGB or grayscale color mode (see page 41). The Flatten All Layers setting works the same way as it does for contact sheets (see step 3 on page 550). The page size options are all photo paper sizes, but you can print the 8" × 10" layout on standard 8 ½" × 11" paper.

- **Label.** This is where you tell Elements whether to put text on the photos. If you don't want any text, leave the Content menu set to None. If you want text, you can use the filename, copyright, description, credit, or title from the file's metadata (page 49), or enter custom text. The other options are for the text itself: font, size, color, opacity, and position. If you don't want black text, click the color square to bring up the Color Picker. The Rotate menu lets you tell Elements to rotate the text so that, if your photos print sideways, say, the text still prints right-side up on the photo. And you can use the Opacity and Position settings to create a watermark.

If all these options aren't enough for you, check out the next section, which explains how to customize a picture package even further.

4. **Adjust the placement of the photos.**

Figure 16-12 explains how to change the contents of a particular placeholder (Adobe calls them *zones*). Keep clicking zones to put as many different shots on a page as there are zones to hold them.

5. **When everything is arranged to your liking, click OK to create the package.**

If your settings required more than one page to fit the photos, then Elements creates a separate file for each page. You can print them or save them in any format that suits you, just like a single photo.

CUSTOMIZING A PICTURE PACKAGE

You're not limited to the picture-package layouts Elements offers. You can customize a layout in all sorts of ways and then save it to use again.

Start by choosing the built-in layout that's closest to what you want. Then click the Edit Layout button in the Picture Package window's bottom right (it's visible in Figure 16-12) to call up the dialog box shown in Figure 16-13.

FIGURE 16-12

To add a new photo or replace an existing one, click any box in the Layout section of this dialog box, and then choose the new photo in the Open dialog box that appears.

(You can't rearrange photos by dragging them from one zone to another.)

FIGURE 16-13

Enter numbers on the left side of this dialog box or just click a zone to bring up resizing handles. Resizing works just like using the Move tool—you can drag or resize a zone, or right-click/Control-click it to see a pop-up menu that includes some standard sizes. To delete a zone, click it, and then click the Delete Zone button.

To start from scratch, click Delete All.

You can choose a preset page size or type in a custom size in inches, centimeters, millimeters, or pixels. And as Figure 16-13 explains, you can also change the size and location of the images in the package. (The boxes for typing in custom sizes are grayed out until you select a zone.)

If you click a zone and then click the Add Zone button, Elements creates an *additional* zone instead of replacing the one you clicked. If there's no space that's big enough for the new zone, Elements just dumps the new zone on top of the existing layout and leaves you to sort things out; simply delete an existing zone to make room for the new one. The Snap To checkbox in the dialog box's Grid section helps you line up the zones.

When you're happy with your custom layout, name it by typing something in the Name box, and then click Save. (Be sure to give your layout a new name so you don't overwrite the *built-in* layout you started with.) Make sure you save it in Applications→Adobe Photoshop Elements 13→Support Files→Presets→Layouts. That way, your new layout will show up in the list of preset layouts.

If this method of customizing a picture package doesn't meet your needs, the box below explains another way to create a custom package.

WORKAROUND WORKSHOP

Creating Your Own Package

You may find that you want a picture-package layout that's different from any of the choices Elements offers. Fortunately, you can easily make your own picture package from scratch on either a Mac or a PC:

1. **Save all the photos you want to use at the same resolution.** See page 40 for more about setting a file's resolution.

2. **In the Editor, create a new document (Ctrl+N/⌘-N or File→New).** Make sure it's the size you want the finished package to be and that it has the same resolution as your photos. You can save time by choosing the Letter preset size from the New dialog box's Size menu; that size is already set to 300 ppi.

3. **Bring each photo into your new file.** Drag the photos from the Photo Bin, and then position them as you wish, or just copy (Ctrl+C/⌘-C) and paste (Ctrl+V/⌘-V) them. Each photo comes in on its own layer, so it's easy to position them individually. Once the photos are in the new

document, you can use the Move tool or Scale command (page 390) to resize them.

4. **When you have all the photos positioned and sized, save the combined file, and then print it.** You can make the file smaller by flattening it first (Layer→Flatten Image), but flatten it only if you don't think you'll want to tweak the layout later.

In Windows, you can also create new layouts in the Organizer for the Picture Package. Go to *C:\Program Files\Adobe\Elements 13 Organizer\Assets\layouts*, and then choose the layout that's closest to what you want. (You might want to audition the different layouts in Elements first and note the name of the one that's most like what you want, so you'll know which file to open.) Open the file in a text editor (like Notepad), save it with a new name, and then make your changes. When you're done, save the changes, and then put the new file into the same folder as the original.

Email and the Web

P rinting photos is great, but it costs money, takes time, and doesn't do much to instantly impress your faraway friends. And to many people, printing is just so 20th century. Fortunately, Elements comes packed with tools that make it easy to prep your photos for onscreen viewing and to email them in a variety of crowd-pleasing ways. (In Elements 13, emailing got a major makeover, making it easier to send photos using any email program.) This chapter explains your options.

■ Image Formats and the Web

Back in the Web's early days, making graphic files small was important because most Internet connections were as slow as snails. Nowadays, file size isn't as crucial; your main obligation when creating graphics for the Web is ensuring they're compatible with the web browsers people use to view them. That means you'll probably want to use either of the two most popular image formats, JPEG or GIF, though PNG is also an option:

- **JPEG** (Joint Photographic Experts' Group) is the most popular choice for images with lots of details, and for ones where you need smooth color transitions. Photos are almost always posted on the Web as JPEGs.

TIP   JPEGs can't have transparent areas, although there's a workaround for that: Fill the background around the image with the same color as the web page you want to post it on. That way, the background blends into the web page, giving the impression that the object is surrounded by transparency. See Figure 17-4 (page 561) for details on this trick.

- **GIF** (Graphics Interchange Format) files are great for images with limited numbers of colors, like corporate logos and headlines. Text looks much sharper in GIF format than it does as a JPEG. And GIFs can include transparency.

- **PNG** (Portable Network Graphic) format was created to overcome some of the disadvantages of JPEGs and GIFs. There's a lot to like about PNG files: They can include transparent areas, and they reduce the file size of photographs without losing data, as happens with JPEG files (see page 73 for more about that).

Elements makes it a breeze to save images in any of these formats using the Save For Web dialog box, explained next.

Saving Images for the Web and Email

If you plan to email your photos or put them up on a website, you'll love the Save For Web dialog box, a terrific feature that takes any open image and saves it in a web-friendly format. It also gives you lots of options to help maintain maximum image quality while keeping file size to a minimum. Save For Web aims to create as small a file as possible without compromising the image's onscreen quality.

Save For Web creates smaller JPEG files than you can get by using the Save As command because it strips out the image's *EXIF data*, the information about your camera's settings (see page 49). To get started with Save For Web, in the Editor, go to File→"Save for Web" or press Shift+Alt+Ctrl+S/Shift-Option-⌘-S, and the dialog box in Figure 17-1 appears.

> **TIP** If the Save For Web dialog box isn't big enough for you, you can make it larger by dragging its lower-right corner.

The most important point to remember when saving images for the Web is that the resolution (measured in pixels per inch, or ppi) is completely irrelevant. You only care about the image's pixel dimensions, such as 400 × 600. If you're working with a photo that you've optimized for print, you almost certainly want to downsize it; Save For Web makes that a snap.

Elements gives you lots of useful tools in the Save For Web dialog box, like the Hand and Zoom tools for adjusting the view. But the main attractions are the before and after image previews in the main image area. On the left is your original, and to its right you see what the image will look like after you save it. The file size is listed below each image preview.

> **NOTE** The Save For Web dialog box's preview panes may sometimes be stacked one above the other rather than side by side, depending on the size of your image and its orientation.

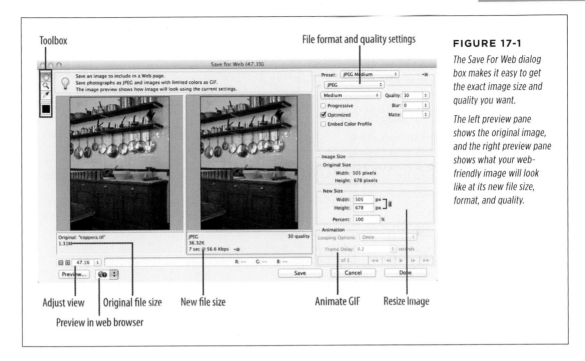

Toolbox

File format and quality settings

Adjust view · Original file size · New file size · Animate GIF · Resize Image

Preview in web browser

Below the left corner of the right-hand preview is an estimate of how long it will take to download the image at that size. You can adjust the download time by modifying your assumptions about your recipient's Internet connection speed, as shown in Figure 17-2. You can also change the zoom percentage (using the Zoom menu in the dialog box's bottom left), but you should usually stick with 100 percent because that's the size your image will be on the Web.

The upper-right part of the dialog box has your file format and quality choices (exactly what you see there varies a bit depending on which format you've chosen). Below that are your options for resizing the image. If you want to create animated GIFs (those tiny moving images you see on web pages), then tweak the settings in the Animation section, which are explained on page 564.

Using Save For Web

When you're ready to use Save For Web, follow these steps:

1. **In the Editor, open the image you want to modify.**

2. **Open the Save For Web dialog box.**

   Go to File→"Save for Web" or press Shift+Alt+Ctrl+S/Shift-Option-⌘-S.

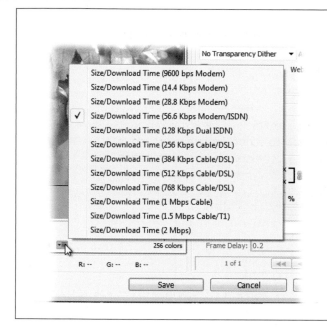

FIGURE 17-2

Below the right-hand preview pane, the Save For Web dialog box displays an estimate of how long it'll take to download your image.

To change the download settings (for example, the speed of the Internet connection), click the four-line square (where the cursor is pointing) to call up this list and pick a different option.

If you're working with a large file, you may see a dialog box stating, "The image exceeds the size Save for Web was designed for," along with dire-sounding warnings about slow performance and out-of-memory errors. Just click Yes to tell Elements that you want to continue anyway. If your computer has enough horsepower to run Elements 13, it won't choke when you use Save for Web.

3. **Choose format and quality settings for your web image.**

   In the dialog box's upper right, use the Preset drop-down menu to choose a format. Your choices are explained in the following section.

4. **If necessary, resize the image.**

   To make sure that anyone can see the whole image, no matter how small her monitor, in the New Size section, enter 650 pixels or less for the longest side of the photo. (650 pixels is about the largest size that fits on small monitors without scrolling. If your friends all have big, new monitors, you can go much larger, but keep in mind that people may look at your images on smartphones or tablets.) As long as the chain icon is visible to the right of the Width and Height boxes, you don't have to enter the dimension for the other side of the photo—Elements fills it in automatically. (The icon indicates that the two dimensions are linked—get it?) If the chain icon isn't visible (meaning the two dimensions aren't linked), there's a break in the line to the right of the two boxes. To relink them, just click the break in the line.

You can also resize the image by entering a percentage in the New Size section. For example, typing *90* in the Percent field shrinks your image to 90 percent of its original size. When you finish entering the new dimensions, press Enter/Return.

NOTE Remember, if any of your friends have dial-up connections, it can take them a long time to download large photos. Elements helps you out by telling you the download times for various connections, as explained in Figure 17-2.

5. **Check the results.**

   Look at the right-hand image's file size again to see if the new file is small enough, and use the Hand tool in the dialog box's left to scoot the image around in the preview area to take a close look at it. Use Elements' file-size optimization feature (explained in Figure 17-3) if necessary. You can also preview the image in your actual web browser (see page 562). There's no Undo option in the Save For Web dialog box, but you can Alt-click/Option-click the Cancel button to change it to a Reset button.

FIGURE 17-3

Save For Web's file-size optimization feature is helpful when you need to send a file someplace that puts limits on your total file size.

Top: Click the four-line square in the upper right of the Save For Web dialog box, and then choose "Optimize to File Size," as shown here.

Bottom: The "Optimize to File Size" dialog box uses kilobytes as its unit of measurement. Simply enter the size you want (in kilobytes) in the Desired File Size box. Below that, picking Current Settings tells Elements to start with whatever settings you've entered in the main Save For Web window, like the format and quality. Choose Auto Select GIF/JPEG instead if you want Elements to decide between GIF and JPEG for you. Once you finish making your selections, click OK, and Elements shrinks the image to the size you requested.

6. **When everything looks good, click Save.**

   Name the new file, and then save it wherever you like.

TIP If you want to process several photos in Save For Web with the same settings, press the Alt/Option key to change the Done button to a Remember button, and then click it. That way, the next time you open Save For Web, it'll have your current settings preselected. (At least that's what it's supposed to do, although it doesn't always work properly.) If you want Save For Web to remember your settings but you don't actually want to *save* the current photo, just click Done and Save For Web should open with the same settings next time you call it up.

■ SAVE FOR WEB FORMAT AND QUALITY OPTIONS

You can reduce an image's file size by changing its length and width, as explained in step 4 above. You can also make a file smaller by adjusting its *quality* settings. The quality options you see in the Save For Web dialog box vary depending on which format you choose from the unlabeled menu in the dialog box's upper right, just below the Preset menu:

- **JPEG**. When you choose a JPEG option from the Preset menu, Elements offers you a variety of quality settings: Low, Medium, High, Very High, and Maximum. You can then fine-tune the quality by entering a number in the Quality box (not surprisingly, a higher number means higher quality). Medium is usually good enough if you're saving the file for Web use. If you're using Save For Web to make JPEG files for printing, then use Maximum instead.

  If you turn on the Progressive checkbox, then your JPEG loads from the top down. This option was popular for large files when everyone had slow dial-up connections, but it makes for a slightly larger file, so it's not as popular today. You can also embed a color profile in the image by turning on the checkbox to do so. (See page 242 for more about color profiles.)

  Since JPEGs can't include transparency, the Matte menu lets you set the color of any area that's transparent in the original (see Figure 17-4). (If you don't pick a matte color, Elements uses white.) By choosing a color that matches the background of your web page, you can make it *look* like the image is surrounded by transparency. You have three ways to select a color: Click the arrow to the right of the Matte box, and then choose from the drop-down menu; use the Eyedropper tool on the left side of the Save For Web dialog box to sample a color from your image, and then choose Eyedropper Color from the Matte drop-down menu; or click the Matte box to call up the Color Picker.

> **TIP** Elements' Color Picker lets you limit your choices to web-safe colors by turning on the Only Web Colors checkbox in its lower-left corner. But do you *have* to stick to this limited color palette for web graphics? Not really. All modern browsers can cope with a normal color range. (Getting colors to display *consistently* in all browsers is another kettle of fish entirely, as the next section explains.)

- **GIF**. The fewer colors a GIF contains, the smaller its file size. Once you choose a GIF option from the dialog box's Preset menu, you can then use the Colors box to set the number of colors, either by clicking the down arrow on the right side of the box to scroll to the number you want, or just typing it in the box.

  If you want to keep transparent areas transparent, then leave the Transparency checkbox turned on. If you don't want transparency, then choose a matte color the way you do for a JPEG (see the previous bullet point). If you turn on the Interlaced checkbox, then your image downloads in multiple passes (sort of like an image that's slowly coming into focus). With today's computers, interlacing isn't as useful as it used to be on slower machines. If you're creating a GIF that you plan to animate, turn on the Animate checkbox. (You need a layered file to make an animated GIF; page 563 has the details.)

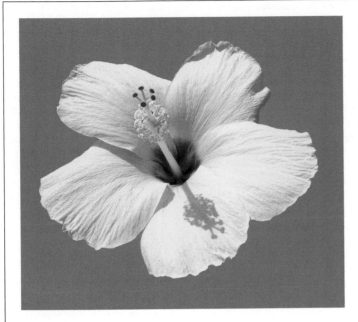

FIGURE 17-4

When you save an image in JPEG format, the transparent areas aren't preserved. But Elements lets you choose a matte color, which replaces the transparency.

By choosing a color that's identical to your web page's background, you can simulate transparency. For example, the purple matte around this hibiscus blossom will blend into the purple background of the page it's bound for.

Dither is an important setting because the GIF format works by compressing and flattening large areas of colors. When you use dithering, Elements blends existing colors to make the image look like it has more colors than it actually does. For instance, Elements may mix red and blue pixels in an area to create purple. You can choose how much dither you want by entering a percentage in the Dither field. Depending on your image, you may not want any dithering; in that case, set the Dither field to 0 percent. (Dithering makes for a larger file, but in these days of large files and fast connections, the difference in size is minuscule, so you'll usually want to use it.)

You can choose the *kind* of dithering Elements uses for the image itself and for any transparent areas by selecting from the menus directly above and below the Transparency checkbox, respectively, although 99 percent of the time you won't need to bother with these settings. But if you're interested, Diffusion, the basic setting, applies dithering in a random pattern that is the least noticeable of the choices. Pattern applies dithering in a square pattern, something like the pattern of a halftone, and Noise is something like Diffusion, except that Diffusion disperses the effect over partial adjacent pixels, while Noise restricts it to staying within pixels. The Transparency dither options affect only partially transparent pixels.

Web Snap and Lossy are both settings that let you tell Elements you want only the antique web-safe colors in your image (see the Tip on page 560). Leave both these settings set to 0—there's no sense in making your GIF lose data.

> **NOTE** If you've used Elements 10 or older, you may notice that in Elements 13, GIF and PNG-8 formats have longer names in the Preset menu than they used to (they have the words "128 Dithered" added to them). They're still the same old GIF and PNG-8 you knew from previous versions.

- **PNG-8**. This option, the more basic of your PNG choices in Elements, gives you pretty much the same options you get with GIF.

  With both PNG-8 and GIF, you get advanced options for how to display colors (specifically, to have Elements generate the color lookup table, which probably doesn't mean anything to you unless you're a web-design maven). The menu below the file-format menu lists your options. You can safely ignore this menu (Elements chooses Selective unless you change it), but if you're curious, here are your choices: Selective favors broad areas of color and keeps to web-safe colors; Perceptual favors colors to which the human eye is more sensitive; Adaptive samples colors from the spectrum appearing most commonly in the image; and Restrictive keeps everything within the old 216-color web palette.

- **PNG-24**. This is the more advanced level of PNG. Technically, both PNG formats let you use transparency, but more web browsers understand transparent areas in PNG-24 files than in PNG-8 files. Your other save options for this format are the same as some of those for JPEGs.

> **NOTE** The Preset menu also includes an Original option, but unfortunately it's not very useful. All it does is make both preview areas show your original image—it doesn't give you a larger view of your photo without the second preview.

Previewing Images

Elements gives you a few different ways to preview how an image will look in a web browser. You can start by looking at the image in any browser you have on your computer; Figure 17-5 explains how.

To add a new browser, in the Save For Web dialog box, click the button shown in Figure 17-5, and then choose Edit List. In the Browsers dialog box that appears, click the Add button and navigate to the one you want. If you want Elements to list *all* your browsers, click Find All. From then on, you can pick any browser in the list to make Elements launch the browser with your image in it.

> **NOTE** If you've used old versions of Elements, you may notice that Adobe has dropped the ability to preview using different color options like Standard Windows or Macintosh Color. That's probably because it was never a very good approximation of what your image would look like in real life. (You need only take a stroll down the monitor aisle at your local electronics store to see what a wacky bunch of color variations are possible.) You really can't control how other people will see your image without going to their homes and adjusting their monitors for them.

FIGURE 17-5

To preview an image in a web browser, in the bottom left of the Save For Web dialog box, click the icon to the right of the Preview button to launch your computer's standard web browser. (Once you've clicked this default icon, Elements replaces it with your preferred browser's icon, or the one for the last browser you used for previewing in Elements.) Or you can click the arrow next to this icon and then choose a browser from the list. The first time you click this arrow, you may need to pick Edit List and then click Find All to use the browser you want; Elements sniffs out every browser on your computer and adds what it finds to this menu.

Creating Animated GIFs

With Elements, it's easy to create *animated GIFs*, those little illustrations that make web pages look annoyingly jumbled or delightfully active, depending on your taste. If you've ever seen a strip of movie film or the cels for a cartoon, Elements creates a similar series of frames with these specialized GIFs.

Animated GIFs are made up of layers, with a separate layer for each frame. The Save For Web dialog box creates the actual animation, which you can preview in a web browser.

NOTE It's a shame that you can't easily animate a JPEG the way you can a GIF. Most elaborate web animations involving photographs are created with Flash, which is another program altogether. (If you want to learn more about Flash, pick up a copy of *Flash CS6: The Missing Manual*.)

The best way to learn about animated GIFs is to create one. Here's how to make twinkling stars:

1. **In the Editor, set your foreground color to some shade of yellow and the background color to black.**

   See page 253 if you need help setting these colors.

2. **Create a new document.**

   Press Ctrl+N/⌘-N. In the New dialog box, set the size to 200 pixels × 200 pixels, choose RGB for the color mode, and then choose Background Color for the background contents. Finally, set the resolution to 72 ppi, and then click OK.

3. **Activate the Custom Shape tool (page 423) and choose a star shape.**

In the Tool Options area, click the down arrow to the right of the Shape field to open the Shapes panel. Then click the drop-down menu at the top of the panel and select Nature. Double-click the Sun 2 shape, which is in the top row, second from the left.

4. **Draw some stars.**

Drag to draw one yellow star, and then, in the Tool Options area, click the "Add to shape area" button (see Figure 5-4 on page 153) before drawing four or five more stars. (This puts all the stars on the same layer, which is important, since that way you won't have a bunch of layers to merge.)

5. **Merge the star layer and the Background layer.**

Choose Layer→Merge Down. You now have one layer containing yellow stars on a black background, like the bottom layer in Figure 17-6.

FIGURE 17-6

This animated GIF has only two frames, which makes for a pretty crude animation.

The more frames you have, the smoother the animation, but the bigger the file, too. On a tiny image like this one, size doesn't matter, but with a larger image, your file can get huge pretty fast.

6. **Duplicate the layer.**

Choose Layer→Duplicate Layer, and then click OK. You now have two identical layers.

7. **Rotate the top layer 90 degrees.**

Go to Image→Rotate→Rotate Layer 90° Left (*not* Image→Rotate→90° Left—that command rotates your whole image, not just the active layer). You should now have two layers with stars in different places on each one.

8. **Animate your GIF.**

Go to File→Save For Web, and on the right side of the dialog box that appears, turn on the Animate checkbox. (If you don't see this checkbox, make sure GIF is selected in the box below the word "Preset"; if it isn't, select it from the drop-down menu.)

In the Animation section on the right side of the dialog box, adjust the time between frames, if you want. Leave the Looping Options field set to Forever so the animation repeats over and over (otherwise your animation plays just once and then stops).

9. **Preview the animation.**

   You can use the arrows in the Animation section to step through your animation one frame at a time, but for a more realistic preview, view the image in a web browser as explained in the previous section. The stars should twinkle. (Well, OK, they flash off and on—think of twinkle lights.)

10. **Save the animation, if you like, by clicking Save in the Save For Web dialog box.**

You can reopen and edit your original files in Expert mode and see all the layers they include. However, it's a good idea to also save them as PSD files to preserve their layers, just in case. If you make any changes, be sure to use Save For Web to reanimate it.

ON THE WEB

Creating Web Buttons

Elements makes it a snap to create buttons to use on web pages. Here's how:

1. Create a new blank file (File→New→Blank File). In the New dialog box's Preset menu, choose Web, and then pick a size you like. In the Background Contents field, choose Transparent. Then click OK.

2. Set the foreground color square to the color you want to use for the button, and then use a shape tool to draw the shape you want. It helps to set your view to Actual Pixels

(View→Actual Pixels) when doing web work, because that shows you the same size you'll see in a web browser.

3. Apply one or more layer styles (page 461) to make your button look more 3-D. Bevels, some of the Complex layer styles, and the Wow layer styles are all popular choices.

4. Add any necessary text using a type tool (see Chapter 14). You may want to apply a layer style to the text, too.

5. Save the file as a GIF.

Emailing Photos

Elements makes emailing photos you have stored in the Organizer a piece of cake. With just a few clicks, the program preps the image(s), fires up your email program, and attaches the image(s) to an outgoing message. (Of course, you can also email images without Elements' help by using your email program, and you may prefer that method since you get more freedom to specify settings like file size.)

NOTE There's one really annoying aspect of sending images from Elements: each message you send includes an ad for Elements.

If you've used a previous version of Elements, you'll be pleased to know that, in Elements 13, you can easily email from any email program without having to hassle around with trying to get the Adobe authentication codes that plagued earlier versions. However, if you were a fan of the Windows-only Photo Mail, that's gone now. Your email options are now the same whether you're using Windows or a Mac.

All emailing in Elements starts from the Organizer's Share menu. Your main choices there are:

- **Email Attachments**. This is the most traditional option, where you send each photo as a standard attachment.

- **PDF Slide Show**. This option creates a basic PDF-format slideshow of your images. All you have to do is name the slideshow (see page 570).

You need to choose the kind of email you want to send before you start. To pick, click the one you want in the Organizer's Share menu. The basic process is pretty similar for both types and is explained in detail below.

Individual Attachments

To send photos as regular email attachments, just follow these steps:

> **NOTE** All sharing starts in the Organizer. So if you don't use the Organizer or you want to email photos that aren't in the Organizer, just use the Attachments button in your regular mail program instead.

1. **In the Organizer, before you email photos for the first time, tell Elements about your email program.**

   Go to Edit→Preferences→Email/Elements Organizer→Preferences→Email. Select the email program you want to use with Elements by clicking the New button to the right of the Email Profile drop-down menu. In the New profile dialog box that opens, if you see your email program in the Service Provider menu, select it; if not, choose Other. Give the profile a name, and then click OK.

2. **Next, if Elements asks, enter your email address, name, and the password for your email account, and then click Validate.**

   If you use Microsoft Outlook in Windows or OS X Mail, Outlook, or Entourage on a Mac, you don't need to enter this information.

   If you chose Other in step 1, you may also need to provide the SMTP server information and the port to use, as well as information on the security needed. You should be able to find this information in the settings for your email program.

   When you click Validate, Elements checks with your email service provider to be sure everything is OK.

TIP You can set up multiple email accounts to use with Elements, but you'll need to go to Edit→ Preferences→Email/Elements Organizer→Preferences→Email and use the menu there to switch from the one you've been using.

3. **In the Organizer, select some photos (this is optional), and then go to Share→Email.**

   You can select photos before you start or add or change them once the Email Attachments panel appears; Figure 17-7 explains how.

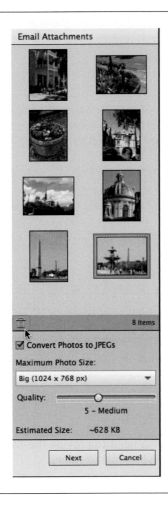

FIGURE 17-7

The Organizer's Email Attachments panel is pretty easy to use. You can start with one photo or a group, as shown here.

To send more photos, just drag the images' thumbnails from the Media Browser into this panel. Remove photos you don't want by highlighting them in the panel and then clicking the little trashcan below the thumbnail area (where the cursor is here). Drag your photos in the panel to change their order

In the Email Attachments panel, below the image thumbnails, is some info that can help you decide how many photos to send and how large to make them:

- **Number of Items.** Indicates how many photos you've selected to send.

- **Convert Photos to JPEGs.** JPEG is the best format for emailing photos, so you can turn on this checkbox to have Elements make JPEG versions of the images you've selected. (If the photos are already JPEGs, then this option is grayed out.) If you want to convert only *some* of your soon-to-be-emailed photos to JPEGs, select their thumbnails before turning on this checkbox.

- **Maximum Photo Size.** This setting tells Elements how large you want the emailed photos to be. Remember that it can take a really long time to download a large image with a dial-up Internet connection, and many email providers have a 10 MB limit per mailbox. If you need to change the size, then use this drop-down menu to choose a new one.

> **TIP** Adobe recommends that you not send email attachments from Elements that are larger than 10 MB. If you try to send a larger attachment, Elements warns you about the size and suggests that you may prefer using a different sharing method, but if you're sure it's OK to send the big attachment, you can just click OK and continue. Most of the time, though, that's not a good idea.

- **Quality.** If you're just emailing photos for viewing onscreen, then you can get away with a lower Quality setting than you can for photos that the recipient is going to print.

Below these settings, at the very bottom of the panel, is Elements' calculation of how large the attachment will be.

4. **Click Next, and then address the email and edit its subject and body text.**

In Elements 13, you have to add your recipients to the program's Contact Book (explained in the list below) before you can send email to them, unless you're using Microsoft Outlook in Windows or Apple's Mail app or Outlook or Entourage on a Mac, in which case you have the following options:

- **Do nothing.** If you're using Outlook (Windows or Mac), Apple Mail, or Entourage (Mac only), you don't need to select any recipients here. Instead, you can wait until Elements is through and then type the address in the completed email before you send it. If you're using one of these email programs and you don't select any recipients, at the end of the email process, Elements presents you with a regular email message, ready for you to address and send.

- **Select Recipients.** Elements keeps a Contact Book—a list of people you regularly email (or all the people you email if you aren't using one of the email programs listed above)—so you can simply select names from the list. (The box on page 569 has more about this feature.) If you haven't used Elements' email feature before, then start by clicking the Edit Contacts button (the little silhouette just above the Select Recipients box) and entering your recipient's contact info.

- **Edit Contacts.** To enter a new recipient or change the information for someone in your list, click the Edit Contacts button (the silhouette), and then enter the new info in the Contact Book.

After you have the email addressed to the folks you want to share your photos with, tweak the text in the Subject and Message fields, if you like. (You'll probably want to get rid of the Adobe advertising—just highlight it and type what you want.) If you aren't using Outlook, Apple Mail, or Entourage for Mac, you have to select at least one recipient before you can go to the next step.

5. **To finish, click Next.**

If you are using an email program other than Outlook (Windows or Mac), Apple Mail, or Entourage, or if you're using one of those programs but you already selected recipients, Elements sends your email. You never see the actual message, only a little window that says "Your files were shared successfully."

If you didn't select any recipients, Elements launches your email program, creates a new message, and attaches the files for you. You can then add recipients and edit the email in the normal way, and then send it yourself.

ORGANIZATION STATION

Elements' Contact Book

The Organizer makes it easy to call up the addresses of people you regularly email by keeping a Contact Book. Anytime you send email to a new recipient, you first have to add the address to the Contact Book by clicking the Edit Contacts button (the silhouette) in the Email Attachments panel. (You can also get to the Contact Book by choosing Edit→Contact Book in the main Organizer window.)

Once you've got the Contact Book window open, click the New Contact button to add an address. Then you can type in a name, email address, phone number, and other contact info. To edit or delete a contact, just select it in the window's list, and then click the relevant button.

You can also create groups of names in the Contact Book, for times when you want to send the same photo to several people at once. To do this, click New Group, enter a name for the group, select entries in the Contacts list, and then click Add. The people's names go into the Members list. To remove a name from the group, select it in the Members list, and then click Remove.

In Windows, Elements makes it easy to coordinate the Contact Book with your existing address book. You can choose to import addresses from Microsoft Outlook or Outlook Express, as well as any that you've saved as vCards (a digital business card format) in other programs. In the Contact Book window, just click Import and then choose your source.

You can also export your Contact Book addresses as vCards to use them in other programs. This is another feature that isn't available in the Mac version of Elements, although OS X's Contacts app can import and export vCards for you.

PDF Slideshows

You can also email a group of photos as a slideshow. Elements uses the popular PDF format, which lets your recipients page through each slide using the free, ubiquitous Adobe Reader program available from *http://get.adobe.com/reader* (or, on a Mac, in OS X Preview, if they prefer). They just open the PDF and view the photos one by one.

To create a slideshow from the Organizer, select the photos you want to include, and then go to Share→PDF Slide Show. In the PDF Slide Show panel that appears, Elements offers you size and quality choices, just as you have for sending photos as email attachments. Name the slideshow, click Next, and then choose recipients and enter a message, if you like, and then click Next again. Elements generates a standard email message with the slideshow attached. At this point, Elements displays a dialog box letting you know the message's file size and approximately how long it will take your recipients to download it. As with regular attachments, pay attention to the size of the PDF that Elements has created to make sure you won't choke your recipient's inbox. If the size looks reasonable, click OK and Elements sends your email or pops up a message with the slideshow attached, just as with regular email (as described in the previous section).

Creating Slideshows

Elements makes it easy to create slick slideshows—even those with music and transitions between the images—that you can play on your computer or send to friends. Slideshows got a complete makeover in Elements 13. The good news is that now, for the first time, you can create slideshows on a Mac. You can also create HD videos and even send your slideshows straight to your Facebook page.

However, making slideshows is now much more automated than it was in earlier versions of Elements. That automation makes the process much easier, but if you're looking for the kind of control and customization options that were in the Windows Slide Show Maker in earlier versions of Elements (like the ability to design your own pans and zooms), it's not available anymore.

NOTE If you find that the Elements' slideshow options don't meet your needs, here are a few alternatives: ProShow Gold from Photodex (*www.photodex.com*) is probably the most popular slideshow program for Windows. On a Mac, if iMovie, iPhoto, and iDVD don't work for you, FotoMagico (*www.boinx.com*) is the next step up. Also, many people create online slideshows using the photo-sharing services mentioned on page 578.

If you prefer the simple life, you can still quickly create a plain-vanilla PDF slide-show in about as much time as it takes to email a photo. PDF slideshows are really straightforward to create, but you can't add audio to them or control how the photos transition. On the plus side, you can send PDF slideshows to *anyone*, regardless of what kind of computer she uses (Mac or PC). As long as your recipients have Adobe Reader (which is free) or another PDF-viewing program, they can watch your show. PDF slideshows are described on page 570.

But, if your friends have even moderately up-to-date computers, the new Elements slideshows are just as easy to create, and they have all the bells and whistles, like fancy transitions and music. Creating them is explained beginning on page 574.

The easiest slideshow of all, though, is the kind you can make in the Organizer's Full Screen view, where it's a snap to create a full-featured slideshow with just a couple of quick settings adjustments. You can create this kind of slideshow in Windows and on Macs, but you can only *show* it to people who can see your computer monitor—you can't save it, email it, or post it on the Web.

Elements also lets you upload your photos directly to a number of popular sharing sites, like Facebook, Twitter, and Flickr. This chapter covers all your options.

> **TIP** For the new type of Elements slideshow, you need to do all your photo editing before you start your slideshow. Full Screen view, on the other hand, lets you edit as much as you like, using the Organizer's quick editing tools.

Full Screen View

Elements gives you a really easy way to create impressive slideshows to play on your computer, which could come in handy if, say, you want to play a retrospective of Mom and Dad's life together during their 50th wedding anniversary party. Whether you're using a Mac or a PC, you do this via the Organizer's Full Screen view, which gives you all kinds of options for music and fancy transitions between the images. To get started:

1. **In the Organizer, select the photos and videos you want to use in the slide-show, and then switch to Full Screen view.**

   If you want the photos displayed in a particular order, put them into an album (page 55) and rearrange them there before you switch to Full Screen view. Then choose View→Full Screen or press F11/⌘-F11 to enter Full Screen View. (If you have a Mac with a short keyboard without the 10-key pad on the right—like on a laptop or the current Apple Bluetooth keyboard—you need to add the fn key to most keystroke combos that use the F-keys on the top row of the keyboard.)

> **TIP** If you'd rather display more than one image at a time, press F12/⌘-F12 instead to start your slideshow in Side-by-Side view, which shows two images at a time.

2. **In Full Screen view, adjust the slideshow's settings.**

   Use the control strip at the bottom of the screen (shown in Figure 18-1) to control how Elements presents your slideshow. (You won't see the control strip until you move your cursor over the photo that's displayed.) Your options are explained after this list.

FIGURE 18-1

In Full Screen view, you can choose background music, transitions, and whether or not to endlessly loop your slideshow.

Just move your cursor over the photo to see this control strip.

3. **Run the slideshow.**

   Click the triangular Play icon on the control strip or tap your space bar to start the slideshow. To pause it, click the Pause icon or press the space bar again.

   To exit Full Screen view and get back to the Organizer, click the Close button (in Windows, the X at the right end of the control strip; on a Mac, the red dot on the left) or press Esc.

Here's what the control strip's buttons (Figure 18-1) let you do:

- **Theme**. Click this button to choose from among four kinds of transitions between slides: Classic (each photo simply gives way to the next), Fade In/Out (the current image fades out as the next one fades in), Pan and Zoom (Elements pans across each photo), and 3D Pixelate (puts an elaborate, glittery dissolve between each image). Move your cursor over each transition's thumbnail to see a demo of it, and then click the radio button under the one you want.

> **NOTE** You can't change the background color in Full Screen slideshows—it's always black (unless you choose the 3D Pixelate transition, in which case it's white).

- **Film Strip**. Click this button to display a thumbnail view of all the images in your slideshow across the bottom of your screen. Click it again to hide the thumbnails.

- **View**. Click this button and then click the appropriate icon to choose between a single-image view or seeing two photos side by side or one above the other.

> **TIP** While your slideshow is running, you can use the F11/⌘-F11 and F12/⌘-F12 shortcuts to switch between Single-Image and Side-by-Side view.

- **Sync**. When you're in a two-image view, this button (whose icon is a padlock) lets you tell Elements to pan and zoom over the two images in exactly the same way. (This button is grayed out when you're in Single-Image view.)

- **Settings**. Click this button to display a dialog box that lets you change the music for your slideshow (or choose None if you don't want any). Elements comes with a few built-in songs, but you can use any compatible audio file (MP3, WAV, AC3, AAC, or WMA format) that's on your computer. If the audio file you want to use isn't in the dialog box's Background Music menu, click the Browse button to find it.

  The dialog box also lets you play any audio captions included in your files, display text captions, and allow Elements to resize the slideshow's photos and videos so they fit onscreen (yes, videos play here, too, if you include them in the show). You can also choose to display a strip of thumbnails of all your photos along the bottom of the screen (the control strip's Film Strip button does the same thing). Use the Page Duration drop-down menu to determine how long each photo stays onscreen.

- **Fix**. Click this button for a pop-out panel that lets you apply all the quick fixes you can apply in the main Organizer window (page 49).

- **Organize**. You can tag photos or sort them into albums right in Full Screen view. Just click this button for a pop-out panel that lists your albums and your most commonly used tags (page 53).

- **Info**. This button brings up the same information about the current photo that you see in the Information pane in the main Organizer window. (If you're using a two-image view, Elements puts a blue outline around the image it's displaying information about.)

- **Exit**. Press Esc or click this button to end the show.

If you click the arrow at the right end of the control strip, Elements contracts the strip to hide the Fix, Organize, and Info buttons.

It takes hardly any time to set up this kind of slideshow, and all you have to do once you get it going is stand back and accept compliments for your impressive display. The disadvantage to this kind of slideshow, obviously, is that you can't share it with anyone who doesn't have access to your computer. But fortunately, as the next section explains, Elements also lets you create slideshows that you can send to other folks.

■ Organizer Slideshows

Elements 13 makes it super easy to create deluxe slideshows that include special effects and music, and are suitable for viewing on today's high-definition screens. These new slideshows are all pre-designed templates that you can't customize as much as the old slideshows included in previous Windows versions of Elements, but now you can create the same slideshows in both Windows and OS X. Elements now does the heavy lifting for you, but your final slideshows are in the widely used MP4 format, which means they're easy to share. You can also send your slideshows straight to Facebook, if you like.

The new slideshow-creation process works exactly the same whether you're on a Mac or a PC:

1. **In either the Editor or the Organizer, go to Create→Slide Show.**

   You have to select at least one photo in the Organizer or have at least one photo open in the Editor before you start. But you can add more photos later, so you don't have to choose everything before you start.

   > **TIP** You can also start a slideshow in the Organizer by selecting at least one photo, and then clicking the Slideshow button at the bottom of the window. When Elements is through playing your slideshow, click the Edit button to customize it.

   If you start in the Editor, you get bounced over to the Organizer to create your slideshow. If you have photos open in the Editor, they get included in your slideshow. If you start from the Editor with no photos open, you just see the Organizer's Media view and have to choose Slide Show from the Create menu again.

   If you have photos open in the Editor that you've worked on but haven't saved, Elements warns you that it will skip those photos when it creates your slideshow. If you want to include them, click Cancel and save your work, and then start again. Photos that you include in your slideshow that are open in the Editor don't have to be in the Organizer, but Elements automatically adds them to the Organizer when you create your slideshow.

   > **TIP** You aren't limited to still photos—you can also include videos in your slideshows.

2. **In the Slideshow window, choose a theme, and then click Next.**

   The window displays thumbnails of the different slideshow options and a description of each. It doesn't really matter which one you choose here, because you can change themes later if you don't like the one you picked.

3. **Wait a few seconds while Elements creates your slideshow and then plays it.**

   If you like what you see, that's it. But you'll probably want to make a few tweaks.

   When you move your cursor over the screen (or when the slideshow ends), a control strip appears. You can use the buttons there to save your slideshow or export it (your choices are explained below). Clicking the control strip's Edit or Exit button brings up the Slideshow Builder, explained below.

When you're happy with your slideshow, use the buttons at the bottom right of the Organizer window to save it for future editing, or export it to your hard drive or to Facebook.

If you decide not to make a slideshow after all, click the X at the Slideshow Builder's upper right.

Elements creates a pretty fancy slideshow with very little work on your part, but there are still a number of ways you can customize your slideshow. In the Slideshow Builder, you can:

- **Add and remove photos**. To add photos, click Add Media in the window's upper left. You can add photos that are already in the Organizer or choose "Photos and Videos from Folder" to add ones that aren't there—yet. Anything you add here gets added to the Organizer, even if you cancel the slideshow. To remove a photo from your slideshow, select it, and then click the Remove button at the window's bottom left.

- **Rearrange your photos**. Figure 18-2 shows you how.

FIGURE 18-2

You can rearrange your slides several different ways. To move slides one at a time, just drag them to their new positions, as shown here, where the painted-post image is getting moved to a position between the ostrich and the alligator.

You can also use the Sort by drop-down menu at the upper left of the Slideshow Builder to choose a sort order. This menu usually starts out set to Custom, but you can also choose to organize your photos chronologically (Newest First or Oldest First).

- **Change the theme**. Click the Themes button at the bottom of the window to bring up a panel showing all the available themes. Just click the one you want, and then click Apply. Click the Preview button at the bottom of the window to audition your new choice, and then click Exit on the control strip to return to the Slideshow Builder.

- **Change (or get rid of) the soundtrack**. Click the Audio button to bring up a window where you can browse through all the music in your catalog to select a different tune, or click No Audio if you don't want any music.

- **Edit your Photos**. If you realize that an image needs more editing, just right-click/Control-click its thumbnail and choose "Edit in PSE." After you're done adjusting things, save and close your image; in your slideshow, Elements updates the image's thumbnail to reflect your changes.

- **Sync the slide display to the music**. Use the Speed drop-down menu at the bottom of the window to tell Elements whether to ignore the audio track when it displays your slides or to sync the slides and the music together, either slowly (Normal) or fast (Brisk). If you turn on syncing, you should see the rate at which your slides appear speed up and slow down along with the music.

- **Turn captions on or off.** You can show or hide any captions that you've added to your photos by clicking this button. You can add captions right in the Slideshow Builder by clicking the area below a photo and then typing what you want. Not all the slideshow themes can display captions. They don't appear in the Minimalist theme, for example, even if you turn them on here.

- **Add slides with text on them.** If you want to create credits, titles, or visual narrations, click the Add Text Slide button, and Elements creates a blank slide that you can type on. Just click the slide thumbnail where it says "Add Text Here." Unfortunately, you have no control over the size, color, or font Elements uses (all that is controlled by the theme you chose), and you can't add more than one line of text to any text slide. If you want to go back and edit your text later, just click the slide again to activate the text so you can change it.

Once you have everything adjusted the way you like, it's time to save your work. If you want to be able to edit your slideshow later, click the Save button at the bottom right of the window and give your project a name. It will be in the Organizer next time you want to work on it. To share your slideshow with other people, click the Export button instead, and choose one of these two options:

- **Export to Local Disk.** Choose this command and then name your slideshow, choose where you want to save it, and select a size. Your choices are 640×480, 720p HD, and 1080p HD. After you click OK, it takes Elements a few minutes to finalize your file, which is in MP4 format. After Elements is through, it asks whether you want to import the completed file to the Organizer.

- **Facebook.** If you want to share your slideshow with your Facebook friends, choose this option, and then wait while Elements finalizes your slideshow. When it's done, you have to authorize Elements to upload to Facebook. There's also a checkbox that lets you download your friends list into Elements' Contact Book (page 569).

Creating this kind of slideshow is a quick and easy way to share your photos in a very professional-looking way.

■ A Few More Ways to Share

The Organizer's Share menu makes it simple to post your photos to several non-Adobe sites so your friends can view your photos online. You can quickly send photos to sites like Facebook and Twitter right from within Elements. (The items in the Share menu change depending on Adobe's current partnerships, so you might see slightly different options from those listed below.) Once you post photos, you and your friends can order not only prints, but also t-shirts, mugs, bags, and other items with your photos on them (exactly what you can order depends on which service you use).

Here's a quick rundown of what you can do with each site and what it'll cost you:

- **Private Web Album**. If you have a Revel account (see page 8), you can select this item to send photos there.

- **Facebook**. To upload photos to your Facebook page (for free), just select photos in the Organizer or open them in the Editor and then choose Share→Facebook. The first time you do this, you're given the option of importing the email addresses of your Facebook friends to your Contact Book (page 569).

NOTE   This list describes the options you see if you've turned off the Premiere Elements options in Edit→Preferences→Editing/Elements Organizer→Preferences→Editing. If you've chosen the setting there to show both programs' options, you see many more choices in the Share menu.

- **Flickr**. This is a really popular photo-sharing site where you can create galleries and slideshows and order different kinds of merchandise featuring your photos. Basic accounts are free.

- **Twitter**. You can tweet your photos from either the Editor or the Organizer. Just go to Share→Twitter. A Twitter account is free.

- **SmugMug Gallery**. SmugMug offers a lot of different gift items that you and your friends can order. You can try it free for seven days, and your friends can order prints and merchandise without a paid account. If you want to maintain a gallery on this site, it's $40 a year for a basic account.

- **Vimeo**. If you have an account with this free, popular video-sharing site, you can upload videos right from the Organizer, even if you don't use Premiere Elements.

- **YouTube**. You can send videos from the Organizer right to your YouTube account. (You don't need a YouTube account to *watch* videos on the site, but you do need a free account to *upload* videos there.) This option appears even if you don't have Premiere Elements installed.

To upload a photo to any of these sites, select the image(s) or video(s) you want to upload, click the Share button, and then choose the option you want. You'll be asked to sign in if you already have an account with the site you chose, or to create one if you don't. Each site has a simple-to-use wizard that walks you through the process of creating an account (and another one for uploading photos once you *have* an account), and they also have tours so you can look around before you decide to join. If you aren't sure which one(s) to try, ask your friends which one they like. Each site has pros and cons, so you may want to try them all before you decide.

TIP If you use a Windows computer and you have an iPhone, an iPod Touch, or an iPad, Elements makes it easy to share photos from your iDevice. If you used your iPhone to take pictures and you want to get them into Elements or if you're using your iPod, iPhone, or iPad to move photos from another device to your computer, just connect your iDevice to the computer and then use the Photo Downloader (page 7) to send them straight to the Organizer, or download them via Windows Explorer and then go to the Organizer and choose File→Get Photos to bring them into Elements. Even better, if you've signed up for Apple's free iCloud service (*www.apple. com/icloud/setup/pc.html*), your Pictures/My Pictures folder should contain a folder called Photo Stream. Your iDevice photos appear there automatically, and you can set that as a watched folder (see the Tip on page 35) for the Organizer, too, so your photos go directly into Elements.

To send photos or albums to your iPod, iPhone, or iPad, either to show them off to your friends or to transport them to another device or computer, if you use iCloud, just put them in your Photostream folder. If not, connect the iDevice to your computer, and then go to iTunes→Photos→"Sync photos from"→Photoshop Elements.

If you use a Mac, the best way to move photos back and forth between your iDevices and computers is still via iPhoto/iTunes, if you don't use iCloud or Adobe Revel. Elements albums aren't recognized by the Mac version of iTunes the way they are in the Windows version.

Additional Elements

Beyond the Basics

So far, everything in this book has been about what you can do with Elements right out of the box. But as with many things digital, there's a thriving cottage industry devoted to souping up Elements. You can add new brushes, shapes, layer styles, actions, and fancy filters. Many of these add-ons are designed to make Elements behave more like Photoshop. Best of all, a lot of what's out there is free.

This chapter looks at some of these extras, teaches you how to manage the stuff you collect, and explains how to know when you really need the full version of Photoshop instead. You'll also learn about the many resources available for expanding your knowledge of Elements beyond this book.

■ Graphics Tablets

Probably the most popular Elements accessory is a *graphics tablet*, which lets you draw and paint with a pen-like stylus instead of a mouse. This kind of tablet isn't a computer like an iPad or Galaxy; it's more like a souped-up substitute for a mouse: You control the onscreen cursor by drawing directly on the tablet's surface—an action that many artists find offers them greater control. If trying to use the Lasso tool with a mouse makes you feel like you're trying to write on a mirror with a bar of soap, then a graphics tablet is for you.

Most tablets work like the one shown in Figure 19-1, where you use the stylus on the tablet just as you would a mouse on a mousepad. Any changes you make appear right on your monitor.

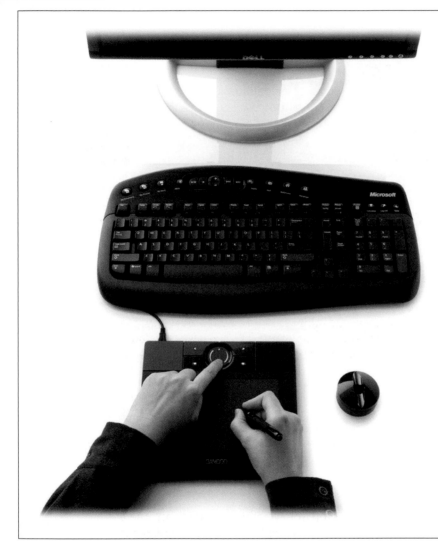

FIGURE 19-1

A Wacom Bamboo tablet in action.

The working area is inside the rectangle on the tablet's surface. The buttons and ring at the top of the tablet let you do things like zoom and scroll.

For basic photo retouching, a small tablet is usually fine. If you want to do more drawing and like to make sweeping strokes when you draw, then you may want a larger model.

You can also buy tablets that let you use your fingers on them, like a laptop trackpad. But for photo editing, you'll be happier with one that comes with a pen-like stylus, since the stylus lets you be more precise when doing things like making selections.

> **NOTE** Some deluxe-model graphics tablets act as monitors and let you work *directly* on your image—but you need to budget close to $1,000 for that kind of convenience.

For most people, it's much easier to control fine motions with a tablet's stylus than with a mouse. And when you use a tablet, many of Elements' brushes and tools become *pressure sensitive*—the harder you press, the darker and wider the line becomes. So a stylus lets you create much more realistic brushstrokes, as shown in Figure 19-2.

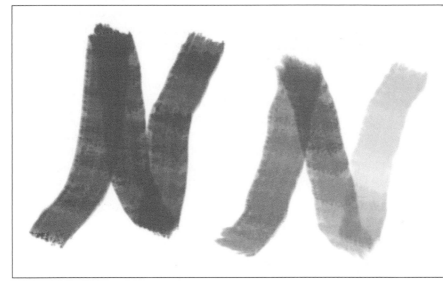

FIGURE 19-2

Two almost identical brushstrokes, starting with fairly hard pressure and then easing up. Both were made using the same brush and color settings. The only difference is that the stroke on the left was drawn with a mouse, and the one on the right came from a tablet stylus.

You can see what a difference the pressure sensitivity makes.

When using the Brush tool, you'll see a Tablet Settings button in the Tool Options area that lets you access the tool's tablet-related options. These settings let you choose whether to let the pressure control the size, opacity, roundness, hue jitter, and scatter for the brushes. (See page 397 for more about brush settings.) Many of Elements' brushes and tools are *automatically* pressure sensitive when you hook up a tablet.

With a tablet, you can also create hand-drawn line art—even if you don't have an artistic bone in your body—by placing a picture of what you want to draw on the surface of the tablet, and then tracing over it. And, if you find constant mousing troublesome, you may have fewer hand problems when using a tablet's stylus. Most tablets also come with a wireless mouse that works only on the surface of the tablet. Or you can use your regular mouse on a mousepad or on your desk the way you always do, and just switch back and forth between the stylus and the mouse.

Tablets now start at less than $100, a big drop from what they used to cost. There are lots of different models, and their features vary widely. If you're choosing one of these entry-level tablets, be sure to select a model that is meant to be used with graphics programs—some tablets are intended more for use with programs like word processors and spreadsheets. Sophisticated tablets, which are more expensive, offer more levels of sensitivity and can even respond when you change the *angle* at which you're holding the stylus.

Wacom, one of the big tablet manufacturers, has some pretty nifty tablet demos on its website (*www.wacom.com*). You can't actually simulate what it's like to *use* a tablet, but the animations give you a good idea of what life would be like if you were to go the tablet route.

Stuff from the Internet

You have to spend some money if you want a graphics tablet, but there's a ton of free (and not free) Elements-related stuff available online: tutorials, brushes, textures, layer styles, and so on. (Most of these add-ons say they work with Photoshop, but since Elements is *based* on Photoshop, you can use most of them in Elements, too.) Here are some popular places to go treasure hunting:

- **Adobe Add-ons** (*https://creative.adobe.com/addons*). This site is the replacement for the old Adobe Exchange, which was a great place to find downloads for Elements. There isn't quite as much here yet, but if you enter what you're looking for (like "brushes") into the search box, you can still find lots of useful stuff, both paid and free. About 99 percent of the items listed are made specifically for Photoshop, but Photoshop's brushes, swatches, textures, shapes, and layer styles work in Elements, too.

- **Simple Photoshop** (*www.simplephotoshop.com*). Home of the popular (but not free) Elements+ add-on tools and some tutorials.

- **The Plugin Site** (*http://thepluginsite.com/products/elementsxxl*). This site hosts Elements XXL, another set of add-on tools similar to Elements+, although quite a bit more expensive. You do get a larger group of tools for the extra money, though. Windows only, no Mac version.

- **The Pioneer Woman** (*www.thepioneerwoman.com/photography/category/photoshop-elements*). Here you can find popular—and free—Elements actions for special image effects.

- **Texas Chicks** (*www.texaschicksblogsandpics.com*). Another site with lots of great actions and tutorials for Elements.

- **Alibony** (*www.alibony.com*). Lots of Elements tutorials, actions, brushes, and effects, many of which are geared toward scrapbooking projects.

- **MyJanee** (*www.myjanee.com/tutorialselements.htm*). You'll find lots of tutorials and free downloads on this site. It hasn't been updated in a while, so some features may be in different places in your version of Elements than in these tutorials.

- **Sue Chastain's on About.com** (*www.graphicssoft.about.com*). Another site with lots of downloads and many tutorials.

- **PanosFX** (*www.panosfx.com*). Panos Efstathiadis produces some wonderful actions for Photoshop, and he has adapted most of them for Elements, as well. Some are free; some cost a few bucks.

- **optikVerve Labs** (*www.optikvervelabs.com*). This is the home of virtualPhotographer, one of the most amazing *plug-ins* (add-ons) for Elements. Best of all, it's free. Alas, this plug-in works only in Windows, not on Macs.

- **Grant's Tools** (*www.elementsvillage.com*). This has long been the most popular set of free add-on tools for Elements. These days, it's easiest to find the most up-to-date version via the forums at Elements Village. Just look for the Grant's Tools thread at the top of the General Elements Discussion forum.

- **ShutterFreaks** (*www.shutterfreaks.com*). This website offers a number of Elements add-ons. Some are free, but most cost a few dollars. You'll find tutorials here, too.

- **CoffeeShop** (*www.thecoffeeshopblog.com*). Offers free brushes, frames, patterns, and tutorials for Photoshop and Photoshop Elements.

- **ActionCentral** (*http://atncentral.com*). Lots of free actions here. Most are for Photoshop, but there are a number that work in Elements as well.

If you're willing to pay, you've got even more choices. You can find everything from more elaborate ways to sharpen photos to really cool collections of special edges and visual effects. Prices range from "donationware" (pay if you like it) to hundreds of dollars for sophisticated plug-ins.

> **NOTE** Elements 13 is based on Photoshop CC (Creative Cloud), so CC add-ons are compatible with it. Plug-ins and other goodies designed for older versions of Photoshop or Elements usually work with newer versions, but not the other way around. For example, a brush made for Photoshop CC works in Elements 13 but not in Elements 3. Also, remember that Mac plug-ins don't work in Windows, and vice versa, but many plug-ins offer two versions, one for each operating system.
>
> When downloading a plug-in, check with the developer to make sure it will work with Elements 13, especially if it costs money. If you're using Windows 7 or 8, check the plug-in's compatibility with them, as well. Mac folks, keep in mind that there's no way to run Rosetta (the old system that let you run software written for PowerPC Macs) anymore, so any plug-ins you buy need to be Intel-native. (This shift away from Rosetta doesn't have any effect on actions, layer styles, shapes, brushes, and gradients—only plug-ins.) So most plug-ins that are more than a few years old won't work with Elements 13.

With so many goodies available, it's easy to get overwhelmed trying to keep track of everything you've added to Elements. Your best bet is to make backup copies of anything you download so you'll have it if you ever need to reinstall Elements. Elements also includes a Preset Manager (Figure 19-3) that can help you keep track of certain kinds of downloads. To launch it, in the Editor, go to Edit→Preset Manager.

> **NOTE** If you download actions, check to be sure that they're compatible with Elements 13. It's safest to use actions written specifically for Elements, but actions for Photoshop will work as long as they don't include steps Elements doesn't understand. (Incidentally, many of the add-on tools you can download are based on actions.)

FIGURE 19-3

Elements' Preset Manager is a nifty feature that lets you see all your brushes, swatches, gradients, layer styles, patterns, and effects in one place.

You can use it to change which groups are loaded, add or remove items, and so on—the same way you would when using the Brush tool.

TIP In Windows, you have to turn on hidden files to see some of Elements' folders. Just go to Control Panel→Appearance and Personalization→Show Hidden Files and Folders.

When You Really Need Photoshop

You can do a ton with Elements, but some people need the full version of Photoshop instead. For example, if you want to write your own actions, or if you have to work extensively in CMYK mode, then you need Photoshop.

When you send a file to a print shop, the printer usually tells you it needs to be a *CMYK* file. CMYK is the color mode used for commercial printing—it stands for Cyan, Magenta, Yellow, and blacK, which are the colors professional printers use. You can't convert files to CMYK in Elements, so if you need CMYK files on a regular basis, it's worth the extra price of Photoshop to avoid the aggravation. (If you only *occasionally* need CMYK files, you might just ask the print shop whether they can convert the file for you.)

Photoshop gives you more of everything: more choices, more tools, more settings, more types of Adjustment layers, and so on. But, for most people, Elements has plenty of features.

▪ Beyond This Book

You can do *thousands* of interesting things with Elements that are beyond the scope of this book. The Help menu gives you access to dozens of tutorials right within Elements. Also, bookstores have loads of titles on Elements and Photoshop, and a lot of tasks are the same in both programs. You can find specialized books on everything from color management to making selections to scrapbooking.

In addition, you'll find hundreds of tutorial websites. Besides those mentioned earlier in this chapter, here are some other popular sites:

- **Adobe** (*www.adobe.com*). You'll find plenty of free online training for Elements here, and you can get to a lot of it from Elements Live (page 22) and the Help menus in the program itself. On Adobe TV (*http://tv.adobe.com*), you can see the same video tutorials linked to in the program's Help menus.

- **Photoshop Roadmap** (*www.photoshoproadmap.com*). This site has tutorials and plug-ins for Photoshop, but there's a big section of Elements tutorials, too.

- **Photoshop Support** (*www.photoshopsupport.com/elements/tutorials.html*). Despite the name, this site *isn't* run by Adobe. It has a whole section of Elements tutorials.

- **YouTube** (*www.youtube.com*). Yep, that's right: You can find videos about almost *anything* on YouTube, including lots of Elements tutorials, including some from Adobe.

- **Photoshop Elements User** (*www.photoshopelementsuser.com*). This is the website for a subscriber-only print newsletter (the only publication specifically for Elements), but it includes some free video tutorials, a forum, and a good collection of links. Its forums, the most active ones out there for questions about creative projects in Elements, are hosted at *www.elementsvillage.com*.

- **PhotoLesa** (*www.photolesa.com/tutorials*). The website of Photoshop maven and Missing Manual author Lesa Snider includes many well-written Elements tutorials.

If you search around online, you're sure to find a tutorial for any project you have in mind. Although many of them are written for Photoshop, in most cases, you can adapt them for Elements. If you get stuck or need help with any other aspect of Elements, there's an active online community that will have an answer for you. Besides the sites already mentioned, try these:

- **Adobe Support forum** (*http://forums.adobe.com/community/photoshop_elements*). This is the official Adobe Photoshop Elements user-to-user forum. It's your best bet for getting answers without calling Adobe support.

- **Digital Photography Review** (*www.dpreview.com*). This site has a bunch of camera-specific forums. You can also get some Elements answers in the Retouching forum if you specify in your question that you've got *Elements* rather than Photoshop (although, sadly, the quality of the posts there has fallen off dramatically in the past couple of years).

- **RetouchPRO** (*www.retouchpro.com*). The forums here cover all kinds of retouching techniques and artistic uses for Elements and Photoshop. They also host frequent webcasts about digital imaging.

- **Photoshop Creative** (*http://www.photoshopcreative.co.uk/*). Another forum for Elements enthusiasts.

Many sites are devoted specifically to *scrapbooking* with Elements. A good place to start is Scrapper's Guide (*www.scrappersguide.com*), a commercial site run by Linda Sattgast.

No matter what you're looking for—add-ons, tutorials, communities—try a Google search, and you'll no doubt find a site that has what you want.

There's no question about it: Once you get familiar with Elements, it's addictive. Lots of other folks have found out how much fun this program is, so you shouldn't have any trouble finding the answer to any question you have.

The only limit to what you can do with Elements is your imagination. Enjoy!

PART

7

Appendixes

APPENDIX A:
Installation and Troubleshooting

APPENDIX B:
The Organizer, Menu by Menu

APPENDIX C:
The Editor, Menu by Menu

NOTE Appendixes B and C are available from this book's Missing CD page at *www.missingmanuals.com/ cds*. (To learn about the Missing CD page, turn to page xxv.)

Installation and Troubleshooting

Elements is easy to install and is pretty trouble-free once it's up and running. This appendix describes some things you can do to ensure a smooth installation, and provides cures for most of the little glitches that can crop up once you're using the program.

Regardless of whether you're using a Mac or a Windows computer, you need to install Elements when you're logged into an administrator account on your machine. (If you've never done anything to change your account and there's only one account on your computer, it's almost certainly an administrator account.) You also need to have an active Internet connection when you install the program, or you won't get past the "enter a serial number" step.

> **NOTE** If you have a previous version of Elements on your computer, you *don't* need to remove it before installing Elements 13. All versions of Elements run completely separately, so you can keep older versions if you want.

Make sure you have your Elements serial number handy before you start the installation process. You can install Elements without a serial number, but only as a 30-day trial; when your 30 days are up, the program stops working. If you have a retail version of Elements (in other words, you bought it as a CD in a box), the serial number is on the label on the install disc's case, or there may be a redemption code on your receipt instead, which you use to obtain a serial number (the directions for how to do this should be listed along with the code). If you got the program bundled with something else (maybe with a scanner you bought, for example), you'll usually find the serial number on the paper sleeve the disc is in. (It's not a bad idea to write the serial number right *on* the disc so you'll always have it around if you ever need to reinstall.) If you downloaded Elements, the serial number should be in an email from wherever you downloaded it.

TIP   Once you install and register Elements, Adobe records your serial number, so if you ever misplace it, you can get it from your Adobe account information. Also, when Adobe releases new versions of Elements, it usually offers a rebate for registered owners of previous versions. And if you agree to let Adobe send you email, you may be able to get discounts on other programs, like on the full version of Photoshop, in case you want to graduate to that program.

Regardless of where you bought the program, if you got the boxed version, the box contains both the Mac and Windows versions of Elements 13; just insert the disc for the version you want to install. You're allowed to install it on two computers—that can be two Windows computers, two Macs, or one of each.

If you downloaded Elements from Adobe or Amazon, you can install the program on two computers but they must both use the same operating system; in other words, two Windows computers or two Macs, but not one of each.

If you use Organizer, Elements stores your catalog of images separately from its program files. That means you can install and uninstall Elements as many times as you like without damaging or losing your existing catalog (if you have one from a previous version of Elements). However, it's a good idea to back up any existing catalogs from older versions *before* installing Elements 13.

If you've used a previous version of Elements, when you first install Elements 13, if the Organizer doesn't automatically find your existing catalog, go to File→Manage Catalogs→Open. Then navigate to your catalog (usually called something like "My Catalog") and open it. (If the Open button is grayed out when you choose your old catalog, click Convert instead.) Elements makes a backup copy of the catalog and adds "-1" to its name (My Catalog-1, for example). The Organizer then uses your existing catalog (the one *without* the -1 in its name). Just remember that any changes you make in Elements 13 won't appear in the backup version of your catalog (the one *with* "-1" in its name).

NOTE   Unlike some previous versions of Elements, Elements 13 *activates* itself (meaning it checks in with Adobe to make sure everything is valid) when you sign in with your Adobe ID. You always have to stay logged in with the Adobe ID you used when installing Elements. If you ever log out, you also deactivate Elements and it will stop working in 7 days. But after you've installed Elements 13 and launched it once, you don't need an active Internet connection to use the program, although you may have trouble using the items in the Graphics panel or the Create templates, since Elements needs to downloaded most of them the first time you use them.

Installing Elements in Windows

Elements 13 is different from Elements 11 and earlier in that you *must* be connected to the Internet during the installation process. So make sure you're online before starting this process.

If you have other versions of Elements on your computer, it's a good idea to make a complete backup of the Organizer catalogs for those versions before you start, just in case (see page 75 for info on backing up). After you do that, here's how to run the installer:

1. **Put the install disc in your computer's drive, or, if you downloaded Elements, expand the file by right-clicking it and choosing Extract All.**

   If you insert the disc, the installer window should open automatically. If it doesn't, then double-click the disc's icon or right-click it and choose Open.

   If you have the downloaded version, double-click the extracted Elements 13 folder. Next, double-click PhotoshopElements, and then double-click *Set-up. exe* to start the installer. (You won't see the .exe extension, but the file type is Application.)

2. **In the Installer window that opens, click Install.**

   If you haven't bought Elements yet (meaning you don't have a serial number), choose Try instead of Install.

3. **Create an Adobe ID or sign in with an existing one.**

   If you have other Adobe products installed on your computer, Elements usually picks up your Adobe ID info from those files. If it doesn't or if you have more than one ID and it offers you the wrong one, just click "Not your Adobe ID?" and enter the correct information. If you don't have an Adobe ID yet, click Sign In, and then click "Get an Adobe ID." Otherwise, click Sign In.

4. **In the License Agreement window, read and accept the license agreement.**

5. **Enter your serial number, and then click Next.**

6. **Choose the language you want Elements to use and where you want the installer to put Elements.**

   Use the Language menu at the lower left of the window to change the language, if necessary.

   Unless you have a specific reason to use a different location (if you install all your programs on a separate drive, for example), just go with the one the installer suggests.

7. **Click Install to begin the installation.**

   If a Windows message box appears asking whether you want to give Elements permission to make changes your system; click Yes.

8. **When the installer is done, click Close to exit the installer, and then restart your computer.**

You don't *have* to restart your machine, but it's always a good idea to do so after installing a new program.

9. **Launch Elements.**

The installer creates a desktop shortcut to Elements. To launch the program, double-click the shortcut or right-click it and then choose Open.

The first time you launch Elements, you see a window where you select your country, and also a note that you may be tempted not to bother to read, but which is very important. In Elements 13, you're *automatically* signed up to let your computer send Adobe info about how you use Elements. Adobe says that this will allow them to "provide you with a more personalized experience." If you don't want Elements to send Adobe this info, click the link that says "To change your preference now, click here," which launches your web browser and takes you to your account page at Adobe.com, where you can change this setting. If you change your mind later on, go to Adobe.com, log in, and then click Manage My Account→Security & Privacy→Desktop App Usage Information.

■ Installing Elements on a Mac

There's not much you need to do prior to installing Elements on a Mac. If you want to remove older versions of Elements, you have to do so them by running their uninstallers. Confusingly, for Elements 6, the *uninstaller* is the same as the *installer*. On the first installer screen, simply choose Remove Adobe Photoshop Elements Components, click Next, and then click Install. (If you don't have the disc or download file to get to the installer, there's an emergency uninstaller in Applications→Utilities, but it's much better to use the Elements disc's installer if you can.) For Elements 8 through 12, you'll find the uninstaller in Applications→Adobe Photoshop Elements [8, 9, 10, 11, or 12]→Uninstall Adobe Photoshop Elements [8, 9, 10, 11, or 12].

To install Elements 13:

1. **Make sure your computer is connected to the Internet.**

You can't install Elements 13 unless you're online. There's no option to wait and let the program connect later on—Elements 13 verifies your serial number by connecting to Adobe during the installation process. You can run Elements *later* without being online, but you have to be connected during installation.

2. **Put the install DVD in your Mac's DVD or combo drive, or double-click the .dmg file you downloaded to expand it.**

Double-click the DVD icon or the .dmg file to see the disc's contents.

3. **Double-click the Adobe Photoshop Elements 13 folder.**

4. **Double-click the Install icon.**

   If you're installing a download version, you see the OS X window warning that you downloaded the program from the Internet and asking if you're sure you want to open it. Click Open.

5. **Decide whether you want to install the program as a trial or a purchased version.**

   If you have a serial number, click Install. If not, click Try.

6. **Create an Adobe ID or sign in with an existing one.**

   If you've owned a previous version of Elements or purchased another Adobe program, you may already have an Adobe ID that you can use. If you have other Adobe products, Elements usually picks up this information from the files on your computer. If it doesn't or if you have more than one ID and it offers you the wrong one, just click "Not your Adobe ID?" and enter the correct information. If you don't have an Adobe ID, click Sign In, and then click "Get an Adobe ID." Otherwise, click Sign In.

7. **Choose the language you want to read the software agreement in.**

   Give the agreement a quick read, and then click Accept.

8. **Enter your serial number, and then click Next.**

   See page 593 for info on where to find your serial number.

9. **If you like, adjust your installation settings.**

   The Install Options screen lets you choose a language for Elements to use and change where the installer puts the program on your computer. Unless you have a specific reason to use a different location (if you install all your programs on a separate drive, for instance), just agree to the one the installer suggests, which is your Mac's main Applications folder. The Elements updater always expects to find the program there, so you'll have fewer problems with updates if you don't change the install location.

10. **Click Install.**

    Enter your OS X account password when the installer asks for it. The installer then does its thing, which takes a few minutes (you can watch its progress in the window).

11. **Click Close to close the installer or click Launch Now to start using Elements.**

    Clicking Launch Now brings up a window where you need to select your country, and also a note that you may be tempted not to read, but which is very important. In Elements 13, you're *automatically* signed up to let your computer send Adobe info about how you use Elements. Adobe says that this will allow them to "provide you with a more personalized experience." If you don't want Elements to send this info to Adobe, click the link that says "To change your preference now, click here," which launches your web browser and takes you to your account page at Adobe.com, where you can change this setting. If you change your mind later on, you can change your settings by going to Adobe.com, logging in, and then clicking on Manage My Account→Security & Privacy→Desktop App Usage Information.

> **TIP** It's a good idea to repair your Mac's permissions after installing Elements. (Repairing permissions is a simple housekeeping task that helps make sure everything runs smoothly.) Go to Applications→Utilities→Disk Utility; in the list on the left side of the Disk Utility window, click your hard drive's name, and then click Repair Permissions. This process can take quite a while, so don't fret, and don't freak out over all the messages you may see scrolling through the window while it's running—they're normal.

To launch Elements, go to Applications→Adobe Photoshop Elements 13, and then double-click the Elements icon (the stylized teal camera icon); or go to the Dock and start Launchpad, and then single-click the Elements icon. Either route opens the Welcome screen (page 4). If you want to launch the Editor directly, rather than the Welcome Screen, it's hidden away in Applications→Adobe Photoshop Elements 13→Support Files.

To keep Elements in the Dock, simply click and hold the program's Dock icon while Elements is running, and then choose Options→"Keep in Dock" from the pop-out menu, or drag the program's icon—*not* the whole Elements folder—into the Dock when Elements *isn't* running. If you add Elements to the Dock and then change your mind about having it there, just drag the program's icon out of the Dock and watch it vanish in a puff of smoke.

▇ Scratch Disks

The calculations Elements makes behind the scenes are really complex, and the program needs a place to write stuff down while it's figuring out how to change your images. If the task at hand is too heavy-duty for your system's main memory to cope with alone, Elements uses what's called a *scratch disk*—unused space on your hard drive—when it's busy making your photos gorgeous.

You probably have just one hard drive in your computer, and in that case Elements automatically uses that drive as its scratch disk. That's fine, and Elements can run very happily like that.

> **TIP** If you use Windows, you can make Elements *really* happy by keeping your hard drive defragmented and making sure there's plenty of free space available for the program to use. To defragment in Windows, go to Control Panel→"System and Security"→Administrative Tools→"Defragment and optimize your drives" (or, depending on which version of Windows you have, "Defragment your hard drive").

If you're fortunate enough to have a computer with more than one internal drive, you can designate a *separate* disk as your scratch disk to improve Elements' performance. Just keep in mind that the scratch disk needs to be as fast as the drive Elements is installed on, or there's no point using it. If you have a USB external drive, for instance, forget it—USB isn't fast enough (even USB 3.0), so just leave your main drive as the scratch disk.

To assign a scratch disk, in the Editor, go to Edit→Preferences→Performance/Photoshop Elements Editor→Preferences→Performance and choose your preferred disk(s). You can select up to four disks to use as scratch disks.

■ Troubleshooting

If Elements behaves badly from the moment you install it, then something probably went funky during installation. That's easy to fix: Uninstall Elements and reinstall it.

To uninstall Elements, in Windows, go to Control Panel→"Uninstall a Program" and remove Elements. On a Mac, go to Applications→Adobe Photoshop Elements 13→Uninstall Adobe Photoshop Elements 13. Then reinstall the program.

Fortunately, Adobe makes good software that looks after itself pretty well. There is, however, one simple procedure you can perform if Elements starts acting funny: Delete your *preferences file*, which is where Elements keeps track of your preferred settings for the program. Deleting this file fixes the overwhelming majority of problems that may develop. You'll most likely need to delete the preferences file when dealing with Editor-related problems.

> **NOTE** There's one downside to throwing out your preferences file: Once Elements supplies you with a replacement file (which it generates automatically), you'll have to redo any changes you made to things like window behavior. Your panels also go back to their original locations, so you'll need to rearrange them again if you pulled any of them out of the Panel Bin. But, on the bright side, deleting your preferences file *doesn't* affect your image files at all.

Deleting preferences is easy. In the Editor, go to Edit→Preferences→General/Photoshop Elements Editor→Preferences→General, and then click the "Reset Preferences on next launch" button. You'll see a rather scary warning that "This cannot be undone." Just click OK; as explained above, it's not a big deal to delete preferences. Then quit the Editor and start it again.

It's much less common to need to reset the *Organizer's* preferences, but if you want to do that, it's easy, too: In the Organizer, go to Edit→Preferences→General/Elements Organizer→Preferences→General, and then click the Restore Default Settings button at the bottom of the Preferences window.

Index

Symbols

8-bit color mode, 41
8-bit images, 288–289, 369
16-bit images, 288–289
32-bit images, xv, 38
64-bit images, xv, 38

A

actions. *See also* effects
  overview, 433, 454
  running, 454–456
activating layers, 206
Actual Pixels view, 101–102, 107
Adaptive Grid view (Organizer), 6,
  43–45
Add Noise filter, 444–445
add-ons, 586–588
Adjust Color Curves dialog box, 332
Adjust Color for Skin Tone feature,
  139–142, 252
Adjust Edge section (Refine Edge
  dialog box), 160
Adjustment layers
  basics, 215–219
  Gradient Map, 476–478
Adjustments button (Quick Fix
  window), 119
Adjustments panel
  basics, 217
  Colorize checkbox, 365–366
  Quick Fix, 122–124
Adjust Sharpness tool, 263–267

Adobe Camera Raw Converter.
  See Raw Converter
Advanced mode (Create projects),
  518–519
Airbrush setting (Brush tool), 397–398
albums
  creating, 55–57
  instant, 50
aligning
  layers, 203–205
  text, 482
alpha channels, 183
anchor points (Magnetic Lasso), 169
Angled Strokes filter, 445
animated GIFs, 563–565
anti-aliasing
  overview, 152
  text, 487–488
artistic text
  overview, 500
  Text on Custom Path tool, 504–506
  Text on Selection tool, 500–503
  Text on Shape tool, 503–504
Asian Text Options checkbox, 488
aspect ratios, 89, 93, 96, 277, 541
attaching photos to emails, 566–570
Auto Analyzer (Organizer), 55
Auto Color (Adjustments panel), 133
Auto Contrast button, 131
Auto Erase option (Pencil tool), 407
Autofill edges checkbox, 86
Auto Levels button, 130–131

Auto Match Color Tone button (Photomerge Compose), 382
Automatic Download checkbox, 32
automatic merges (Photomerge Exposure), 294–295
Auto Red Eye Fix (Quick Fix), 126
Auto Sharpen button, 135
Auto Smart Fix command, 27, 130
Auto Smart Tone, 142–143, 229
Average Blur filter, 444, 452–453

B

background color square, 253–255
Background Eraser, 418–420
Background layer
   basics, 189–190
   opacity of, 197
backgrounds, choosing, 41–42
backing up files, 75–78
barrel distortion, 385–386
Basic mode (Create projects), 512, 518–519
Basic Workspace (Expert mode), 10–11
batch-processing photos.
   See processing multple files
Before & After views (Quick Fix), 124–125
bit depth, choosing (Raw Converter), 288–290
Bitmap mode, 41
black-and-white photos
   colorizing. See colorizing black-and-white photos
   converting color to, 349–352
   Convert to Black and White command, 357–358
   layer mask view, 214–215
   tinting, 362–366
blemishes, fixing
   with Clone Stamp, 318–322
   with Content-Aware Fill command, 321–324
   with Healing Brush, 315–318
   overview, 309–312
   with Spot Healing Brush, 312–315
blending exposures
   manually, 299
   overview, 292–294
   Photomerge Exposure.
      See Photomerge Exposure

blend modes
   basics, 411–413
   overview, 198–199
Bloat tool (Liquify filter), 493
blown out photos, 231
bmp (Bitmap) files, 72
bokeh (blurring), 447
bordering selections, 176
borders
   adding to prints, 542
   drawing (shapes), 428
bounding boxes (printing), 539
bracketed exposures, 229
brightness
   adjusting in Quick Fix, 130–132
   Brightness/Contrast controls, 229
Brush tools
   Brush Settings palette, 400–402
   Impressionist Brush, 406
   making custom brushes, 405–407
   overview, 395–396
   Pencil tool, 407–408
   saving modified settings, 403–404
   settings for customizing, 397–401
   Special Effects brushes, 404–407
Burn and Dodge tools, 409–413
buttons, Web, 565
B&W Color Pop effect, 355

C

calendars, photo, 521–522
calibrating monitors, 131, 239–240
Camera Raw Converter. See Raw Converter
cameras, digital. See digital photography
canvases
   adding to images, 112–113
   adding with Crop tool, 91
   Canvas Size dialog box, 113
captions, adding to multiple files, 306–308
card readers, 30
cascading windows, 100–101
catalog databases, 78
catalog (Organizer), 44–46
categories, album, 57
categories (Organizer), 53–55
CD/DVD jackets/labels, 523

clarity (Raw Converter)
adjusting, 283–285
Clarity setting, 269
clipping layers together, 206–208
Clone Overlay button (Healing Brush),
317
Clone Stamp
fixing blemishes with, 318–322
overview, 311
cloning, 310–311
CMYK files, 588–589
collages
Collage option (Photomerge), 370
photo. *See* photo collages
Color Curves tool
enhancing tone/contrast with,
331–334
overview, 251
colorimeters, 239–240
colorizing black-and-white photos
antique images, 361
Colorize checkbox (Hue/Saturation
dialog box), 364–366
with many colors, 359–361
with single color, 361–362
tinting whole images, 362–366
color modes
changing to Grayscale, 352
types of, 41
Color Picker tool. *See* Eyedropper tool
colors
adjusting in Quick Fix, 133–134
balancing (Adjustment panel), 134
color channels, 352
Color Halftone filter, 440
Color Lava app, 255
color management, 131, 539, 542–545
color sliders (Adjustments panel),
133–134
color stops (gradients), 471–472
correcting color cast, 250–253
correcting with Average Blur filter,
452–453
correcting with gradients, 478
correcting with Smart Brush, 233–237
saturation. *See* saturation (colors)
colors, adding/removing
colorizing black-and-white photos.
See colorizing black-and-white
photos

converting images to black and
white, 349–352
overview, 349
removing color, 352–354
spot color. *See* spot color
colors, choosing
Color Picker, 255–257
Color Swatches panel, 258–259
Eyedropper tool, 257–259
overview, 253–255
colors, controlling
calibrating monitors, 239–240
Color Settings dialog box, 241
color spaces, 240–243
creating Smart Brush presets, 238
overview, 237–239
colors, replacing
Color Replacement tool, 343–346
Hue/Saturation Adjustment layer,
340–341
overview, 339
Replace Color command, 341–343
Comic filter, 414, 441–442
committing text, 486
Constrain Proportions checkbox, 108,
111
Contact Book (Organizer), 569
contact sheets, printing
on Macs, 549–551
in Windows, 546–548
Content-Aware Fill command
fixing blemishes with, 321–324
overview, 311
when to use, 329
Content-Aware Move tool
basics, 180–183
overview, 311
when to use, 329
contrast
adjusting in Quick Fix, 130–132
enhancing with Color Curves,
331–334
Convert to Black and White
command, 357–358
dialog box, 350–351, 352
Cookie Cutter tool, 96, 429–431
copying
images in Editor, 26
layers, 194–196
copyright symbol, 307

Correct Camera Distortion filter, 86, 382–387

Create feature, 509–510

Create projects
Basic/Advanced modes, 518–519
CD/DVD jackets/labels, 523
Facebook covers, 523–525
Graphics/Favorites panels, 526
greeting cards, 521
photo books, 519–521
photo calendars, 521–522
photo collages. *See* photo collages
saving, 515

cropping photos
Cookie Cutter tool, 96
Crop tool, 90–94, 122
to exact sizes, 93–94, 96–97
with Marquee tool, 94–97
overview, 89–90
for printing, 535–537, 541
in Raw Converter, 277–278

cursors, precise, 400

Curves tool. *See* Color Curves tool

customizing
brush shapes, 405–407
Brush tools, 397–401
picture packages, 552–554

Custom Shape tool, 423–424

Custom Workspace (Editor), 12

Cylindrical mapping (panoramas), 370

D

Deardorff, Scott, 415

Decontaminate Colors checkbox, 161–162

Defringe Layer command, 171–172

deleting
Adjustment/Fill layers, 219
brushes, 404
effects, 458
favorites, 527
files from memory cards, 32–33
filter layers, 439
layer masks, 213
layers, 192
layer styles, 464
place tags, 65
preferences, 599
presets, 266

Depth Map settings (Lens Blur), 449

Depth of Field effect (Guided Edit), 459

desaturating colors, 335–337

Despeckle filter, 318

Detail Smart Brush, 233

dialog box links (Help), 21–22

Digital Negative (.dng) files, 73

digital photography
Camera Calibration tab, 286
Camera Effects (Guided Edit), 459
changing camera default settings, 285
Correct Camera Distortion filter, 382–387
digital blending, 292
DNG Converter, 276
DNG files, creating, 291–292
EXIF data, 556
importing photos from cameras, 29–35
JPEG compression options, 73
Lens Blur filter, 447–451
photo filters, 299–300
processing multiple files.
See processing multiple files
Raw Converter. *See* Raw Converter
shooting tips for panoramas, 372
white balance settings, 279

Display Calibrator Assistant (Mac), 240

distortion
Correct Camera Distortion filter, 382–387
Distort command (Transform), 388–391

distributing layers, 203–205

dither setting (GIF files), 561

Divide Scanned Photos command, 79–81

DNG Converter, 276

DNG files, creating, 291–292

Dodge and Burn tools, 409–412, 413

downsampling photos, 111

drawing
outlines/borders, 428
with shapes. *See* shape tools
straight lines, 400

duplicate layers
applying filters to, 436
erasing color from, 357

duplicate photo searches, 34, 68–69
duplicating
    layers, 193–194
    layer styles, 464
Dust & Scratches filter, 318
dusty photos, 318

E

Eazel app, 395
Edge Detection section (Refine Edge dialog box), 159–160
editing
    Edit mode (text), 484
    gradients, 470–472
    layer masks, 213–215
    layer styles, 462
    metadata in Organizer, 49
    photos
        Auto Smart Fix command, 27
        Guided Edit, 23–25
    photos in Quick Fix. *See* editing in Quick Fix
    place tags, 65
    saved selections, 184
    text, 486–488
editing in Quick Fix
    adjusting brightness/contrast, 130–132
    adjusting exposure, 130
    color adjustments, 133–134
    overview, 124–125
    red eye, 125–129
    sharpening, 134–136
    Smart Fix command, 128–130
    suggested workflow, 137–138
    whitening teeth, 136–137
Edit in Progress error, 37
Editor
    copying images in, 26
    modes, 8–10
    vs. Organizer, 4–5
    Photo Bin, 13–14
    rotating photos in, 82
    Tool Options, 13–14
effects. *See also* actions; special effects
    basics, 456–458
    Effects button (Quick Fix window), 119
    Effects panel (Quick Fix), 143–146

    overview, 454
    text, 491–492
Elements 13
    add-ons/plug-ins, 586–588
    determining version of, 4
    development of, xiii–xiv
    Elements Agent feature, 59
    installing, 3–4, 593–594
    learning tips, xviii
    new features in, xv–xvii
    vs. Photoshop, xvii–xviii
    training/Help resources, 589–590
    troubleshooting, 599–600
    uses for, xiv–xv
    Welcome screen, 4–6
eLive (Elements Live), 8, 22
Ellipse tool, 425
elliptical areas, selecting, 149–150
emailing photos
    Contact Book, 569
    as individual attachments, 566–570
    overview, 565
    as PDF slideshows, 570
    resizing images for email/Web, 105–109
emailing slideshows, 570
Embed Color Profile checkbox, 242–243
Equalize special effect, 347–348
equalizing images, 477
Eraser tool, 416–417
Events view (Organizer), 66–67
EXIF data (cameras), 556
Expert mode (Editor)
    basics, 10–12
    fixing red eye in, 126–129
    History panel, 25
    overview, 9–10
    Panel Bin, 14–18
    Tools panel, 18–21
exporting
    Export New Files window, 531
    photo collages, 514
    slideshows, 577
exposures
    adjusting in Quick Fix, 130
    blending. *See* blending exposures
    blown out photos, 231
    correcting parts of images, 233–237
    fixing major problems, 229–230

overview, 228
Shadows/Highlights command,
230–233
symptoms of poor, 228–229
extracting objects from photos,
171–172
Eyedropper tool
eyedropper method (Levels),
247–248
sampling colors with, 257–259,
345–346

F

Facebook covers, 523–525
face-recognition technology, 60–63
Faces tool (Photomerge), 372–374
fading
effects, 200
Fade Amount setting (sharpening),
265
Fade setting (Brush tool), 401
Favorites panel, 526, 527
feathering edges of selections, 149,
152
files
backing up, 75–78
changing format of, 75
creating new, 39–42
format options, 72–75
processing multiple. *See* processing
multiple files
saving as version sets, 26
Fill layers, 215–219
filters
adding noise with, 443–446
Average Blur, 452–453
categories of, 440–442
Effects panel, 436–437
Filter Gallery, 437–440
Filter menu, 435–436
Gaussian Blur, 446–447
Lens Blur, 447–451
overview, 433–434, 435
performance tips, 439
Radial Blur, 450–452
removing noise with, 442–443
Surface Blur, 453–454
finger painting (Smudge tool), 415
Fit on Screen command, 101

flattening layers, 209–210
flipping
photos, 83–84
selections, 324
floating panels (tabs), 17
floating windows, 97–101
folders
Folders panel (Organizer), 50–51
storing photos in, 30
watching (Windows), 35
fonts, 481, 485
foreground color square, 253–255,
257–258
frames
Frames button (Quick Fix window),
119
Frames panel (Quick Fix), 143–146
for photo collages, 516
Free Rotate Layer command, 87–89
Free Transform command, 392
fringing, 487
Frye, Jodi, 396
Full Screen view
Organizer, 51–53
slideshows, 572–574
Fuzziness setting (Replace Color), 343

G

Gaussian Blur filter, 446–447
**Geometric Distortion Correction
checkbox (Photomerge),** 371
GIF files
animated, 563–565
overview, 72
posting on Web, 555–556, 560–562
transparency and, 472
gradients
color-correcting with, 478
creating noise, 473–475
definition of, 435
Gradient Editor, 470–472
Gradient Fill layers, 468–470
gradient maps, 475–477
Gradient Map special effect, 347
Gradient palette, 475
Gradient tool, 465–468
overview, 465
saving, 475
text, 491–492
transparency in, 472–473

Graphic Novel filter, 414, 441–442
graphics
    adding to photo collages, 516–517
    tablets, 399, 583–585
Graphics panel
    basics, 526–528
    effects in, 456
    Frames section, 430
    text effects, 491–492
    tint effects, 363
grayscale
    changing color modes to, 352
    images, 41
greeting cards, 521
grids, 86–87
Group Shot tool (Photomerge),
    375–376
groups, layer, 191
Guided Edit
    B&W Color Pop effect, 355
    mode (Editor), 9
    Photo Effects, 355, 450
    Selective Black and White effect, 355
    special effects in, 458–461
    using, 23–25
guides, 86–87

H

Hand tool
    basics, 103–104
    in Quick Fix toolbox, 121
Hardness setting (Brush tool), 402
HDR (high dynamic range) programs,
    299
Healing Brush
    Content Aware option, 314
    fixing blemishes with, 315–318
    overview, 311
    Pattern mode, 325–326
    in Quick Fix, 122
healing damaged photos, 310–311
Help sources, 21–24
hexadecimal codes (colors), 256
hidden tags, 56
hiding
    filter layers, 439
    layers, 196–197
    layer styles, 465
    Photomerge Exposure panel, 298

    photos, 34
    selections, 149
    Welcome screen, 6
highlights, adjusting (Levels), 132
High-Pass filter (sharpening), 267–269
histograms, 245–247
History panel, 25
hollow outline text, 500
Horizontal Type tool, 480–484
Hue Jitter setting (Brush tool),
    401–402
Hue/Saturation Adjustment layer
    changing colors with, 340–341
    removing color with, 358–359
Hue/Saturation dialog box
    basics, 335–337
    Colorize checkbox, 364–366
    desaturating colors with, 353
Hue slider (Quick Fix), 133

I

ICC profiles, 242
iDevices, sharing photos from/to, 579
images. *See also* photos
    changing sizes of, 105–109
    converting to black and white,
        349–352
    correcting parts of, 233–237
    equalizing, 477
    flattening, 209–210
    formats for Web posting, 555–556
    Image Capture program (Mac), 80
    Image Size dialog box, 106
    image windows, 18
    moving objects between, 219–223
    opening stored, 35–39
    positioning for printing, 539–541
    rotating, 49, 82–84, 390
    saving for Web. *See* saving images
        for Web
    setting in text, 496–501
    special effects, 346–348
    straightening contents of, 84–90
    turning into brushes, 405–407
    views of, 97–102
importing photos from cameras, 29–35
Impressionist Brush, 406
input sliders (Levels), 249–251

installing Elements 13
  on Macs, 596–598
  overview, 3–4, 593–594
  in Windows, 595–596
instant albums, 50
Instant Fix button (Organizer), 49
Intersect mode (selection tools),
  153–154
inverting selections, 172–173
Invert special effect, 347
Iris settings (Lens Blur), 449–450
irregular areas, selecting, 151–154

J

JPEG files
  artifacts, 318, 443–444
  bit depth and, 290
  layers and, 191
  overview, 72
  posting on Web, 555–556, 560
  saving photos as, 73–74

K

keyboard shortcuts
  Auto Smart Fix command, 27
  clipping masks, 207
  closing files, 37
  closing photos, 138
  Color Settings dialog box, 241
  comparing photos, 51
  Convert to Black and White, 350
  copying/cutting layers, 195
  copyright symbol, 307
  Create Keyword Tag dialog box, 54
  duplicating layers, 194
  filters, 435
  Free Transform command, 388
  Healing Brush, 325
  hiding photos, 34
  inverting selections, 172, 417
  Levels Adjustments panel, 249
  merging layers, 208, 366
  moving selections, 183
  new files, 39
  new layers, 191
  opening stored images, 35
  Paint Bucket, 408
  Photo Downloader, 30
  printing files, 534
  Raw Converter, 274

  rearranging layers, 200
  Refine Edge dialog box, 158
  Remove Color command, 352
  resizing photos, 105
  Save for Web, 556
  saving files, 70
  saving options, 74
  screen views in Organizer, 121
  Select All, 148
  Selection Brush, 162–164
  selections, 149, 153, 155
  Slide Show button, 51
  slideshow views, 572, 573
  Smart Brush, 356
  Smart Fix commands, 129
  Stamp Visible command, 210
  straightening image contents, 84
  Undo/Redo commands, 25–26
  White Balance tool, 280
  Whiten Teeth tool, 136
  zooming, 100, 103
  Zoom tool, 102
Kuler app (Adobe), 255

L

labels
  attaching to multiple files, 306–308
  CD/DVD, 523
Lasso tools, 166–172
layers
  activating, 206
  adjusting opacity of, 196
  Adjustment and Fill, 215–219
  aligning/distributing, 203–205
  arranging with Move tool, 202–203
  Background, 189–190
  basics, 185–187
  blend modes, 198–199
  clipping together, 206–208
  copying/cutting from, 194–196
  correcting exposure problems with,
    230
  creating, 191–193
  deleting, 192
  duplicating, 193–194
  erasing color from duplicate, 357
  file formats for saving, 191
  filter layers, 438
  flattening, 209–210
  Free Rotate Layer command, 87–89

Gradient Fill, 468–470
hiding, 196–197
layer masks, 210–215
Layers panel, 187–188
linking, 205–206
locking, 197–198
merging, 208–209
naming, 195
rearranging, 200–202
Stamp Visible command, 210
layer styles
basics, 461–466
editing, 462
overview, 434
Style Settings dialog box, 463–464
leading (text), 482–483
Lens Blur filter, 447–451
Levels adjustments
basics, 243–245
correcting color casts, 252
eyedropper method, 247–248
histograms, 245–247
in Quick Fix, 130–132
slider method, 248–250
libraries
Brush tools, 397–398
color swatches, 258–259
gradient, 475
Revel, 58–59
Line tool, 426–427
linking layers, 205–206
Liquify filter, 493–496
List view, 50–51
locking layers, 197–198
Lomo Camera effect (Guided Edit), 459
lossless file formats, 73
Luminance Channel sharpening (Mac), 136
Luminance slider (Raw Converter), 288

M

Macs
installing Elements 13 on, 596–598
printing multiple images on, 548–554
printing on, 536–538
Magic Eraser, 417–418
Magic Wand tool, 165–166

Magnetic Lasso tool, 169–170
manual merges (Photomerge Exposure), 295–299
maps, gradient, 475–477
marching ants, 148
Marquee tool, cropping photos with, 94–97
masks
clipping, 206–208
layer, 210–215
Masking setting (Raw Converter), 287
Mask mode (Selection Brush), 162–164
Unsharp Mask, 260–263
Media Bin, 67
Median filter, 318
Media view (Organizer)
basics, 6, 47–50
tagging places in, 65
viewing tags in, 43–44
merging
layer masks, 213
layers, 208–209
metadata
editing in Organizer, 49
searching photos by, 69–70
midtones
adjusting, 132, 247, 250
Midtone Contrast slider, 232
monitors, calibrating, 131, 239–240
Monochromatic setting (Add Noise filter), 445
motion blur angle setting, 265
Move tool
arranging layers with, 202–203
in Quick Fix, 122
relocating objects with, 182–184
moving
objects between images, 219–223
selected areas, 179–183
Multiply layer blend mode, 229–230
multisession discs, 76

N

naming
groups of files, 303–304
imported files, 31
layers, 195
Navigator panel, 104

noise
    adding with filters, 443–446
    creating noise gradients, 473–475
    reducing, 264
    reducing in Raw Converter, 286–288
    removing with filters, 442–443

O

objects
    changing color of. *See* colors,
        replacing
    extracting from photos, 171–172
    moving between images, 219–223
    object searches, 68
    raster, 209
    relocating with Move tool, 182
    turning into brushes, 405–407
opacity
    of brushstrokes, 399
    of layers, 196
    opacity stops, 472–473
opening
    PDF files, 38
    specific file types, 37
    stored images, 35–39
    unsupported formats, 75
Organizer
    Adaptive Grid view, 6, 43–45
    applying Quick Fixes within, 121
    avoiding on Windows computers, 46
    backing up files in, 76–78
    basics, 42–44
    catalog, 44–46
    categories and tags, 53–55
    Contact Book, 569
    creating slideshows in, 574–576
    Edit in Progress error, 37
    vs. Editor, 4–5
    Email Attachments panel, 567
    Events view, 66–67
    Folders panel, 50–51
    Full Screen view, 51–53, 572–574
    Media view, 47–50
    overview, 6–7
    resetting preferences, 599
    Revel online service, 57–60
    rotating photos in, 82
    tagging people in photos, 60–63
    tagging places in photos, 63–66
    using on Macs, 48

Orton Effect, 450
OS X, printing in, 536–538
outlined text, 498–500
outlines, drawing (shapes), 428
Out Of Bounds effect, 460
Output Levels sliders, 250
**Output section (Refine Edge dialog
    box),** 161–162
Overlay blend mode, 413
oversharpening images, 262

P

padlock on image, 37
Page Setup dialog box (printing), 541
Paint Bucket, 408–409
paintings, turning photos into, 414–416
panels
    opening/closing, 53
    overview, 11–12
    Panel Bin, 14–18
panoramas, creating, 368–372
pasting
    Paste/Paste Into Selection
        commands, 151
    text into Elements, 486
paths, text on. *See* artistic text
Pathway effect, 457
patterns
    Healing Brush Pattern mode,
        325–326
    overview, 324–325
    Pattern Stamp, 326–327
PDF files
    emailing as slideshows, 570
    opening, 38
    overview, 72–73
    saving PSE files as, 515
Pen and Ink filter, 414
Pencil tool, 407–408
perspective
    Perspective command (Transform),
        388–391
    perspective distortion, 86
    Perspective option (Photomerge),
        370
    sliders for controlling, 387–388
Pet Eye checkbox, 127
photo collages
    adding graphics and text, 516–517
    adjusting photos/frames, 514–516

Basic and Advanced modes, 518–519
creating, 511–515
overview, 509–511

Photo Downloader
basics, 30–35
overview, 7–9

Photographic Effects layer styles, 363

Photomerge
Faces tool, 372–374
Group Shot tool, 375–376
overview, 367
panoramas, creating, 368–372
Photomerge Compose feature, 219,
379–383
Scene Cleaner tool, 376–379

Photomerge Exposure
automatic merges, 294–295
manual merges, 295–299
overview, 293–294

photos. *See also* images
albums, 55–57
auto-stacking, 34
batch-processing. *See* processing
multiple files
blowouts, 231
colorizing black-and-white.
See colorizing black-and-white
photos
combining with Photomerge
Compose, 379–383
cropping. *See* cropping photos
editing. *See* editing
editing in Quick Fix. *See* editing in
Quick Fix
editing with Editor. *See* Editor
emailing. *See* emailing photos
flipping, 83–84
hiding, 34
importing from cameras, 29–35
moving objects between, 219–223
Photo Bin (Editor), 13–14
photo books, 519–521
photo calendars, 521–522
Photo Effects (Guided Edit), 450, 459
Photo Filter Adjustment layers, 216
photo filters, 299–300
Photo Fix Options panel, 49
Photo Play effects (Guided Edit),
460–461
printing black-and-white, 354

recomposing, 326–331
removing color from, 352–354
resampling, 111–112
Restore Old Photo Guided Edit, 310
scanning, 38–39
searching. *See* searching photos
sharing online, 578–579
straightening scanned, 79–82
turning into paintings, 414–416

Photoshop
vs. Elements 13, xvii–xviii
features beyond Elements, 588–589
Photoshop Masking & Compositing,
215
Photoshop Restoration and
Retouching, 310

Photoshop Elements 13. *See* Elements
13

Photostream folder, 579

picture packages (printing)
on Macs, 551–554
in Windows, 548

Picture Stack effect (Guided Edit), 460

pincushion distortion, 385

Pixar files, 72

pixel dimensions, 106–108

Places view, 63–65

plug-ins
for Elements, 586–588
filter, 442

PNG files
options for Web posting, 562
overview, 72, 556

Polygonal Lasso tool, 170–171

Polygon tool, 425–426

Pop Art effect (Guided Edit), 460

portraits, fixing (tutorial), 454

Posterize special effect, 347

precise cursor, 400

preferences
Adobe Partner Services, 532
Asian Text Options, 488
Auto Smart Tone, 143
Clone Stamp, 322
Color Picker menu, 256
cursor, 400
Elements Agent slider, 59
external editors, 36
floating documents, 99
guides and grid, 87

History States setting, 26
Move tool, 483
preferences file, 599
RAM memory, 371
Raw Converter, 281, 285
Revel accounts, 58
saving files, 74
scratch disks, 599
Supplementary Editing Application
checkbox, 47
Undo/Redo commands, 25
units and rulers, 87
zooming with scroll wheel, 103
presets
Adjustments panel, 123–124
creating (Adjust Sharpness dialog
box), 266
creating for Smart Brush, 238
Preset Manager, 588
previewing
images for Web posting, 562–563
Preview checkboxes, 227
printing
black-and-white photos, 354
contact sheets
on Macs, 549–551
in Windows, 546–548
multiple images
on Macs, 548–554
in Windows, 546–548
ordering prints, 530–533
panoramas, 368, 372
Picture Package feature, 548
preparing for, 529–530
Print Size view, 101
resizing images for, 109–113
printing at home
color management, 542–545
More Options, 541–542
in OS X, 536–538
overview, 533–534
photo paper experiments, 546
positioning images, 539–541
from Windows Organizer, 539
in Windows, 534–537
processing multiple files
Adjustment layers for, 216
applying Quick Fix commands, 306
attaching labels, 306–308

changing image size/file type,
305–306
choosing files, 302–303
overview, 301–302
Process Multiple Files command, 216
renaming files, 303–304
profiles, camera (Raw Converter), 286
psd (Photoshop) files, 72, 191
pse (Photo Project Format) files
overview, 72
saving Create projects as, 515
saving photo books as, 521
Push mode (Refine Selection Brush),
178

Q

Quick Fix
Adjust Color for Skin Tone command,
139–142
Adjustments panel, 122–124
applying commands to groups of
files, 306
applying corrections in Organizer, 121
Auto Smart Tone command, 142–143
Before & After views, 124–125
editing photos in. *See* editing in
Quick Fix
effects in, 456
Effects/Textures/Frames panels,
143–146
overview, 8–9, 117–118
Quick Fix toolbox, 120–122
Quick Fix Vibrance slider, 335
Quick Fix window, 118–120
Quick Highlight setting (Recompose
tool), 328, 329
Quick Mask, 215
Quick Selection tool, 121, 154–156

R

Radial Blur filter, 450–452
Radius slider, 159
Rainbow Map (Smart Brush), 492
rasterizing vector shapes, 424
raster objects, 209
ratings tags, 56
Raw Converter
adjusting clarity/vibrance/saturation,
283–285

adjusting sharpness/reducing noise, 286–288
adjusting tone, 280–283
adjusting views, 276–277
adjusting white balance, 277–280
basics, 273–275
camera profiles, 286
choosing bit depth, 288–290
DNG format, 291–292
fixing red eye, 277
non-raw files in, 289
overview, 272
preferences, 281
profiles in, 286
rotating/straightening/cropping, 277–278
saving images, 290–291
saving settings, 284–285
raw format
converting to DNG, 292
pros and cons of, 278
rearranging layers, 200–202
recomposing photos, 326–331
Rectangle/Rounded Rectangle tools, 425–426
rectangular areas, selecting, 149–150
Rectangular Marquee tool, 96, 149–150
red band on image, 37
red eye
automatically fixing, 34
Auto Red Eye Fix, 126
fixing in Quick Fix, 125–129
fixing in Raw Converter, 277
Red Eye Removal tool, 122, 127–128
Reduce Noise filter, 442–443
reference lines (camera distortion), 384
reference points (transformations), 390
Refine Edge dialog box, 156–162
Refine Selection Brush, 177–178
Reflection effect (Guided Edit), 460
Remove Color Cast command, 252–253
Remove Color command, 352–353, 357–358
Rendering Intent setting (color management), 544
Replace Color command, 341–343
Reposition option (Photomerge), 370
resampling photos, 108, 111–112

Reset icon (Quick Fix), 125
Reset Tool option, 322
reshaping selections, 177–178
resizing images
adding canvas, 112–113
for email and Web, 105–109
Image Size dialog box, 106
overview, 105
for printing, 109–113
resizing selections, 173–176
resolution
font sizing and, 485
Max Print Resolution (Organizer), 539
monitors vs. printing, 40
overview, 105
for printing, 109–110, 530
Restore Old Photo Guided Edit, 310
Revel, Adobe, 8, 57–60
RGB colors
overview, 41
printer profile, 545
RGB color spaces, 241–243
rotating images
in 15-degree increments, 390
basics, 82–84
Free Rotate Layer command, 87–89
in Raw Converter, 277–278
Rounded Rectangle tool, 425–426
Roundness/Angle settings (Brush tool), 402
Rule of Thirds (cropping), 92–93
rulers, 87

S

sampling colors
Color Replacement tool, 345–346
with Eyedropper tool, 257–259
saturation (colors)
adjusting in Raw Converter, 283–285
adjusting with Sponge tool, 338–339
Hue/Saturation dialog box, 335–337
overview, 334–335
slider (Quick Fix), 133
saving
changing file formats and, 75
colors in Swatches panel, 259
Create projects, 515
files as version sets, 26
gradients, 475
images in Raw Converter, 290–291

layers in supported formats, 191
modified Brush tool settings,
403–404
options for, 74
photo books, 521
Save As dialog box, 70–71
Save As formatting options, 72–75
saved searches, 69
selections, 183–184
settings in Raw Converter, 284–285
saving images for Web
overview, 556–557
previewing images, 562–563
Save For Web dialog box, 556–557
Save for Web format/quality settings,
560–562
using Save for Web, 557–559
**Scale slider (Correct Camera
Distortion filter),** 387
scanned photos, straightening, 79–82
scanning photos, 38–39
Scatter setting (Brush tool), 401
Scene Cleaner (Photomerge), 376–379
scrapbooking projects, 430
scratch disks, 598
scratched photos, 318
Screen layer blend mode, 229–230
searching photos
basics, 67–68
for duplicates, 34
by metadata, 69–70
selecting
irregular areas, 151–154
overview, 147–148
rectangular/elliptical areas, 149–150
Select All, 148–149
Selection Brush
basics, 162–165
Mask mode, 342
in Quick Fix, 121
selections
adding text to, 500–503
controlling selection tools, 152–154
extracting objects, 171–172
feathering edges of, 152
inverting, 172–173
Lasso tools, 166–172
Magic Wand tool, 165–166
moving selected areas, 179–183
Quick Selection tool, 154–156

Refine Selection Brush, 177–178
refining edges of, 156–162
removing color from, 357–358
reshaping, 177–178
resizing, 173–176
saving, 183–184
sizing, 150
smoothing/bordering, 176
Transform Selection command,
173–176, 392
turning into brushes, 405–407
**Selective Black and White Guided
Edit,** 355
shadows
adjusting (Levels), 132
Shadows/Highlights command,
230–233
shapes, outlining with text, 503–504
shape tools
basics, 420–423
Cookie Cutter tool, 429–431
Custom Shape tool, 423–424
Ellipse tool, 425
Line tool, 426–427
Polygon/Star tools, 425–426
rasterizing vector shapes, 424
Rectangle/Rounded Rectangle tools,
425–426
Shape Selection tool, 427–428
sharing photos/videos online, 578–579
sharpening images
Adjust Sharpness tool, 263–267
High-Pass filter, 267–269
in Quick Fix, 134–136
in Raw Converter, 286–288
Sharpen tool, 269–270
Unsharp Mask, 260–263
Shutterfly online service, 519–521,
530–533
Side by Side view (Organizer), 51–53
simplifying text, 487
sizing
brush cursors, 398–399
files, 40
multiple files, 305–306
selections, 150, 173–176
text, 481–482
sizing images
adding canvas, 112–113
basics, 105

for email, 108–109
Image Size dialog box, 106
overview, 105
for printing, 109–113, 540–541
for Web, 105–108, 558–559
Skew command (Transform), 388–391
skies, blown-out, 408
skin
    adjusting tone of, 139–142
    improving texture with Surface Blur
        filter, 453–454
slider method (Levels), 248–250
slideshows
    creating in Organizer, 574–576
    emailing, 570
    overview, 571–572
    running in Full Screen view, 572–574
Smart Brush
    colorizing black-and-white photos
        with, 361–362
    correcting color with, 233–237
    limitations of, 339
    making presets for, 238
    overview, 156
    painting away color with, 355–357
SmartCurve add-on, 334
Smart Events, 66–67
Smart Fix command (Quick Fix),
    128–130
Smart Objects (Create projects), 517
Smart Radius setting, 159
smoothing selections, 176
Smudge tool, 414–416
Solarize preset (Color Curves), 335
Spacing setting (Brush tool), 401
special effects. *See also* actions; filters
    basics, 346–348
    in Guided Edit, 458–461
    Photo Effects, 355, 450
    Special Effects brushes, 404–407
    text, 491–496
Specular Highlights settings (Lens
    blur), 450
Spherical option (Photomerge), 370
Spin mode (Radial Blur), 451
Sponge tool, 338–339
spot color
    erasing color from duplicate layers,
        357

painting away color with Smart
    Brush, 355–357
removing color from selections,
    357–358
removing color with Hue/Saturation
    Adjustment layer, 358–359
Spot Healing Brush
    Content Aware option, 314
    fixing blemishes with, 312–315
    overview, 311
    in Quick Fix, 122
stacks, photo, 34
Stamp Visible command (layers), 210
Star tool, 425–426
stored images, opening, 35–39
straightening
    contents of images, 84–90
    photos in Raw Converter, 277–278
    scanned photos, 79–82
    Straighten tool, 84–86
straight lines
    drawing in selections, 168
    drawing with Brush tool, 400
    Line tool, 426–427
Style Settings dialog box (layer
    styles), 463–464
styling text, 483
Supplementary Editing Application
    setting, 47
Surface Blur filter, 453–454

T

tabbed view, 18
tablets, graphics, 583–585
tabs (floating panels), 17
tab views, 97–100, 101
tagging
    people in photos, 60–63
    places in photos, 63–66
tags (Organizer), 53–56
teeth, whitening (Quick Fix), 136–137
temperature adjustments (color), 134
text
    adding to photo calendars, 522
    adding to photo collages, 516–517
    anti-aliasing, 487–488
    artistic. *See* artistic text
    creating, 484–486
    creating outlined, 498–500
    editing, 486–488

effects, 491–492
gradients, 491–492
liquifying, 493–496
overview, 479–480
pasting into Elements, 486
resolution and font sizes, 485
setting images in. *See* Type Mask
  tools
Type Tool Options settings, 480–484
warping, 484, 488–491

textures
improving skin, 453–454
Smart Brush, 236
Textures button (Quick Fix), 119
Textures panel (Quick Fix), 143–146

themes
collages, 511
Facebook covers, 524–525
slideshows, 576

Threshold special effect, 347–348

thumbnails
contact sheets, 550–551
Thumbnail Contents setting (Layers
  panel), 189

TIFF files
overview, 73
saving layers as, 191

tile display, 99

Tilt-Shift effect, 450, 460

tinting
black-and-white photos, 362–366
black-and-white tint effect, 351
tint adjustments, 134

tolerance setting (Magic Wand), 165

tonality, correcting automatically,
  142–143

Tonal Width setting (sharpening), 265

tone
adjusting in Raw Converter, 280–283
adjusting skin tone, 139–142
enhancing with Color Curves,
  331–334

Tool Options, 13–14, 480–484

Tools panel, 18–21

Transform commands
Free Transform, 392
overview, 387–388
Skew/Distort/Perspective, 388–391
Transform Selection, 173–176, 392

transparency
in gradients, 472–473
JPEGs and, 560–561
of layer masks, 214
overview, 42

troubleshooting Elements, 599–600

Tsume setting (text), 488

Type Mask tools
activating accidentally, 480
creating outlined text, 498
overview, 496–497
using, 496–498

Type tools
in Quick Fix, 122
Tool Options settings for, 480–484

U

Undo/Redo commands, 25–26
uninstalling Elements 13, 599
unlinking layer masks, 213
Unsharp Mask, 260–263
upsampling photos, 111

V

vector shapes, rasterizing, 424
version sets (files), 26
Vertical Type tool
Asian Text Options, 488
columns, 482–483
Tool Options settings, 480–484

vibrance (color)
adjusting in Raw Converter, 283–285
slider, 133

views
adjusting in Raw Converter, 276–277
image, 97–102
View Mode (Refine Edge dialog box),
  158

vignetting
correcting, 386
creating with Correct Camera
  Distortion filter, 383
removing, 370
Vignette Effect, 152

visual similarity searches, 68

W

Wacom Bamboo tablet, 584
warping text, 484, 488–491
watching folders (Windows), 35

watermarks, 306–308
Web
creating Web buttons, 565
image formats for, 555–556
resizing images for, 105–109
saving images for. *See* saving images
for Web
websites for downloading
add-ons/plug-ins, 586–587
CD/DVD label templates, 523
Color Lava app, 255
exposure blending programs, 299
Kuler app (Adobe), 255
noise-reduction software, 443
programs for obscure formats, 75
slideshow program, 571
SmartCurve add-on, 334
Snapfish online prints, 532
websites for further information
blend modes, 412
Deardorff, Scott, 415
Digital Photography Review, 414
Eazel app, 395

Fry, Jodi, 396
Help/training resources (Elements),
589–590
iCloud service, 579
resolution, 105
smudging, 414
Wacom tablets, 585
Welcome screen, 4–6
white balance (Raw Converter),
277–280
whitening teeth (Quick Fix), 136–137
Windows, Microsoft
defragmenting, 598
installing Elements 13 in, 595–596
printing in, 534–537
printing multiple images in, 546–548
window views, 97–99, 101
workspaces (Editor), 10–12

Z

Zoom Burst effect (Guided Edit), 450,
460
Zoom tool, 102–103, 120